PRINCIPIA OR BASIS
OF
SOCIAL SCIENCE:

BEING A SURVEY OF THE SUBJECT FROM THE MORAL AND THEOLOGICAL, YET LIBERAL AND PROGRESSIVE STANDPOINT.

BY R. J. WRIGHT.

Second Edition, Crown 8vo., Cloth, Price, $2.00. 8.00

Published by J. B. LIPPINCOTT & CO.,

715 and 717 Market Street, Philadelphia.

The following notices of this work are selected from a larger number that might be offered.

The Philadelphia "PUBLIC LEDGER" *says*,

"A work which is the result of an evidently long and patient study of Comte's, Carey's, Paley's, Spencer's, Mulford's, Mill's, Guizot's, and Fourier's writings on cognate subjects, although it differs essentially in method and matter from all of them."

The Philadelphia "EVENING BULLETIN" *says*,

* * * "It is evidently a work of immense labor, and of a good deal of originality. But to give any idea of its character would be difficult in a newspaper notice, and we content ourselves with calling attention to it as a work that deserves examination by all those who take an interest in that very capacious and comprehensive branch of modern philosophy which goes by the name of social science."

The Philadelphia "PRESS" *says*,

"We cannot begin to give even the briefest summary of a book which not only differs in many points from Comte, Carey, Paley, Herbert Spencer, Mulford, J. S. Mill, and Fourier, but is also the first of a series."

Der deutsche "PHILADELPHIA DEMOKRAT" *sagt*,

"Dies Werk ist in seiner Art eine Novität in der Literatur der Social-Wissenchaft. * * * Der Verfasser sagt, dass man bisher die Social-Wissenchaft, obgleich sie in ihrem innersten Wesen 'Moral' sei, ausschliesslich den 'Ungläubigen' und den Socialisten überlassen habe; dass er dagegen sein national-ökonomisches Werk im Interesse der offenbarten und überlieferten Religion verfasst, es aber nichts destoweniger von einem liberalen und progressiven Standpunkt aus geschrieben habe. Die Quellen aus denen er am Meisten geschöpft, und die Autoren, deren Werke" [ausser den obengenannten,] "er vorzuchsweise seiner Arbeit zu Grunde gelegt, führt er in der nachstehenden Reihenfolge auf, nämlich: die Bibel, Appletons' Encyclopädie, Wheaton, Ruskin, Tennison, Guizot, De Tocqueville, F. Cooper, Schleiermacher, Mc'Cosh;

und Nordhoff's Monographie der Communisten Gemeinden in den Ver. Staaten.

"Wenn auch von unentschieden religiösen, und zwar christlichen Standpunkt aus geschrieben, hält sich das Werk doch gänzlich frei von Mysticismus, und es gipfelt das System des Verfassers folgerichtig in Communismus; allerdings nicht in dem von Cabot, und noch weniger in dem der Pariser 'Commune,' sondern in einem durch 'Religion' und 'Moral' limitirten Communismus.

"Obwohl der Verfasser schwerlich National-Oekonomen zu seiner neuen Lehre bekehren wird, so ist sein Werk immerhin interessant und verdient gelesen zu werden."

TRANSLATION. *The* "PHILADELPHIA GERMAN DEMOCRAT" *says,*

"This work is in its manner a novelty in the literature of Social Science. The author says that until now Social Science, although moral in its inmost nature, has been left * * * to the infidels and Socialists; but that he, on the contrary, has composed his national-economical work in the interest of revealed and traditional religion, but that, nevertheless, he has written it from a liberal and progressive standpoint. The sources from which he has derived most, and the authors whose works he has principally used as a basis for his labor" [in addition to those above mentioned,] "he gives in the following order, * * * namely, the Bible, Appleton's Encyclopedia, Wheaton, Ruskin, Tennyson, Guizot, De Tocqueville, J. F. Cooper, Schleiermacher, Mc'Cosh; and Nordhoff's Monograph of the Communistic societies of the United States.

"Though the work has been written from an undetermined" [or undenominational] "religious, and, certainly Christian standpoint, yet it remains entirely free from mysticism; and it logically crowns the system of the author with Communism;—to be sure not with the Communism of Cabot, and still less with that of the Paris Commune, but with a Communism limited by Religion and Morality.

"Though the author will scarcely convert National-Economists to his new doctrine, yet his work is nevertheless interesting and deserves to be read."

The Philadelphia "CHRISTIAN INSTRUCTOR" *says,*

"This large and well-published work is evidently the result of much thought and labor on the part of the author. It is an earnest discussion of the whole subject of Social Science, and while in many of his views he is of the school of Comte, Fourier, Spencer, John S. Mill and the like, he stands on far higher and better ground every way, and gives one of the most instructive and inviting presentations of the subject, and one of the least exceptionable that has probably been laid before the public. In preparing it he says his earnest desire was to contribute his mite towards the Christianization of politics, the promotion of real freedom and progress, and the improvement of society. * * * While however we say all this, we think the book is one of the best of the kind, and may well be read by any who are interested in the subject of which it treats."

The "PRESBYTERIAN" *of Philadelphia says,*

"This is a weighty book, not easily read, and not easy satisfactorily to notice. The writer believes in the possibility of a 'Social Science,' but differs in many respects from Comte, Spencer, and other writers on the subject. He believes in the scientific value of Ethics, Metaphysics, and Religion, which Comte declined to consider parts of Positive Science. He also believes in communism, but not in a vulgar communism, but communism placed on the basis of Christian kindness and benevolence. * * * The sayings of Jesus on the mount and other of his discourses, the writer thinks applicable only to a Christian Commune, and in his ideal commune, all these principles are to be predominant."

"THE FRANKFORD HERALD" *of Philadelphia says,*

"Principia or Basis of Social

Science. By Robert J. Wright of Tacony. This volume, which bears the imprint of Messrs. J. B. Lippincott and Co., has the following dedication: 'To the memory of my dear departed sister, Josephine Amanda Wright: by whose self-sacrifice, unto death, I was enabled to survive, and to work, and to produce these and other writings: this work is affectionately and reverently dedicated by her living monument R. J. W.'

"The author reviews the works of Comte, Carey, Paley, Spencer, Mulford, Mill, Guizot, Fourier, and others. He gives his object in publishing this volume as follows." [Then follows page VII from the book itself.]

"THE FRANKFORD AND HOLMESBURG GAZETTE" *says*,

"We have received a copy of the above interesting work. A hasty glance over its neatly-printed pages, reveals many new and perhaps strange doctrinal points to us, but are nevertheless based upon reasonable grounds, and are indicative of the deep study and research of the author. The latter has subdivided his work into five sections or books, to wit: I. Summary Introduction to Social Science; II. The Precinct; III. The Nation; IV. Corporation; V. Limited Communism. There is much in its pages to interest the theorist, and we therefore ask for the reading of the book, in order that its true merits may be known."

PROF. GEORGE ALLEN, *of the University of Pennsylvania, at Philadelphia, says*,

* * * "I was hardly less surprised than gratified, by the presentation of your remarkable work. Your book so attractive in its table of contents, and obviously upon the merest inspection, so original in its treatment of each topic, * * * has attracted me * * * powerfully. * * * I have been able to gratify my eager curiosity only in part. I hope to do better for myself soon. In the meanwhile allow me to express my gratification at the prominence you give to your firm and full belief in Revelation, and at the fairness and liberality with which you speak of religious organizations not your own * * *."

REV. D. C. MILLETT. D.D., *of Philadelphia, says*,

"I have not read it through as yet, but have gone far enough to appreciate its value, and hope some time to talk it over with you in propria persona."

REV. D. S. MILLER, D.D., *of Philadelphia, says*,

"I am glad to hear of you as still engaged in study and speculation upon great themes. * * * I do not doubt it to be the fruit of earnest labor and thought; and the affectionate dedication of it to the memory of your dear departed sister, and my friend, is very grateful to me."

REV. THOMAS MURPHY, D.D., *of Philadelphia, says*,

"I have derived a great deal of information from your book."

REV. Z. M. HUMPHREY, D.D., *of Philadelphia, says*,

"It bears the marks of most careful preparation, and I have no doubt that it will prove of great value. * * * A more leisurely examination of the work may call out a more mature expression of opinion as to its merits."

REV. ABEL C. THOMAS, *of Philadelphia, says*,

"I hope to read your disquisition with both eyes open. Confessedly it will require close attention in the perusal."

MRS. M. L. THOMAS, *of Philadelphia, says*,

"Allow me to express the great interest I have found in reading your Principia. * * * Your views of the great problems of human and divine government are broad and many-sided, and such as mark the profound scholar and the earnest thinker. Hoping that the world you are striving to enlighten may yet enter into a comprehension of the eternal principles of truth as you present them, I am," &c.

HENRY J. WILLIAMS, ESQ., *of Philadelphia, says*,

"I thank you very sincerely for the beautiful book. * * * I have not yet read it, but hope soon to do so; and will then transfer it to a public library which I have established at Chestnut Hill, where it will be preserved safely."

Ex-Mayor Alexander Henry, *of Philadelphia, says,*

"I * * * shall take pleasure in its perusal—and judging from a glance at its contents, doubt not that it will afford much valuable information."

D. W. Sellers, Esq., *of Philadelphia, says,*

* * * "from the reading of which during the coming fall I anticipate pleasure and instruction."

John B. Colahan, Esq., *of Philadelphia, says,*

* * * "from the perusal of which I expect to derive much information on the subjects treated; * * * a valuable addition doubtless to the sources of knowledge."

John D. Lankenau, Esq., *of Philadelphia, says,*

"I am very much obliged to you for the tender of your book on social science. * * * My best acknowledgments for your courtesy.—With the greatest respect," &c.

Wm. F. Guernsey, M.D., *of Philadelphia, says,*

"I am pleased with your views arguments and conclusions. All is free from censure or egotism. I wish it might be read by all. You have my thanks for the volume: and thanks for your labors in producing so valuable a work."

H. J. Doucet, M.D., *of Philadelphia, says,*

"Allow me to congratulate you on the completion of your great undertaking: hoping that your health and life may be preserved so that you may be able to fulfil the promise * * * I shall take the liberty at some future day to make some criticisms."

R. Patterson, Esq., *of Philadelphia, says,*

"I am sincerely thankful for your sending me your work on Social Science, which I doubt not I shall read with deep interest. Already I have concluded a study of the special division of 'Limited Communism,' which I find full of suggestions and originality in treatment."

M. W. Woodward, Esq., *of Philadelphia, says,*

"The dedication of it affords me a very gratified remembrance of your lovely but not forgotten sister."

Charles Santee, Esq., *of Philadelphia, says,*

"I doubt not it will amply repay for all the time necessary to become fully acquainted with its contents. The dedication of it to your departed sister has revived my recollection of her faithful labors * * *."

Ellis Clark, Esq., *of Philadelphia, says,*

"I promise myself great pleasure in a more thorough perusal."

The Pittsburgh "Christian Advocate" *says,*

* * * "So far as we know, the author of the present volume is the only man who has pretended to consider this science from a distinctively Christian point of view. As the Positivists have hitherto given it the most attention, it has received a skeptical turn. The author calls special notice to his point of view. His volume, the first of a series relating to Social Science, contains five books, entitled respectively, Introduction, Precinct, Nation, Corporation, Limited Communism. In it he has written for the people rather than for philosophers, and has adopted a style at once simple, direct and forcible. There is little in it that an ordinarily intelligent reader will not understand, and *must* understand before he can see the causes of the complications and corruptions of our political and social life."

The Pittsburgh "Presbyterian Banner" *says,*

"This is an elaborate work, evidently prepared by one earnestly anxious to instruct his fellow-men and do good to them. He grapples with the most complicated problems in social and political life, and sets forth the remedy for many of our present ills in a life which he himself admits to be an ideal one. Much of the reasoning is sound," * * *

WM. E. BARBER, ESQ., *Westchester, Pa., says,*

* * * "I have been impressed by the perspicuity and systematic arrangement of its contents, and the originality of your views upon the topics discussed, and I am satisfied that you have opened up veins of thought which are fraught with results of the highest importance to the well-being of society. * * * I earnestly trust that you will be spared to continue your thoughtful investigations * * *."

REV. PROF. JOSEPH STEVENS, *Jersey Shore, Pa., says,*

* * * "Your elaborate work on Social Science * * * I feel gratified as the result of my examination, to be able to commend your work highly. It must have cost you much time and labor; and the department of science which it handles, being comparatively new and undeveloped must have rendered your task all the more arduous. But you seem to have accomplished your undertaking thoroughly and well."

REV. A. A. LIVERMORE, D.D., *Pres. Meadville Theological School, Pa., says,*

* * * "Your learned and elaborate work Principia. * * * I am sure by a look at its table of contents that it will repay a careful examination."

PROF. J. H. DILLINGHAM, *of Haverford College, Pa., says,*

"I much regret the long delay apparent in sending thee the acknowledgment of the receipt of thy very interesting work. * * * I hope soon to obtain time to read the work, connected as it is with my own department of instruction."

REV. W. F. P. NOBLE, *Chester Co., Pa., says,*

"I hasten to acknowledge your noble book, * * * You thinkers should publish *minutes*, like ecclesiastics, telling where you can be found."

PROF. TRAIL GEREN, M.D., *Lafayette College, Easton, Pa., says,*

* * * "I am glad to find so much that points to a higher relationship of the subject than I have seen in the works of other writers on Social Science. I shall have occasion to return to it when I have more leisure."

REV. SELDEN J. COFFIN, *Prof. of Mathematics Lafayette College, says,*

* * * "A beautiful volume. 'Principia,' bearing your name so modestly on the title-page * * *. Dr. Green and I were each touched by the Dedication. You are to be congratulated on the serviceable completion of so solid a piece of labor."

The "NEW YORK WORLD" *says,*

"The author of this remarkably original treatise informs us in his preface that among the * * * effects of the great rebellion was the turning of his attention to politics, and the stimulation of his ambition to promote the Christianization thereof by producing 'a volume that could safely be recommended to pious young men.' He differs from Comte in holding that 'metaphysics, ethics and religion' are branches of a really 'positive philosophy;' from Carey, in subordinating mercantile or financial to metaphysical considerations, and in foreseeing dire consequences from the increasing price of land and the approaching over-population of the world; Paley, whilst commendable for writing in the interests of revealed religion, fails to give sufficient weight to moral instincts; Spencer thinks too much of secular science and not enough of religion; Mill 'takes too much the commercial view of everything,' and is 'too essentially English;' Fourier alone takes a wide enough scope, and even he has adopted an ideal 'too high for the common world, and too low for the higher life.' Above physicists and statesmen, as teachers of social science, are placed theologians, and next to theologians are ranked the various sorts of communists. * * * His ideal is * * * Christian communism in incomes, labors and general life, doing to others perfectly as we would be done by. * * * Human society is divided into six component units—individual, family, social circle, precinct, nation, and mankind; * * * nations should be split up into very small precincts, each of which should have the utmost internal liberty and self-government, only being restrained by a præterpluperfect national government from trespassing on the equal liberty of other precincts. Law and war are to be replaced by arbitration and moral suasion; * * * and certain plentiful commodities adopted as the media of exchange. All these and many other details are elaborated with an infinite amount of philosophical argumentation."

The New York "HEBREW LEADER" *says,*

"J. B. Lippincott & Co., Philadelphia, have just issued a valuable work, entitled 'Principia; or Basis of Social Science.' * * * The author has spent several years of profound thought in the preparation of this work, patiently investigating kindred subjects by such writers as Comte, Carey, Paley, Spencer, Mulford, Mill, Guizot, and Fourier, and showing wherein he differs from them."

The "LIBERAL CHRISTIAN," *New York, says,*

"On page 19 we are told that 'Social Science may be defined to be the Philosophy of Politics;' and on page 20, that 'The science of society is the science of the dispensations of Providence.' Then on page 22 we are asked to 'observe the rank and grade of social science among the four most general sciences, namely: Theology,Metaphysics,Sociology and Mathematics.' We regret that Mr. Wright has not furnished a classification of the sciences; but he complains of want of space. * * * He hopes 'that if the public cannot tolerate these writings as a work of science, they will, at any rate, tolerate them as a kind of sermons to politicians and statesmen.' So mote it be."

REV. HENRY W. BELLOWS, D.D., *New York, says,*

"I * * * hope to have time in the course of my vacation to look into it. * * * I hope to receive instruction from your book, and am gratefully yours," &c.

CHARLES GOEPP, ESQ., *New York, says,*

"You have grappled with the most interesting of all subjects, collected most valuable facts, and made close research into recondite principles. * * * I believe that the best grade of German scholars would appreciate your work as well as, if not better than any English ones. * * * It would translate well."

E. STEIGER, ESQ., *New York, says,*

"It is encouraging to see that the momentous questions treated in your book have still sufficient attractions for superior minds in these material days. I trust that the great labor you have undergone in writing the work will be duly appreciated by the select and discriminating public for whose information it was written."

The Brooklyn "NATIONAL MONITOR" *says,*

"Social Science is yet in its infancy, and he who fosters it into maturity, or searches out its essential principia underlying the multiplicity of defective social systems, and brings them to the front, for foundation stones on which the ideal social system of nature and reason and revelation may be reared, will ever be remembered with gratitude by society, and handed down to succeeding generations as society's greatest benefactor. * * *

"Not however for this renown does the author of the elaborate work before us seem to have written. His Principia is the offspring of higher motives. * * * Each book is appropriately divided into chapters and sections, thus taking up every distinct theme in a separate chapter and section, so as to afford easy reference as a text-book on social science. * * * Upon the whole, the author has given to the public a book on social science that will be to society a strong push in the right direction."

REV. THOS. K. BEECHER, D.D., *Elmira, N. Y., says,*

* * * "is not mistaken in supposing me to be specially interested in such lines of thought and observation. From a reading of the first

35 or 40 pp. I perceive already that you and I have many things in common. My only hesitation is based on what may be called the inertia of ignorance. When you and other thinkers have solved the problem of a perfect social order, you will then have come only to where Jesus Christ was Eighteen Hundred years ago. * * * I assure you of my thanks * * * for a work of such scope and Christian wisdom."

REV. AUSTIN CRAIG, D.D., *Pres. Christian Biblical Institute, Stanfordville, N. Y., says,*

* * * "Outwardly as well as inwardly I find it a beautiful book. * * * It is full of good thoughts—worthily expressed. * * * Your spirit seems excellent everywhere; and (I believe) your work was (from the first) an offering to God and man; and so may man receive it, and God follow it with his blessing."

REV. PROF. C. W. NASSAU, D.D., *Lawrenceville, N. J., says,*

"You have my sincere good wishes for success to a work which has cost you so many years of patient labor."

PROF. R. P. STEBBINS, D.D., *Cornell University, says,*

"I shall read it during my vacation. The table of contents gives some very important topics."

REV. PETER B. HEROY, *Bedford, N. Y., says,*

"I was never more surprised than to receive your valuable book. * * * It must have been the work of your life. I intend, as I have time from my ministerial labors, to read it; and the more so as coming from the heart and intellect of one so well beloved in other days."

REV. CHARLES A. BECK, *Milford, N. J., says,*

"I consider the subject as one of the highest importance. * * * If there are errors in treating it, still we are to be thankful there is struggling toward the right. * * * I have no doubt I will be deeply interested in reading it."

REV. WM. H. PITTMAN, *Hopewell, N. J., says,*

"It is a book of great merit, a valuable addition to American and Christian literature: it is a book that every minister and statesman ought to have. * * * Every subject and division is made plain."

The Boston "ZION HERALD" *says,*

"This volume * * * is a conscientious and thoughtful effort to solve the problem of the best conditions for man's social well-being. The writer has read widely, and criticises without hesitation the systems of Comte, Spencer, Fourier, and J. S. Mill. He illustrates freely his own themes from the whole breadth of social science literature. The outcome of all his thinking, large portions of which are very suggestive and valuable. * * * The evident sincerity, honesty, and hearty conviction of the author constantly impresses you; * * * the book amply repays the reading, by its wholesome suggestions upon many subordinate themes relating to social development, public health and morals, international intercourse, and the removal of the great evils that now press upon society."

The "BOSTON GLOBE" *says,*

* * * "The author admits that Herbert Spencer is the King of the Social Scientists. * * * Fourier's Ideal is said to be too high for the common world and too low for the higher life. The author considers that society is held together by and happiness in it depends upon, Love of the other sex, Acquaintanceship, Material or business interests, Education, its interests and its literature, Goodness, namely, doing justice to others, and forbearance under injustice, real or apparent. There are some excellent ideas in this volume. * * * The book is well worth reading, though its advanced views will hardly find acceptance among practical statesmen."

The "BOSTON TRANSCRIPT" *says,*

* * * "In his preface the author briefly compares the principal characteristics of his work with those of Comte, Carey, Paley, Spencer, Mulford, Mill, Guizot and Fourier, stating wherein he differs from the

theories advanced by them, and acknowledges his indebtedness for encouragement and aid, to the Bible, Appletons' Cyclopedia, Wheaton, Ruskin, Tennyson, Guizot, De Tocqueville, J.F. Cooper, Schleiermacher and Mc'Cosh, and to Ballou, Nordhoff and various writers, Catholic and Protestant, on natural theology, theism, communism, and the higher life of the Individual Soul. * * * Enough has been stated to show the formidable nature of the task which the author has undertaken. To explain and illustrate his manner of executing it would occupy columns instead of paragraphs."

The Boston "LITERARY WORLD" *says*,

"A very formidable-looking volume is R. J. Wright's 'Principia; or Basis of Social Science'. * * * To ascertain by careful perusal the character and purpose of this work would be a task of no little magnitude, and to record one's discoveries would be a still greater one. We despair of conveying an adequate idea of the contents of this ponderous volume, and refer our readers to the book itself."

The "BOSTON JOURNAL" *says*,

"The author * * * explains in his preface the points on which he differs from Comte, Carey, Paley, Spencer, Mulford, Mill and Fourier. The last named he regards as wide, rambling, and almost wild in his analogies and range of topics; and the scope of the other writers is too contracted. * * * The author's purpose is to consider in this volume the fundamental political organic principles, which in succeeding volumes he will apply to the solution of various social and political problems. The work is plainly the product of sincere and laborious thought, * * * it has a certain freshness and earnestness of statement which will incline the reader to overlook its obvious faults. * * * His sub-divisions are numerous, but well arranged and calculated to assist the reader."

WENDELL PHILLIPS, ESQ., *says*,

"Your interesting looking volume came yesterday. I have only time now to scan its table of contents—a rich carte—and I hope soon to find leisure to test your arguments. Accept my sincere thanks for the opportunity. These are to be *the* questions of the coming fifty years, and every contribution to their discussion is valuable,—indeed, as you suggest, the highest duty of a citizen."

MRS. JULIA WARD HOWE *says*,

"I am much obliged for the valuable gift * * * your 'Principia.' The perusal of the preface * * * has shown me that its scope and object are in sympathy with all that I most reverence in the present, or desire for the future. I intend to study your work carefully * * * what appears to me so well planned * * *".

REV. ADIN BALLOU, *Hopedale, Mass.*, *says*,

* * * "your able, instructive and valuable work. It is freighted with thought, knowledge and suggestion. * * * I have read what little I conveniently could of it since its receipt, but not enough to criticise worthily its manifold evolutions of data, much less to master its system of principles, reasonings and conclusions."

The "LOUISVILLE COMMERCIAL" *says*,

* * * "Of a work so elaborate as this, written in such a spirit and treating of such a large subject, we prefer not to express a decided opinion without a more careful and thorough examination than we have been able to give it. * * * This volume is designed to give the 'fundamental political organic principles.' * * * He has tried to write such a book that all liberal-minded people, whatever may be their religious or political views, may read it without pain or disturbance. * * * A book written in such a spirit and for such an object deserves careful consideration, no less than its size. * * * Whatever fate Mr. Wright's theories may meet at the hands of masters and competent critics in social science, he has certainly produced the most elaborate and high-reaching and thoughtful work on his subject that has appeared from an American pen. He apologizes for his style, * * * As a whole, it is a valuable contribution to our political

literature, and it would be a good thing if others of our men of mind and leisure would devote themselves to such studies as those of Mr. Wright, to which we owe this volume."

The "CINCINNATI TIMES" *says*,

* * * "A ponderous volume. * * * We wish the author could have held himself until cold weather—the book is too big a job for us at the present state of the thermometer."

The "CINCINNATI GAZETTE" *says*,

"Mr. Wright * * * asserts * * * that the progress of the human race in the highest aims of life, is too uncertain of proof, to be made the basis of a positive science. He * * * aims to elevate politics from the low ground which they have occupied, in our country especially, by pointing out the great truths which lie at the foundation of national existence.* * * We can only sketch the outlines of the author's design, and call the attention of thoughtful readers to his volume."

"HERALD OF GOSPEL LIBERTY," *Dayton, O., says*,

"A review of this book leads us to commend in it these valuable features: 1. The importance of the general subject. 2. Its numerous but appropriate subdivisions, embracing the whole field of Social Science. * * * 3. The author's thorough, steady, patient, and complete investigation of his theme. 4. His peculiar, natural, and acquired talents for investigating and discussing the subject, and for reducing it to practical rules of Christian ethics. 5. The evolving from the metaphysical and the abstruse of his subject, the simplest and most practical moral rules in all social, civil, and religious relations. 6. Such an arrangement and relation of subjects, as well as that full discussion and presentation of all its features, as adapts the book to a general want, and renders it of great worth — the book embracing 524 pages, and no repetition. Other points deserve commendation, while in a few things only is the work open to criticism. * * * But, compared with its many points of excellence, these few features of criticism sink almost from sight."

Contribution to "HERALD OF GOSPEL LIBERTY" *says*,

"The subject of which the book treats, * * * is at present commanding the attention of the most thoughtful and studious minds of this and other lands. * * * Wright has evidently devoted much careful and patient study to the investigation of the whole range of subjects embraced in his theme, and has talents which fit him in a peculiar manner for such a work. From a cursory examination of its pages, we are led to believe that this book possesses merits of a high order, and which should create for it a wide demand. * * *."
D. E. MILLARD.

"THE INTERIOR," *Chicago, says*,

"The Principia is a voluminous work on an immense subject. The subject embraces all the relations existing in society, and thus covers the sciences of Law, Government, Political Economy, and Moral Science, with many other lines of thought, which lie in the field of Philosophy. The author pursues the most of these more or less persistently, and always independently of the recognized leaders, Mill, Guizot, Paley, Comte, Spencer, etc., and in combating all of them he brings out a great variety of suggestions. Indeed the work under the author's plan of treatment became a kind of cyclopedia of social science. * * * From this it will be seen that the author is radical in his views throughout. And yet it is just this type of character whose works it is most interesting, and in one sense most profitable, to study. His devotion to a theory, and the earnestness and zeal of his researches which result from that devotion, give his discussions the interest of novelty as well as originality, often giving the reader, by suggestion, an entirely new view of an old subject. The style is strong and compact, and the work will be found a good investment for the student of politics, law, or any of the sciences included under the general subject."

The "CHICAGO JOURNAL" *says*,

* * * "The writer covers a great deal of ground, giving a vast amount of valuable information. * * * It contains the elements of a good book."

The Springfield "DAILY REPUBLICAN" *says*,

* * * "The quality of his culture may be seen from his chapter on theology as a prerequisite to the study of social science. Among his arguments to establish this relation is the statement that 'of the eminent men of the Christian world, a far larger portion of them are found to be the children of clergymen than of any other professionals;' also the fact that the theologians, Ximenes, Wolsey, Richelieu, Cranmer and Talleyrand became the best and foremost political statesmen of the world, and that the statesmanship of Rome, although clerical, 'is acknowledged to be the most far-reaching in the world.'"

The Chicago "TRIBUNE" *says*,

* * * "The arrangement * * * of the contents is unique; so is the style; so is the punctuation. * * * He calls especial attention to it. The following sentence, the end of the preface, may serve as a fair example: 'And finally, borrowing an idea from Paley, but revising it, we may say,—that we cannot see why, our having done, however feebly, yet as well as we were able, a work which seemed to be very much needed,—should hinder any other person from doing it as much better as he would choose to.'"

REV. G. C. HECKMAN, D.D., *Pres. of Hanover College, Ind., says*,

"Principia has just arrived. Many thanks. I will read it with great interest and care."

The St. Louis "GLOBE DEMOCRAT" *says*,

"This is an able and comprehensive survey of social science, from a moral and theological, and yet an exceedingly liberal and progressive stand-point. * * * Besides its voluminous character, it is a deeply-philosophical dissertation, and we adopt the author's suggestion not to judge it positively until it has been carefully considered, * * * we are inclined to look upon it as a valuable addition to the many valuable treatises which we already have upon the engaging subject of social science."

GOV. C. C. CARPENTER *of Iowa, says*,

* * * "So far as I have been able to examine the book, I find it original in thought and style, and I believe it will be calculated to promote thought and investigation, and to greatly increase an intelligent comprehension of the special subjects upon which it treats. I hope it may be generally read by thinkers upon social questions, and that you may have the pleasure of witnessing the results of your study and labor in the improvement of the social philosophy and practical methods of the age."

PROF. DANIEL SCHINDLER, *Prof. of Metaphysics in Michigan University, says*,

* * * "I have not yet had time to do more than run over the table of contents, and here and there to open and look at your book. I have seen and read enough, however, to assure me that your flow is individual, and your discussion positive, and that you have made genuine contributions toward the solution of some of the vexed problems of Social Science. I shall take pleasure in giving the Principia a careful perusal during my vacation. * * * I hope God may give you life and health to complete the flood of work you have marked out for yourself."

L. C. DRAPER, ESQ., *Sec'y of the State Hist. Soc. of Wisconsin, says*,

"Our librarian has acknowledged the receipt of your fine volume. We are always glad to add such to our library. * * *

"I have the honor to inform you that at a meeting of the Exec. Com. of the State Hist. Soc. of Wisconsin held this day, you were unanimously elected a corresponding member."

REV. GEORGE D. STEWART, D.D., *Omaha, Neb., says*,

"I think the book evinces much

careful study and mastery of the problems of sociology. * * * The object and aim are worthy of yourself, and should commend themselves to every man who lives and works in the Christian spirit. * * * It is a fine specimen of American book-making as regards the mechanical execution. It is good for tired or strained eyes. The dedication is very touching to all of us who know the facts."

The Baltimore "METHODIST PROTESTANT" *says,*

* * * "Anything like a faithful and exhaustive notice of such a volume would require the space of a quarterly review. * * * The author, in his preface, has outlined our labor in a brief but clear dissection of its contents. * * * In this volume he gives only the fundamental political organic principles. He professes to write free from prejudice as to existing parties, and to have prepared a volume which can be safely recommended to pious young men and students for the ministry, who desire to keep abreast with the age on this subject. In this light especially, our own examination of it leads us to endorse the work as the most compact and yet comprehensive of the science of which we have knowledge. It should find a place in the library of every minister who would cultivate enlarged views of a thinking period. It is most thorough in its treatment. * * * It is a book for study and reference, and a most valuable addition to the discussion of an eminently important subject."

The Baltimore "EPISCOPAL METHODIST" *says,*

* * * "It is philosophical in its scope of thought and modes of inquiry, and after giving the author's definition of social science, endeavors to show its relation to other sciences. It proposes to carry into social science the same wide spirit of harmony and generalization that Schleiermacher carried into theology. Recognizing the Divine character and renovating influence of Christian truth, it proposes to bring its influence to bear upon the political system of the world, and thus contribute by its reflex bearings to the moral regeneration of mankind."

The "BALTIMORE AMERICAN" *says,*

* * * "This volume is presented to the public in the humble, but earnest desire of being able to contribute his mite to the Christianization of politics, the promotion of real freedom and progress and the improvement of society, firmly believing that the promotion of freedom and progress in this world is aid to the salvation of souls in the next world."

The "NEW ORLEANS BULLETIN" *says,*

"The author * * * offering his work as a mite contributed towards the promotion of real freedom and progress, and the improvement of society. He defines Social Science as the 'Philosophy of Politics,' and therefore specially worthy the thoughtful consideration of American citizens, to whom we therefore commend the work."

The "LONDON SATURDAY REVIEW," *England, says,*

* * * "We have three works on political science, none of them entirely without claim to attention. Mr. R. J. Wright, in his Principia, undertakes to reconstruct not merely the basis of social science, but that of political society itself. His political order is to be founded on the aggregation of a multitude of Precincts, * * * with a population ranging from that of a village to that of a moderate-sized town. Each of these is to constitute itself, by force of social affinities and the attraction of like to like, of families in the same state of moral advancement, intellectual education, refinement, and general social character; room is also to be made for societies of special tenets and tendencies. * * * This is the basis * * *:—the general construction of the edifice, the details of each successive enlargement of the self-governing area and corresponding reduction of the powers of government, and the distribution of different functions among the different ruling bodies, we must leave the reader to study in the volume itself."

ADDITIONAL NOTICES.

HERBERT SPENCER, *London, Eng., says,*

"I have to thank you for a copy of your Principia, etc., brought over by my friend Prof. Youmans. * * * I am glad to see a work which, though in some respects divergent from my own views, is in others coincident with them. All such efforts to diffuse larger conceptions must be beneficial."

T. W. HIGGINSON, *Newport, R. I., says,*

"I have read with especial interest that portion of it relating to the organization of labor by association. * * * Your book must represent a great deal of study and work, and you deserve much credit for putting so much sincere labor into it, and carrying it out so thoroughly."

The "PRINCETON REVIEW" *says,*

* * * "Whatever success the author may have attained or failed of, * * * he has given out no second-hand or hackneyed views. His book is the fruit of long observation, careful study and profound thinking. It abounds in reasonings which are original, often just and generally, even when obnoxious to criticism, highly suggestive.

* * * "The author shows a breadth and depth of view quite beyond that of average specialists and writers on it, or its different branches, in the importance which he assigns to theology, metaphysics, psychology, ethics, in short all the mental sciences, as a needful propædeutic for mastering sociology. Here he is *toto cœlo* above, as well as different from, Comte, and the entire school of positivists, sensualists and materialists. * * * Mr. Wright justly says: 'The study of theology is the scientific study of religion, and, therefore, calls into exercise the higher faculties of the mind. Hence, it is one of the best preparations, for earnest original study in any of the sciences.' * * * — * * *'

"The above quotations will be found scattered, from pages 31 to 36, inclusive, and will suffice to give a taste of the book, which may lead some to a further examination of it. While we highly value it, we dissent from some of its positions.* * *

"We regret that the foregoing notice, prepared for a previous number, has been, by inadvertence, delayed until now."

The "INDEPENDENT," *New York, says,*

* * * "The subdivision of topics * * * is exceedingly minute. * * * Mr. Wright regards social science as 'a kind of high politics.' He makes it so high and at the same time so comprehensive, as to embrace nearly all the other sciences. * * * Mr. Wright shows much reading on the subject of which he treats and large industry in collecting materials, while he is scholarly and generally lucid in his style."

The "EVENING TELEGRAPH," *Philadelphia, says,*

"An introduction to a new system of philosophy, which shall be distinctively American and distinctively Christian. * * * A work like Mr. Wright's, that is so full of carefully-digested information on a large number of important topics, can scarcely be perused otherwise than with profit. The topics discussed * * * are all, or nearly all, of an eminently practical character which have a bearing upon the governmental problems which we are endeavoring to solve in this country, and as such they merit the attention of those who desire to understand and to perform with the best effect all the duties of citizenship."

The "BANNER OF LIGHT," *Boston, says,*

"Mr. Wright has in this large volume shown himself the master of all the schools, whose peculiarities he exposes in a full and fair manner, desirous of nothing but arriving at the truth. * * * How faithfully he has done this can only be learned from a studious perusal of his volume, upon whose pages are to be seen the proofs of patient and well-directed thought and the most painstaking investigation. * * * To be welcomed by all such as are in earnest rather for the truth than for the support of any preconceived theory. The author, after all, pretends to have done no more than lay down the principles of the science in this volume, but in mastering them a key is obtained to the whole subject."

The "CHRISTIAN ADVOCATE," *New York, says,*

"This is the work of an author with whom we have not heretofore been acquainted—which fact, however should not be construed as proof that he has been unknown. We suspect that he is somewhat of a solitary student, and much more conversant with books than with men. * * * In his religious philosophy he seems to be of the best Christian type, and in his political philosophy he is purely and broadly American. * * * There need be no hesitation, however, to say that it contains a vast amount of valuable materials, and to the intelligent reader who looks beneath the surface of things it will prove provocative of valuable thoughts."

The "PITTSBURGH COMMERCIAL" *says,*

"Very many will be surprised to find this such a sensible work, judging it by its title. * * * The unique style, correctness and freshness of statements, make the reader lose sight of the mode of reasoning and peculiar forms of thought. * * * Without concurring in all the author's opinions, we find much in the work to admire, and particularly the high tone and conscientious effort to solve the problem of man's social well-being."

The "CHRONICLE AND NEWS," *Allentown, Pa., says,*

"The work is one of advanced ideas, the author differing materially upon many points with writers upon kindred subjects. The vexed problems of social life are discussed so honestly that the reader cannot fail to be impressed with the writer's earnestness in his expressed desire to be able to help promote progress, improve society and benefit mankind. * * * We advise those interested in the subject to read the book itself, assuring them that it will well repay perusal."

The "CHRISTIAN ERA," *Boston, says,*

"In the fullness of its table of contents, * * * in the cyclopediac range of its topics, embracing 'high politics,' theology, metaphysics, moral philosophy, political economy, the science of government, the science of physical man, and miscellaneous topics relating to the development and progress of the race; in the minuteness of its sub-divisions, * * * in the originality of its punctuation marks, * * * in the singularity of its syntax, * * * this 'Principia' is not merely an imposing and curious, but a ponderous and unique book. As an illustration of a peculiar method of literary work, * * * it is the most extraordinary volume we have ever encountered."

The "CHURCHMAN," *New York, says,*

"At the first glance this seems an imposing work. The size of the book, the very title, and a glance at the table of contents, filling nearly twenty pages, and embracing almost a cyclopedia of topics, impressed us as only things of vastness can, and we prepared ourselves for solid reading and close thinking. * * * We venture to suggest whether principles so very vague as those which he proposes to make the basis of Social Science, including theology and morality, can be of much use in preparing young men for the Ministry. 'High Church, Low Church, and no Church' are all the same to him. * * * As to the work itself we have little to say."

The "EPISCOPAL REGISTER," *Philadelphia, says,*

"We do not feel ourselves prepared to enter into any full review of this work. The author has made his subject a study, and writes in the interest of religion."

MISS E. P. PEABODY, *Cambridge, Mass., says,*

"The book * * * is very interesting; but I have not read it carefully enough to speak of it worthily. * * * A gentleman friend of mine has your volume now STUDYING it. * * * He says it is very interesting."

JOHN JORDAN, JR., ESQ., *for the Historical Society of Pa., says,*

"I am directed by the Society to communicate to you their thanks * * * for Principia. * * * We gladly welcome * * * this exceedingly interesting work as an acquisition to our collection. * * * We will be happy to receive your visits here."

REV. J. F. GARRISON, *Camden, N. J., says,*

"The subject is one of supreme importance. * * * It concerns the church even more than the state. * * * One statement gives me much assurance of a satisfactory discussion; and that is your purpose to make use of metaphysical considerations in settling your principia * * * —the right point of view from which to approach the whole subject.'"

WM. WELSH, ESQ., *Philada., says,*

"Mr. Wright will please accept my acknowledgments of his kind remembrance of his old neighbor." * * *

"On the receipt of your Principia I hoped to get time to study it carefully."

REV. T. J. SHEPHERD, D.D., *Phila., says,*

"I thank you very heartily for the volume, and I should be glad, when leisure offers, to read it. * * * I will be happy to see you and to express my acknowledgments in person."

T. W. WORRELL, ESQ., *Frankford, Pa., says,*

"I anticipate great pleasure as well as profit in the reading."

JOSEPH MOORE, *Pres. Earlham Col., Richmond, Ind., says,*

* * * "A book which from what I have observed thus far, promises to be of great value in my profession (teaching)."

E. F. STEWART, ESQ., *Easton, Pa., says,*

"You seem to have taken a broader and more philosophical view of the subject than any of your predecessors or compeers."

REV. J. P. WATSON, *Troy, O., says,*

"I am truly grateful to you, and have, so far, much enjoyed its examination."

REV. J. E. NASSAU, D.D., *Warsaw, N. Y., says,*

"A handsome volume, a sort of thesaurus on Social Science. * * * I am glad to see that the Alumni of Lafayette are making their mark in the literary and scientific world, as well as in other avenues of usefulness."

REV. O. O. WRIGHT, *Fall River, Mass., says,*

"I have been studying it carefully, that I might tell you what it is to me. I find a deep interest and much profit in it. * * * I feel that it is calculated to do great good."

REV. J. D. NORMANDIE, *Portsmouth, N. H., says,*

"I shall read it with much interest as soon as I can."

The "INQUIRER," *London, England, says,*

"Writers on Sociology * * * may be and frequently are very able and accomplished men, like the author of this volume. * * * Although * * * perplexed * * * we have yet formed a high opinion of the author as an earnest and sincere thinker, animated by a generous desire to correct some of the miseries and evils of the social state under the existing forms of civilization. * * * The author seems to have bestowed an immense deal of labor on his work; * * * but we doubt much if any one knows or can know, within the compass of earthly life, all the elements —not even all the fundamental ones —that belong to * * * human society. * * * As for their number they are just as likely to be six hundred as six. These inner mysteries of human nature may be sneered at by practical men as 'airy nothings,' but without them none of the so-called facts of life would have 'a local habitation and a name.' * * * Our author * * * does not invest his ideal communities with *couleur de rose* and an atmosphere all blessedness and joy. * * * Society needs change, and society will have it in time. * * * We hope such of our readers as are interested in the science of Sociology will look into this volume."

PRINCIPIA

OR

BASIS

OF

SOCIAL SCIENCE.

BEING A SURVEY OF THE SUBJECT FROM THE MORAL AND THEOLOGICAL, YET LIBERAL AND PROGRESSIVE STAND-POINT.

BY
R. J. WRIGHT.

SECOND EDITION.

PHILADELPHIA:
J. B. LIPPINCOTT & CO.
1876.

DEDICATION.

TO THE MEMORY OF MY DEAR DEPARTED SISTER,

JOSEPHINE AMANDA WRIGHT:—

BY WHOSE SELF-SACRIFICE, UNTO DEATH, I WAS ENABLED TO SURVIVE, AND TO WORK, AND TO PRODUCE THESE AND OTHER WRITINGS:—

This Work is Affectionately and Reverently Dedicated

BY HER LIVING MONUMENT,

R. J. W.

PREFACE.

FIRST. In presenting a new work on any subject, it seems proper that the writer should commence his preface to it, by pointing out wherein his work differs from, or is called for by, the characteristics of other and abler works, already in the same field. Therefore we will briefly compare the principal characteristics of ours, with such works.

From Comte we differ;—First. In adding metaphysics to his merely physical sciences, and in maintaining the idea, that metaphysics, ethics, and religion, are branches of a really "positive philosophy." Second. By denying that the progress of the human race in the highest aims of life, is anything like so well proved in history, as to be made the *basis* of a "Positive Science."

From Carey we differ;—First. In making much more use of metaphysical considerations, and less, of merely mercantile or financial ones. Second. In believing that the price of land IS increasing with fearful rapidity, and bringing evils on earth, as yet but little anticipated. Third. In admitting that the population of the world IS approaching, and will approach, a density that will puzzle social science, morality, and religion, to provide against the evils thereof. Fourth. Mr. Carey has too much animosity, and is too bitter against England.

From Paley we differ, chiefly;—In our estimating the moral instincts, as on a PAR with reasonings from expediency: and in regard to views arising from the differences between monarchy and democracy; and about the pre-eminent value of the British Constitution. But we agree with him particularly, in that our work, like his, is written avowedly in the interests of revealed or traditionary religion.

As to Spencer; we admit he is *the* King of the Social Scientists; but think, First, that unless by his metaphysical argumentation, he does not differ from Comte so much as he appears to think he does: except that Comte was avowedly atheistic, but Mr. Spencer is rather deistic. Mr. Spencer seems to work chiefly in the interests of secular science; but *we* work chiefly in the interests of religion, and of scientific statesmanship. And our work differs so much from his, in ideas, conclusions, methods, classifications, and spirit,—that we can only refer the reader to the whole course of the works, respectively.

From Mulford we differ, chiefly;—In objecting to the predominance which he gives to the rights of Nation, over all the other Elements of humanity, and of social science; and object, that his work has a less wide scope than either Fourier's, Comte's, Spencer's, or Mill's.

With regard to J. S. Mill;—He is a valuable writer, and we often quote from him, as confirmatory proof, but he does not allow enough for the demands of human *feeling;* besides, he takes too much of the commercial view of everything. Furthermore; Mill is too essentially English, and European,—in the plans which he proposes, and in those which he opposes; and in the arguments which he adduces.

Guizot's "History of European Civilization" is a first class work, and has been well abridged; but its scope is only historical, and European; and its *form* is not scientific, but rather narrative.

None of these writers, except Fourier, takes a wide enough scope. Comte and Spencer omit the *true* moral and theological bearings. Paley omits the Physico-Scientific.

As to Fourier; He is so wide in his analogies, and range of topics, as to be almost wild in those respects. Besides, his IDEAL is too high for the common world, and too low for the higher life; and requires a larger number of persons for a single "phalanx," than can easily be obtained for such experiments.

SECOND. The authors or works to whom this writer is most indebted for encouragement and aid; besides those above mentioned,—are, the Bible; Appleton's Cyclopædia; Wheaton, Ruskin, Tennyson, Guyot, De Tocqueville, F. Cooper, Schleiermacher, and M'Cosh; also to Ballou, Nordhoff, "The Circular" and other writers on Communism, and to the various works on Natural Theology, Theism, etc.; and to various writers, Catholic and Protestant, on the higher life of the Individual-soul.

And besides this general acknowledgment, the endeavor has been made all along, to give the authorities and exact quotations, in their respective places. A general acknowledgment is also due here, to a host of American historians, statesmen, and commentators on the Constitution of the United States,—whom he has read and heard and admired from early boyhood.

THIRD. The writer's own aims in, and view of this volume, may be stated as follows: Politics, which, previous to the Great Rebellion, he had considered as, in this country, but little more than party squabbles for place, and for words,—rose up before him, after the war, as *the* object to which he desired to devote some of his best time and thought. And this volume is a part of the results. It is one of a series, taking a survey of the subject from the moral and theological, yet liberal and progressive stand-point. The series has been several years under thought, and in preparation. And this volume gives only the fundamental political organic principles. The writer's scientific thoughts are generally arranged as arguments for one and another of his proposed ideals. Because an ideal is a theory. And, "not to have an ideal higher than ourselves," or than our common institutions, is to let ourselves and our institutions go downwards by the gravitating force of inherent evils. Yet he has endeavored to write in such a spirit, and to produce such a volume, that all liberal-minded and liberal-hearted persons, might read it, without pain or disturbance; either to their religious convictions, whether high-church, low-church, or no church: or to their political feelings, whether Democrats, Republicans, or whatever else they might be:—and furthermore, a volume that could safely be recommended to pious young men, especially to students for the ministry, who really desired to be useful, and to be abreast of their age, on this subject. In that spirit he presents the volume to the public, in the humble but earnest desire, of being able to contribute his mite, towards the Christianization of politics, the promotion of real freedom and progress, and the improvement of society: firmly believing, that the promotion of freedom and progress in this world, is aid to salvation of souls in the next world.

Its method of discussion aims to be, by reverting constantly to general fundamental principles, instead of to the passions or prejudices of the day, or age, or country. It endeavors to see the inside of its subjects impartially, and to harmonize contending truths; and on new, and American principles. It attempts to carry into Social Science and Politics, the same wide spirit of harmony and generalization, for the sake of conciliation, that Schleiermacher so successfully carried into Theology.

The work will sometimes have occasion to censure the faults and sins of governments, of our own, as also of others. And like all other rebukes to wrongs and evils, the more opposition the censures meet, or the less welcome their reception is, the more it would prove that they *were really needed:* At any rate, the work is published from a sense of duty to God: and bearing in mind Froebel's words, "come let us live for our children."

FOURTH. As to the title, we call it "*Principia* or Basis of Social Science," as referring, *not* to our treatment of the subject; but to the five great heads or topics here treated, and to their superior and more general relation to the several other topics, which we propose to publish at some future time,—in other volumes, with *other titles*. Therefore, this volume needed *some* appropriate title appended to the term Social Science, to distinguish it from them. And, should the remaining volumes of this series be published, they will be less abstract, and more immediately practicable, than this one.

FIFTH. As to the Form and Style. The form of the book, and of its Divisions and Sub-Divisions, has merely grown up gradually out of the subject, and of the author's method of studying it, namely, first analytically and inductively,—and afterwards synthetically and deductively.

As to the Style. The endeavor has been, to make it intelligible and unequivocal, to thoughtful readers with a tolerably fair English education, who are without much technical knowledge on the subjects treated. But still it seems true, that a study which ranges through most of the sciences, culling the gems, and extracting the essence, from many of them, cannot be *fully* understood, until *after* acquiring something, both of the general knowledge, and of the general discipline of mind, that are acquired by those studies. Moreover, for instance, Primers, or even early schoolbooks of any science, *cannot be produced until after* the principles of the science become pretty well established; so that *then* many preparatory arguments may be dispensed with. To make a work on this subject intelligible to all, would therefore be, to make it, either, so primer-like, or so prolonged and diffuse, as to cut it off from the sympathies and attentions of those who, in reality, were most likely to study it. As to such matters, and in the present early condition of Social Science, all works concerning it, ought to be compared, *not* with works on Chemistry, or Astronomy, or even Moral Philosophy, or Political Economy; but rather, with works on Geology or Metaphysics.

For the defects of style; and lack of thorough revision, both previous to, and whilst going through the press,—the writer must beg the indulgence of the public,—especially on the grounds of advancing years, and of much enfeebled health.

As to the *punctuation*,—IT is, generally, according to the author's own rules; and he therefore relieves all other persons from responsibility for its general deviation from the ordinary customs thereof. For, in his view, punctuation should be adapted to suit readers, and students, rather than hurried reviewers; and should principally aim to give most of the pauses for reading, and for making the meaning distinct and unequivocal, and, even obvious to the unlearned; and especially so, in abstract writings; also remembering that it is *easier to remove* punctuation marks from stereotyped plates, *than* to insert them therein.

SIXTH. But after all, there may be deemed necessary, some excuse for the writer's presuming to publish his work *at all*, on such an *exalted* topic.

Well: He does not pretend to class this work, as at all on a par with the works of the other great names already mentioned. He does not claim any pre-eminent ability, but only, patient study and laborious thought. Yet he remembers, that as Spencer himself says, (Westminster Review, vol. 67, page 243): "In science, as in life, every man, strong or weak, carries his burden but a little way, and then gives place to a younger." And perhaps this remark may apply even to the great names above mentioned, as well as to others, as also to his own. However, he hopes that his thoughts, at any rate, will at least serve as *suggestions* to others, and that they will stimulate others to produce better and more readable works on the subject, whilst also retaining soundness in Morals and Theology. And he hopes also, that if the public cannot tolerate these writings, as a work of science, they will, at any rate, tolerate them as a kind of sermons to politicians and statesmen. And he is quite willing that no persons other than those who are given to these kinds of studies, or who desire to become so, will read his book at all.

The concluding words of one of Mr. Wheaton's prefaces, seem appropriate here; and are:—"The knowledge of this science has, consequently, been justly regarded as of the highest importance to all who take an interest in political affairs. The Author cherishes the hope that the following attempt to illustrate it, will be received with indulgence, if not with favor, by those who know the difficulties of the undertaking."

Accordingly, we ask critics to be indulgent, and to let the volume have time to be clearly understood, consistently in its various parts,—before they extinguish it utterly. And finally; borrowing an idea from Paley, but revising it, we may say,—that, we cannot see why, our having done, however feebly, yet as well as we were able, a work which seemed to be very much needed,—should hinder any other person from doing it as much better as he would choose to.

TABLE OF CONTENTS.

BOOK I.

SUMMARY INTRODUCTION TO SOCIAL SCIENCE.

PART I.

PRINCIPLES OF THE STUDY.

PART II.

PRINCIPLES OF SOCIETY ITSELF.

BOOK II.

THE PRECINCT.

PART I.

GENERAL VIEW OF THE THEORY OF THE PRECINCT.

PART II.

SPECIAL ARGUMENTS FOR THE THEORY.

PART III.

CONCLUSION OF THE PRECINCT:
PARTIAL APPLICABILITY BY CHARTERS.

BOOK III.
THE NATION.

PART I.

THE NATION AS A FUNDAMENTAL ELEMENT.

PART II.

INTERNATIONAL LAW.

PART III.

THE DOCTRINE OF NATURALIZATION.

BOOK IV.

CORPORATION.

MAIN DIVISION I.

ARGUMENT FOR POLITICO-GOVERNMENTAL CORPORATIONS.

SUB-DIVISION I.

ANTICIPATIONS OF GOVERNMENTAL CORPORATIONS.

SUB-DIVISION II.

RIGHT OF GOVERNMENTAL CORPORATION.

SUB-DIVISION III.

ADVANTAGES OF GOVERNMENTAL CORPORATIONS.

SUB-DIVISION IV.

PRACTICABILITY OF GOVERNMENTAL CORPORATIONS.

MAIN DIVISION II.

GENERAL SURVEY OF ALL KINDS OF CORPORATIONS, ACCORDING TO THEIR SEVERAL NATURES.

SUB-DIVISION I.

RELATIONS TO THE OTHER ELEMENTS OF SOCIAL SCIENCE.

SUB-DIVISION II.

MISCELLANEOUS CORPORATIONS.

MAIN DIVISION III.

CORPORATIONS WITH POLITICO-GOVERNMENTAL FUNCTIONS.

SUB-DIVISION I.

PRELIMINARIES.

BOOK V.

LIMITED COMMUNISM.

MAIN DIVISION I.

NATURE OF COMMUNISM.

SUB-DIVISION I.

IDEA OF COMMUNISM.

SUB-DIVISION II.
FOUNDATIONS OF COMMUNISM.

MAIN DIVISION II.

THE COMMUNITY'S PRECAUTIONS AND GUARDS AGAINST INDIVIDUALS.

SUB-DIVISION I.

WAYS AND METHODS OF PRECAUTION.

SUB-DIVISION II.

APPLICATION AND RECEPTION OF NEW MEMBERS.

SUB-DIVISION III.

GENERAL TESTS AND QUALIFICATIONS.

MAIN DIVISION III.

THE INDIVIDUAL'S GUARDS AND PROTECTION AGAINST THE COMMUNE.

SUB-DIVISION I.

FROM THE COMMUNE AS A SOCIETY.

SUB-DIVISION II.

PROTECTION OF THE INDIVIDUAL MEMBERS FROM THE RULERS AND OFFICERS, AS PERSONS.

MAIN DIVISION IV.

USES, INCLUDING ARGUMENTS AND STATISTICS, OF COMMUNISM.

SUB-DIVISION I.

ARGUMENTS FROM SCRIPTURE.

SUB-DIVISION II.

ARGUMENTS FROM THE UTILITIES OF COMMUNISM.

SUB-DIVISION III.

STATISTICS.

BOOK I.

SUMMARY INTRODUCTION.

PART I.

PRINCIPLES OF THE STUDY.

CHAP. I. IN GENERAL.

THIS article (namely "Book I.") proposes to give the theory of Social Science in its *Universal* Principles. These principles (or laws) of Social Science, may be divided into two sorts. One sort relates to the progress of the SCIENCE; and the other sort relates to the movements of SOCIETY itself. Accordingly, this Summary Introduction is divided into two parts; corresponding to those two sorts of laws. It proposes, in its first part, to consider the nature and laws of Social Science as a STUDY: and then, in its second part, endeavors to point out some of the fundamental and spontaneous powers and principles of society itself. And in this second part, the Introduction proposes to touch *only* the formulæ and laws, which are too general for any other position in the science: because all the remainder of our books on this subject, will be devoted to the FURTHER elucidation of those objective principles of SOCIETY. But as to the laws of the STUDY, we shall but seldom ever refer to them again, after we shall have passed through the first part of this Introduction.

CHAP. II. DEFINITION OF SOCIAL SCIENCE.

Social Science may be defined to be the Philosophy of Politics. It is a kind of *high-politics*, and ought therefore to be in the front rank of the sciences for Americans; yet, from its relation to morals and metaphysics and class prejudices, it cannot be studied with the same degree of disregard of subjective and personal feelings and notions, with which other sciences may be pursued. In this respect it is like its kindred studies history and theology. Hence, more than in any other study, the *animus* of the writer must be borne in mind, and be duly allowed for. Social Science is moral in its very nature; although hitherto it seems to have been abandoned to the "infidels" and the socialists.

The fundamental conception of Comte's work, after eliminating its atheism, is a conception at once not only of the highest generalization, but also of deepest insight. It is the conception that Social Science comes in place of an obsolete ecclesiastical and metaphysical positive theology, and tends to produce a new intellectual hierarchy. This conception arises from the insight, that just as Social Science is now practically the most general and the most all-embracing of the sciences, including even theology and religion itself; so, in the preceding ages, theology had been the most general of them all. Hence it was, that it had absorbed the greatest and best minds of the Middle Ages: and hence too it was, that the churchmen of those days were the greatest statesmen, and that the statesmen of the Roman Church are seldom surpassed, even at this late day. And our Bolingbroke calls religion "The First Philosophy," which is true in more senses than he meant it.

But in assenting to Comte's assertion, that Social Science comes in place of an obsolete metaphysical theology,—we are to be understood, as only referring to their functions in the organization of *church* and of *state;* but not at all as referring to their functions in the contemplation of religion *by the Individual.*

The science of society is the science of the dispensations of Providence. Because, so far as Providence is only general, and is fulfilled by regular laws, and in the order of cause and effect, so far it must be fulfilled by the progress and laws of society, as much as it is fulfilled in this life at all. This is the same thing in effect, as to say that Sociology is the study of the laws of Providence. All history and all Social Science abound with facts illustrative of this idea. And yet, most religious people seem to think, that Providence will take care of things so well that there is no se for Social Science; yet one of the very ways whereby Providence *does* take care of things, is by the teaching of examples. And these examples, it is the special business of Social Science to study and to classify. And some religionists even fling the insinuation against Social Scientists, that they are trying to "help God govern the world." But the same objection lies equally strong, against the followers of every science which has for its direct object to benefit man; and especially against doctors of medicine. And the objection lies much stronger against theologians and churchmen, that THEY are trying to help God govern the world. Yet St. Paul expressly says, "We are laborers together with God." (1 Cor. iii. 9, and 2 Cor. vi. 1.) And the fact is, that everybody, so far as he uses his faculties aright, helps God govern the world. And the only pity is, that religionists do not study divine Providence better; so that they would help God *more,* to govern the world.

If we turn now to practical applications, we will find that Social Science runs nearly parallel to Christianity, and often coincides with it. On this subject we will quote from Wendell Phillips, who will surely be held free from the charge of partiality towards religion. And observe, that what he says of the Church is equally true of the State; and THAT is the application we desire the reader to make, all through the quotation.

In his speech before the Free Religious Association, May 28, 1868, he says, "The records of Christianity hold, it seems to me, a very large measure of the lessons that Social Science needs. In the first place, *the Christian records are principles;* but the church is an alleviative. It approaches evils to alleviate them, not to cure them. THAT is not the New Testament method. There are two ways of touching evils. If the gas was escaping in this room we should open the ventilators and relieve ourselves. That is *relief.* To-morrow, the superintendent would send for a gas-fitter, and he would stop the leak. That is *cure.* Now, as I look at it, all action of the church approaches poverty to make it comfortable: it approaches crime to endeavor to soften it: it approaches prostitution, to shield it from temptation. *That* is relief. That is opening the windows to get rid of the leaking gas. But Social Science and the religious philosophy of the New Testament, while they attempt all that, prescribe that the really religious intellect should seek not relief, but cure."

Indeed, Social Science and Christianity run parallel to each other, most of their length: Social Science doing for society, in most things, what Christianity is doing for the individual.

CHAP. III. SCOPE OF SOCIAL SCIENCE.

§ 1. *In General.*

Now observe the rank and grade of Social Science among the *four* most general sciences; namely, Theology, Metaphysics, Sociology, and Mathematics, (Moral Science being here regarded as composed of elements or extracts, partly from Theology, and partly from Metaphysics;) and observe also, that their generalness is in the order above named, and that we only claim for our science, a position as *third* in this order of generality. But we have not space to enlarge upon this comparison.

§ 2. *Locus of intersection with the other sciences.*

We are now to consider the *locus*, that is to say, the principal points or properties, of the *intersection* of Social Science with the other sciences that are most nearly connected with it. We may consider criminal law, civil law, constitutional law, and international law, as separate parts of one general science, under the name of *the Law*. Then we may consider Political Economy as the science of producing and distributing property, or rather, as the science of industry. Then, by taking these two sciences together, namely the Law and Political Economy, we have the substance of Political Science. But, inasmuch as Political Science looks too much to *polity*, and to the present, it becomes necessary to consider the Philosophy of History, and thus, to perfect the politician into a statesman, by introducing the experience of the past. Now the Philosophy of History becomes the "History of Civilization," only when we assume a continual progress of civilization in all the past; and as this is a somewhat disputed question, the Philosophy of History is to be preferred as embracing the others.

But the statesmen produced by all the sciences just mentioned, have their ideas limited too closely to the facts and changes that are occurring in the present, or that actually have occurred in the past,—but without any philosophical conception of the radical changes that *might* occur. Their solutions and remedies are consequently too special, and have no scientific or absolute expressions or formulæ. Now the business of Social Science is, to investigate the changes of society by *general* principles, and to hold the results in general formulæ, of which all past and present facts are only particular instances.

Then it happens that statesmen sometimes find that morality and doing right are a safer guide than the highest wisdom of experience; and sometimes they would prefer to do right, whether it was expedient or not, as far as they can see. Here then, it becomes necessary to appeal to Moral Philosophy; but we consider Moral Philosophy only in the light of a combination of parts selected from Theology and Metaphysics. In considering formulæ so very general as they *then* become, Metaphysics is applied to also, because it treats of the most important laws of the very beings who constitute society. By this time the formulæ have become so very general, that the common classifications of historical facts become of less importance. Resort is then had for analogies to all the sciences, from Gravitation up to Zoölogy. The most general laws of universal nature are then found to be applicable.

In this respect, Social Science acts much like Natural Theology. It ranges through all the sciences, culling the general principles of each, digesting and assimilating them to itself. And while it omits not any one of the sciences, from the lowest to the highest; it nevertheless finds *most* of its nutriment in the higher ones, such as Zoölogy, Anatomy, Physiology, Instinct, Metaphysics, and Morals. And so wide is its range, that it touches all the sciences which earnest men think and feel about, in their deepest and most serious moments.

CHAP. IV. USES.

§ 1. *Implied in its Definition and Scope.*

Many of the uses are so plainly implied in its definition and scope, that they need not be repeated now, having been sufficiently touched above.

§ 2. *Magnitude of Civil and Political Evils.*

Nowhere are the intentions of men so often and so utterly frustrated, as in legislation. Here truly, "things are not what they seem." In this country, laws intended to preserve morality, to shut taverns on Sunday, or to close bawdy houses,—generally have as their main result, the causing bribes to be paid to policemen or other officials. Laws intended to limit the power of corporations, end with putting bribes into the pockets of the leaders of the legislature, or else of the judges. Laws intended to help a weak company, only help its directors to *help themselves* at the expense of the community. Laws intended to prevent gambling, only drive the gambling into commerce, and so, corrupt the channels of ordinary trade. Laws to compel specie payments, only shut up the banks altogether. Laws intended to befriend renters at the expense of owners, only drive honest and cautious men out of the business of renting entirely, and increase the competition among, and the risks to be paid by, the renters. Laws to oppress any class of people, first drive them to deception, and next drive them out of your jurisdiction, and next tend to raise up friends for the oppressed. Even fashion, intended originally to separate the great from the little, tends instead, to produce unusual extravagance, and finally becomes the mark of disreputableness. Customs intended to secure honest men, become only traps to catch the simple, or barricades to shield rogues.

The THEORY of politics and of trade and of the public press, is, OPEN knowledge or open market, and competition, and gradual changes: the PRACTICE of politics and trade is, false news, secret combinations, and sudden revolutions. Hence it is necessary, as Spencer says, to enquire, not only what is to be done, but also how to do it. A man intending to reach the moon, might rupture himself, and he would still reach his aim sooner than some legislators or leaders will reach *their* objects, by the means they are using: and the same will apply to some of the philosophers, and their proposed "*laws.*" And although most of these remarks apply more directly to statute law *only*, and not so plainly to those deeper and spontaneous social laws, which work, both over and under and within and without government,—yet in their spirit and principle, they apply *also* to those deep and spontaneous social laws. Thus there arises the necessity and the use of a true SCIENCE on the subject.

And then furthermore, our politicians and statesmen need such an enlarged scope of ideas as will set them to guarding against COMING evils, rather than to be forever providing against antiquated and worn-out ones. It is the misfortune of some peoples and of some governments, to be always guarding and fortifying themselves against old dangers, and in fear of a return of exploded errors. They are forever making constitutions and laws, to protect themselves from those evils which the progress of society, or its new form of government, has already rendered impossible; but yet, working in the midst of a verbiage of literality and legality and of cares and fears about "*the worn-out*,"—they are neglecting to see or provide for the very evils that are surrounding them, and it may be, even sapping the foundation of their rights, liberties, and happiness. This danger and evil, which is liable to befall any country, is especially the bane and hindrance to our own. In the midst of dangers from bribery by vast railway and other corporations, we provide against those only of individuals. In the midst of all the evils of demagogism, we are forever providing guards against monarchy. Governed and tyrannized over, by secret cliques of unprincipled and rapacious politicians, and their colleagued contractors,—we are continually guarding against an aristocracy of birth or honest wealth. Endangered by the scum and dregs of vice and prison degradation of all the world, we are forever providing against aristocracy. In the midst of a tangle of laws, allowing almost all criminals to escape, we are always providing more guards for the liberty of unknown and unsettled individuals, and thus fostering and covering individual secrecy.

One of the uses of Social Science, is to enable us to foresee great revolutions and rebellions; and either to avert them, or to provide means for personal escape or relief, when we cannot influence or prevent them. The Saviour says, "When they persecute you in one city, flee ye to another."

§ 3. *Philosophical Basis Wanted.*

Comte truly says, "In the present stage, philosophical contemplation and labors are more important than political action, in regard to social regeneration; because a *basis* is the thing wanted; while there is no lack of political measures, more or less provisional, which preserve material order from invasion by the restless spirits that come forth during a season of intellectual anarchy. The governments are relying on corruption and on repressive force, while philosophers are elaborating principles; and what the philosophers have to expect from wise governments is, that they will not interfere with the task while in progress, nor hereafter with the gradual application of its results."

We may observe, how much the need of Social Science is

shown and proved, by the mistakes and defects of the very men who have of late produced works on this science, including also Comte himself. We might mention their ignoring generally, the depth and reality of sin, and the real moral spontaneity of man. Also, Spencer's idea of the spontaneous evanescence of evil; also Spencer's idea, that the deadly and killing spirit was an absolute necessity to enable mankind to clear the world of the noxious animals; Comte's idea, that the social feelings wisely enlightened, are capable of enabling man to overcome and outgrow his own selfishness; Comte's idea of the power of physiological knowledge to overcome all evils; Buckle's idea, that society has derived *no* benefit from metaphysics; Mulford's idea, that nation is the only politico-social unit or person; some theologians' idea, that orthodoxy or conversion is alone sufficient to enable men to overcome evil;—and finally, that perversion of morals, which assumes that because social evils are the ordinance of Providence, therefore the effort to do away with them is contrary to Providence.

Social Science is passing through, or must yet pass through, its period of criticism, even as the other sciences do. Just as Comte has shown, that the critical "*régime*" in civilization and in social affairs, must necessarily only be transient and preparatory; so (to turn the tables upon him) *we* say, that the criticism and rejection of religion from science, will be found to be only a temporary and preparatory stage, although perhaps a necessary one; but that afterwards the critics will criticise away their criticisms, and so, God be restored to nature and to science, more fully and more truly than ever.

§ 4. *Improvement of Humanity consistent with free-will.*

There is in the minds of many persons, a lurking doubt of the use of Social Science; on the assumption, that the general course of human events is a fixed destiny. But to this we answer: the same objection might be made to the use of means, in many other matters of which we may believe the end to be fixed. And a still better answer is, that the objection is an unjustifiable inference from the facts adduced by it. It alleges the uniformity of certain very general facts found in statistical tables, such as that the number of deaths per year, on the average, is the same in different years, by each particular disease, and by suicide, and even by suicide in each particular occupation. But these facts only prove the doctrine of *chances;* the *law* of our BELIEF, but NOT the CAUSATION of events. And according to the doctrine of *infinity;* of an infinite number of really free acts, all will *not* go one way; for the larger the number of really free acts, the stronger is the certainty of our belief that their diversities will be exactly in proportion to their absolute freedom in each particular case. But this universality does not introduce any new element of *power*.

However, true knowledge lessens the power of, and hence lessens the freedom of evil. Thus Social Science benefits mankind by lessening the temptations, and by bettering the conditions.

We affirm that the improvement of humanity is consistent with free will. Temptation is a probationary and a proportional power. We set it down as a certain moral truth, that the greater the temptation to which Mankind are exposed, the greater will be the sainthood of those who overcome, but the fewer will be the number of the persons who *do* overcome; and vice versa. Even suppose that Social Scientists may not expect to make people religiously better, or even morally better, considered as to their heart or intention; yet they expect, by lessening the powers of temptation around people, to make them ACTUALLY both better and happier. For we all know that man is to some extent the creature of circumstances.

§ 5. *Influence on Other Sciences.*

Another use of Social Science is, that it brings improvements in all the various sciences, even in Mathematics; and this it does by their *reciprocal* influences, and from the very generalness of Social Science. This, Comte points out theoretically, and also illustrates it by his own example frequently, in pointing out improvements in the other sciences, evidently suggested by this one. Thus the study itself is most thoroughly made up of wisdom and progress.

When we consider the great elements of human progress, how indissolubly they are found to be connected with one another; we find that one will bring on another, as Comte remarks in regard to the relations of truth and beauty,—that while in the lower stages of civilization, the fine arts lead to intellectual culture, so in a higher stage of civilization, intellectual culture seeks at least its recreation in the fine arts. Thus, of inseparable elements, either one may be cause, and the other effect; so then, Theology and Social Science are related together so inseparably, that it may be hoped that in the future, Social Science will lead men back to Theology.

Comte himself, in his latter days, avows a Deity to be the ultimate compound and integration of humanity; and the doctrine of Deity, to be a necessary result of Sociology; thus showing, both by his experience and his theory, the intimate connection between Social Science and Theology.

Comte also teaches, that Social Science, in turn exerts a vastly improving power on the natural and biological sciences; so also we may hope it will, in turn, exercise a greatly improving influence on Theology itself, which is a pre-eminent branch of the Highest Biology!

§ 6. *Summary of Uses.*

In general we may say,—the use of Social Science is to point out how really to benefit mankind by law and voluntary benevolence, instead of by merely well-intentioned but vain and actually injurious attempts; to point out the natural rights and duties of all, and how really to accomplish them. The pursuit of Social Science would always be found to furnish "new themes to the Protestant clergy," and to all other clergies, and to all kinds of moral improvers. It would tend to the promotion of virtue and health, the prolongation of life, and to the general morality and happiness of mankind.

The sum of all the uses of Social Science is, that without its aid morality itself cannot prevail permanently among mankind. Accordingly, Comte (Pos. Phil. p. 787) says, "*A universal sentiment of duty can prevail only through the culture of the most general ideas, and thr ugh the rule of the spirit of generality.*" But observe, that the spirit of generality found only in Social Science, is just a new name for the prevalence of a morality founded on universal utilities, that is, a spiritual morality; as the spirit (in Metaphysics) is necessary to the prevalence of theoretical Theology. Again, Comte truly says, "The Theological sanctions of morality have become inefficient on the popular mind; yet morality itself, expressing as it does the feelings of humanity, craves, or is ready to receive, some other sanctions; and in cultivated civilization especially, is ready to receive intellectual sanction, that is, will welcome Social Science as the best substitute for *metaphysical* Theology."

§ 7. *Modes of Influence.*

Social Science in its application to the improvement of society, operates in two ways; one, by improving and enlightening the men who lead society; and the other, by enlightening contenting and keeping in order, the mass of the Individuals of which society consists, so that the natural laws of society's life have opportunity to develop and produce their results. And the science teaches all men more and more, the impotence of man in self-will, and the necessity of all to wait on Nature more reverently and patiently.

Furthermore, the improvement of the science affords the means for improving society itself, just as the improvement of *any* science, prepares the way for the improvement of all the arts that depend upon it.

Here it might be asked whether the influences of this science can ever become practically and politically available in a Republican government, especially in this country? We answer: the general knowledge which Social Science requires, (it being that science which takes only the general elements of all the sciences) —shows most readily to the general public, the real learning and the mental discipline of the study, and of its successful students. Moreover, the great principles of each of the sciences can be made very plain to the popular mind, according as one person or another has natural aptitude for each of the particular studies to which the general ideas belong. And by selecting and grasping several or all of these general ideas only, a Sociologist may be comprehended and appreciated by the masses, and exert an influence for good, even if the people were not able to comprehend his plan or theories AS A WHOLE. And the fact is, the GENERAL elements of the sciences are just the ones that are easiest remembered, and are the most beautiful, and the most interesting to the common people. So that the minds duly trained to perceive and select such elements, will be the minds well trained and well adapted to interest people generally, and thus exercise such influences as would be permanent.

CHAP. V. PREPARATORY STUDIES.

§ 1. *In General; and Methods.*

Much has been said as to WHICH are the most suitable studies. But the inquiry, HOW the student should pursue the preparatory studies, is quite as important as what ones they are in particular. The first and most striking peculiarity is, that the student must bestow his attention, not on the usual, but on the most unusual facts or phenomena in each science. Thus, monstrosities, as well as extraordinary excellencies, are to be studied. Hence it is necessary for the Social Scientist to consider such subjects as sudden conversion, war, and the arts and tricks of speculators, and of professional politicians; also such peoples as Quakers, Pitcairn Islanders, also soldiers, sailors, and others, whose mode of life is very unusual, also the successful communities, including many Catholic and a few Protestant ones; also the various *informal* corporations of trades, guilds, rebels, school-boys, professional criminals, and so on. Furthermore, it is very desirable that the methods should be pointed out by which the sciences have progressed, and the kind of circumstantial evidence, and succession of hypothesis after hypothesis, continually hedging the certainty within narrower limits, without ever obtaining mathematically absolute certainty. For, even in the higher branches of mathematics, in the transcendental functions and in the Calculus, it is not the *a priori* demonstration that satisfies the mind; but the fact that the results and formulæ following from the hypothesis, solve all the questions, and in all the applications to which they can be put, especially those whose results were previously known.

In the selection, then, of the sciences which should be preparatory to Social Science, one principle of the selection should be to choose those that will most readily allow or encourage their being pursued in the analytical methods; approximating, as closely as is convenient, the actual processes of relevant thoughts that really produced the results as we have them.

Of *Mathematics* nothing need be said, because it is the discipline and transcendental form or type for all the sciences.

§ 2. *Theology.*

We observe here, that the study of Theology, by any person who is open to conviction, and is anxious to judge impartially for himself, and who is also anxious for his soul's salvation, is peculiarly analytic, and presents in each one's own mind a history peculiarly his own. And often that history is a life-long history, reaching to what is deepest in human nature, drawing out its capacity and sincerity to the utmost, and furnishing a discipline peculiarly excellent for enabling the mind to judge of the recondite truths of human and divine activities. Such a study of Theology now-a-days, bears the same relation to other studies, as the study of Theology itself, in the days when the student's life depended on his opinions, bears to its common study now.

The study of Theology is the scientific study of religion, and therefore calls into exercise all the higher faculties of the mind. Hence it is one of the best preparations for earnest original study in any of the sciences. The success of the German and Scotch metaphysicians is chiefly owing to this cause. And even of the pre-eminent mathematical and physical scientists, Candolle's statistics show, as to the professions of their sires, that Protestant clergymen are more numerous than any other profession. And of the eminent men of the Christian world, a far larger portion of them are found to be the children of clergymen than of any other professionals.

The *peculiar* fitness of the studies of the Theologians, as discipline and preparation for Political Philosophy, is further proved by the fact that at various times they have become the best and foremost political statesmen of the world. Ximenes, Woolsey, Richelieu, Cranmer, Talleyrand, and others may be mentioned. And then also the fact, that the statesmanship of Rome, which is conducted entirely by clergymen, is acknowledged to be the most far-reaching in the world. Remember also those old Puritan statesmen of Cromwell's day, who knew their Bibles and catechisms even better than their laws,—how readily they were turned into generals and statesmen whom all the world wondered at, and who out-generaled and out-witted even the Romans themselves.

Furthermore, both Fourier's and Herbert Spencer's writings show that they have been well disciplined with Theology, and particularly with its relation to Metaphysics. And Fourier spent the last hours of his life on his knees, voluntarily alone with God. And even Comte's ideal social power, is only a grand paraphrase of the church as a free spiritual power, in somewhat that general way that we may for instance speak of, —the church of the United States. But the fact is, that the church, or some outgrowth from it, although perhaps not always under the *name church*, has generally been found in advance of the state, even in mere *forms* of government. For the church is typical of all human society, and produces the foremost corporations. Dr. Craig suggests to me to say, that Theology includes the study of "the kingdom of heaven's aims and struggles, to issue finally in the perfect social state."

But when we speak in favor of Theology as a scientific and theoretical preparation for Social Science, we must not by any means be understood as if saying, that statesmen practically ought to be selected from among clergymen. The experience of the Middle Ages, culminating in the Inquisition, is against the selection of governors, with civil or coercive powers, from among professional Theologians. The government of the church in the Middle Ages, was almost the only important popular form in Europe; and it therefore absorbed much of the then existing turbulent and ambitious educated material, which, finding itself shut out from civil power, concentrated in, and gave vent to itself in the church.

On the other hand, in civil affairs, the modern change of form of government, from hereditary and aristocratic, to popular, does not show its highest uses in civil affairs, but in church affairs. And this it does by operating as an extra inducement to draw the most ambitious and turbulent materials of society *away* from the church into the state. Hence, under popular civil governments, the church itself is the greatest beneficiary—the party most benefited. And hence also, the church of modern times is not so likely to become so cruel or bigoted in its coercions, as was the old church. But this is no argument for the selection of statesmen from clergymen. And because the evil would be LESS now than formerly, is not any argument why we should resort to the evil at all. The prevalence of fanaticism and of religious bigotry, in all pre-millennial times, is an unanswerable objection against any return, before the millennium, to such old methods of selection; and so also is the reflex corruption thereby produced in churchmen and in church. And the modern principles of the division of labor, and the very different kind of energies required in statesmen, from what are required in clergymen, are both unanswerable arguments against returning to those old methods.

§ 3. *Metaphysics.*

We would now argue for the predominance which must be given to Metaphysics over some other studies, as preparations for Social Science. This is proved by the following reasons, which are cumulative. Metaphysics forms a considerable element in two other of the principal preparatory studies, namely, Theology and Moral Philosophy. It is the science of the most important faculty and part, of the individual creatures who make up human society. These Individuals themselves, each separately, are types of society, from which as types (as we shall hereinafter see) we form our most valuable judgments and arguments in social actions,—the human Individual being one fit type of human society, and the laws of the Individuals therefore, being fit types of the laws of society. And it is the science for the self-criticism of the scientist himself, whereby to criticise away his own personal aberrations.

Psychology itself, so far as independent of supernatural considerations, is nothing more than a small branch of Metaphysics.

The fault of the old theorists was not that they reasoned Metaphysically; but that, having some special one-sided doctrines to establish, or particular feelings to gratify, they perverted Metaphysics. And it has been found also that some of our moderns who use statistics and figures, can make perversions equally as great as the old metaphysicians did, and as difficult to overthrow, and which sometimes indeed, cannot be overthrown at all, only by resorting to the metaphysical laws of our being, and to common sense.

The attempt to ignore Metaphysics on grounds of physical philosophy, is much the same as to deny sensation to an animal, because not possessed by a vegetable.

Comte's idea is, that mental science can only be pursued by observing the operations of the mind, and that, the moment we stop thinking, to observe those motions of the mind, the motions themselves must stop; and then there would be *nothing to observe.* (See Introduction to Positive Philosophy.) But this doctrine entirely mistakes the mind's true course of proceeding in the case. The truth is, that the science of Metaphysics does not proceed essentially or chiefly by direct observations of the actions of mind, as and when they are influenced by its immediate causes (external or internal); but it proceeds by observing the MEMORY of those states of mind afterwards. And therefore it can be just as correct as the memory. The simple question is, as to the reality and faithfulness of memory. For, granting this, we can afterwards write down the actual occurrences of our minds; for all writing is just exactly noting down the facts of our mental processes, and if we will be faithful and write them *all fairly,* we then have a statement of facts as to the mind's operation, which we can consider and reconsider, ponder and analyze, to our hearts' content, the same and as fully as we could do with any record of any other natural or experimental phenomena.

In respect to self-consciousness, individuals are types of society. A society, like an Individual, cannot understand itself by an effort of direct self-consciousness of its own characteristics. It can only understand itself by observing its history; having previously encouraged the faithful narration and publication of that history, by interested and morally as well as mentally competent persons. And the better any society is, the more it will criticise and improve its own characteristics, by the light of its own experience, in defiance of its passions, its prejudices, and its theories.

There is one other science to be mentioned here as an important preparation, namely, the science of Medicine; but as this is a somewhat new position, and as it is desirable to avoid repetition, the evidences of this should be postponed to the head of "*The Individual,*" and of "*Health*" and "Life."

CHAP. VI. PROMOTERS AND TEACHERS.

§ 1. *Not the Classes generally supposed.*

The question now occurs, whom are we to look to for Social Science? No great advance can be made in this science, except in an entire and sympathetic willingness to receive light from all sources. But as to what classes of persons to look to for Social

Science, we observe, that they are certainly NOT the inferior classes of infidels. Great reasoning powers, great culture, may enable a few of them, as in the case of Comte, to rise to a valuable height in the comprehension of all those parts of the subject that are not expressly spiritual. But *inferior* minds must be guided by sound instincts, rather than by intellectual speculations.

Furthermore, we are not to look to the REGULARS, whether politicians statesmen or lawyers. For these, by devoting their minds wholly to their own particular branch of the science, are not competent to take a liberal or unbiased view of the whole subject.

Another reason is, the habit of studying political questions chiefly for immediate action and application, begets the habit of endeavoring to found and build merely temporary contrivances on everlasting foundations, and then of reasoning backwards, and from the permanency of the foundations, rashly assuming the permanency of the superstructure. Statesmen and lawyers, anxious to have the strongest possible arguments for present measures, work powerfully to argue and convince Mankind that their measures are absolutely required by the eternal nature of things. What is wanted is,—that such certain eternal and ever applicable principles should be discovered and elucidated, as should be both flexible and comprehensive enough to apply to all temporary and varying real necessities,—without at all implying, either that the institutions or the logical arguments for them, were absolute or permanent. The devotees to any science or business are the great obstructions to progress in it; except perhaps they be the GREAT discoverers. And it is strictly in accordance with these facts, that little hope of governmental improvement is to be expected from professional politicians.

M. Comte preceded us in a similar conclusion; yet it is a part of his theory, that government *is finally* to be placed at the disposal of scientific men, although not of the savans of any particular science, but of a class of savans not yet arisen, and whom he does not think it possible to point out beforehand. As to the world's physical scientists generally, notwithstanding the valuable aid their previous studies have given them for fitness to encounter the great problems of social life, yet they are generally so absorbed with hobbies, so ambitious of scientific fame, so unmetaphysical in their methods of thought, and often so half-skeptical religiously, and so conceited in their own opinions of the true principles of that science of society which they have not yet studied, that there seems but little hope as yet of their doing much for it. Perhaps it will be soon introduced into the colleges and universities, as a branch of the regular course. And then we might expect it to attract the attention of the pious scientists. But what is usually studied as Social Science in those institutions, is little more than enlarged Political Economy.

§ 2. *The Real Promoters.*

As yet, those who have done most to aid Social Science, are probably, Socrates (or Plato), Fourier, Comte, and Herbert Spencer, who are the most profound scientific generalists of all time.

A more likely class than either the ordinary statesmen or the ordinary physicists, to look to for Social Science, would be the true scientific Theologians, if they had the time to spare from their other avocations. But this seems seldom to happen; since most of them either have the charge and the daily labor of large church congregations, or else of educational institutions. These latter, namely, the theological head officers of the secular institutions, may contribute much towards our science, when there arises a sufficient public demand to turn their business attention to it, and when more leisure is afforded them. Theologians are, by their training, best fitted for universal or general study. Wells, whose occupation is the examination of heads, says, "As a class they (the Theologians) have the best heads in the world." (Physiognomy, p. 488.)

Another evidence that Theologians are to be looked to for Social Science, is found in the fact of the success of their communities. The founders of the successful communities have nearly always been Theologians originally, even if uneducated ones, or if they had afterwards deserted their Theology. Actual successes of this kind evidence practical knowledge of Social Science, and also ability in new developments.

The only regular students of Social Science of moderate caliber, who have yet done much for it, are the communists. These, by evidencing their faith in their own theories, by lives of communism and self-sacrifice, present new elements, namely, profound sincerity and self-sacrifice, powerfully co-operating in their study of the science.

Here also should be added all those classes of persons, who, upon principle, like the primitive Christians, the original Quakers, and some more modern peace-men and innovators, personally and individually disregard tyrannical laws, whether of government or of fashion.

Another reason why Theologians, religious and benevolent persons, are necessary in the improvement of Social Science, is, that they alone proclaim to any rulers (whether kings or peoples) the peculiar portions of truth that they respectively need. Other professions will flatter their kings, if in a monarchy; or will flatter the people, if in a democracy. The epithet for the leaders and politicians of the old Jewish people was, "they who call the people blessed,"—as any one may see by merely referring to the marginal renderings in our usual large Bibles. Thus, in Isaiah iii. 12: "O my people, they which lead thee," (marginal reading, "they which call thee blessed"), "cause thee to err, and destroy the way of thy paths." Again, Isaiah ix. 16: "For the leaders of this people," (marginal reading, "they that call them blessed") "cause them to err; and they that are led of them are destroyed."

We must not omit to enumerate the brave and devoted missionaries scattered over heathen countries, and various explorers geographical and scientific, who are sending home new ideas and new truths of social philosophy, gathered by experience and on the spot, of such various social systems as they necessarily encounter and naturally study and appreciate.

There is also another class who are doing noble but sporadic work, in aid of our science. They are generally retired statesmen or professionals, or retired merchants, or Christian men of considerable means, some of whom are to be found almost everywhere. They turn their attention generally, each to some one or few special points in the study or the practice.

Dr. Craig suggests that clergymen and physicians COULD be of great use to Social Science by their facilities for collecting statistics of such a private and moral nature, as it is scarcely possible could be derived from any other sources.

CHAP. VII. MEANS AND DATA.

§ 1. *Observation.*

We have now to consider the means and data of the science of society. This can consist only in a very small degree of personal observation, and only in the persons of leading statesmen, and in times of peculiar contemporaneous national events. And such observation will be far less applicable to the government of great Nations, than to the government of small Precincts. The larger and more populous the territory, the less can its affairs be observed by one human mind, or conducted in one age of life. Social observation therefore mainly consists of history. The great want here is for brief histories which shall represent principles rather than events. Such works would be nearly the same thing as "histories of civilization" of each particular country. They should prove, as to the case of each Nation for itself, the *general rules* and general consequences of the various principles of national action. This is what Paley's theory proposes, but for a different purpose, namely, for his proposed basis of morals.

§ 2. *Experiment.*

If Social Science is ever to become a real science, experiments must be encouraged in it, as really as in all the other sciences. But almost the only experiments of any thoroughness we have of late years are communistic, except a few experiments on some peculiar methods of settling unoccupied lands. Our Precinct system affords much the best basis for experiment. This system consists in forming very small Precincts of, and in, some one great Nation, and allowing within each Precinct, the utmost internal liberty and self-government, consistent with the general prosperity of the whole; in fact, an establishment of a United States of Precincts, on the general principle of "mind its own business" so long as it allows every person to leave a Precinct, if he does not like it, and does not interfere with others' equal liberty, nor with the general welfare.

This system, indeed is almost the only hopeful or desirable basis. Because, if large national experiments preceded the precinct experiments, vast ruin might follow in case of non-success. And the consequences also might be not rapid enough to teach the living generation who actually try the experiment. Furthermore, this Precinct system is one which in itself would be the germ of all subsequent continuous peaceful and agreeable experiments.

The next best kind of experiments are well organized voluntary corporations, as for instance, the moral communes. These ought to be encouraged by law, and be by every other reasonable facility allowed to organize into townships or counties, or whatever other local government their extent or prosperity might enable them to attain; always holding the commune or corporation responsible for the reasonable care of its women and children. No communes have succeeded unless they have been governed by good and wise men. They ought to be protected therefore, because according to our theory, government ought to be in the hands of wise men, namely, those who possess the transcendental elements most fully. Furthermore, all communes, even bad ones, are types and miniatures of society at large! and the evil ones teach us lessons at their own expense, and by their own free choice. Only keep them apart, so as not to contaminate the rest of society.

In all sciences we must keep in mind the conditions. And one of the conditions of any desirable social experiment for a free people is, of course, that the persons who enter upon it should do so VOLUNTARILY, and from real conviction. Otherwise it is no experiment of the natural workings of free or desirable society; but it is a mere experiment in tyranny, in corruption, or in punishment. Hence arises the great necessity for allowing to all social experimenters, the fullest possible liberty consistent with the equal rights of others, provided they will keep themselves from intruding their objectionable features before and upon the rest of society.

In regard to the use of experiments, we may observe that they give, not merely a balance of contradictory arguments, when some great and good principle or plan is found to succeed in some one or more cases, but not at all in others. On the contrary, wherever a great and good principle or plan has triumphantly succeeded, even only once, it is a sure proof that the principle or plan is PRACTICABLE FOR HUMAN NATURE. And thus, every new attainment is the advancement to a new position by the vanguard of improvement. In other words, a principle established for one, is established for all. Mankind, some of them at least, are improving, and are gradually becoming fit for better and better social conditions. And the exact amount of this fitness, is entirely too complicated an answer, to be obtained by any theoretical or *a priori* argument. The net total resultant of the many conflicting and variable forces, acting from time to time, can only be ascertained by trial itself.

And what, after all, is the history of any nation, and of its laws and wars and government? what, but a series of experiments, now with one object and now with another, yet having scarcely any more of the scientific conditions of a USEFUL experiment, than an eclipse or an earthquake.

This is the era of political experiment all over the world, and this fact probably shows one of the final causes for the division of Mankind into nations or races, namely, the better to compel them to try different series of disconnected experiments, as to the structure and laws of society: then, that process having continued for ages, the present stage of civilization and universal exchange, serves to point to a time having arrived when each Precinct and Nation is to study all the others, and to try whatever it finds in any of them that would appear beneficial to it. This, then, is the era of universal experiment in social and political, as well as in the other sciences, when each Nation is trying experiments from suggestions derived from any or all of the others.

§ 3. *Modification of Expediency Doctrine.*

Another one of the data for social science is, a modification of the doctrine of expediency; namely, a reasoning from general consequences and general rules, in such a way that the general consequences are used to obtain general moral rules, not independent of, but only in connection with, the moral instincts. Such general rules are substantially the same as Dr. Paley's Principles of Moral Philosophy would become, by taking the moral instincts into its connection *formally*, as indeed he often does materially essentially and instinctively, in the course of his work. No doctrine of expediency can be received, altogether regardless of the moral instincts, nor can these be taken without the other; but right and expediency always go together, with the privilege, amid contending principles, to prefer that which happens to be the clearest in any given case; and never swerving from the great foundations of morality, namely, the sanction of God and the equality of the rights of men under the same circumstances.

§ 4. *Return to First Principles.*

Allowing now, that reasoning from cause and effect, and from general theories of society, based upon cause and effect alone; or starting with theories that can just as well be turned into exactly opposite directions and developments,—that such reasoning is altogether insufficient of itself to invent or discover the true social system or true Social Science:—nevertheless, we must always be ready in our reasonings, to return to the first principles of things; and not wander far off into answers to arguments, and then replies to answers, and then objections to replies, and the removal of the objections, and then answers to those removals, and so on as may be done endlessly.

There is a class of Social Scientists, (with whom, it is to be regretted, Spencer has almost enrolled himself), who argue that government ought not to do nor to attempt to do, scarcely anything except to keep the peace among its own citizens, and organize for fighting with the citizens of other governments. They argue for letting natural laws take their course, as fully in all sanitary matters, as in sumptuary ones; and they ask us to let death multiply until Individuals will of their own accord provide for the health of a city; they ask this, even with the same pertinacity that they ask to let men eat and dress extravagantly until checked by their reaching the bottom of their pockets. This leads to the necessity of showing, that we must resort to first principles in order to answer these arguments.

Let us consider some instances of the kind of proof required; —discretionary power is given to trustees, agents, representatives, judges, governors, in order that the discretion may be used for the cause of truth and justice, as against the impossibility of government making exact and perfect rules beforehand. But when those officers use a "hook or crook" of exact rule, to authorize a violation of truth or justice, and would plead their discretionary powers, they violate the *first principles* in the case, and must return to first principles, in order to see the error of their argument.

Again, it is admitted, private charity is better than public;

the first principle being, that private character is able to be investigated more truly by the benevolent and on the voluntary principle, than by government. But, when we find Individuals *failing* to do a necessary work, when we find whole tribes and districts and scattered millions, famishing, and no sufficient private aid coming, the public must come to the rescue, and justify itself by recurring to first principles.

Again, when the elective franchise is given, and decisions are made according to majority, all is intended for the reason or first principle, that it is supposed that the possession of that franchise by all, is a needed means for the protection of their own rights. But when they would use the idea of the majority, to take away the rights of others, their arguments should return to first principles. And the mere *will* of a majority, can find no arguments to defend it, in trampling on the rights of a minority.

Now, when some would allege, very restricted powers to government,—that it must in fact do almost nothing, but (that which, by the way, it cannot do at all, namely) protect life and property, they are fond of assuming or trying to prove, that government was not instituted for any of those other purposes. They think they then recur to the first principles of the thing. But; —Do they? Or shall we ask, what was man himself instituted for? Was man made for Sunday, or Sunday made for man? Was man made for law, or law made for man? If *this*, then, is the first principle of the thing, the do-nothing governmentalists are in the wrong theory;—who would let one set of unthrifty idle poor starve, in order that others might learn more foresight; or one set of strong passioned men and girls rot, that others might learn to avoid the danger, &c., &c. Some Sociological arguments favoring the absurdest conclusions, can be fully and satisfactorily answered in this manner, which might take whole volumes to refute in any other manner; so complicated and abstruse is the whole science, and so mixed up with local prejudices and visionary theories.

The fact is, that for practical application, all abstract principles must undergo a degree of concrete integration; and the definite quantities and "constants" which had been dropped in differentiation, must be restored. This is readily accomplished by a resort to the first principles of things.

§ 5. *Analogies of Natural Laws.*

Then we have the analogies of natural laws, beginning with the laws of inorganic matter, and ascending to those of the vegetable, and finally of the animal. And as we rise in the scale of existence, always of course, pay more and more respect to the analogies which gradually approach the human being himself. In the application of this principle, Comte made great advances beyond Fourier, and Spencer, still greater advances beyond Comte, and Carey also has made some use of natural laws for analogies, but only or chiefly of those drawn from the inanimate world. It is the introduction of these kinds of analogies into Social Science, that seems to be its strongest attraction to the modern physicists. And by their influence, analogies which formerly were considered to be nothing more than very pretty figures of speech, are now admitted to be fundamental laws of the Science.

The great Social Scientists, such as Fourier, Comte, Spencer, avow a causal connection between the lower order of creatures, organic and inorganic, and the nature of man, individual and social. Even Plato, Swedenborg and others, who do not appear to accept the doctrine of a causal connection, make free use of the resemblances.

§ 6. *The Tribe-Principle.*

There is another principle upon which we build much of our Social Science. It is the theory of the tribe; namely, the theory that the tribe-element of primitive stages of mankind, disappears as to its form, in modern or developed society; but yet, as to its essence, reappears therein under several different forms. This we call the tribe-principle. The developments of this, will be found frequently recurring in the progress of this work. We have not met with any work on Social Science, hitherto, which makes any practical application of the tribe-element, to modern society.

§ 7. *The Type-Theory.*

We have the type-theory; according to which, the Individual human being is regarded as a type of Family, and of all the other personal units more complicated. And then, the Family is likewise regarded as the type of the Precinct, and of all the other Units more general than it; and so on, up to the Nation, and even to Mankind. This is a very different idea, from merely using the Individual man or any other animal, as the type of society at large, as has been done by Plato, Hobbes, Spencer, and many others. Besides the increased complexity and development of our use of the thought, ours has a less outward, but a more moral, origin and nature. See that other view pretty fully treated in the *Westminster Review*, January, 1860, in Spencer's article, "The Social Organism." Extracts therefrom will be found under the head of *Individual*.

The substance of our theory, as has been mentioned already, is the typicalness of each and all the different personal elements, or units of society: and this in such a sense, that each one is typical of all those that are more general than itself.

The way whereby we came to alight upon this theory, was this.—In the course of the study of Social Science, it soon became apparent, that, amid such a conflict of different theories and contending suggestions, it would be simply impossible to weigh and consider them all fully and in detail; and that consequently, the disputes in Social Science could never be settled in that way. The question then almost became, either to give up the science in despair, or try to find some more practicable method of proof. At last it appeared, that in nature there are certain objects and circumstances, that, when used by a proper instinct and not superficially, at once and by analogy show forth results and consequences, with more certainty and truth than the deepest or most complicated reasonings.

The case is, as Howson says, "When an important change is at hand, God usually causes a silent preparation in the minds of men; and some great fact occurs, which may be taken as a *type* and symbol of the whole movement."

For the proof of our theory of types, we appeal, partly to the existence of typical forms in general, and to fundamental analogies as existing in common sense, and as the data and basis of the judgments of common sense.

It is a wonderful fact, that we often find in common life, and even with inexperienced persons, a degree of common sense that is truly surprising. And among the uneducated classes generally, there seems to prevail more wisdom about many matters, than can be found among those given to the deepest researches of reasoning.

One of the best, and probably one of the first cases, of the analogy of the individual with human society, is given by St. Paul, (1 Cor. xii.), and applied to the church. But evidently, the principle is applicable to every form of human society, from the Family upward.—" For as the body is one, and hath many members, and all the members of that one body, being many, are one body: so also is Christ. . . . For the body is not one member, but many. If the foot shall say, Because I am not the hand, I am not of the body; is it therefore not of the body? . . . If the whole body were an eye, where were the hearing? . . . But now hath God set the members, every one of them, in the body, as it hath pleased him. And if they were all one member, where were the body? . . . And the eye cannot say unto the hand, I have no need of thee; nor again, the head to the feet, I have no need of you. . . . And those members of the body, which we think to be less honorable, upon these we bestow more abundant honor. . . . For our comely parts have no need; but God hath tempered the body together, having given more abundant honor to that part which lacked; that there should be no schism in the body, but that the members should have the same care one for another. And whether one member suffer, all the members suffer with it; or one member be honored, all the members rejoice with it."

Fundamental analogies may be further perceived among abstract subjects and questions. Consider now, such questions as the right and principle of civil government *at all;* or the true principles of church organizations, or the relation of church to state. The discussions on ordinary principles seem endless. But, by fixing our minds on some of the simple but essential elements of society,—say, the Individual, or the Family, or even on some one locality or Precinct,—we obtain a type or basis for a class of analogies which are not only suggestive, but to a certain extent also, logically conclusive. Further illustrations will be found at the commencement of the part on the "*Individual,*" and especially at the commencement of the part on the "*Family.*" And the chief type and illustration is the Family; even as Comte says, that it is both the unit and the type of society at large.

The doctrine of fundamental analogies, harmonizes somewhat

with the old Platonic thought of the real existence of general ideas and general forms. And it would seem that all creation is but an evolution from, and a development of, these general forms. Yet still our idea is not so much *that*, as this other thought, that all life repeats itself more or less, and produces microcosms; that everything re-types itself, and that some of these fruits are so closely and truly microcosms, that they may safely be taken as typical forms.

Swedenborg also agrees, that by "correspondences" the animals have their instinctive knowledge, and that man is like them therein,—(*Heaven and Hell;* 108 and 110),—that uses are the same in all worlds, but the same use takes different forms in different worlds; and that the *correspondence* in forms, results from the *sameness* of use. (H. and H.; 112.)

When the greatest philosophers and anatomists of the world, were vainly endeavoring to reason out a great archetype, or general outline-skeleton for all animal life, the poet Goethe perceives, that a leaf is the archetype wanted. Prof. Owen has enlarged this idea into a system of creation according to an "ideal typical vertebra," as in the Divine mind. But Owen, having confused this capital thought with a very different one, namely, the purely mechanical "*old fogy*" undevelopment-idea of creation, laid himself open to cavil.

The basis of these fundamental analogies, seems to rest in the very ultimate beginning principles of inanimate matter. In general, perhaps the theory is admissible that many of the primal conglomerations or organizations in nature, are in the forms of their totalities or ultimates; crystals, in the form of their totality, and the primal parts of seeds and germs, in the form of their completed wholes, and the parts of the brain in the form of the whole. And even all motion might be the result of the original rotary motion, supposed to have existed in the beginning of creation. Everywhere, from highest to lowest, in the movements of being—nebula, suns, planets, electricity, stomach, blood—EVERYWHERE we find the great element of circuitous motion. However, it is beyond our depth, to give "positive" knowledge of the foundations of fundamental analogies.

§ 8. *Ideals.*

(*a*) *Historical Ideals.* Imaginary and ideal original states of society, are experiments of some kind, on our own minds, and are efforts to reach the great archetypes within our own minds, are latent activities on the basis of an inward type theory; so that, among the data for Social Science, and among the scientific means of improving it, may be mentioned this inevitable tendency of the human mind, to imagine peculiar states of society in its most simplified forms:—Thus, the church-hypothesis, of one original pair for all Mankind, and they created in a state of moral and intellectual perfection:—Also, the opposite hypothesis, that Mankind were originally a set of barbarians, but little if any, superior to the unreasoning animals. Each of these opposite hypotheses answers to explain different phenomena of society. The church-hypothesis explains the laws of the moral nature of individual man; whilst the barbarian hypothesis serves to explain the scientific, social, and governmental progress of Mankind as a race or as a whole.

Then, again, imaginary conditions of society, and imaginary positions of Individuals may be conceived; and these may serve to show the superior worth of man and life, above all fashions and property and earthly distinctions. They also help us to form a judgment as to what are the strongest passions of human nature. The principle is just like the great advice, to do unto others as we would that they should do unto us: it is an experiment upon our own moral consciousness.

(b) *Prospective Ideals.* This sort of reasoning is the foundation of ideals for the future of human society; and thus, of *hopes* for society, and thus becomes a guide of struggles for the improvement of Mankind. But imaginary states are, in the main, necessary to the pursuit of any study, in a truly analytical method; for the subsequent re-integration that is necessary to form science, cannot follow without ideals as to mental aim.

Nor is *our* ideal to be supposed to be a reach at absolute perfection. On the contrary, it is an ideal modified so as to come within the writer's ideas of present human possibilities. And it is by no means supposed to be the end of all progress or of all ideals, on this subject. As for its scientific value as an aid to study, we hope to place our ideal at least in the same category as Plato's Republic, More's Utopia, Fourier's Association, and Ballou's True System of Human Society; and that is not saying very much for either of them. Its practicability is altogether another question, and is reserved for its proper place in a separate "book." Our ideal is such a universal coöperation as would have to be called Limited or Christian communism. By communism, we mean, not freedom of sex, but coöperation and mutuality,—in religion, in self-government and in industry,—in incomes, and labors, and general life,—in all things moral and lawful,—and by doing to others perfectly as we would be done by,—as only can be done in "association"-life.

Judaism owes much of its power to its having its *ideal* kingdom of the Messiah, as its central point, which it was its *duty* constantly to seek; and which it was certain it would finally attain.

§ 9. *Efficacy for solution of phenomena.*

But the greatest and best proof of the excellence of our theory, is of the same kind as presents itself in every science, namely, the success of the applications of our individual theories, to the solution of *all* the facts, and to the general classification of the subject *as a whole.* This argument is of such a nature, that we hope it will gradually increase, even to the end of the last division, where it comes to be applied to the difficult problems and relations of civil government, of religion, communism, and human life. But yet, so thoroughly is the nature of this sort of argument understood in the physical sciences, that we scarcely need mention it again.

CHAP. VIII. THE METHOD.—ANALYTICAL.

In a new and undeveloped science, some greater attention to preliminaries of method and arrangement, may be excused, and is even demanded, than in the case of the more developed and better ascertained sciences.

There are two main methods of pursuing any science,—the analytical and the synthetical. The synthetical consists in laying down the subject in a regular and connected order, so that what follows is generally based upon what precedes, simply as possible, and sustained by demonstrations of the truth of what has been said. The analytical, is the handling of the constituent parts of a subject in the various ways POSSIBLE. It consists, first, in taking the subject all apart and considering each part separately, then combining those parts together repeatedly, with a view to forming some synthetical arrangement. But, as first attempts are generally unsuccessful, the first forms of synthesis will be unsatisfactory. Then the whole subject must necessarily be re-analyzed. And this process continues to be repeated, with an increase of knowledge and experience gained by previous operations; and all this, in regard both to ideas and to general classifications. And, in the sense in which we are here using the words analytical and synthetical, they are both included in the term inductive, as distinguished from deductive. And the term deductive applies to the synthetical, chiefly as to the deduction of the classifications. We deduce mostly forms, not substance nor inferences, by this method of thinking.

Another feature of the analytical method is, that we pursue our studies in regard to all the different parts of the subject at the same time. In fact we do this in the same manner, to some extent, as if they were entirely different subjects, but constantly are on the watch for every suggestion that may arise, of comparisons with or relations to, any of the other parts of the subject as a whole. We seek ideas within our own minds, half ramblingly it may be, just as a physicist wanders over the earth for glacier-stones, fish-bones, and stone hatchets. And this is exactly the point of the process where new ideas arise.

Another point of contrast between the two methods is, that the synthetical usually aims to be argumentative, in such a way that argumentative conclusions are constantly intended and looked for, in such works as admit of argument; so that they are valuable chiefly in proportion to the soundness and variety of the arguments adduced. But the analytical process is generally *corrupted*, at least at first, in proportion as it has in mind any particular theory or object to prove. So that, while synthesis aims to prove this or that particular truth already believed in, analysis hunts and seeks for any truths it can find that appropriately relate to the subject.

One word as to the manner in which this work has been wrought out:—The manner has been purely analytical. After storing the mind with much that others had written; and writing short notes or essays on various points as they occurred,—writing perchance on the same day, short essays or notes on parts of the subject the most distant or the most unlike: we found that the facts or doctrines thus having been cut up and analyzed, suggested other points or positions or questions, which all had to be noted down immediately, to be afterwards further examined. And subsequently, all these suggestions had to be arranged and compared and collated together. This part of the process was synthetical, and made further suggestions, whereby the work became what it is. And all these various changes took place, as well in regard to the methods forms and classifications of the ideas, as in regard to the ideas themselves.

CHAP. IX. THE CLASSIFICATIONS.

§ 1. *The Classifications in general.*

One objection to most Social Sciences is, that their writers, each has his own peculiar pet scheme or theory, and frames his whole work so as to be a special pleading in favor of some such theory. Now, to have a theory is no objection; but to twist the classification to suit it,—to have only ONE theory, and to stake the treatment of a whole philosophical work, to favor such a one theory, is a thing not done in other sciences claiming to be inductive or philosophical.

The first great desideratum in Social Science, would be a work which would give such a scientific and truthful general outline of the subject, as could be easily used in any of the different theories on the same subject. Thus it would be a real analysis of the subject itself, objectively, as to its generally ascertained facts and principles. The originator of such a classification, containing at least a compend of the principal ideas on the subject, would be a lasting friend to posterity; even should it not add any single new idea to our stock of knowledge about it. For classification is the foundation and essential of all the sciences.

Now, it seems that the principal merits of a scientific classification of any book, besides those already mentioned, are that it be such as to avoid repetitions as much as possible; that it arrange the different parts in such an order of succession, that what precedes will facilitate the understanding of what follows; and that *that* which precedes, will also serve as argumentative premises, for reasonable conclusions in the parts that follow.

This latter attainment, however, is rarely possible, consistently with the other two, and in an analytical work of this kind, can hardly be expected. So then, our classification may be considered successful, in proportion as it avoids repetitions, and arranges the parts that precede, so as to make intelligible those that follow,—trusting to the consistency of the whole, as one of its main arguments.

We will now endeavor to do what is certainly a very hard thing to do, namely, to *classify the classifications* of this very abstract subject.

§ 2. *Zoölogical Classifications.*

(*a*) *Zoölogical,—By others.*

The Zoölogical classifications of Social Science, trace analogies with the various parts of a man, or other animal.

Spencer in Westm. Rev., and in Ills. Prog., has shown many of the advantages and disadvantages of this form of treatment. Plato adopts the correspondence of reason, will, and passion, for the divisions of society. Hobbes adopts "that Leviathan great man called the commonwealth," and its parts. Swedenborg makes the societies of heaven and hell, to be in the "forms" of a man, and carries out the analogies into the very minute parts. It has often seemed to the writer, that Spencer's splendid classification for vegetable and animal Biology, might, with slight adaptations, be equally splendid for Social Biology; namely, for Social Science itself.

(*b*) *Zoölogical,—By us.*

The writer's first classification was MEDICAL and biological, as follows: and in the subdivisions of each of the five main parts, all the *ones* (1^s) correspond with or relate to each other, and all the twos (2^s) with each other, and so on, with the 3^s and 4^s.

(I.) *Social Physiology.*

1. Sensible System.
2. Vital System.
3. Motive or Mechanic System.
4. Life-power in its totality.

(II.) *Social Therapeutics.*

1. Theory of Medicine.
2. Practice of Medicine.
3. Pharmacy.
4. Hygiene.

(III.) *Sociological Powers and Organs.*

1. Mental, Moral, Psychological, Mysterious and Philosophical.
2. Vital, Circulative, Unseen, Scientific.
3. Motive, Mechanical, Material, Structural, Obvious, and Political.
4. Harmonious, Completed result, Perfect cure, and Limited Communism.

(IV.) *Classes of Society.*

1. Moral and Religious classes.
2. Intellectual and Educated classes.
3. Physical classes.
4. Holy Instinctive classes (?)

(V.) *Departments of Government.*

1. Constitutions.
2. Laws.
3. Usual Offices.
4. New Offices.

§ 3. *Abstract Ungeneric Classifications.*

Albert Brisbane classifies thus: Education: Industry: Social Laws and Institutions: Government: Religion: Accessory Branch, including Fine Arts and Sciences.

The Chinese "Statutes and Rescripts of the Great Pure Dynasty," are arranged thus:—General: Civil: Fiscal: Ritual: Military: Criminal: and Public Works.

Carey suggests as main divisions, simply:—Political Economy: and Jurisprudence.

Mulford in his preface, implies a classification which may be expressed thus:—Political Economy: Jurisprudence: Statistics (or Statics?): Political History: and Political Science in general.

Here follow classifications by five great institutions: and then follow two of our Summary ones. (A) is of the British Assoc. of Soc. Science. (B) is of the European International Association. (C) is of the American Assoc. of Soc. Science. (D) is of the Western Social Sci. Association. (E) is of the School of the French Empire, for its course of studies. (F) is our Summary of these five, made for a comparison of them with one of our classifications, to be given hereinafter. And (G) is ours, modified here for the comparison.

The perpendicular lines vary, so that the spaces between them, will carefully exhibit the comparative *scopes*, of the works and of the sub-headings of their respective authors; *i.e.*, Law in (B) means more than in (A), but less than in (C).—Finance in (D) means more than in (E) but less than in (F).—And the whole line or scope of (B, D, E or F) means more than in (A) or (C) and less than in (G). And crime in (A) consists of a *part* of what (B) calls "Law," and a part of what it calls "Health and Charity."

A	Social Economy	Law	Crime . . .	Health . .	Education
B	Pol.-Economy	Law . . .	Health and Charity . .	Art & Literature	
C	Finance . . .	Law	Health . .	Education	
D	Finance . . .	Law	Health . .	Education	Fine Arts
E	Finance .	Political Economy	Law	Statistics	. . ? . .
F	Financial . . .	Political .	Legal . .	Philosophical . . .	
G	Property	Politicals	Philosophicals	Personals	

§ 4. GENERIC CLASSIFICATIONS.

(*a*) *Generic,—By others.*

Fourier's ideas may be classified thus:—

(I) Universal laws of matter and mind. (1) The series distributes the harmonies. (2) Attractions are proportioned to Destinies. (3) Analogy is universal.

(II) Fundamental passions of human nature. (1) Sensuous desires. (2) Moral-Social affections. (3) Intellectual and distributive impulses. (4) Unity-ism.

(III) Fundamental elements of society. (1) Capital. (2) Science. (3) Labor.

(IV) Attractive industry; chiefly by means of groups within series, systematically and harmonically arranged.

Both Comte and Spencer divide Social Science into Statics and Dynamics; but disagree as to what are the lines, or even what the principles, of the division.

Comte's view of Social Science is given as his Social Physics, and may be condensed thus:—Principal Philosophical Attempts at a Social Science: Characteristics of the Positive Method in Social Phenomena: Relation of Sociology to Positive Philosophy; Social Statics, or Theory of the Spontaneous Order of Society, including the Individual, the Family, and Society in the abstract.

Social Dynamics, or Theory of the Natural Progress of Society: First Theological Phase, Fetichism,—Beginning of the Theological and Military System: Second Phase, Polytheism,—Development of the Theological and Military System: Third Phase, Age of Monotheism,—Modification of the Theological and Military System: Metaphysical and Critical Period of Modern Society: Final Tendency of Modern Society: Final Action of the Positive Philosophy.

Spencer's "Social Statics" is divided as follows:—Fundamental Principles: Personal Rights: Political Rights: Connection with Social Dynamics.

His proposed new work, which seems to be his Dynamics, is, (like Comte's,) to consider historical progress mainly; but is to be divided as follows:—Data of Sociology: Inductions of Sociology: Political Organization: Ecclesiastical Organization: Industrial Organization: Ceremonial or Custom-Organization: Lingual Progress: Intellectual Progress: Æsthetic Progress: Moral Progress: Consensus.

(b) Our Generic Classification.

Table II.

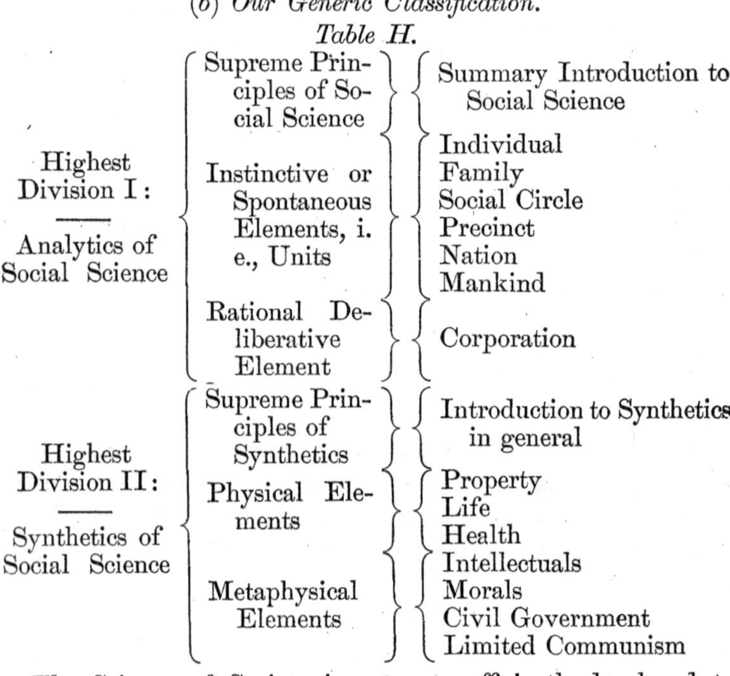

Highest Division I: — Analytics of Social Science	Supreme Principles of Social Science	Summary Introduction to Social Science
	Instinctive or Spontaneous Elements, i. e., Units	Individual Family Social Circle Precinct Nation Mankind
	Rational Deliberative Element	Corporation
Highest Division II: — Synthetics of Social Science	Supreme Principles of Synthetics	Introduction to Synthetics in general
	Physical Elements	Property Life Health
	Metaphysical Elements	Intellectuals Morals Civil Government Limited Communism

The Science of Society is not yet sufficiently developed, to *express* its two main divisions accurately; although the general conception seems clear enough. The division into Statics and Dynamics, (of Comte and Spencer,) is evidently too materialistic, inorganic, and lifeless. But Primary and Secondary, speaking in a figure from Geology, might answer. Or Anatomy and Physiology; or Structure and Functions. Or we might say, Pure Social Science, and Applied Social Science; because, in the degree of abstractness, the Analytics is related to the Synthetics, somewhat as Pure Mathematics is to Applied Mathematics. But we prefer the terms *Analytics and Synthetics.* And then subdivide as annexed.

(*c*) *Some Higher Comparisons.*

This classification (H) by summing it up differently, namely, as our (G) in the ungeneric classifications previously given (IX. 3), may be compared with the one (F), there suggested as a summary of the classifications of the five great institutions there cited. This comparison may be made thus:—

Economical or Financial = Property.

Political, includes, Precinct, Nation, and Corporation.

Legal is Health, Civil Government, and Communism.

Philosophical only touches Summary Introduction, Individual, Family, Social Circle, Mankind, Introduction to Synthetics, Life, Intellectuals, and Morals.

Approximating the three in tabular form, thus;

F	Financial	Political	. Legal . . .	. . . . . . Philosophical . .	
G	Property	. . . Politicals		Philosophicals	Personals
H	Property	Precinct Nation Corporation	Health . . . . Civil Government Limited Communism	Summary Introduction Mankind Introduction to Synthetics Life Intellectuals Morals	Individual Family Social Circle

Compare with the outline of Mr. Spencer's PROPOSED Sociology. In which of course we can only *guess* where he would place them.

Spencer's.		*Ours.*
Data of Sociology Inductions of Sociology	. . . .	Life Individual Introductions
Ecclesiastical Organization		Corporation Morals
Custom Organization		Social Circle
Political Organization	. . . .	Precinct Nation Corporation Civil Government
Industrial Organization		Property
Lingual Progress Intellectual Progress		Intellectuals

Spencer's.	*Ours.*
Esthetic Progress	Intellectuals Morals
Moral Progress	Health Individual Family Morals
Consensus: and interdependence of structure and function.	Introductions Mankind Communism

(*d*) *Some Transcendental Analogies.*

The general relation between our Analytics and Synthetics, is analogous to the two kinds of primal forms of solid matter—"Matter has two solid states, distinguished as crystalloid and colloid; of which the first is due to union of the *individual* atoms, and the second, to the union of *groups* of such individual atoms; and of which the *first is stable* and the second unstable." And again those two primal kinds are typical of the still more primal fundamental kinds, namely solid and gaseous; (because liquidity is only a transient state of matter, in its passage from solid to gas or from gas to solid.) Our Analytical Elements are supposed to be socially the individual atoms; the Synthetics are supposed to consist of *groups* metaphysically, and hence are more complicated.

Next observe two ascending series, resembling the *octaves* of the major scale in music, (do, re, mi, fa, sol, la, si, do,)—one of which takes in the whole eight parts of the analytics; and the other, the whole eight of the synthetics. They are to be read from the bottom, upwards. Musicians will understand them.

Analytics.	*Synthetics.*
8 Corporation.	8 Limited Communism.
7 Mankind.	7 Civil Government.
6 Nation.	6 Morals.
5 Precinct.	5 Intellectuals.
4 Social Circle.	4 Health.
3 Family.	3 Life.
2 Individual.	2 Property.
1 Introduction.	1 Introduction.

In the following four classifications, let all the ones (1^s) be compared with each other, and all the twos (2^s) with each other, and so on; and some resemblances will be observed, besides the more obvious ones between 3^s and 4^s and between 7^s and 8^s.

Comte's Final Outlines.	*Our Analytics.*
1 Introduction.	1 Introduction.
2 Mathematics.	2 Individual.
3 Astronomy.	3 Family.
4 Physics.	4 Social Circle.
5 Chemistry.	5 Precinct.
6 Biology.	6 Nation.
7 Sociology.	7 Mankind.
8 [Ideal Humanity.]	8 Corporation.
Our Synthetics.	*Oken's Outlines of Biology.*
1 Introduction.	1 Organosophy.
2 Property.	2 Phytogeny.
3 Life.	3 Phyto-physiology.
4 Health.	4 Phytology.
5 Intellectuals.	5 Zoögeny.
6 Morals.	6 Physiology.
7 Civil Government.	7 Zoölogy.
8 Limited Communism.	8 Psychology.

We have many other such analogies, but have concluded to omit them.

§ 5. *Our Order of Publication.*

As in music the tunes are made by *generally* deviating from the order of the gamut, so in the actual publication of our ideas, and for convenience' sake; because those ideas will have to be published only gradually and in parts, as separate works, we will adopt a different GENERAL grouping. But what that general grouping may be, we do not know in advance; only this much. Our New Theory of Social Science would be pretty fairly represented by (I) Summary Introduction, or Theory of Social Science in General. (II) The Primary Fundamental Politico-organic elements, namely, Precinct, Nation and Corporation. And (III) The Ultimate Ideal, viz. Limited Communism. These subjects (we say nor mean not, our treatment of them) make up a real Principia of Social Science.

SUMMARY INTRODUCTION TO SOCIAL SCIENCE.

PART II.

PRINCIPLES OF SOCIETY ITSELF.

CHAP. I. PRELIMINARY.

THAT part of Social Science which treats of the fundamental principles of society itself, taken as a distinct part from the principles of the SCIENCE, goes on the assumption, that society, like any other part of nature, has its own rules, its own principles, and its own laws,—a set of higher laws which embrace and over-rule all that governments and governors and individuals do; whether they will, or not. And, to investigate these higher laws, is one of the principal objects of Social Science, and is the particular object of this second part of this Introduction. Those laws which are too general for any other part of the work, are collected in the Introduction. They are arranged, not so much in the order of subject or matter, as in the order of their abstractness and generality.

CHAP. II. MOST GENERAL SOCIAL LAWS.

§ 1. *Differences of Degrees of Things.*

In the higher organizations of the world, whether material or social, differences of degree are often more important than differences of kind. For instance, the difference between the most improved and the least improved men, of any one and the same race, is greater than the difference between the most improved of the lowest race and the least improved of the highest race; and the higher you rise in the scale of being, the more important the difference of degrees becomes. Hence, we are never to be disturbed, in the separation of things widely different, because of there being a difficulty or even an impossibility, of *exactly* expressing or drawing the line, between them.

In every question relating to the subject of governmental

action, the question of the degree of interference, is more important than the abstract one, of interference at all. And this holds true as to every kind of government, from that of a man over his dog, to that of the Supreme Being over the universe. Moreover, it is as important a question, when referring to the differences of the elements of materials of organic worlds, as to the differences between moral rights; as we will now try to show.

This introduces the consideration of the functions of the infinities,—the differentiations and integrations in the "calculus," whereby infinite differences in the degrees, make entire differences in the kinds, of the things considered. In a subsequent work we may perhaps show, that creation itself was probably a process of infinite integrations from nothing, and that the importance of degrees pervades all creation, in regard to the first principles of things.

The solution of the analogies between the physical and the intellectual world, can be found in only one or the other of two alternatives; namely, either in the Doctrine of Universal Correspondences, or in our doctrine of creation by integration. But yet, these two alternatives are not incompatibles. For, if the doctrine of correspondences is true, our doctrine of creation by integration does not interfere with it, but affords the only rational explanation of it.

All the other explanations of creation are utterly unsatisfactory. For, materialism is merely a hiding of ignorance, behind a cloud of scientific classifications. And Pantheism, whether true or false, is of no practical use in the solution. For, whether God created matter out of nothing, or whether He himself only takes the form of matter; neither alternative explains how mind becomes matter, nor how matter becomes mind. And the doctrine of the eternal self-existence of matter, cannot explain how matter becomes mind, only by going back to Pantheism. In fact, both the materialistic and the Pantheistic philosophers, meet and stop at this point of the harmony of the physical with the social laws.

Spencer's great idea, and what runs through all his works, is, the idea of EVOLUTION from homogeneity into heterogeneity; and that when unity becomes differentiated into plurality, each factor becomes an outward condition tending to produce changes in the other factor. But yet he utterly ignores and denies the idea, of inherent or spontaneous power, in any factor, to change itself. (See Biology, § 373, and elsewhere.) How strange it is, he cannot see, that if the germ of an animalcule, for instance, has no spontaneous power to change itself, neither could the original nebula of the universe have had any such power, either by the principle of "infinite chances," or by any other principle.

§ 2. *Analogies with Physical Laws.*

In addition to what have been previously given, we now give some of Carey's "General Social Laws," (abridged edition, pages 526 and 527.) "The simple laws which govern matter in all its forms, and which are common to physical and to SOCIAL SCIENCE, may now be briefly stated thus:—"All particles of matter gravitate towards each other, the attraction being in the direct ratio of the mass, and the inverse one of the distance." . . . "All matter is subjected to the action of the centripetal and the centrifugal forces; the one, tending to the production of local centres of action; the other, to the destruction of such centres, and the production of a great central mass obedient to but a single law." . . . "The more perfect the balance of these opposing forces, the more uniform and steady is the movement of the various bodies, and the more harmonious, the action of the system in which they are embraced." . . . "The more intense the action of these forces, the more rapid is the motion, and the greater the power."

"Such are the laws which govern masses and atoms [i.e. respectively]; but there are other laws, in virtue of which, masses are reduced to atoms ready to enter into chemical combination with each other; the tendency towards combination, existing in the direct ratio of the perfect *individualization* of the particles." These laws are:—"That heat is a cause of motion and force; motion being, in its turn, a cause of heat and force." . . . "The more heat and motion produced, the greater is the tendency towards acceleration in the motion and the force." . . . "The more the heat, the greater is the tendency towards decomposition of masses, and individualization of the particles of which they are composed, thus fitting them for entering into chemical combination with each other." . . . "The greater the tendency towards individualization, the more instant are the combinations, and the greater the force obtained." . . . "The more rapid the motion, the greater the tendency of matter to rise in the scale of form." . . . "At every stage of progress, there is an extension of the range of law to which matter is subjected, accompanied by an increase of the power of self-direction, subordination and freedom, keeping steady pace with organization."

"Studying man, we find:—"That, association with his fellow-man is a necessity of his existence." . . . "That, his powers are very various, and that the combinations of which they are susceptible are infinite in number, there being throughout the world, no two persons who are entirely alike." . . . "That, the development of those infinitely various faculties, is wholly dependent upon the development of individuality." . . . "That, the greater the diversity, the greater is man's power to control and direct the great forces of nature, and the larger is the number of persons who can draw support from any given space, and the more perfect the development of the latent powers of both earth and man." . . . "That, the more perfect the development, * * * the more rapid is the societary motion, and the greater the force exerted."

§ 3. *Metaphysical operation of Social Laws.*

The Social Laws in general, operate, not like physical laws, regardless of men's faith or opinions about them; but to a great extent, they operate like the spiritual and religious laws of conscience; that is, they operate according as men have faith and expectation. At any rate, many of the laws of Social Science produce their effects, only *as* they are apprehended, and *by being* apprehended, by the reason and feelings of men. Thus, Distrust will bring a financial revulsion or "panic," whilst calm trust or heedless indifference or even ignorance, will sometimes avert one. Thus it is that speculation interferes with the legitimate operation of so many of the laws of Political Economy, and thus makes the study become one of human nature and of metaphysics, instead of a study of finance. The metaphysical conditions which modify laws, and often even reverse their supposed effects, are not the mental states of those by whom the laws are made, but of those by whom and to whom the laws are to be applied. Hence, it comes to pass, that the intentions of law makers are nothing towards the success of civil laws; nor commonly are the intentions of voters or electors much towards the success of getting either the candidates or the measures they want.

§ 4. *Condensation of General Social Laws.*

Spencer's four great principles are, (1) That evil is the result of non-adaptation of character to circumstances. (2) That the better, both of principles and races, are the stronger and will gradually prevail over the worse, and thus evil tends gradually to disappear. (3) That every person has a right to entire liberty, so far as his liberty does not interfere with the equal liberty of other persons. (4) That this principle of equal liberty is the principle of justice, and must be supplemented by an additional principle of "negative beneficence:" (Soc. Stat. p. 98) namely, "voluntary abstinence, for the sake of others, from the full exercise of our just rights." But we do not think he succeeds in showing how this latter will be accomplished.

Miraculously or else traditionally Revealed Religion, alone can save society, as well as the Individual. It saves by general principles and general means, which are real causes. These causes are already introduced into human nature, history and society. Nevertheless, God still has a connection with, and personal rule over those causes, and also over persons,—so that the ignoring of God, is rebellion against him, and so, necessarily produces a false philosophy. To ignore God, even in the spontaneous disappearance of evils, is to put stops to the working of the *Cause* of the spontaneous disappearance, and, therefore, stops to the disappearance itself.

The spontaneous elimination and evanescence of evils, is only of WEAK evils; unless, onthat ETERNAL and infinite plane, unknown to mortals, where evil itself may be shown to be weakness.

It is true yet, and must continue true for a long time, that morality and government must be the chief reliances, as substitutes for that animal instinct which guides brutes; and, for that science of humanity which is not yet known.

"All force expended in one direction, is lost in some other direction. No force is without its reciprocal action." The earth holds the moon in its course, but yet the moon makes the tides on the earth, and even draws the planet itself, some measure, out of its regular course. Compulsion spoils those who use it.

"Man, can neither create nor annihilate," passions nor social powers, any more, than physical ones. "All that he can do, is to direct these forces," and to set them to balancing each other.

Within certain but only narrow limits, wants create facilities and inventions and discoveries. This, it may be hoped, will occur, accordingly as men are brought more and more to see that they have great and real social needs, and to see the evils of their own systems.

The social organism is like the individual, in being subject to a law, whereby there takes place a process of adaptation of personal character, to the conditions of Nature and of circumstance. But still, it is the duty of Society's doctors, "to AID Nature." As Spencer (Biology, § 377) says, "In civilized man there is going on a new class of equilibrations,—those between his (own) actions, and the actions of the societies he forms. (First Prin. § 135). Social restraints and requirements are forever altering his activities, and, by consequence, his nature; and as fast as his nature is altered, social restraints and requirements undergo more or less re-adjustment."

The higher the being, whether vegetable, animal, or society, the more true it is that it will have a separate organ for every different vocation or function.

The makers, judges, and executors of laws are human; and hence, selfish and shortsighted. And therefore we must constitute our laws accordingly; remembering the unreasonableness, &c. of the men who are to administer them.

Government of all kinds, whether civil or communistic or family, must be absolutely free—in proportion to the number of individuals involved in the application of any principle of law, and to their distance in space, and to their nearness in morality and intellect.

The rights of the great divisions or Units of society, must ever be held inviolate. And in mature society, there are principles evolved which are of equal rights with the units.

Laws have more than one effect; and any designed effect requires a simultaneous law-arrangement of two or more laws, to accomplish it; like compounds in medicine, and like the correcting lenses of the telescope.

The more fit concrete and nearer, any function, instinct, or organ is, to its proper direct action, the less must be the application of balances or checks; and *vice-versa.*

We must remember the dualism, of even the good powers and orders, that exists everywhere in nature; and which, in Sociology, divides the representative powers, and requires laws to be double, to counteract each other's refractions.

Duality runs through nature; in sexes; in centrifugal and centripetal powers; in growth and decay; in attraction and repulsion; in mind and body; in church and state; in two parties; in two kinds of chemical affinities; in two kinds of electricity; in good and evil; in day and night, &c. The duality we are speaking of, is not like that which Fourier speaks of, namely, one of alternation and subversion; but it is a duality of concurrence and production, and is like the duality of sex which pervades all nature, and which perhaps originates from the same deep and hidden causes as sex itself. Everywhere, the world is propelled, and both things and thoughts begotten, by the duality of Resemblance and Contrast.

CHAP. III. EQUILIBRATA OF SOCIETY.

§ 1. *Spontaneous combining powers.*

The spontaneous combining powers in society, act to combine both those that are alike, and also those that are opposite. These combining tendencies consist of two entirely different kinds. On the one hand, persons whose interests and feelings are alike, will join together more or less permanently. And on the other hand, those classes and races which are very opposite to one another, will naturally seek each other's society; because of the good that each can do to and for the other, and because each supplies qualifications that the other lacks. This is the relation between the highly educated and the entirely ignorant. This also is the relation between the very rich and the very poor. It seems even to find a counterpart in the tacit peace between Roman Catholics and Quakers; when they both perhaps are at "outs" with nearly all the other denominations.

These sorts of combinations sometimes or frequently take a political form, and result in some of the most unexpected and reactionary movements in government. The Tories and the Radicals of England often unite with such results. These results seem to follow also from other causes. Oftentimes men are found who take special pains to convince the world, that they themselves are free from the prejudice that might naturally be expected in their class. Thus, the Commoner will take extra pains to show by his manners and sentiments, that *he* is not a "Plebeian"; and with a similar ambition, the nobleman will espouse the interests and the measures of the poorest and most needy. Sentiments thus espoused in the first place out of mere love of approbation,—become in time the sincere convictions of their hearts, or at any rate, the permanent policy of their lives. The result is also aided by this, that there are always some persons who will become peculiarly disgusted with other persons, for the very prejudices and errors with which they themselves have been most familiar, namely, those of their own class. And to become disgusted with our *own* evils is rather a good sign.

A careful observer of society, soon perceives the mutual attraction between the highest and lowest classes. The American internal war, and indeed most other such wars, have been produced by a union of the very opposite classes of society. In fact, these two classes generally act together in England, as well as in this country. That same worldliness which is generally the cause and effect of splendid success in the fortunate, produces in the unfortunate, indolence and vice, which soon sink them to the lowest strata. That same worldliness produces, also, an inability to appreciate that which is best and most interior in morals and religion, and a tendency to the showy and the external; hence there come certain moral sympathies between these opposite classes, far stronger and deeper than are commonly found from either, towards the middle classes. Then also, the distance is so great, that friction, collision, and even emulation and envy, are precluded. And then again, each of these classes can do for the other, what the other is most apt to need or to want, both in things that are right and also in things that are wrong.

On the other hand, the highest and lowest live more nearly to *nature*, than the middling classes. The lowest live so, as a matter of course. The highest live so, because they are elevated above the comparative necessity for those restraints, both on passion and appearances and generosity, which trammel the middle classes. Neither party being much afraid of "society," and both being strongly set in their own way even by principles, the world fears them, respects them, and even tolerates in them, vices and oppositions which it would set itself against with crushing force, in the middle classes.

The good order of society, requires the ultimate supremacy of the middle classes, in the *actual* administration; but at least the equality with them of the highest and the lowest, in the constitution and laws. But we know, that the exact opposite is often the real state of the case, and government is too often administered by secret coalitions between a handful of the *very* highest, and the leaders of the mobs, and thus with the mobs themselves.

§ 2. *Spontaneous quarreling powers.*

The quarreling powers depend somewhat, upon the oppositions of the combining powers just above mentioned. As human nature has so many faults, and as the faulty are least apt to bear with the faults of others, it soon arises that those persons and those classes ages and races, who are quite near together, both in interests and feelings, become prejudiced against each other personally, or become rivals in pursuits, and perhaps both. This occurs as soon as outward pressure is removed. And then, unless the relationship between them is maintained by very close bonds indeed, so as to form personal or corporation-friendships, the parties will become bitter enemies. Hence, ages races and classes who are near each other, are apt to quarrel among themselves, and form cliques in social intercourse, or parties in politics.

§ 3. *Spontaneous Reactionary powers.*

There is a class of latent, corrective, and oscillating, social powers. But the PRINCIPLES of the reaction lie deeper in nature than we can very easily explain. But one of its elements evidently is a love of novelty, or rather, a tendency to be fatigued by sameness, even of the best things; and of course, much more so, by the worst things. By this law, an age of infidelity will sooner or later be succeeded by one of belief; an age of sham and form, by one of sincerity and spirit. Things after long disuse, will sometimes come up again with all the charm of novelty, added to their natural beauty.

This is probably the same law that Comte hints at, when he

mentions *ennui*, as one of the bases of hope for the improvement of society.

A notable instance of this law is, that "one of the latest novelties in French journalism, is to make considerable use of the New Testament. Alexander Dumas so thoroughly appreciated the love of novelty, which characterizes his countrymen, that, in one of his novels he incorporated a large part of one of the Gospels, with great effect. To many of his readers it was the *newest* part of his book."

Again, take the case of children. Children suffer in consequence of their parents' faults, both by general consequences, and by the particular consequence of the entailment of a hereditary tendency to the same fault. This, under Christianity, causes the children to dislike the fault as a kind of inherited slavery. The sin in the parents, having been more or less voluntary, was guilt: but in the child, at first, the tendency or the fault not being of moral freedom, is not guilt, and so makes room for the possibility of more or less of self-developing cure, which, real guilt would perhaps not be able to accomplish.

In human nature there are certain sympathies for the injured and the down-trodden, that will sooner or later arouse influences for their relief. Even if a class are so far down in the social and moral scale, as seldom to furnish to outward observers any instance of the nobler or better powers of human nature,—if they are so low that FACTS can say but little in their favor; then FICTION will take up their cause, and fancy will imagine and paint specimens of their imaginary heroes in unknown circumstances.

The lower and more degraded the class really is, the more strange, the more picturesque, the more startling, and the more effective, the fiction will prove. It is in strict accordance with these great principles, or metaphysical laws of society, that the book called Uncle Tom's Cabin has had such a powerful influence in counteracting slavery. Similar tendencies worked in the Middle Ages, aiding in the emancipation of the European serfs.

One of the principal features of *modern fiction* consists, in the exhibition of unexpected goodness in that unfortunate class of women, for whom general society seems to have no practical sympathy, and in regard to whom, those who have sympathy seem almost hopeless of any method to produce much practical good. But observe,—the rise and prevalence of this kind of fiction, is exactly and immediately preceding a strong feeling among the leaders of some of the benevolent *societies*, that something can, and ought to be done for them, more than can be done by merely *individual* charity. The efforts of these benevolent persons, are as yet a mere imperceptible item in the hidden recesses of society, doing little, and scarcely hoping much from any means at their command. But they are types and prophecies.

The natural sympathy of society here at work, must be strictly distinguished from that morbid sympathy, which feels only or chiefly for the murderer or the criminal, and little useful sympathy for the victim; a mere self-righteous sentimentalism sometimes, or an affectation of singularity. The fact is, that confounding the poor outcast women,—the *victims* of society,—with those who make society their victims, namely, the robbers and swindlers and real criminals, is one of the principal reasons why the criminals themselves cannot be ferreted out and punished. The defensive natural sympathies and powers of society, can only be claimed for criminals in so far as crime is the *necessary* result of misfortune and oppression; which is not the case with most criminals in the United States. Moreover, the defensive natural powers of society, cannot be appealed to in any such a manner as to exclude society from the right to defend itself *effectually*, and by whatever means *necessary*, from its aggressors,—those who are enlisted in a selfish habitual and professional war against it, and against every victim, unfortunate enough to fall under their skill or power.

§ 4. *Evils balancing each other.*

Evils will produce their effects in some manner. They often counteract each other: but not without producing special evils that would not follow from counteracting evil by good, or by the power of justice. This is well illustrated by McCosh on the Divine Government, and by a late book, "The Gospel of Good and Evil," of which some extracts are here quoted from "The Radical" for May, 1869. "Gambling is a species of mental exhilaration. The spirit of adventure is inherent, and bestows that peculiar nerve which risks, encounters, and overcomes." "*The petty vexations* of life, and ebullitions of ill-humor, keep the passions in daily drill; just as soldiers in peace keep up the martial spirit by drilling, by petty quarrels, duels, and wrangling brawls. *Family-miffs* are a grand institution for giving needful repose and after-exhilaration, to overtasked affection." "Tobacco narcotizes the baser passions and appetites,—it lulls the BEAST to repose. Many an angry word and violent action are diverted from the wife and children, by the soothing action of the pipe." "The uses of *fashion* and vanity are found in their conservative influence upon morals; and their propulsive power in human progress, makes them indispensable agents for good." "Slander springs from useful exuberance of the organ of self-esteem. What an ingenious contrivance is scandal, to give ebb and flood and never-ceasing movement, to the moral atmosphere! With easy grace would unwatched virtue yield to temptation, and a sorry condition of society would ensue." "It is to the criminal propensities of man that we owe civilization. Crime first suggests and compels men to organize, that a system of defense may be adopted against this evil."

Alas, that the Radicals cannot make a better *basis* for civilization, than the foregoing crime-begetting one.

§ 5. *Equilibrity of sentiments.*

Another of the general social laws, is a certain instinctive tendency of the opinions, of an individual or of a society, towards a certain ideal equilibrium. In other words, one set of opinions tends to equilibrate another set of opinions; that is to say, the dangers of one part of one's opinions are counteracted by the eccentricities of another part. The why and wherefore of this, it is not so easy to explain. Some might attribute it to their peculiar theory of the equilibritiveness of human character itself. They tell us that at bottom, there is very little difference of inward moral character between different persons notwithstanding the differences of their outward characters. But, while this may be true of the spontaneous characters of *races*, of neighborhoods, and of all hereditary classes,—it can scarcely be true of those classes which are self-selected. However, the position is probably true as to the mere opinions and sentiments, (apart from the passionate actions), of the generality of men, in any given *status* of civilization. And, being true of the individuals generally, and the generality of individuals making the ruling sentiment of a locality,—we may say that the aforesaid position is true of natural societies, precincts, and nations; and this may therefore be a sufficient explanation of this equilibritiveness of the opinions and sentiments, that we are now speaking of. But it applies LESS directly to a corporation considered by itself.

§ 6. *Calculus of Variations.*

The spontaneous reactionary powers, also the self-counterbalancing of evils and of opinions, and all the equilibrata that we have pointed out, seem to show how the distant branches of mankind can never fly off from the general course, beyond certain limitations. In this respect, the study of these reactions is like La Grange's calculus of variations, which was invented purposely and applied to show, that the variations in the orbits of our planets,—which some astronomers feared, would sometime "endanger the stability of the solar system,"—had *limits*, within the very same mechanical forces that produced them,—sufficient to prevent those dire results, and in due time, to cause a reaction and return to former curves. There are limits, probably, even to the distance that lost souls can make, of separation from the race. The Psalmist says, although he "make his bed in hell, God is there." (Psalm cxxxix. 8.) And, *vice-versa*, what concerns us more to know,—there may be limits to the distance, the saved can rise above the lost.

CHAP. IV. CONSTITUTION OF SOCIETY.

§ 1. *Real bonds of society.*

Society is held together by, and happiness in it depends upon, the following things,—*Love of the other sex,*—*Acquaintanceship,*—*Material or business interests,*—*Education,* its interests and its literature,—Goodness, namely, doing justice to others, and forbearance under injustice real or apparent:

Limitation of the habitable Earth. This becomes a stronger bond gradually, as population increases, and as barbarism and isolation become less possible, and thus the geographical limitations force men into some society or other.

Government and Laws. The comparative power of government, as a bond holding society together in peace, decreases with the increasing limitations of the Earth by increase of population; but its power FOR GOOD OR EVIL, correspondingly increases, as the possibility of escape from it decreases.

The question how far we *can* have good government, depends, in part, on the amount and force of error and human infirmity, and not only on wickedness or sin, and hence there is special use of light and knowledge on the subject.

Patriotism as a selfish NATIONAL feeling, is only a temporary bond, of isolated nations and of unsettled ages. Its *foreign* effects are as bad as its *domestic* are good; therefore these nullify one another, and make it of no account morally in the highest view of the ultimate results. But the spirit of patriotism can easily be stimulated to act for one's own immediate neighborhood, as well as for one's nation; and so, be made to act for both the centrifugal and centripetal forces of society. Yet still, its evil foreign effects entitle it to but little approbation.

But patriotism as a self-sacrificing feeling of human love, such as naturally expands always to be co-extensive with national and human intercourse, is a very necessary element.

In ordinary times, the offices whether of church or state, do not fall to the best men, but rather the reverse. All affairs when they become ordinary, are apt to become matters of business; and business matters are,—well, we need not say what. But at any rate, there are necessary and higher elements, both in church and in state, than can possibly be made matters of business. Every one sees, this is true as to religion. But it is not so generally seen as to politics. And yet, it is just as impossible to conduct political affairs, without a high degree of patriotism, as it is to conduct religious affairs without a high degree of piety. And this high degree of patriotism in the one kind of officers, is just as necessary as the high degree of piety in the other kind.

In ordinary circumstances, the conduct of political affairs becomes the net resultant of contrasting interests, embodied in conflicting parties, sects, avocations, and classes of society. Now, just imagine what a bedlam or pandemonium, a church is turned into, when it becomes merely the resultant, the prize, and the theatre, of such conflicting embodiments, or even of such contending spirits. And the state becomes turned into its own peculiar kind of a bedlam or pandemonium, when its living spirit, patriotism, is suppressed, and the embodiments of the other great passions and interests of men, rise to the top and swim in corruption, or sail in a hurricane of war; or both.

§ 2. *Tests of a good social condition.*

Comte's general test of a true social system is, that it must be in harmony with itself, in all its parts, in all its details, and in all its consequences, as reasoned out by the finite mind. So impracticable indeed, is such a test, that Comte himself, in his arguments, treats it as if it must not only be consistent with itself; but that all its advocates and believers, as also its hypocritical assumers, must be in harmony *with one another* about it. But we will try to present a more practical view.

(*a*) *General Tests.* The true objects of a government, and the true tests of a good social condition, are not form but spirit; not any particular "——ocracy," but the physical and moral good of the people in the long course of ages. The general aim is the greatest amount of permanent *individual* happiness to all, with the least suffering to any. For national without individual happiness is mere vanity. Special regard must be paid then, to all the conditions that contribute to the happiness of the Individual Unit:—Increase of population, early marriage, family harmony, respect for age by youth, vegetable diet in dense populations, tillage, health and longevity, productiveness not too much in advance of the amount of productions wanted;—Economy in consumption, moral and physical improvement of the race, manifestation of the unity of interests between Individuals, classes, and societies; men doing the right things from attractions, or freedom in motives and feelings,—Independent benevolent study, as well as physical labor, made attractive,—"Indirect concurrence of the passions and inequalities which are now discordant,"—Feelings and ideas trained into habits in harmony with true interests,—Variety of occupation, turning labor into exercise,—Labor in groups or companies,—Worthy and moral enjoyment for honest wealth,—The settlement of new lands, regulated in so orderly and gradual a manner as to carry the comforts and blessings of civilization with it,—Righteous distribution of rewards or payments to and among, capital, industry, intellect, and morality; honesty and peace, giving the greatest inducements to industry; and the lowest rate of interest for capital.

(*b*) *Tests in Morality*:—Faith, reverence, truth, and utility, being appreciated and held in the highest and in equal values,

—Certainty of rewards according to individual deserts,—Infrequency of dishonesty and falsehood, and their ill-success,—Amount of common virtue being enough to cause men to continue moral, whilst there is an ever increasing release from the need to labor,—Harmonizing liberty with the qualifications to use it well, so that neither may be too far in advance of the other,—General contentment with station and circumstances, consistent with religion, virtue, and education,—High moral tone, especially for honesty and peace, both of officers and of laws, and of national conduct and character.

(c) *Tests in Fashions*:—Artificial refinements and consumption, so far as are necessary to furnish employment for all. These are necessary in the proportion that the land can support more than it employs to work it; and also in proportion to the human imperfections that need labor to prevent vice and waste of health.—Fashions that will make honesty and industry, marriage and healthy children, honorable,—A fashion that will adopt as its luxuries, *science*, beauties of *taste*, and in general, "the products of much labor rather than of expensive material;" where the luxuries shall be in home-arrangements, "pictures, furniture," &c., rather than in outward show,—Where the *number* of the unnecessary things, and not their value, is the greatest, and where the things themselves are least injurious,—Where the idle and luxurious persons (who *require* these luxuries), are the fewest in number, but where the many *could* get them honestly, if they did not already prefer better customs.

(d) *Tests as to labor*:—That all parties who are engaged in any work should have the fairest share of the profits; that is, where labor, capital, science, and morals, come nearest to having each an equal share; where the co-operative and mutual principles are carried out to their fullest extent *to those who will reciprocate,* whether domestic or foreign parties, so far as can be, without receiving their vices,—Where wages are remunerative, and the times of work reasonable, especially for women and children,—Where the prices of products and the times of labor are least, in proportion to the cost of living, including both the necessaries of nature and the artificial innocent demands of custom.

(e) *Tests as to government*:—Where taxation is incidentally a means to the furtherance of all the aims mentioned above,—Where government attempts especially to mitigate the evils of its own production, the inevitable results of the social organization; rather than to interfere with individual or local liberties,—Where government coöperates in these good ends, by its own examples, officers, and laws,—Where there are natural checks and balances *really* operative, and where the antagonistic forces of government are in due moral equilibrium,—Where government has the convictions of all classes of the people with it,—Where government is a true representation of the feelings of all, and recognizes in due proportion, all the distinctions, and guards against all the prejudices actually in existence. Government is a falsity, in proportion as it ignores (or pretends ignorance of) the distinctions and prejudices which society itself spontaneously develops. (In a republican government, all that is meant is, not class representation, but suitable laws to provide against any one class doing injustice to a weaker or less active or less numerous class; and suitable forms to the same end)—A proper representation and balance between the personal Units and Analytical Elements, namely Individual, Family, Precinct, and Corporation. (Freedom of Individuals is not possible, unless they have the privilege of segregating themselves, both in Precincts and voluntary corporations of their own preferences)—Where government if republican, secures that the people shall be educated and trained properly for the functions of citizens. This requires, first, good family government; second, that education shall be of the judgment, and produce social wisdom, rather than be of all knowledge, or merely for worldly success; third, that the true science of society should be held of the highest importance, and most properly taught, not only to the young, but also to the general public.

§ 3. *The spirit, not the form.*

More importance is usually attached to *forms* of government, and forms of election and forms of society, than is consistent with social prosperity. The *spirit* or principle *should* be the ultimatum. Any Nation or any society *could* be governed by an administration, partly composed of all three forms of government, as well as of one, provided such a society were characterized by harmony and fraternization within, and by peace outwardly. Common sense instructs us, that the truth which applies to denominational distinctions of churches and forms,—the truth that creeds or forms do not alter *true* Christianity, also applies to civil and political distinctions. So that, if we WILL idolize the forms, then our politicians and demagogues WILL make us pay for it. But there is no reason to hate or be jealous of other governments: only in that secondary sense that our jealousy causes them apprehension of aggression from us.

The form should be allowed to develop from, and thus to suit the spirit. And the greatest care should be taken to preserve, in society and in government, a right spirit. But the *ultimate* intentions or aims, are not by any means what constitute the spirit. The spirit of any party is far more plainly exhibited by the means they are willing to use, than by their intentions or aims. And the higher a true civilization becomes, the more men must and will adhere to right and fair *means*, as well as to right and fair *ends*. Thus, the character of the means is the best test of the character of the spirit.

Now, the means used are generally represented by *forms* of organization. For, in social affairs, the very first and mildest and most specious development of the wrong spirit, probably, takes place in an idolatrous attachment to usual forms. Such a refusal to progress, at once becomes a disease, and ends in social or political death. Hence, all forms of organization must undergo changes,—and all old organizations must pass away and be followed by new and different ones,—if we would allow society to progress really. Nor will these changes be always nor usually a return to former ones, but often to entirely new ones, utterly unconceived of until the time towards their appearing. This applies of course, not only to voluntary societies, but also to all the forms of government.

Says Wendell Phillips, (May 28, 1868); "It seems to me that organization is a mile-stone, which represents how far opinion had traveled when it crystallized into an organization. You cannot expect of * * * organization, necessarily in its shape as an organization, an acceptance of any NEW idea. As long as it can recognize its own place, and let you take yours, it is to be fellowshipped, not as a force in the movement of society, but as a breakwater and anchor to keep what we have gained."

§ 4. *The New Reliances.*

Our new theory of Social Science may be compared with the old, as to its main dependencies, in the following respects. Instead of relying chiefly on lengthy details in profuse constitutions and laws; our theory relies, partly, on a proper and national representation in laws and government, of all the principal active *powers* and constituencies; and partly on more and more constituting special and voluntary organs for each particular kind of duty; and partly on constituting the framework of government on the truly analytical Elements of human society, that is to say, on the philosophical Units of our Social Science. Or, to sum it briefly, our theory relies chiefly on the real powers, instead of on mere verbiage. And this, not so much by checks and balances of power, as by leaving to each its proper and natural duties.

This new basis of reliance differs from the old in this respect: The old basis, exactly prescribing *how* everything shall be done proved and finished, is exceedingly simple in theory, but inextricably complicated and uncertain in practice; and is ever becoming more and more complicated, and more and more entangled, and is felt to be more and more defeating to the very objects of government: But the new proposed basis, whilst complex in theory of organization, is simple in its practical application, and ever tending to become more and more productive of the true ends of government. Like as in medicine, a philosophical analysis of diseases, enables the practitioners to have easy work in their applications; but the brief axioms and phrases of "quacks," are apt to require all guesswork in their particular application. And what evils would happen under a scientific system, would manifest clearly and at once, where the fault or cause was to be found. Men and institutions would manifest their peculiar character with more simplicity, and thus they would each bear their own burden, whether of praise or blame, and would be revised accordingly.

CHAP. V. THE DOCTRINES OF PROGRESS.

§ 1. *In General.*

For reasons previously stated, we cannot, as some do, make the theory and doctrines of progress swallow up the whole theory and classification of Social Science; because those doctrines are only to be obtained as the last and highest results of the science. Here it happens as in the case of Astronomy. At a certain advanced stage, the science came to a stand-still for want of more abstract analysis. Hence, the Differential and Integral Calculus were devised. Just so, the Dynamics which Comte and Spencer were seeking, cannot we think be found until some new and transcendental method of social analysis is arrived at.

All that Comte argues for, can be accomplished by and in our Precincts. And after that, most of what Spencer argues for, may be applied to a national government including such Precincts. And in the mean time, many of Mr. Mill's views may be regarded as eminently practical for the transition state.

"Order and progress both come from one and the same set" of suitable conditions of the corresponding forces. And of the two forces whose resultant is order and progress, one consists of imitativeness, the customary, and the moral, including the rational; and the other consists of the governmental forces.

"Between different stages of progress, there is a time of confusion and chaos," either of forces or of ideas or of both. And this is true, not only in general, but also in regard to progress in each particular point.

The progress of society, is a process of life; only to be examined, by the principles and sciences of life. And divine morality is a process of world-wide and eternal life.

In the early stages of society, the direct or immediate causes of action may be interests; but the indirect permanent and deep causes are feelings. Nevertheless, the more society becomes enlightened intellectually, the more will interest become one of the real motives at the bottom, in all the contentions between the different classes of society, and between different localities. And interests work *subtly* in existing feelings passions and false reasonings. Animosity against the "owners of cheap labor," had as much to do with the cry for union and abolition, as sympathy for the colored race.

§ 2. *Spencer's Limitations.*

One of Mr. Spencer's principles is, that all evil results from the non-adaptation of constitution to circumstances. Admitting this, yet we ask, who shall say that education and charity and religion, are not some of the "circumstances" which are the conditions of man's happiness? and who shall say how much governmental interference in business or social details, might also be necessary to adapt him to his "circumstances" thus interpreted?

Again, Mr. Spencer says, Every man has freedom to do all that he wills, provided he infringes not the equal freedom of any other man. The principle is pretty, but we must watch the inferences. The error of the inferences as to the do-nothing theory, may be shown by an example,—thus, Virtue is a necessity and antecedent to social improvement. Virtue consists of three parts, namely, the outward action, the belief in the reasonable utility thereof, and the moral internal will. Now, whilst government cannot reach the moral internal will, yet it *must* often touch the outward action, Why then, may it not also touch the intermediate thing, namely, the reasonable utility of virtue, and teach and encourage virtuous "rights," as well as encourage patent rights and copy rights, the latter of which Mr. Spencer is strongly in favor of. Not forcing good, but *encouraging* good, is what is asked for.

But again,—we say that Mankind and God have some rights in the matter of civil society, and that therefore, one man's freedom is not the only limit to another man's freedom. But this extensive subject must be postponed until we consider the relation of government to religion, which will perhaps form part of a future work.

Yet Mr. Spencer thinks that "the order of nature without law, should be left to decide these questions." If so, why may not the same order of nature without law, be left to carry on the whole business of government? "Do away with disturbing of arrangements," says he, "and allow things to take their natural course, and the best men will EVENTUALLY draw to themselves, respectful obedience." But we answer, sin and ignorance ARE "DISTURBING ARRANGEMENTS," and who shall say how many thousands of years yet, it shall be before their disturbing influences shall be removed, and the best men will draw to themselves respect? And what is to become of mankind with all their miseries, in the mean time?

Nevertheless, there is a great truth underlying Mr. Spencer's theory;—and it must be fully granted and kept distinctly in mind, that a human government should only interfere with human liberty, in the proportion to which itself and human nature, approach to perfection and righteousness; at least of those who control the government. The restrictions over the liberty of the citizen, should be only in proportion to the perfection of the ruling classes, individually and socially.

Another principle to be demonstrated and acted upon is, that large and ample provision should be made to enable those persons who feel themselves aggrieved by human society, to separate themselves from it, or, as Mr. Spencer says, to exercise the "right to ignore the state," yet in such ways as that they should not endanger or disturb those who are satisfied. The necessity of some resources for dissenters and theorists to escape the interference of government, becomes all the more necessary in our system or theory, because we advocate considerable interference by proper Precincts and Corporations, in affairs of education, morality, religion, &c., as will appear in the chapters on those subjects. The great error of government in all time, has been, attempting to force individuals to conform to its own peculiarities, instead of merely to prevent individuals from disturbing others.

In this connection appears one of the great uses of our small Precincts, also of voluntary communities and political corporations. To such, special privileges might be allowed according to circumstances. Just as the old Roman law allowed persons of the same various views and feelings, in certain cases, to inhabit their own special Precincts and districts, and there to administer their own laws in their own way. Either our system for Precincts, or our system for Corporations, affords all the right possibilities for individuals to "ignore the state": but we cannot imagine any other systems that would.

§ 3. *Periods of human progress.*

The elementary stages of human civilized society, must be characterized by vast accumulations of facts and of words, and by great memories. In this respect society must be like the individual. The infantile process of learning, is to perceive ideas intuitively or "by guess," and THEREBY to learn the meaning of words. But the adult process of learning, when the meanings of words are known, is to learn ideas *from* words. In the transitional age the two methods are more or less confused,—and then the vivid memory of words is of value, to keep down the infantile process of guessing the meaning too soon. Hence, in the very early stages of a progressive society, considerable attention to words and MAXIMS must be expected, and some degree of excess thereof may be overlooked, as long as its heart is right, and its desire to learn is active.

The critical or metaphysical stages of human progress, both individual and social, come next to be considered. The critical or metaphysical period of the individual mind, as also of society, is a necessary transitional period (as Comte observes, but in regard only to society at large). It is the period of self-criticism,—a period intervening between that improvement which is produced by other powers, and as it were by constraint,—and that still more subsequent period, when habits have become second nature, and when the involuntariness of obedience, is not like it was in the first stage, a mere instinct and ignorant innocence,—but has become in a degree positively virtuous, without being distinctly conscious that it *is* virtuous; because, by reason of confirmation by habit, it no longer needs deliberate efforts of the will, or even self-conscious struggles against a contrary inducement.

The fourth stage is one of confirmed good moral and intellectual habits. It is also to be noticed, that the metaphysical stage is not possibly consonant with the highest or fullest efforts of the human mind, individually or socially; because it continually interrupts the thoughts of their objects, by intruding thoughts and feelings about the person himself, the thinker; and thus in an intellectual point of view, hinders concentration. Moreover, the metaphysical stage or habit, whilst it lasts, is necessarily productive of pride and thus of evil. But so far as the evil thus produced is necessary, it is not guilt; and will in time reach towards its own cure.

§ 4. *Progressions to be homogeneous.*

Practical suggestions for improvement, whether of the science or of society itself, should be offered in series or sets. Each set of improvements should be worked or taught a while, before going on with the next set. Each set should include references to all or most of the matters wherein improvements are wanted, so far as they are apprehended. As one set of improvements may be necessary to prepare for others, or make them practicable; just so, the suggestions of the one set may be necessary to prepare people's minds to receive or judge of the next set. Hence it is, that in Social Science the historical facts themselves, are essentially connected with and must be coördinated with the science of them, in order to make desirable progress. To that end it is necessary, that improvements be suggested in somewhat like the order and proportions that society needs them. And equally so, it is impossible for the sociologists to foretell particular events far ahead, or in general terms to advise in advance, the true methods; because the sociologist himself can only progress in his science practically, in something like the same proper order and proportions that society itself must follow.

§ 5. *Who the coming leaders will be.*

One of the most general principles of the social motion is, that leaders will arise, and the generality of men will follow them. This will be so, whether any civil law exists or not. We see this in the power of fashion, and in the influence of example, all this world over. Here then we ask, what hope is there of good leaders arising to benefit society? And leaders are a very different class of persons from rulers or drivers. They are an order of spiritual powers, like the old religious powers, as to morality; but very different from them in their breadth and culture, both as to ideas and as to liberality. Comte has some good thoughts on this point.

The new order of spiritual powers will be unlike the outgrown order of the ecclesiastical, in another respect,—"they will be humble." This consequence results from several causes, but chiefly these:—the progress of all scientific investigation, is not one of absolute certainty, but avowedly only one of probability and of theory. And then, from this further cause, that these powers would obtain and maintain their influence and supremacy, not by material forces nor by supernatural terrors, but by educating the people, cultivating their faculties, and disseminating truths, tending ever more and more to bring the people up even with the advancing front of the leaders themselves. In other words, the very method by which Social Science rules, is, by ever lessening the moral and intellectual distance between its professors and the public. Thus the new order of spiritual powers, it is hoped, will be humble.

When Comte comes to the question, who the new leaders will be, or how they will arise,—he gives up the problem as insolvable. But we suspect, that much of what has been said in the first part of this Introduction, can be readily applied to this part, and therefore need not be recapitulated here. Many of the persons of whom we have already spoken as the helpers of Social Science, are only so indirectly as it were, or unintentionally; inasmuch as the works in which they are directly and intentionally engaged, are frequently the improvement of society itself, rather than of the science.

Furthermore we suggest, perhaps the coming leaders, like the best preachers, will be those who can succeed best in inducing society to hate its sins and evils most, and to forsake them most abidingly. In such work, not only good spirit good talent and virtue are necessary, but also a good example, and a good life toward society,—an abnegation of self, by devotion to Mankind. Perhaps the great practical social reformers of modern times, may be indicative of something about the origin of this class of the spiritual powers; also the founders of Roman Catholic houses in various ages, the modern co-operating capitalists, and all earnest thinkers and sympathizers on the great social problems, who have faith enough in their theories, to live up to them, and to sacrifice present self for others and for the future self. In the long range of history, the lessons of failure become almost as instructive as the lessons of success. Whenever the generality of such leaders would arrive at one general and uniform theory, there would arise a profoundly respected social power; and *so* in proportion as they *tend* towards such a general theory. At any rate, the main *impetus* of their influence need not await until after educating *all* the people highly, for the generality of people are moved more by feeling or affection than by reasoning.

CHAP. VI. THEORY OF THE SIX UNITS.

§ 1. *In General.*

We have now come to what we suppose to be one of the most original and valuable parts of our theory, namely, that human society and therefore Social Science, each consists of six fundamental elements, or Units; namely, Individual, Family, Social Circle, Precinct, Nation, and Mankind.

Both Aristotle and Hegel seem to admit, with almost the force of our idea of Units, three great ideas, the Family, the Precinct [or commonwealth] and the Nation,—and Mulford seems to regard them as THE three "distinctive" forms of society, (chap. 16), the Family having "organic," and the commonwealth, "formal," but yet necessary relation to the Nation.

Mulford, however, does not neglect to place the Individual in some degree of prominence. Thus, if we may call his first thirteen and last two chapters, the *abstract* relations of the Nation, then the intermediate chapters are the *concrete* relations of the Nation. These (concrete) are given in the following order,—Individual, Family, Commonwealth, Confederacy, Empire. According to Mr. Mulford as we understand him, the "Nation is the friend of the first three, namely, Individual, Family and Commonwealth," but (as we understand him) the antagonist of the other two. This is coming very near to the doctrine of fundamental elements or units; nevertheless, the idea does not seem to have suggested itself to him. On the contrary, p. 276, he says explicitly, "The Family is not the unit of society,"—and nothing but the Nation has his high term "moral personality," which is his equivalent for our term Unit.

Others also, have singled out Family, Church and State merely, as the great divisions of Social Science, with such preeminence as shows they unconsciously regarded them as tantamount to our idea of the Units, yet without connecting these divisions by any general theory, or by the relation of fundamental elements. But church is a corporation and not a natural person, and State is only an abstract term for the Science.

But not only the Individual and the Nation are natural persons, but every one of the essential elements of our analytics is a natural person, namely, Individual, Family, Social Circle, Precinct, Nation, and Mankind.

On the contrary, the assumption by a Nation, that *it* is the source or origin of *all* political power, is high presumption before Heaven, and a usurpation of the rights of the Almighty and Divine Creator. And this is so, whether the presumptuous government is of Belshazzar or of Nebuchadnezzar, or of a democracy.

Of one thing we may be sure; government, to be permanent, must be homogeneous in its essential elements. If Precincts were only recognizable as artificial persons or corporations, then there could be no permanent peace and order in society, until the Nation itself were recognized as only a corporation. So, on the other hand, the Nation, as a local organism distinct from corporation, can never be satisfactorily dispensed with, unless all the under or local departments, namely, the Precincts, can also be dispensed with. This would mean, a people joined together as a grand corporation instead of as a Nation, and consisting exclusively of sub-corporations, abstract from locality,—a conception too indefinite and too general to be judged of, without further experience in the parts of the system separately. And again on the other hand, a Nation can never enjoy its full rights as a God-given "moral personality," only as it recognizes the moral personality of the Precinct also. The law of personality is, as Mulford says, "be a person and respect other persons"; and we add,—respect them, however small or humble they may be.

§ 2. *Origin of this Theory.*

It may be appropriate here, to state simply how our theory of the Units originated. The Units, (or most of them) were arranged as the best possible division of the subject we could devise, merely as divisions of the study, before their functions as units were clearly conceived. And here arises one strong argument for this number and classification of the units, namely, that the arrangement is necessary, in order to classify the materials of Social Science.

But our theory not only makes our divisions logical or subjective divisions of the science, but also fundamental elements of society itself.

Comte had stated that the Family is the true unit of society,—and not the Individual. This struck us at once, as a favorable idea. But when we reflected, as Paley says, that all that nations and societies suffer or enjoy, is not felt in the bulk, but only in the Individuals, we perceived that the Individual cannot be given up as a unit; hence, then, we have at least two units, namely, the Individual and the Family. And when once the fact, that there must be a PLURALITY OF UNITS, was assumed, and what the first two are, the way was opened to reach the true and full number of them. Nation and Mankind soon occurred, as two other units at the other extreme. Then the rights of States or minor localities, and of voluntary corporations, had to be placed somewhere between the extremes already ascertained. This problem was insoluble, except by a theory of the Tribe which should make the principle or spirit of Tribe survive in modern society, under differentiated forms, namely as Social Circle and Precinct, as natural unalterable elements, and Corporation as an artificial element and therefore as a distinct genus from all the six previously obtained, not itself a unit but a type of a unit. See CORPORATION, for a fuller account.

§ 3. *Some Singular Sixes.*

We present here a few classifications of nature, by sixes, which by analogy tend to show that we have hit upon and discovered the right *number* of, and the right particular units, of which society really and virtually is composed. Most of these classifications presently to follow, are numbered so that all the 1's may be compared together, and all the 2's, and so on. And we hope none of these our analogies, will be thought to be any wilder than some of Fourier, or Comte or Hobbes or others who have labored in this department of imaginary thought.

The figure which gives the maximum amount of internal content, with the minimum amount of external surface of similar bodies joined together, is a HEXAGON; as, for instance, the cells of the bee.

In developed civilization, there are six great classes of society. They help in forming Social Circles, and they give the bases of limits of, and highest moral shares of property, in distribution. These will be portrayed in another book.

The errors and vices of Mankind, have instinctively and spontaneously alighted on our six units, as the fundamental motors of human passions. Nearly all the "respectable" crimes and great enormities, are committed for the sake of, and under the perverted infatuation of, one or the other of these ideas that we have singled out and generalized under the name of units of society; namely, either for the rights of (1) the Individual, or of (2) the Family, or of (3) Social Circle, class, and clan, or of (4) one's own Precinct or Neighborhood, or (5) of Nationality, or for (6) the welfare of Mankind, including under Mankind, as we do, religious action in society, which plants itself on that wide human ground, for the justification of social compulsion and religious persecution.

Roget classifies his "Thesaurus of English Words" into six Main Divisions, thus, Abstract Relations, Space, Matter, Intellect, Volitions, Affections.

Ballou (in Practical Christian Socialism, p. 108) has six infinities; namely, the Deific spirit, the soul-spirit, matter, space, duration, diversity.

Paley's Divisions of Moral and Political Philosophy, are the following:—

1 Preliminary Considerations.
2 Moral Obligations. Origin of, &c.
3 Relative Duties of Persons and Property.
4 Duties towards Ourselves.
5 Duties towards God.
6 Elements of Political Knowledge.

Spencer's lines of progress, are readily made into six, thus:—

1 Advance from Qualitative to Quantitative.
2 Advance from Concrete to Abstract.
3 Application of abstract to new orders of concrete.
4 Simultaneous advance in generalization and specialization.
5 Increasing subdivision and re-union.
6 Constantly improving Consensus.

Our classification of the sciences:—

1 Perceptible Mechanical Powers.
2 Imperceptible Mechanical Powers.
3 Imponderable Powers.
4 Animal Powers.
5 Human Transcendental Powers.
6 Supernatural Powers.

Our Units.	*Systems of Crystallization.*	*Astronomical Systems.*
1 Individual	1 Monometric	1 Satellites
2 Family	2 Dimetric	2 Planets
3 Social Circle	3 Trimetric	3 Suns
4 Precinct	4 Monoclinic	4 Groups
5 Nation	5 Triclinic	5 Clusters
6 Mankind	6 Hexagonal	6 Nebulæ

Organs of sense.	*Religious Society.*	*Plato's Sciences.*
1 Sensation	1 Adam	1 Arithmetic
2 Temperature	2 Adam and Eve	2 Geometry, Plane
3 Taste	3 Patriarchy	3 Geom. three dimen.
4 Smell	4 Israel in Egypt	4 Astronomy and Motion
5 Hearing	5 Israel in Palestine	5 Harmonics
6 Sight	6 Christian Church	6 Real Existence
Spencer's Universal Data.	*Mental States.*	*Mental Faculties.*
1 Force	1 Physical Emotion	1 Consciousness External
2 Motion	2 Conception	2 Consciousness Internal
3 Matter	3 Idea	3 Association of Resemblance
4 Time	4 Thought	4 Association of Contrast
5 Space	5 Metaphysical Emotion	5 Abstraction
6 Unknowable Power	6 Will	6 Generalization
Suggestions from Oken's Classification.	*Hegel's Classification.*	*Comte's Classification of the Sciences.*
1 Living Nature	1 Logic	1 Mathematics
2 Creations of Elements	2 Mechanics	2 Astronomy
3 Functions of Elements	3 Physics	3 Physics
4 Cosmogony	4 Organic Physiology	4 Chemistry
5 Material Totalities	5 Psychology	5 Physiology
6 Immaterial Totalities	6 [The Idea]?	6 Sociology

§ 4. *Combinations of the Six Units.*

(*a*) *Combinations in Concatenation.* Each personal unit of society, contains a subdivision or principle which points to, or connects with, the unit next above it. The Individual has sexual functions, and these point to the Family. The Family has grand-parents, and gives out brethren and sisters to make new friendly Families,—these give rise to Social Circles. And these seek to reside in near neighborhood, and thus become Precinct. And these again, multiplying, constitute Nation.

In the development of society, society comes to self-consciousness and to the understanding of itself, only by means of the light which each one unit throws upon the character of the others. By spiritualizing Goethe's great saying, that man knows himself only as he knows external nature, we will readily see how, in the origin of human society, the individual man or woman only knows himself or herself, *after* organizing into the Family relation. And likewise, one Family alone does not (or would not) know itself, only by becoming a Social Circle or a tribe, viz., only after several Families had come to exist in the same neighborhood, and thus spontaneously to have formed a tribe—So likewise, the tribe could not understand itself fully nor be really developed, only by coming into relation with several tribes, that is, by becoming part of a Nation; or, the one tribe growing and dividing into several tribes. So likewise, the Nation cannot understand its true functions, only by realizing its position as a part of the great Family, Mankind.

And now, in the advanced stages of society, when new organs are put forth, and new settlements and new developments resolve the tribe into two distinct branches,—one, the preferred acquaintance (namely, the Social Circle)—and the other, the Precinct of nearest or lowest degree of local government, we must reduce our argument to adapt it to modern conditions, and then say thus:—The Individual knows himself only by coming to the Family; and both Individual and Family know themselves only by coming both into the Social Circle, or into the local organization or Precinct; and all these again, comprehend themselves only by their relations with the Nation; and it again, can comprehend itself only by means of its relations to Mankind.

Furthermore, as Nation and Precinct, Social Circle and Family, are all Individual human beings, these general principles will hold when applied beginning with the Nation and going *downwards*. Any organization of men can understand itself only by understanding and appreciating the elements of which it is composed, and with which it most constantly comes into relationship and contact. So then, the Nation can understand itself only by appreciating Precinct, Social Circle, and Individual. So also, the Precinct can only understand itself, by appreciating all the units below it; and so on for the rest. Thus it is, that the very principle which runs through the development of all human society, has only to be viewed from the opposite side, to be seen to confirm the great doctrine of the right of some government influence being vested in all the units of society severally.

(*b*) *Combinations in Solution.* We now come to combinations of a more complex and versatile kind.

In the development of Society, society combines its elements variously; hence we observe that three of them, namely, Precinct, Nation, and Mankind, involve the idea of locality and are dependent upon the location, and so might be called the local units or units of locality. But the other three units are entirely independent of the idea of locality, and are purely personal, namely, the Individual, the Family, and the Social Circle.

Again we observe, that these six naturally divide themselves into three pairs, in each of which pair, one unit is a part and the other a whole, namely, Individual and Family, Precinct and Nation, Social Circle and Mankind. Furthermore, in each of these pairs, one unit is related to the other, not only as part to whole, but the relationships are evidently much alike in several metaphysical and moral respects, one pair being personal, one political, and one, moral or voluntary.

And then again, we have three pairs by a different combination, such that the two of each pair are connected closely together by metaphysical and moral relations and considerations; thus, one pair consists of Individual and Mankind. Another pair is of Family and Nation. And the third pair is of Social Circle and Precinct.

We observe also three dualities. First, the whole six are divided into *two* threes; next, the whole six are divided into three *twos;* and third, the division itself of these two views is the third duality.

(*c*) *Analogy in Chemistry.* All the elements of chemistry may be divided into two classes, and in three different methods. One, is into Metals and Metalloids, another, is into Acids and Alkalies, and the third is into Electro-negative and Electro-positive. We have here as much of the divisions of our six units, as could be expected to survive under chemical analysis, under which NO LIFE can continue. Here in chemistry we have, not three pairs of classes making six classes, but only three WAYS of pairing classes.

(*d*) *Analogy in Geography.* Here is another class of natural analogies of our six units, found in the relations of the six great geographical divisions of the world, called continents. In the northern hemisphere we have three continents, namely, North America, Europe and Asia. And then we have three southern continents, South America, Africa and Australia. Then in another view, we have them in pairs thus, North America and South America, Europe and Africa, Asia and Australia. Thus much Steffens and Guyot have observed; but we add some other twos and threes. Thus, as to the shape—three of them (North and South America and Africa) are shaped like "legs of mutton"; and the other three of them (Europe, Asia, and Australia) are nearly like irregular oblongs or trapezoids. Again, viewing them in pairs, one pair, Europe and Asia, are joined together arm in arm or side and side, by a range of mountains. Another pair, North America and South America, are joined together by a long narrow isthmus. And the third pair, namely, Africa and Australia, are alike only in being unlike the others in that respect; just as Individual and Mankind are unlike each other, and unlike all the rest of the units,—for Africa is joined, not to the continent immediately north of it but to the one on the east, and not by an isthmus so much as by a broad flat territory, and by a long narrow sea: whilst Australia is unlike the others, by being solitary. Then, leaving Australia out of the question as solitary, and corresponding to the Individual (as was done by former geographers,) we have all the rest of the earth divided into two parts called the old World and the new World, having the very peculiar contrast, as the geographers have remarked, that the new World is long and narrow, and has its greatest length running north and south; and the old World, although much larger in one direction than the other, yet cannot be called narrow, and has its greatest length east and west. The old World has its long slopes and plateaus towards the north, and the new World has its long slopes towards the east.

And now, if we count the Individual, as the solitary one corresponding to Australia, we have five other units. Three in the old World, namely, Family, Social Circle and Precinct, and two in the new World, namely, Nation and Mankind.

Again, observe another analogy of peculiarities, a solitary one at each end of the six; and two closely connected pairs between them. Individual and Mankind are two extremes, which in a certain sense are different from society; one is a *no* society, and the other is an ideal that is never completed. But the other four make two pairs closely connected, namely, Family connected with Social Circle, and Precinct connected with Nation.

Now, let us observe this geographical analogy, in mere figures, expressing the ratio of coast lines to each 1000 square miles of continent; and on the proportion of which, intercourse and civilization so much depend. (See Mankind.) The figures stand thus, $6\frac{3}{8}$; 4, $3\frac{1}{2}$; $2\frac{5}{8}$, $2\frac{1}{8}$; $1\frac{5}{8}$. Europe's figure is $6\frac{3}{8}$, and Africa's $1\frac{5}{8}$. But, between these, there are two pairs, whose figures come pretty nearly together. Thus, one pair is North America 4, and Australia $3\frac{1}{2}$: the other pair is South America $2\frac{5}{8}$, Asia $2\frac{1}{8}$.

The foregoing analogies of course, are only to show in a *cumulative* way, a probability of our six as an important number of a true classification in social science.

CHAP. VII. BALANCES OF THE SIX UNITS.

§ 1. *In General.*

We have now come to express formally that part of our theory, which is the doctrine of the necessity of the perpetual balance of the units, in order to make a happy people, or a good and righteous government. What we mean, is no Pantheistic or development-idea, that these units WILL *ultimately* balance each other. But we mean, that the duty of society is to *make* the balance, and to give to each unit its due proportion of influence; and that, only in proportion as society does this, can it produce either a happy people, or a good government.

The necessity for preserving this balance, might be legitimately inferred from their nature as units; so that the establishment of the theory in general, of the units, involves in it the necessity or duty of their balance. This necessity and duty may also be inferred from their combinations. For, in all the departments of nature, we cannot have substances composed of elements, only when these elements are in their *due proportions* to each other, and also are existing in the *necessary contiguity.* Unless the parts are real, the whole cannot be real.

But these, as positions are very abstract; and as it is very important to establish this doctrine of the balance of the units, upon clear and well-known grounds, we desire the reader's attention to a few direct arguments and illustrations on this point. And to the elucidation of which, we propose to devote most of the remainder of this Introduction.

§ 2. *Individual and Family as Types.*

If our type theory (already illustrated) is as good as we suppose it to be, it ought to help us to solve the still more difficult theory of the balance of the units. And the analogies are at hand. Just as the heart the lungs the stomach and the brain, are each a vital organ, and act each independent of the others; yet life and health absolutely depend on the free action of each exerting its own due balancing power, so it is with the elements of society. So again, for another illustration, to refer to the Family as type of society, the masculine and feminine elements must co-exist in harmony in their mutual work, and yet, each must maintain its own individuality, in a due balance.

§ 3. *Resemblances to Gravitation.*

The power of association it is true, draws men together like the law of gravitation, with a force in proportion to their numbers or mass, and in inverse proportion to their distances. But this law, when transferred from inanimate matter and applied to humanity or to living beings, requires several modifications. And even among the astronomical bodies, there is a centrifugal power always exactly equal to the centripetal.

If we turn to the sidereal systems for illustrations, then Nations will answer to solar systems, prettily and truly. Planets will revolve around suns, moons and satellites around planets, and so on; each in its own orbit, and doing its own work; and each kept from centrifugal disorder, by the attracting power of its own immediate center, namely, the next highest orb in the generalizations. But still, it is in vain to look for exact analogies of life-processes, in the laws or actions of inanimate matter. Saturn's ring may illustrate the relations of Families to a tribe; but we have no binary systems in our solar system,—nothing to illustrate the Family organization in the relation of male and female. Although in the binary systems of far distant stars, the suns of other systems, we have the beautiful arrangement of two companion stars revolving around each other, or rather, revolving around an ideal center, the ideal point of their mutual attraction; and each being of the color needed to complement the other in the spectrum. And in some cases, there appear to be more than two, sometimes even several suns, occupying these relations to each other. But not in the simple organic matters substances or minerals, do we find any trace of male and female, other than electricity. It is only where we enter into the living world, vegetable as well as animal, that we find sex running throughout all or nearly all life; but we find the *Family* organization, only in a few of the very highest animals.

Now, let us remember that in the natural formation of society, after the formation of Families and tribes, the centripetal and centrifugal forces are not exerted and felt, so directly between the Individuals as between the Families, or the tribes. Nations are formed originally and in all history, not by Individuals but by Families and tribes. Thus, even the centripetal force itself is not so much directly between Individuals, as it is directly between Families and tribes. And the sun over our heads does not draw us away from the earth, but draws us along with it.

Where the two forces of human society, the centripetal and the centrifugal, are most perfectly and independently balanced in all their forms,—where the national, the neighborhood, the Family, and the Individual, all have the powers of each in the best balance,—there will be the most rapid and true prosperity. And this is brought about in accordance with one of the laws which Mr. Carey has announced in only one of its relations, namely, in the relation of city state and Nation, rather than to its full extent. This law might and should be enlarged, as I have enlarged it, to the other units. That law thus enlarged is, that in proportion as this balance of all the parts is preserved, the rapidity of human diversity or individuality is promoted; and in proportion to that individuality, will be the feeling and consciousness of human responsibility intellectual and moral; and in proportion to the responsibility both intellectual and moral, will be the activity and morality; and in proportion to the activity and morality in such a condition of balanced freedom and order, will be the universal prosperity.

§ 4. *Resemblances to Chemical affinity.*

But the relation of persons in small districts, is much better illustrated by the powers and laws of chemical affinity. Here we see that the attraction between molecules or Individuals when placed very near together, becomes an entirely different power from gravitation, as far as we can yet perceive; and one that exceeds it beyond all possibility of comparison. So that although all bodies undergoing chemical changes, are also subject to gravitation, yet we cannot perceive that the chemical changes themselves are at all affected by gravitation. Here we have illustrated the absolute independence of neighborhoods within Nations.

This principle of elective affinity illustrates another feature, both of man and of society, or of close neighbors to each other, whether in space or in relationship; and this is, that molecules or Individuals can unite with each other, only within certain definite specified and limited proportions. So it is with Individuals; each one has his own peculiar character and his own proper rights, such that other Individuals cannot understand him nor his true character or responsibilities, beyond certain degrees. And these degrees may vary in different subjects, so that any two persons may have more and closer affinities on some subjects than on others. Here we have illustrated the eternal rights of Individuals, in the recesses of their own hearts, and to their own hearts' secrets, as well as to combinations and sympathy with other persons.

As Comte well observes, the attempt or even the hope, to reduce all the operations and laws of nature, to one law, is and will be a vain attempt. And the fact is, that the laws and powers which attract men into Nations, are not the same as far as we can analyze, as those which cause them to seek the society of and organization with their immediate neighbors. The one is gravitation, the other is affinity. And hence, the national principle and the neighbor principle, are much better illustrated by what are recognized to be two entirely different natural powers, and to be working by entirely different laws.

One obvious inference from this view is, the evident and much greater importance of the neighbor-attraction, than of the nation alone, in itself considered as the ultimate object sought, the end of the means; and including in the term neighbor, not only Precinct, but also social acquaintance and business circle or chartered company.

By reference to Mr. Carey's law regarding the balance of centralization and decentralization, it will be observed, that all turns upon individuality and personal responsibility, that the national power itself is useful, only as it develops or allows the development of these. Whereas, the chemical affinities are the immediate and direct operation of these individualities themselves.

§ 5. *Natural History of Society.*

One element of the centrifugal force of society, is the innate feeling of human liberty, and the necessity in order to happiness, for each individual to follow his own bent or inclination. The more condensed society becomes, and the more varieties of occupation study and training are introduced, the more different the various persons' bents or inclinations become, and the more absolutely essential for each one's happiness, becomes his right to have great liberty in those respects. And the same holds true both for Individuals and for Families. And thus the centrifugal forces become electrical repulsion, nay more, they become biological and medical, and instead of centrifugal forces we have incompatible characters.

Another law is the attraction of the sexes. Here we have an attraction, often not in inverse but in direct proportion to distances, and *according to* the great differences and co-ordinating needs of each sex for the other. Distances, in space or in social position, are little in comparison with the power of this great attraction. Then again, when this attraction becomes chemical, and finds its combination and fulfills it with the rising Family, it forms the very strongest tie and gives the very strongest combination in human society. Now, it is here too, that there arises the very strongest centrifugal and repulsive force. Each Family tends to repel every other Family. This is chiefly the result of the antipathy or dread, of men for men, or women for women, in regard to those of the *other Families.*

This centrifugal tendency also results, from the autocratic influence which parents naturally desire to exercise upon their own children, and from their dread of or opposition to the influence of other Families on their children.

Out of the necessities of Families, there soon arise Social Circles Precincts and Corporations; the consideration of which is deferred a few pages, namely, until we come to the subject headed "The Tribe Principle." (Chap. VIII.)

Oftentimes in history, conquests have been useful in causing tribes or Precincts that were previously at war and entirely under centrifugal influences, to submit to a centralizing attraction. But no such centralizing force as is compulsory, can be justified, until after tribes Precincts or Nations placed in juxtaposition by providential circumstances, refuse to enter *peaceably* into such confederation as is necessary for peace and order, refuse to conform to the centripetal attractions required by circumstances. Then, the arising of the strongest tribe or of some foreign power, as a centripetal power, seems justified by the necessities of the case, and by the interests of Mankind.

An overwhelming tendency to centralization seems now to exist all over the civilized world, except temporarily in the Southern states, where the decentralizing movement was made evidently for a special and exceptional purpose, namely, of forming a *new center* of despotism over a part of its own people; and was not a movement made upon any well founded principle of decentralization. Its theories of Precinct rights were held good only for the white man's, not for the negro's Precincts. And its theories of state rights were only held to be good against the *old* government, and not against the *new*. Its power against its own parts, was far more threatening, than that of Great Britain towards the American colonies in the Revolution. Its people had forgotten about ninety years of history. They had forgotten that the early colonists mostly had been driven to a new country by persecution or distress. Whereas the settlers in the Southern states had been invited and encouraged and aided by the general government, in every way, and fostered to become great and prosperous states.

The advent of the constitution of the United States, therefore, was a return to the original and natural balance of society. It speaks of "We, the people," as well as states; and thus acknowledges a double power in its very inception,—the people the Nation as a whole, forming the centripetal force; and the former tribes or colonies, now states, forming the independent or centrifugal powers.

One of the great practical problems in Social Science, is to determine how much Individual and Family liberty, each ought to resign and assign to the governing powers, and especially to the tribe, or district or company. Another of the great practical problems in this relation of centrifugal to centripetal forces, is, to find how much power and liberty the tribe or district or company should assign to the central government, and how much it should retain for itself. The safe general rule seems to be, that so far as the *principle* is concerned, men, Families, or tribes, only resign to government those rights which are necessary and only *so far as* necessary, to the accomplishment of the general and mutual objects. But yet, that in the practical and actual administration of government, the superior power (that is, the more general) must be the judge, as to the actual administration, in cases of doubtful rights, and also in cases of expediency not conflicting with rights. Because, the contrary supposition would be unreasonable; that is, it would be unreasonable to suppose, that if the right were doubtful, or the expediency remain to be proved, the more general power should be subordinate to the less general. Whereas, as to absolute and undoubted rights, it is simply absurd to suppose *them* to be irrecoverably and upon principle, transmitted to any second party or second Unit, whatever be its power.

In speaking as above, of assigning or resigning power to government, it is not meant that government actually arose in that way, nor to ignore the authority of God in civil government; but only to exhibit that method, as one of the means of arriving at what the ordinance of God is in the matter.

CHAP. VIII. THE TRIBE PRINCIPLE.

§ 1. *In General, and classifications.*

As in the Unit the Family, we have to consider it in *two* entirely different aspects, so in the tribe, we have to consider IT in *three* subdivisions, each of which, now comes logically to be viewed as a fundamental and essential element. Now, when we take this tribe principle as thus analyzed, and apply it to modern civilization, we see that there arise three different functions or kinds of organization, namely, (1) Precinct or Neighborhood, (township, ward or county, as the case may be,) (2) Social Circle or acquaintance, consisting in friendship, and providing for and looking towards new families, (3) organized voluntary association, that is, lawful corporation for special purposes, corporations for business and corporations for politics, &c.

The casual reader will here observe a kind of confusion in our treatment of Corporation. For, in our main original classifications, we place Corporation, not among the expressly ascertained units, but as a separate class. The confusion arises from the subject,—consists of the confluence of the things in tribes, and is explained by the fact, that our theory anticipates, that in the future the corporation will more and more take the place of, and fulfill functions of civil government; or at least, that there is a possibility and a practicability that it *may* do so, and that all the three elements of the tribe, tend towards a re-integration in their primal form, but in a renewed and Christian spirit.

§ 2. *Permanence of the Tribe Principle.*

The Tribe, as an element of society, although a unit in the early ages of Mankind, and of each Nation in particular, yet soon disintegrates or differentiates into heterogeneity; and as to its form, so far disappears from visibility in modern society, as to require to be considered as a PRINCIPLE rather than as a unit.

In general, the tribe, according to ancient history is the original foundation of political government, being the immediate successor of the patriarchy. Nor does it ever lose its power (in a transcendental sense), as a unit and element of modern society. But its power and spirit ever survive in all societies, although the forms of its manifestation change. This idea seems not to have occurred to any previous writer that we remember.

We are shown the IRREPRESSIBLE activity of the tribe PRINCIPLE, by its continual reappearance in modern society, even where we should be apt to expect it least,—as in the early tendency of every religious denomination to change insensibly from a voluntary to a virtually hereditary association,—especially is this the case with the small denominations. We see the same thing also, in the various dignified occupations and professions, even those of politicians and statesmen. The Corporation becomes a Social Circle led by the same Families.

§ 3. *Natural History of Tribe.*

This tribe principle has a very complex origin in human nature, and fulfills various different functions.

First, it forms tribes identical with Social Circles. It supplies Individuals to form new Families. Incest is decided to be objectionable, not only on physical grounds but also because after arriving at puberty, it is well on account of mental peculiarities, for people to have a new start in life; as it were, a sort of being born again into a new world, by bringing together different elements from different Families. And in love, it is not more certain that we choose our resemblances in some respects, than it is also certain that we choose our contraries in certain other respects. Thus instinct, as usual, anticipates physiology and other sciences. Incest therefore needing to be avoided, a circle or collection of Families, that is, a tribe, becomes a necessity even to the happiness and perfection of the Family itself.

Then again, the natural desire and tendency for friendship in the same sex, of persons of similar ages and sympathies, require a collection of Families. Otherwise, the parents would have no friends of their own sex, as here mentioned. And in the younger ones, friendship craves more variety than the relation between the sexes, and hence there is a stronger reason for the tribe existence, for these early ties, than even for the Family relation itself. Then we have occasional or only temporary coöperations needed, in greater works than can be accomplished by any one Family. These give rise to tribes. There is first, temporary organization, next social organization, next business corporation, next political corporation, and next tribe.

In primitive times the tribes are often migratory, and so the Precinct idea or even the neighborhood idea, is only temporary at first.

Even if we assume, Mankind arose from one pair, the increase of Families would soon give rise to social sets and cliques; and these again would soon result in the formation of separate companies and of separate locations, thus, of tribes. There would be no centralizing power, no central force of attraction after the first parents had died, or at any rate, not long after the successors appointed immediately by them had died. And thus the result would soon be Social Circle, Corporation and Precinct, together forming an independent tribe. Therefore it is, that we must commence the theory of society as now understood, and as related to politics or to government,—with the tribes as *already* existing.

For the central power which could exist any length of time, *only* under a patriarchal form, has no relation to anything that goes to exercise power in modern society. It is a power (in Family isolation), of personal and parental affection, which can never afterwards be repeated except under similar circumstances. Hence it is that the theory of society as a political government, must begin with the *centrifugal* force of rival tribes, as well as their coöperative force. Indeed, it seems almost certain in our historical vision, that the centripetal force arose only by an afterthought, namely, the combination of two or more tribes to resist some other one tribe or combination of them.

The Social Circle and the Corporation are different means of overcoming *new* evils; they are new organs put forth by the life of society in its growth,—but mark! *not* to fulfill functions *better* than the now grown tribe, but to fulfill functions which the now grown tribe cannot fulfill *at all*. The grown tribe may, it is true, do the material work to be done, in an inferior manner; but is utterly incapable of accomplishing the mental harmony, the moral work. Without the corporative organ, the tribe may build a road, but it will only be either one of universal necessity, or else one of favoritism to a few, at the expense of the others. Again, without the Social Circle functions, the tribe may produce marriages, but they will not be happy ones. They will either be marital servitude, as in primitive conditions; or marital wars, as in modern civilization, where fashion now does the forcing which the barons and fathers used formerly to do.

§ 4. *Mutual relations of the three constituents.*

(*a*) *Balance of the three constituents.* We maintain, that one of the necessary balances of power, must be a balance between these three elements, as if units,—as indeed between all the six units of society, namely, Individual, Family, Social Circle, Precinct, and Nation, and morally, Mankind also; each taken as one alone. In a harmonious government, each of these six units must have its full influence, namely, each unit must have an equal influence; and each unit one undivided influence. And similarly, the three elements of tribe, as if units, must be brought into and kept in a balance with each other,—just as the three prismatic colors, all must be weaker or all stronger, in order to combine in a pure white light.

Here then arises the necessity of having each element brought into harmony with itself,—with all parts of the same element.

(*b*) *Corporation.* Formally, our theory does not argue for so much fundamental necessity, prominence or importance, to the Corporation, as it does to the Precinct, Social Circle, and those other instinctive elements we call units; but assigns it to a separate order, called artificial or rational. All we have to remember here is, that the right of all citizens to form simple corporations *within the Precinct*, is a right involved in the fundamental elements of society, namely, the tribe element. It is therefore as eternal and indefeasible, as the right to form partnerships or any other contracts ought to be: but of course not including any natural right of monopoly; for this perversion into monopoly, is the very matter that has destroyed the rights of all men to form corporations at their own will and judgment.

The greatest peculiarities about corporations, appear to be those which follow essentially from the nature of the case, and relate mostly to those corporations whose very objects and nature require them to have a greater local extent than *one* Precinct,—such as corporations for roads, or travel, or general purposes, or politics, or for larger divisions of territory than the Precinct. But still these should always if possible, be chartered by one or more Precincts, rather than by the Nation. It is chiefly thus that corporation-honesty and moral responsibility can be revived. And the Precincts may combine for special purposes; either to do certain works themselves, or to unite and charter some corporation to do the same directly, but not through the medium of some other corporation. The chartering of one corporation by another is unnatural, especially for political purposes.

(*c*) *Social Circle.* The differences of Social Circles, are more natural and inherent metaphysically, than of location or Precinct itself; but those of Corporation are less so; and when corporations are absorbed by, or become made up of Precincts, still the differences of Social Circle will continue.

But the only Social Circles which can found their true defence in the tribe principle, must be those in which the elements of kindred, friendship, affinity, and immediate occupation, are likely to be active and prominent. Hence, merely voluntary even if organic associations,—called "classes" of society, cannot be considered to be a fundamental element of government. They are ghastly bodies without souls, and the cause of great civil woes. In other words, differences of social position pertain to the Precinct, but *not* to the Nation: and their physical forms should be either Corporation or Precinct. And the Precinct being the material or bodily form, is the one with which daily government has more to do. Yet the government which is founded on ignoring any fundamental element, is that far, a falsity. But Social Circles, enlarged and *de-souled* into "classes of society," should have no recognition as fundamental elements of the unit we call Nation.

Now in the case of the true Social Circles, as their character and object will be spiritual, so also should be the *power* used, namely, spiritual moral and voluntary. And in their case there seems no easy task to find any existing satisfactory American method, of giving honest and peaceful Social Circles any open influence in government; or of preserving in any honest manner their rights, except perhaps in the organization of juries, and in two or three other applications which are to be considered in another place. But the greatest present means for the virtuous Social Circles to preserve their fair and equal rights against the *vicious* Social Circles, and against inimical prejudices, is, by society spontaneously forming into small Precincts with original state rights, as shown in that part of the subject. In fact, all minorities must look to the full right and freedom of forming themselves or collecting into state-Precincts, as their principal method of obtaining either property-rights or personal freedom, in the United States. The common corporations ought not to have, and Social and religious Circles cannot easily have political rights, as such, in this country, except as in Precincts. Hence, the tribe principle practically becomes the Precinct element. Nevertheless, new kinds of corporations can be devised, to accomplish all that is necessary under this head.

In this country, property-holders, like all other minorities, can look for their rights to the spontaneous formation of civil corporations, or else of collecting in small Precincts where owners' rights will be guarded simply on the ground of the fundamental rights and independence of the *tribe*-elements, and of the tribe principle. Property is only one of the constituents of Social Circle. The other constituents equally as important and active, are, morality, intellect, education, and sometimes even personal acquaintanceship and good manners.

(*d*) *Precinct.* Just as in the Individual, improvement requires that each person should become more in harmony with himself; his affections, his reason, and his will, all harmonizing together: and just as in the Family, its two objective principles must be in harmony and in unison with each other, that is, the parentage principle in unison with the sexual, in one unit the Family; just so, the three different elements or principles of the tribe, namely, Precinct Social Circle and Corporation, should in a perfected social system, be found all in the same one unit; that is, the *usual* Precinct should be ever tending, more and more, to become or consist of only *one* Social Circle, and to be but one corporation for its own special purposes.

But all Precincts need not be thus constituted. For the most beautiful music is made not by all the sounds being the same, but by some of the notes being far distant in the scale, yet duly related to each other, and so, harmonious. And the prettiest of all the accords, and the *only* one that nature makes, is the octave, (the natural harmony of the male and female voices). Thus one kind of Precincts would consist of *sames* or equals as to intellect, morals and property: the other kind would be of accords, where the differences of intellect morals and property would be *organically* recognized. But the tendency of even these two kinds of Precincts would ever be towards each other morally and metaphysically; namely, towards each other in resemblance, and towards each other in friendship.

It would therefore appear, that most of those powers of Individual freedom, which the Individual-liberty theorists advocate for private persons, we advocate for the three differentiations of the tribe principle, namely, Precinct, Social Circle and Corporation. And we prevent these from abuses and tyranny, by two principles. One is, the equal rights of all other similar bodies, as established and guarded by the central or general government; Spencer's principle for the Individual, extended to these three social bodies. The other principle is, by making the Precincts so small comparatively, and by so securing the freedom and security of persons and property, in changing from one Precinct to another, that the free choices become indefinitely various.

Precincts being material things,—visible material divisions of the earth,—must ever be the forms and bodies, of which social differences and voluntary associations are the souls. Precincts are the fundamental organizations for human liberties, and for the rights of minorities. Then, by the voluntary principles of competition, interest, urgency and utility, whereby Individuals and parents are now able to regulate themselves and their affairs, the Precincts would then be obliged and be taught, to regulate themselves and their affairs for the general good. And this, too, without their necessarily having any more really benevolent intentions, or much more Social Science than they now have; but all be brought about by those spontaneous natural principles of social order, which the liberty and "let alone" theorists advocate for Individuals. Thus Precincts, like Individuals, would all be acting however ignorantly yet surely, for the good of all the others.

CHAP. IX. BALANCES OF ALL THE ELEMENTS OF SOCIAL SCIENCE.

§ 1. *Balances of the Analytical Seven.*

(*a*) *Law of proportions of power.* The balance of elements, implying an equality of political power in each, requires that the activity and perceptibility of the *power* of each should be in inverse proportion to its extent or greatness. In other words, the larger and the more complex and less voluntary, any political organization is, the less compulsory power should it exercise over the elements below it; in other words, the greater the tribe or Precinct or company, the less power should it exercise, over either the Families or the Individuals who compose it. And the greater the Nation, the less power should it attempt over either the Precincts, companies, Families or Individuals, who compose it.

(*b*) *Natural tendency to over-centralization.* Nearly all the political evils of government come from violating the foregoing law,—come from applying to tribes and Precincts, principles applicable only to Families, and then applying to Nations, principles that are only applicable to tribes or Precincts. This we shall find to be the cause and process, not only in theory, but in the actual history of the origin of society and governments.

Even the Chinese empire, now consisting of one-third the population of the earth, was once a small tribe; and then its patriarchal form was quite appropriate. The only mistake it has made is,—just like that of our individual states, namely, merely retaining the old form under the now entirely different circumstances. And this too, with the same excuse as we, namely, that the change of extent is too gradual to be exactly marked as to any precise time.

Just as Individuals generally have a tendency to excess of all social indulgences, and to giving the social customs of society unrighteous sway; so have governments and Nations the tendency to excess of the social principle in centralization. Just as the stronger sex has sway, to the neglect of the feelings of the weaker, so in political constitutions, the stronger unit, that is, the Nation, is prone more and more to have its own way, even with the free consent of the lesser ones. The thorough reform must come, not from the Precinct, but from the Nation. The tendency is towards too much compulsory society throughout. In Families, it comes to neglect the rights of Individuals, and makes social slaves. In the Precinct or neighborhood, it comes under the guise of fashion, to nullify the rights of Families and Individuals. In the Nation, it comes absorbing all the rights of the Precinct, and finally reverses the true order of nature, and assumes with true feudal despotism, that the rights of the Precinct flow downwards from the Nation. In like manner no doubt, if a universal or general empire of many Nations could be established, *it* would also have the temerity to assume, that all rights had originated from it; although Mankind had been without it in fact for thousands of years, and it itself were but of yesterday, the mere success of tyranny or of brute force.

With the Chinese and about three-fourths of the population of the globe, the two elements which the governments chiefly recognize are, first, the Family element, through its head the father; second, the Mankind-element, in the limited form of a universal empire of its own race entirely secluded from all other races.

In the other and smaller part of the human race, the Family as a governmental element is scarcely recognized at all, and the national and race ideas, are not isolation from all other Nations, but are conquest over them; and among the Nations themselves, the idea is not confederation, at least not permanent confederation, but each one struggles to maintain such a balance of power, as will give itself a moderate *advantage* over each of the other powers in the *equilibrium!* Yet all the while, the idea of a Precinct as an element of governmental power, has never had its balanced exhibit among civilized or semi-civilized Nations, except perhaps in some parts of the German empire, in India and Japan. But among savages and barbarians, the idea of the Precinct-power, has been held with such tenacity as absolutely to prevent nationality.

(c) *Fields of physical and metaphysical power.* In the spontaneous and inorganic relations of Nations to Mankind, and in corporations, the more developed and intellectual parts obtain mastery over the others. Whereas, in the compulsory, very formal, organic and ordinary relations of Precincts to Nations, the most physical and *least* cultivated morally, whether persons or Precincts, are the classes which are strong, and do practically succeed in governing the whole Nation. Thus the South governed the North,—and now the West governs the East.

The submission of Individuals and of Precincts to Nations, is different from that of Nation to Nation, or of Nation to Mankind. The principles are different.

Hence, each locality, and every minority, should have its rights protected by some practical and social means, at least *as* effectual in their sphere, as the barriers of race, which include language, religion and permanent intellectual and physical development. And it is evident that there is no possible arrangement short of human perfection, that can accomplish this end, except that radical constitution of Precinct, which our theory proposes; or that of voluntary political Corporation, subsequently to be more fully explained.

(d) *Different elements represent different rights.* There are three moral theories of social rights, essentially different, namely, the cosmopolitan, the national, and the neighborly. These three moral theories are all true in their proper locations, but outrageously false, *out of* their locations.

The cosmopolitan or universal-brotherhood theory, is that which properly applies to the internal affairs of the Precinct, and of the Corporation, except to such affairs as are inconsistent with the peculiar organization or object thereof. But the national theory applies to affairs outward of the Nation, and establishes chiefly, the self-protecting rights. The Nation's chief operations are with other Nations, it being the protector of Precincts and Corporations, and being the organ expressly for foreign affairs. The chief uses of central or national government, are to guard against the forces, tricks, tariffs, &c., of other national governments; and to prevent the internal Individuals, Families, and tribes, from resorting to force, tricks, tariffs, &c., in hinderance of internal freedom and intercourse. The Nation, as to other Nations, is to be an active power in principle; whilst in regard to the internal parts of which it is composed, it is to be negatively active, namely, active chiefly to anticipate and prevent probable disorders; Nations being supposed to be at selfish competition with other Nations, and to favor peaceful coöperation within their own borders.

To consider, then, the most active and efficient functions of right daily government, we must go to the Precincts or small bodies, and consider THEIR rights and powers.

As to the Nation's influence WITHIN the Precincts, or within the corporations, THAT must be founded upon cosmopolitan or universal brotherhood principles, with the additional idea of a paternal governing and unifying principle. Whereas, the Precincts themselves, and the corporations also, each one for itself, will be the administrator of the aforesaid world-wide principles of brotherhood, to all such persons as properly and of right compose it, or ought to continue to compose it. To all others, it must be a self-protecting institution, that is, be conducted on the national theory. The same is true, also, of Social Circles, Families, and Individuals,—every one for itself, the Nation for them all.

The difference between national and Precinct rights, may be summed up thus; national government is fulfilled by securing the two rights,—internal *liberty* and removal. Precinct government is fulfilled by securing internal *strictness*, and by free removal. And voluntary Corporation can fulfill many of the functions of both Precinct and Nation, but not *all* the functions of either.

§ 2. *Balances of the whole Fourteen.*

(*a*) *In General.* The foregoing doctrines of the balance of the units are now to be explained in a wider sense. Hitherto we have referred them only to the elements of the analytics, but now they are to be widened so as to include the elements of the synthetics also: and these balances are to be understood chiefly in a moral and metaphysical sense.

Society, as we have already seen, analytically consists of six instinctive units and one deliberate element, together making seven fundamental elements; also we have seen that synthetically considered there are seven departments of thought and administration in government (whatever be the analytical elements which administer it or are subject to it),—namely, Property, Life, Health, Intellectuals, Morals, Civil Government, and Communism. And a complete Social Science must include the treatment of all the fourteen elements as *fundamental:* and therefore, a balance must be maintained between them. But the term balance must now be understood in a more abstract sense. The first seven elements are *typical* of the last seven. Thus, all we have said of the theory and balance of the first seven, is, by a little enlargement of principle, applicable to the theory and balance of the whole fourteen also. But the balance now, is rather a balance of opinions and of scientific departments, than of political powers.

Here belongs the explanation of a law of facts that has often been observed, namely, that the attempts to suppress some moral evils by force, or by direct legal action,—turn out in fact to really increase the evils, besides producing other and greater ones. Attempts of this kind generally come from efforts by some more general Element, to take away the rights of some less general one. The explanation then is, that the rights of each element *will* find vent in its own sphere, so that no one element CAN profitably interfere with the rights of another element. No other explanation of the curious law of facts above mentioned, has been given that we know of, which does not tend in substance, either to take away the value of law altogether, or else offer itself as a mere isolated and empirical explanation of some single fact. But what is wanted is an explanation which will be both general and definite.

(c) *Balancing powers, to be homogeneous.* Moral powers must balance moral ones, and political powers, balance political. For, in regard to the balance of the elements, it is not always necessary that the equilibrium be maintained by political or civil power, neither is it possible always to maintain such equilibrium by moral or intellectual means *only*, without civil or political power, but sometimes the one kind of power must be relied upon, and sometimes the other. All that this part of the theory requires is, that the equilibrium should SOMEHOW be actually maintained.

It will however be evident on reflection, that to establish a theory which will be simple and homogeneous,—the political power of one element must always be balanced by the political power of the other elements; and so also with the moral powers. Thus for instance, the moral or intellectual powers of a *district* should be balanced by the same kind of powers in the Individual, the Family or the Nation. And on the other hand, just in proportion to whatever political power may be granted to a *Nation*, so also should balancing political power be bestowed upon the Individual, the Family, and the district. For while it is true that one kind of power in one element, may possibly be greatly counterbalanced by another kind of power in the other elements, yet the problem or case for human calculation is thereby made indefinitely or infinitely complex: so that on the one hand, human reason can never fully understand the equilibrium, even if an equilibrium could be obtained; and on the other hand, the chances are almost infinite against there ever being an equilibrium under such conditions.

It would follow from this theory; as Mankind or the race as a whole, is a real unit; that government can never be perfect until some limited balance of political power is vested in Mankind, and some suitable political form discovered whereby that power may be exercised. And as long and as far as the power of mankind as a whole, is exercised only by moral and intellectual means, so far and so long it may be kept in due equilibrium, without any other powers in the other elements than the moral intellectual powers; and *vice-versa*.

Some principles of social duty are dependent entirely upon conditions of mutuality, for instance, the Free Trade principles.

So also are all theories of equality. They must be recognized by both parties, or they are not justly obligatory upon either. Yet, there are Christian duties of supererogation, to a limited degree, in Social Science. But on ordinary principles, no Nation, Precinct, locality or corporation, can be expected to act unselfishly to others, nor to cease to strive to maintain or obtain mastery, when it knows that the others are striving to maintain or obtain the mastery over it.

Although the balance of power and of rights between all the fourteen elements, is to be equally maintained, yet property is not to be counted directly, except in communism, where the very nature of communism counteracts the evils of an honest property influence or representation within a commune. In other words, a regulated and limited common property can (and alone can) firmly establish a property-representation for those who have contributed it. This doctrine of course precludes, until a more perfect human nature comes, that absolute communism which the so-called socialists imagine. And on the other hand, it excludes all vain and hopeless attempts to obtain for property, some political power indirectly in ordinary civil government.

(c) *Delegation of Powers.* Each element must be considered as delegating a portion of its powers to the political governments of the Precinct, Nation or Corporation, *so far as* necessary for the preservation of the rest of the rights and interests of the *same element;* but *not,* as is generally thought, be required to make this sacrifice for the rights and interests of some *other* unit or element. For *that* would be a sort of metaphysical generosity, not to be expected in government affairs.

Good government cannot be obtained without delegating strong powers to some party or organ, whether Unit, Element or Individual. But the difficulty is how to apportion the different powers to their proper Elements.

The right of government to operate in various miscellaneous affairs, not directly necessary to preserve equal rights and property (such as education, maintenance of the poor, post offices, &c., &c.,) has been questioned. But we maintain that the important tests are, not the kinds of work, but the amount and object of the interference, and especially the unit by which the interference is to be accomplished.

We must grant the right of each unit to take direct care of the parts next under it, and of which it is composed. But excessive centralization cannot be justified by authority of this principle, because excessive centralization attributes to a Nation the right to violate the equal rights, all at once, of all the other units.

Another point to touch upon here, relates to all the departments of government. This point is the right of government to an adequate share of property-accumulations, bearing some proportion to its share of influence in the production thereof. Nearly all property is owing largely to civilization, and that again is largely owing to the peace and order produced by good government. This claim comes, not for officers nor Individuals, but for the thing itself,—government. Good government cannot be obtained without paying well for it openly and honestly, both in money and in honor; to some persons money, and to other persons honor, and to others, both. And if the *large* payments were made honestly and *openly*, the real expense would be less in the end than where the remunerations are taken underhandedly; and then better men also would be secured.

(*d*) *Typicalness of the Series.* In the series (as given in the Analytics) of the seven elements, each of the six units as a whole is typical of all the units above it in generality; and the developments of each unit are therefore to be considered as typical of higher social phenomena,—as a flight of six stairs, rising higher and higher. But Corporation placed solitary as the seventh element, has *all* the six units typical of and leading to it, not as stairs, each to and by means of the other, but each for itself leading directly to it, like doors and windows on the first floor of a building. Consequently, the reader is requested to give that turn to whatever articles we may publish of that analytical series, so far as their nature admits; and thus to read them with both meanings. For it is by such methods of study, applied to each unit, that the writer entertains hopes of some of the many future unexpected, but indisputable, developments in Social Science. And it appears to him that the very same relations, but in a more transcendental sense, may be traced in the seven elements of the Synthetics also.

CHAP. X. ARBITRATION-JURIES.

§ 1. *Indirect Balances in General.*

There are some very simple indirect methods of approximating the general balance of all the fourteen elements. The first is, investing the male sex alone with civil powers. But of that, we would treat under Family. The second consists in investing age with a counterbalancing power in government. This may be accomplished by placing the *powers* of age and youth in separate legislative bodies, so as to counterbalance each other;—making greater age a qualification for voting for senators, than for voting for members of the lower house. The mere age of the *official* representative, (as now ordained) is of very little consequence in this connection. This topic will be treated under "Civil Government." Another method of indirect balance, is by arbitration-juries, the full and practical details of which are reserved for "Civil Government." But here we give a general statement of the idea.

§ 2. *Arbitration.*

Here, a few words may be allowed upon the propriety of arbitration in civil affairs. Often, both parties in a suit are to blame: in which case, judges and juries ought to prescribe *compromises* where practicable. But our laws do not fulfill any such function, except the parties themselves voluntarily agree to it: which is not at all what we mean. For the law, in many cases ought to fix compromises, rather than decide entirely on one side.

The next argument in favor of compromises, is, that all law and all order and all society are founded upon compromises. An instance is found in the new law to settle the difficulties of the land-tenancy in Ireland. It is to be administered by courts of arbitration specially instituted for the purpose. Because it is evident, that common law remedies for a grievance so deep, among a people so poor as the Irish are, would be useless to them. And if arbitration be good for them, why will it not be equally good for us and for all? Thus it is, that the necessity of arbitration in civil affairs, is beginning to be perceived. And even in criminal affairs, the Scotch have a compromise verdict, namely, "not proved."

§ 3. *Juries in general.*

Juries, originally in former times, were only of the middle class. They were an institution established to protect the middle class from the tyranny of the landed aristocracy. The middle class is of course the most suitable if *only one* class is to be represented therein. But *any one* class will take too much care of itself. The right to vote, and the right to serve on juries, were co-existent at the first; and then, when the right to vote was given to all in the United States, the right of juries went with it, although not deliberately as a specific or intended object, but incidentally, and even perhaps inadvertently, jury work being considered as a duty rather than as a right.

The idea of trying a man "by his peers," originated in criminal trials, when *political* offences were held to be the same as criminal ones, and when the defendant was considered as the only person interested (the commonwealth being considered as the plaintiff), but that idea does not apply to property cases, for in these, there are involved the interests, at least of two other Individuals. But even in personal and criminal cases, the feelings of the injured and the sympathy of *his* friends, have a right to be and ought to be heard, at least as fully as those of the accused. Only thus can private revenge be prevented. Moreover, to give one class, trials by their own sympathizers only, tends to put other classes at their mercy as to life and limb, and destroys the general feeling of security. Now in principle, the idea of trying a man by a jury of his own class alone, is just as absurd, as it would be to try men by a jury composed only of the sympathizers with the injured party or with the accusers. Hence, both in criminal trials and civil suits, the jury ought to consist of men from both sides or classes.

§ 4. *Classes of Society.*

Juries, if they are ever to be impartial and under equal influences, must recognize existing classes, and provide against inequality in the jury box. As long as petty jealousies do exist between elements of society, and the sympathizers of each decide for its own class; and as long as oaths have so little effect in doubtful matters of opinion; and as the decisions of juries often of necessity have to depend upon doubtful, obscure and difficult points of facts and of law,—so long every government should, in some measure take cognizance of and provide for the differences which do exist; and the government which so fails to recognize the real differences, is so far founded upon a falsity, and so far is in itself a despotism. And if government persists in such oversight, and persists in practically maintaining that minorities have no rights that majorities are bound to respect; such selfishness and unfairness in the government, will surely also select unfair men for its officers, and men not above taking bribes; and the consequence will be, that the minorities will persist and increase in their practices, of considering that majorities have no rights that minorities are bound to respect if they can avoid them by bribery and trickery. The present anarchical and selfish condition of the moral sentiments on these subjects, is very acceptable to those who are willing to give or to receive bribes, but is rapidly corrupting the moral tone of the Nation, and throwing the wealth of the country into the hands of immoral tricksters or reckless gamblers; and unless checked, must ultimately result in driving honest poverty out of politics, and honest wealth out of the country. Let all classes have their dues, but let them use the means of honesty, compromise and arbitration. Then politics will become synonymous with patriotism; and wealth become synonymous with virtue and utility.

Taking juries indiscriminately from the people, gives the refined, the educated, and the wealthy circles, but a small minority, seldom even one in each jury, and in cities, not one for several juries. Now, in trials where large amounts of property are in dispute between contestants all wealthy, this habit of submitting them to the decision of men most of whom have little or no property, and whose personal character is unknown, is a habit quite as erroneous in principle as it is unjust and corrupting in practice. Moreover, juries in reality are a sort of arbitrators, and ought to be so considered and arranged for, in order that both plaintiff and defendant, and all parties interested, should have an equal representation therein. And it is well known that in the large cities, the juries very often are *packed*, and made to consist of men of little character, and who are either watching out for *jobs*, or glad to glut their clan-animosities and partialities.

§ 5. *Principles of the Methods.*

The methods for constituting juries which we would propose as the true ones, are founded upon the three following principles. (1) A wise recognition of, and so an efficient provision against, the evils of the different classes of society. This recognition might ascertain the classes of society, either on the basis of voluntary association, or of Social Circles, or on the basis of their taxation, or on the basis of expenditures. (2) The second principle upon which our proposed method is founded, is a modified arbitration, namely, simple arbitration modified by this, that the parties are to choose, not the individual arbitrators, but the class thereof; or at any rate, the law to choose such a class for them as they would naturally choose for themselves. That is to say, the law chooses a portion of the arbitrators from their natural class. (3) The third principle upon which juries should be founded is, the principle of counting the *public* a third party, needing its share of arbitrators in trials for crimes or public wrongs, also in civil cases of direct public interest; so that the public would have one-third of the arbitrators, and the plaintiff another third, and the defendant another third.

CHAP. XI. PRINCIPLE OF VOTES.

§ 1. *Expression of Averages.*

As the universal balance of all the elements of Social Science, is supposed to be the highest attainment of human government, —so, in a republican government, or in a deliberative body, this balance of elements may be popularly supposed to be attained by and in the AVERAGE will of the ONE element, namely, the Individual. At any rate, a government can only be truly republican, even as representing only the one element Individual, when it represents the opinion and the will of the AVERAGE OF ALL; not of a majority only. The true will of any voting assembly is not its majority-will, but its average will.

The discovery and expression of averages by elections, is a problem requiring considerable mathematical ability to *understand, when stated briefly:* therefore a fuller treatment of it is reserved for "Civil Government." But the *process of voting* under it would be quite simple enough. It is a process which is also commendable for its other advantages, besides the mere feature of its expressing averages, and is merely one case under the general formula of the ideal ballot now to be mentioned.

§ 2. *The Ideal Ballot.*

(1) *Ideal Ballot in general.* As a brief abstract statement would scarcely be intelligible, the accompanying concrete formula is furnished. This general formula ticket is given in a very low number of names, merely to exhibit the principle. The names of persons may be either written or printed. The grade figures below 100 must be *written* by each voter. The rest of the ticket is supposed always to be printed. It exhibits ORDERS of choice and also DEGREES in those orders. In the proposed article "Civil Government" we shall show how to simplify these ballots and the degrees of choice for practical purposes; but here we treat them only *generally* and for mathematicians, to show the theory.

TICKET.

CANDIDATES' NAMES.	GRADE VALUE.	
— Adams	First Choice	**100**
— Brown	Second Choice	*95*
— Clark	Third Choice	*92*
— Dunn	Fourth Choice	*70*
— Evans	Fifth Choice	*66*
— Flipp	Sixth Choice	*62*

This formula would probably be the actual ticket, only in four cases; namely, either for six choices by each voter, if only one officer were being voted for,—or three choices, if a board of two officers were being voted for,—or two choices, if a board of three officers. (Or six *votes* for four officers.)

For small boards however, three choices for each officer should be allowed to each voter. And even for large boards there should never be less than two choices for each officer. So that in cases of large boards, the ticket should be enlarged to double the number of the board to be elected. For instance, a board of ten officers would require a ticket with privileges of at least twenty names, by each voter.

This ideal ballot gives at once and altogether, all the advantages of all possible improved plans of voting, whether by constituencies, or by representative bodies. All the other proposed improvements are valuable, only in proportion as they practically approximate the same results as this, or else, as they may tend to prepare for and lead to its adoption. This most general formula for a ballot, namely, our ideal ballot, is one which expresses all the following principles at once:

((*a*)) Applicability to any number of persons, for one office or board of officers, whether one or many.—((*b*)) Expressive of alternate choices, and of the degrees thereof, both as to candidates and as to PARTIES.—((*c*)) There are here supposed to be only such legal restrictions to its absolute unlimitedness, in respect both to choices and to the degrees thereof, as are necessary for practical convenience of counting; and therefore applicable to exclude any immense count of useless scattered ballots. No other restrictions are now made than are thus or otherwise scientifically expressed.—((*d*)) Restriction *c* to *a*. Let each voter vote for not more, say, than five alternate choices when for one officer,—four alternates, for two,—three alternates, for three or more officers to be elected in a board.—((*e*)) But no voter need vote all the number allowed him, unless he chooses to, but should never vote less than three alternates, nor ever more than ten alternates, except when a board of more than five, and then two alternates for each officer.—((*f*)) All the expressions must be placed on one ballot paper,—whether for a board of officers, or for only one officer.—((*g*)) Restrictions *c* and *d* to *b*. Let the highest grades of alternates be, say 100, and let the lowest grades of alternates be never less, say, than 50. And let the voter at will, divide all the grades of his alternates between 100 and 50.

((*h*)) *Illustration.* Case *d-e-f.* Suppose for one officer. Each ballot would contain five names. Then a voter's first choice would be 100, his second perhaps might be 90, his third might be 80, his fourth, 75, and his fifth 70,—or with differences whether fixed by law or not, any how, so the fifth choice was not less than 50.—((*i*)) *Illustration.* Case *d-c-f.* Suppose for a board of five officers. Then each voter has the privilege of his highest number, namely, 10 names on his ballot.—((*j*)) But if voters would write no more than five or six names, this omission would have the same effect as (but no other effect on the names omitted than) if the voter had remained away from the polls, *as to those names.*

((*k*)) If three parties were up, and if each voter would vote for two persons of each party, then the sample ticket would represent a case of a voter grading ALTERNATIVE PARTIES, as well as grading alternative candidates.

((*l*)) Now, the summing up of these grade numbers of all the candidates would represent numerically, the comparative total grade values of all the candidates.—((*m*)) In the case of election of one officer, the one highest total in *l* would be the one successful candidate.—((*n*)) In case of several officers being voted for, as one board, say five, then the highest five totals in *l* would be the five successful candidates.

(2) *Ideal Ballot for ideas.* The same principles which have been given above, for voting for individuals, are also applicable to voting for laws, clauses of laws, motions, amendments, &c., &c. But the methods of and the restrictions in their application thus to ideas, are among the highest and latest attainments of forms in Social Science. They will be treated of in a subsequent work, under the head of "Civil Government."

CHAP. XII. PRINCIPLE OF CURRENCY.

Another transcendental use of averages is, their ability to express the true principle of currency; and their consequent applicability as an actual basis for the only currency that ever can approximate to *honesty* and flexibility *both ways*, or to permanent security. We can only here hint at this basis; and postpone the methods of its application, and the arguments for its propriety, to a subsequent work. Well then, this proposed currency, first must not falsify,—must promise to give nothing but what it can and will give when demanded; and second must promise to give a portion of all the commodities usually bought or sold in trade. Because every sale of any article possessed by us, is essentially an exchange of some one article for the privilege of reinvesting the same in ANY OTHER article; and this requires that the said privilege should be represented by an *abstract* currency, but yet one that can always and at once be made concrete at the option of the holder. The element of AVERAGES in this currency is transcendental, yet theoretically absolute, and consists in this, that the trade transactions in each one commodity during a long average time, are considered as one element of those constituting the idea of the currency. And the commodities and their proportions are selected with a view to represent fairly, the collective average of the different commodities—by averages taken separately for the same fair length of time. And such a collective average must (just as in the case of votes) be the true total average of the commodities bought and sold. And then a convenient amount of that average of commodities could be taken as the unit (instead of Dollar or Pound), and then convenient fractions of that must be taken for smaller amounts. But of course in practice, only a certain select number of commodities could be taken, but fairly, so as to represent the whole—these representative commodities could be taken in the practical application for a real and actual currency.

Every currency that redeems promises to pay one thing by paying another thing, or by promises to pay another, and so on, can be nothing but a vicious gas for ballooning out into the unfathomable regions of financial space, unless *somewhere* at the bottom or end of the promise upon promise, there be a something real and unalterable. And furthermore, every step of promise upon promise, complicates the matter almost indefinitely, both as to the ability of the human mind to comprehend its chances, and also complicates almost indefinitely the opportunities of the currency law-makers to "see-saw" it to suit themselves, and with injury and injustice to a whole community.

Another point is that the amount of silver and gold is not a tenth nor perhaps a hundredth part sufficient to meet the demands made for it in crises and panics; and the sticklers for a purely gold and silver currency can never do any better with this part of the argument than to *say* that such a currency is the best that can be established. But, is it the best?

Now the *seemingly* probable expedient to avoid the difficulty, is to introduce the function of time and credit, and to give all currency-promises a right to require some specific time of notice before payment can be demanded. But suppose, when the time of payment comes, the old panic still continues or a new one arises, what becomes of this probable expedient? Another extension (called suspension)? And another? And so on? Thus we see our balloon gas has only changed its form. Previously it consisted in piling promise upon promises, now it consists in piling time upon time.

But a currency of commodities, taking a sufficient number of plentiful commodities, would always allow of redemption at the option of the holder. One objection is that commodities are inconvenient to carry, and may not be the ones we happen to want. This objection is easily removed in the present state of civilization and credit, by warehouses, and by pledges of actual stocks of goods. And surely a credit system that can be trusted to make *irredeemable* currencies, or to make extensions and postponements *at will*, can be better trusted to make a credit currency based upon commodities demandable at will. As to the other objection of fluctuations and scarcity of some kinds of goods at certain times; this would be overcome by taking a large variety of the commodities most used, and of standard mercantile qualities. Suppose some thirty different articles were selected, as Wheat, Rye, Corn, Iron, Lead, Copper and so on. Then if any one or two of these happened to be unusually scarce when panic came, or payment was demanded, let the payor have the privilege of objecting and excepting to said one or two articles, and then let the payee have also the privilege to except to an equal amount *in value* of any other articles he might select as being unusually plenty. Thus the average would be maintained. The proportioned values for such purposes would have to be fixed when the currency itself was established. And let NO ALTERATION of the currency be made except by an alteration of the Constitution of the Precinct or Nation; and only by the constitution let such a currency be established.

The unit should be taken as near the value of a gold coin dollar as may be convenient, and then the constitution should settle the *exact* value of the dollar in comparison with the new unit of averages. Then whilst the standard was fixed in the constitution, the details might be left to ordinary legislation but requiring perhaps a two-third vote for alterations even thereby. And *after* the relation of the dollar to the unit of averages had been fixed, *then* part of the Real Estate and surplus old stocks and loans of corporations, held by the banks, or part of their fixed capital *above* what they had loaned out for the component articles of the averages, might be allowed by an alteration of the constitution, to enter into a new and enlarged list of components but unaltered in average value. *Then* first class Rail Road mortgage bonds, as also national state and municipal bonds, thus translated into the new units of currency averages, might be allowed to form a small or reasonable part of the banking basis.

Or it would be possible to make all these changes by one alteration of the constitution, if it could be done fairly so as not to make it a subterfuge to debase or alter the real value of the currency-units. This transition itself would not be more dangerous than the present system, nor than the old system of state banks.

And it would be better to make the whole change at once perhaps, so as not to entirely throw out the government bonds that are now the basis of banking. Indeed the very same amount of government bonds that are now required as security, ought and might continue to be required. Our whole proposed change refers not at all to the bonds as security, but only to the substitution of pledges of commodities *instead of the* artificial present *legal tenders and bank notes.* And it would not be right to release all those bonds at once and have them thrown on the market at a ruinous reduction, which would at once spread distress and ruin throughout the country, and only to the benefit of foreign purchasers.

The reader understands that all bonds would then be estimated for any and all purposes, at and only at their value in the new units of the currency averages.

It is also understood that no property or commodity pledged as the basis of currency, should be sold or removed unless by substitution of some other lots of the same *kind and amount*, or by repayment and withdrawal of that much currency. Such a currency, in effect would be simply "orders" for goods in such kinds and proportions that everybody would want them, and everybody could readily convert them into the *particular* commodity wanted.

All is made both convenient and practicable, by the introduction of systems of warehouses, and by giving the new system to banks based upon warehouse and other commercial contracts for commodities *actually in store*, whether in public or in Individual's own warehouse. And what such banks would promise to pay would be certain definite quantities in the prescribed ratios of each of the kinds of commodities previously prescribed, when demanded in certain specified amounts: having previously issued out or loaned these currency averages in agreed amounts, for any of the component specified commodities, or rather for pledges by the customer, of the certificates of warehouse for the same, as might be agreed upon.

There would also surely arise a class of dealers, some, merchants, and some, brokers, who would deal exclusively or very specially, in only those articles which were required in the Averages. And some of these would be wholesalers, and some retailers. And to these each Individual customer could bring in his currency, and obtain only just the one or two articles that he wanted,—and thus obtain them at only the usual and regular market price, and without any loss. But in case of panic before the arising of such a class of dealers, of course, holders of small amounts of currency would have to sell it to brokers or merchants, who would thereby accumulate the required amounts for presentation for payment. But the details must be reserved for the proper place in "Property," one of our proposed future works on Social Science.

The only fluctuations or discount, such a currency would be capable of, would be the aforesaid brokers' charges for buying up *small* amounts to consolidate; and the slight expenses of the charges and freights to *near* places deemed more safe; and the *difference* between the *quality* of the commodities which the banks would really pay, and what the *knowing* ones would *expect*, and that would not be much, for whatever difference in quality they would previously expect, would be the permanent depreciation of it, and not the expense of redemption.

CHAP. XIII. CONCLUSION OF INTRODUCTION.

The objection is often made against Social Scientists, that there is *no practical* use in their kind of discussions, and no hope that any special attention will ever practically be given to their conclusions.

We answer, that this question of practicability depends entirely upon what the particular plans are that may be offered, and in what spirit. If good plans and sound arguments can be offered, in a good spirit, their practicability will depend on the intelligence, patriotism and justice of the people. Under such circumstances, to doubt the practicability of the suggestions if good ones, is to doubt the intelligence and patriotism of the people. And when once any plans began to be tried in one or two localities, and were found to produce, in a pre-eminent degree, the benefits expected from them; then to doubt their adoption more and more by the people, would manifest a deeper infidelity in the fitness of the people for self-government, than would be worth while to argue against, in the United States. Where would be the fitness of a people for self-government, if they were going to be forever insensible to the demonstrations of sound arguments confirmed by undoubted experience; and if truth and justice must never dare to show their faces until after their practicability is shown?

Besides; the World is wide; and there are other peoples in it beside those of the United States. And in these higher problems of Social Science, there can and will be emulation among Nations, as well as, and perhaps sooner than between the Precincts of the same Nation.

The suggestions of Social Science are sometimes alleged to be impracticable, because not put forth by any great politician or political party. But that was equally true once, of every reform that has ever been accomplished. Reforms *begin in moral* powers, but after being morally successful, they are adopted by political parties,—by one party or by several. Those who are best to think, are not the best to act.

Moreover, scarcely anything can be more censurable, than this habit of always crying out at every suggestion of improvement,—impracticable! impracticable! Would it not be better for our "wiseacres" to spend their energies in the consideration of *principles*, and of what things *would* be useful, and *how* to make them practicable,—rather than in this eternal speculation about what *will be* successful? And hardly any minor matter hinders improvement so much as this eternally choking down every thought of, and every aspiration for, something better,—under the chilling contempt of impracticable! impracticable.

And after all, we beg to remind our readers, that *we* have

very little concern about practicability. The law of right, as Spencer says, will not be still nor be altered, by our imperfections, or present inability to fulfill it. Our business is to endeavor to study out what is *right,* and what *ought* to be; and then to leave practicabilities to Time, to God, and to the statesmen,—deeply feeling however, that all that moralists can do in regard to men individually or governmentally, is to point out and urge upon them, their duties, and then pray for them: and those societies which after all, *will not* do the good, will certainly reap the evil, socially as well as individually. Social Science proposes to accomplish its good effects, only *indirectly.* In this respect it is like the relation of Theology to piety. Nothing but the Divine spirit, working in the patriotism and equity of the people, can peacefully develop the *powers* which would be able and willing to accomplish thorough reforms.

There are many other points that might have been touched upon in this Introduction, but we have endeavored all along, to defer them to their respective places in the subsequent parts, and to retain in the Introduction only such thoughts as are either too general, or too complex, to find appropriate places anywhere else. Hence its parts sometimes may have seemed fragmentary. And so on the other hand, of the ideas that have been set forth in the Introduction, but few will be touched upon in the remaining parts, and but seldom,—except when giving them as the topics of further elucidation.

BOOK II.

THE PRECINCT.

PART I.

GENERAL VIEW OF THE THEORY OF THE PRECINCT.

CHAP. I. PREFACE.

IN order now to understand our idea of a Precinct, all the usual legal idea and identification of Precinct with Corporation, must be entirely banished and annulled. And almost every thing that a Corporation is, a Precinct, according to our theory, is NOT. See Corporation I. (A) & II. I. I to V. But a Precinct is as much a fundamental Element or Unit of society, as Individual or as Family or as Nation. Furthermore, in order to get the true idea of a Precinct, we must presuppose a general knowledge of the Individual, the Family and the Social Circle; which Elements, for convenience' sake, we postpone the consideration of for the present.

Precincts are neighborhoods organized into civil governments; they are territories *within* territories; they are *parts* of a tribe or Nation, and are not self-existent. In other words, Precincts are the organizations of the neighborhood principle, in civil government. They might be compared with the "states" of the American Union, by calling them very small and REFORMED "states."

The Precinct is the fourth fundamental Element or "personality" of society, as determined in our Analytics. It is also the fourth UNIT as mentioned in the ascending series of the six great Units. That series is thus: Individual, Family, Social Circle, Precinct, Nation, Mankind.

But Precinct must be completely distinguished (in our theory) from Corporation, which is of a different genus, and is the seventh Element of the Analytics. Yet Corporation is ever tending towards becoming a Unit, that is to say, a fundamental element, but yet cannot be assumed to be entirely fundamental, at least this early in the science, nor this early in the progress of the human race.

As was said before, the Tribe-principle of human society, is, in the early ages, undeveloped and unanalyzed; but in the later ages, this Tribe-principle develops into heterogeneity, and takes three distinct forms, namely, Social Circle, Precinct, and Corporation. The Precinct therefore, is a fundamental element both of Developed Society and of the Tribe-principle.

Of our great six Units of society, only two are political in the full sense of the term, namely, Precinct and Nation. Of these two, which may therefore be called the fundamental political elements of society, the lowest, or the first one in order, is the Precinct, namely, the element now immediately before us. Again, of these six Units, three are Units of Locality, namely, Precinct, Nation, and Mankind; and of these three, Precinct of course is the smallest and lowest. To determine the size of the Locality and the extent of the population of a Precinct, are problems attempted in a subsequent part of this article. But an exact definition of a "Precinct" in our theory, cannot be given intelligibly, without further knowledge of the theory itself.

We will now give;—First: A general view of the Theory of the Precinct. Second: Some special Arguments for this Theory. Third: A conclusion pointing towards some partial Practical applications of the Theory, possible in, (without an alteration of the Constitution of,) the United States.

CHAP. II. HISTORICAL STATEMENT.

§ 1. *In General History.*

The history of states and Nations in a living progression, constantly tends to meet the changing problems of a larger population, for the same territory and for the same representation. And this produces fundamental changes of some of the principles and rights of the governments themselves. And the greatest cause or source of social and political evils, is, adhering to "worn out" systems, whose utility is more and more passing away by the merely natural growth of society itself.

Non-subdivision for fundamental Units, and especially for Precincts, seems to us to be the greatest general cause of social decay.

The decay of Nations in general, it is true, is attributed to various causes: but writers seem to have passed by with little or no attention, that great cause which has operated *in* and *over* all the others.

At the spontaneous origin and foundation of government, we find the separate Localities or Precincts to have great power within themselves and over their own territories. But in the course of time, population increases, Precincts which had small populations come to have large. Thus it follows, that laws which were suitable for the former, are no longer suitable for the latter; the country and the government become rife with cruelty and corruption; new and more stringent laws are added, in the vain hope of stemming the tide of new evils. Also, *old* and bad laws which could not be enforced at all, because of the sparseness of population and its uncivilized independence, and whose crudity was balanced by their impracticability,—now become practicable against honest and orderly citizens, and become enforced against *them;* whilst the dishonest, the disorderly and those who still continue uncivilized in heart, escape. Thus vice is rewarded, and honesty and virtue punished; and thus, classes of outlaws are fostered and nourished in the midst of civilization.—Then, *more* laws are tried, and laws are heaped upon laws; as the Precincts, now called states, become more and more populous.

The state, in each case at first, is merely a little band of acquaintances. But gradually the population increases, the "state" becomes a great and complex political body; it never subdivides, but the overgrown and still growing enormous complexity, and distant and unfeeling organization, still continues to regard itself as *the* fit source of all absolutism, and the fountain of all civil power. For convenience' sake to be sure, counties and townships are organized; but not as subdivisions of the state, or of the original fountains of right, but only as mere organs of the overgrown state, and dependent upon the absolute will of the great power, as to every thing IT chooses to exercise that power for.

All the while, the simple common sense expedient is overlooked,—of merely dividing and subdividing the states, as fast as necessary to keep pace with the *increase* in the numbers of, and also with the increase in the *density* of, the population. For, simple increase in *density* of population, increases the opportunities both to conceal crimes and to commit them; and hence, as the population increases at *one* rate, the subdivisions should increase at a *greater* rate,—thus, to counteract the increased facilities for evil, made numerous, partly by mere density and its attendant subdivision of occupation, and partly by mere numbers; the necessity caused by competition, of each one's attending more and more exclusively to his own business, and consequently neglecting public affairs and general culture; and the necessarily increasing ignorance as to the character of the individuals, and as to the secret aims and motives of the various politicians and their parties.

If now, on the other hand, the subdivision into new states had more than kept pace with the increase of population, and had also been regulated in proportion to increased density, then the natural ingenuity of men would have devised *practical* and successful methods, ever new, and ever varying, as might be necessary, to counteract the new and old evils aiming to grow up or to hide themselves in the new phenomena of progressive society and advancing civilization.

This subdivision of Precincts (or states) is just as necessary as the subdivision of Families. Here again the Family is the type of society. And we notice this to be the case, even in the peculiar points relating to density and to advanced civilization. In the early stages of society we find married children remaining with their parents, and the Family consisting of two or more sets of sub-Families, and quite numerous; but as the numbers and density increase, this complication of the Family becomes less and less frequent; but gradually, the formation of every new Family, or even the attainment to maturity without marriage, causes men, as they become able, to go out and form new Families or new social connections of some kind. Thus, the natural history of the Family, typifies what that of the Precinct *ought* to be.

§ 2. *In United-States-History.*

The average population of each of the states, at the time of the American Revolution, was not greater than 250,000. Several had but 70,000. The present average is over one million (1,000,000). Some, as New York, Pennsylvania, &c., have from three to five millions. And the course of things has the same bad tendency.

The population of an average congressional district is at present about 150,000, and will increase; because the number of representatives is limited by the nature of things. Contrast these numbers with the numbers represented in the early stages of our Republic, and we find that now, each representative district contains about ten times the number of persons it then did.

And furthermore, considering affairs *within* the Precinct, we remember that some of the little colonies of America, settled by our forefathers, and consisting of only a few hundreds of inhabitants to each, were carefully and well managed, by the principle of direct Democracy, and the submission of the laws to the direct vote of the people, who all resided within convenient distance of each other. Thus our constitutions were made, only providing for states with populations of an average of only about 70,000, and they a scattered plain industrious country people, living close to nature and to social realities, and not used to "shams." But now the states have become so large that the citizens cannot possibly have any intimate knowledge of, nor much feeling of intimacy towards, each other. Yet we ignore the fundamental changes involved, we give the same rights to these larger bodies that the smaller originally possessed; and this, without the knowledge, the neighborly feeling, the mutual observations, or the sincere naturalness, inseparable from small country populations and communities living and working in close neighborhood.

The states and their constitutions were originally reactions against civil, feudal, and religious tyranny. And against *absentee* government,—so generally worse than a present government. The settlements also had a peculiar origin, having been made chiefly by peculiar classes, viz.:—adventurers for gold, persecuted religious sects, &c.

And subsequently to the *revolutionary* war, the Constitution of the United States, was itself an apparently necessary reaction against entirely independent and quarreling states; not necessarily confederated *too little*, but *without power* to administer their confederation-laws AT ALL. This reaction, like the reactions of society generally, is an extreme. It has failed in what it sought, namely, the permanency of Union without internal war. But, the consolidation or centralization which it shunned, is coming upon us by the natural growth of so large a body, and by the necessary circumstances of purchasing new territory, and maintaining the Union by war, and the extreme reactionary *theories* consequent thereupon.

The rights of Precincts are inalienable in principle, and unquenchable in feeling. And the violation thereof is almost sure sooner or later to bring bloodshed. The real cause of the American Rebellion, was a neglect of Precinct and corporation rights by both North and South. The Northern free-men WOULD go among slaves and preach insubordination; and the Southerners demanded to go and to take their slaves with them *any where* they pleased. It was not the demand of the Southerners to take their slaves to the *new* territories, but the claim to go North to *arrest* fugitives, and even to take the slaves with them through and into the free North, that really "fired the Northern heart."

These views might, at one time, have seemed to imply a vain claim of every little Precinct to "secede." But now, the contrary doctrine being settled by war, makes this question less difficult. The arrangement into small states, such as our theory proposes, would have prevented any great attempt at secession; and the present "United States," if organized into very much smaller states, would make even the IDEA of "State-Right Secession" quite preposterous. And the smaller the Precincts are made, the more preposterous would be such a claim. But this subject is considered subsequently in this book.

The real justification for interference by the Nation, with the affairs of the Slave-Precincts, is that these latter totally ignored the rights of the colored race either to Precincts or to Corporations. I mean this would be a justification in time of peace.

CHAP. III. RELATIONS TO THE OTHER ELEMENTS OF THE ANALYTICS.

§ 1. *Relations to the Six Units.*

We have endeavored in the Summary Introduction, to establish the doctrine that there are six natural Units or measures of right, or as Mulford might call them "Moral personalities," inherent in the constitution of society, namely, Individual, Family, Social Circle, Precinct, Nation and Mankind; and that each unit is typical of all those above it, and *vice-versa.* Accordingly, no one unit has any such superior right over the one next below it, but what *that* in turn has a similar right over the one below IT; and so on. If there are any exceptions to this, they are in favor of the two extreme units, namely, one, Mankind, as the whole and absolutely the superior; the other, the Individual, as the ultimate social atom not capable of any further social subdivision. Therefore nationality cannot absorb Precinct-rights, any more than Family can absorb Individual rights, or any one element absorb the other's rights. It is therefore error, to endeavor as some do, to take away the natural rights of Precincts and to enumerate them as if they were mere corporations, and to single out the Nation as the only unit having real and original governmental power. Because all Precincts are "free and equal" *in their sphere*, as Individuals are so, or, as Nations are.

The sovereignty of a Nation over its Precincts consists, not in any wizard power or talismanic right of the idea, Nation,—but simply in a VASTLY superior DEGREE of power over the same locality; hence, of the same sort of power, and with the same sort of right, as would be exercised by any very large, say Continental Coalition of Nations. We have had foreshadowings and intimations of such coalitions in the past history of Europe,—but only intimations. The empire of Russia is also an exhibit of the principle in a more permanent form. Degree in biology and in sociology it is true, (as was said in the Introduction), is more important than kind. But in this case it is also true, that the KIND of power which Nation exercises over Precinct, is the same as Coalition, Confederacy or Empire exercises over Nation. And the vast difference in the DEGREE of power between the inferior and the superior, is what constitutes the right in each case, and therefore Nation cannot plead it, as against Precinct.

We may add, that the coalitions and empires above mentioned, are themselves, to the Nations, foreshadowings and intimations of the Unit Mankind. And, should the time ever arrive when Mankind itself would form into a Coalition or Empire, IT would exercise much *more* power over those other Coalitions and Empires, than those Coalitions had exercised over Nations (for coalitions are not Units), and would exercise at least AS much power and right over the Nations, as they were doing over Precincts. Whether such a union of all Mankind is possible or not, before the coming of that Great Man "who is Lord of the whole earth," we cannot say, but suppose not. Yet the reference illustrates the principle.

Again—as to the relation of counties and townships to provinces, and of provinces to states, and of states to Nations,—we may derive the true light from the basis of our fundamental analogy, namely, the Family. A single Family occupies a certain locality, several such Families form a neighborhood, several neighborhoods a township, and so on, up to the general Nation.

We cannot find here, any such clumsy arrangement as a province a State or a Nation, (that is, an institution nearly at the end or summit of the political scale), being regarded as the foundation and source of all government rights, and upon which all others must depend, whether above it or below it. The Family-analogy carried out, shows us that what are called "state-rights" begin with the Family, and must gradually lessen with each step as you go up, till the general government itself is reached. In other words in general, each neighborhood must have the same power to freely fulfill its own methods, as a state itself has, so far as consistent with the rights of other Precincts; and still more generally we may say, that such are all the rights that any state has, or any Nation, or even, any World.

It may be observed that largeness of power in Precincts, by no means involves the theory that they must be regarded as the *superior* source or *origin* of governmental powers. For instance, the feudal system, in its origin, most clearly and fully was based upon the theory that all power descended from the supreme or national government downwards; and yet, it gave the utmost amount of liberty to each of its subdivisions of powers; so that the inferior was only required to make acknowledgments of the inferiority, and to aid the superior in war. This is analogous to the Divine Government itself:—all power coming down from God in theory, yet the utmost liberty is given to the Individual in practice. [Blackstone, B. I. ch. 4.]

But of course, the general or national government is to exercise the same restraining power over Precincts, that it does over Individuals; that is, power restraining them from trespassing on the rights or "equal liberty of other" Precincts, or on the rights of removal of all Individuals who either are or ought to be citizens of other Precincts.

The Precinct or Neighborhood principle, is the main modern enlargement of the tribe-idea. And the tribe-idea is originally the essence of the state. A familiar example is found in the Scottish Nation, which was composed of many clans, each having a separate government under its chief, although they were subservient to the authority of their king. Tribes then are the original elements of Nations. And the centralization principle, carried to the extreme of claiming the Nation to be the source of civil power, is the result merely of military power and monarchical marriages. (See Paley's Political Philosophy, Bk. 6, ch. 1.)

Our theory is not at all the theory of the Paris Communists; for *their* theory ignores the elementary necessity of the Nation, and desires to recognize only Precincts confederated throughout the world, independently and irrespectively of the principle of nationality. Another point of difference, is, that the Paris Communists ignore the elementary character of the Social Circle, and aim to destroy all such circles. Other points of difference are, that the Paris Commune ignores the elementary character and fundamental rights of the Individual and of the Family. It denies the freedom and rights of Corporation. It also ignores THE DUTIES of Corporation, and the intimate relations existing between LARGE cities and their Nation, as pointed out in another part of this article on the Precinct: for the totality of a large city is, in essence, a national corporation, although the separate Precincts of which a city consists are not so. Furthermore, the Paris Commune subverts all the elements of society except only one, namely, an iron bound, tyrannical and special form of the Precinct. Furthermore, that Commune is so utterly at variance with our whole theory, scientifically, metaphysically, morally and religiously, as scarcely to be susceptible even of comparison with it.

Our theory of the relation of Precincts to the Nation, namely, many centers instead of one, is the same principle applied to government, which Carey applies so successfully to economy. Indeed, his system of decentralization of the places of manufactures and commerce and intellect, would be greatly promoted by ours, of decentralizing the places of government. Nevertheless, the bases of the two theories are different: *his* basis, is, upon property and utility; *ours*, is, upon personality and human rights.

§ 2. *Excess of centralization.*

A work has lately appeared by Mr. E. Mulford, on "The Nation." Although learned and conceived in an Orthodox spirit, and having a similarly high moral aim as our work, yet it seems to ignore the fundamental rights of the Precinct. It recognizes but one political unit or integer,—that of the Nation. It seems in some places to use the word commonwealth in a sense approximating that of our word Precinct. It maintains that the "Nation is the institution of rights," even including the right of property therein, (pp. 94 and 95.) This is a fearful "variation" on Paley's perverted but yet general assertion, that the foundation of the right of property (at least in land) is "in the law." It claims a right of the Nation to interfere even with the Family relation: and yet it says, "the Family exists in an organic relation to the Nation," (p. 284.) And yet small as the rights of the Family are admitted to be, it reduces the rights of the "commonwealth" to an indefinitely lower degree. Thus it says, "In the processes of society, the Family exists in an *organic*, and the commonwealth in a *formal* relation to the Nation." And again, in table of contents it says, "the commonwealth is the civil corporation." And again (p. 307) it says, "the commonwealth is a formal organization."

We answer, that Mr. Mulford continually through the work, confuses the idea of government, with that particular part or organ of government called the Nation, and claims for IT all the blessings and benefits that are usually claimed for any department of government. Our whole work and general theory are so very different from his, that we cannot even contrast one with the other in any better way than by saying, that ours is founded on *six* foundations, and his on only one. We could easily prove that all he says of the substance of the Nation, is equally true of the substance of the Precinct, in its due proportion. (See his first chapter.) We argue that the Precinct also "is founded in the nature of man, is a relationship, is a continuity, is an organism, is a *conscious* organism, is a *moral* organism, is a moral personality:" and all quite as truly so, as the Nation.

Mr. Mulford's theory in another part is, that the distinction between the rights of a commonwealth (or Precinct) and those of the Nation, consists in this, that the Nation has the political, and the commonwealth the civil rights. But what is the *guarantee* of civil rights, when political rights are denied? This question may be asked, as well where the rights of Precincts are ignored, as where those of individuals are so. And the pretence that civil rights are sufficient without political rights to guarantee them, belongs to a past age. Accordingly, all the military rights of the Precinct, except as police, are ignored by him: thus (p. 299) he says, "When the *governor* is represented as the 'commander-in-chief of the army and navy of the commonwealth,' the office is not further defined." * * * The title he says "is a name for which there is no reality, and except for lawyers it leads beyond all soundings." * * * "And the governor in this character, on the streams to which he may be confined, is like Wordsworth's fisherman, 'tricked out in proud disguise'" (!)

But then again, this distinction between "political" and "civil," is insufficient, even according to Mr. Mulford. And not only does the Nation possess concurrent civil powers, but also superior ones; and this he argues, even to the extent of interfering with the Family, which even he admits to be a separate integer (or unit) of society. Accordingly (pp. 297, 298) he says:—"The administration in divorce * * * passes consistently to the commonwealth, but the Nation has an immediate obligation in the maintenance of the Family, * * * and if it fails to attain this, in its action through the commonwealth, it is imperative that it shall assume its immediate authority." Again, in regard to education in the public schools, he says, "while the administration of a system of education may be referred to the commonwealth, its institution is of national importance, and also of national obligation; and in the defect of the commonwealth, its authorization should proceed from the Nation."

In another place (p. 315), Mulford draws the distinction between "State" and "Nation" to be between "civil" and "moral"; making the Nation the moral organism. (I suppose he means, moral unit.) According to this theory, the Nation is both the political and moral unit of supremacy. But as a whole, Mr. Mulford's theory is all summed up in the distinction of a "central *government* and a local *administration*;" but yet he refuses to accept *that* as the statement of his theory, and he devotes one page (viz. 317), to arguing against a theory that underlies and is the foundation of his whole book; for there are but three other possible theories of state-rights, as he says, (p. 309,) and he objects to them all; and endeavors to avoid the difficulty by saying (p. 309) that "the relation (between State and Nation) is fundamental—that it is a necessary conception," but that "only in their substance" this relation is realized; and charging that these other theories comprise mainly the phases which the subject has assumed in "abstract speculations and legal presumptions." This is as if the discussion of an abstract principle was adjourned in the supreme court, and transferred to the patent office to find a model! For it is with "abstract speculations," that we are dealing: and the charge of "legal presumption" belongs to the other side.

"We agree that the relation is fundamental," and that "this relation is realized only in their necessary conception." But the question is, *which* relation is fundamental, and *what* is the necessary conception of it? A re-perusal of his preface, more especially of pp. V and VI, seems to show that much of his difficulty arises from confusing the laws of social science which treat of its progress as a science, with the laws which treat of the progress of society itself. We have endeavored to point out the distinction between these things, in our Introduction even from its very beginning. But we also feel that he is systematically and upon principle, *partial* to the claims of nationality; because, when giving the rights of a Nation, he claims for it a right to acquire foreign territory without paying much attention to the wishes of the territory to be acquired, but in giving the rights of a State he does claim for it a right *not* to be alienated or transferred. And what else does this mean, but that *we* have a right to acquire peaceably a state from Great Britain, Spain, Germany, &c.; but that *they* have not a right to acquire a state from us? And what is this but the old egotistic Americanism, that said, foreigners had a right to be naturalized into the United States, yet that a citizen of the United States could not be naturalized into any other Nation? But later decisions of our Supreme Court have reversed this old egotism, as to the Individual; and Social Science is reversing this theory as to States. The same unwritten constitution which allowed us to acquire Louisiana and Florida, without even precedent, would also allow us, if great necessity arose and the consent of a state were given, to transfer it to some other Nation, or to give it total separation. But of course, the *expediency* is quite another question. Nor would our principles apply to the alienation of any state except what was on the borders, as Louisiana and Florida were.

This much, however, we grant to Mr. Mulford's claims for the Nation. If a Precinct neglects its duties of education, or morality, the Nation has a right to use reasonable MORAL means, instruction, persuasion, &c., to produce improvement therein. And furthermore, the Nation has a right to enforce, that no Individual or Family or Social Circle shall be forcibly and unjustly deprived of its rights by a Precinct. Yet still these rights may sometimes be nothing more than a right to compensated emigration.

Furthermore we admit, that after Precincts were restored to their natural rights, as fundamental Units; then much of what Mr. Mulford says of "commonwealths" would be true. For then commonwealths would be, what LARGE cities also ought to be regarded, namely, organs of the Nation: but their parts, absolutely as Precincts.

CHAP. IV. ABSTRACT AND DIRECT STATEMENT.

§ 1. *In General.*

Our theory may be stated in its most general expression, thus: —Every Locality should be independent of surrounding Localities, except in things which are incompatible with the rights of other Localities, or of Individuals, or with the general progress of the whole.

The idea may be presented in another way, and one that accords with the common politics of the day, as if foreshadowing a true Precinct self-government. One man advocates, allowing each township to decide for itself, its method of voting, another, its police organization, another, its question of liquor, another, of dogs, another, of sheep, another, of flowers or grain, another, of tobacco, another, of Sunday, another, of church, another, of school, another, of woman suffrage, another, of marriage or divorce, another, of customs of dress and equipage, and so on. Now our theory is, to arrange to let each Precinct judge all these questions together, for itself. And this would merely be a practical acknowledgment of the freedom and rights of the Precinct.

§ 2. *Adaptations.*

Our theory of Social Science reconciles into one, the two principal contending theories. That theory like Spencer's which reduces the powers of government to a minimum, we apply to the supreme government of the whole Nation; or the highest generalization and largest organization of the people. Whilst the other theory, which like that of Comte and many other Frenchmen, gives to government the maximum amount and diversity of powers, we apply only to the very smallest local or Precinct organization, whose powers are somewhat analogous to those of our individual states in the United States.

And now in order to secure individual liberty as far as possible, these Precincts are not only to be made as small as possible, but provision is to be fully made by the general government, for the free safe and practicable removal of every citizen, with the proceeds of his property, except in case of crime as set forth by said general government or at least within limits allowed by it.

In order to accomplish this result, it would seem necessary to commit to the courts of the general government in each Precinct, a concurrent power of Habeas Corpus, and of the sale of property for persons ordered to emigrate, or who perhaps were merely desirous to depart voluntarily. Or else peculiar courts might be organized, composed of one-half Precinct-judges and powers, and one-half general-government-judges and powers;

with the provision that in case of disagreement, the party should have right to sell and leave, under the general government's authority.

This arrangement allows every sort of persons to find their like, and to reside together and carry on their government on plans that would very nearly enable them to be unanimous, and in Precincts so small as would make it easy for persons to travel from one to another. It is obvious however, that under this arrangement, the banished party should come under heavy penalties for re-entering his former Precinct without permission; and extra care should be taken to prevent this result.

It is easy to see the logical and philosophical relation here, of general-government-authority, to the special Precinct-authority; because the words *government* and *Precinct* might be omitted, and we could treat of the subject by simply saying general authority and special authority, and consistently give the general powers and those for direct general influence, to the general authority; and the special power or power for special local purposes, to the special or limited authority. Thus the mere statement of the thing, seems a good argument for it.

§ 3. *Resemblance to international relations.*

The minutiæ of rules and regulations for inter-Precinct affairs, would be the same in substance, as those for international affairs,—excepting of course, variations occasioned by the differences that necessarily exist between Precinct and Nation. And these minutiæ would arise in nearly the same manner as international law: accordingly the reader is referred to that subject and to NATION, for a consideration of them. The true system of reciprocal law for Precincts (when exhibited) will be very *nearly* the true system of international law, when once that system has attained any thing *near perfection;* ignoring of course the inadmissible pretensions of secession. In fact, the best proof of the perfect arrangement and analysis of international law, will be its applicability nearly all through, to the Precinct, and its allowing both subjects to be treated together,—pointing out their general sameness, and their occasional differences.

A prominent feature of the theory is or should be, that Precincts should be allowed to form new confederations among themselves, under certain restrictions. The progress of society demands, that all circles or Precincts or associations of men, who are desirous or willing to do better to one another than human nature at large will as yet justify, must necessarily enter into mutual arrangements. This is the basis of all our great national and international beneficial orders, such as Odd Fellows, Masons, &c. Of course, nothing secret is meant or implied, in the Precinct-organization. This way of doing more justly and truly to one another, can only become general, by first exhibiting its superiority, by being adopted on the condition that each shall do so to the other. Therefore the preventing of such combinations in small Precincts, is absolutely preventing the progress of society in its best moral features.

In forming these leagues, no restriction is mentioned that they must be adjoining, nor need they be, because their smallness is the protection against rebellion. A limit might be placed to the number that should enter into any one league, *so long as* any danger was apprehended from such a source.

CHAP. V. THEORY OF AMALGAMS.

§ 1. *Description of Amalgams.*

By an Amalgam we mean a small Precinct with fundamental natural powers; but yet so leagued with each of its IMMEDIATELY contiguous Precincts that its power is partly limited by them, and on the mutual condition that each of the other Precincts is limited by the same PRINCIPLE, but of course not limited by exactly the same identical Precincts, for that would be geographically impossible with the principle. As the idea appears to be original with us, we will try to make it plain.

The legislature and government of each Precinct, (which we might call its Amalgam-Directors,) might consist of one or two or four or of some *even* number of persons, chosen by each adjoining Precinct, together with a number chosen by the Precinct itself, equal to the total of those chosen by all the adjoining Precincts. Thus for instance, if a Precinct were surrounded by and contiguous to, say *four* adjoining Precincts, which is about as small a number as is usually probable; and if each such Precinct furnished two directors, that would be eight, and the Precinct itself should appoint the other eight, and thus the smallest common Board of Amalgam-Directors for any Precinct would be sixteen.

Almost the only cases in which the number of Precincts in any one Amalgam, would be *less* than *four*, would be the cases of Precincts on the *frontiers* of any Nation. In these cases, each given Precinct would have at least one side, namely the foreign side, which would not be adjoined by another Precinct of the same Nation. In such cases, the wisdom of a national government would be to plan the division, of the Precincts on the frontiers, with special reference to this difficulty, so that no Precinct need ever have less than three others, and seldom less than four others adjoining it. On the frontiers the Nation should appoint a share of the Amalgam-Directors.

A regular rectangular division into Precincts, similar to the plan of government surveys of public lands, would make every internal Precinct to be surrounded by eight others, and then the minimum of Amalgam-Directors would be sixteen: or if two from each,—then thirty-two.

The special reason for an even number from each Precinct is, that thereby some balance of power might exist, say one half of each may be elected by the elder persons and the other half by younger persons; or any other balance that might be proper.

The number might be increased to four, and then a possibility would arise of having majority votes of each Precinct, if that be considered any advantage, although it is not so considered by the writer.

The total Directors elected by the Precinct itself, should be so arranged, that each (say) two of them, together with the corresponding two from the any one of the other specified Precincts in regard to and with which there was any particular matter,—should be a joint committee to superintend and arrange all minor difficulties, intercourse and joint operations, exclusively concerning and between their own two specified Precincts themselves; subject of course, in important cases, to the confirmation or refusal of their proceedings by the Amalgam-Directors of either or both the Precincts concerned, and to other legal action.

§ 2. *Argument for Amalgams.*

The description already given seems to contain a pretty good argument of itself. The spirit to "do unto others as you would that they should do unto you," must have its governmental form. Leagues of an original and peculiar kind between ADJOINING

Precincts, are absolutely necessary. Every Precinct, as it is LOCALLY the centre of a neighborhood of Precincts, and also is a part of the neighborhood of every contiguous Precinct, so it should be made LEGALLY such. In other words, every Precinct should be the centre of a small Amalgam, or small council of amalgamated political and civil authority, exercising proportions of the power of all the Precincts in the Amalgam, but yet exercising that power on only the central one of each Amalgam.

The Amalgam, in the first place, is necessary for the sake of police uses chiefly, and to prevent offenders from escaping with impunity into adjoining Precincts before a proper police can be called. But there are also other advantages. The Amalgam would also prevent any one Precinct from deviating too widely or too suddenly from its immediate neighbors; such overwide deviations shocking the consciences of neighbors, or producing riots or other great evils.

Society is not a manufacture nor a building, but a growth and a life. Hence the old method of counties subdivided into independent Precincts, which make a merely mechanical structure, can never be a proper or perfect form for life-processes. What we propose here, is strictly analogous to the interchange of processes of living bodies. This organization is entirely different from the common one, whether of States or Nations, and is perfectly analogous to the life of Individuals and also of Families. Each one is the centre of one life, and at the same time, is an adjunct in the periphery of every contiguous one. But yet, the Amalgam is not itself a Fundamental Unit of society. But the Precinct is that Unit. *Nor* is this theory of Amalgams any *essential* part of our general Theory of the Precinct; but is only one of its higher susceptibilities, and one which would be likely to develop out of necessary inter-Precinct *police* organizations.

CHAP. VI. COMPARISON WITH STATES UNDER THE CONSTITUTION OF THE UNITED STATES.

§ 1. *The most obvious points.*

(*a*) *In general.* The comparison of the Precinct-system here proposed, with the present states under the U. S., may be summed up by saying, that some of the powers of each individual state (i.e., small Precinct,) would be assigned to the Precinct, or to the Amalgam with its surrounding Precincts; and some of these powers would be assigned to the Nation: whilst on the other hand, some of the powers of the Nation would be assigned to the individual Precinct, or to its Amalgam with its surrounding Precincts.

No Precinct would be in amalgam or league with only *one* set of Precincts; because every one of them would form a part of as many different Amalgams, as it touched Precincts which surrounded it, plus one more necessary Amalgam, namely, the one of which the Precinct was itself the centre; and perhaps, plus such additional leagues, as under the national permission, it might form voluntarily with Precincts not touching it: but this latter is much less natural than the other.

In this comparison with the States of our Union, we may say in general, the difference between the system of Precincts, and that of the States in the Union, consists in the vastness of their number, smallness of their size, and the consequent facility of individual removal, secured by the national guarantees, commanding that Individuals should be compensated by the Precincts ordering removals. By these differences, free choices are secured for all, a new element of government is introduced, new organs created, new functions performed, and harmony and peace secured in the consciousness of personality in every Individual, joined with mutual respect for the personality of all other persons.

Every Precinct or small neighborhood, possesses by nature, and should have granted to it by law, the same rights for the most part, that the constitution of the United States grants to its States severally. But the very diminished size of our proposed states, makes necessary a number of alterations or exceptions from the state-rights granted under the constitution; and some of these alterations are diminutions of local power, and some are increases thereof; in other words, some "state-rights" should be allotted to the Nation and others to the Precincts. We may illustrate our general theory, by pointing out in detail, a few of these differences from the present government of the United States,—upon the following named subjects.

(*b*) *Inter-Precinct affairs.*—The first class of differences consists of inter-Precinct relations. The first difference, however, might become very radical in nature. We do not regard any one Locality as being independent of the Localities which immediately adjoin it. The Precinct itself can only have a legitimate government, by admitting more or less political power to be exercised within it, by its immediately adjoining Precincts; and *it* in turn exercising a reciprocal power on each of them in Amalgams such as we have described above.

The exact amount or proportion of this kind of inter-Precinct power, is not easy to determine, previously to experiment, unless by instinct. To us it appears that each Precinct should have an exactly EQUAL amount of political power to that of the SUM of the powers of all its immediately adjoining and contiguous Precincts. But to carry out this idea rigidly, according to the arguments we shall hereafter pursue, would make it necessary to have each Amalgam or *congeries* of Precincts, as small as we there advocate for the single Precincts; and would indeed make the single Precinct so small, as to make the theory at present appear visionary.

For the "present distress" therefore, we need only advocate a congeries of *police* arrangements for Precincts. The police of each Precinct should be allowed to enter its adjoining Precincts when in pursuit of offenders immediately after the offence. Or still better, a consolidated police should be chosen for each Precinct, by an authority consisting, one-half of delegates from the immediately adjoining Precincts, and one-half by the Precinct itself in which they are to act more immediately, with the privilege of extending their pursuits of criminals freely into the immediately adjoining Precincts. Some clauses of the constitution of the United States, have only a formal but not a spiritual opposition to our theory; that is to say, their objects are good, but their methods are incompatible with our proposed theory. For instance, "No state shall enter into any treaty, alliance or confederation.—And no state shall, without the consent of Congress, enter into any agreement or compact with another state," &c. *Incompatible:* Because, no great moral improvements can be made, either by Nations, Precincts or Individuals, only so far as they are allowed and encouraged, to treat their friends or those who do well,—better than they treat those who are not their friends or who do not well; and only as they are allowed thus to treat one another better, on the condition of mutuality or special reciprocity.

That part of the constitution of the United States, which in spirit is most at variance with our proposed radical theory, is its Article IV., especially the following extracts, § 1: "Full faith and credit shall be given in each state, to the public acts" &c., "of every other state." But under our theory, Precincts, like Individuals, would need to prove their credibility, to the satisfaction of other Precincts. And § 2: "Citizens of each state shall be entitled to all the privileges and immunities of citizens of the several states." But under our theory nothing of the kind would be possible long. For every Precinct would establish its own conditions for citizenship within itself. And § 3: "No new state shall be formed within the jurisdiction of any other state, * * * without the consent * * * of the Congress." But under our theory, Precincts must ever continue to subdivide, with the increase of population. Yet still, the consent of the congress is so far necessary, that it should provide the GENERAL laws and forms of proceeding for such subdivisions. Immigrants and sojourners should be judged by the Precincts into which they voluntarily come. Fugitives should be judged, not by the Precinct whence they escape, but by the Nation. The *return* of fugitives by force, except for causes approved by the Nation, is absurd: but by treaty with adjoining Precincts, is reasonable.

In order that each Precinct might have a reasonable opportunity to know that the inter-precinct regulations were carried out fairly, and to assist therein; each should allow one Precinct-consular-agent from each of the immediately adjoining Precincts, to reside therein, at his own convenience, who should have all the immunities of person and Family that foreign consuls have. And the same privilege would have to be granted, of course, to a reasonable number of the agents of the general government.

Disputes between residents of different Precincts should be settled by parties selected from both, and should be decided according to the principles of arbitration. All disputes wherein a Precinct was interested, should be settled by principles and laws *more general* than those within the Precinct itself, yet still, according to the principles of arbitration; whether the contending party were another Precinct, or whether it were the Nation itself; provided, that constitutional questions, in cases wherein the Nation is a party, should of course be determined by the courts of the Nation itself. Furthermore, all cases of dispute, as to whether any matter belongs to the Nation or not, should be carried *by appeal* to the national courts.

There should be provided by the Nation, general laws for the declaration of national roads, &c., for the charter of new roads running through, say three or more Precincts; but the details should be executed by the Precincts themselves through which they are to pass. But roads between only two Precincts could safely be left to the discretion of the Precincts concerned.

Rivers and water courses, would come under the law of roads.

All regulations of travel on roads declared national, should be retained by the Nation, or assigned to the Nation. But not so as to give any traveler a right to halt in objectionable places times or manners, nor remain long nor depart far from the road itself, without the consent of the Precinct. New roads not declared national, entering more than three Precincts; and changes of the location of such, should require the consent of say three-fourths of the Precincts through which the road or changed location is to be made.

(c) *Affairs within the Precinct itself.* The other class of differences that would have to be pointed out, in this comparison with the constitution of the United States, relates to matters within the Precinct itself.

Any Precinct should be allowed to establish for itself, as its own legal tender, a solvent paper-currency representing fairly *any* specified commodity or commodities of general use in the United States; *provided* that no refusal to liquidate, according to the actual promises, should be allowed.

The Nation should not assume to pass any bankrupt, or any other law releasing debtors, or otherwise interfering in such matters, except to secure the right of change of domicile.

No Precinct should be allowed to make any general assignment or forfeiture of private property to the public, under less than 50 or 100 years' notice, without compensation. This rule is needed to prevent agrarian outrages. And on the other hand, to prevent speculators from procuring such agrarian legislation and notices,—merely that *they* might lay up property; and then after a time, get the notices repealed.

The right of Individuals to remove from a Precinct with the proceeds of their property, and the right to a free sale or transfer of such property to the highest bidder in or out of such Precinct, should be guaranteed, except for crimes recognized by the Nation or by the genuine principles of morality. And then the penalties should not, excepting banishment, be in excess of those allowed *by* the Nation from time to time, for offences of a similar degree of criminality.

There is one foundation for certain special Precincts, namely, a peace-foundation, which would require some further special enactments and principles; and which no doubt would be granted to them by the national government,—namely, Precincts established on a peace-basis, should not be required to violate *that* basis by draft or otherwise; and on the other hand, the voluntary formation and existence of such Precincts, would much facilitate the administration of the rules of war, in the other Precincts generally. Indeed, so clear are the rights and so important the uses of Peace-Precincts, that even before the institution of any GENERAL system of Precincts, these rights should be granted by easy *charter* from congress, or by general laws.

(*d*) *Temporary restrictions* of the Precinct-powers, would be necessary, for such a length of time as would preserve rights and secure safety under state-authority, until the plan could be safely and fully instituted, and the necessary changes and removals could be made. But to make the matter more plain, we will give a few details of those exceptions and reservations.

States could pass laws for intercourse with contiguous states, and relating to contiguous operations; but only to go into force at a certain *future* time, and on *condition* of the contiguous states adopting similar laws previous to that time.

No person at any time, should be punished for offences against religion, in the exercise of freedom of conscience, by any other punishment than by requisition to remove from the district after 12 months' notice. But in the beginning, this class of permitted orders of removal, should be suspended for 5 or 6 years after the adoption of the general plan, to allow plenty of time for the settlement of present interests, and vested rights, and for due deliberation. And all persons removing by order, at any time, should be paid a sum sufficient to enable them and their families, if any, to travel to the nearest Precincts or neighborhoods where they would be allowed to remain, so far as a knowledge of their character possessed at that time, would render their stay admissible. Rates of compensation should be fixed by the national government; unless otherwise agreed between the particular Precincts respectively concerned in each kind of removal, —namely, the one forsaken and the one adopted.

Also some special provisions of a greater length of notice, (say 21 years) would be required for the affairs and the government of minors, and for fiduciary property; or such property might be sold according to existing state or national laws, if any, and be held by Trust Companies accordingly.

To prevent injustice in the beginning, the Nation's Criminal Law and perhaps also its whole Civil Law, should be carefully improved, not by tricky "digests," but by all known necessary statutes:—And then by a clause, that it should remain unaltered for say 10 years. This would allow political and social dissenters, time to sell out and remove.

It might also make the transition seem safer and more satisfactory to some persons, if, for the few years during the transitions, the privilege of appeal to the Supreme Court of the Nation were allowed and reserved for all important cases. But the suggestion is only to satisfy the timid, and to be temporary in its nature, for obviously, the permanent existence of such a rule of appeal, would become, or at any rate, *might* easily become tantamount to the entire nullification of all the essential rights and benefits of the plan itself.

§ 2. *Points of the comparison needing further illustration.*

(*a*) *Commerce and the Legal Tender.*—In comparing the proposed Precinct-system with the constitution and system of the United States, there are several points which seem to need further elucidation than what could be given to them in the foregoing *general* views. Let us now proceed with them.

It may be doubted whether the legal tender ought to be entrusted to the Precinct. Now we admit that while law, whether of Precinct or Nation, may for extraordinary reasons, extend the time of fulfillment of contracts reasonably, or even depreciate, the common old currencies, by altering the legal tender, yet when the emergency is past, the old tender should be promptly restored: But that has hardly ever been done. We may also admit, that changes of so great a nature may arise, that a permanent alteration of the legal tender may become necessary. But obviously no such alteration should be made, otherwise than by alteration of the constitution itself. But experience proves, as we show under Property, that the question of changes in the legal tender, cannot safely be entrusted to national governments, because their control is too absolute, and competition too entirely slow in its effects thereupon. And all the serious troubles that have arisen from LOCAL currencies have arisen from their being irredeemable. Hence, all that the Nation ought to prescribe on the subject of the currency, is, that all promises of currency should be redeemable in the legal tender promised, with only such extensions of time as were duly provided for by law:—otherwise, should be payable, one half in the currency of, and under the regulations of, the promisor; and the other half in that of the promisee, or of the Precincts of residence thereof. But the Nation has a right to see that no Precinct shall have *one* legal tender for its resident debtors, but a different one for its resident creditors; nor that any other differences should be made except those which pertained strictly to Locality, such as, to the nearness of and known reliability of guarantors, when guarantors were necessary, in extensions of time.

On the other hand, to the Nation, legitimately belong, the regulation of the subjects of WHOLESALE Commerce, domestic and foreign, and even the regulation of intercourse between Precincts so far as they had not entered into special agreements of their own. All the other matters must come under a merely general supervision of the Nation, so far as to see that neither Individuals nor Precincts, were brought under the application of laws to which they had not first actually knowingly and freely consented. Furthermore, these rights may safely be given to Precincts, because the right is guaranteed, of removal to such other Precincts as will receive the Individuals in question.

b) *Divorce.* The most difficult cases to understand the precise effects of our theory in, are divorces, especially when there are children. We may explain this difficulty thus: It is a part of our theory. (1) That no Precinct should receive immigrant strangers, without evidence of the legitimacy of the immigration, satisfactory to its government. (2) If persons removed to other Precincts merely in order to get a divorce, and then to return to their original Precinct or some other, they, by this right of Precinct to examine character, would be excluded from all Precincts which disapproved of their course. (3) Few Precincts would be silly enough to allow divorce to new comers, especially where there were children to be supported, because such children would come upon the Precinct for support. (4) It is no part of our theory, to prevent persons who deliberately intend to try any social experiments, from assembling in Precincts *by themselves*, and reaping the full effects of their experiments, whether they be good or whether they be evil. But the Nation has the right to compel the support of the children &c. (5) It is a part of our theory, that the question of marriage and divorce is of too private a nature for the law to judge understandingly, especially without the concurrence of the Social Circle, and the moral and religious organizations. (6) That whether divorced or single, all women are entitled to special assistance from government, and especially divorced women; and that the better class of Precincts, would voluntarily, and the others should be obliged to, provide for this right; and those Precincts which did not so provide, would not be very inviting to the women. (7) That the rights of Precincts we are advocating, are rights over their own citizens, not rights of contracts in which one party is a citizen and the other not.

Still, we must admit, that length of residence, in order to have full rights, must have some reasonable limit. But even this is more safely left to competition among the Precincts, than to the monopoly of a distant central power, whose policy would continually fluctuate, with its probable influence on great totals of voters, and the probable need of such influence. Furthermore, the unlimited gift of such power to the Nation, might easily result in breaking up nearly all the advantages of the Precinct theory. But, for the further discussion of the principles of the Family, the reader is referred especially to that Element, and also to some parts of the discussion on Property.

Here we observe this much however. The states which have led in hasty divorces, have been chiefly the *new* states with very sparse populations. The foundation-fault therefore has been, that same that we have to encounter every where in our national history ar.d politics, namely, the over hasty partitioning out of our new lands so much sooner than the wants of Mankind, or of civilization or morality, either required or permitted.

The new system would require power to *enforce* the Precinct-principle, in cases of desertion of marital or family obligations.

The right of free migration should be restricted then, if it could be, when the Precinct itself should render some aid to deserted women, and efficient aid to deserted children. The women, to be sure, should have the same chance to follow after their deserting husbands, that they now have under the ordinary constitutions. But whether they should be allowed to take away young and helpless children, into all sorts of risks and dangers, is another question. If a Precinct fulfills its duties to its women and children, it naturally has the right of guardianship over deserted children, until they attain to full age. Our theory is, that it is the duty of governments to care for the children, and even to aid the women. But the causes of divorce are sometimes very private and very sacred. Nor can any civil government judge of such questions. But still, every Precinct should be allowed to try its own plan, under the national rules. And the Precinct's license of divorce, would and must be made to be held in balance by its duties to aid and protect the deserted women and children, which should be made obligatory, at least, as the condition of Precinct-divorces.

It is almost certain, that the rule would soon become general among the Precincts, to require of immigrants, certificates or other evidences of good character, coming from other Precincts, at least those within the Nation. And these certificates would vary according to the nature and predominant ideas of the Precinct into which the immigrant would remove. Moral Precincts would require moral certificates; Hygienic Precincts, hygienic certificates; Secular Precincts, secular certificates; and so on. But probably most of them would soon require duly attested certificates of faithful performance of Family-obligations. Some would require such, for the sake of principle; and some for the sake of preservation from a rush of social parasites, unwilling to maintain their own Families or be responsible for their own doings.

(c) *Punishment of crime.* Precincts must be required to hold their own criminals in duress, or else transfer them to a *superior* authority. The principle should be established, that although no Precinct should be required by superior government, to punish criminals beyond its own idea of justice and expediency, yet neither should any Precinct be allowed ever to avowedly permit great criminals, or even *any habitual* criminals, to emigrate to other Precincts. And this latter can only be avoided *in some cases,* by the Precinct passing all such criminals regularly over to some more general authority. Hence, the Precinct should not banish for any real or enormous crime, thus turning criminals loose on other Precincts. And in the case of certain specified crimes, should not even allow the criminal to go at liberty. But if the Precinct does not approve of punishing him by holding him in duress securely enough or *long enough,* it must then pass him over to the more general authority, the Nation. Precincts, even as Nations, should be held accountable, if they permit their inhabitants to "raid" against adjoining or neighboring ones, or against any others.

The foregoing principles, would make necessary an exact reversal of the rule of the Constitution of the United States (Art. 4, Sect. 2) in regard to the restoration of fugitive criminals, and the usual jurisdiction only by the Locality of the offence. Every government, Precinct or other, has the *natural* right to punish its immigrant criminals, even for crimes committed elsewhere; and that was often the rule in ages of simplicity and *nature.* Precincts like Nations, would require to make their own special treaties, in order to place themselves under a different order.

(d) *Division of Precincts.* The just principle is that each Precinct should be allowed to divide at will, whenever, BUT NOT BEFORE, it had a population sufficient to make two or more Precincts, each having an AVERAGE of population of the rest of the Precincts of the Nation. This rule should apply even more strictly to the admission of new "states" or the transformation of mere rural territories into states, than to the division of already existing ones; because the Nation evidently has more right over and more claims upon a state which and WHEN it makes, than upon one already existing. And while two senators are admitted from each state, the state itself should be divided into two separate senatorial districts, arranged expressly with a view to the probable subsequent division, and modified from time to time, to suit the changing probabilities of the expected lines of division.

Most of our states that have been admitted, since the first ones, have had less than 100,000 inhabitants, at the time of their acknowledgment as states. And the average of most of them is 50,000. But several that have lately been admitted as states, have had only about 10,000 (!) But in the census of 1870 New York has 4,382,000; Pennsylvania, 3,522,000; Ohio, 2,666,000; Illinois, 2,540,000 ; and so on (!)

The seven states which inaugurated the great rebellion, had at the time only 82½ per cent. of an average state-population; and only 51 per cent. of an average state-voting-population. And the thirteen which finally composed the rebellious confederacy, contained but 92 per cent. of an average state-population, and only 66 per cent. of an average of the voters. Thus the statistics warn us of the danger of giving so much preference to square miles rather than to population, in admitting new "states" to the Union. Furthermore, the late financial panic helps prove the same conclusion; for that panic was brought on chiefly by the over haste and consequent rottenness of the western Rail Road building. And if there is any one thing corrupting the Congress of the United States more than any thing else, it is this preponderance given to Locality, and its connected speculation for "grabbing up" the new lands.

(e) *Rebellion of Precincts.* One of the principal defects in the constitution of the United States, is the omission to provide expressly for the contingency of rebellion by states. But our comparison shall be very explicit on this subject. Rebellion by a state or Precinct, forfeits the *political* rights of that *state* or Precinct, as such. And the more united the Precinct had been, in its rebellion, the more just would this punishment be. Let us illustrate this.

Nothing is clearer, than that the whole subject of the internal government of each of the states is, by the constitution, left to the government of the state itself. IF then, when a state rebelled, it REALLY continued to be a state, it is evident that the general government would have no authority to administer the affairs of the Nation, so far as they involved that state, even during its rebellion, nor to settle its affairs any time afterwards, even after complete conquest. Such a conclusion would place the Nation at the mercy of a few states, and would be absurd. What part of the secession argument, then, it may be asked, is false? Why, that which assumes that a state continues to be a state after it rebels. The fact of rebellion by a state as such, that is, by the state government as authorized and upheld by the regular majority of the voting people of that state,—that fact per se, annuls the political rights of the state as a state, and remands it to the condition of a "territory" or "district." Just as certainly as the fact of an Individual's rebelling, naturally takes away his political rights, just so, the fact of a state rebelling by full authority of its political rulers and voters, takes away the political rights of that organization of voters, and of that moral charter or state sovereignty which it possessed. Unless this were so, you would establish as a principle, that a rebellious state, after being badly beaten, had nothing to do but to disarm its fighters, and return to the halls of congress to obstruct legislation, withhold pay of the war debt, withhold pensions for the killed and wounded, and throw all its influence to injure the general country and provoke wars with other countries; and then rebel again.

If a state does not forfeit its rights as a state by rebellion, then the general government must have disbanded its armies at once, after the fall of Richmond, and allowed the Southern rebels to resume their seats in congress, vote for ALL their Blacks, instead of for the $\frac{3}{5}$ of them, which was all they were allowed to vote for before the war. This is just the kind of a settlement that might have been expected, if the result of the war had been exactly the opposite to what it was, and if the South had come off conquerors instead of the North, yet without accomplishing an entire dissolution. In fact there is no way to justify either Congress or the President, requiring any stipulation or constitutional alteration to be accepted by a rebelled state, which does not imply that the rebelled state has lost its political rights, and is no longer a state at all, in the eye of the law or of the constitution. It is an established principle that war annuls all previous political contracts, except *otherwise mentioned.*

Rebellion does not take a state out of the Union, but it takes its political constitution out of the constitution of the United States. Its territory remains as property, and its roads to be taken and traveled on;—its inhabitants remain to be governed and protected, as may be wise and reasonable; the rights of citizenship of loyal Individuals as Individuals remain unimpaired, in the same manner as if residents of territories; but their political state rights are gone, for the state is no more a state, but a territory or District like the District of Columbia, or like any western territory not yet admitted by congress. All the world over, wherever one part of a country rebels, and is defeated and conquered, the governors of that region lose their political rights, until restored by the conquerors:—and in this country, the governors of the rebellious states were the majority of the voters of those states, except perhaps in one or two of them. The political rights of that dynasty, therefore are forfeited. The President's pardon cannot affect that subject, because it is not an Individual affair, but an affair of office, of majorities, and of the state government itself.

Nothing in this argument, however, is to be so construed, as to deny the *right* of Precincts to rebel, upon *sufficient* cause. The conflict of arms results in general from the uncompromised conflicts of opinion, and which are useless to discuss any further. It is a resort to which every living thing which believes in fighting, has a natural right, upon just occasion. But after the resort to arms has been made and concluded in conquest, the *rights* of the conquerors are limited only by the laws of nations and by Christian morality. But the *expediencies* are a different question.

(*f*) *Separation of National from Precinct politics.* To avoid confusing local interests and local parties, with national ones, no council or legislative body elected for Precinct affairs or Precinct purposes, ought to be chosen to select officers for national affairs; but such ought to be selected according to a different division of parties, grounded upon an entirely different classification of ideas, and relating to an entirely different class of concerns. But to this, must be excepted questions concerning the division of a Nation or Precinct, or concerning the relative degrees of power or administration belonging to either. But, as every returning to such a discussion and division on this branch of the subject, tends to confuse inextricably the separate businesses and functions of the two great organs of government, it follows that something ought to be done to prevent constant or long continued political struggles, in this matter of the relation of Precinct to Nation. This might be accomplished perhaps, by having conventions held, for the express purpose of remodeling the constitution of the Nation, at only certain *regular* intervals, say, every ten or fifteen years, in hopes that in the interim all question relating to the subject might have rest. Moreover and still better, to keep the different businesses and the two functions separate, the elections for National officers ought to be at as different times as possible. And as annual elections are frequent enough, it would be best that the elections for Precinct or Nation were held in alternate years or not oftener, and not any nearer together respectively. And the longer time that could be allowed, consistently with other reasons, to intervene between the different kinds of elections, the more distinct they would be kept, and the better therefore would be the results.

CHAP. VII. STATEMENT AND DETERMINATION OF THE SIZE OF PRECINCTS.

§ 1. *Conditions in general.*

Under this head we will first give the *formulæ*, with some general arguments; next, a few further thoughts on the conditions of population; and then a few on the conditions of locality. The object here however, is not to go through the whole argument for small Precincts, which is reserved for the Second division of this Part, of the work. But assuming the general doctrine to be established, the particular problem, is to determine exactly how small the Precincts should be. This consideration is placed before the other, in order the better to *explain the nature* of our theory.

Precincts should be no larger in territory or population, than would admit of all the adult people, or at least all the voters, meeting conveniently in one assembly. And no larger than would allow the heads of Families as residents, to be generally acquainted with each other, at least by hearsay, yet not so small as to preclude the chances of reasonably furnishing the proper proportion of qualified governmental officials.

This minimum of smallness is called for, because each Precinct of a perfected system, is required to derive considerable government authority from its adjoining Precincts, and be an Amalgam therewith; so that to have large Precincts, would require this Amalgam to be larger than would accord with the safety of individual personal liberty. Thus, each Precinct is the centre of one life, and at the same time, is a part of the circumference of life of every other Precinct adjoining it.

The second idea to determine the size of Precincts, is the necessity of keeping local and national politics distinct. However small the legal organization of any territory or company, there will always be formed a few and never more than a few caucuses, cliques or parties; voluntary subdivisions or suborganizations to affect the legal one. These subdivisions or suborganizations are formed on purpose to affect the legal organization, and grow out of it and cannot get far from it. This is the reason why there never can be more than a few of such parties, because as their number increases arithmetically, their power decreases geometrically. That there will always be at least two, or a few such subdivisions, is, because different human minds do not see or feel alike. From these considerations it follows that the Precincts ought to be small, so that the suborganizations which will arise in each, shall flow out of it voluntarily, and relate to the concerns of each immediate neighborhood itself; and for similar reasons, the amount of power and business given to the national or large organ, should be a minimum, or the smallest possible, so as thereby to cause the least amount of interference with the business and concerns of the Precinct. In other words, these things should be so, in order to prevent local parties being formed upon national interests, or *vice-versa*. For instance, if Precincts were so small as to consist of only *one* Family each, and as Family questions would seldom be introduced into national politics, therefore such divisions would furnish the minimum of confusion of the two kinds of politics. Again, if

Precincts became a little larger, so as to consist of only a few Families each, the confusion would become rather more frequent, yet still would be comparatively rare, because the questions for consideration, would be still very local and very personal. Hence, the larger the Precincts are made, the greater will be the confusion of the two kinds of politics, and *vice-versa.*

§ 2. *Conditions of population.*

As to the actual size of these Precincts, the most important consideration by far is density of population. The general theory points at from 10,000 to 20,000, as being the highest number that should constitute a Precinct, as this gives from 1000 to 2500 adult men or voters to each, which is the highest number that can conveniently meet and consult.

Election districts should not consist of a larger population, than would allow of all old or established residents, being tolerably well acquainted with each other's personal and business character, either by direct acquaintance and observation, or by common hearsay. If Precincts are larger than this, then their officers should be chosen by electors each of whom represents and is from an elective district as small as herein mentioned. But the smallness makes the direct voting by the people more practicable. For the larger the district or population, the less direct can the election be. And a vast deal depends upon the "*Primary*" elections. And our idea is to make the Precincts as small as the smallest district of primary elections, or as near that as possible.

The utmost population should be such that all persons entitled to vote for any one branch of its government, should be able to meet in one building under cover, and so that any ordinary speaker could be heard from one end to the other. Thus, its size would vary with the number of voters. And whenever their number became too large to meet as described, either the Precinct would have to be divided, or an additional division be made of its representative houses, or an increase of age or other qualifications for suffrage.

Smallness also secures to each of the people, mutual knowledge of the other, and mutual *good feeling,* so that government is more practicable, and happiness more complete, all being agreed.

On the other hand, it is desirable that the population of each

Precinct, should be sufficient to enable it to select one representative to the national legislature or congress, for itself, without being joined in a congressional or senatorial district with any other Precinct, so long as it remains possible to avoid it. At the same time, the congress itself must not be larger than can conveniently meet, debate and consult. Now, a national population of Fifty Million, would require that each Precinct should contain at least Twenty Thousand average population; because if less, then the congress would have to consist of more than Twenty Five Hundred members. Hence arises the necessity of not making the Precincts smaller than are required by the fundamental conditions before mentioned.

The only possibilities for allowing larger populations to the Precincts, lie in the direction, either of increasing the age of suffrage, or otherwise democratically lessening the number of voters, or else in the direction of the electoral colleges or houses of delegates, for the special purpose of electing all general officers. And these delegates must be FREE,—not pledged to vote for any particular candidates. For, our fundamental principle is, that the number of direct voters for any candidate must always be within the limits of probable personal acquaintanceship, both with the candidate and with each other, and of conveniently assembling in consultation. To accomplish this object, Precincts might be subdivided into wards; but the voluntary and spontaneous division of the people themselves (within the Precinct) into Corporations as shown under that head, is much the better plan; and any delegate-system, really such, would be more acceptable to the people in that way. But the consideration of that way, must be deferred to its proper head.

An obvious corollary from the foregoing principles, is, that woman-suffrage is so far an erroneous movement, lessening the probabilities of decreasing the size of Precincts to the proper and necessary smallness.

§ 3. *Conditions of Locality.*

As to the extent of ground or territory to be embraced in a Precinct, it should not be larger than would allow each man, or each voter, to travel by the usual methods, to and back from the place of meeting, conveniently in one day. In case the population was too scattered for such a limit of territory, the theory then would be,—that some merely *temporary* arrangement, analogous to the principle of United-States-territorial government, be made, until the population became sufficiently concentrated on such a tract, say of not more than about fifty miles diameter, the place of meeting being central, and not more than twenty-five miles from the circumference or boundary.

As the essential idea of Precinct is neighborhood,—both population and locality must be small enough to admit of the usual feelings of real neighbors. Therefore the word neighbor, in common usage, as it contracts or expands for different localities, is an excellent definitive for the varying size of Precincts.

If largeness of territory be offered as a reason why a state should be recognized as such, relying upon the *hope* of an increase; then that reason is equally as great, why it should *not* be so recognized, for it is so sparsely settled that the inhabitants live too far apart, and consequently are too little acquainted with each other. And if it is really going to increase so fast, it will not have long to wait.

If it be said that the idea for the maximum size of the Precinct here presented, would not answer for the settlement of our new lands: we answer that our method of settling them has been too unscientific, and entirely too extravagant and diffuse. This we shall endeavor to prove at large in the article on land, under Property. It is the land-treatment that is wrong, not our Precinct system. Besides, even if modifications were necessary in the wild woods, that would be no argument for them, where they were not necessary.

In regard to boundaries, it is of course desirable that natural boundaries should be preferred, where they can be obtained;—by natural boundaries we mean Rivers, Creeks, &c.,—but in modern times and small Precincts, we can seldom have anything better than roads or streets; fences or walls. But these latter can be made the best of all possible boundaries. At any rate, street boundaries are poor ones, because they call for double jurisdiction in the places most frequented; and rivers do somewhat the same, in thickly settled localities.

PART II.

SPECIAL ARGUMENTS FOR THE THEORY.

CHAP. I. PREFACE.

§ 1. *Classification of Theories.*

The dispute about the relative rights of State and Nation, may be *spun* out almost indefinitely, by writers who have no scientific system wherein to place them; according as they hold to one or another of various theories, which no one knows either the origin or the evidences of. These various theories of the fundamental relations between State and Nation, may be summed up into three classes, which are here presented as a convenient outline for meditation on the subject, and for the classification of all the arguments upon it; for the use of persons who may wish to pursue the subject in detail, further than we can spare time to do:—Only remarking that ours, is what is here called the III. THEORY.

(I. Theory).—Supremacy of the Nation. States are Corporations with charters from the Nation alone.

(1) (*a*) Either:—Temporary, at the option of the Nation:
(*b*) or:—Perpetual.

(2) (*a*) Either:—With Definite limited charters:
(*b*) or:—With Indefinite charters altered by time and circumstance.

(II. Theory).—Supremacy of the States. The Nation is a confederate Union:—

(1) (*a*) Either:—Temporary, at the option of the States:
(*b*) or:—Perpetual.

(2) (*a*) Either:—With Definite and written charters:
(*b*) or:—With Indefinite charters altered by time and circumstance.

(III. Theory).—Balances of State and Nation: Both as coexistent in the people, as distinct Units:

(1) (*a*) Either:—Alterably:
(*b*) or:—Unalterably.

(2) (*a*) Either:—With Definite written charters:

(*b*) or:—With Indefinite charters altered by time and circumstance.

(3) (*a*) Both:—For all Internal peace, order, and fraternity between Individuals and States, within the limitations of State-rights.

(*b*) And:—For all External International relations, without limitations of State-rights!

§ 2. *Limits of the special or collateral Arguments.*

In the foregoing article, THE GENERAL VIEW AND STATEMENTS *of our theory*, are really a general argument for it. Moreover, most of those statements contain special parts that are direct and formal arguments for various portions of the theory, as they pass along. Thus the historical statement contained arguments, some drawn from the general course of history, some from the history of the United States. The scientific statements consist entirely of analogies which are arguments in substance. The comparisons with the constitution of the United States, presented the reasons for differing in a few places from that great and as yet unapproached political document. And the discussion of size was a direct argument for our system, because in this country where we are so familiar with the principle of state rights, and of independent sovereignty within limits, the question is more one of size than of any thing else.

Furthermore, we will find some arguments when we come to the discussion of NATION, and determine its true location, and that it is not the sole unit, nor even the most active unit of political society; and that it does not occupy any such a position of absolute power toward the Precincts, but what in the progress of history the power of Mankind over IT should be similar. Indeed, that position is almost drawn (in the Introduction itself) in the discussion of the Units, and their necessary balances.

Many of our arguments for the Precinct are better considered under Corporation; for while they apply equally to both, they are better considered under the latter; because in the common theories, it is the more familiar organ, and still more, because the arguments are true in their own nature, entirely without respect to any ideas of locality. And for these arguments, the reader is referred to that Article.

In arguments of this kind, it should always be borne in mind that the question is, not whether what one advocates is perfect, but whether it is better than what the opposing disputants advocate. The question is, *not* whether the government under small Precincts is infallible, but whether it is not better than a government of large states, or an entirely consolidated one.

The neighborhood is the real germ of the state, and of its rights of government, both theoretically and historically. This proposition appeals to the human heart as well as to history. Hence, the burden of proof ought to be upon those who maintain the preference of large states as against small Precincts. This would be so, even if the doctrine of small Precincts were not essential to the sound general theory of government, and even if there were no particular arguments to show the superiority of the rights and of the effects of the small Precincts: for it is in the Precinct or near neighborhood, that civil government necessarily BEGINS, and will always spontaneously reorganize after distractions or interruptions. But nevertheless, we will proceed with other arguments as we may be able.

CHAP. II. THE GEOGRAPHICAL ARGUMENT.

§ 1. *Forms of the Continents.*

It is a remarkable fact observed by the great geographers, that progressive civilization has been almost entirely confined to the countries, the most indented by seas and oceans. Thus Europe has 6$\frac{3}{8}$ miles of coast to each 1,000 square miles of continent, whilst Asia has only 2$\frac{1}{8}$. What is thereby gained, is not merely an increased extent of coast line facilitating commerce, but many abrupt and long peninsulas, which *preserve the individualities of tribes and districts.* Thus Guyot (p. 46, "Earth and Man") says: of Europe: "Its principal mass is deeply cut in all parts by the ocean and by inland seas, and seems almost on the point of resolving itself into peninsulas. These peninsulas themselves, as Greece, Scandinavia, repeat to infinity the phenomena of articulation and indentation of coasts, which are characteristic of the entire continent. The inland seas and the portions of the ocean, its outer limits enclose, form nearly half of its surface. * * * Thus it is the continent most open to the sea for foreign connections, at the same time that it is the most individualized, and the richest in local and independent districts." It is true that Asia has extensive peninsulas; the places of origin of the ancient civilizations, Arabia, the two Indies, Mandchouria and China. But the influence of these peninsulas was overcome by the immensity of the unbroken continent, to which they in comparison formed only small extremities. Thus Guyot (p. 46) says: "Asia is a mighty trunk, the numerous members of which, however, make only a fifth of its mass. In Europe, the members overrule the principal body, the branches cover the trunk," and (p. 45): "The extent of this continent [Asia] is such, that, in spite of the depth of the indentations, there yet remains at its centre a greatly preponderating mass of undivided land, which commands the maritime regions, as the body commands the limbs." These all (p. 296) "are so many new Individuals, exciting each other reciprocally to animation." Moreover, other geographical conditions co-operate to make true Precincts. "The ground is everywhere cut and crossed by chains of mountains, moulded in a thousand fashions in such a way as to present, within the smallest possible space, the greatest number of districts physically independent." Again: "No continent is more fitted, by the multiplicity of the physical regions it presents, to bring into being and to raise up so many different nations and peoples." And (pp. 313–14) he says: "The assimilation of the peoples of Europe, stops far short of confounding their distinctive qualities. Not long since the world saw them, * * * protesting against the complete fusion, seemingly about to annihilate their individual existence, and threatening to carry them back to the chaos of a homogeneous unity. * * * Each of the great physical districts composing that continent, in reality sustains a people whose moral and intellectual character, aptitude, talents, differ as much as their language, from those of their brethren. Each of these Nations plays, in the great drama of history, a special part in accordance with its particular gifts, and altogether, they form in truth and reality one of those rich organic unities, which we have recognized as being the natural result of all regular and healthy growth." Again, reasoning from the greater to the less, and observing that even the continents themselves are great types of the uses of locality itself, however small, Guyot says (p. 323): "That the three continents of the North are organized for the development of man. * * *

That each of these three continents, by virtue of its very structure and of its physical qualities, has a special function in the education of Mankind. * * * That the entire physical creation corresponds to the moral creation, and is only to be explained by it. * * * It is not perhaps without some surprise, that we behold privileged continents and races almost unalterably smitten with a character of inferiority. And yet, why be surprised at this? Is it not the attribute of God to dispense His gifts to whom He will, and as He will? Do we not know that in every organism, there are needed divers members, clothed with functions more or less exalted, but alike necessary? We shall see that this great contrast of the historical continents, and the continents of the inferior races, seems established by Providence AS A STANDING INVITATION ADDRESSED TO MAN, BIDDING HIM UNFOLD A NEW ACTIVITY. * * * For the law of contrasts in the order of nature, is the law of love in the moral order."

§ 2. *Geographical course of Civilization.*

Again, Guyot (pp. 300–1) says: "The first glance we cast upon the annals of the Nations, enables us to perceive a singular but incontestable fact, that the civilizations representing the highest degree of culture ever attained by man, at the different periods of his history, do not succeed each other in the same places, but pass, from one country to another, from one continent to another, following a certain order. This order may be called *the geographical order of history*," (or of civilization). * * * "Tradition universally represents the earliest men descending, it is true, from the high table-lands of Europe." "The traditions of the Chinese place the first progenitors of that people on the high table-land, whence the great rivers flow; they make them advance, station by station, as far as the shores of the ocean. The people of the Brahmins come down from the regions of the Hindo-Khu and from Cashmere, into the plains of the Indus and the Ganges: Assyria and Bactriana receive their inhabitants from the table-lands of Armenia and Persia."

Again, speaking of the ancient civilization of China, Hindoostan, Syria, Arabia, Egypt and even Judea, Guyot says (pp. 306–7): "During the long centuries of these first ages, man has therefore learned but one thing, that he depends on the will of a master, but that master is an inexorable despot devoid of love. He can only fear him; if he obeys him, it is as a slave; he loves him not nor adores him, for love presupposes liberty. Men cannot remain thus. A cry of liberty makes itself heard; it re-echoes to the depths of that East which groans in its chains. In a small corner of the earth, neighboring still to the East, but admirably organized, in that small peninsula of Greece, where all the varied contrasts of the whole continent seem to be repeated in a narrow space, under a climate blessed of Heaven, a new people arise, upon a new land, a free people, a people of brethren," (and we add, a people consisting of several small and perpetually distinct tribes and Precincts.) "With them the period of youth commences; human consciousness awakes with energy; man recovers himself. * * * Who can describe all there is of fresh and youthful energy, in that people of artists and philosophers, whose efforts open to us a world entirely new? This is no longer the world of nature; it is that of the human soul. Everything, in fact, with the Greek, bears that eminently human character which betrays the preponderance of human personality, and the energy of individual character. * * * The Greek no longer goes to the outer world of nature in search of wisdom, but descends to the depths of human consciousness. With Socrates and his school, philosophy has passed from the realm of nature into the realm of man; she has become a moral philosophy. In the social life of the Greeks, no more * * * of those hard despotisms * * * which by regulating human existence in detail, hinder its improvement; but communities of free and equal men, and the predominance of democracy,—of Individual and local life; these are its characteristics."

All history and all experience corroborate these truths. But in order to apply them to present times, we must remember that those localities anciently contained but small populations comparatively, in their days of intellectual progress and development; and that they prove our theory of the Precinct, as well as, or even more than they prove the necessity of nationality. The political cause of the downfall of the Greek democracies, was *not* their preservation of the rights of the Precinct, but their being without ANY adequate or permanent *central* government, whereby the nationality would be politically expressed.

The experience of history is against the cultivation of nationality, to the extent of the subversion of all local rights. The Romans allowed the natives of different Nations, to have their own laws in their various places of foreign residence. The recognition of a few Precinct-rights, has come down even in the modern laws of England, both in special local customs and in general powers, as in Isle of Man and of Jersey, and several other places. There are also specialties, not confined to one locality only; as Burgage, Gavelkind, Copy-hold, and Villein-socage. These specialties relate chiefly to the titles of real estate.

Even the poor inhabitants of India, were as happy with their Precinct-system as their false religion would allow them to be, until England swallowed it up in a vast gulf of centralization, and sunk the people into poverty and dependence. (See Carey's Soc. Sci.)

Small states, especially small free republics, are the best governed, both our own, and some foreign ones: as the Republic of San Marino, the Cantons of Switzerland, the small German free cities and states. Nor do we have to go from home to find examples; for our own small states are better governed, politically speaking, than the larger ones. Rhode Island, Connecticut and Delaware, are much better governed than New York or Pennsylvania. And life is more respected in our small cities than in the large ones in the same neighborhoods. The colonies of the United States were substantially states at first, yet with but limited populations for many years; and they were the best governments of their age in the world, and were the germs of a great and we hope good future. Also, there are many late experiments which prove the great moral uses of increasing the powers of small districts; as for instance, Bethlehem, Oberlin, Vineland, also several large "communities."

CHAP. III. ANALOGIES WITH PHYSICAL NATURE.

§ 1. *Variety in God's Creation.*

All that infatuation for absolute uniformity of religion, which used to prevail in the Middle Ages, seems concentrated, in the United States, into the one idea of producing sameness of political organizations. And yet the story goes, a certain great bigot could not make a few watches keep time alike. And whence indeed comes this insatiable desire among *Americans* (we call ourselves so), to force all political organizations into some one pet form, and under one central human power; suppressing all variety, and blotting out all individual independent development? It does not come from nature. Behold the infinite variety of creatures, both in the vegetable and animal worlds. Says Dr. Dick: "What an immense space in the scale of animal life, intervenes between an animalcule, which appears only the size of a visible point, when magnified five hundred thousand times, and a whale a hundred feet long and twenty broad! The proportion of bulk between the one of these beings and the other, is nearly as thirty-four million million million to one. Yet all the intermediate space is filled up with animated beings of every form and order! A similar variety obtains in the vegetable kingdom. It has been calculated that some plants which grow on rose-leaves and other shrubs, are so small that it would require more than a thousand of them to equal in bulk a single plant of moss, and if we compare a stem of moss which is generally not above one-sixtieth of an inch, with some of the large trees in Guinea and Brazil of twenty feet diameter, we shall find the bulk of the one will exceed that of the other no less than about three million million times, which multiplied by 1000 will produce three thousand million million, the number of times which the large tree exceeds the rose-leaf plant. Yet this immense interval is filled up with plants and trees of every form and size! With good reason then, may we adopt the language of the inspired writers,—'How manifold are thy works, O Lord!'"

And we add; the same variety pervades the whole stellar universe, so far as telescope or Mathematics or light itself can reach. And yet, all vegetables, animals, stars and comets, in infinite variety, are working in one connected system of law, even in the control and government of the infinite God. And shall puny man present us *one* uniform system of political motion?

§ 2. *From Homogeneity to Heterogeneity.*

In Spencer's writings, a philosophical basis for our Precinct-theory, may be found in physical philosophy; and the proof also that it is perfectly consistent with the laws of universal nature, animate and inanimate; and furthermore, that as the Population and Power of a Nation increase as a whole, the power and independence of function, of the separate parts must increase also, and also the number of the subdivisions of the parts, —(thus constituting a philosophical basis for our Precinct-theory, stated in universal terms). That these things are so, and that the violation of them must produce political disease, disorder, and finally national death, is quite accordant with the very scientific generalizations by Spencer (*First Principles*, § 187): as follows:

"By the aggregate Solar System, as well as by each planet and satellite, progressive concentration has been and is still being exemplified. In each organism, that general incorporation of dispersed materials which causes growth, is accompanied by *local* incorporations, forming what we call organs. Every society, while it displays the aggregative process, by its increasing mass of population, displays it also by the rise of dense masses in special parts of its area," [cities]: "And in all cases, along with these direct integrations, there go the indirect integrations by which parts are made mutually dependent." [That is, Voluntary associations, Federations, Corporations, Societies, States and Provinces]. "From this primary re-distribution, we were led on to consider the secondary re-distributions, by inquiring how there came to be a formation of parts" [i.e. Precincts] "during the formation of a whole. * * * It turned out that there is habitually a passage from homogeneity to heterogeneity, along with the passage from diffusion to concentration. While the matter composing the Solar System has been assuming a denser form, it has changed from unity to variety of distribution. Solidification of the Earth has been accompanied by a progress from comparative uniformity to extreme multiformity."

"In the course of its advance from a germ to a mass of relatively great bulk, every plant and animal also advances from simplicity to complexity. The increase of a society in numbers and consolidation, has for its concomitant an increased heterogeneity, both of its political and industrial organization. And the like holds of ALL super-organic products—Language, Science, Art and Literature. But we saw that these secondary distributions are not thus completely expressed. At the same time that the parts into which each whole is resolved, become more unlike one another, they also become more sharply marked off. * * * Further consideration made it apparent that the increasing definiteness which goes along with increasing heterogeneity, is not an independent trait; but, that it results from the integration which progresses in each of the differentiating parts, while it progresses in the whole they form. * * * As fast as there results variety in the sizes and forms of aggregates, and their relations to incident forces, *there also results variety in their movements.*" And we add,—unless these various new organs and new functions be allowed to develop naturally, diseases and disorders must follow.

The Precinct-principle is the only principle whereby every separate function of society, may have its own new special and appropriate local organ. Its effect is just opposite to the national system; for the national system presents all inducements to make all offices mere functions of the Nation itself as the *one* organ of governmental rule. Whereas the Precinct-principle makes that idea absolutely impossible; and presents the idea of special organs for each special work, as the only manner in which such special work can be accomplished, at least beyond the Precinct. Then the alternative becomes either, special organ, or not special work, of which the practical result is only one organ for all functions, as in *sponges* and *star*-fish.

§ 3. *Concentration versus Diffusion of Power.*

Centralization or concentration increases power at *particular* points. But diffusion of power increases the *total* amount of *usable* power as a whole, by liberating more and freer motion, and by increasing the spontaneous activity of all the parts, and, at the same time lessening the power lost partly in friction, and partly in the central cohesion.

But these good results can only follow of course, after centralization procures and maintains general peace and general freedom; that is to say, whilst it prevents the Precincts from interfering with each other, or with the private rights of Individuals, and preserves them from being interfered with by foreign Nations.

This Precinct-system will give large power to a greater number of persons; and this dividing power, whilst at the same time stimulating to its faithful exercise, will also render a posthumous fame, of more relative activity and importance as a motive, because it will present a far larger number of vacancies for it. For, the great and good men of little states, are remembered as long as (and often loved more affectionately than) those of larger ones.

§ 4. *Sociological Experiment.*

The absolute necessity for Sociological experiment, in order to the improvement of society, has already been sufficiently spoken of, in the Summary Introduction. Therefore, the most that could be done here, is briefly to point out that our Precinct system affords one of the finest possible fields, and the very first practicable one, for the trial of such experiments.

The Precinct-principle opens the way for true and voluntary sociological experiments. If one Precinct commits errors, it will soon suffer the natural consequences thereof, and others can avoid the error. If one discovers or invents or introduces any good, others can freely follow.

In the case of Individuals finding themselves not in sympathy with the Precinct wherein they reside, the fault may be, either in the Individual or in the neighborhood itself. The sympathies and feelings which are disturbed by the residence among them, of an Individual out of harmony, may be bad feelings or they may be good ones. It is presumption for others to pretend to judge in most cases. Who is to decide? The answer is, that as long as the resident is free and able to go to some Precinct where he *will* be in harmony, and to take his possessions or their value with him, in such case, no decision of the mind is needed to be made upon the subject as to who is right. Only let the Precinct enjoy its own liberty, without infringing the equal liberty of others. Only let it continue on its own plan awhile, and the fruits will evidence plainly who was wrong, —the Individual or the Precinct. Small Precincts that are wrong will not long go on harmoniously. The smaller the Precinct, within reasonable limits, the sooner will the result manifest its moral quality. This manifestation however, will prove, not the correctness or incorrectness of any *one* of its principles, but only of the net-resultant of the whole. These understood principles will soon work themselves fully into results, and show their true character. Only thus can the science of society become much improved. Neither good nor evil can be made plain to the minds of the people in general, otherwise than by allowing systems to work out into light, their own natural and true results.

In general, with regard to all the domestic changes and improvements, recommended in this book on Social Science, or in any other book, or from any other source, it is possible to try them, better, by means of small Precincts than by any other method. And not only so, but it is the only method whereby true sociological experiments can be made, or whereby any society can, either attain ideas any considerably advanced before its age, or prove such an advance even if it had attained it. Even most national and international questions would not be altogether impossible of settlement by Precinct-trial, as many such questions can be solved as readily by distant Precincts of the same Nation, as by different Nations.

CHAP. IV. OBJECTS AND USES OF "LAW."

§ 1. *In General.*

All laws may be divided into two sorts; as they regard either the thing commanded to be done, or, the sanction to enforce it. The first sort of laws may be regarded as counsels of wisdom, the second, as punishments for the violation of those counsels. The first, are the primary and ultimate design, the second, are only incidental to the accomplishment of the others. A large part of human laws are only the re-enactments of the laws of nature and morality; of such, the violation will always and ultimately be followed by their own natural and spiritual consequences. Why then does the law of the land affix and add any arbitrary punishments? The answer is, that the natural and spiritual punishments are so often disbelieved, so seldom appreciated, and often so long in coming, that they are entirely insufficient as safeguards of human society.

Another large class of laws are not re-enactments of the laws of nature or morality, but only the settlement of points indifferent in themselves, or not clearly limited in nature or morality; but yet necessary to be settled definitely in some manner, in order that all persons may know beforehand, how to regulate their affairs in regard to them. In these cases, the necessity of having arbitrary sanctions to the prescriptions of law, becomes all the more evident, but *as yet* those sanctions are hardly any more necessary than in the cases of the violations of natural and moral law. We say, *as yet*, for in proportion as humanity improves, if indeed it will improve sufficiently, the necessity of arbitrary sanction to natural law will become less and less urgent. For the more men see their true duties, and feel the obligations of them, and have faith in the certainty and importance of natural and spiritual consequences, the less will they stand in need of arbitrary ones. And this again, greatly favors the principle of self-government in Individuals, which by promoting solid virtue, tends more and more to render government unnecessary. Thus and only thus, can the highest and best civil liberty be attained. The "forces" of arbitrary punishment, and of government by others, can only be generally disused, as Individuals become gradually more and more perfect in *self*-government.

The same principles evidently apply to Family-government, the type of and preparation for the state government. And *here* we must look for the great test and measure, of the varying needs of men for more or less natural strictness and arbitrariness of government, namely, whatever is found to be the decrease or increase of necessity for arbitrary Family-government, and whatever the degree or the lack, of the power of voluntary self-control in the Family, especially among the children; THAT will be found to be both a preparation for, and best measure of, the amount of fitness for their being entrusted with similar degrees of self-controlling power in the affairs of the world. In other words, it is only in proportion as men become fit for freedom individually, and in Family-relations, both as parents and children, that they will become fit for release from law and force, in civil and political relations.

Another idea in this connection is, that if laws must be uniform for all persons in the same Precinct, it follows that all its residents ought to be in nearly the same moral degree of self-control and moral civilization; that is, should be substantially in *moral homogeneity*. Hence, in an old Nation with settled and fixed habits and general homogeneity, (which however can only be the case in a lower state of civilization,) it would not seem to matter so much, whether a government were a great consolidation, or a union of small Precincts. But in proportion as moral civilization increases, the moral and intellectual differences increase, and the necessity of Precinct-freedom increases, together with a greater degree of liberty for each to select the Precinct best fitted for him; and, each Precinct to select and invite the Individuals best suited to IT.

The most effectual punishment that can be administered for most offences, is that which society administers spontaneously, through the loss of social standing among one's companions and associates. But this kind of punishment is greatly modified, and in many cases almost nullified, under the present condition of large territories. This nullification comes about in two ways. In one way, the citizens so frequently reside in a different territory from that in which they transact business, that they seem to have two lives and two representations, almost entirely distinct. The other way in which this nullification of social punishment is also brought about, is the facility with which offenders may remove from one territory to an adjoining one, and the certainty of finding about the same assortment of social conditions, and opportunities for companionship, that they had found in their former residence; so that the change is merely one of persons, but not of the *kinds* of persons. But if the Nations were constituted into the very small Precincts which we propose, persons of similar moral dispositions would collect in Precincts together; and offenders would often find it very difficult to find acceptance elsewhere, if they made themselves discreditable in their own Precinct.

§ 2. *Multitude and Minutiæ of affairs.*

Another argument for the Precinct theory is; there exist too many and too minute affairs needing the interference of law, to be entrusted to a large state or Nation. Governments ought to do so many things which yet it is obviously unjust to tax unwilling or dissentient persons for, or compel such to co-operate with or conform to,—and furthermore, there are so many different views of rights, that the difficulties can only be obviated by encouraging people of similar views to reside and do business in the same neighborhoods, and thereby, in conformity to their own rules. The following are some of the subjects which belong more especially to the Precinct, either because of its inherent right over them, or because of the uncertainty of their being proper objects for government interference at all:—Rights of Conscience, including religion and church,—Rights to Alcoholic Liquors and to Luxuries,—Right and duty of Governmental Education,—Right and duty of Governmental maintenance of the poor, the care of the sick and infirm,—Questions of Health not affecting localities or Individuals beyond the Precinct,—Right of Marriage and Divorce—including aid to widows and needy children,—Right of Women to avocations, to property, and claims to suffrage,—Age of Suffrage,—Right of Individuals to ignore Government when aggrieved,—Questions resulting from War, such as Drafting into compulsory service and compelling to pay war taxes,—Control of Farming Lands, Mines and Mining operations,—Streets and Roads within the Precinct, Manufacturers and Retail Trade,—Paper Currency.

Many persons will doubt the legitimacy of some of these rights being given to the Precincts,—but even omitting the subjects of currency and divorce, and perhaps of ignoring the state, enough other matters have been mentioned above, too minute and too multitudinous in their nature, to be accomplished by national power or under national laws.

In general we may say that many things, from their *local nature*, should require the agreement especially and only of the neighborhoods, townships, &c., that are directly interested. And mostly, the interference of one locality with another, should be in proportion to their geographical and other nearnesses. Therefore this question depends on the size of the Precinct; the degree of right interference being in inverse proportion to the size of the Precincts. But the difference of their interferences, is to be more as to the smallness of the specialty or matter, than in the principles to which it relates.

The duties and consequent rights of a Precinct are what were chiefly in Comte's mind, in the structure of his theory of government. And it accordingly exhibits the fact of its origin from the little plan of St. Simon (or Fourier) applied to a French or other vast empire, comprehending minutiæ of regulation, and details, that cannot be either justly or successfully applied to or by a large consolidated government, especially to or by sinful or even imperfect beings, as men are. Plato and some other manufacturers of ideal governments, have made a similar confusion of the rights of the different units. And Mulford and the other centralizers are following in their wake.

§ 3. *Competition in Government.*

Then again, the numerousness of these little Precincts would introduce the principle of competition among governments, as a practical motive, for daily use. Viewing large Nations, we can find no such competition for citizens, at all worth mentioning: except that between Nation and Nation, as the United States against Germany or Great Britain. And in the United States we cannot find any traces of a competition of this kind worth mentioning, except in the very new States competing for settlers, or in the cities competing for this or that particular kind of trade or honor. There is but little governmental competition among us except for short-sighted or *immediate* results.

Now, if any could introduce this principle into operation among and between some thousands of adjoining townships, villages and Precincts, we can scarcely doubt that its effects would be equally as good as they are among private individuals. Of course we do not mean to exalt competition as a very good thing *in itself;*—we fondly hope for and look forward to the day when it will be greatly superseded by co-operation. But so long as competition is needed among the mass of Mankind, individually, so long and for that very reason, it will be needed among Precincts and localities. Even if it were possible for communes to exist, from which the principle of competition would be effectually shut out, still there would remain a necessity to have competition between different communes. For competition is necessary somewhere in everything, during the present incomplete civilization. And the monopolizing and repressing spirit and policy, are just as bad in government as they were in trade and manufactures.

CHAP. V. POLITICAL OBJECTS AND USES.

§ 1. *In General.*

Smallness of territory produces mutual knowledge of each other, as well as mutual good feeling, so that government is more practicable, and happiness more complete; the people being agreed in their general opinions. Smallness of Precincts also makes a direct vote by the people more practicable: the larger the district or population, the less direct can the representation be. Thus, the people have both a better opportunity to know their representatives and officers personally, and also a better opportunity to express their own views and intentions. Such are the schemes and cliques constantly forming to deceive the people, both in trade and politics, that ordinary citizens cannot possibly know them before they are accomplished; and hence necessarily have to depend on the characters of the leaders, and therefore should know their characters well.

§ 2. *Corruption.*

The notorious and general selfishness, partisanship and corruption of officials, whether in political, or fashion-making, or social governments, drive men to the resort of having small districts with a maximum of self-regulating power, that thus there may exist the plainest and most direct responsibility to the people, and the least amount of government by absentees and strangers. Thus all the motives of Social Circle and personal acquaintanceship, will be added to the ordinary motives, in order to induce official faithfulness.

Small Precincts, making up the whole Nation as we propose, by the greatness of their number, and by the smallness of the amount of revenue they could afford to waste, as well as by the check which would constantly be held over their officers, by the mere fact that their doings were observed *in particulars*, by all their constituents,—would afford the best possible political checks against the success of all attempts at corrupting the legislative bodies, as well as against the value or amounts that would or could be obtained by success and skill in bribing.

§ 3. *Specialties.*

We are all the time having special acts of superior Legislatures, now for some county, now for some town, giving control, now over temperance, now over its plan of voting, now over this thing, now over that. But special legislation has been one of our greatest curses, whether in regard to corporations, counties or towns. Perhaps it is not generally known among the people, that nearly one fourth of the counties and Precincts in the State of Pennsylvania, have had granted to them special privileges, or, been put under special restrictions; one thing to one, and another to another, not applied to any of the other Precincts. The Speaker of the Pennsylvania Senate, in his Inaugural, Jany. 1871, says: "Special legislation has become the vice of our system. The prevalence of a general rule of law over our whole territory, upon subjects usually within the scope of legislative action, is now the EXCEPTION,—and special enactments and special privileges are found upon almost every page of our voluminous annual statute book." Let us have no more need thus to extend human rights *drop by drop*. Give every Precinct its local rights in ALL respects, without any more specialism. For the true Precinct-theory is the first step into a truly GENERAL legislation.

Some moral or literary qualifications might be highly useful in cities, to counteract the influence of mobs; and also especially because cities are in advance of the country in some other kinds of culture, so also it would seem ought they to be in advance in the culture and qualifications required for political franchises. At any rate, it would be well to allow such Precincts (within a city), as chose, to try some such qualifications, and see how they would compete with those that refused any such revised qualifications. This, however, is to be understood, only after the *general* Introduction of the Precinct-system.

Our Precinct-theory contains the only method whereby, under the tenure of land by the public, as advocated by Spencer (and the present writer), the tenants can be induced to improve, with permanent buildings, as thoroughly as under the private ownership tenure, or so very nearly as to answer present purposes. This can be accomplished by allowing the tenant to erect whatever permanent buildings, mainly of brick, stone or iron, he chooses, subject to general rules of common sense and expediency, under the sanction of officers for the judgment of the case; and then the public giving the tenant a *mortgage* for the amount, to run various lengths of time, from 50 to 100 years, according to the nature of the case. Absolute proofs of the actual cost, would be required. But where is the governing power that could now be safely trusted with such judgments? We may answer, nowhere but in small districts of an honorable, moral, and well-cultivated people.

CHAP. VI. HUMAN HAPPINESS.

§ 1. *In General.*

Government and civilization are only valuable as they promote human happiness. Human happiness depends more on the multitude of *little* things of daily life, than on the occasional great events. And connected with this also, human happiness rests largely on closeness of sympathy, sameness of view, tenderness of feeling, with those with whom we are most frequently in contact. The most ultra liberty, in association with a people with whom we were not in sympathy, would be loneliness and desolation. A solitary man is not so lonely in an uninhabited wilderness, as is a stranger in a strange city, not even speaking the language of the people.

There can scarcely be a question, that small isolated Christian populations are the happiest, and morally the best. The Pitcairn-Islanders, the Republic of San Marino, the Welsh, the Scotch, the Irish, and the voluntary associations of religious communities in America in modern times, and the rush into religious communities in the early ages, all co-operate to prove this idea.

The Pitcairn-Islanders, are a splendid proof of the utility of the independence and isolation of Precincts, so also are the few cases of successful civilization of the North American Indians,—only made successful by isolating their Precincts. And partly in the same manner perhaps, may be explained the unexpected virtue and happiness of the Mormons in Utah, and of some of the free communists. "Evil communications corrupt" the *best* manners; and even vice, in isolation, loses much of its power.

The fact in nature and providence, that men are involved in the sufferings and partake of the joys and honors of their own Nation, and their own Precinct, proves, that Nature intends, that men should depart from localities whose sentiments or principles they radically dissent from, and should seek other localities whose principles they approve of, and thus become justly entitled to and affectionately participant in, the sufferings and the joys of their localities, whether Nation or Precinct. But still, the obligations and natural "indications" for removal from Precinct to Precinct, are much stronger than for removal from Nation to

Nation, because the removal from Precinct to Precinct is comparatively so very much easier than the other.

As Comte has done much to show how great respect a government ought to pay to its thinkers, and why and how it ought to take care of them; so Spencer has done much to show the unalterable nature and inviolability of Individual liberty, as against majorities, equally as truly as against aristocracies. But when it comes to the application of their own principles, neither of those writers seems to have hit upon the happiest method. We have now however, only to do with their theories so far as they relate to Precinct-rights and order. And there is no method for securing the independence, happiness and rewards of good thinkers, so successful as the Precinct-system.

§ 2. *Individual Liberty.*

The fullest possible allowance for Individual rights and freedom, as far as is consistent with other men's equal freedom, can only be attained, either in a state of isolation from society, which is the road to barbarism, or else in such a variety of Precincts, as will allow each Individual to find some one or more persons sufficiently near his own ideas, as to justify being regarded so for the usual practical purposes of life. And this variety is possible, only by making the Precincts very small, so that they shall be numerous, and the variety, brought within convenient or accessible distances. And the great "emancipation" question among all highly civilized peoples, is the question relative to the Emancipation of the Precinct.

The Precinct-system is the best method whereby to enable men as Individuals, to avoid "government control," (as Spencer demands, meaning of course, national control.) Instead of liberty to "ignore the state," we would have liberty to change one's Precinct residence. Spencer, it is true, not thinking of the Precinct-theory, carries his idea of "ignoring the state" to an extreme, when he describes this right as "the attitude of a citizen in a condition of voluntary outlawry." But remember, Spencer was thinking only of outlawry from the *Nation.* And Mulford's reply (p. 274) to Spencer is not sound. Thus his reply says: "If then * * * Mr. Spencer assert and exercise his rights, and while maintaining his right to ignore the state, is robbed by some vagrant, of course he cannot recover through the aid of the government, the property which he has lost; or the vagrant, not having determined himself to ignore the state, may bring the power of the government, being the agency in his employ, to secure him in his actual possession,—IT of course refusing to admit the claim of one who had ignored the state." Now this reply to Spencer is not sound; first, because it does not follow that a state must of course "refuse to admit" a person's claims, merely because it was not bound IN DUTY to recognize them; but second and chiefly, because the *vagrant* is by the supposition, under the state and bound to obey its laws, and therefore has no right to rob or murder anybody. The fact is that Mr. Spencer's idea simply is, that the person who ignores the state is in the relative condition to the state, somewhat similar to what a foreigner was held by ancient national law, and is still held by barbarians, namely, at their *government's* mercy:—but it does not follow as Mulford has it, that such person is at the *individual* mercy of any one who chooses to maltreat him. Both these writers are possessed by Nationality; the one feels the tyrant's goad and would tear its heart out, the other is pleased, and "licks the rod." We conclude, Mr. Spencer is right in the principle at bottom, although not to the unlimited extent he argues; and that, only a system of Precincts can be trusted to carry it out.

CHAP. VII. HUMAN NATURE.

Personal attractions have strength like the chemical forces, so also have home and locality; whereas, the artificial states or districts, and even the Nation itself, have comparatively only the strength of gravitation. Thus it is, that Social Circle and Precinct have, in actual life the strongest power on man naturally, and the first government claims upon him that he voluntarily yields to.

Human nature itself makes more account of Precinct than it does of Nation. There may be one man in ten thousand, or even one in one thousand, who in a time of great excitement, may be willing to give his property or even his life, for his Nation. But there can be found nearly everywhere, and in ordinary times without extraordinary excitement, one man in a hundred, perhaps one in ten, who may be willing, according to his means, to deny himself dollars, more or fewer, for the benefit of his own immediate neighborhood, and even to risk his life for it if necessary. And even in great sacrifices for national patriotism, the motive at bottom often is to please one's friends, neighborhood and Social Circle.

Again, we find that the riotous and disorderly, do in fact and naturally congregate and reside together in small localities, in which they would not allow orderly citizens to reside in peace; we find also that the outcasts and criminals have their localities, through which it is not only repulsive but dangerous for respectable, or even respectably dressed persons to pass alone. Why, then, should not quiet and orderly citizens be encouraged or allowed to form into localities of their own, and to exclude others from settlement there, and from all unnecessary intrusion? or are vice and disorder to be allowed always and everywhere, *systematically* to enjoy privileges ever denied to the virtuous and orderly?

It is a general doctrine of Swedenborg, a philosopher of rare insight, that it is the universal Law of Heaven and Hell and Eternity, that men should continually be striving to find their exact sympathizers, and will ultimately arrange themselves in groups and societies, exactly according to the genera and species of their moral and intellectual characters. And the idea seems both natural and philosophical. From which it would seem a proper inference, that the same tendency is justifiable in, and should be amply provided for, by the laws and arrangements of earthly society. And this exactly confirms our Precinct-theory.

CHAP. VIII. MORALITY AND RELIGION.

§ 1. *In General.*

The Precinct-principle is further proved, by its consistency with the Saviour's maxim to "love thy neighbor as thyself." The interpretation which some put on the word neighbor, making it mean all Mankind, is mere jugglery; for it takes away all the meaning of the word "neighbor", and therefore takes away the "point" of the passage. No doubt the ultimate object of Christianity is, and the result will in a perfect state be, to make all Mankind love each other as themselves; but it is hardly fair to force that interpretation on to every passage in the Bible, nor even upon every passage which says *love.* The truth of the passage is this, namely, that loving the neighbor as one's self is the place where this universal love *begins,* so that if perfect there, it will gradually work outward through circle after circle, unto all Mankind. The fact is that this passage is very sociological, for, being requested to explain it, the Saviour gave the parable of the good Samaritan, the exact point of which is, that persons living in one Precinct, when traveling in the adjoining one, are bound to fulfill the duties of charity in distress, even although the adjoining Precincts be religious enemies to each other. It seems to be diametrically opposed to burning heretics, at least when they live in the next Precinct. If you may *perhaps* burn them out, you must not go out to burn them.

Another very proper interpretation of our Saviour's maxim of loving the neighbor, is, that duties are to be performed to the persons whom we actually meet, and especially whom circumstances make needy, rather than that we should be filled with sentimentality, and go hunting over all creation for opportunities to do good. Now, this inward doctrine, when it takes an outward form, seeks to take some form of the social structure, and that form is emphatically the Precinct. It would be almost impossible, otherwise, for men generally to know what to do, or where to do it.

It is rather a happy accident, if accident it be, that our "constitutional" word designating Precinct, namely, the word *common-wealth,* should be so very expressive of communism. One cannot escape the feeling that this is a prophetical anticipation in language, that the Precinct is the especial container and political form of communism. The old Roman word republic meant public *affairs,* not common-*wealth.*

§ 2. *Unity of Local Enterprises.*

The system of small Precincts affords opportunity for religious unity, and success in benevolent enterprises; and thereby can be realized the great and truly Christian idea, that all the Christians of a place are the church of that place. And so long as men differ widely on doctrines, and on the degrees of their importance, this desirable result cannot be realized to any considerable extent in any other way.

The plan of having all the Christians of a place organized as the church of that place, gives rise to the practicability of placing all the benevolent operations in one Precinct, under one arrangement of visitations and management; the advantage of which is well known to all engaged in benevolent enterprises, both in preventing deception, and in promoting virtue, and counteracting vice and crime.

Perhaps it may not be desirable that each Precinct should be made up entirely of one religious persuasion at present, nor until the coming times when Mankind have become so fit, and intelligence been so disseminated, as to prevent the dangers. Yet even now we find that many do get into Precincts consisting almost exclusively of their own religion or class. As the Catholics settle among their churches, also the Quakers, the Chinese and the colored persons; whilst the aristocracies also get by themselves in their own neighborhoods, to a considerable extent.

Mr. Ruskin has drawn a beautiful picture of the duties of a state, and especially of its "moral overseers." But it is evidently a picture that is only practicable as yet, by and in such Precincts as would adopt it,—such Precincts being so small that all persons who "loved darkness rather than light" could readily move to the places of their choice; or possibly it might be adopted by general corporations like any of the various Associations. In "Time and Tide," p. 80, he says: "Putting however, all questions of forms and names aside, the thing actually needing to be done is this,—that over every hundred (or some not much greater number) of the Families composing a Christian State, there should be appointed an overseer or bishop, to render account to the State, of the life of every Individual in those Families, and to have care both of their interest and conduct, to such an extent as they may be willing to admit, or as their faults may justify, so that it may be impossible for any pers n, however humble, to suffer from unknown want, or live in ιn-recognized crime,—such help and observance being rendered without officiousness, either of interference or inquisition (the limits of both being determined by law) but with the patient and gentle watchfulness which true Christian pastors now exercise over their flocks."

As a remedy for and a prevention of the vice and degradation of cities, some regular plan of visitation might be very efficient. The great difficulty to be overcome, is the difficulty of getting the voluntary moral and religious forces of society to combine, for such a purpose, into one harmonious organization. But the good of these plans can never be obtained permanently, only when there is but one religious and benevolent organization for the same objects in one given locality, which in fact is the beginning of either our Precinct or our Corporation system.

One of the arguments for our theory is to be found in the difficulties attending the matter of the Bible and religion in the public schools, or indeed in schools at all, whether public or private. This whole question we will endeavor to examine when we come to Education and Public Schools, under the head of the Intellectual element of Social Science, only remarking now, that any religion or non-religion whether Chinese or whatever, which asks for its own schools or school-fund, in countries where it has *not* the rule, *ought* to be able to show that it grants separate public schools or school-funds in countries where it *has* the rule. But if they cannot do that, why still let us give them their rights here, and trust to the good effects of justice and to other means, to correct what seem to us their errors. Provided however, that no denomination should receive as its share, more than it contributes to the *general* fund for the same *purpose*.

§ 3. *Persecution.*

The Precinct principle explains the political rights of small minorities, for instance—the Mormons; and so long as social distinctions press hard upon women as a sex, so long will any *tribe* be politically justifiable which will improve the condition of woman. And this explains the moral but temporary justification of "Mormondom." Their political success is explained by the inalienable right and indestructible power of the Units, and in particular of the Precinct-unit. As Dixon says, we with our tremendous majority and ample appliances, revenues, preachers and so on, ought to be willing to use and to rely upon moral and religious influence alone, to convert or reform the Mormons; only demanding freedom for *our* moral influences to operate there, and for *their* people to admit those influences. But more probably, we ought not to demand anything more, than freedom for all Mormons who desired to, to return to the other parts of the United States, at the expense of the Mormon Precinct.

Calvin burning Servetus in the little Precinct of Geneva, or the New England Puritans hanging Quakers in the little colony of Boston, are very different things, from the king the emperor or the republic, trying to extirpate heresy throughout *all* their dominions. The spirit in the heart of the rulers may be the same, but the spirit of the people that upholds it is very different; and so also are the sociological principles involved. And what, during the Reformation, saved Germany and Switzerland so quickly, from long dissensions such as disturbed France and the British Isles, were their independent Precinct systems.

Here we must offer an argument which may perhaps not be popular, but its weight of importance presses it on us. It has always appeared to the writer, that the old Catholic argument for persecution of dissenters, has never been fairly answered. The same argument is used by Mahometans, and even by some evangelical Protestants. They argue thus,—the salvation of the soul is more important than that of the body, yet nearly all admit, it is justifiable to defend our bodies with mortal weapons, and to put murderers to death,—much more therefore would it be justifiable to put heretics and infidels to death, whose doctrines are supposed to kill, not the body only, but the immortal soul. To this argument, it is no answer to affirm dogmatically that religion is a province beyond the control of human law, for that is the very point in question. Nor is that argument ever practically regarded, when any one religion becomes tremendously in excess of all opposing ones, for instance, in the case of the United States against the Mormons.

But there is a ground upon which this argument for persecution may be thoroughly avoided, namely, by the rights of the Precinct. Let all who work in religion or morality, to cultivate practices utterly at variance with the fundamental determination of their neighbors, remove to localities by themselves, where the other citizens may feel that their children and Families are safe from the contaminations of what they conceive to be soul-damning doctrines. This doctrine of Precincts would have saved the early Christians from persecution by the Jews. Our Saviour commanded his disciples, saying, "When they persecute you in one city flee ye to another." This principle carried out would have ultimately driven those Christians into localities by themselves, where, by their works they could have proven to the civil governments, that they were not evil-doers; and, what is more to the argument, where Rome would have allowed them their own "cultus," according to her established rules; and when once the recognition of such a "cultus" had been made by law, the time would have soon arrived when the Christians would have been allowed to found their own local Corporations anywhere throughout the Roman Empire, mingling with the common citizens in the day, and retiring to their own localities at night, according to the Roman laws, but all the while deciding disputes between themselves by their own rules.

We have seen something like this, when the persecuted Moravian *puritans* fled to the estates of Zinzendorf and were there tolerated.

§ 4. *Scripture-Type, in the Hebrew Nation.*

Here may be placed an argument from the Scriptures,—the divinely authorized example of the Hebrew Nation instituted by the special authority and care of God. The Hebrew Nation was divided into tribes, and great care was commanded to be taken to preserve their distinctness. This authorized example combines with the type-theory, as elaborated in the Summary Introduction and other parts of the work, and should (it seems) be admitted as a precedent. Mulford very properly claims the authority of the Hebrew precedent for the divine authority of the Nation, but it is equally as quotable for the divine authority of the Precinct. Some objections that might seem valid against this argument will be treated of under the head of "Special Objections Answered," at the conclusion of this the second PART of Precinct. (See Chap. X.)

CHAP. IX. TRIBE-RELATIONS.

§ 1. *In General.*

Resemblance and sympathy form the chief elements of the Family circle. And in primitive states of society, the same similarity of views feelings and interests, in a degree also, takes place in a whole tribe.

But when we come to a mixed people, one mixed with immigrants from various countries, of persons of various races and of the most opposite views of religion and morals, there remains but one possible method of completely applying the tribe-principle to the case. And be it remembered, the tribe is a natural unit of society; the *principle* therefore upon which it is founded, must always exist, and be made fundamental in the constitutions of government. The only way then, of applying the tribe-principle, is, by allowing each Individual to select his own tribe; and each tribe to fix its rules, and to say whom it will receive and whom not. There must be a plain agreement, either expressed or implied, between Individuals and Precincts, that both parties are in the main satisfied with each other.

In modern times, the fundamental unit of the tribe-principle, finds its own first development in *material* things. We find men, in all the various classes of society, subdividing themselves spontaneously into social and political and business circles. But until government can understand and embrace this principle, and legally recognize the tribe-element, it must necessarily be a failure, for it ignores one of the essential elements and one of the essential conditions, of the organization of society. Here then, two alternatives present themselves. First, an effort to organize the religious, moral, social and political circles, into the tribe-unit or tribe-element, by constituting them with the general powers of government. That this is positively practicable, and so far desirable as a subsidiary aid, may perhaps be shown under the head of Corporation. But the main alternative evidently is the second one, namely, regarding the Precinct-division as the unit or holder of the common government-powers. For no voluntary circle, unless it occupies its own territory for itself, can completely answer to the idea of a tribe. The aim of government, here, is to make both principles unite into one, to make each Precinct become the voluntary union of the same circle, or of two or more harmonious circles.

§ 2. *Relations to Social Circle.*

Laws are necessarily unjust which do not acknowledge and provide for existing facts, and existing grades in society, which are as distinct as different religions, or different Nations. And among the facts thus necessary to meet and provide for, one is the Social Circle. So great is its importance that we have classified it as one of the Units or fundamental analytical elements of human society.

The very origin of Tribe was historically a Social Circle,—some particular set of friends voluntarily associating with each other in preference to others. And as our theory takes the tribe to be the origin of the Precinct, it follows from the theory, that the idea of Social Circle is inherent in that of tribe. And when tribe becomes Precinct, it equally follows from our theory, that the idea of sociability and Social Circle, must be an eternally essential idea of the Precinct, not necessarily of every Precinct in particular, but of the idea in general, and of some in particular.

Reverting again to historical origins, the tribe would not continue always to be of *one* Social Circle only. Differences would arise gradually within the Precinct itself, from various causes; and then occasionally other persons would join with it from other Precincts, whose occupation made it mutually agreeable or mutually advantageous to do so. The instincts of Mankind often produce the co-existence and very near residence in the same Precinct, of the very richest and the very poorest, because such are essential to each other constantly. Whilst the middle classes seek neighborhoods by themselves, despising those who are below them in the Social Circle, as much as they envy those who are above them in the same artificial distinctions.

Hence it is possible for more than one Social Circle to exist in one Precinct; but not for more than one social set to have the government thereof: nevertheless an equal arbitration between all, is possible. But in the matter of the rule of a Precinct, nothing is more certain than that the rule generally falls to the control of one Social Circle; and not only so, but also into the control of some one set or clique of that Social Circle. The instincts of men are constantly exhibiting this tendency. The aristocracy will seek one neighborhood; the respectable orderly working people, another; the rowdies, another. Let the fighters get together and fight one another; this is the providential arrangement for the self-cure of these evils. But let good and orderly citizens, have the control in their own localities.

It is not for a moment supposed that Precincts are to consist of persons necessarily all in the same social equality, but only, that they should be in a state of mind whereby they would have the same views of the rights and duties flowing from social distinctions, if any. Neither, that they should all be employees or all employers; but only that their ideas should be in harmony as to the mutual rights and duties of employees,—no more than that they should all be either males or females, but that they should have the same opinions and feelings and habits, as to the relative duties of Family-life. Thus it is that the question of equal freedom without disturbing the rights of others, becomes practically, the equal freedom without disturbing what others have learned to be their rights, or what they have become fitted to enjoy, up to that time. *Hence, perfect freedom for the Individual in society, in practice really means* a perfect or indefinite variety of small and near Precincts,—each Precinct in itself as far independent, as is consistent with the important utilities and rights of the others.

§ 3. *Relations to Races, Species, and Breeds.*

By our Precinct principle, it becomes possible for different races to be in separate Precincts, as indeed they are in duty bound to continue, unless they can live amicably and usefully together. And where they can thus live amicably, they also can form Precincts of mutual service, and thus exhibit one of the Creator's designs in ordaining different races of men, as well as different races of animals or vegetables. It would of course be found, that the higher the development of reason in the superior race, and also the better and higher the moral developments in both races, the more amicably and easily they could live together, and the more they would voluntarily organize together. Whereas, the lovers of fine arts and amusements, of war, and of ignorance, would naturally be found repelling each other, and forming Precincts each of their own kind. Thus the great problem of different races co-existing in one Nation, which is looming up with very unsatisfactory proportions in the United States, might be easily settled. Europeans, Catholics, Protestants, African descendants, Chinese, and Indians, need give no further theoretical or scientific uneasiness.

The principle is, that these opposites will voluntarily seek each other for mutual good, as soon as they are fit to live together in peace and charity; and will *consent* to arrange themselves so that neither *can* domineer over the other. But until that time comes, they may either, one be in submission to the other, or else each seek its own separate neighborly locality voluntarily.

Small Precincts are required by the Moral and Physical Advantages, of marriages between persons of blood and race not far distant. Modern researches tend to prove that bodily health also, is best promoted by inter-marriages of persons not much further removed from each other, than sufficient to keep clear from the dangers of marriage within close or traceable degrees of kindred. Amalgamations between races very different, as between the whites and blacks in this country, and as between the English and the Hindoos in India, are said by the Physiologists, almost always to become barren in the third or fourth generation, and to end the race.

Mankind, when removed to climates very different from their natural ones, become enfeebled in health, and decrease in fruitfulness. But Jews, Gipsies and some others, seem to be less subject to these influences, apparently because of possessing better constitutions; and this superiority may be owing to their being close tribes, and answering our theory here in regard to neighborly marriages. It is admitted that marriages between races of close resemblance, have been productive of some benefits.

The superiority of the English in many respects, is attributed to the fact of that Nation being a compound of the blood of several Nations who in ancient times occupied the Island, and who yet contribute some of their still separated elements from Ireland, Scotland, and Wales, and from the isolated retired hamlets of England itself. And the rapid progress of our country in so many respects, is attributed by many, to similar causes,—namely, our great intermingling of the blood, not only of the original British tribes, but also of the various German tribes, with a little tincture from almost every Nation in Europe. Yet neither the mingled English nor the Americans are so healthy as the separate tribes, either morally or physically.

These facts would tend to show, that whilst the intellectual and material progress may be the results of unions of varieties that far distinct; yet that moral progress, and especially physical health, are deteriorated thereby. And this deterioration of health has become such an alarming phenomenon in this country, that any general principle for its improvement should receive every possible encouragement.

Among Mankind, as among "other animals," it is necessary

from time to time to raise new and improved breeds. And distinction and separate development of Precincts, is one method, and the very best one, to accomplish this end. In improving the blood of human beings, we cannot of course expect to proceed as with animals, in disregard of the moral conditions and moral feelings; because these are the most important parts of human nature. And it is in order to improve these, quite as much as or more than, to improve any intellectual or physical characteristics, that it is desirable to produce improved stocks of human beings at all. And of course, the idea of attempting to produce this kind of improvement, in a formal, outward or prescribed way, is inhuman. But the natural and instinctive operations of our Precinct system, would spontaneously produce some of the most radical improvements of this kind, that could be desired; and that too, by the marriages of persons sufficiently near alike, who being located near together would spontaneously and instinctively select each other, better usually than formal science could advise.

CHAP. X. SPECIAL OBJECTIONS ANSWERED.

§ 1. *Intermingling, Useful in the Past.*

It may be objected to our theory of Precincts, that great advantages have followed the past policy of the United States, in the intermingling of all classes. We answer, that in arguing for the *future*, for persons of different religions politics and classes, to form Precincts by themselves, we must admit that great advantages have accrued in the *past*, from arranging so that all intermingled freely, thereby breaking down "caste." We may even admit that if the balance of advantage is yet in favor of the present plan, nevertheless we may see, that in many places we are approaching a class of evils of an opposite kind; that, anarchy and irreligion are being established, and parental rights swept away by the *extreme* of the intermingling which we in the United States are accomplishing; and that we are now just about the turning point, when, though the intermingling policy of past years, still may have the benefit of the argument in thinly settled country places, yet in cities, towns, and even in thickly settled agricultural and mining regions, the old method has evidently passed its greatest point of usefulness, and the new order is absolutely demanded by the balance of influences. In general therefore we may infer, that the intermingling era is passing away by tacit but common consent; and that the time is coming for re-organization.

What is now far more to be guarded against, is the *friction* of the different classes or colors, in the same localities. For, the nearer people are together, the more they hate each other for the small differences of daily life, as those small differences bring them into more and more disputation and variance; and consequently they are more and more stimulated to and upheld in those oppositions, by those of the same class or color, than when apart from the others at their homes or recreations. The case is the same as with the progress in machinery. At first, friction is not thought of at all; but in the later and higher developments, the study how to lessen friction, becomes one of the most important of all, both to the mechanic and to the inventor.

The intermingled modes of life, in mixed Precincts as now most commonly found, are doubtless unobjectionable, so long as the friction is but small, and as their citizens can live harmoniously together, and retain a good degree of mutual sympathy and mutual regard for the rights and feelings of their neighbors. But unfortunately, this is becoming a less and less frequent case. Pride and tyranny on the one side, and pride and envy on the other, are stimulating men everywhere into antithetic positions. Everybody wants to be despotic to his inferiors, "superior to his equals, and equal to his superiors." Hence a universal deep undercurrent of discontent. And this gives rise to the necessity of allowing persons who are unhappy under their present conditions, to form new relations and new residences, upon principles which seem promising of contentment and peace.

It might be apprehended that the collection in the same localities, of persons of the same character, would produce narrow-mindedness, and prevent general improvement, as it formerly has done. But times have much altered. Now the art of printing, the diffusion of education, the dissemination of public presses, and the addition of the telegraph, are bringing all parts of the world into such close acquaintance with each other, that the old dangers of localization are not to be feared. The union between characteristics and ideas of whole peoples, which formerly could only be accomplished by union of blood, and mixture of tribes, can now be largely fulfilled by the transmission of ideas, and the spread of cosmopolite sympathies.

Such is the intimacy of distant localities, that merely *geographical* distinctions alone, in a nation, especially in ours, are ceasing to be real checks or balances in the working of government. And since the abolition of slavery, the old geographical checks are passing away insensibly, leaving no balances in our government at all, of any value for good; but rather oppositions and old enmities, without sufficient moral powers to balance them.

If however, the time is not yet near for a change of policy in these respects, or even if our argument against intermingling be deemed entirely and eternally erroneous, then let it be remembered that our proposed Corporation-system, would not interfere with the usual intermingling, but still would furnish most of the political advantages of the Precinct-system. See Corporation.

§ 2. *Danger of Secession.*

If the objection were raised, that the dividing up of a Nation into Precincts would make the chances of secession easier, we would reply, that it would have just the opposite effect; and this would be the case in two entirely different ways. (1) For, the larger the number of Precincts the Nation was divided into, the less would be the chances of corrupting Individuals, and obtaining their votes by cheating; for it could not possibly be known beforehand, which way each Precinct would vote, when there was such a large number of them; and therefore it could not be known which ones to cheat in, or how many. In the late war, this corrupting and cheating were actually done in several instances; and states were said to have given majorities for secession, which had not done so at all, but the true votes had been concealed and false returns made. It will be seen at once, that where there is such a large number of Precincts as we propose, the number of Individuals required to give false returns will be largely increased.

(2) And besides this there is another reason: the more Precincts a Nation is composed of, the less the population of each will be, and the less the number of voters; and therefore false returns would surely be detected, and that being foreknown, they

would be prevented. For where there is any doubt, the returns can at once be examined, and every real and authorized voter can be reached and examined.

The true doctrine of our "American "states" is, that they are Corporations. This we will endeavor to show under Part III., speaking of the relations of Precincts, Cities, and States, to Corporations. This shows at once the absurdity of that theory of state rights, which, involving secession with it, too, viewed those merely chartered organizations called states, as being the original sources from which all power was derived, both above and below them. In their origin too, as colonies, most of them were *actually* chartered organizations. But having gradually absorbed from and robbed, the Precincts, of their natural and proper rights, and having allowed the growth of the body to dispel the soul out of one social unit, they aimed next, to suck the soul out of the other unit, that is, the Nation. The pride that grew up out of the first usurpations, led directly to the ambition that aimed at the second.

But now let us ask, will it help the matter any, to transfer that usurped power from state to Nation, and allow one natural element at one end of the scale, to exercise all the powers belonging to the other end of the scale? Whilst the states were lifting up their heads, there was a superior power over them which they well knew and feared. But if that superior power itself assumes their functions, where is the power to check IT? There is no human power, but foreign.—Hence, let us now return to first and sound principles, and restore power to Precincts.

Another argument against the danger of secession, is found in the fact, that adjoining localities generally form spontaneous political REACTIONS to each other. And as every Precinct is, by our theory, balanced by its Amalgam with the sum of its adjoining Precincts, there would generally exist a spontaneous balancing power to the extreme tendencies of any Precinct in particular. The most unlike in property, would often go together,—namely, the richest and the poorest. And *in between* pairs of such Precincts, would generally be intermediate ones for mechanical purposes, stores, &c., because they would be needed by the adjoining Precincts. All the Precincts of one kind would not be formed in contiguity, partly because of business demands, and partly because of the expenses of removal to great distances, and partly because of the ties of relationship refusing to be broken by very great distances. No such great diversity of geographical interests or feelings, could take place, as now exists between East and West, or between North and South.

The natural tendency of localities to form political reactions with adjoining localities, may not be easily explained, but is nevertheless very easily proved to be a fact. For instance, at the breaking out of the Southern rebellion, the rabid pro-slavery Eastern Virginia was surrounded by Maryland, Delaware, Western Virginia and North Carolina. The rabid pro-slavery South Carolina was touched by the staunch old Whig states of North Carolina and Florida, and only by the moderately pro-slavery state of Georgia. The fire-eating state of Mississippi was touched by Whig Louisiana and Tennessee, and by the moderately pro-slavery Alabama. And the same similar general law is found to hold in the case of the old Whig states, which were surrounded by or chiefly touched by rabid pro-slavery sections; for instance, South Carolina by North Carolina and Florida, with moderate Georgia,—Louisiana touched by rabid Mississippi and Texas. Sometimes, however, it is necessary to take two states or parts of states together, as one locality, to show the effects of the principle in every case. But enough has been said to show the principle. It must be remembered that the politics of the Southern States were very different before the war, from what they are now: the metaphysical *reactions* being from pro-slavery to freedom, of some, and from old union to everlasting grumbling of the others. The *soldiers* in rebellion became the soldiers in submission.

But the principle is, there would be quite as much danger of civil *war* between adjoining Precincts, in their reactions against each other, as there would be of the secession from the Nation, of Precincts in combination. But now what shall we say:—that our proposed system is liable to BOTH these objections, namely, civil war between Precincts in some places? and secession of combined Precincts in other places?—Or shall we not say, that both these anticipated evils only COUNTERBALANCE each other, and thus nullify each other? Besides, we have the power of the Amalgams, which would be quite as efficient and even more efficient, to check riot and to prevent civil war between the Precincts of which an Amalgam was composed, than they would be in preventing secession from the Nation. But now, the simple truth is, that in any case of disorder, whether towards secession of, or towards intestine war between, Precincts, every Precinct and every Amalgam of Precincts, would have the same right to call for support from the Nation, as any state now has, or as any county now has to call upon its state for aid. Both Precincts and Amalgams, would have direct recourse to the aid of the national government; and the complex relations of the subordinate parts of the Nation, would have nothing whatever to do with the question, in case of any kind of resort to arms.

Another safeguard in our theory, against any attempt at secession, is the doctrine already laid down under our general idea of the SIX UNITS, and especially under the head of "Rebellion of Precincts," in which place we endeavor to show that Precincts have no rights of *sovereignty*, and no other right of rebellion, than what every living creature has when sufficiently aggrieved. The sovereignty of the Precinct is no part of a theory of SIX units, any more than that of the Individual, or of the Family, or of any other of the six.

The real dangers of secession, are not at all in the direction of formal local subdivision, but in the direction of too rapid increase of population,—that is, too rapid for our science as yet; and in too great a *diffusion* thereof; and in rebellions being fostered by foreign Nations, because of our audacious violations of the laws of Nations,—subjects which are treated under the head of "International law" and in other appropriate places.

§ 3. *Confederacy, or Nation?*

There is one objection that may possibly be offered, which, in its assumptions is so contrary to the whole theory, as scarcely to deserve mention, and yet it may perhaps be better to anticipate it directly. The assertion may be made that our theory tends to produce a confederacy instead of a Nation. Now the answer to this is, that we have all along maintained, that a part of the "State" powers must be assigned to the Nation,—that our theory upon the whole, does *not* increase the totality of the "State" powers, but only *re-arranges* them, giving more power in some respects, but less, in other respects. And as to the mere difference in size of the Precincts, although we may say, that as a tendency of human nature, the larger the size and therefore the smaller the number, of states, the more their junction has the *appearance* of a mere confederacy, and *vice-versa;* nevertheless, size of subdivisions does not affect the principle at all, and need not be discussed.

§ 4. *Objections from the Scriptures.*

It has been objected to our theory, by some who attach greater comparative importance to Nation than to state or Precinct, that the very frequent use of the word "Nations" in the Scriptures, in reference to the original inhabitants of the neighborhood of Judea, is against us. But "Nations" in those cases only mean what they do when applied to the various *tribes* of American Indians,—as for instance, the "Six Nations." But the *thing* meant by Nation in these cases, evidently comes much nearer to our idea of Precinct, than to the thing now meant by Nation as that word is now understood. And the same is also the case generally, in the histories of primitive times.

Another objection from the Scriptures might be, that the final secession of a large part of the Jewish Nation, speaks unfavorably for the permanency of tribal Precincts. But this secession is another argument from Scripture, to the contrary. The Hebrew Nation, it is true, was divided into tribes, and great care was taken to maintain the distinctness and completeness of each one. But it is also true, that in the course of time, excessive power became vested in the central government, namely, the kings, and this did not arise from its nature as a Nation, but from the ancient *absolutism* of Eastern feelings and Eastern Monarchies. But in the original structure of the Hebrew polity, and after its war-polity under Moses and Joshua ended, the Nation possessed *no physical* power or physical organ expressing its unity. This unity depended exclusively on the moral powers, especially the moral Corporation of Levi, and the moral power of the prophets, and the sense of nationality. And these moral powers had been more efficient in preserving the union, than the despotic power of the kings was subsequently. In fact, the real cause of the civil war that finally broke up the Hebrew Nation, was, each party in its turn endeavoring to control the centralizing power, and thus to force its own views and polity upon all the Precincts; and calling in foreign aid for that purpose. And to speak more generally, the falling away of the more distant localities, has always been one of the steps in the *decay* of states, Nations, confederacies, and empires.

CHAPTER XI. MINING DISTRICTS.

The general principle of law hitherto has been, that mines of *precious* metals belong to the Nation, and that even the sale and title to land do not naturally alienate the Nation's right to *precious* minerals. And we know now that *all* minerals are precious. The principle is good; Justice to all, as also the historical troubles in many mining districts, help to confirm the principle. Mines therefore, like sea-coasts, and like Large Cities, which we shall treat of in the next chapter, should be amenable to the Nation *directly*. Strictly mining districts, if thickly populated, ought, like "States" and Large Cities, to be considered as *double* Corporations, having one of their charters from the Nation itself. But if thinly populated, they ought to be treated like "territories" not yet admitted to be full State-Precincts, but only preparing so to be, and meanwhile be under the control of the Nation alone.

CHAP. XII. SPECIAL RELATIONS TO "STATES" AND LARGE CITIES.

§ 1. *Federative Corporations.*

(*a*) *Classifications.* When we came to the consideration of large cities, those which according to our limitations of population would consist of several Precincts, we were halted for a long time, unable to decide where to place them. We had long decided to ignore altogether, what are commonly in America, called "States,"—thinking that all their functions could properly be analyzed and divided off, partly to Precinct and partly to Nation. But the consideration of large cities soon re-opened the question about ignoring "States," and showed plainly that they and large cities *both*, must come under the same closely related category; the only difference in principle being the geographical extent of the states, and even this difference being counteracted in many cases, by the much greater population of the cities. It was furthermore evident, that states had providentially served to counteract the cities by furnishing a sufficient country population for that purpose. But still, the doubt was as unsettled as ever, where to classify BOTH of them.

It was evidently possible according to our theory, to take two entirely different views of states and large cities. On the one hand it was possible to consider them as a sort of inter-precinct-*federations*, a sort of *inter-national-like* federations between Precincts: and on the other hand it was possible to conceive of them as Corporations chartered by the *Nation*. A prolonged inability to decide between these two possibilities, at last draws us to accept a compromise between them, and we will call the resultant name Federative Corporation. This compromise may be stated thus:—States and large cities are SPONTANEOUS corporations with DOUBLE charters, one charter from the Nation above them, and the other charter from the Precincts below them. There is no more difficulty in conceiving this thought, than in conceiving the thought of a railroad deriving its charter from two different states, which is a very frequent occurrence. But we must remember, that AS Corporations they are spontaneous, and have their right of charter given by nature, without the artifice or deliberation of man; and therefore it would be quite as true an idea to conceive of states and cities, as confederations of Precincts, duly authorized by the Nation.

The only difficulty is, to see how the old "Colonies" or "Settlements," which previously and historically had been natural and valid Precincts, should have gradually and insensibly *lost* that character, and have become Corporations. And furthermore, some which had at first been actual Corporations, and then changed into real Precincts, then again gradually changed back into Corporations,—of our present "State" kind. The solution is to be found in the Tribe-principle. Because Precinct and Corporation are two of the elements of the Tribe; and as has been previously stated, one of the peculiar traits of all the three elements of the Tribe is, their tendency to and facility of, interchanging themselves, one for the other. And this very tendency and facility, are some of the reasons why those three elements had to be co-ordinated into one in our general theory.

Reasonably therefore, it was deemed best to place this subject at the end of the treatment of the Precinct. And this was especially necessary, because without it, the theory of the Precinct would be incomplete and unsatisfactory. Nevertheless, we retain a place and heading for this subject in the classification of Corporations, for the satisfaction of those persons who would prefer the latter place for it. We might perhaps ourself have preferred CORPORATION as the best place for it, were it not that that subject, as an element of government, is less familiar to the reader and much more difficult and complicated in its own nature; and therefore it was deemed best to keep it as unencumbered as possible.

We say then, all political or governmental organizations or divisions, superior to the small Precinct, except the Nation, may be regarded as federative Corporations constituted by the *union of Precincts.*

(*b*) *Right of Precincts to form into Federative Corporations.* The necessity for an express charter or legal permission for the existence of any Corporations, whether financial or political, is not at all inherent natural or necessary to the matter. This necessity has arisen under English laws, and because of a *lumbering* clumsy artificiality of our laws, which arbitrarily stand ready to construe a union for any special purpose (except purchasing or holding of Real Estate) as an unlimited partnership for *all* purposes. In nature, (as indeed *ought* to be the case in the law) all voluntary partnerships are limited, which do not expressly assert the contrary; yet in law, the reverse is the arbitrary principle. But now, when the voluntary association becomes greatly co-extensive with any one neighborhood, there arises a Precinct business interest, and this interest, in the accidents of history, was necessitated to obtain charters and become Corporations, as in the free cities of Europe. And this again, not because of any inherent necessity, but because these Corporations had arisen among the industrial classes, who were then serfs, only gradually becoming either free in person, or capable of holding property or of self-government, and only gradually asking their rights from the landed and feudal aristocracy. And thus the charters of these free states, were in a degree, obtaining freedom, property and self-government, all at once, for such Precincts. Thus it often happens, that an artificial or secondarily derived Corporation, namely a State or Barony, gives the legal status or authority to a natural and original Corporation, by acknowledging to it the return, of a measure of the rights to which it is rightfully entitled by natural principles of justice and Social Science.

We see there are several kinds of Corporations, commonly so called. One kind, the Precinct itself, *we* do not count as a Corporation, but as an eternal spontaneity and natural unit of society. But those subsidiary Corporations that may be created within its limits, are *our* first kind. The other kinds are secondary, consisting of those which are more or less outside of the individual Precinct. Now, our theory regarding the Precincts as the original elements or units of power, requires us to admit, as of agents, the equal rights of such Corporations as consist of either two or more Precincts, and also of such voluntary associations as two or more of them may incorporate or constitute: We mean the equality of their rights with those of Corporations organized or constituted by central national powers, so that these again must at any rate be classified into a third kind, or tertiary Corporations, and on entirely different principles from the former two kinds.

And then again, there is a kind of corporation which is, as it were, a delegate authorized by a delegate, namely a corporation authorized by a previous yet continuing corporation. Such are all the corporations which are chartered by those mongrel institutions we call states. For these states themselves, being only corporations of a peculiar kind, present this singular phenomenon, of one corporation authorizing and chartering another for political functions, and also for other businesses. Such are nearly all the railroads, canals, and business corporations in the United States. The only powers that ought to pretend to *charter any thing*, are the Nation and the small Precincts; and charters ought to be as easy and as free as partnerships.

If we admit, for states as well as cities, only the status of corporations, and not that of fundamental instinctive elements or units of society, we would not undervalue them thereby; because our theory elevates corporation itself, from the position of a mere creature of government, to that of a fundamental, although artificial or rational element. By thus elevating the corporation, we would not degrade the city and state. The thing that our theory really does affect, is the Precinct, which it raises at one bound, from the low position given to it by the low theory of corporation, to the high position of a fundamental instinctive unit of society.

(c) *Temporary uses of "States."*—Although the division of Nations into provinces and states, has no foundation in the fundamental principles of government; yet, so long as Social Science is in its infancy, and Mankind so imperfect, the division is of very high importance as a provisional one for temporary purposes. For one thing; a province or state serves providentially to counterbalance the large city, by a power that will do the least evil in proportion to the amount of good; for there is no other power that can be proposed for such a counterbalance, except the Nation. But inasmuch as corruption increases in direct ratios, to the sum of the population, the size of the country, and the distance of the party governed from the party governing; but is in the inverse ratio to the restrictions of power;—it is inferable without doubt, that in general, the national power operating *directly* as a check to the city, would be overwhelming, and thus be a worse balancing organ than some intermediate political power, which should be similar in one of the two great elements constituting the divisions; for instance, similar in population, as it of course could not be similar in geographical surface. But you may ask, why should surface have *any* thing to do with it? We answer, because surface, although little for aggression, is every thing for defence; and because surface scantly occupied, belongs to futurity.

Another use of states, so long as they are maintained, has been for state prisons, and might be to make punishment-cities more practicable. In order to form such cities large enough to be useful, they would need to be the receptacles of the criminals from many Precincts. And this would require, either, state or national co-operation, unless indeed it were deemed better to let the Precincts themselves make special leagues or *confederations* for such purposes. But this would require a very high degree of Christian civilization, to justify it, or to make it successful.

§ 2. *Cities equivalent to States, in rights and responsibilities.*

One of the foundations for State, in distinction from Precinct and Nation, is the existence of metropolitan cities, which, states sometimes claim as the property of the one in which they are located. But such a claim is generally spurious, and in the case of large cities, always so. For instance, the city of Philadelphia belongs as much in its business relations, and also socially and financially, to New Jersey and Delaware, in proportion to their size, as it does to Pennsylvania. Likewise New York City belongs to New Jersey, Rhode Island and Connecticut, as well. But the fact is, that all these large cities belong to the Nation, socially and financially. It is the national trade and tariff that has built these metropolitan cities. It is the trade both domestic and foreign, of the separate parts of the whole Nation. Hence, such a city has a better claim on principle, to be an original unit, that is, a state, than any one of the several United States themselves. And as long as the mongrel distinctions of State are kept up, these metropolitan cities ought to claim as a right, that they should be co-equal states, and no longer subject to the fleecings and petty tyrannies of state legislatures, but responsible only and directly to the general government on the one hand, and to the people who inhabit, and to the Precincts of which they are composed, on the other hand. But, until government becomes better, perhaps all these complications are, merely difficulties in the way of greater evils. But the plea of a certain great city, to be elevated into a state, in the midst of a great war which it had indirectly done much to produce, was not just. Let it stay, and take its share of its own evils; and "never swap horses in crossing a stream."

Cities therefore, especially large ones, should be under the control of some supervisory larger country power, either of state, as at present, or rather and especially under the national government; because they are morally and metaphysically the product and property of the whole public, or Nation, and profit by the Nation's trade and progress pre-eminently.

But besides these things, also their powers over the state, their ability to sustain taxation, and their special corruptibility, and the fact of the invariable collection of special wickednesses that voluntarily flow into them, all require their submission to a superior agricultural or country power.

And such a submission has its logical justification or basis, in this, that cities are the offspring of and dependent upon, a large agricultural or country district, for their very existence.

It is quite apparent to all thinking persons, that the manner is grossly unjust, in which, for instance, the Legislatures of New York and Pennsylvania, tyrannize over their great Metropolises. It is equally apparent, that it would be productive of immense evil, to allow New York City to begin now to govern itself, and, that the government would be administered in the interests of the lawless and disorderly. In fact, the legislative aid of the state has been invoked by the order-loving citizens, to preserve their city from evil; although the case is different in Pennsylvania. Hence we see that neither the state nor the city itself, can be trusted to govern a metropolitan city. That the national government could not be trusted with the *internal* administration of such a city, is evidenced by the mal-administration of Washington City for many years.

The only alleviation is, to have the city divided into a large number of small Precincts, each of which shall have its own internal newly apportioned state rights, and each be responsible to the general government, by itself. Then the Precincts that would allow the disorderly to rule, would soon be forsaken by the orderly and peace-loving citizens, who would naturally fall into Precincts by themselves; and the disorderly and riotous might perhaps murder and fight one another to their hearts' content, so long as they did not interfere with their neighboring peaceable Precincts, nor with migrating out of them, nor the transit through them; as, in that case they would come under the defence and military possession of the National or General Government, the same as any other Rebels.

The experiment of allowing the "state" governments to control the affairs, and alter the charters, of large cities at will, has been tried and found wanting and abandoned, both in Pennsylvania and New York. A state should have no more right to prescribe the width, direction or other circumstances, of the ordinary streets or City-Rail-Ways &c., IN the city, than the general government itself.

On the other hand, any particular neighborhood or township, has as good a right to say, whether it will support any religion, whether it will allow Sunday travel, (of course except the travel under government sanction of the larger district or province, for instance the Mail), what the conditions of Divorce of its own citizens, and whether it will license liquor or brothels, and whether it will make all real estate return to a general fund, (of course compensating all the present holders), and what communistic or other moral experiments may be allowed:—Each neighborhood has the same political right to do these things for itself, under certain restrictions, as the state itself is now allowed to have; and with the new apportionment and balances of power; more right. The business of a "state" is not arrogantly to assume all these rights to itself, but only to prescribe and define the reasonable limits, within which, each neighborhood and township and county may regulate these matters for themselves.

This theory, it will be seen, claims for neighborhoods, many rights which the advocates of ultra-individual liberty, claim for the Individual, and is thus a compromise between theories that hitherto have seemed to be in radical opposition. It is also a compromise in various other respects. And here a word might be dropped quietly in the ear of the new society advocating God and religion, &c., in the national constitution. Supposing for argument's sake that they are right from their stand-point, as to their religious principles, and as to the general idea of the relation between religion and government; still they fail entirely to discriminate between the Precinct and the Nation, as organs of accomplishing the Divine will in government. And the same want of discrimination seems to be made by their opponents, whether high church or non-church men, of whatever affiliation.

In cities, the close proximity of the population of many Precincts, without any geographical lines or distances between them, constitutes their chief peculiarity: thus, the peculiar functions of cities require the putting forth of new organs. And the idea that sums up all these organs, under which they must classify themselves, is, special organizations of all these small Precincts, of which they are composed. Besides being divided into small Precincts, the same as said above, the special organization of the whole city should have special powers, the exact limits of which are not easy to give fully, until after some experience shall have been had, and further study given to its details. Nor is it necessary to discover all the details of a plan, before perceiving the utility in general of the plan itself.

A consolidated municipal Police and Board of Health would at least be necessary; whilst the Fire Department and Boards of Trade, Water and Gas, might be either municipal powers, or special corporations. Probably the city government might be best accomplished by an equal number of rulers, chosen partly according to its own general municipal principles and by its own members; and partly by the state, so long as such mongrels as our states are tolerated, or instead thereof, by the national government. This is proposed as a constitution for the general city power; and of course is not intended to disturb the Precinct-powers, reserved to each of the many small Precincts which the city is to be considered as consisting of.

We need not depend on theory alone for the settlement of these questions, but on actual experiment. The city of Philadelphia, for 150 years, that is from its origin until about the year 1850, consisted of several distinct corporations or boroughs, as distinct as Philadelphia is from Pittsburg. Afterwards they became consolidated into one corporation, and that experiment has been tried for fifteen or twenty years. The subsequent amount of corruption and destruction of private rights, clearly proves that the larger the political organization, the more corrupt it becomes. The only objection to the old organization of independent boroughs, was the facility which it gave for rowdies and criminals to escape from one borough into another. But after suffering for many years, the boroughs adopted an organization of consolidated police, and this effectually corrected the evil. The city had not been governed nearly so well for twenty years before, and has never been better governed since. Although Mayor Henry did as well as mortal could do. This consolidation of police, cured the evil; and is one illustration, among many that might be given, why Precincts with state-powers, should be allowed to form special leagues with each other.

Another instance is the city of London, which, during all the hundreds of years of its existence, and to this day, although the largest city in the world, consists of a number of distinct and separate corporate boroughs.

§ 3. *Special Needs in Large Cities.*

(*a*) *In General.* Cities are entirely an artificial product, and city life is not entirely an instinctive one; therefore men, like animals when out of their instinctive life, are unable to help themselves by their unaided ordinary instinctive powers. Cities therefore require a high degree of social science. Yet Spencer makes no radical allowance for city organization. His theory will not answer for "Corporations." He requires such a persistent adherence to the "let alone" doctrine, as to advise even that the streets should be allowed to become foul, until by producing diseases and annoyances, and affecting the prices of Real Estate, and the standard of the neighborhood, capitalists may ultimately be induced to form voluntary corporations for the purpose of cleaning them, without the aid or prompting of the city government.

Up to a certain point of size, cities or towns improve the health and morality of Mankind. Just in proportion as men get nearer together, their intercourse becomes more frequent, and general intelligence increases. Brought together for business or occupation, they yet derive, incidentally, other and very different advantages, from the very frequent intercourse of social life, increased opportunities and inducements for intellectual and moral culture, and for religious exercises. The very fact itself of a larger circle of personal acquaintances, contributes to the general improvement of the inhabitants.

Nevertheless, it must be deeply felt by every practical social scientist, that large cities present many features requiring special treatment, and produce many special vices dangers and sufferings, difficult to cope with successfully, by any treatment yet imagined. Statistics drawn from some of the old cities of Europe show, that the population actually dies out every few (say six or seven) generations, and that they are sustained only by the influx of new blood and new persons from the country. This course of things shows there is something radically wrong, either in city life itself, or in the lack of discovery as yet of the true principles of city government. We shall have occasion to examine into this matter at some length, under the heads of "Health" and "Life." At present, all we can delay to consider is, the relation of this subject to our Precinct-theory, namely, to constituting cities into small Precincts for their political administration. We may remark then, that all the general arguments for our theory are, like everything else, intensified, when applied to large cities. We may also remark that the growth of very large cities ought to be discouraged; and their connection with the whole national power, might tend in that direction; but that "state" powers foster the LARGE cities. Because no state has more than one such, and therefore encourages concentration; but the national policy would be, as it generally has been, to encourage the dissemination of population. In fact, the function of new cities is just as much a part of our national policy, as the settlement of new farms.

(*b*) *Residences and Occupations too far Apart.* Next, coming to the special arguments; the great political object is to induce citizens to reside within the Precincts where their occupation lies. To this end the following reasons may be given. Yet the *great remedy* is the Precinct-system. Minor remedies may come up under "Civil Government." But at present all we can do, is to give some reasons or arguments for this uniting of residences and occupations in near neighborhood.

(1) Under the present scattering system, the number of inhabitants becomes so great, and the Individual persons so fluctuating, that the citizens become less and less watchers or critics of one another, whether for preventing wrong doing, or for arresting criminals. Then the criminals can find hiding places in obscure lanes and bye-ways, and under the cover of acquaintances whose occupations are unknown; *then* morality begins to deteriorate, temptations increase, and the powers of counteraction proportionately decrease. (2) Another point of decrease of honor and general morality in cities, is reached, when their residents in large numbers become so fashionable or so enfeebled in health, that they must remove their residences to some different and distant parts of the city, from those in which they fulfill their daily occupations. This works badly in several ways. In one way, it has a similar effect to increasing the transient and fluctuating part of the population; it gives each resident so much less time and so much less interest in the neighborhoods, both of his residence and his occupation. Furthermore, some of the best hours of the day are lost in the travel to and fro. (3) The head of the house is absent from his home, when he may be wanted in case of family disputes, and, needed correction of children. The women become more

and more given to trifling; the sanctity of marriage is more and more endangered. All the better feelings of family life are more and more interrupted. (4) Another way in which this increasing size and incidental residence, distant from the places of occupation, does injury, is, that the business districts, after being forsaken as abodes by those who ought to continue near or in them, often become occupied by the lowest classes of society,—in that interim between the time of their being aristocratic enough for residences, and the time of their becoming wanted for grand stores and offices. A large Precinct of this kind, containing the largest portion of the city's wealth, will sometimes be inhabited chiefly by Individuals who have neither property, reputation, nor permanent residence in the locality. Our Precinct-theory would not at all apply to such cases. To prevent the political and party evils arising from these causes, the wards in Philadelphia are often found divided so as to be, say, two miles long, and only one-eighth of a mile wide; which is a violation of the first principles of the geography of the Precinct-system, and increases the social and moral evils working at the bottom.

(c) *Growth of Cities too Rapid for Social Science.* The evils in large cities may be classified according to two principles of separation. One, according to their origin, as physical, metaphysical, and moral,—the other according to their degree of permanence—into removable, and irremovable, or as the New York Council of Hygiene, in regard only to physical health, says, "preventable," and "not preventable." But after all, the classification of removable or irremovable, is very defective for Social Science, in the question regarding the size of cities; because size itself has all imperceptible degrees, and because the relation of size is complicated again with, and ever varies with the capacity of Social Science to cope with the subject.

It must be admitted, that the tendency of men to concentrate in cities, has ever been in advance of the morality and the sciences that are necessary to govern them. So that even under despotic governments, they become pests morally and socially; whilst in republics, in addition to these evils, there are the evils of riot and mob-ocracy. Hence, one of the necessary methods of preventing the evils is, checking the growth itself, until social and political science can come nearer to catching up with the evils. Hence then, it becomes prudent to discourage the too rapid influx of human beings into ONE locality. And this is best effected, in the usual and most approved manner of social retardments, especially by direct taxes, and sufficient in amount to effect the objects aimed at.

Accordingly, taxes should be imposed in cities on the male population over the age of 18. Also, a tax per acre on the amount of ground built upon, not counting the yards or areas not built upon. Also a tax per *cubic* foot of all buildings, except residences of small tenants; tax to be paid by the owner. Also a tax on all living expenditures over certain specified amounts per person of any age; tax to be paid by the head of the Family. These extra taxes should be commanded, and their total Precinct amounts, or else their percentages, should be specified in general, by the government of the state or Nation; but the PROCEEDS should be collected and *expended* by the Amalgam of the city Precincts, and be expended solely for the physical and moral improvement of the city itself, and be fairly apportioned to *each Precinct* therein,—instead of, for instance, on the principle of having all in one grand park, and that perhaps, 3 or 4 miles from the city's centre where fresh air is most needed. Furthermore, all private persons who have open lots duly planted, should be accounted benefactors, and so much of their lots as were thus planted, should be exempt from all taxation.

In these and all other possible ways, the rules and expenditures which tended DIRECTLY to discourage the increase of the city, should INCIDENTALLY tend to make it more healthy and more moral. But there are so many evils to be counteracted, that only faithful and long continued experiments, can prove what are the best methods of counteraction.

One of the most important views of the advantages of small Precincts, will be found in connection with cities: because the advantages of the system will be most apparent among them; both because *there* is the most *need* for this principle of subdivision, and also because, by the facility of removals, the plan would the *more easily* be put into actual operation. Indeed, perhaps cities are the places appointed by Providence, for the trial of most kinds of practical "experiments;" for therein the results become quickly visible to a multitude of "observers."

(*d*) *Plan of treating Fallen Districts.* Here is a plan for benefitting Five Points, Bedford street, Sink, and other such places, and is a sort of exception to other general rules.

A Precinct of this kind, would bear a somewhat similar relation to the city, that a city now under the old theory, bears to the state, which in fact is somewhat similar in principle, to what a conquered province bears to the conquering country, after the return to a condition of settled peace. It is a kind of absolute dependence of the smaller upon the greater; exercised partly for the good of the province itself, and partly for the good of the whole. The fall of any Precinct into the condition of a rendezvous for social outcasts, must be regarded as in principle, a sort of rebellion against the general city, however sincere, however mistaken, however ill-treated, the rebels may be, or conceive themselves to be. But on the other hand, as these kinds of rebels have the right to live, the rebellion must be treated rather as one by a Locality, than as one by Individuals. It is a rebellion whose essence consists, not in violence against human wills, nor in warring against the citizens generally; but rather as a taking away of the public land. The world's plan is, to turn the poor creatures out of doors, every once in a while, to please fanatical zeal.

Our plan is as follows.

Let the neighborhood within prescribed limits, be legally constituted, separately, into a *Reformatory Precinct* under the immediate control of some sufficiently general and superior power. This would naturally draw many respectable people out of it. These should be compensated, in all cases where the law is applied, either suddenly or soon after the time of the enactment thereof. Constituting the locality into a Reformatory Precinct, would give special powers to make special regulations binding on property holders, to keep the places decently clean and healthy. The power of the municipal government, when fully applied, should, extend to *confining the residents within the Precinct.* But not to exclude honest citizens, having known and visibly honest means of support &c. from entering and returning. Special permits might be given to the most deserving and improving residents, to go out to work, or to gather fragments. It should also prevent any other persons from moving into it, *to reside* therein. Stations of work, and of gratuitous supply of the absolute necessaries of life, should be located there. All spirituous liquors should be kept out, and dram shops closed up therein. The women and children should be specially cared for, with more minor comforts than the men. Schools for teaching, not only the rudiments of reading, writing, arithmetic &c.; but also for teaching the common sense principles of success in every day life, the principal *motives and uses* for common self-control, common morality, and the rudiments of responsibility and gratitude to God and man; as enforced by suffering and as taught by nature. Free encouragement should be given to the various religious missions, to maintain their good works; and suitable buildings or rooms should be furnished to them by the city, without charge. A small prison should be arranged within the Precinct itself, and a special police arrangement to suit the peculiar people. Small sums of money should be given to them as *rewards*. A portion of the houses should be taken to supply *free lodgings* of the *plainest* kind, sexes apart. Also free medical attention and medicines, and as many things free as possible, but under advices as to what and when.

But this subject runs into that about the Punishment-Cities, which are to be considered under the head of Government. The chief difference is, that criminals and all who cannot pretty fully clear themselves of suspicion of felony and similar offences, should be carefully and thoroughly *excluded*, even from occasional entrance anywhere within the bounds of these "fallen districts." The entire separation of professional criminals from openly fallen women, is one of the only means of either, detecting, punishing, or preventing general crimes; as well as a necessary means of preserving or restoring the women and their children. Nor is it socially *just*, to confuse the open sexual immorality of women, with the secret crimes of felony. And as to the deeper moral and religious questions involved, this is not the part of the science in which to consider them.

PART III.

CONCLUSION OF THE PRECINCT: PARTIAL APPLICABILITY BY CHARTERS.

CHAP. I. IN GENERAL.

It seems an appropriate method whereby to conclude both this whole article on the Precinct, and also this part about the relations of states and cities to Corporations,—to introduce a topic, which although entirely different from either of them, and from our whole theory of the Precinct, yet nevertheless has no other so proper a place in the work, and yet has much intrinsic and PRACTICAL importance, namely,—the topic of how far, and by what principles, the *general advantages* of our theory of the Precinct, could be realized by one or more Precincts, by means of charters merely, and not upon grounds of general rights; and without an alteration of the constitution of the Nation, although they might involve an alteration of the constitution of the particular state. Because, there are late decisions in Pennsylvania, that "the state legislature cannot delegate to the people the power to enact laws." But of course this is only a dodge of the "*legists*," for the charters of all boroughs and cities, involve the right of those corporations to make certain kinds of laws. And if they can delegate to the borough, why not also delegate to the people of a "ward"?

This topic to be sure, might be postponed to CORPORATION. If so, it would come under the head of corporations exercising governmental and political functions; and under the lower or derivative order, exercising functions under present governments, and under the subdivision, for *general* functions. But the reservation of this topic to that element of society, would interfere too much with the very general abstract and theoretical mode of thought there pursued.

In general we may remark, that persons who cannot receive the PRECINCT-theory in the fullness of foundation we give to it, may probably be able to admit the rights, as *grants from a superior power*. This would be, in effect, to rank Precincts as Corporations, in which case, nearly our whole argument on freedom of Corporations, would become a part of the Precinct argument, and would counterbalance, by extent, what was lost in the depth, of the foundation. But we have aimed to place the rights of Precincts upon more durable reasons, regarding as we do, Precincts to be spontaneous and instinctive units of society, with inalienable rights, concurrent with the rights of all the other units, Individual, Family, Nation, &c. But after all, it is not so important now, and practically, what grounds we place the rights upon, as it is, how extensive we will grant those rights shall be.

CHAP. II. BY CHARTERS FROM THE NATION.

The simplest and best method would be, by charters from the Nation itself. But this could not be constitutionally effective within the limits of already existing and completed "states," unless by *their* consent. The general government alone, could only furnish such charters for its "territories," or such parts of them as it chose so to do. But of course, no such charter could convey any more power, than what the general government *might* convey to any other of its "new states." These powers would be more ample, however, than any yet conveyed to a new state. But no thoroughly ample grants could be given by charter, even by the Nation, without a previous alteration of ITS "constitution."

In "old states," even granting ample charters to Precincts within them, considerable facilities would be obtained by the grant of charters from the general government also; so that each Precinct would thus have two charters.

If charters were given by the Nation, whether alone or concurrently, the principles hereinafter mentioned, would most generally apply with equal suitability.

There are some objects, which, for their complete attainment, or even for their satisfactory trial, would require the subsequent co-operation of the national government, for instance, Peace-Precincts. And the United States government should be petitioned to excuse such Peace-Precincts from all military burdens, both personal and financial. The United States government should also be petitioned to confirm the relief of some of the Precincts, by amendments of the national constitution, so as to make their privileges more permanent, and their independence more real,—somewhat like the Free Cities of Germany, which having been established even in the Middle Ages, still preserve their freedom, and give us specimens of the best, happiest, and most effectual governments in the world.

Even Russia had granted such freedom many years ago, to a large peace settlement of protestant Mennonites ; but lately revoked it. This drove the Mennonites to emigrate to the United States, whereupon the Russian government restored the grant. But grants revocable at will, will not answer, nor anything *less* than irrevocable charters. Consequently the Russian Mennonites still continue their emigration into this country. They are slightly communists, as they hold their pasture lands in common, and perhaps some other things. They had a difficulty in finding suitable lands. For the United States government, with its all extravagant waste of public lands, has no method it seems, to encourage settlements either in joint or in common ownership. It has lands for Mormons, and "squatters," and reservations for Indians, but not for communes,—until paid for in severalty.

CHAP. III. BY CHARTERS FROM A "STATE":—PRELIMINARY SUGGESTIONS.

Here we are to consider how near an approximation could be made to our Precinct-system, by *any one* "State," without any alteration either of the constitution or laws of the Nation.

If nothing better nor more can be done, it would be something at least, if each state would give to its townships or smallest Precincts, at least the *county* powers of sheriffs, &c. Because, a very general and thorough diminution of the size of counties, even without any radical increase of the powers, would be a first step towards the proposed new order; yet as it would not provide compensations for removals, it would lack one of the advantages of the more radical plan.

It is certain however, that any State might give to any one, or a few adjoining Precincts, a charter so as to embody the principles herein set forth, *as an experiment.* And the experiment might be made with such limitations, either of time or space, as would avoid running excessive risks by untried plans.

Of course any change should be made gradually, and have a few years of notice, that all persons might remove to the district of their choice, who were not satisfied with the ruling majorities or powers in their own Precinct. Another feature in the starting of this plan is, that no Precinct should be *forced* into this arrangement. But each one should have the choice, to take its Precinct-freedom, or to remain under the old state-machinery, as some perhaps would do at first; the main idea being, to increase freedom, not to diminish it.

CHAP. IV. THE CONSTITUTION OF THE UNITED STATES AS A FORMAL BASIS FOR A "STATE."

§ 1. *In General.*

In order to put the proposed theory in operation in the United States, it would not need to be adopted by the general government at first; for it is practicable for each state itself to make an experimental approximation to the general idea. To produce this change, all that would be required would be,—first, for any state to adopt the constitution of the United States for its own state-constitution, substituting therein the words "state," or "each state," for "United States;" and "Governor" for "President;" and instead of "Governors," the word "Sheriffs:" also, to use some reasonable precaution against local oppression; and to make a few other verbal alterations which would obviously be necessary. And second, to provide by general law, to allow any city or borough which would accept the alteration, to accept the constitution of the United States, as its borough charter, with a few obvious and necessary restrictions; or the same might be granted to separate Precincts severally. And to make the matter more plain, the following suggestions are offered; showing how any one or more states might give to any one (or more) county or township within it, such an enlarged charter, as would enable any such Precinct to exercise generally the powers which the state itself now has, but with such exceptions as will presently be mentioned. Or the state, by general law, or alteration of its "constitution" affecting *all* its Precincts or townships, might so enact and provide. The idea is, that each Precinct should have the same powers in relation to the state, that each individual state now has, in relation to the Nation, under the constitution of the United States:—with the exceptions now to be mentioned.

§ 2. *Exceptions.*

The exceptions or reservations to the state, of its present powers, might all be comprised in general, under the following five classes.

(*a*) *Excepting:*—Limitations of Time.—If the means whereby the change was effected, were charters incorporating Precincts, the charters need not be perpetual, but might be made either for a limited time, or else revocable at any time by a prescribed amount of majority of the voters of the state. But if the means were a general law, it would naturally be revocable by the state, the same as any other law; nevertheless, some definite amount of majority should be prescribed, under which the law should not be revocable; or rather, the means of the alteration should be what is commonly called an alteration of the constitution of the state.

(*b*) Excepting:—that no property-qualification should be required of voters, for any *State*-representative or officer. This exception is necessary to guard against anticipated logical objections, rather than to accomplish the general system of the theory.

(*c*) Excepting:—all matters relating to the government of the individual state in its totality, and in its relations to the Nation. For, its state government would need to be continued, both for the sake of its own general internal affairs, and also for the sake of its relations to the Nation.

Of course, in our plan, when adopted by all the Precincts of any State, the old state-machinery would be largely reduced in number; and the business of those officers that remained, would also be vastly reduced. The only absolute necessity for retaining the state-organization at all, would be to maintain and fulfill its relations to the general government, that is the Nation. But if the main object cannot be accomplished throughout a *whole* state, and if only a few scattered Precincts, or perhaps only one, could get such a charter, then, instead of adjoining Precincts in every Amalgam, having equal power in the election of the Precincts' officers, the *state itself* might have to retain those powers also.

(*d*) Excepting:—those few particulars wherein our proposed system differs essentially from that of the United States, in the apportionment of powers. These items have been already mentioned in a former part of this article, where we drew a comparison between the two systems. Accordingly, the state might give by charter to its individual Precincts, and to their Amalgams, all the rights which itself possessed; but it *could* not give those which the Nation ought to give: and it would be folly for it to give to the Nation, the rights which, under a perfect system, should return to the Nation, because there are other rights which ought then to be returned from the Nation to the Precinct, which yet the state has no power to take. Hence, the rights which, in the former comparison were assigned to the Nation, should be retained by the states, under the plan of state-corporations here suggested; otherwise the Nation would or might acquire more than its share of power in the alteration.

(*e*) Excepting :—all affairs and officers having relations to, and representatives to or in, the government of the United States. No alterations of these relations and officers can be made, without the consent of the United States government. That, although desirable, has already been considered. But it would be a higher alteration than we are now considering, as required by the very nature of the plan by state-corporations, and for separate state-adoption.

CHAP. V. SIMPLE AND DIRECT FORM OF CHARTER FROM A "STATE."

A still better method of charter, (for experiment) than the adaptation of the constitution of the United States, would be, to grant a charter expressing *directly*, a complete but brief outline of what the Precinct rights ought to be, with the usual reservation,—"so far as the same does not conflict with the constitution or laws of the United States." A form of charter of this kind, adopted by any state subdividing itself into small localities, and by amendment to its state constitution, would afford the most direct and most satisfactory experiment that is possible, without the direct co-operation of the Nation revising its own constitution.

What would be wanted would be, not a huge volume ot interminable details; but a real "magna charta," a simple "bill of rights," a charter with little words, but big ideas.

However, this whole subject of chartering Precincts by "States," is only incidental, and is no essential part of the theory of the Precinct.

In conclusion. We now leave this theory to the reader's careful consideration; if it shall seem to him to deserve it.

BOOK III.

THE NATION.

PART I.

THE NATION AS A FUNDAMENTAL ELEMENT.

CHAP. I. PRELIMINARIES.

THE Nation is the FIFTH Unit or fundamental Element of society, as determined in our Analytics. So much however, is said of this topic by other writers, that comparatively little remains for us. And according to our theory, its proportionate importance is over-estimated by most other writers. In a true analysis, some part of what is usually attributed to it belongs to Mankind, and another part belongs to Precinct, and another to Corporation; so that only a fourth, is its real place. We have Precinct on the one side, Corporation on the other, and Mankind above it. The internal affairs of Nation, we consider mostly under the heads of Precinct and Corporation and "Civil Government;" the higher external affairs we consider partly, under the head of Mankind, including Nation as of course *one* of its fundamental elements. Hence, in this article we have comparatively rather to consider the theoretically lower or intermediate affairs, commonly called international law, but in a wider sense than usual.

In fact, one of the great works which Social Science has to accomplish, is to analyze into its real elements, what is called "The Law of Nations," and thus to appropriate to each department, its appropriate share. For the custom has been, to collect under this term all the *general* principles of law, and even of human rights, which seem to have no more suitable place in the field of thought. Thus in the Roman law, the phrase, authority right or law, of Nations, (jus gentium),—generally was used to express that sense of right which is common to most or to all men, and which is in conformity to common instinct and reason, and which is called by us the law of nature. Such a combination is all very well in an address by "counsel," but is not exactly the true course for a scientific work. The absolute law of right, the relative rights of established usage, the law of God, the modifications by voluntary contract, all ought to be somewhat considered, in the treatment of any branch of practical morals, or of applied law; but yet, properly belong to a more general and higher department of thought, than any one of them. Thus also we may take Grotius' sources of international, and generalize them as the true foundations of all law, namely, nature's law, divine law, custom, and compact: and in both departments, custom and compact may be put together, and again generalized into, "Consent," as we do in II. I. 2, of this article.

Interesting also are the questions, how far voluntary contracts or agreements modify, what otherwise *would* be natural laws, or God's law. For instance; is it right to use *explosive* bullets in a war between Nations who agree to do so? And is it right for human beings to marry for a *limited* time, even if they agree to do so? And is it right for Nations or Individuals to lie, cheat and steal, even if all sides agree to do so? But if not, then how would that decision affect the question of war at all, or of the methods of conducting war? But these questions belong rather to Moral Philosophy and to Theology.

One of the evils of so confusing Law and Right in general, with international law, has been to pervert universal principles, partly in favor of war, and partly to indulge Nations with privileges to do wrong. For, until the last few years, perhaps we may say until the work of Mr. Field, the law of Nations has been *chiefly* occupied with matters about war, providing for, or conducting, or concluding it. Thus, pharisaically strict rules of non-resistance, have been taught as if they were eternal principles obligatory on Individuals and Provinces &c.; whilst war at the same time has been held forth, as if it were very wise and good between Nations; nay as if it were their most glorious achievement. Accordingly, the claims of Nation over Individual, have been stretched to a tension beyond common sense, chiefly to justify the claims of Nations on their citizens, for war-services and for war-taxes, and for the forcible collection of excessive internal taxes even in time of peace. In fact, nearly all the old despotic notions about the divine right of kings, have passed down into modern Society, transmigrated into the idea of the divine and UNLIMITED right of Nation; together with absolution from all sin (in advance)—or even the other royal doctrine transmigrated, namely, the *Nation* can do no wrong. In such a fog, there can neither be a true Moral Philosophy, nor a true Theology.

The ready susceptibility of the usual ideas on the Law of Nations, to higher generalizations, will appear also from the following extract from Appletons' Cyclopedia, on this subject. "It was the object of Grotius to show that Nations are governed by a law distinct from the natural law, to wit, by a code or body of rules, founded indeed in the law of nature, but proceeding immediately from universal *consent.* 'Those right deductions,' he says, 'which proceed from the principles of reason, point to the law of nature, while those which proceed from common consent, proceed from the law of Nations.' Puffendorf rejected the distinction which Grotius had drawn, between the law of nature and the law of Nations; he denied that the latter was founded upon express consent, but considered it merely the law of nature applied to Nations." Both sides admitted, that, as "aggregate bodies of Individuals, Nations must be in some degree subject to the law of nature," from which we may, with Wolf and Hobbes, properly maintain "that, in their collective capacity, Nations acquire a new character and being, different from that of the Individuals of whom they are composed; therefore in its applications to societies of men, the law of nature must undergo some changes and modifications, and thus is derived the voluntary law of Nations."

Thus do these writers dimly and confusedly anticipate the idea of Nation as a Great Social Unit; but only of IT, ISOLATED, and not as one of several Units. But modern Science is disintegrating these conglomerations, and out of them we may hope to see differentiated, three different degrees and grades of thought, and three different branches of study, namely; One, of the Nation as one of the several Units of Society: The Second, The (higher or real) Law of Nations, that is, that law of nature, which consists of the principles which every civilized Nation is presupposed to hold in common, and to be applicable to affairs *within* as well as outward of itself: And the Third, what is now called Law of Nations; but which should then simply be called *Inter*national Law.

CHAP. II. RIGHTS OF THE NATION IN RELATION TO THE OTHER ELEMENTS.

§ 1. *Rights in General.*

It is generally admitted, that in all their legitimate organizations Mankind have, in their collective capacities, rights which they do not possess as Individuals. This admission seems to be an indistinct anticipation, that society consists of a plurality of Units, each of which has its own peculiar rights. But unfortunately, those writers who have taken this ground in regard to Nations, have too much ignored the rights of citizens as Individuals and as Families, and of the other Units. These collective rights however, may be analyzed so as to be resolved into only two, namely, one, the right of *many* rather than of *one* person, that is to say, the right of numbers; and the other, which is better,—the right of peculiar position or relation of any organization, person, or locality,—which has claim when there is no alternative resource to it, for the maintenance of its rights in question, in any particular case.

Vattel, as quoted and referred to by Twiss, the standard English author on the Law of Nations, (in their Chaps. I.), says: (§ 4), "Nations being composed of men naturally free and independent, and who, before the establishment of civil societies, lived together in the state of nature,—Nations or sovereign states, are to be considered as so many free persons, living together in the state of nature." Again (§ 5) "Men being subject to the laws of nature, and their union in civil society not being sufficient to free them from the obligation of observing these laws, since by this union they do not cease to be men; the entire Nation, whose common will is *only* the result of the united wills of the citizens, remains subject to the laws of nature, and is obliged to respect them, in all its proceedings. And since the law arises from the obligation, as we have just observed (§ 3), the Nation has also the same laws that nature has given to men, for the performance of their duty." Again (§ 10 and 11): "The experience of communities * * * confirms what the instinct of the Individual-man suggests. There is accordingly, in human nature, a tendency towards society, and whenever opportunity presents itself, men are found to associate themselves together for the purpose of mutually aiding and assisting one another. There thus grow up spontaneously, relations of natural society amongst men. The law of this natural society is, that each Individual" [whether person or Nation] "should do for the others, everything which their welfare requires, and which he can perform without neglecting the duty which he owes to himself [or itself]: and this obligation of natural society is coextensive with the human race. The Universal Society of the human race, being thus an institution of nature, all men are bound to cultivate it, and to discharge its duties: and they cannot release themselves from that obligation, by any convention or private association." Vattel also (§ 10) says,—"a law which all men ought to observe, in order to live agreeably to their nature, *and in conformity to the views of their common* CREATOR." Mr. Twiss omits this latter part, but we are happy to find somebody saying something about the rights of the CREATOR, in relation to National duties and rights. We are also happy to hear about human race and *human nature,* in this connection.

What Mulford says of the inviolability of the Individual and of the Nation, is equally true of the Family, the Precinct, and of all the other Units or "moral personalities" of society. Thus, p. 268, he says: "The conception which defines either the Nation or the Individual, as subordinate and secondary, is, in its error, the postulate of an inevitable antagonism. If either be held, not as an end in itself, but only as a means having the other for an end, there can be no principle of unity, and no form of reconciliation." And we affirm that the same may be also said of the relation of the Nation to the *Family* and to the *Precinct*, and to *Mankind*: and whether to the Social Circle or not,—remains to be investigated.

Accordingly however, we cheerfully admit the same rights to the Nation: so that every Nation has a right to modify and limit the powers of the Precincts within it, so far as called for by its particular genius and mission, and to provide against the special dangers of its own time and position; as against Turks, Barbarians, Aristocracies, Demagogeries &c.

Writers generally, and Mulford also, include among the *special* rights of the Nation, the following: (1) "The right of self-preservation;" as if anything whatever could exist, without that right; and (2) "The right to declare war and conclude peace;" as if everything that had a right to defend itself, did not also have that right; and (3) "The right to form INTERnational relations;" as if Individuals did not have the right to form inter-individual relations, and Families, inter-family relations, &c.; and (4) "The right to coin money;" as if the manufacture of money had not been already proved by Spencer and Mill, to be more safely bestowed upon Corporations, than aught otherwise; and (5) "The right of Eminent Domain;" as if *Mankind* itself had not superior right thereunto, which must some day be re-established, at least metaphysically and morally re-established.

The right of the Nation over the domain, is the same as its right over persons, namely, a restricted one, limited in principle by the rights of all the other Units; and limited in practice, only by the rights of superior powers when they shall normally arise. When the question comes up, of division of a Nation into two or more Nations, the subject of the rights of isolated or singular Precincts, has nothing particularly to do with it; neither has the question of Eminent Domain. The question of Domain is included, as a minor matter in that of subdivision of the Nation, and puts to rest all argumentation based upon property rights, just as a legitimate divorce *a vinculo*, allows not the usual claims on property, arising out of the marriage law, nor of arguments upon that ground.

As was said in our Summary Introduction: every Unit, whether Individual, Family, Social Circle, Precinct, Nation or Mankind, has its own rights, which are inalienable, indefeasible, and indivisible. Therefore in general we may say, the sovereignty of the Nation over the Precincts within, and over relationships to other Nations and Mankind outward, IS LIMITED BOTH BY THE ETERNAL NATURE, AND BY THE INALIENABLE RIGHTS, OF THE UNITS.

Nevertheless, in cases of conflict of authority, or of difference of opinion between Precinct, (or other lesser unit,) and Nation, the former must of course yield to the latter. For, although *in principle* the Units are equal,—Precinct, and so on, to Nation,—yet in doubtful cases the *practical* decision must be allowed to the superior power. This has been shown in the Introduction, under the head of "Resemblances to Gravitation." Therefore all the lower ones must give way before the unions of many Nations, whenever such unions are formed; but still, each retains its own share of eternal *rights*, inalienable and indefeasible, as any other of the elements. The lesser elements can not be deprived of their rights avowedly or upon principle, but only by mistake, or by the *necessities* of arriving at definite conclusions. The case is somewhat the same as between man and wife; both have equal rights; yet as there must be somebody to decide in doubtful cases, that right is conceded to the man, but only to be exercised honestly and faithfully.

Our doctrine as to the Rights of a Nation may be summed up thus:—the sovereignty of the Nation consists, as to Precincts, Corporations, Individuals and Families, not in superior rights but in superior power; but with the right of judging in doubtful cases of jurisdiction; and on the other hand,—in reference to the Unit above it, namely, Mankind, the Nation has only its rights as one of the Essential Units,—*all* being subject to their *peculiar* conditions of *position* and locality.

These peculiar conditions of position however, are sometimes very important. Thus, a few miles of ocean near the land belongs to the Nation, not to the adjacent Precinct. So Mining Districts, also Large Cities, and what are called "States" (see Bk. II. Pt. II. Chaps. XI. and XII.) must hold a part, at least, of their rights, as fiefs of the Nation, and so far be in direct subjection to IT.

The Nation, mainly, is the power of negation to the Precincts, just as Mankind is to the Nation. Yet the Precinct acts on all below or derivative from it, just as much positively as negatively. But the relation of these is sufficiently treated under Precinct, and need not be enlarged upon now.

The rights of a Nation would be well set forth by Spencer's *general theory* of government, supposing the Nation first to have been subdivided into Precincts, and the Precincts to have had constitutionally granted to them, their real share of rights as set forth in our theory on that subject. But the theory of the *do-nothing* and *no-power* of government, is utterly untenable in any small government, or among any ordinary set of men living in close neighborhood. And the theory itself, as set forth by him, exhibits plainly the facts of its origin in a large strong and consolidated government over a free and practical people. It endeavors to maintain the consolidated nature of government, by entirely denying rights and duties that are absolutely essential to *every* small or immediate *local* government. In these respects Spencer's view is diametrically opposite to Comte's: so that each one's theory contains a large amount of truth and wisdom, when we know to what field to apply it.

Inasmuch as Precinct is a Unit of society as truly as Nation, it follows that the general principles of nationality and internationality, are applicable to Precinct, as truly as to Nation, but in a less degree. Hence, the reader, in going through this part of the work, is requested to bear that relation in mind; and to observe that we are pointing out *principles* that are equally as applicable to Precinct, but in a *less* degree, and in regard to a *different* class of affairs. Because Precincts bear the same relationship in form and law, to the Nation, that Nations bear in spirit to Mankind. And then again, the Precinct, being the next lower Unit to Nation, and being the only other one which is Local, and being with it also fundamentally a political Unit, —is pre-eminently the type and guide for National arguments and National ideas.

The rights and duties of the Nation, and indeed of any organ or department of Civil Government, in relation to the Individual, the Family, the Social Circle, the Precinct and the Corporation, are better considered under those five heads respectively, than in this place. But the best place to consider them, in our classification, is under our head CIVIL GOVERNMENT, in the SYNTHETICS; under which head, controversies between Nation and particular Precincts should be provided for, whilst of a peaceful character. Controversies of a warlike nature, are provided for under Nation, in Birth and Size of Nations, and in Rebellions,—which will be treated presently. The relations to

Mankind will also be considered presently; next the general relations of one Nation to another, and to ITS citizens, namely, International Law; and afterwards the Doctrine of Naturalization.

Some countries are cursed with a deficiency of nationality, and some with an excess of it. Guizot, (p. 309), speaking of Greek Civilization, says: "The Greek who carried the individual culture of man to so high a pitch, knew not how to establish the social relations on a *solid* basis, nor to organize a national body, nor to combine the peoples subjected to his influence, into a *system* of Nations strongly united together. I wish for no other proofs than that terrible Peloponnesian war,—that fratricidal struggle, from which dates the decline of Greece, and the lamentable history of the Empire of Alexander and his successors." And we may add, that what distinguished the Peloponnesian war from the domestic war in the United States, was not only the length of time of the former, but also the fact that it was *not* so concluded as to settle any great principle, nor to establish any great policy.

On the other hand, there is sometimes an excess of nationality. Nationality is made the basis and instigation of most wars. The idea constitutes the strongest intrenchment and the highest glorification, for the hidden selfishness and the secret animosities of Mankind. Under its sacred veil, as also under the delusive garb of fanatical religions, human beings have, for ages, turned the worst passions of a fallen nature, into honorable and worshipful attributes. The time we hope must come, when patriotism as usually understood,—rallying for one's country merely because it is one's OWN country,—will be accounted with that narrow-minded selfishness, that rallies for section or party or society or Family or even person, because it is one's *own*. But the time has *not yet* come. It cannot come, unless on conditions of mutuality, and by or with new national brotherhood-views and feelings, in several of the leading Nations; and thus make a new clause in international law. It is the peculiar function of Christianity to cause this metaphysical organ, Patriotism, to be re-absorbed, and more and more to disappear from being an *exclusive* organ of nationality. This it does, partly by furnishing a renewed spirit to Individuals, and partly by diverting a portion of the vitality of patriotism, to other elements, say to Precincts, Corporations, and Mankind.

§ 2. *Duties of Progress.*

Here; just between the general rights of the Nation, in regard to all the other elements of Social Science,—and the special and superior rights of Mankind,—may be placed, as partaking partly of the nature of both of those departments,—the present topic, namely, the duties of a Nation *to progress;* and especially *not* to retrograde: for these are duties which it owes alike to all the Individuals, Families, and other internal elements which it contains; as well as to all its surrounding and related Nations.

For instance. If any serious attempt were made to reinstate slavery in the United States, it would arouse a universal cry of horror throughout the civilized world: and would probably soon lead to a great war; foreign Nations also joining in it, for the sake of mingled policy and humanity.

The interventions of civilized Nations, in the affairs of the uncivilized, and semi-civilized, are justifiable rather upon grounds of the uncivilized tending to retrogression, than upon any other grounds. For, when the less civilized ones come into frequent intercourse with the more civilized, the former lose their barbarian virtues, and retrograde, unless they adopt our higher developments and thus progress. This explains the European interventions in Asiatic affairs, as of Turkey, China, &c., and also in African affairs. The justification is, their aim to check slavery,—to check despotism, now being used chiefly to prop up their falling religions,—and to check their general retrogression towards barbarism.

These also are the real reasons which justify most of the usual protectorates, and armed interventions, of some Nations, in favor of others. These are the reasons which justify the protectorate of Europe over Greece, and of the United States over Mexico, and over various other American states; namely the protectorate which is embodied in the Monroe-doctrine.

Very different justifications are of course generally *alleged*, and often believed in: and especially often is alleged the old doctrine about "Balance of Power." But if this were the chief reason, it would be expressed in a claim to force all Nations to modify themselves, so as to become as nearly equal in size and strength, as human Individuals, or Families are, each to each. The demand for retaining the balance of power, when there is NO balance, must necessarily mean merely a demand that no one shall increase itself, or its influence: but that absurdity has never been attempted. The real chief reason, more probably has been, that the grasping Nations were the physical ones, the least civilized of Europe, and were tending to retrogression, and to forcing that retrogression upon other Nations. In regard to this subject, Wheaton § 62, says,—"questions of the greatest difficulty arise, which belong rather to the *Science of Politics* than of public law,"—(that is, they belong especially to our Department, namely, Social Science). And again, § 63, "Encroachment * * * overt acts * * * ambitious purpose," &c. "Such were the grounds of the confederacies created, and the wars undertaken, to check the aggrandizement of Spain, and the house of Austria, under Charles V. and his successors;" But everybody knows the really retrograde moral and religious impetus, which was the most active and most dreaded element of those wars. Thus again Wheaton § 63, says, "The repeated interference of Austria and Spain, in favor of the Catholic faction in France, Germany, and England; and of the Protestant powers to protect their persecuted brethren in Germany, France, and the Netherlands, gave a peculiar coloring to the political transactions of the age." We may also add, that the same principles underlaid and justified Cromwell's European policy.

But it is *not* hereby *assumed*, nor is it necessary to prove, that the real grounds for foreign intervention, were always justifiable, nor always consisted of sound principles in Ethics, or in Theology. All that is necessary to assert is, that the peoples believed them so to be; or thought there was some reasonable probability that they did so consist. For instance, referring to the French revolution of '89; Wheaton § 64, says, "The successive coalitions formed by the great European monarchies, against France, subsequent to her first revolution in 1789, were avowedly designed to check the progress of her REVOLUTIONARY PRINCIPLES, and her military power." And we add that there would have been little reason to fear or check that military power, had it not been really and chiefly animated by the desire, to spread throughout Europe, those revolutionary principles, which out of

France and at that time, were generally believed to be ruinous to all interested, sovereigns and peoples alike.

And so, in regard to the British Opium-War in China; and to her wars in India. The British and other commercial peoples *thought*, that the progress of commerce forbade such retrograde policies as China and India were constantly inclined to follow. But in Japan, and the Sandwich Islands, and elsewhere, where the native policy has been persistently progressive, and seeking to catch up with the civilization of the age, no wars have been inaugurated.

Poland was partitioned, really because it had an active tendency to retrograde towards barbarism.

Ireland was conquered by, and has still to be retained under special control by England, chiefly because it had and still has, the same retrogressive tendency.

Bismark's policy, although subversive of the old talk about "Balance of Power," has been sustained by the sympathies of the most advanced Nations of the world; because his policy is abreast of this age of progress. But he is overdoing the centralizing work, and is subverting the Precincts of which Germany consists, and which have been the bulwark of freedom and thought, for ages. And therein lies his danger. Yet still perhaps those who have a nearer, and inside view of the threatening dangers, may know that his policy of centralization is necessary temporarily. "And necessity knows no law."

All the great powers of Europe, have acquired accessions of territory during the last century, at times, without producing serious objections, or war;—particularly and lately, France, Italy, Germany, and Russia. The great war against Russia (about Turkey), was partaken in *only* by England and France, and by them chiefly because they really coveted various parts of the Turkish dominions for themselves:—and as one incidental reason, because those dominions contain Palestine; for the old hankering for Palestine, which kept up the great Crusades for several centuries, is not entirely dead yet. Moreover Russia baffles England in India; and is so much greater than any of the other powers, that they naturally may have special fears from her. And the ruling dynasty in France, sometimes engages in foreign war, to entertain and divert her people at home.

But no Nation has ever thought of warring against Russia merely because of her immensity, although one fifteenth of the population of the Earth: nor against China, *for that reason*, although being one third of the Earth's population. Russia, although warlike, is progressive and emancipatory. She has neither needed a great war, to bring her to her senses; nor exhibited general enormities arousing the sympathies of the civilized world against her. She also allows great freedom to her Precincts. But the time may come, when the Nations will fear her: yet the first Napoleon's prophecy was so premature, as to be almost absurd: for he thought nothing about the great functions of her Precincts—because Precincts make a weak government for aggression; although a strong one for defence.

The principles elucidated in all this § 2, ought to aid in forming a right idea about the present affairs of Spain. Spain became a Republic, wise, peaceable, not disturbing other Nations, and attending well to her own affairs. But a reaction has come. The Republic has gone down. And now the question is, shall the thousands of Individuals and Families and Precincts, of Spain, who have learned what civil, moral, and religious liberties are, be forced back against their enlightened consciences, into a darkness and servility that would now render them miserable?

Rights once given should not be taken away. The first and eternally right plan, therefore, is to adopt a true Precinct-system; and thus to allow the citizens of all the various different opinions, religious and political, to arrange themselves spontaneously, into the political and religious associations that, they conscientiously believe will make them happy. And the Nation itself should pay the expenses of their removals, thus made necessary by its own changeable policy. But if the Nation will *not* do that; nor even allow the people to rearrange themselves into their own Precincts at their own expense (which doubtless they would only be too glad to do),—then somebody or something may be held accountable for such tyranny and oppression. Shall the accountable thing be held to be the Form of the Civil Government;—or the Religion?

If the form of government is to be held accountable, then all the monarchies of Europe are interested, and have right to intervene, in some manner, to rescue their own form of government, from such disgrace. If the religion is to be held accountable, then all the liberal Catholics of the world, are interested to rescue their religion from such disgrace: and the unrelenting Catholics, with the dark-age spirit, if there be any such in these days, and if they aid and encourage such unlimited retrogression,—should be held morally accountable; and might be denied what would otherwise be their religious powers in other countries. How can Catholics ask for division of school funds in Protestant countries, when the countries of their own faith, drive out and persecute Protestants; and if, as by our *supposition* above, it is not the Civil Government that is to be held accountable, but only the religion? The Catholic church is a world-wide CORPORATION, and as such can be held accountable for its doings, when it is admitted that the affairs are its doings: just as truly as any Nation can be held accountable.

But however little or much that Corporation is to be held accountable for the retrogressions in Spain, *that* does not exculpate the Civil Government thereof: because *that* is the Arm of power which is *actually* doing and executing all this mischief. Governments therefore have a right to urge on Spain, the establishment of some humane relief: and first of all, some true system of Precincts, as may be most according to her own peculiar nationality. Or does the right of other Nations to intervene, consist only and selfishly in the measure of danger which they can *perceive* to threaten themselves, by or from the reaction? The smothered cry of the most advanced peoples of the world, is, that the reaction and retrogression ought to be *limited* and restrained, by the importunities, the protests, the non-intercourse, and if need be, by the arms of those who believe in war,—of the free peoples of the world.

The only other alternative, and the *least* that the rights of the human race, Mankind, or human nature, can demand, is, that Spain should allow all her dissentient citizens, a free emigration, after plenty of time to dispose of their property; and furthermore, that Spain will pay the expenses of their migration, and all reasonable charges and *damages* for the injury her policy is doing to them. In other words, the least that can be demanded for those oppressed by a Nation, is about what should be demanded for the oppressed of a Precinct; but also a little *more;*

namely, damages, because an emigration *entirely* from one's native country, is a much greater damage, injury, and unhappiness, than merely from one's Precinct.

§ 3. *Rights in Relation to Mankind.*

No position can be more untenable, than the claim for immunity of individual Nations, which some writers advocate. If any Nation, abounding in coal or iron, or other necessary article; possessing superabundance of wealth, with "interest" at very low rates, with labor unemployed or doubly taxed; leading the fashions of the world with extravagant and constant fluctuations, so that nothing but swift transportation would answer for any commodities,—if any such Nation should arise and fall under the combined control of its shipping and mining capitalists, the result would be long continued and fearful waste to the world, of the limited commodities, iron and coal. At the same time, the iron-working people of that Nation, owning no land, and at the mercy of the combination, might be grossly demoralized in general, and finally forced to emigrate to other countries. In such a case, the right of Mankind to intervene cannot be disputed,—if they know not better than by war,—then by war,—if they know better,—then by legislation, and discriminations, laid directly against the offending Nation, its trade, its literature and its emigration.

Or, again: if any Nation should persist in maintaining immense standing armies, after all other Nations wished to disarm,—such persistence would force all the neighboring Nations, either, to continue to maintain all their armies idly, or else to discriminate by legislation, and perhaps finally to use their armies once for all, effectually, on the warlike nuisance whose threatening attitude persisted in retarding the civilization and peace of the world.

The rights which Nation once had as the *representative* of Mankind, are passing away to empires and confederacies. But these latter cannot, according to our theory, be permanent, because the next and only Unit above them is Mankind; nor can they eventuate in an organization of Mankind into ONE permanent government; because *that* is the function of Jesus Christ only, for His visible return and reign on earth. And the idea of one confederation of compulsory government for all Nations, previous to His reign, seems to us even more chimerical than the idea of one consolidated *church;* because the church is an organ of only *one* class of interests and feelings, but Civil Government is an organ of all classes of interests and feelings.

It was a bold thought of Charles Goepp in his essay headed "E pluribus unum,"—that this United-States-Government would one day embrace all the Nations of the earth. This thought, although not admissible in that application, is well worth considering in the *principle.* But as to the *confederability* of all the world in one representative body, IF it could be shown to be *practicable,* it would do something toward showing that a confederation thereof is natural and probable. And from this difficulty we may infer that confederations are not to be permanent, but only transitional to the higher Unity. And there might be a *number* of world-wide conventions which would represent various Corporations for various interests; but hardly any *one* Civil Government especially for Localities.

Of the various grades of government possible, the following calculation of maximums is suggested. Assuming, as we have elsewhere done, that 2500 is the largest number of persons that can properly and conveniently assemble for the performance of political functions, whether for primary voting, or for representative legislation; and supposing that number to be the highest that can conveniently do the primary voting in a Precinct of thirty thousand inhabitants, that is to say, supposing twelve persons to each voter, then we would have the following series:—

Precinct, Population, - - - -	30,000
Nation, - - - - - - - - -	75,000,000
Third Grade, - - - -	187,500,000,000
Fourth Grade, - -	486,750,000,000,000

The second grade here, gives the highest maximum desirable for any Nation. The third grade here, would be able to answer for the political organization or confederation of the whole Earth, with a population of 4½ Individuals per acre of the land (exclusive of the waters); and that is a density about as great as can possibly subsist upon it, by any known methods. The fourth grade would represent a population of 11,000 per acre, or 2 persons of the present size to a square yard of land; that is to say, *only* just room for all to lie down on.

Any Nation, being resolved into the higher kinds of political Corporations, and supposing the Corporations within the Precincts, to be transposable into four uniform and homogeneous classes,—would be susceptible of four times the population above given, namely 300 Million, or one-fourth the present world; and the Third Grade would represent a population of 18 to the acre.

On the other hand, some writers think that an assembly ought not to consist of more persons than can meet together and converse, without straining either the voice in speaking, or the ear in hearing; say 300 persons each. Then the grades would be thus. First grade 3600 population. Second grade 1,080,000. Third grade 324,000,000. Fourth grade 97,200,000,000. Thus the fourth grade would be about half as much as the third grade, on the first named supposition. And the introduction of homogeneous Corporations would proportionally increase the possible numbers.

CHAP. III. RIGHTS IN RELATION TO CONFEDERATIONS.

§ 1. *Right to form Confederations.*

The whole subject of confederations is generally placed as a part of international law; but the position most of it occupies in relation to our Unit, Mankind, requires us to locate most of it here. Nationality is the only elementary civil and state power, that as yet has represented, or can represent directly, the interests of Mankind. But, up to this time, Nationality, through international law, has not been much exercised in that use, beyond the matter of lessening wars, and promoting commerce in physical things. The true representative of Mankind, at present, is Confederation. But this is only temporary, and transitional to something higher; moreover, confederations themselves are not permanent, as Nations are, nor as Mankind (metaphysically speaking) is conceived as being.

Confederations between Nations may be defined to be, the ASPIRATIONS of Mankind toward political unity,—toward one law and one government. And international law is the *legal* expression of *some* of those aspirations.

What directly and practically distinguishes a Nation, (even when organized into military Precincts or feudal system), from a Confederation, is, that the latter acts on the people only

THROUGH its constituent local parts, namely, through the Nations,—but the Nation acts on its people directly, as truly as the Precincts do, because it is an instinctive Unit as well as they.

A combination of two or more Nations into one, with the INTENTION or desire of being PERMANENT, constitutes a confederacy (or confederation): and if the confederacy is to be governed by a hereditary monarch, it is called an Empire. Mr. Mulford (in "The Nation,") regards a confederacy as consisting of a union between "commonwealths" [or Precincts] *only;* ignoring the fact that a confederacy is based upon the assumption that its component commonwealths are *independent* states, and therefore are self-dependent Nations, in principle; and it expressly disavows the idea of the confederacy itself being the Nation. Confederacies therefore commit the equally great mistake, of establishing a theory of government upon one unit or one integer only, and ignoring an equally important unit. We have the Confederacy ignoring Nation, and Mulford ignoring Precinct. Mr. Mulford also argues against the right of real Nations to form confederacies. This he argues by confusing confederacy with Empire, and arguing against the advantages of unions, because the government of such unions has usually been hereditary and vested in an Emperor.

Our argument here however, does not fully discuss the merits of the question, of the right or expediency of Nations to form confederacies; but merely discusses that confusion which only conceives of a union between Nations, as an Empire, overlooking the possibility of such a union being a popular and elective government. And it is the confusion consequent therefrom, of applying the word confederacy, to a union between Precincts only, to which we are *now* objecting. Mr. Mulford's book is a lamentable instance of great principles of eternal truth, being deflected, in order to apply to the narrow exigencies of some one good cause—of a good cause, namely, the nationality of the United States, upholding it by fearful perversions of fundamental social principles. Although his book is in many respects, a highly valuable one, and has done good service in a good cause.

Mr. Mulford has an indistinct apprehension of the growth of the international confederative power, when (p. 254) he says: "Since the Nation has its vocation in a moral order, and its end in the realization of the destination of humanity in history; the Nations exist in an international relation, which has for its condition a moral relation; and the system of international laws is definitive of the moral order in which these relations come forth. The Nations, in the attainment of their necessary end, are constituted in a moral order. They cannot therefore, in the development of national life, remain in isolation and indifference. * * * As the relations consist in the moral order of history, their ampler expression will come, in the higher realization of the being of the Nation, in the moral order of history. * * * And as the Nation advances in the realization of its being, the science which has for its province the definition of the law of international relations, will become constantly the expression of a development in wider and more varied relations."

Again, (p. 256), he says: "In the realization of the being of the Nation in history, there will be manifest among Nations a deeper relationship. * * * It is therefore no dream, but the coming of a new life, which holds the prophecy and the realization of the fraternity of Nations. In the development of history, this relation is becoming more perfectly apprehended; and as Mankind recognizes more deeply the universal fatherhood, there is manifested in the Christendom of Nations, the Family of Nations."

Some of the foregoing phrases, as, "vocation in a moral order," "moral order of history," "attainment of their necessary end," "expression of development," "fraternity of Nations," "Family of Nations," are pretty much all *we* could ask either for Nations, or for Precincts; and show the common or similar relations between them; and that the same may be represented in international law, as we said under Precinct.

The true doctrine is, that the right of Nations to form moral and useful confederacies, is as eternal as the right of Individuals to enter into partnerships; but the confederacies themselves are not eternal in their nature; for, if they were permanent in their nature, and permanently voluntary, they would cease to be called confederacies, but would really be Nations, and be called so. Because Confederations, Leagues and Empires, bear the same relation to the particular Nations of which they consist, as the Amalgams of neighboring Precincts, bear to the particular Precincts which compose them. The principles of this relation are treated under the head of Precinct. But Nations cannot be admitted to be capable of forming themselves into Corporations, nor *vice-versa;* because they are not elements of the Tribe-Principle.

By the term confederacies here, we of course understand, not confederacies between "States" or parts of a Nation, but between separate Nations. And our American states are shown by us, under Precinct, to be only a kind of higher Corporations, with double charters,—one, from the Precincts of which they are composed, and the other from the Nation.

§ 2. *Uses of Confederations.*

Nothing but confederation between the common sized Nations, can be any balance at all against the rising power of the empires. There is the Chinese Empire, containing $\frac{1}{3}$ of the population of the globe; and there is the Russian Empire, containing nearly $\frac{1}{15}$ of the population, and $\frac{1}{7}$ of the land of the globe. The power of such Nations, sometime will and must be felt disproportionately pre-eminent over all others, taken singly, or connected by only temporary and fluctuating combinations.

The trouble in empires, confederacies, and "unions" of different Nations, is, the attempt to make the fundamental constitutions of their parts, that is Nations, *uniform.* But, as Humboldt in his latest days said,—"to elevate the constitution of *one* Nation to the rank of an *ideal,* is to ignore the necessary historical modifications, and, to a certain extent, to call in question the importance of the *peculiar* development of every nationality. The English constitution especially, with all the conspicuous elements of freedom, which it may embody, is still essentially an insular, oceanic product, which can be only partially imitated by the Continental States, which are rather of volcanic origin."

One of the principal wants of modern times, is an international congress for the great and especial purpose of preserving the peace of Nations, and also for marine law, and for international affairs *not otherwise* agreed upon between any particular Nations.

The balance-of-power theory, was not anything better than an exhibition of instinctive fear against changes that necessarily are always being made, and so, was only a promoter of war. But it answered a temporary purpose, as an excuse, until men could see a better, for refraining from religious wars, and as a defence against wars for increase of territory. Yet it could not continue. But now, by constituting a world's congress, or one special organ for this one function alone, we reach a higher step in living civilization, and insure its greater success. As such a congress would depend, for the execution of its decisions, partly on their moral effect, all sagacity should be employed for its constitution. This sagacity will exhibit itself in relying, not on the form of selection, but on securing a fair representation of the real and actual powers of the world, or of its leading Nations, at the time. But it need not depend only on its moral power, nor even chiefly thereon, but may easily find a ready method for the enforcement of its decisions, without war. Declaration of partial or complete non-intercourse with those Nations who *would* actually resort to war, instead of submit to the congress's decisions, would soon bring the offenders to terms. This is the method which the congress of the United States so successfully used, instead of war, to bring Rhode Island into the Union, at the adoption of the constitution. In fact, non-intercourse is the usual resort of educated and refined society, towards bullies and fighters. We find it successful in Precinct and in Corporation government, as well as in that of Individuals.

As to the question whether such a congress ought to be permanent, intermittent, or remittent,—whether it ought to abide always in session, or only at intervals; and if the latter, whether the intervals should be regular; or whether it ought to be assembled only upon requisite occasions,—these are questions not essential to be settled at the first.

Perhaps still another plan might be employed for some purposes, namely, a st nding committee to act in the interim of the sessions, with some limited powers, and especially the power of convening the congress upon requisite occasions. For, of course it would not be safe to entrust the decisions of disputed international questions for immediate action, to any ordinary committee of such a congress. Such a standing committee with limited powers, is a constituent of some of the most perfectly organized churches. And in this matter we see another instance where the world might learn from the churches, even as to mere forms of government.

CHAP. IV. CONTIGUITY, PHYSICAL AND METAPHYSICAL.

The intercourse between Nations must vary according to their many essential differences. The greater difference which distance ought to make, is evident in this, that a Nation is bound to prevent, and may be held responsible for, incursions made from the borders of its own territory, into a foreign one immediately adjoining: but as to miscellaneous expeditions against distant countries, no Nation can be expected to do any thing more, than merely to use *reasonable* endeavors to prevent them. "Love thy neighbor as thyself" applies to Nations as well as to Individuals.

It can hardly be doubted, that distance, either as to space or as to civilization, requires a different set of international laws for persons nearest, than for those farthest off; just as our theory of Precincts has special regulations for those Precincts that are immediately contiguous. But such differences of international law, could only be made by treaties; and such treaties, oft repeated and long continued, would naturally become leagues, and these in time, confederations, especially where the Nations were contiguous.

Nations, as well as Precincts, tend ultimately to form each its own particular character; and LIKES flock together,—"*likes*" that is, inward resemblances, although perhaps outward contrasts.

As it is the tendency, that all the persons of a Family should gradually become assimilated, and like to each other, so also all the Individuals and Families of any society, are tending to become alike. So also, all the Individuals, Families and companies of a Nation, have a tendency to become more alike,—Individual to Individual, Corporation to Corporation, and Precinct to Precinct. Even the social sets which are organized purposely to express differences, gradually take the same *outward* resemblances of customs, &c., as far as means will permit. Furthermore, all the Nations of the world having commerce and intercourse, also are tending to resemblance or uniformity in their outward forms.

Through all this outward uniformity, we find that the stronger law, is an inward law, that *likes* flock together with like—that

Families tend to express one spirit, and draw together those who are similar. So also with Precincts, companies and social sets. So also with Nations; and in the course of time, and with free travel, immigration and emigration,—this segregation may be expected to continue, until all the communicating Nations of the earth, will become possessed more and more fully and firmly, each of its own peculiar life and inward character. Thus it is, that real heterogeneity develops out of homogeneity, as time advances.

In ancient times and among barbarians, the special national characteristics were formed by isolation and barbarism. And in modern times, we see each Nation forming its own peculiar national character, by the very opposite means, namely, by intercourse and civilization. In ancient times, the outward circumstances were mostly different, but the inward spirit mostly the same. In modern times, the outward circumstances,—all those things which can be seen, imitated and learned by rote, or by diagrams and models, are being imitated; and the Nations are thus becoming alike. But in the inward things of the heart, Nations as well as companies, social sets and Individuals, will become more and more *unlike some* others, and must be more and more attracted to those with whom they most sympathize. In some Nations, where the spirit of love and mutual regard for each other's rights, exist, much happy communism may develop; whilst in those Nations and peoples who are clamoring for equality and fraternity,—violating the relative duties of station ability and age, and puffing themselves up with pride and self-will, their desired communism and equality will not come; but instead thereof, all the vice and luxury that dishonest wealth can buy, after honest wealth is driven away; and all the results of refined enmities, when the peace men and the unimpeachable citizens, are driven, either into obscurity, or into foreign lands. The example of France is a warning to humanity.

CHAP. V. DEFINITION OF NATION.

No definition of the Nation can be accepted, which denies that "God hath made of one" continuous "blood," *at least many* "Nations of men," (Acts xvii. 26.) But some writers have carried out the radicalness of the idea of Nation, to the extent of supposing that nearly all of the many great Nations of Mankind, are indigenous, spontaneous developments, from the regions they inhabit; without allowing for the facility with which men change their abodes, and commingle nationalities; a facility which is well known in history, as well as on reflection might be expected. Even if we admit more than one original or spontaneous race, still under no supposable theory, can there be admitted to be more than three, or at most five, such original or spontaneous races.

Let us give here (chiefly from Twiss, vol. i. pp. 2 and 3), a definition of a Nation (People, or State)—which has an interesting history attached to it. Coming from Scipio Africanus, it is first quoted by Cicero (De Republica, i. 25.) This work, the "De Republica," was lost in antiquity, to the great regret of scholars and statesmen. But the definition therein, of a State, was preserved and transmitted by St. Augustine, in his great work, "The City of God." Indeed, those best able to judge, (including Cardinal Mai,) think that St. Augustine derived his first suggestions for his "City of God," from reading Cicero's "De Republica." From St. Augustine, Grotius derived the definition we are speaking of.—And now at last Cardinal Mai has found and deciphered from an old Palimpsest, a large part of the identical old Ciceronian "De Republica;" and among the saved fragments of which, is this very definition we are now to give.

Cicero gives it thus: "Therefore said Africanus, Public affairs are the affairs of the People; but not every collection (cœtus) of men, however congregated, (or aggregated), is a people; but the collection (cœtus) of the multitude, associated by consent of justice (juris, right, or law), and in the (communione) communism (fellowship) of utility."

St. Augustine adds: "Therefore surely, where that righteousness or right-ness (justitia), is not, *there* the collection of men is not associated by the consent of justice (juris, right, or law), nor in the (communione) communism (fellowship) of utility." (City of God, xix. 21.)

Grotius gives the definition thus: "The State (civitas) is the complete collection (cœtus) of free men, associated for the sake of enjoying justice (right or law), (causa,—juris) and of the common utility."

If the reader does not like the writer's translations, as above given, he can refer to the places in Twiss or elsewhere, and translate them for himself. Observe this much, however; as to the great *substance* of the ideas; that Scipio, Cicero, and St. Augustine, fully coincide in their representation of the definition; and that their words apply equally as well to a city, or a Precinct, or even to a Corporation, as to a Nation. And so does Grotius's *civitas*, although IT is usually translated State; and was by Grotius applied also to the free cities and small Precinct-States of Europe. One of Ainsworth's definitions of *civitas*, and his *first* one, is, "Corporation." But of course in the later Latin, *civitas* usually meant state or city, but it mattered not how *small* the state was, nor whether it was part of another state, or of an empire, or not: and the small ones answer to our "Precinct;" and the large ones, to our idea of Nation.

But, let us resume our attempt for a developed definition of Nation.

Recognition does *not* constitute the Nation. Mulford, agreeing with other writers on the Law of Nations (pp. 252 and 253), well says: "The sovereignty of the Nation has its immediate," (but only its "*external*) manifestation, in the *recognition* of Nations. It is the moment in which there is a conscious realization of the historical power of a people; and each (Nation) stands toward the other, in a recognized sovereignty of the world. * * * The Nation recognizes in another, that which it is conscious of possessing in itself, in its own necessary being. * * * This recognition presumes then, respect toward the Nation recognized as a Nation. It must concede to it the rights, which in its own necessary existence it asserts for itself. There is the application, here, of the fundamental law of rights,—*be a person, and respect others as persons.* This law is implied in the being of the Nation as a moral person; it is the necessary postulate of rights and of duties. From this, then, proceeds the recognized right of a Nation, to determine its own political end; the right to establish its own political form."

But "a people may exist with a manifest unity and sovereignty, and with entire independence and freedom, and be in reality a Nation; although it receive no recognition from other Nations. Whether it be *in reality* a Nation, is to be determined only by its content,— * * * but its recognition depends only upon the determination, in the judgment of another, whether it be a Nation." Here then, we may ask, how shall we determine just how much a Nation separating from its past, shall depend upon the recognition of that past, for the right of its separate nationality?—for its right "to be a person"?—And when doth arise the duty of that past, "to respect others as persons" in such a case? And how much depends on present qualifications alone?

Mulford, (p. 253) well gives the "content" of a Nation, or that by which its nationality is to be determined, as follows,—"the internal sovereignty which is manifest in law and freedom; and the external sovereignty which is manifest in independence and self-subsistence." Nevertheless, the latter condition is too much of a *de facto* and not enough of a *de jure* one, to serve as the basis of nationality in our Social Science. It is a condition which directly leads to the extremest war. For the existence of a "*moral* personality" we must seek moral conditions of justification; we must find those conditions, not in the mere fact of the birth, much less, in the violence of it, but in the moral legitimacy of it. We speak of this subsequently, under the heading "Birth and Size of Nations."

Mulford, (Index to Chap. I.) defining the "substance of the Nation," says—"The Nation is founded in the nature of man,—is a relationship,—is a continuity,—is an organism,—is a conscious organism,—is a moral organism,—is a moral personality." Furthermore, (in Index to Chap. IV.) he says: "The origin of the Nation is of Divine foundation,—in its moral being and personality,—in its government,—in its authority and powers,—in the facts which indicate the consciousness of the people,—in the facts which indicate the conscience of the people." This is all very true and excellent, but is equally true of the Precinct, and of the church, and sometimes of other Corporations perhaps.

Moreover, Mulford all through, confounds State with Nation; and this he does deliberately; for, he says in his Preface, p. viii.: "The words 'Nation' and 'State' are used synonymously." And, by him, "a particular State in the United States, is written 'State,' and is described as a commonwealth; as, the commonwealth of Massachusetts or Virginia," &c. He thus develops things and principles, that are equally as repugnant to the natural rights of Empires, Confederations, and Republican Unions, as to Precincts. By his centralizing theory, even the rights of the Individual and of Mankind are glossed over, and Social Circle is not thought of; and no basis remains but Family and Nation.

Neither Comte nor Mill, identify the Nation with either State or Government, but carefully avoid even the appearance of doing so. Comte's word usually is "Society," sometimes "Government." Mill's word is "Government." Yet both Comte and Mill overlook the distinct rights of Neighborhoods, as such, (i.e. Precincts.)

Wheaton does not commit the error of identifying State with Nation. Wheaton (§ 17) thus defines the State:—"Cicero, and, after him, the modern public jurists, define a State to be a body political, or society of men, united together for the purpose of promoting their mutual safety and advantage, by their combined strength. This definition cannot be admitted as entirely accurate and complete, unless it be understood with the following limitations:—It must be considered as excluding (such) Corporations, public or private, (as are) created by the State itself. * * * Nor can the name State be properly applied to voluntary associations of robbers or pirates, the outlaws of other societies. * * * A State is also distinguishable from an unsettled horde of wandering savages, not yet formed into a civil society. * * * A State is also distinguishable from a Nation, since the former may be composed of different races of men, all subject to the same supreme authority. * * * So, also, the same Nation or people may be subject to several States, as is the case with the Poles."

Thus Wheaton's idea evidently is, that the State is sometimes above the Nation, namely, in Empires and confederations, —that in all other cases, legitimate supremacy is what constitutes nationality. But the very word state, "status," standing, implies something having the quality of permanency, and therefore cannot rightly apply to confederacies.

When we come to Corporation, we shall find that IT can perform many of the functions of Nation, as well as that element can, and some of them better. Yet still, there will always remain some of the functions of Nation, that are not performable by any other element than itself. And this is true, also, of all the fundamental elements of the Analytics.

In our opinion, a Nation may be defined to be, one of the spontaneous, natural Elements or Units of human society; a governmental union of Individuals and Precincts, possessing or being distinguished by, most, if not quite all of the following characteristics. (1) One Head or Government. (2) Having the Government continuous, internally and historically, either direct or revolutionary. (3) Being apparently the development from one tribe, by similarity of Language, Customs, Religion, &c.: yet divided into several or many tribes. (4) Inhabiting contiguous Precincts or districts. (5) Having a Special Metaphysical organ or centre of attraction, called patriotism. (6) Having the *real* interests of all the parts, to consist in the maintenance of the national union. (7) Being distinguished from Confederacy or Empire, by having had a spontaneous, instead of a deliberative origin. (8) Being distinguished from Precinct or "State," by superiority or sovereignty over the other. (9) Being distinguished from Corporation, by having had an instinctive origin, and by *necessarily* embracing and referring to *all* the inhabitants of a Locality.

The point of the definition, is, that whilst every Nation will be found to contain NEARLY ALL of the characteristics mentioned, yet many Nations will be found to lack one or another of them; nevertheless the element lacking will be different in almost every case. This form of definition, we, in our inward thinking, often adopt in the higher realms of thought: because the *tout ensemble* of the thing defined, remains a "constant"; yes, so constant as not even to disappear in "differentiation."

CHAP. VI. REBELLIONS.

Whenever the forms of government become so perverted, that they essentially hinder the real *objects*, then rebellion becomes justifiable, if it is expedient. If the rebels have no reasonable ground to think themselves right, and if they are really rebelling for immoral or criminal purposes, then they are simply criminals or rioters. But if the rebels think they have reasonable grounds for their rebellion, then they should be treated as recognized "belligerents." But when rebels are justly entitled to be treated as belligerents, then arise two cases, as follows:

Case (1.) If the rebellion be an attempt to change the order of the government, the solution of its justifiability is the net average resultant of two questions, namely, the question of the amount of grievances, and the question of the power of the persons or parties aggrieved, because power is a right when no higher law intervenes.

Case (2.) If the rebellion be an attempt to separate from the Nation, then the two questions just mentioned, still come up, namely, the amount of the grievance, and the power of the parties aggrieved: but other questions also come into the solution. There is the necessity for, and certainty of, the birth and the arising of new Nations, during all the course of time, past, present and future: there is the probability that no such birth of a new Nation ever will take place upon the mere abstract grounds of its necessity, without having some grievance as the immediate ground of it: there is the certainty that the greater a Nation becomes, the less willing its rulers are to have it severed, and the greater is their power of evil, and the more severe they are apt to be, towards dissenters or rebels (excepting the severity when two religious *parties* are nearly equally balanced, and are determined "to war to the knife"): then again, there is the certainty that, as long as human nature continues sinful and imperfect, Nations cannot happily attain their maximum theoretical size, previous to division; charity must make allowances for the imperfections of both sides; and neither can the best nor the most competent rulers be obtained, for the largest possible governments, nor can peoples be made capable of submission to all, that charity might ask them to endure.

CHAP. VII. BIRTH AND SIZE OF NATIONS.

§ 1. *In General.*

Nations are begotten by three processes; one is, by outgrowth from one Family and tribe; another is, by the mingling together of elements from a plurality of Nations; and the third is, by direct separation into parts. The first process is the slow and gradual work of ages, and seems to have been nearly confined to antiquity. The second process has occurred only in a few cases, the principal of which are, the ancient English, and the modern citizens of the United States. The third process is like that in Zoology, termed by the physicists, *agamogenesis.*

Nations in a living progression must, ever and anon, be subdivided. This is the same law we saw operating in the case of Precincts, which are the chief types of Nations. The ever increasing population of the world, creates the necessity in both cases. The generation of all new *Local* political bodies, must be by actual spatial subdivision.

Just as in the case of Individual beings, (according to Spencer), we have two kinds of generation, *gamogenesis and agamogenesis ;*—that, in which fructification takes place indirectly, by means of germs or seed; and that, in which there is mere growth of parts, and then mere visible subdivision of parts. The generation of *Corporations* may be more or less by gamogenesis, so also is the generation of special organs, but the generation of the new *geographical* bodies, can only be by agamogenesis. Now, while both kinds of generation operate against growth, yet the agamogenesis has almost an indefinitely greater degree of such opposing force, than gamogenesis. (See Spencer's Biology, §§ 334 to 346). Hence by analogy we infer the necessity of national subdivision, in opposition to indefinite growth. The only questions are, *when* to divide, and by *what* means. Any person who is acquainted with history must know, that the present division of Nations is not eternal,—that in times back, there were fewer Nations than now, and that the antithesis between Growth and Generation has been confirmed by history; so that when the division has been prevented by force, the growth has been restricted; and when the growth has been left free, the division has occurred. The only questions therefore are, at what density of population to divide; and by what means, whether peace or war. (See above, and Mulford,—that recognition does not constitute th Nati

Our problem here is only to determine the *maximum* size of a Nation, taking its forms of government and all its relevant conditions, all of the most favorable kind. Hence, every item *less* favorable than the ones we are about to give, will, or *should,* justify subdivision at a *less* size than is found in our problem.

The maximum size of a legitimate Nation, depends partly

upon its form of government, and partly upon the average population and qualifications of suffrage in its Precincts, and partly upon local conditions.

§ 2. *Conditions of Population and of Politics.*

If there exist any form of popular representation in a Nation, not consisting of the higher Corporations, the size must be limited strictly by the average population and qualification of suffrage in the Precincts; because each Precinct ought to be entitled to send one representative, at least; and the whole number of representatives should not exceed 2500. These principles, applied, will give a population of from twenty to one hundred million as the utmost legitimate limit for a democratic Nation, under a system like that prevailing at present in the United States, or elsewhere; or practicable otherwise than by suitable political "Corporations" of the higher kinds.

What science points to in general formula, may be expected certainly, although it may not come exactly in methods that science anticipates, nor for this or that particular reason. Hence, patriots have no reason to suppose they can avert the results, by refusing to arrange into small Precincts; because, false divisions and false "State" corporations of five million, and all other unnatural methods, only hasten the evil results, through metaphysical or moral causes, the exact forms of which of course cannot be foreknown. And social science has no ability to look into the FAR distant ages beyond, to inquire if any other subdivisions may become necessary; because, as said in the Introduction and elsewhere, the science of society can never be very far in advance of society itself. And new subdivisions would bring their own evils, which only the science of their times can treat.

The only practicable method the writer can see, whereby it is possible to enable Nations to hold together, with larger populations than are mentioned above, is the adoption of some of the higher Corporation-systems proposed under that head. Possibly, Nations might grow to as much larger size than the foregoing representation of Precincts, admits, as the Precincts were divided into political Corporations of the higher kinds, UNIFORMLY; that is to say, the same number of Corporations, and on the same bases. But the practicable differentiation of such Corporations, seem to be only a limited few; consequently, the principle can only be expected to retard, but not absolutely prevent, national subdivisions.

§ 3. *Conditions of Locality.*

Again, the size of Nations depends not only on population, and political organization; but also on conditions of Locality; and on the relation of population and organization *to* Locality. The larger the total Locality, the less the coherence of the parts. Two kinds of condition of Locality enter into the question. One, is the total space included, namely, the actual number of square miles; for by it, the number of diverse interests and forms are increased, and the possibilities of population, also. Nevertheless, the other condition of Locality is quite as important, namely, the linear distances of the extremes. This is important both for military and for civil administration. Whether a country be 1000 miles long and 4000 wide, or whether 2000 miles in each direction, makes no difference in the total content; but it makes a vast difference in its adhesiveness,—the 4000 miles linear distance giving perhaps only one-tenth the cohesiveness.

But the linear condition becomes still more important, when its direction of latitude or longitude is brought into consideration. Because sameness of latitude, gives sameness of all the natural productions, and therefore produces rivalry in all the departments of industry. But linear direction along lines of longitude, giving differences of latitude,—so long as they are on only one side of and not too near to the equator, give differences of all the natural productions. These tend to produce the harmony of industry. Incidentally also, they produce other vastly important harmonies,—namely, the harmonies arising from interchanges for health, and for variety in study and in pleasure. Isothermal lines have nearly the same effects as lines of latitude.

§ 4. *Applications to the United States.*

The population of the United States is now (A.D. 1875) about forty million, and doubling in about 17 years: hence, about the year 1900, the population will probably have reached its utmost scientifically legitimate limits. Even the present forty millions is the highest limit, with our present political arrangements, and with universal male suffrage at 21 years of age. Science can give, except the higher political Corporations, only two alternatives here, either; to lessen the number of voters by increasing the age or other qualifications required; or to prepare to divide the country amicably, by formation of a new Nation,—of course not between North and South; dissimilar climates; and making territories three thousand miles long, and only five hundred broad,—but between East and West, making two, averaging about fifteen hundred long, by one thousand wide. All our extra stimulation to immigration, and all our hurry in "developing the resources of the Great West," are tending to this result. If you remove the seat of government west of, or even nearly to, the Mississippi; then when the division came, the West might claim to be the original trunk, and charge the East with seceding! The effort of the Westerners to move the Capital to the West, reminds us of the efforts of the Southerners to capture Washington. The tendency of increasing the numbers, races, classes or sexes that vote, is obviously in the same direction.

Although increasing the age required for suffrage, may retard the division for a generation or two, and our "Corporation"-system, retard it much longer; nevertheless, the result seems certain to come, sooner or later. Nor is it to be denied that not only the good methods we propose, but also overwhelming despotic power in the central government, might for a time continue to hold the Union FORCIBLY together. But the evils of such a despotism would probably be far greater than its good.

Improvement in public and private morality would also help us. Because there is no doubt, that our increase of population, and our increase of *spread* in distant localities, faster than Social Science is able to provide for, or morality to purify,—are the great causes of our Southern, and Indian and Mormon wars, and of the general demoralization both private and official.

These truths all combine to prove, that those ambitious persons, who, in neglect of the true conditions, are working so hard to "develop the resources of the Great West," and roll a tide of immigration thither, are "cutting their own throats," as Union citizens, and hastening the very dissolution they say they are endeavoring to prevent. The fear of vast solitudes of forest and plain, seceding!—What an idea!

Some writers are so *full of hunting eternal or absolute arguments, to maintain the* justice of our *late* war against the Confederates, and are so full of palaver about the *absolute* indivisibility of a Nation; that they seem to have entirely forgotten that less than a century ago, "*our own Nation*" was only a *province* of the Nation of Great Britain!—and that we have acquired a large proportion of our own territories, by purchase and by conquest from other Nations. And such writers seem to have no conception of the difficulties which their theories, could they be believed, might produce, to Great Britain's giving us Jamaica, or Canada; or Spain's giving us Cuba; and so on. And if their views are sound, neither purchase nor treaties nor conquest, could make a just or morally obligatory transfer of territory.

Most great Nations have repeatedly practiced on the principle, of dividing their own or other Nations. And our Nation has repeatedly acted on the principle that other Nations have a right to divide; why then should not our national constitution, as a matter of theory, acknowledge the same right? Our constitution grants the right of its "States" to subdivide, on certain conditions; and can it be that the superior power has really less right than the inferior, in matters for which it is the *legitimate organ?* The only peaceable method at present provided, is an alteration of the constitution itself: but even that would be disputed by the advocates of certain higher laws of nationality. True, the time is far away yet for a proper division: but constitutions ought to look far ahead; and one of the good ways to preserve a union peaceably, is to make a separation *legally possible*, and thus let men feel they are not held altogether by force. When will Mankind learn, that not in religion only, but in all the deeper interests and affections, force is not the best reliance, nor legal inability the best promoter of contentment? And our object in treating this subject, is to promote the means which will really tend to preserve the Union.

§ 5. *Provisions for Peaceful Subdivision.*

The principal means for introducing the Christian process of subdividing in peace order and friendship, are, firstly, Social Science, and secondly, written constitutions.

The works on SOCIAL SCIENCE or International Law, which omit to recognize and provide for the necessity of the peaceful subdivision of Nations,—are as far behind the age's *wants* in Social Science, as the old statesmen, who think all disputes between Nations must be settled by the sword, are behind the age's wants in moral and religious science. The scientific provision for such subdivisions, when they become necessary, is one of the incidental lessons to be derived from our idea of the nature and origin of Nation, as set forth in the previous part of this subject.

The remainder of the topic about the subdivision, contains *no theoretical* difficulties, but only the practical difficulty and "unpleasantness" of blood and war. Because, if subdivision can only be accomplished by war, then the doctrine that rebels are to be treated as "belligerents," brings them always under the principles of international law, since they have then to be considered as Nations "pro tem.," no matter how unjust or unreasonable their attempt at separation might be.

From what is above said, it is inferable that the usual arguments are unsound, which, against subdivision, plead such ideas as the Nation's right of eminent domain, or its right of the person, as against expatriation, and all those other minor kinds of rights usually treated under international law. Such pleas are unsound,—because they all belong to a minor department of the science; and during an acknowledged "belligerent" rebellion, are all held also in suspense, as only "pro tem."; and then are all revoked "per se," by the success of a revolution having subdivision for its object.

These views seem highly proper to be expressed now, because nothing hinders the good cause of our national Union more than specious but unsound arguments for it,—and especially, such arguments as would go to show that this or any other increasing Nation, must continue ETERNALLY undivided.

What remains for science to accomplish, is, to dispel the superstitions, ghosts and hobgoblins, about the subdivisions of Nations, and to provide for their *peaceable* accomplishment, in and by the recognized constitution of each Nation respectively, and by the doctrines of international law DE JURE. And *vice-versa:*—And this is the beauty of science. It is a good rule, "it works both ways." The ascertainment, beforehand, of the true principles and grounds of the subdivision of Nations, preserves society from premature and unnecessary divisions, and from the vain attempts thereunto; and places such unnecessary divisions, or the vain attempts thereunto, in the category of *seditions*, to be recognized as such by international law, and all the world over.

PART II.

INTERNATIONAL LAW.

CHAP. I. PRELIMINARIES OF INTERNATIONAL LAW.

§ 1. *Classifications.*

Most of what has been said already, on *the Nation* as a Fundamental Element, is applicable to this part of the subject, but need not be repeated; the relations to Mankind, particularly so. And these latter relations will be further considered, when we come to that Element of Social Science. Corporations also have relations to the subject:—because their full benefits cannot be obtained without some modifications of international law: and also because each is type of the other reciprocally; namely, Nation is type of Corporation, and Corporation is type of Nation; and because the reciprocal relations of Corporations, under our proposed system, would be necessarily more *intimate*, and more similar to international relations, than even our inter-precinct ones,—and would therefore call for a more complete development and accurate statement, of international law, as type for inter-corporation law, than even the inter-precinct relations did. And so on the other hand, the inter-corporation law would throw light upon, and develop and improve, international and inter-precinct law.

This our Part II. of Nation, being a brief treatment of International Law, may be prefaced by saying, that since it was written, Mr. Field's valuable work upon the subject has been published; and to it the reader is referred. Let us introduce our treatment of the subject, by giving the classifications and outlines, from three long established works; the first, French; the second, English; the third, American,—namely, Vattel's, Twiss's, and Wheaton's: slightly modifying the classifications however, in order to perspicuity and homogeneity. For the sake of these modifications, and perhaps also for the sake of saving the trouble of references; the reader will pardon the selection of such familiar matter.

Vattel's work, although old, is perhaps the most interesting and generally instructive, of any work on the subject extant. Although, like the other old works, it contains a considerable amount of matter which belongs to other and very different departments of Social Science.

Vattel divides the subject, about as follows. (I.) Preliminaries.—(II.) Nations considered in themselves.—(III.) Nations considered relatively to Other Nations.—(IV.) Of War.—(V.) Restoration of Peace :—And of Embassies.

(I.) *Preliminaries.* Idea and General Principles of the Law of Nations.

(II.) *Nations considered in themselves.* State-Sovereignty and its modifications. A Nation's duties to Itself. The constitution of a State. The Personal sovereign. The succession of the sovereign. Objects of a good government:—(1) To provide for necessities;—agriculture;—commerce;—highways and artificial watercourses;—money and exchange:—(2) Individual and general felicity;—piety and religion; justice and polity:—(3) Self-defence;—national glory;—protection from or submission to other Nations;—vacant countries. Public and Private Property. Alienation of Domain. Rivers and Lakes. The Sea.

(III.) *Nations considered relatively to other Nations.* General duties of humanity. Mutual commerce. Dignities and Equality of Nations. Preservation of their security. Mutual justice. Regard for Individual citizens. The Domain. Rules as to Foreigners. Changes from the primitive communism. Modifications of the right of Domain. Usu-caption and Prescription. Public Treaties. Other Public Agreements and Conventions. The Faith and Obligation of Treaties. Sureties therefor. Interpretation of Treaties. Termination of Disagreements.

(IV.) *Of War.* In General. Means and Officers of War. The Just Causes. Declaration of War: and War in form. The Enemy and his property. His Allies and Subsidies. Of Neutrality. What is right to do in War. Of Unjust War. The Voluntary Law recognizes both parties as having an equally just cause. Acquisition and Conquest. Individuals in time of War. Conventions and Agreements in time of War. Civil War.

(V.) *Restoration of Peace: and of Embassies.* Peace and the obligations thereto. Treaties of Peace;—Formation, Observance, and Breach thereof. Embassies, Ministers, and Ambassadors.

Twiss's works divide the subject as follows:—

(I.) The Rights and Duties of Nations in time of Peace. —And (II.) The Rights and Duties of Nations in time of War.

(I.) *The Matters of Peace* are divided thus. Nations as subjects of Law. Incidents and modifications of international Life. National State-systems of Christendom, and of Mahometandom. Sources of the Law of Nations. Right,—of Self-preservation:—of Acquisition:—of Possession:—of Jurisdiction:—of the Sea:—of Legation:—of Treaty.

(II.) *The Matters of War* are divided thus. Settlement of International Disputes. War and its Characteristics. Commencement of War. Rights of a Belligerent within Enemy-territory. Rights of a Belligerent on the High Seas. On Blockade. On Contraband of War. On the Enemy-characteristic. On Capture and its Incidents. Privateers. Rights and Duties of Neutral Powers.

Wheaton's work divides the subject somewhat as follows:—

(I.) Scope.—(II.) Absolute Rights.—(III.) Relative Rights.

(I.) The Scope comprises, the Definition, Sources, and Subjects of international law. The Subjects are Nations, and Sovereign States; which are described as two different classes of Subjects.

(II.) The Absolute International Rights, comprise, Self-Preservation and Independence; Legislation, civil and criminal; Equality; and Property. And Property includes both the right of a State to own for itself, and the right to rule over the property of its citizens.

(III.) The Relative Rights, comprise Legation; Negotiation; War; and Peace. And War may be considered, either as to its Immediate consequences; or as to its Subsequent ones; and, in its relations, to Citizens,—to Enemies,—and to Neutrals.

Now, regarding the various works of writers on this and on other departments of "Law," and considering the distinctions they continually draw, in the courses thereof, as well as the main classifications which they make,—we find that the subject *might* be divided in all the following several different

17

ways:—after allowing, in all cases, some one head for General topics not classible under any other. Moreover, perhaps there might be, in every classification, a place also for matters whose position was doubtful; but this we only suggest. We might however divide into:—

Absolute, and Relative rights:—

Public, and Private rights:—

Rights of Persons,—Rights of Things:—

Natural, and Positive Laws:—

Principles depending on Locality, and Principles abstract from Locality:—

Internal, and External Affairs:—

Affairs in Peace, and Affairs in War.

At any rate, all these distinctions ought to be discussed, and applied to the subject, in the GENERAL Part of any *thorough* work on it; which of course, our little article makes no pretension whatever, to be.

The classification we have adopted for the present essay, is as follows:—

FIRST: The Preliminaries of International Law.

SECOND: The Most General International Laws.

THIRD: Affairs in Peace.

FOURTH: Affairs in War.

And of these again, we make only a few brief subdivisions, which will appear in their proper places; and we introduce, in due course, some of the antitheses above mentioned. The reader will observe, that our *General* classification, differs from all the others, principally in this, that ours provides *one* general head, for all such matters as should properly be gathered together under the term, Most General International Laws. The *minor* differences of our classification, from the others, can only be made plain, by comparing with them, our heads, as they will arise in the course of our treatment. And if we succeed in selecting the most salient points of the subject, and in condensing and generalizing them sufficiently and clearly, we shall have accomplished the utmost that we can hope in this field, —a field which is not peculiarly ours, and has been so ably and diffusively treated by many writers.

There is no difficulty in applying all these principles of classification, except War, to the relations between Precincts also. Indeed, these principles, for the most part, and dropping formalities, obviously appertain to every form or division of *Local* government, from Empires down to townships, each to each.

In other places, we have suggested that this subject ought to be considered in such an *order*, and by the consideration of such general principles, as would in the main, apply to Inter-PRECINCT relations, and also to Inter-Corporation ones, as well as International; and at the same time, point out the differences between them. Because, much of what we propose on this subject, especially what relates to *neighboring* Nations, is equally applicable in principle, to the regulations between Precincts established according to our theory: and excepting matters of Locality, is also equally applicable to our proposed Governmental Corporations. We therefore need to dwell on this subject of international law, at some length; yet, can spare but little space for it, except so far as it is connected with some one or other of our special theories: and, *rejecting discussions about official persons, or diplomatic or other* FORMS; *rejecting also, technicalities, "positive" or arbitrary regulations, and other details*, aside from general principles more interesting to the general reader. Indeed, the great want of the age, in regard to all "law," is improved and really scientific and righteous classifications,—namely, real GENERAL-izations and SIMPLIFICATIONS. Because vice, error and stupidity, hide their heads behind "musses," SPECIOUSNESS, and complication; and so the genius under words, appears as if it was the genius over things. But we are, in this PART, seeking for such very general principles, as will underlie Inter-Precinct and Inter-Corporation Law, as well as International.

§ 2. *Foundations.*

The real foundations of the law of Nations, as also the foundations of all laws, are threefold. First, moral principles. Second, arguments of utility. Third, consent; and consent includes both custom and compact. But when apparent differences arise between these three principles, they can only be settled by recourse to a higher science than this, namely, by recourse to Moral Philosophy. But in our social science, the arguments that may be based merely and only upon consent, are of much less importance than those based upon moral principles, or those upon utility; because one of the very *objects* of our science, is to point out how the established order existing by consent, is wrong; and how and why it ought to be improved; yet with due respect to the transitional duties. And when the question becomes merely one between Principle and Utility, our theory decides to use Principle as the highest rule; Utility as only subservient thereto. But it decides thus, for the sake of practical certainty and truth, whilst at the same time, it upholds the idea that utility is always coincident with moral principle; but it feels itself incapable of demonstrating this coincidence perfectly, in every particular case. And *here* is where our work differs from most others, namely, in making comparatively much less account of argumentation from apparent utility. Our supreme preference for principle over utilitarian argumentation, receives however, an indirect corroboration, by the fact, that all the languages of Modern Europe, as well as the old Latin, do *not* use the term "*Law* of Nations," but the term "*Right* of Nations," as the phrase whereby to designate international law.—(Wheaton, § 12). Mere consent in international law, is no more than common law or statute law in the civil municipal; and is liable to be improved as reason, morality and progress require, yet always with due regard to lawful expectations by usage.

A practical difficulty arises here however, namely, to say HOW the law of Nations is to be revised or improved. It will not do to hold with Puffendorf, that usage is of little account against theoretical argument; neither will it do to hold with some others, that special treaties are the only methods of reforming international law. The true method of the reform, is, always to have recourse to the *principles* involved, but yet always to remember that usage, present expectations, and past contracts and arrangements, are necessary to be taken into the account, *in order to judge what* IS the voice of the natural principle or "natural law," in the case. And this is a mode of thought, that most of the regularly trained "legists" seem unable to indulge in. And yet, only thus can the distinction be stated truly, between "natural law" and the law of Nations. The legists study how to make laws unalterable and unavoidable, the social scientists study how to make laws progressive and improvable; and since between the old and the new, there always is a degree as well as a time of transitional confusion, so far it must happen, that the social scientists come indirectly in conflict with the legists. But this conflict is proportionally very limited, because the occasions and objects of it, form but a very small part of the aims or occupations of either class, either the legists or the social scientists.

The following classification (which is a different one from the foregoing) will, perhaps, do something towards harmonizing the different classifications that others have made, of the foundations of International law,—by referring them to their different relations to Consent: as Express, Presumed, Moral obligation to, and Pressure to, Consent.

First. Express Consent. This embraces treaties, also the manifestoes of one Nation to another, also the opinions and the decisions of the officers and judges, in any particular Nations, who have to meet international questions.

Second. Presumed Consent, in other words, Tacit Consent. This includes Custom, or, as the English say, long usage; it also includes general interest or general convenience, as new occasions arise in which custom has nothing to say; it also includes a certain high degree of self-interest or convenience, which no Nation could be expected to relinquish, even for the general good, without compensation.

Third. Moral ofligation to consent. This constitutes what in our theory, are called the claims of Mankind; so that we should trace arguments upon this foundation, directly to Mankind, as one of the original and eternal Units. This division of international law includes, what others call the law of nature and justice; it also includes the divine law, or equity, which is the amelioration of justice by kindness, on the condition of mutuality. Both of these lead to the consideration of moral progress, for the condition of mutuality means progress; and the opinions of what justice and equity are, vary with progress. And this subject of progress, both by reversing old laws, and also by presenting entirely new circumstances, constitutes one of the greatest practical difficulties of international statesmanship. The other greatest difficulty, and that which seems to be pushing more and more for settlement, is the relation of the highly civilized and

Christian Nations, to the heathen, both semi-civilized and barbarian.

Fourth. Pressure to consent. This part of the subject is what other writers would probably consider, under the head of, the means of execution of international law. But we may retain the reference to consent; inasmuch as inflictions on Nations, according to international law, are not intended as punishments, but are intended as forces to coerce consent; and inasmuch as it makes a neater and more uniform classification, to retain some modification of consent, as the basis of this Fourth division, as well as of the preceding three; and also because the fear of recourse to pressure, is often one of the leading motives whereby backward or selfish Nations, are induced to accord with improved laws, although nothing is said about such fear; and, therefore, pressure may be classed as one of the foundations. For, the theory of the equality of Nations, only extends in practice, to etiquette, and hardly to that.

These pressures to consent, consist partly of reprisals, and partly of treaties excepting the offending Nation from some of the usual privileges or honors of Nations, or excepting its citizens from the common privileges of travel or trade; also entire non-intercourse, and in the last resort, war. Although in the Synthetics we are to take pretty strong moral ground against war, yet in the Analytics we must treat it as a reserved right.

§ 3. *Sources.*

The sources of international law, namely, its law *documents*, are summed up (by Wheaton § 15,) into six, and may thus be condensed:—(1) "Text writers of authority,—showing what is the approved usage of Nations, or the general opinion respecting their mutual conduct, with the definitions and modifications introduced by general consent. * * * They are generally impartial in their judgment. They are witnesses of the sentiments and usages of civilized Nations. * * * (2) Treaties of peace, alliance and commerce, declaring, modifying or defining the pre-existing international law. * * * (3) Ordinances of particular States, prescribing rules for the conduct of their commissioned cruisers and prize tribunals. * * * (4) The adjudications of international tribunals, such as boards of arbitration and courts of prize. As between these two sources of international law, greater weight is justly attributable to the judgments of mixed tribunals, appointed by the joint consent of the two Nations between whom they are to decide, than to those of admiralty courts established by and dependent on the instructions of one Nation only. * * * (5) Another depository of international law is to be found in the written opinions of official jurists, given confidentially to their own governments. * * * Where an opinion has been adverse to the sovereign client, and has been acted on, and the State which submitted to be bound by it was more powerful than its opponent in the dispute, we may confidently assume that the law of Nations, such as it was *then* supposed to be, has been correctly laid down.* * * (6) The history of the wars, negotiations, treaties of peace, and other transactions relating to the public intercourse of Nations."

Here is to be mentioned another source of international law, namely, the moral and benevolent organizations, especially the religious ones. Ancient Rome had, as it were, a special band of officers to supervise and execute international law. It was a sort of religious body, as it also performed the religious and sacrificial rites of the occasion,—viz., the *collegium fetialium*. During the Middle Ages, the Popes were often appealed to as authority in international affairs. And probably after all, science will not dispense with, but rather point us back to, calling into exercise some organs of the church, as the best and truest cosmopolitan judges, and the most reliable representatives of the rights of MANKIND. International disputes can be settled, and wars prevented, only by reference to the highest principles of human nature, and under decisions by the most reliable men. The Christian church, therefore, may be enumerated as one of the undeveloped organs or sources of international law.

Another source of international law, would be the literature and the legal decisions, that would arise, in the actual development of the system of Precincts, such as we have proposed. This system develops fresh from nature, and ever receives fresh life and direction from nature, aided at the same time by all the other organs and sources of international law; all acting spontaneously and closely in unison with nature, but with the element of war or physical force excluded, by the peace functions of the Nation over them.

Our proposed system of Corporations, would also develop the same principles, as international law, and would thus be another source of it.

We do not pretend to state what the law of Nations *actually* IS, so much as, what it OUGHT to be. Our sketch, then, is rather an *ideal* of what natural and Christian international law ought to be, as to its *substance*, but of course not, as to its form. But this ideal is to be all along subjected to such modifications as mutuality may require. The Christian ideal when presented as a political rule, generally depends in part upon the condition of mutuality. Mutuality of international obligations, is secured by two means,—one is negotiation or treaty, the other is the actual law, as the same is acknowledged and made unequivocal. Hence in international law, there is comparatively less respect due to the ideal, than in municipal law; and more respect due to the actual. For municipal law, being more thoroughly instituted into the common thought and common life, of Individuals, is supposed to occupy, and does in fact occupy, much of the position of a moral ideal. Another reason of the difference is, that the municipal law forbids battle among its subjects, and presumes peace as its ground of operation. But international law acknowledges war, and provides for it, and is chiefly occupied either in preventing, or conducting, or concluding war. Nevertheless, we present our sketch of this ideal in its radical form.

Now, coming down from the abstract to the concrete, of course, the Law of Nations, among European, and even among Christian Nations, has had a *historical* origin. Nations having had a common origin, traceable by history, or having had intercourse for many centuries, will have a connection between their Law-s of Nations, their laws of *mutual intercourse,* more than in any thing else, at all common to them. Historical divergencies in language, in religion, in customs, in dress, &c., will all be marked, and generally tend to *farther* divergency: but the Law of their mutual intercourse, must necessarily tend towards a constant approximation, after they emerge from that obscurity and mutual repugnance which envelop their origin as Nations. Hence, as regards the Law of Nations, there is more agreement, than as to what compose the fundamental principles of Christianity itself. So that this Law is a "positive" law, but yet an "imperfect" one, owing to its having neither a legislative, a judicial, nor an executive power to enforce it; nor is any such likely to arise justly and properly.

But in this Law, just as much as in Christianity, we ever have right to appeal from history to the original authorities, and thus to discuss what it OUGHT to be, as well as what it actually is. And whilst most writers discuss chiefly or only, what it is, surely here and there an isolated one, has right to discuss what it ought to be.

CHAP. II. MOST GENERAL INTERNATIONAL LAWS.

§ 1. *Leagues.*

The right of Nations to form leagues or confederations, has been sufficiently advocated above, under the Relations of Nation to Mankind. But such confederations, if for offensive operations or offensive war, would belong to the *War* part of the subject. But defensive alliances would belong to this General part, because their principal tendency would be towards peace. Yet defensive alliances could not be considered as belonging to this part, if the privilege of Individuals to do, much as they please, in other countries, continues to be maintained. Because, under that theory, invasion or Offensive War, is sometimes the only method of *defence* of citizens accounted abused by foreigners. But viewing the privilege otherwise; consistency with our own theory requires us to mention this subject of alliances in *this* place, so far as it belongs at all to international law.

§ 2. *Treaties.*

In International Law, Treaties fulfill nearly a similar extensiveness of function, that Trusts do in the civil law, or that "state-rights" do in the Nation; namely, they can accomplish every thing not specially and clearly forbidden by some higher law. And therefore we need not enter into particulars. The most difficult part of the subject really, is, what relates to the continuity of treaties, namely, what reserved rights remain in either party *alone* to annul them, and the *effect* that war has upon them.

In regard to the *reserved* right of revoking them, the fact or element of coercion in forming them, cannot be pleaded as a sufficient ground for non-obligation, because then, the means of peace would be greatly weakened,—for as Dana says, "coercion * * * is of the essence and idea of war."

On the other hand, absolute perpetuity of promises for the future, cannot be included, because in history, the changes of Nations are too great, and their lives too long, to allow any such preposterous claim. Perhaps the best rule would be, to adopt a limit of time for promises of future action, a new sort of "statute of limitations," say the average length of the life of Individuals, namely, 33 years, as the duration of the obligation, because then the average race of Individuals would have changed. It would not be admissible to allow the express use of the word "forever," or other similar term, or other dodge of the legists, to interfere seriously with this rule, because the unscrupulous conquerors would always insert such terms. At this point however, the decision of a congress of Nations might be allowed, as a new sort of "seal," sufficient to lengthen the duration of the promises of a treaty, perhaps to a century, but scarcely any longer,—excepting, of course, treaties for the permanent *transfer of territory;* including within this exception, also, the treaties which acknowledged the birth or independence of Nations, or any thing else which from its very nature implied perpetuity.

The question is raised, how far war, the mere fact itself, annuls treaties. In general we would say, war revokes the contents of previous treaties. But to this there are several exceptions, namely; stipulations in regard to the conduct of the next ensuing war; stipulations as to actions that had been accomplished and finished before the breaking out of the war; stipulations in regard to which disputes had arisen and had been prominent causes of the war. This last mentioned exception is disputed by some modern authorities; still, it depends upon the obvious principle, that the differences which had caused the war, would naturally be, either provided for at its conclusion by treaty, or else were to be dropped; which could only be the understanding, by regarding the previous treaty stipulations revoked, and the questions then at issue, to be solvable only according to the general principles of the law, apart from specialties of treaty.

Other disputed points will be settled by adopting the principle, that the effect of war on a treaty, is to be judged, not by the general nature of the treaty, but by the particular stipulations therein, each such stipulation requiring a separate judgment. For instance, the treaty of peace and recognition of our nationality by England, in 1783, contained also a stipulation granting certain rights of fishery in the British dominions. Now the question is, whether the war of 1812 revoked that stipulation. Politicians and "patriots" say, no! But the writer, contrary to the common American assertion, must *admit* that this stipulation was annulled by the War of 1812. But, had the dispute in question been one relating to a previous stipulation about boundary, or title to property, or other *finished* fact, IT would not have been revoked by the latter war.

If, however, the war were *caused* by a Nation's express refusal to continue fulfilling stipulations, which it had previously and evidently performed,—and it should throw down the gauntlet of war as the alternative,—such a Nation would of course revoke its assent to the treaty, and would thereby forfeit all its rights and claims under it. And if, in the struggle of war, it should be permanently defeated, this defeat would revive the rights and claims of the conquering Nation, without reviving those of the defeated Nation, any further than the conqueror voluntarily allowed, or than the general law of Nations, apart from the treaty, required.

Again, if a part of a Nation rebels, and sets up its own independent government positively, it thereby ceases to have any rights other than if it were a really independent Nation; because such action binds itself, but it does not bind the other party. Hence, if the revolted part, is positively and permanently defeated, the very best view that can be taken of its rights, is, that they are only the rights of a defeated Nation. In such a case, the old constitution occupies the same relative position, as an old treaty, namely, binding upon the defeated party, but not so upon the conquerors.

The most that can be asked for a "belligerent," is the right of a Nation "pro tempore." But if the "belligerent" *succeeds*, and treaties of peace and acknowledgment are made by the military authorities, in good faith to all, then such treaties are binding upon the old Nation, no matter what the old constitution or laws may have said. Because, if the old Nation is defeated as to the *object* of the war, then treaties made with its military power, *must* be binding upon it, *as to that object;* and all old articles and laws to the contrary, can now be considered as having been only " pro tempore" as to IT.

The next question about treaties is, whether one Nation contracting, is bound to look to all the *concurrent* powers of the other, which are necessary to *complete* the treaty. The answer would seem justly to be, that the first named Nation is as much bound to know the one part of the other Nation's rules and powers, as it is the other part. This question comes up in a serious difficulty existing in the constitution of the United States; inasmuch as the President and Senate are invested with the treaty-making power; but yet, if the treaty require the payment of money, or any *positive* legislation, it cannot be *completed* without the co-operation of the House of Representatives. But that house does not always accord with the other. What then is the right principle? The answer according to fairness and equity would seem to be, that " the house" has the right to refuse its concurrence, when, and only when,—either the President or Senate, or the foreign contracting power, had reasonable evidence *to believe* the house was in fact AVERSE to the measure. The contrary rule would take away the independence of the house, which is one of its essential elements. Not the question of constitutionality, but the question of *opinion* of constitutionality, may be brought in, as well as of expediency. This seems plainly to be equity in all cases where the powers of parties are concurrent, as also in the case of Individual partners, in any of the common businesses of life.

The case is, as if three partners are engaged in any business, under a general agreement, giving each his appropriate functions to perform,—then, any two partners are not bound to hesitate in every performance of their proper function, to STUDY whether the other *one would* approve,—but, on the other hand, neither have they any right to do that which they KNOW is against his approval,—especially when his active co-operation in some subsequent act, in his own appropriate department, is necessary to complete the transaction.

But to give *less* right than the above, to the treaty-making powers, would be to trespass on the rights of the Senate and

President; although in matters that really would allow of long postponement, and of uncertain conditions; it would be the duty of the treaty-making power to insert an express condition, "providing that the House of Representatives concur." But, the question whether any matter would allow of such postponement and conditions, the Senate and President are the proper judges of, provided they exercise their judgment in good faith.

§ 3. *Eminent Domain.*

The subject of Eminent Domain, perhaps, belongs to the consideration of the rights of the Individual-Nation, which have been argued above; but so long as there remains any part of the Earth, of which the claim of Eminent Domain is not yet settled, nor granted to some of the civilized and recognized Nations,—so long it may be proper to retain the subject under this head. Other writers would find another reason for considering Eminent Domain under international law, namely, the consequences of their theory of "do as you please in *other* countries," which continually brings the believers of it, in conflict with the "eminent" rights of foreign Nations.

The right of Eminent Domain comprises;—(1) The spontaneous right of ownership to all property not personally, nor otherwise appropriated, whether land or water, navigable or otherwise, appropriable by Individuals or otherwise;—(2) The right to purchase fairly, and to build, manufacture, improve and hold, all property real and personal, necessary for the performance of its functions of government;—(3) The right to collect all reasonable and necessary taxes, for the due performance of its functions;—(4) The right within its own boundaries, of government, as excluding other Nations; and the right of fixing its own external boundaries, exclusive of Precinct-interference;—and (5) The right of reasonable and necessary, but only very general control, over all governmental proceedings within its geographical boundaries, even as against its own Precincts. (6) But when the question of division of the Nation arises, this of Eminent Domain has no power over it; as has been shown above; for the question itself INVOLVES A DIVISION OF THAT RIGHT.

In all these rights, we can readily see, that in due submission to nationality, Precincts have, or ought to have, in regard to other Precincts, similar concurrent rights,—each within itself.

Nations far in advance of others in civilization, assume on discovery, the right of government, and even of the property of the land, especially of nomadic or roving tribes. The right to the land, as to its settlement and cultivation, depends upon the rights of the unit Mankind, and especially upon the need that arises, because of the filling up of the Earth with population. The right of government by the very superior Nation, depends partly on that of the land, and partly upon an almost universal superiority, intellectual and moral.

Now, the "Monroe-doctrine," is a partial claim to Eminent Domain, as against all the other civilized Nations of the Earth. Striking indeed is the coolness and assumption of ten or twenty or forty millions of people, saying to all the rest of the civilized world,—we take one whole quarter of the Globe as our heir-loom; and no other Nation shall send its national organ into this Quarter, to rule the savage and half-civilized tribes, that we are not willing to rule, and not able to receive without ruining ourselves; nor indeed do we know what to do with them. *All* the *Individuals* of your civilized Europe, may indeed come here *as Individuals,* if you will go through the political sieve of our uniformity, and swear allegiance to our nationality, and to our claim to this Quarter of the Globe-heir-loom. Such a mode of discussion may be patriotic or democratic, but it can hardly find either precedent or justification, in *eternal principles* of International Law. But as a *temporary* expedient, to prevent wars between Ourselves and Europeans, the position may be tolerable, until better policies than War shall prevail, and better civil governments, in Europe and elsewhere. But what a doctrine to be proposed as an *eternal principle* of Social SCIENCE! And yet, it is our non-interference in European affairs, that reconciles Europe to refrain also from interference with us. Besides, European Nations have nearly all of Africa, and large parts of Asia, convenient for them to carry their power and civilization thereunto; and this gives us an equitable claim to a similar development on this continent.

On the other hand, the right must be admitted, of every civilized Nation to establish restrictions sufficient to prevent foreign Nations, not at all homogeneous or friendly to it, from establishing themselves too near it, or in a part of its probable dominions.

But these questions of homogeneity and friendliness, involve the subjects of religion and morals and race, as well as forms of government; and our government cannot cope with these topics.

The recognized right of taxing foreign commodities, together with the necessities of defence, justify every Nation in a claim of exclusive control over several miles width of the sea-coast: the rest of the sea is held as common property. Since this law follows a coast as it fills up, instead of giving a fixed line,—it seems to be expressed in the best manner.

§ 4. *Arbitration.*

This topic is placed here, merely because its great prominence in the public mind at present, would be apt to lead readers to look for it somewhere under the head of Nation. But in our classification, the proper place for arbitration is under our head "CIVIL GOVERNMENT"; where arbitration comes up, together with juries, and the other methods of settling controversies and administering law. Nor is arbitration any better fitted for national affairs, than it is for Precinct or Corporation or Individual; howbeit, it is the best method in all cases:—and one of the great problems of government, is to devise methods of making it practicable and regular, more or less in all. We have touched upon it in Summary Introduction II. X.

§ 5. *Naturalization* (*Indicated*).

In this general place, perhaps, rather than elsewhere, the subject of naturalization, and its counterpart, de-naturalization, ought to be considered. This seems to be the case, because naturalization, although generally accomplished in time of peace, is generally *disputed*, if at all, in time of war. Another reason is, that according to our theory, the right of naturalization in a neutral Nation, ought not to be interrupted in time of *war*, if the consent of the adopting country can be obtained; because it is often needed, then, both by Individuals and Families, rather than at any other time. But since the discussion is lengthy, and would interrupt the course of thought we are pursuing, and because it takes a wider range, we have treated it as a separate Division, namely, Part III. of the Nation.

As to the right sometimes assumed, of a Nation, to recall its citizens from a foreign country, the claim is simply a preposterous tyranny against the rights of the Individual, if interpreted to mean anything more, or the disobedience to the command, to be punished any heavier than by a mere de-naturalization of the absentee, and perhaps by an order *not* to return.

§ 6. *Forms.*

No settlement of great international disputes can be made, until all questions of form become absorbed in the great questions of spirit and truth. A people may dispute among *themselves*, whether a case shall be decided by forms or not, in disregard to truth and righteousness; but may not dwell much upon such a consideration, in a discussion with a foreign Nation. The question with us, for instance, is, not at all, whether the Alabama got to sea in due form of law; but, the *facts* of our injuries. And on the other hand, when a criminal escapes from one country to another, as from England to this country, the question is, not whether he ought to be held by *our forms*, but the question is, whether he is probably guilty.

The question about *forms of proceeding*, in international law, may be settled simply thus: that all forms valid in their Locality, should be valid in other Localities, as to all acts and proceedings previous to war, or litigation, as the case may be; but that after war or litigation, and for the proceedings therein, the forms must all conform to those of the government for the time being, of the Locality where the property lies, if the case be of property; or where the persons are held, if the case be of persons.

CHAP. III. AFFAIRS IN PEACE.

§ 1. *Property in General.*

Having thus touched upon the consideration of the most general international laws, we consider next the particulars, separately:—Of Affairs in Peace:—And, of Affairs in War.

We come now to consider that part of the law, which relates to affairs in Peace:—also in two parts:—Of Property:—And, of Persons.

The general rule of property is, or should be, that all property real and personal, must be awarded according to the laws of the location wherein it is situated. To which there are two classes of disputed exceptions. One class of disputed exceptions, is, where both the litigants are citizens of a foreign country. But even this exception *cannot* be pleaded for "real" or immovable property, and therefore it *should* not be for personal property; because, according to our theory, there is *no* longer any *radical* political distinction of right or expediency, between those two kinds of property, in most modern and civilized countries.

The other class of exceptions, is that of the estates of deceased persons. In this case, justice seems clearly to say, that where the deceased leaves a will, it should be held valid if legal EITHER in the place where it was made, or in the place where it was to take effect. For we cannot know which rule the testator aimed to conform to. This should be the rule, except that particular bequests *in conflict with* local laws, should be construed as if of an intestate there; and that when the deceased dies intestate, the property should be awarded,—one half according to his own Nation's laws, and the other half, according to the laws of its location.

In all cases regarding property "situate" in one country, when the decision made in another, requires for its execution the aid of the one in which the property is situated,—the voluntary concurrence of this one, ought to be obtained. And it is the undoubted right of any Nation, to judge of the justice of any decision which it is required to forcibly or legally execute; and if any of its own citizens are affected thereby, it is its *duty* to judge thereof.

§ 2. "*The Tariff.*"

The right of tariff on foreign trade has been universally recognized: but this subject will be considered under the element PROPERTY. We may however say here, that international law only requires mutuality; and mutuality consists, not in uniformity of particulars, but in mutuality of spirit. It must have regard to the past proceedings, and also the present condition of both countries. It must also embrace the consideration, of the tariffs of all the other countries with which each has commerce. All these considerations combine to make the resulting decision possible, only in a general spirit of friendliness and reciprocity.

§ 3. *The "Person,"—in General.*

The claim of any Nation, to prevent its citizens from emigrating, although still maintained, is entirely contrary to our whole theory, and especially to the principle of Individual selection, and to the Christian spirit, as well as to the wisdom and progress of modern times. We can only regard Nations as having the same essential rights as Precincts, allowing for the increased size, and for other evident facts and necessities. It was formerly held, that a Nation had a right to recall its own citizens from a foreign country; but the United States have exploded that claim as made by foreign Nations. Nevertheless in the Great Rebellion, laws were enacted forbidding citizens to leave; and a public spirit was fostered, that it was even the *duty* of good citizens to return!

The Nation, you say, has the right of control or guidance over all residents, whether its own citizens or foreigners. If so, then other Nations besides the United States have this right. But the government and people of the United States are continually trespassing on this right, and thus making and maintaining enmity among foreign Nations. But the right itself, if claimed by a semi-civilized people over a fully civilized one, would be disputable. Moral considerations cannot be ignored on this subject.

But alas! what shall we say, when a religious teacher enters a foreign, highly civilized country, but of an opposite religion; and there publicly teaches his religion, contrary to the laws of his then residence? The answer of modern civilization must be, to *allow* this teacher, providing his religious sincerity is admissible,—even if his religious teachings seem to us to savor of immorality. Any other doctrine would have been good against Christ, and his apostles; and against religious reformers generally. And the same principle might partly apply to INTER-PRECINCT travelling preachers. The case is involved in much difficulty.

In cases regarding PERSONS, no division or apportionment, such as occurs in regard to PROPERTY, is conceivable, except in the claims of marriage.

In regard to the claims of husbands or parents, in a foreign territory; no country ought to be held bound to deliver up a woman or child, contrary to its own principles; for such a course is horrifying to the best feelings of human nature, destructive of the human rights of the persons forced, and to the national rights of home. And the same may also be said of claims for personal services, in order to a condition anything like slavery.

§ 4. *Specialties in Marriage and Divorce.*

In cases where the marriage is disputed, in a different country from where it is alleged to have been contracted, the ordinary international law seems utterly at fault. And judges and juries, in response to the voice of humanity, sometimes decide such cases according to the principles of justice and common sense, in defiance of all "law."

One very hard case is something like this. A Protestant man A is openly married to a Catholic woman B, by a Catholic priest in country *A-B*. They live together (and have children) many years in honorable marriage,—no one questioning their honor or virtue, although an old antiquated law existed, that required the Catholics, in such marriage, to go through some formalities of deference to the other religion, ruling in the said country *A-B*. Well, after a time, A marries a woman who is perfectly aware of his former marriage, and then removes to country *C*, without his first Family. Then B, with the Family, follows, and claims alimony for herself, and maintenance for the children. In such a case, the usual international law seems entirely against justice, and on the side of the second alliance.

But our whole theory easily settles the question differently, and upon several grounds. Firstly, our Summary Introduction demands that we jump out of the tangle of prescriptions, and go back to first principles. Secondly, our theory of international law demands that forms be absorbed by the essence, spirit, and truth. Hence, forms can only be introduced into the methods of *proving* the marriage, but not into the methods of its original contraction. Thirdly, the Family, according to our theory, is an eternal, absolute Unit of human society. Hence, the voluntary and deliberate act of the competent parties, as intended to be understood, each by the other, is binding upon them personally, no matter what positive laws may say to the contrary. Forms or "positive" laws can only be binding upon other persons, or for real estate in and of the country concerned. Fourthly, the law of country *A-B* in such case was a law promotive of fraud. And if the man A, from the first did not intend to continue bound by the alliance, then he was culpable of fraud, and the law as to *him* was a law of fraud; and we know that in "law," fraud vitiates any transaction. Therefore no international or treaty law, can bind to uphold for any Nation, such a law of fraud. Fifthly, whatever disobedience of form, against the laws of their own country, A and B and the priest committed might be punished in their own country, even to the loss of citizenship there, if that Nation chose; (but cannot reach as a crime, unto international relations, in any manner;) yet not to the destruction of life, of the Individual nor of the existence of the Family relation, because of the eternal rights of the Six Units.

The subject of foreign marriage and divorce, resolves itself into two parts, which have just been treated of separately, namely, Property and Person. But to be more particular:—the case occurs, of citizens of one country marrying within another country, whether emigrating thither purposely to marry in contrariety to the laws of their own country, or not. The French law ignores such marriages. But according to our theory, as mentioned elsewhere, such disobedience, instead of affecting the marriage, should affect the *citizenship*. In brief, all disobedience of one's own Nation, and recourse for exemption to another Nation, should be held to be an irrevocable, or at least an absolute, abandonment of the former citizenship.

But in cases of DIVORCE, more complicated questions arise. When person A resides in country *A*, and consort B gets a divorce in country *B*, contrary to the laws of *A*, such a divorce should have no more authority over person or property in *A* than waste paper; except by a statute of limitation for the relations of "person" only.

The question, what authority should such a divorce have in country *C*, is answerable by only one of two principles, namely, either by a compromise, such as acknowledging the divorce as to the person, but partly refusing it as to property; or else by establishing some "positive" or arbitrary rule. But such positive rule, however, should be of the essence of the compromise above mentioned, or it would be an "arbitrary wrong."

The civil law seems to regard removal from one Locality to another, made *purposely* to obtain either marriage or divorce contrary to the laws of the first place,—as fraudulent, and therefore as vitiating all the proceedings in the view of the first place. It may be admitted that such a ruling would be sound, under a system of laws founded directly upon nature and moral right, and not upon prescription. But such a ruling, under present "law," is merely a technical dodge of the legists. Purpose to avoid law, fraudulent! when yet the *thing to be done* itself, and all the proceedings step by step, are *according* to law! The fact is, it is only when the things themselves, for instance, cheating the creditor, gambling, &c., are themselves wrong under *any* proceedings, that the charge of fraud arises under the *special* proceedings. And the assuming that a divorce, for instance, was itself wrong, is ignoring the right of all other Localities to form their own opinion thereon.

§ 5. *Transgressors.*

In regard to transgressors of law, whether criminal, civil or political,—the writer cannot see why it has ever been doubted, that in general among admitted equals, every Locality has a right to keep its own peace, by its own laws; and that if foreigners do not like those laws, they should keep away. The contrary cannot be maintained, only so far as the Nation interfered with, is held to be *far inferior* to the other, in civilization and rights. And even then, the right of the inferior, should only be interfered with, so far as its exercise was actually barbarous. But alas! this rule would "interfere with trade and travel" and "manifest destiny," and so on!

The idea that the "flag" should protect persons engaged in transgressing the laws or comities or equities between Nations, is absurd as well as unjust, and if thoroughly carried out, would establish and protect *piracy*, as effectually as the laws and customs of Tripoli, which produced our war with that power. The public may rest assured, that quite other than the apparent or alleged reasons, are the *real* reasons for our national policy and dogmas on this subject.

It is disputed whether a Nation is bound by natural law, to surrender fugitives from justice, to the Nation in whose jurisdiction the crime was committed. Now, supposing laws to be intended to prevent crime, the solution is,—if the forsaken country inflicts the greater punishment, that is, if it regards the crime as of a deeper kind, the duty of return might be more easily admitted in logic, but would be less likely to be allowed in practice; but if the adoptive country inflicts the greater punishment, evidently it is not morally bound to give up the fugitive, upon the old principles; else, where is the right of a country over all its residents, or its right to defend itself from criminals? Yet, in this case, the claim would be more likely to be allowed in practice. But in fact, the question depends at least equally as much on the citizenship of the *injured person*, as on the nature of the *injuries*, and also on the contiguity of the countries in question. The foregoing very general principles may readily be understood so as to apply to political offences, as well as to natural or moral ones; except when the forms of government or political and religious structure, are essentially different, and *antagonistic* in their nature.

The principal justifiable reason for the return to the forsaken country, is the greater facility of conviction and punishment. But the facility does not always depend on such a condition as foreign or not; but partly on conditions of local distance, and partly on many metaphysical and moral circumstances. Even the expenses of witnesses, depend more on distances and modes of travel, than on flags or nationalities. The great desideratum is the establishment of such procedures, as shall *insure* the punishment of criminals, by *some* power and *somewhere*, by law, no matter much, where or by whom. Furthermore, in some countries, and even in some Precincts, conviction and execution of a sentence for crime, are very uncertain, whatever may be the evidence; whilst perfect evidence is rarely to be obtained anywhere.

On the other hand, when the forsaken country accounts deeds as crimes, which the adoptive country does not account so,—the rule of course would be, not to surrender the fugitive at all. Upon this principle, *political* offenders are not subject to return. But this exception should apply only when the offenders are citizens of the country wherein the political offence is committed: because we must allow to the citizens of every country, a degree of right to revolution therein, which we ought not to grant to other persons, whose very object in going there, perhaps was to aid in revolution,—and above all, this exception should not apply, when the offenders are *proper citizens* of the country to which they *return* after committing political offences in a foreign country; because the exempting, such offenders, is in effect, making every country a kind of base for military operations against, and for revolutions in, every other country.

What then shall we say of the amity or friendship exhibited, when a great Nation, not only pleads for the release of persons imprisoned in a foreign country, for attempts to excite insurrection there, but actually passes a resolution welcoming their return, and allows its largest metropolis to give them an official reception and ovation, on their return home? And what would we have said, if the government of England had urged in that manner, for the release of our Southern rebels, and then having succeeded,—the city of London should have given them an official ovation? and that too, at the very time they were bullying us to pay some disputed private claims arising in a previous war, and had even just recalled the second of two Ministers, because of their not pushing such claims with sufficient vigor? The term "Insult" would not *begin* to express our indignation. And the question becomes really contrary to all scientific explanation, when we remember that the persons so offending, had been originally citizens of the country wherein the offences were committed, but had become naturalized in and sworn allegiance to this great country, and then had gone back from it, *full of true love and patriotism for their* ORIGINAL *country*,—to stir up rebellion against *its* government!

It is here to be remarked, however, that leagues among *contiguous* Nations, to be durable and peaceable, ought to contain stipulations to return, at least the worst or most visionary *political* fugitives, as well as civil criminals; otherwise the territory of either party, is at all times liable to be made the base of voluntary or private operations against the other. This is true, whether the contiguity is physical or *metaphysical.* These are some of the cases in which special confederations are needed, between such contiguous Nations. And if the rule could not be made to apply to all the LARGE rebellions, it might at any rate, apply to the petty rebellions, that have no pretence of claim for *recognition as belligerency.*

Perhaps the refusal or reluctance of a Nation to surrender to its neighboring Nation, the political fugitives who had needlessly disturbed its peace, might be circumvented lawfully by the following method:—The Nation liable to such disturbances might enact a law, that all such persons should be held to a certain length of service in its military or naval forces. Such a law ought to be sufficient, because even the United States government acknowledges that its naturalization is not valid against the foreign Nation's claim to individual military service. Besides, if the law of the disturbed Nation provided no other punishment (than here mentioned), for such returned offenders, the adoptive country would be more willing in time of peace (of which we speak), to surrender them.

CHAP. IV. AFFAIRS IN WAR.

§ 1. *In General.*

Our third and last great division of international law, is, Affairs in War.

Although war is a great and almost unpardonable evil, nevertheless, it is a *common* fact, and has to be provided for. Every probable and reasonable course to prevent it, should of course be pursued. We mean, not merely that every expedient should be adopted, to escape from war *after* provoking its appearance; but that the regular course and policy of every Nation, should be carefully framed purposely, to avoid exciting war, or exciting those feelings, either of cupidity, rivalry or fear, which generally provoke it.

Spencer's assertion that the position merely of no recourse to *offensive* war, would be equally as productive of peace, as more radical peace-ground, is erroneous; first, because people differ as to what constitutes offensive war. It is erroneous also, because it does not tend to a thorough disarmament, nor to the discouragement of war-principles, war-glory and the war-spirit, so fully as the more radical grounds. But this subject must be postponed to a subsequent volume, except as incidentally we here touch upon the arguments for ameliorating the severity of war, and for maintaining the rights and independence of human personality.

The rights of Individuals and of neutral Nations demand, that timely notice of several months, be always given previously to commencing active hostilities: But this rule cannot easily apply to the immediate spots of sudden ebullition, nor to "civil" wars. To make it practicable for the latter, would be quite a feat for social science.

Hardly any doctrine seems likely to become so practically efficient, in hindering or suppressing war, as the doctrine, that quarreling Nations have no more right to disturb the peace of the world, by their quarrels, than rowdy Individuals have to disturb the peace of a municipality, with their personal fights:—or than selfish Precincts called states, would have, to interrupt the harmony of the Nation, with Inter-Precinct wars. And this doctrine may be made practical, by the gradual strengthening of the assertion of the rights of neutrals, in all possible ways.

The International rights of War come next for consideration. We will treat of them under the following divisions:—First: As related to the rights of Individual-persons, whether citizens, or enemy-citizens, including all three as moral persons; and consider those rights of the Individual which concern *himself*, his soul, and his happiness. Second: The Rights of War as related to the Ways and Means of conducting it, the policy, the modes of warfare, weapons, and ameliorations. Third: the Rights of War, as referring to contrabands, both things and official persons; and as depending on or related to Locality, whether in the Neutral's own Locality, or in Localities common to all the parties. In treating of these subjects, we, in the first two Divisions, touch property only in a casual way; because the rights of persons are so much more important, and so much less regarded, by writers generally. In the third Division, we treat more of property, because the usual classifications for that subject, serve also to arrange the ideas in regard to persons.

§ 2. *Relations to the Individuals of the Belligerent Nations.*

First, as related to the rights of Individuals as persons. In the first place, we object entirely to the old theory, that because the governments of two Nations, make war,—therefore all the people of both Nations, must also become enemies and war against each other. We also object to the old theory, that the Nation warring has a right to whatever control it can obtain, over the Individual persons of its Enemy-Nation, restricted only by that indefinite idea, Christian or human civilization. We protest absolutely, and in the name of *the Individual*, against all such interpretations of nature or morality. The old days of brute instinct and blind impulse, are passing away, and the rights of the Individual are coming up into notice. Nowhere perhaps, is the right "to ignore the state," more needed, but less easy to be obtained, than in regard to war. So important are the rights of Individuals, that we consider them, abstract from the distinctions between citizen or alien, Enemy-Nation or Neutral-Nation. And even property is considered and felt to be, rather a means of happiness to the *Individual*, than as a subject of abstract and complicated rights. Can it be possible then, that we, having been nominally *Christian* Nations a thousand years or two, and Protestant three hundred,—shall yet persist in forcing men to say, "Our country right or wrong"?

Of course it is easy to see, how very *opposite* these views are, from Mulford's, and the high imperial German theories,—that in war, the Nation has right to the services of ALL its citizens; and that, in brief, "the army is the Nation."

While we advocate thus in theory, the rights of the individual person, we must confess we do not see very clearly HOW these rights can be fully and practically recognized by Nations at war,—except through Individuals concentrating in Peace-Precincts, or organizing into political Corporations, as will be explained under that head. At least, these must be the preliminary methods, because it seems a long while away, before Nations will be so Christianized, as to allow their own citizens who enjoy the advantages of peace, to decline the responsibilities of war; and seems only attainable as the other ameliorations of war that have been introduced, namely, *gradually and mutually.* Although doubtless the good time might be hastened by treaty stipulations, so that even long before wars cease altogether, their most oppressive effects may cease to fall upon those who repudiate, either war in general, or the particular war in question at any particular time.

Citizens of Enemy-Nations can be exempted from the hypothesis that they are actually enemies, and from the consequent disabilities of that hypothesis,—only as the progress of cosmopolitan liberality, shall make proportional changes in men's feelings and habits, so that the exemptions would be reasonable and safe. And therefore it is only gradually that Individuals of Enemy-Nations, can be exempted as fully as the citizens of Neutral-Nations are,—from the rule forbidding them any intercourse or trade whatever, with the Individuals of the opposite belligerent.

Nevertheless, throwing aside mere impulses, and appealing to reason alone, we can find no objection to such trade, except along the lines of belligerent operation; and even there, the good feelings promoted by light trade, would do more to produce just peace, than continued war. This has been illustrated by the petty trade between soldiers of the two opposing forces, in the late rebellion.

On the other hand, just in proportion as Individuals are held bound to the WAR-duties of their own country, so also should they be held bound to its peace-duties as neutrals; and therefore bound not to interfere individually, in the quarrels of enemies or belligerents. Hence, the violation of such peace-duties and claims, should be considered quite as much an offence against one's own country, as is the violation of its *war*-duties or claims. Accordingly, "fillibustering" ought to be held as a high offence against our own country.

Great latitude must be allowed to all Nations, to judge for themselves, of the sufficiency of the reasons of war, so long as they only provide for injuring persons who *voluntarily* enter into the contest. But Christian civilization must more and more place NON-combatant Individuals, even when citizens of an Enemy-Nation, on a par with the citizens of neutral Nations. Scarcely anything was more annoying to our own citizens during the rebellion, than being drafted into compulsory service themselves, whilst foreigners were quietly taking their ease under the "protection" of their respective consuls. The rights of the Individual Unit must be RE-ASSERTED, in the face of the Nation, the Precinct, or even Mankind itself. And the lesser Units have the more need, to RE-ASSERT their rights, because they have NO power to enforce them.

According to these principles it is, that the law of Nations is more and more exempting neutrals from all the annoyances of war. Christian civilization not only strengthens its position, that unconcerned NATIONS shall not be disturbed by the fighters, but equally as fully maintains the rights of the Individual, not to be disturbed by them. Indeed, the change itself is owing quite as much to the rise of value of the Individual, all over the world, as to the rise of peace-principles. It will not answer here, to introduce jugglery of words about a Nation being a moral personality, for however that may be, there cannot be any question that a human being is a moral personality, and entitled to the rights of opinion and conscience; especially in non-interference with other people's fights. At first, to be sure, the persons of neutral Nations are exempted, because of prudential reasons, or of fear; but that which has been begun from policy, ought to be confirmed upon principle, and the rights of the Individuals of all other Nations, confirmed for the sake both of Justice and of Conscience. Hence the investigation of the rights of neutrals, has for us also the double use of an investigation also of the rights of the warring Nations over citizens. Observe however, that the right of the Individual here spoken of, is a right to be not disturbed from his own peace, by the wars of others; but is *not* a right to aid in disturbing others' peace.

Of course, every amelioration of war, that decreases the number of persons or *classes* who are expected to become combatants, or the amount of the property at risk, is a great advantage when *mutual;* whether the amelioration be of sex or age or of professions, as physicians clergymen &c.; so also, of condition, such as sickness or wounds. The same good principles call for, and the same good principles follow from, those improved laws that exempt foreign Nations from interference, and exempt also the property, persons and businesses of foreigners, from the vicissitudes of war. But this very amelioration which hails with joy every exemption of sex or classes, must condemn neutral Individuals interfering with belligerents, unless in retaliation for similar interference against us, that has not been compensated for. We would increase the rights of Individuals, but also increase the punishment for admitted transgressions. And any Individuals transgressing after due notice, should forfeit their citizenship for life, *without chance of recall.* And similarly punished should be, all conduct tending intentionally to excite wars or insurrections in other countries. The citizenship of foreigners, instead of being considered as granting immunity for such offences, should be considered forfeited thereby; because such conduct destroys the freedom of all the citizens of the offending country, of travel in the other, and tends also to excite war. This offence is generally committed by the naturalized citizens of another country, or by the adherents of extremely opposite religions or politics;

and either in revenge for past vexations, or in hopes of future religious or political power by annexation; and is often the indirect means of introducing religion into politics.

§ 3. *Ways and Means of War.*

Having thus endeavored to speak for Individual personal rights, and protesting that no methods or means of war, which avowedly and upon principle violate these rights, should any longer be tolerated,—we come next to such Ways and Means as do not conflict with the rights of Individuals.

The propriety or admissibility of different war methods, is not to be judged chiefly by their *war-consequences*, but by their *peace-consequences.* Hence peaceable Nations should not, by treaty, resign their right of recourse to *extraordinary* war measures; because a reliance in time of peace, for recourse to them in war, will promote peace, and free men from warlike thoughts and cares in common times. For, in these days, peace is the rule, and war the exception. The proper application of this principle, instead of the usual method of referring arguments to war-conditions, would make a great change in the international war argument. And as to domestic wars, this principle aids the side of liberty, because it tends to lessen the preponderance that those who are *in* power, naturally have, over those who are *out:*—and as to foreign wars, the constant reference of arguments to times of peace, promotes the interests and progress of Mankind. This principle of reserved rights, refers to several means, for instance, privateering, minute-men, ready militia and guerrillas; provided the same be citizens, or really intend to be, of the Nation in whose cause they are occupied, or of an Enemy-Nation.

Although Privateering need not be forbidden, it ought to be brought more under government naval discipline and control. This might be accomplished, by requiring a government-deputy to be employed on each privateer, as a witness, with liberty to protest, and in desperate cases, to take away, or to publish the revocation of, the government's charter and clearance; the deputy of course to be responsible for his conduct. This would place the commander of the privateer, on his own responsibility, if he acted against a protest. A somewhat similar power is [or was] possessed by surgeons in the British army, but with them, it was only for the protection of their own men. Sea-warfare differs as much from land, as does the mercantile sea-service differ from the ordinary land mercantile business, and must have a corresponding absoluteness of power. Reliance on privateering, assists peaceable Nations to omit war-cares during peace, and this is of great importance. So also, does reliance on Militia, "Minute men" and Guerrillas.

The infliction of sufferings on Individuals, or on collective bodies of persons, by way of retaliation,—is contrary to the rights of the fundamental element the "Individual," and cannot be justified, unless, on the particular persons who have either voluntarily assumed such a risk, (as for instance, who have made an unconditional surrender, or have placed themselves expressly as hostages); or else on persons who have individually deserved punishment, as those who in some manner have so far violated the usages of war, that their lives and persons are deservedly at the mercy of the party who holds them. For, the attempt to justify individually-undeserved retaliation, upon the ground of the assumed rights of the NATION, or upon any other ground,—can only be successful, by also assuming that the liability and chance of any Individual's suffering such retaliation, is one of the GENERAL chances of war, foreseen and voluntarily undertaken by the individual soldier; but the fact is, that such chances are not expected nor undertaken voluntarily, by the individual soldier, because such an infliction does not occur to one soldier in a hundred thousand. And any chance which is so small as that, only operates upon a very few of any people; and there will always be a large number remaining, upon whom it will not operate. Another reason why retaliation should generally be discontinued is, that it is going back to barbarism, and is on a par with that old mode of warfare, which bound prisoners to the stake, and for the flames, and spared NOT the women and children.

Possibly, retaliation may be just, when sufficient previous notice shall have been given, that if such or such an *outrage*, contemplated by the other party, should actually be perpetrated, then such retaliation shall be made. In this case, the refusal of the other party to refrain from the outrage, might be interpreted as a constructive *committal by them*, of evils as great as the threatened consequences whatever they might be, and as a voluntary assumption of the responsibility thereof. But even this rule can only apply to the particular Individuals who compose the body which perpetrates the offence, or runs the risk,—and not to persons who are entirely free from such interpretation, and from such indirect participation.

Thus, the rule in regard to the effects of war, on *persons*, should be exactly the reverse of what it is, as it affects *property;* because property is NOT an elèment of the ANALYTICS of human society, and has no rights itself, although its possession may entitle *persons* to rights; and because injuries to property may easily be compensated for, but injuries to persons, of health or limb or life, cannot be.

As concerning corporeal personal movable property, belonging to a citizen of a belligerent, it belongs in justice and by nature, to the other party, if that party can seize it without infringing seriously upon the rights of a neutral. A compensation to the citizen, from *his own Nation*, is due, if he can show conclusively that he was acting in accordance with its laws, and had used all proper means to protect his property. But so long as proof of this kind is very difficult to obtain, and, so long as Nations do not consider themselves bound to make up the losses of their own citizens, in such cases,—so long the growing tendency to spare the property of private Individuals, is a high evidence of Christian progress, although not a matter of justice.

But the difficulties of proof may be partly obviated, as follows. A practice might easily be introduced, whereby one enemy would give to Individuals of its opposite, as well as to its own people, certificates of the value of supplies taken, or damage done. Such certificates, although not conclusive of the value, would be additional testimony thereunto. The present rule of compensating neutrals, but not their own citizens, and of sparing the Enemy-Individual's property, but not their own citizens',—seems too unreasonable to endure very permanently. At any rate, the belligerent who gives such certificate judiciously and sincerely, should be free from all further moral responsibility, in the case, as to the citizens of an enemy.

Incorporeal and landed properties are excepted from absolute transfer to a captor, simply because they cannot be either carried away or destroyed.

While speaking of the ways and means of war, we cannot forbear to suggest here, the following improvement. Let Nations in peace provide by treaty, where their battle Localities shall be, in case of war; just as Individuals in health and safety, lay out their "cemetery-lots." If possible in these treaties, let all combinations of war-alliances, be anticipated and provided for, as nearly as possible. Let Nations, when they determine to indulge in war, give a certain number of months' previous notice, and then let them resort to the appointed Localities, and confine the war therein. In other words, let the same refinement be attained by Nations, that has been attained by Individuals in the DUEL, whereby disputes, instead of being fought out, *whenever and wherever* occasion or opportunity admitted, to the disturbance and danger of the public,—are adjourned to set times and places, where the injury to unconcerned parties will be none at all, or at least a minimum, and, previously provided against.

§ 4. *The Rights of Neutrals according to Localities.*

(*a*) *In General.* Having thus treated of War, firstly, in relation to the rights of Individuals, and secondly, in relation to the Ways and Means of conducting it, so far as these do not intentionally conflict with the rights of persons or property; we come, thirdly, to consider it in relation to the rights of Neutrals, on their own and on common Localities; so far as these rights have not been considered incidentally under the foregoing two heads. This part relates both to private and to public property, and to official persons of Enemy-Nations; *except* their agents or ambassadors accredited to each other, or to neutral Nations; because such persons, with their attendants and property, are almost universally exempt from the ordinary vicissitudes of war, and are not to be understood as included in our treatment of the subject.

The rights involved, are summed up in two conflicting principles: one, that "neutrals shall not interfere in the war," the other, that belligerents shall not interfere in the neutral's peace. These principles are of course partly conflicting, hence a compromise has to be effected between them. Regard can only be given to *principal* effects; which are of two kinds: one, the principal effect of any given *circumstances;* the other, the principal effect of a *rule* applying to them.

Here the distinction becomes prominent, between a Neutral

Nation as an organism, and the Individuals who compose it. The Nation as an organism, must preserve its neutrality strictly, and in every particular; but to expect such an absolute control over its individual citizens, would be absurd, in this age of the world.

We will consider first, the matter of passage through the territory of a neutral; because the neutral territory is analogous to the neutral ship when considered apart from its contents. It is generally admitted that enemies have no right to passage through the territory of a neutral, much less any right to conduct hostilities therein: (Wheaton, §§ 426 and 427) and, by modern writers, it is coming to be admitted, that a neutral has no right to grant permission of passage to a belligerent. (Dana's note.) Nor can the neutral territory be rightly used, in any manner, as the *basis* of belligerent operations. But it should not follow from this, that a neutral Nation is bound to oppose such passage, by force of arms, without the co-operation of other powers, who may be as much interested in the maintenance of the principle, as itself. Furthermore, the active Individuals of an enemy, have no right to passage across the territory of a neutral; and their doing so ought to be punished as an offence tending to involve the neutral into the war feelings, and hence into the war consequences.

The next question is, what articles (and persons) are, and what are not, contraband of war. The common principle is thus stated by Dana: (notes to Wheaton, §§ 505 and 501) "One cardinal rule is, that the neutral may trade with the enemy. Another is, that he shall not intervene in the war. The practical result of the conflict of these rules is, that, in trading with the enemy, he must not break an effective blockade, and shall not take to the enemy, merchandise which is of such a character as to afford *direct* military aid, or which will help to relieve or avert the pressure of actual siege or blockade." * * * These various "considerations have led to a practical adjustment of the question of contraband, to the effect, that the neutral may carry merchandise to both belligerent markets, subject to this condition,—that, if it be contraband, it may be taken from him, at sea, and converted to the captor's use." * * * But "as to what things do or do not come into this category: The test is variously described, and more or less strictly; but it seems to amount to this,—Is the primary and ordinary use of the *article* military, when in the enemy's possession, *in time of war?*"

But this, the actual rule, is both unjust and unnecessary. The "primary" use of the article in time of war, is often not the use in time of peace; and then the rule interferes with the rights of neutrals. Again, it is not merely the directness of the use of any article, which constitutes its importance, but it is the special need the enemy may have for it, and the special vicissitudes and emergencies of times and seasons, which of course constantly vary.

Strictly speaking, according to natural justice, the belligerents have no right to interfere *intentionally* with the rights or interests of neutrals at all: but the vicissitudes of war are so great, that this rule cannot be maintained.

In the vicissitudes of war, opportunities are frequent, wherein the advantages of small trade with a neutral, would be counterbalanced by serious interruption of the course of the war, and followed by immense losses of property and lives,—such, for instance, as in a siege or blockade. The liability of vicissitudes justifies this rule of war. But on the other hand, the common doctrine, that directness of the utility of the articles of trade, for military uses, also constitutes the contraband, is not sound nor reasonable; for when there exists *no special* exigency, the general injury to the trade of neutrals is far greater than the advantages to the belligerent. Besides, the refusal to pass these minor articles, so long as food and any kind of clothing are allowed, not only has but little effect upon the war, but it has great effect in producing personal discomfort to the soldier; so that the rights of the Enemy-*Individual,* as well as the rights of neutrals, are needlessly disregarded. But the generally received policy is different.

Now, we shall generalize yet more completely, if we understand "article" to include, besides property, any government official person, excepting *perhaps* a non-combatant; and apply the same principles accordingly. This generalization is sound, because the principles involved are the same, whether persons or property are the agencies employed. For instance, *persons intending* to enlist or engage in the enemy's service, are quite as much material of war, as chattels are; so also are persons intending to carry war-material or dispatches, or to purchase contraband materials. The difference consists chiefly in this, that property, when captured, can be applied to the use of the enemy; but, usually, Individuals cannot be so applied. But this difference is quite limited, because guides, pilots, surgeons, interpreters, and even mechanics and laborers, can be *forced* to apply themselves to the indirect uses of their captors.

We may now consider more in detail, these rights of neutrals in their own or in common Localities, under the following divisions:—Firstly: Of affairs involving articles and officers on the territory of a Neutral. Secondly: Of affairs involving articles and officers on neutral or common Localities, namely, on the high seas.

(*b*) *Affairs in the Locality of a Neutral.* The generally accepted rule is, that the people of a neutral Nation, in their trade with a belligerent, must *not* furnish him with the particular articles called contraband, but *may* furnish him with any other articles. The restriction in this rule ought to be repealed, for the following reasons:—It is impossible to execute. It causes irritating interferences in other governments' affairs, and thus constantly endangers the peace of neutral Nations. It prolongs wars, and increases their expenses both of life and property, without altering the decision. The analogy between forbidding enlisting soldiers, and purchasing war-materials, does not give a sound argument, because the soldiers, being persons, are usually supposed to be of the neutral citizenship; and thus the foreign belligerent, if allowed to enlist soldiers, would be drawing our citizens into ruin and death, to the injury of their Families, and of the country at large. But the purchase of materials has the opposite effect, stimulating trade, and thus benefiting the country furnishing the supplies. Hence, the *general* rule should leave the domestic trade of every Nation "free" to both enemies,—for cash or bona fide immediate trade, but not for any form of credit to, or for, mere "belligerents," and not for loans, nor for any longer than the *usual* mercantile credit to or for non-belligerent Nations. Because the extension of credit is made to *both* the belligerent Nations equally, and thus lessens the *immediate* effects on both of them, and thus prolongs or stimulates the war, without any great advantage to any parties concerned.

Nevertheless, this general rule ought to have one sort of exception, namely, the export of war-materials, and of all the *direct* means of transportation. Instead of excepting to the manufacture or sale of many articles used in peace, we should except rather to the means of transportation, to either enemy. In some cases, the means would be freight-wagons, horses, oxen, and so on. In other and in most cases, the means would be boats or vessels. This exception is not much liable to the objections, the other was. It is practicable in domestic policy, and does not cause general irritation. It is analogous to the principle of export duty; which, in turn, is the same according to international principles as an import duty. Governments do not pretend to inquire into everybody's store, to tax his foreign imports, but tax them once for all, at their entrance into the country. The place, and the only proper place, to interfere with foreign trade in common articles, is, at the importation or the exportation of the commodities. "Rowdy" Nations disturbing the peace of the world, ask too much of all, when they demand that other Nations shall institute new legal proceedings, interfering with the course of their own internal affairs generally.

Hence, we infer, that the people of a neutral Nation, of right can unrestrictedly manufacture and sell, except strictly war-material, and entertain war-officers purchasing materials, &c.; and that trade with a neutral is not to be interrupted; so that the only questions with us, relate to the transportation, and to arms and ammunition. As to arms and ammunition, which are the only things we can admit are strictly war-material; the duty to watch their manufacture and sale, is no hardship, neither is it a special task imposed upon neutrals *only* in the case of war,—because Nations, for their own internal peace and safety, need to have constant regard to such things, and *ought* always to have such a knowledge and registration of them, as they have of all other *dangerous* occupations.

Yet our principles would allow the foreigners to come *only* into the few large markets, on or near the borders of the neutral, and with publicity to their actions; but would not allow miscellaneous travel through.

Again, the voyaging or departure "must not be allowed to interfere with the war"; therefore, in case of means of transportation, wagons, cars, or other vessels for either belligerent, having been built in a neutral territory, the neutral is bound to forbid their departure; then if they depart by stealth without due clearance, or by false representations, the duty of all Nations, and particularly of the neutral escaped from, and whose "state" was thus "ignored," is to treat such a vessel as an outlaw, forbidding it entrance into their ports or seas: and doubly so, if a vessel of war. Hence, in such cases as the Alabama, not only England, but all other neutrals should have forbidden its entrance into their dominions, not as a vessel of war of a belligerent, but as the *outlaw of a neutral.* And in case of such entrance, the vessel should be forfeited. Such ought to be henceforth established as a rule in the Law of Nations. The conception, to be sure, of an outlaw who is not a pirate, is somewhat difficult to get; but not any more difficult, than the conception of a "recognized belligerent" who yet is not a Nation.

(c) *Affairs in Common Localities.* As to affairs involving articles or officers in *common* Localities, and on the high seas. Here comes in for consideration, *the ship.* The ship is the abode of human beings; it is an "*arrondissement*," a Precinct, with a recognized government of its own, under the sanction of some recognized Nation. Here are two complicated questions. The road is mutual, but the vehicle or *car*, is of the one Nation. The inference is, that the principles involved are exactly the same, as those in the case of the Locality of a neutral on land, except, that the travel must not be interfered with; nor the special rights of humanity refused, in the distresses that men who travel by sea are particularly liable to. With these limitations, the voyaging ship has no rights other than it possessed in its own territory. In other words, the neutral's *voyaging* itself, or any part thereof, must not be entitled to immunities that will directly aid either of the belligerents. A neutral, on board ship, may manufacture spars or sails or guns, if possible, and may carry them to another neutral, but has no right to carry them to any belligerent place, person, or vessel.

But now comes the more difficult question:—the contraband property which any neutral sells to a belligerent, or the belligerent official whom he entertains,—has some *other* belligerent a right to transport, on the high seas? Of course not, *from his own,* nor *from* the shores of either, nor *to,* any belligerent place, person, or vessel;—but, has the neutral a right to carry such "article" or person across the seas at all? The entire denial of this right, would often refuse a neutral vessel the right of sailing from one part of his own country to another. From this reasoning we may justly infer, that Mason and Slidell MIGHT have required to have been returned to Nassau "as they were," or else forwarded, so as to reach their ultimate destination at the time they would have reached it, by LEGITIMATE means, if undisturbed by a neutral,—UNLESS, instead of only running our blockade, in one of their OWN vessels, they had come through, in a *neutral vessel violating blockade,* or had run *through our* lines or our country. And as *this is so,* their case comes under that we treat in the next paragraph. Because it has come to be a settled principle of international law, that blockade is nothing to belligerents, only as it is effectual in particular; but is obligatory on neutrals, when effective in general.

The case then, was really thus. Rebel emissaries were constantly embarking on board foreign steamers from New York, and as soon as at sea, would openly insult our citizens, and glory over their success in getting on board. Now, all such persons (having been spies in the United States, according to the laws of war, and also being warlike emissaries, and having obtained their passage surreptitiously), the foreigner had no right to transport; neither would the foreigner have had right, to transfer them to the United States authorities for punishment. Therefore, the officers of the ship should have confined the passage-takers, to the vessel until its return; and then sent them through the United States lines to their *Confederate* home,—a proceeding very similar to that, by which the United States sent both Mason and Slidell to *Nassau.* The passages of the emissaries at New York, were obtained by *deception;* the capture of Mason and Slidell was by *force.* A friend or neutral has no more right to allow the deception, after it becomes known, than to allow the force, after its *illegality* becomes known,—to aid either belligerent.

We may add to this thought, the general rule, that the more indirect or circuitous, the aid rendered by a neutral, the more freely, such aid is permitted by the law of Nations. But this *ought* to be true, *only* for the reason and *in the degree*, that the circuitousness obscures the true state of the case, or complicates it with the relations of innocent parties.

The Virginius, in the Cuba affair, affords another instance of a dispute settled erroneously by both parties, and on principles which will not stand the test of time.

The claim of the United States amounts to this: That a foreign government has no right upon the high seas (namely in *common* Localities), to interfere with a vessel bearing the American flag and American clearances, even although such vessel may have been, with those old clearances, engaged for several years in fomenting discord and aiding rebellions in various neighboring countries; and at the very time of interference, also be engaged in carrying arms and ammunition to rebels, even when *their* belligerency has *not* been admitted; and may have repeatedly escaped capture by the injured country, through means of false representations and false oaths, in foreign ports! And furthermore, that the fact of the said rebels not being recognized even as belligerents, LESSENS the rights of the injured government, in the case! Whereas in the case of the Alabama, it was the recognized belligerency ALONE, that saved her from capture in or near neutral ports. And furthermore, that the vessel when discovered to have borne a flag and papers, to which she had no right, as the *means of injuring the foreign* country, and when captured, belongs, not to the injured government, but to the United States, which had all the while fostered the irregularities, and protected the vessel! And furthermore, that when the injured government might have redress against the United States, for *direct* damages, if any such could be proved (which of course is next to impossible in such a business)—yet it has no redress for *indirect* damages, (namely therefore none at all). And finally that the assent (although only after persistent objection), to these principles, by a very weak power, under threats of immediate war or reprisal, and of taking territory of immense value, from the weak and injured government,—that such assent is proof of a principle of international law! The whole conclusion is so improper as ought not to need any argument.

It must be admitted, that Spain, in her hasty execution of the men engaged, violated the rights (not of American citizenship, because the Virginius crew, according to our theory, had forfeited those rights), but had violated the rights of HUMANITY and of just international law; but this gives to the United States government *no more* than to any other government, the right to punish the violation of the laws of humanity. And yet the United States government takes those men to its bosom, and the people publicly honor them, just as England treated the "confederates" against the United States. Although the offence being political, cannot be punished or recognized by foreign governments in *their* Localities. But the case is different in *common* Localities, for in them one Nation has as much right as another.

Now the truth is, that all the question relative to the right of the vessel to bear any national flag and its papers, in injuring another government, is just as much (or more so) a question for decision by the *injured* government, as by the one whose flag and papers are falsely assumed—And in disputed cases, belongs to neutral Nations to decide; either by diplomatic notices, as when the foreign ministers at Washington notified our government, that the execution of the Confederate privateers as pirates would be held as a public outrage; or by arbitration.

The real motives of our government thus treating Spain about the matter were:—first, our sympathies were with and for the Cuban rebels, and the other rebels whom the Virginius had aided, although Spain was a republic itself at the time; second, our desire to get Cuba, and all other territory we can get near us; third, a truckling to the popular impulse that burst out, when the news of the capture and proceedings were first received. Alas our government is in danger of doing as republican France did in her revolution of "'89", namely, allowing popular clamors to drive us into the violation of international law, and thus stirring up all Nations against us. But in the case of the Virginius, democratic republicanism overreached itself, and seems to have caused the downfall of Castelar, and of our struggling sister republic of Spain.

The growing principle of international law, that more and more exempts neutral Nations from the effects of war, ought justly to be so applied as to exempt, not only from interference *by the Enemy-Nations*, but also from *all entanglements therein by* private Individuals, who undertake to aid either of the belligerents. In other words, the privileges and legal opportunities of private Individuals, to entangle their neutral countries into war or war-complications, must decrease equally with the decrease of the privileges of Enemy-Nations to interfere with neutrals; and then, Individuals who interfere with the war-affairs of other Nations, must be allowed to do so at *their own* risk, clear alike from punishment as outlaws or pirates by neutrals, and clear also from their protection; and their country, clear of all responsibility for them. In short, neutral Nations must not be easily disturbed, either by Enemy-Nations, nor by belligerent dynasties, nor by the individual abettors of any of them. Still, humanity and Mankind must be heard, in limiting the punishment of political offenders, within the bounds of civilization and Christianity; as also of all other offenders.

CHAP. V. CONCLUSION OF INTERNATIONAL LAW.

This subject, namely, international law, is connected with that of Universal Empire, and of Races, and of the influence of Christians and of Christianity; and hence, should be finished under the head of Mankind; not, indeed, in any one part especially, but in various connections.

PART III.

THE DOCTRINE OF NATURALIZATION.

CHAP. I. CLASSIFICATIONS.

This subject is generally treated as a part of International law: but with us it has to take a wider range of discussion. Its place of consideration under that head, and one or two general principles of it, are there given. (See II. II. 5).

Naturalization may be *defined* to be the transfer of personal nationality, from one Nation to another. It is a subject which cannot be fairly nor fully understood, without referring to the Nation itself as one of the great fundamental Units of human society: otherwise, the lengthy consideration of the subject, would belong to the division of "Civil Government" rather than to this place. Much that has been said above, can readily be brought to bear upon this subject, but is left to the reader's own ingenuity and reflection.

Naturalization has been divided into COLLECTIVE and INDIVIDUAL.

CHAP. II. COLLECTIVE NATURALIZATION.

Collective Naturalization, namely, the naturalization of the inhabitants of the whole of any given territory, takes place usually when any territory becomes transferred from one government to another. And if the transfer is made with the voluntary co-operation or concurrence of the inhabitants, it generally accomplishes the transfer of a full and equal citizenship, without even those special reserves that are usually made in case of Individual-naturalization; such exceptions, for instance, as not being allowed the possibilities of becoming a member of parliament, or privy council in England; or of becoming President or Vice-President of the United States.

This transfer of full and equal citizenship, along with the comparatively small territory or district, that is separated from one Nation and joined to another,—being founded in justice, and in a knowledge of human nature, and on the feelings of birthplace, home, &c.,—is an incidental but strong argument in favor of our Precinct-theory. Because it shows, that history and international law, regard and treat the human feelings for, and attachments to, the immediate Locality of one's birth and home; as being superior to, and more reliable than, the more general Locality of one's native Nation. In fact, this argument belongs more properly under the head of PRECINCT, than under Nation.

In the transfer of Alsace, we have lately seen a pre-eminent instance of the superiority of Precinct-attachments to National ones: Because *there*, a people who had originally been part of Germany, but conquered and retained by France, some centuries, then when re-conquered by Germany, demonstrated the utmost aversion to returning to it.

Collective naturalization is generally provided for fully by treaty, although it could equally as fully be accomplished by conquest, or by secession; since all that is really needed, is the concurrence of the inhabitants of the territory whose allegiance becomes changed. And such a transfer is evidently more effectual by a secession, or an *accepted* conquest, than by a transfer between superior powers, which might be more or less against the will of the inhabitants of the transferred territory.

Collective naturalization might better be divided thus:—that which takes place by the annexation of new territory; and that which takes place by the recognition of *classes* of denizens who had not previously been citizens. But both these subdivisions of collective naturalization, depend mainly, on the same principles of morality and right as does Individual-naturalization, except, that the attempt to obtain *special* proofs of individual-character, is *not* made, nor any special oaths or promises obtained. There is also another, and even more important difference, in the case of annexing new territory. For in such cases, whichever way the territory goes, so also go the feelings of birthplace, home, &c. But, on the other hand, if the annexation has been produced by conquest, the evils and dangers of naturalization are greater, and the subject more difficult. With these and similar modifications, the PRINCIPLES involved in the whole subject, will be sufficiently discussed under the subject of Individual Naturalization,—as we soon propose to do. But as far as we are correct on the point, that for the annexation of new territory, collective naturalization depends largely on the same principles as Individual, our theory tends to discourage such annexation; unless of territory where the inhabitants are already nearly similar to ourselves, in moral and intellectual condition; or are acknowledged so far inferior, as to consent to and produce, a territorial government over them by the superior; to be able and willing to do the latter of which, is one of the great needs of the United-States-government. Otherwise it is hard to see how we can deal safely with the Indian problem, or with the Monroe-doctrine; which latter, even if fully assented to by European powers, is threatening this country with great difficulties in the future,—practical difficulties, of how to deal with peoples who cannot govern themselves, who need and want our protection and police over them; but yet are, for those very reasons, unfit to enjoy the *full* rights of American citizenship, and whose overwhelming numbers, if equal voters, would first be a balance between all parties, and then, the ruling party themselves.

CHAP. III. INDIVIDUAL-NATURALIZATION.

An Individual may obtain naturalization, either by conforming to some general law, or by special grant of the government. But we will consider the subject in relation: first, to the rights of the *Individual* human being; second, to the rights of the *Nation renounced;* and third, to the rights of the *Nation adopting* (or, as the phrase is, "the *adoptive* Nation.") And we wish all the *principles* here exhibited on this topic, to be understood *generally*, and as equally applicable to change of citizenship from Precinct to Precinct, under the reformed constitution we have proposed, as to change from Nation to Nation. But whilst the same principles are applicable, they must yet be modified in their application, to suit the altered circumstances. The *double* value of the principles thus treated, must be our excuse for some things that might otherwise seem unpatriotic, in this "Part III." of this article; and for giving undue length and prominence to a subject, which for the Nation has already been settled by history, and seems out of date.

§ 1. *The Rights of the Individual.*

The abstract right of an Individual, to change his nationality, and to remove from a country where he is not happy, to a country where he thinks he will be so,—cannot reasonably be denied. But yet there are many *conditions* to which he may be bound to subject himself, in making the transfer. All the reasonable claims of his native country and of its citizens, upon him, for any proper length of time, ought to be granted first. But what standard is to be used, to judge of the reasonableness of the claims? Not that alone of the government and people about to be renounced, nor that alone of the people or government about to be adopted and re-inforced. Therefore the standard must be one which might be considered a sort of compromise between the two parties; and the judgment rendered, should be one which we would suppose would be given according to that standard, by impartial persons, that is, by arbitrators or referees, being persons or Nations who fulfilled an *intermediate* character between the others, and who were so far removed from the scene of action as to be entirely disinterested. This rule is of course partly ideal, because the actual judges are primarily the two peoples and governments who are *directly interested* in any given case. But the rule is an ideal, suggesting to both parties in a dispute, what kind of a standard *they ought* to adopt, and what kind of a judgment they ought to render; always deferring to the maxim of the *Chief Ruler*, "Do unto others as you would they should do unto you," with this natural limitation, namely,—so long as the other Nation will do so to you.

Another moral principle tending to illustrate this part of the subject, is this: Every innocent Individual has a right to live *somewhere*. The Nation of his birth has no right to expatriate him, without providing some other reasonable home. And this brings up the still more general proposition, that in the last resort for principles, every human being has a right to reside among the people whom he most resembles, taking into consideration all his characteristics, physical, metaphysical, and moral. This, we theorize, is a still more general principle than even birth itself; and at all events, is the only fundamental principle of direct application, when once the operation of the law of birth is laid aside. And the practical standards and rules for deciding in particular cases, are the same as those just above mentioned, namely, Compromise, Fraternal Equality, and the Condition of Mutuality.

And these principles are true, and the freedom demanded is just and necessary, on the ground of the rights of the INDIVIDUAL UNIT; and equally *as* true or more so, in time of war, as or than in time of peace. And the only exception, or limitation to the right of free emigration in war LESS THAN in peace, would be, that the emigrant should not remove to the ENEMY-NATION; but might, to any other one he pleased, that appeared to be a suitable one, and to which he seemed to desire to go in good faith there to abide.

But this principle is not to interrupt any rights of a native country, which are valid in *peace* as well as in war. Of which we speak next.

§ 2. *The Rights of the Renounced Nation.*

"Mr. Wheaton, while Minister at Berlin," stated one of the true and fair principles of naturalization, when he "declined to interfere to protect from military service, a Prussian subject who had been naturalized in the United States, but had returned to Prussia. Mr. Wheaton said to him: "Had you remained in the United States, or visited any foreign country EXCEPT PRUSSIA, on your lawful business, you would have been protected by the American authorities, at home and abroad, in the enjoyment of your rights and privileges as a naturalized citizen of the United States. But, having returned to the country of your birth, your native domicile and national character REVERT, so long as you remain in the Prussian dominions; and you are bound in all respects to obey the laws exactly as if you had never emigrated." Dana's note, § 86.

The reason of the justice of such a decision is, that the contrary rule might easily be so employed as to seriously impair national rights. Because, when a citizen returns to his native country, he has its accent, its manners, and its personal relationships; all of which tend both to bind him thereunto in feeling, and also tend to prevent the national authorities from distinguishing such foreigners from citizens. If returning to their native country were indulged in by large numbers of foreigners of that kind, a country would have scarcely any escape from requiring, at every important crisis, tests of allegiance from ALL its inhabitants—an almost endless task, as also very expensive and very unsatisfactory. The only easy plan to allow self-expatriated foreigners to return as the citizens of another Nation, would be, for the original country to command methods whereby every such person, immediately on his return, should register himself as such, in some Locality, and confine himself thereto.

Leaving one's country and changing citizenship, is something like a woman's leaving her husband, and afterwards marrying another; and if the leaving was FOR GOOD CAUSE, the new husband would still naturally be averse to having his wife returning to friendship with the former husband, however willing he might be for her to form friendships with other men.

If the past disorders are not abandoned, foreign Nations may, at last, be driven to absolutely forbid their self-expatriated citizens from ever returning; or forbid their original departure, either entirely, or until they have taken oaths and given security, *not to return*. Or our policy of forcing our ideas of nationality on other governments, and thereby provoking their secret animosity, may, some day, by the aid of our internal dissensions, have very disastrous consequences.

The plea by which the United-States-government endeavors to repudiate these sound principles, and to deny that nationality reverts to a foreigner upon revisiting his native country, is, that the general claims of foreign Nations under *general* laws, are of no application,—and that only when the claims have become individualized, so as to call for, and to apply to the immediate duty of, the Individual,—do they have international force. But this is merely ignoring the foreign system altogether. True, the writer's private theory, claims, that no government has a right to forbid its citizens to remove to another country; but neither international law, nor the United-States-government, acknowledges this principle. And our government has no right to act upon it on one side of the question and *not* on the other.

The foreign system giving us trouble in this respect, may be compared with our own system thus. The foreign, instead of drafting men from its mass for military service, only during war,—designates a certain proportion of its young men for *annual* discipline, and to be called out *first* in case of war. Now if we, every few years, were to draft a portion of our people for such purposes, we would then have a class of citizens for, and a method of comparison with the foreign ones. In times of war, there have generally been formed in the United States, bodies of volunteers called "minute men," "home guards," &c. Such bodies of men resemble young foreigners in their own country, except in the variable matter of having volunteered. The two systems are entirely different; and our decisions and policy presumptuously violate the foreign internal classification of citizens, instead of only attempting to have it modified reasonably, by equitable limitations.

But we may conduct this discussion of the rights of the Nation renounced, by a resort to higher grounds. Now, when we bear in mind the distinctive characteristics of national independence,—that between Nations, the simplest reciprocities of justice require previous treaty stipulations, and that the return of an escaped slave, even between Precincts (states) of the same Nation, requires constitutional provision; we infer at once that when an Individual escapes or removes to another government, the government abandoned has naturally no further national rights over him. Now, only apply this same principle to the reverse case, and the question of naturalization would be at least half settled. Only say, that the actual migration from and leaving of one's adoptive country, and entrance into the former, release a person from the *protection*, as well as from the claims, of the last country left; and hold-to the principle,—and the question is half settled. Certainly, if leaving one's native country is an avoidance of the laws, then a return to that country is a revival of its laws.

In fact, the question may be argued on still broader grounds, and without reference to any previous naturalization. It may be maintained theoretically in general, that if leaving one's country, whether native or adoptive country, is a virtual forsaking of its claims, so therefore it must be a virtual forsaking of its protection;. *unless there are treaty stipulations to the contrary.* And, on the other hand, if leaving a country is an escape from its laws, so therefore a voluntary and Individual entrance *into* a country, is theoretically a submission to or acceptance of its laws. And if there are any just exceptions to these principles, let them be considered and settled *as exceptions;* but let not the universal principles of justice and fairness, be perverted, to excuse the exceptional cases. If the highly civilized Nations of Europe, claim the right for their citizens to reside and trade in the barbarous countries of Asia and Africa, yet without subjecting those citizens to the barbarous and superstitious laws and customs of such degraded peoples; let it be SAID SO, at least to ourselves scientifically; and let not the great laws of Mankind or of equality, be perverted. And again, if Democracies and Republics are going to claim as much superiority of rights, over Kingdoms and Empires, as civilized Nations claim over the uncivilized, or the half-civilized ones, let that claim also be scientifically expressed; and let the inside world of our own citizens know, that if the Nations of Europe are jealous of us, they are so, in consequence of the direct avowals of some of our leading men, and of the long continued aggressive policy of our national government: and, a change of our policy would soon allay their jealousy.

It is strange, and wonderfully inconsistent, that a people who have such strong and centralizing views of nationality, as those of the United States, should have such loose views of the transfer of citizenship from one Nation to another. It is a subject by which, more than by any other, in this era of the world, our foreign relations are liable to be disturbed, and universal war and disorder, provoked.

The theory and decisions of the United States government, so far as they have been developed, until after the great rebellion, were peculiarly selfish and one-sided, in regard to alienism or expatriation. Thus, the right of an American-born citizen to become naturalized into any foreign government, had been denied by us, whilst the right of the citizens of *all* foreign governments, to leave their own countries and become naturalized in the United States, had been fiercely maintained. Yet the right had even been conceded, of a foreigner once naturalized in the United States, to renounce and again become a citizen of his native government. And the whole set of our laws on the subject, was evidently intended to allow and encourage the greatest possible amount of seduction of the citizens of other governments, away from them, together with the minimum of desertion from our own; and without regard to consistency or national equality. That our policy was clearly demagogic, and tended to incite disturbance throughout the world, is fully proved by the fact that when the very foreigners whom we had received as citizens, and upon oaths of allegiance abjuring all attachments to foreign governments, departed from us, to incite or participate in the struggles of their native countries, we still retained over them the fostering and protecting care of our flag, and thus indirectly excited and stimulated them to foreign aggressions. But this was one-sided; for a citizen who proves by his acts, that his warmest political affections are still in and towards his native country, thus proves that in heart he has not become truly naturalized-out from the land of his birth. The proper course for our government to take, is to openly and fully warn our citizens, that interference with the affairs of other governments, will be taken as the virtual renunciation of citizenship in the United States; and if any difference, this interpretation will be more surely given to acts of foreigners returning to their native lands and interfering there, than in regard to any other kinds of interference; on the principle that return revives citizenship there. And these warnings should be repeated, and republished thoroughly, when circumstances seemed to call for them; and then, if our Individuals *would* persist in interfering with other countries, and in efforts and tendencies to embroil us in foreign disturbances, then we had no more care for them than any other neutrals had; and the consequences of such expatriation, should be allowed to fall upon those who so persistently bravadoed all the Nations interested, subject only to the claims of common pity and humanity. The whole principle of our past conduct, reminds one of the course taken by the French Republic of 1789, which ended in stirring up all Europe against it. The only supremacy which can be granted by international law, to one government or people, over others, is a supremacy founded upon intellect controlled by morality and goodness; and only that kind of supremacy will *ultimately* prevail: and *that* is a supremacy which will come about more by general consent, than by force or threats.

Since the great rebellion of '61–65, we have, to be sure, seen that our policy was to amend our principles, but the amending has only been of the *theory* chiefly, and not much, if any, of our practices. But since England has settled the Alabama claims liberally and promptly, and is treating us fraternally in the affair of our centennial; it is time for us to let our old enmity against her drop forever.

§ 3. *The Rights of the Adoptive Nation.*

We may say, in general, that although our theory utterly denies the right of what our government did during the rebellion; namely, denies the right of a national government to forbid the departure of its citizens, yet it by no means forbids Nations the right of discretion, as to the reception or refusal of immigrants. For instance, compare the Nation with the Individual Unit. An Individual has liberty to go where he pleases, although he has no right to intrude into the company of those who do not want him. But this restriction is counteracted by the rights of another unit, namely, Mankind. For, where population is in excess of the capacity of the land to sustain it, and whilst there are immense territories of other Nations uninhabited, it certainly is the duty of *some* of those Nations, to receive the immigrants. But whose duty is it? We answer, that treating the question now as a *moral* one, we are to consider not only the extent of uninhabited territory, nor the abundance of its wealth and productions; neither are we to consider only the choice of the immigrants, when that choice depends merely on the consequences of such things as cheap land and high wages; but we are to consider moral and intellectual relations. So that the duty of receiving the immigrants, will devolve upon that Nation which, having the most ability to do it, is yet nearest like them in intellectual, moral and religious character. This principle may be modified to favor the reception of such classes of persons as are scarcely fit in morals and intellectuality,—the better, when such persons are of a *mild* and *peaceful* and obedient disposition, so that they will readily place themselves under the guidance of their adopted country. For, among Nations as well as among Individuals, self-preservation is the first law of nature. And no theory in this case can be more unreasonable, than the supposition that everybody has a right to go everywhere, and exercise political supremacy, and the consequent powers of *governing others* ON THEIR native soil. And on the other hand, the right of the immigrants to be free from imposition or tyranny of their adoptive country, is involved in the necessity and the fact of their coming, and in the duty of the other party to receive them.

Now here is another place where our Precinct and Corporation theories come in so admirably. In order then, to secure the rights of all parties, probably the most satisfactory plan would be, for immigrants to be allowed to form their own Corporations, for their own government and rule, without control over, or even without the ordinary subjection of their internal personal affairs to, the government of the adoptive country. The feasibility of this will be deducible from our general principles of Corporation, although no special allusion need be made to it there.

But the Precinct-system offers really the most perfect and best plan, for foreigners to enjoy their own rights customs and religion, with the least amount of interference with those of other persons, or, of the adoptive Nation itself. But inasmuch as it is sometimes inconvenient, the Corporation-system would give the most general satisfaction to them. Yet both systems can be employed, some in some cases, and some in others. But the Precinct-system is most effectual, both for releasing minorities from the power of majorities, and also for releasing majorities from control by turbulent and cabalistic cliques. And the same principle applies to keeping up the distinctions between Nations; that is, avoiding too much mixing of utterly heterogeneous elements.

§ 4. *Personal Conditions.*

(a) *In General.* We have already considered in part, the rights of the adoptive Nation, by comparing them with the rights of the Nation *renounced.* The remainder of this part of the subject, embraces the reasons for requiring important *conditions* of naturalization. These may be comprised in two divisions. One, is, to prevent errors that may arise out of the changed relations. The other, is, to procure and prove real fitness for the transfer to the new nationality. The means relied upon in the United States to accomplish these two objects, are, Length of residence, Oath of allegiance, and Legal Registration under Judicial sanction. Something is *said* about good moral character, but nothing is really done about that qualification, except in case of having been publicly convicted and imprisoned lately for felony. Some of these questions will come up again for a little consideration, under the head of Qualification of Voters, in "Selections," under "Civil Government," and such of them as should come up there, are omitted here.

(b) *As to Preventing Errors.* The naturalization laws of the United States are entirely right, in accounting that the citizenship of a husband, of *itself*, naturalizes the wife; but this is the opposite of oppressing women, and is hardly granting them that *equality* of rights which some are so loudly demanding. In regard to the difficulties about aliens holding real estate, when privileged to hold personal estate; in a country like this where real estate confers no special political privileges, the distinction is utterly useless, and is a mere result of the retention of antiquated distinctions derived from the feudal law; and the retention of such distinctions is mere *pettifoggery.*

(c) *As to Proving or Producing Fitness;* there is no evidence to believe that oaths of allegiance are worth the few moments spent in making them, or the paper they are written upon. As to *length of residence*, IT is the most practicable reliance for producing or proving, feelings and convictions suitable to the changed nationality. But we find that blind attachments to native land are, not only life-long, but even hereditary. It is probable, that a reasonable knowledge of the theory and principles of the society and government INTO which they had come, taught to and exacted from foreigners, in order to naturalization, would be of great use. The *nominal* condition of good moral character, ought to be made a *real and vital* condition. But even after all, the greatest difficulty, namely, the predilections of birth and early training, continue; and of these, the influences of early training and *clan*-sympathy, are greater even than the mere fact of birth itself.

Special antipathy to any foreign government, is quite as fully an UNfitness for naturalization, as partiality for the adoptive one, is fitness; and in fact the antipathy is, generally, only another form for home-partiality, or some other prejudice, under a different condition of things. But at any rate, the antipathy is productive of more evil than the partiality is of good; because such is the general character of human nature that hatred is more active than friendship.

Just as *Nation* is an eternal Unit of Society, so nationality is an abiding element of human character, and is not capable of being laid aside by an effort of will, nor by papers of naturalization. This is constantly proved by the fact, that some of the immigrants in the United States are continually at work endeavoring to influence the peoples, and revolutionize the governments from which they came. And then their quite innocent and proper publications and "organs," and societies for mutual benevolence, &c. have necessarily, although unintentionally, the effect of constantly keeping alive their old partialities and their old animosities. If the immigrants came from a greater variety of countries, and in more equal proportions from each of them, their animosities, and the troubles and difficulties therefrom arising, would be apt to balance each other, and so be less, generally.

But the wants of the United States for population at first,

and the inducements our country could present, were so strong, that an easy system of naturalization laws was natural, and almost inevitable, under the peculiar circumstances. All that can be done, is to educate their minds and hearts to truth and goodness; and then, trust to their own sense of honor justice and kindness. All that we want is to preserve peace and justice. No clamor about patriotism or "native" land, should bias the matter. And it is well to receive foreigners as fast as we can digest them, politically, socially, and morally.

But we ought not to be in too great a hurry to parcel out all our public lands. In some of the states and territories, foreigners are allowed, even by the United States courts, political privileges *before* naturalization. But this is contrary to some of the fundamental principles of nationality. For nationality presupposes that its Precincts are parts of itself, not only geographically, but personally. And this allowance therefore, is only another part of that system which aims to draw immigrants from foreign countries, and stimulates western emigration and *scatteration*, wildly, and prevents our unoccupied lands from being held forever by the public as landlord, and for the profit of *all* the people (see Spencer on the tenure of land),—and puts them into the private ownership of the sort of gentlemen, whose energy for taking care of "number one" is not the least of their qualifications, and who are always ready to accept from the Nation, a few hundred square MILES of good land, to "develop our resources."

BOOK IV.

CORPORATION.

CHAP. (A) PREFACE TO CORPORATION.

OUR definition of Corporation is, that it is a something entirely different from, either Precinct, or Nation, or borough or town, or any other Locality-government whatever. Just as is the case with churches; the members of the same Locality belong to different churches; and members of the same church, belong to different Localities: so there have been, and it is as conceivable that there may be, different civil governments for different Individuals in the same Precinct; and that such Corporations for civil self-government, may embrace members from two or more Precincts. But the main point of the difference is, that different Corporations for the self-government of their own voluntary members, may be formed WITHIN THE SAME PRECINCT; just as persons may be members of different other voluntary societies therein. The members would select themselves, on the ground of metaphysical and moral resemblances or adaptations. There would be intermingling of all classes, individually, personally and socially; but the civil government for each Individual, would, in most cases, be administered by the civil or political corporation of which he was a member. Differences between members of different Corporations, would have to be settled by arbitration, or in some other equitable manner, between the authorities of the Corporations, or in methods prescribed by them. Nevertheless, matters *strictly* referring to the geographical concerns of Localities, whether of Precinct or Nation, would have to be settled by those Local governments respectively; and *only* such matters; except that all FOREIGN affairs must be left also to the Nation.

We have had more difficulty and more labor, over our article on Corporation, than over almost any other part of the work. One reason was, we had found no books that had afforded us any material aid. True; Mr. Carey's Large edition, in vol. 3, chap. lii. § 3, pp. 415 to 423, has eight or nine excellent pages upon the subject, in a miscellaneous way: but unfortunately, these have been *entirely omitted* from the *Abridged* edition, (see its chap. xliv. §§ 2 and 3), which is the one I have generally used. The reader is referred to the Large edition itself. Calvin Blanchard, an old *chum* of Greeley, has also published considerably on this subject; but I have never seen any of his writings thereon; and as represented in the New York Tribune, his theory is very different from mine, as will appear in chap. ii. § 2, ensuing. Also, a Mr. Sinnickson has written some little, but well, upon this subject; yet not until my article was pretty well under way, at least I did not meet with anything from him previously, and only a few scraps, then.

Another reason of the difficulty and labor over this subject of CORPORATION, and this latter principally,—was the fact, that the *variety* of *possible* or even useful Corporations, is almost indefinitely great; and even the variety of the political ones, which are the kind we design specially to treat, is also so great, that real difficulty arises, both as to the classifications of the whole, and also as to the kinds to select for illustration,—to enable the reader, without undue complication or prolixity, to have, both a glimpse of the whole field, and yet a sight of minutiæ sufficient to be intelligible and unequivocal. It was also desirable, to endeavor to avoid such a repulsive dryness, as would insure there would be no readers of the article at all. Hence, it has been deemed best, to arrange its Main Divisions or Parts, in a rather different order from what has usually been pursued by us. Accordingly, the Argument,—Anticipations in history, and the Anticipations by some other Social Scientists, and some formal Arguments for the Right and Expediency,—are placed *first:* Then, the General Survey of them, according to their nature; the Definitions and Classifications: And last of all, are placed the more Exact Investigations of the general theory, rising gradually to the most general conceptions of the subject, and then falling to the more practical ones.

In this First Main Division, which we call the ARGUMENT,

we only give a few Anticipations, and a few miscellaneous evidences for the rights; and a few of the miscellaneous advantages, whether common to it with the Precinct, or peculiar to it alone. We give these miscellaneous arguments in this Main Division, simply because they seem out of place, in the two subsequent ones.

Many arguments for Corporations, are adducible also, either for Precinct or for Nation; and are thus common to two Elements. Those common to PRECINCT and Corporation, will first and frequently be treated. But for those common to NATION and Corporation, the reader is referred back to that Element, namely Book III.; or forward to the investigation of "Corporations exercising inherent political functions,"—as treated in the Third Main Division of this present Element or "Book."

MAIN DIVISION I.

ARGUMENT FOR POLITICO-GOVERNMENTAL CORPORATIONS.

SUB-DIVISION I.

ANTICIPATIONS OF GOVERNMENTAL CORPORATIONS.

CHAP. I. ANTICIPATIONS BY FACTS.

§ 1. *In Religion and Morals.*

The earliest Corporations we find in history, whether connected with the civil power, or independent of it, are the religious organizations. Bretano expressly says, they followed immediately after the "frith guilds"; and the frith guilds are essentially our elementary Precincts, and not merely artificial or deliberative Corporations. And the religious organizations of most countries and ages, are either virtual or actual Corporations.

The tribe of Levi was a legally instituted national Corporation. It occupied a very different position, from that of all the churches in the United States, taken *collectively;* and different also from any modern national church. Its position was like that of the bishops of the Middle Ages, possessing secular dominions. Hence, it exercised civil authority, by virtue of its religious office. The Levites, besides possessing the dignities and exemptions enjoined as *religious* officials,—were also the ordinary *civil* judges, of the country around the numerous cities allotted to them.

The Christian churches have always been Corporations. Just as the reformation and freedom in the churches, in the 16th century, were, as Guizot says, the precursors and first steps of reformation and freedom in the intellectual world; so also the commencement and persistence of independent Corporations, by churches, may be the precursors and first steps of civil government by Corporations in general.

The monastic institutions of the Middle Ages, possessed a very considerable degree of municipal power upon their own territories; and were also allowed more or less political, as well as ecclesiastical representation, in the Nations. Of Monasticism, Comte (Pos. Phil. 608) says:—"We must also recognize the political bearing of the monastic institutions, which certainly were one of the most indispensable elements of the vast organism, * * * the cradle whence issued by anticipation, the chief Christian conceptions, dogmatic and practical; * * * the foundation whence issued the reformation of orders; a provision for the beneficial exercise of political genius, which it has been impossible to appreciate since its inevitable decay. * * * The Catholic system could not have preserved * * * the attribute of generality, * * * if these contemplative train-bands, who were placed by their very nature at the universal point of view, had not been forever reproducing direct thought, while exhibiting an example of independence which thereby became more generally practicable."

It is a Corporation of the most respectable citizens of Gothenburg, Sweden, who are now executing the most successful plan against intemperance, ever devised. They pay all its profits into the city treasury, appoint all the retailers, furnish them all the liquor at wholesale, allow no profit whatever to be made by the retailer, out of the strong liquors sold, but only the profit out of malt liquors, coffee, tea, cigars, and victuals, which they are *required* to keep on hand, and to sell reasonably. Also the Corporation requires the sales-rooms to be pleasant places; and does not allow any liquor to be sold either on credit or on pledge.

Our respectable Indian commissioners might succeed as well as the Swedish Temperance-friends, if only they were duly organized into a suitable Corporation. But otherwise, the "rings" against them are too strong for them.

§ 2. *In Politics and Parties.*

All the political parties, great and small, are virtual Corporations; so also are the organized "rings" and cliques *within* these other organizations, whether of church or state. Several of the "United States" were started by, or soon transformed into, Corporations. Indeed, all Corporations, when they become great and important, are drawn more or less into politics, even if not intentionally so. But generally, they turn their *realized* greatness voluntarily, into political channels. Even the Temperance-societies and the Peace-churches, sooner or later, and more or less, find themselves acting according to this tendency.

Carey has enumerated some valuable Corporations of antiquity, to which the reader is referred; namely his Large Edition, vol. 3, chap. lii. § 3.

The legislative and judicial authorities in the Middle Ages, were cosmopolitan. They were Councils of virtual *compromise*, acknowledging the representation of Corporations such as we propose in the latter part of this article; and some remnants of which, still continue. The parliaments or national assemblies of the European governments, contained representatives of the Free Cities, the Churches, the Monasteries, and the Universities. But these were in such small proportion, as to avail but little before the grand controlling power of the Great Localities. But even so far as these corporate representatives *did* retain *real* power, the power itself gradually ceased to be free in its operations; besides, the choice of the representatives also ceased to be free. But worse than all, the Corporations themselves became antiquated; and the system contained no principle of recognizing Corporations as such, nor of reorganizing them; and therefore new kinds as demanded by progress, were not formed; and of course, when the Corporations ceased to have general political value, their rights lost their defenders, even among the unlearned laity. Nevertheless, those legislatures were sufficiently analogous to these we propose, to entitle them to be here cited.

Several of the earliest and most prominent attempts at settlement, in the United States, were made by actually chartered Corporations. Such was the case with that at Jamestown, which was the earliest of all. The Jamestown Corporation was divided into two companies, each having its own part of the territory to manage. This Corporation, eleven years subsequently, allowed its colonists to elect delegates to a legislative assembly, whilst retaining itself the appointment of its governor and select council; but in a few years more the Corporation dissolved: and that was the origin of democracy in the United States. Then the "Plymouth Corporation" obtained, in 1620, the grant of the United States, between Maryland and Canada; and from that Corporation the "Pilgrim Fathers" obtained their lands; whence came the grants of Massachusetts, Rhode Island and Connecticut. The settlements at and near Philadelphia, were begun by a Swedish Corporation in 1638, many years before Penn came. The first settlements in New York were made in 1610, by a Holland Corporation, "the Dutch West India Company." And the principal impetus to the settlement of Georgia, was given in 1732, by the charter of incorporation under the leadership of Oglethorpe. It must be admitted, that all these Corporations ultimately failed of their corporate designs; partly because the colonists had but little gratitude to the Corporations who had brought them over from the Old Country, and given them lands; but chiefly, because, being foreign and non-resident Corporations, they were no more able to govern the Colonies, than were the respective kings, or other civil authorities, of the countries whence they had come. And that the colonists were able to throw off the yoke of the Corporations, so much easier and sooner, than the yoke of the kings, and that the Corporations yielded so to the force of circumstances, is proof of their value, if only rightly constructed. And all that kept them from yielding more readily, seems to have been the hope of regaining their financial losses therein,—an opposition that might have been easily and justly met, by the colonists compensating them fairly.

§ 3. *In Education.*

The Universities and Colleges of modern Europe, possessed for centuries, a limited degree of municipal authority. The word "collegium" itself meant association, and included the ideas both of partnership and Corporation. "The word university, in the code Justinian, is used to designate a Corporation. Thus there were in Rome, in the 7th and 8th centuries, universities of tailors, bakers, &c." (App. Cyclop. xv. 836). The universities soon found it necessary to have some sort of municipal government, by instituting their members into Corporations for that purpose. For administering their authority, the universities were subdivided, sometimes into colleges, and sometimes into DIVISIONS OF SEVERAL NATIONALITIES; yet each of these divisions included several different nationalities. It was this necessity, perhaps, quite as much as respect for learning, that caused the universities to be allowed various kinds and amounts of political power, both representative and judicial.

Several of the European medical colleges, "have both a power of police over matters pertaining to the public health, and the privilege of examining candidates for medical degrees," and without whose authority they cannot practice. (App. Cyclop. v. 468).

Oxford University in England, and so also Cambridge, is a federal Corporation, consisting of several distinct colleges, each of which, within certain limitations, is an independent organization, having its own private property, and having control over its own students within its own boundaries.

Of the Universities, Comte (Pos. Phil. p. 726) says:—"At a time when national divergences were still very great, and when the Catholic bond was dissolved; the Universities threw open their doors to foreigners; so as to mark the new speculative class as European, and to afford the best testimony to the *cosmopolitan* character of the scientific spirit."

Most of the communes and communities, at least the Protestant ones, are and have been, without actual charters, but yet are virtual Corporations, exercising a limited degree of governmental power. And they may as well be enumerated here, under education, as anywhere else; because their principal use to the world thus far, has been to teach by example and precept, what can be done in their way; and thus they are instances of what Corporations have done in education.

§ 4. *In Trade.*

Plutarch relates, that in the early ages of ancient Rome, Numa organized the citizens into societies or Corporations, according to their occupations. Some of the modern *savans*, however, say that Plutarch was wrong in this story; but how *our* savans should have so much more certain knowledge about it, than Plutarch, is not so easy to see. But it *is* very easy to see, how this very variance from the present customs and ideas, might raise doubts as to the ancient facts. According to Plutarch, (App. Cyclop. v. 467): "The original design was to prevent the danger of any general conspiracy, by organizing separate assemblies, festivals, and finances, for different portions of citizens." But in fact, these institutions had rather the opposite tendency, and became so disorderly that they were repeatedly suppressed by the Roman government. But in modern times, we find such organizations arising spontaneously. All our trades, wholesale and retail, Employers and Employes, are forming themselves into partial Corporations for their particular self-interested purposes.

The Guilds of Europe in the Middle Ages, remnants of which continue to this day, were virtually, political Corporations. Of these Guilds, Comte (p. 695) says:—they "incorporated the members of each craft, and protected Individual-industry *at first;* however they might oppress it at last." Bretano, in his history of Guilds, says: "The trade-unions of the present day, were the successors of the 'craft-guilds' of the Middle Ages. These again succeeded to the town-guilds or guilds merchant, which were local rather than professional, and included the commercial rather than the producing class. These were preceded by a yet more ancient sort of guilds,—the religious or social guilds; for they were a mingling of both characters; and before these, came the original guilds,—the frith-guilds of the Anglo-Saxons, which seem to have been associations of neighbors for mutual help and defence", [namely, Our Precincts]. "Within the craft-guilds, the institution of apprenticeship grew up. This institution was then accompanied with much formality; for it was not merely the introduction to a business, but to CITIZENSHIP."

Of merchants making their own laws, Comte (p. 694) says:—"During the medieval period, when industrial communities legislated independently, before the formations of the greater polities, there were commercial tribunals and regulations, which do great honor to the Hanseatic merchants, whose jurisdiction contrasts very favorably with others of that age." And we add, that the old Dutch Bank notes, founded upon and representing always, the exact amounts of coin actually deposited and reserved,—were the only legitimate paper-currency, the world has *yet* seen: and, the departure from which system, has entailed a financial curse upon the world, which, in all probability, will continue to weigh heavily upon it, as long as the ordinary course of human things shall endure.

The greater part of the mercantile law in England, may in spirit be regarded as the work of Corporations; for it is chiefly a digest of mercantile *usages* of late date. Mr. Mill, while strongly condemning the common law of England, yet commends the mercantile part of it highly (Pol. Econ. p. 534), as follows:—"Fortunately for the prosperity of England, the greater part of the mercantile law is comparatively modern, and was made by the tribunals, by the simple process, of recognizing and giving force of law to, the usages which, from motives of convenience, had grown up among merchants themselves; so that this part of the law at least, was substantially made by those who were most interested in its goodness."

Of this class of Corporations, the most interesting and the most hopeful kind, are those which we often find men spontaneously forming, in order to avoid the corruptions and inefficiency of the ordinary law; and thus to perform spontaneously and very satisfactorily, the particular functions for which they are organized; for instance, associations such as the Boards of Brokers, Boards of Trade, Chambers of Commerce, and various kinds of Trade-Exchanges, Trades-Unions, and Employers' Unions, which are found more or less in all the large cities of the world.

§ 5. *Cosmopolitan and Migratory.*

Several Corporations are cosmopolitan, and almost world-wide. The Jewish people have ceased from being a Nation, for 2000 years; yet have continued to live as a virtual world-wide Corporation. The Catholic Church is another cosmopolitan Corporation. So also are the Moravian and Quaker Churches; also, several of the great Foreign Missionary Societies. So also are the Free Masons, and perhaps some other Societies.

Then also there are various migratory or TRAVELLING Corporations. The settlers and colonists on new territories, are always virtually, and often actually, incorporated Companies. Sailors and soldiers are travelling Corporations, both virtually and organically. The Gypsies also are a notable exemplification, exercising politico-governmental functions among themselves, by voluntary organization; entirely independent of all other "civil powers"; and almost entirely abstract from particular Locations, whether Precinct, Nation, or even Continent

Some of the Corporations established for making foreign settlements, are also cosmopolitan, and almost *world-wide*, in their nature. The British and Dutch East India Companies, begun for trade, exercised political government, and produced settlements. So also several other organizations, which in former centuries helped to settle the newly discovered Continent. California received many of its best early settlers from the East, by means of Corporations; and now it is receiving its vast additions from the "Celestial" Empire, by the same means. All the classes of society and all the Social Circles, are VIRTUAL Corporations, and may be enumerated under the head of cosmopolitan, as well as anywhere else.

Chivalry was another cosmopolitan institution. Comte (p. 621), says: * * * "Mohammedanism had, even before the Crusades, originated something like the noble associations, by which Chivalry affords a natural corrective of insufficient Individual protection," * * * yet "their free rise is attributable to the Middle-Age-spirit." The examples of Chivalry show some of the principles, whereupon the peace-men may build their theories of the most absolute non-resistance: because there will rise up FOR SUCH, when oppressed by fighting men, other fighting men, actuated by mingled duty, compassion, combativeness, and love of glory. And for such, the Corporation-method is the best.

CHAP. II. ANTICIPATIONS BY WRITERS.

§ 1. *The Ancients and the Idealists.*

Plato, in his Model Republic, bases his whole theory of government, upon the conception of a Corporation. For, as Spencer (Ill. Prog. 391), says, his (Plato's) ideal of a body politic, is to be put together by men, in parts, as a watch might be.

The Scripture places the Corporation of the Christian Church, on a par with a Kingdom or Nation. It is often, in the Gospels, called the Kingdom of God. And in Matt., xxi. 43, is expressly called A NATION. And the Prophet Daniel speaks of it, as a kingdom which should ultimately absorb all the other kingdoms of the Earth.

Hobbes, not only implies but actually asserts, the corporate nature of bodies politic,—and this, notwithstanding his whole system is based upon the analogy of society to a living animal. "'BY ART,' he says, 'is created that great Leviathan, called a Commonwealth.' And he even goes so far as to compare the supposed social contract, from which a society suddenly originates, to the creation of a man by the divine fiat." (See Spencer's Ill. Prog. 391.)

In fact, the general principle that pervaded most writings on Society and Government, in all ages previous to the utterance of McIntosh, that "constitutions are not made, but grow,"—was the idea of virtual Corporations. But in our day, the principle is being ignored in all directions. Even Spencer, whose theory would be greatly aided by our principle of Corporations, says, that the fact "that this Apothegm of McIntosh should have been quoted and requoted as it has been, shows how profound has been the ignorance of Social Science." But how he can reconcile this, with that other great doctrine of his, namely, "that all science is but the extension of common knowledge," we do not see. Yet perhaps we are in the darkness that "pervaded through all previous time"; for we are convinced, that if hitherto it has been true, that "constitutions grow but are not made,"—it is high time they *were really made.*

Also, all other of those writers who have proposed ideals of government, (as Sir Thomas More, Fourier, and so on,) proceed on the same virtual Corporation-Hypothesis of government.

Even the framers of the constitution of the United States, proceeded on the same hypothesis. The whole theory of "delegation of rights," as the origin or essence of government, proceeds upon the same hypothesis.

§ 2. *The Modern Scientists.*

(*a*) *Spencer.* That all civil governments, whether of the Nation or Precinct, partake of the nature of a Corporation, seems indeed *almost* to have occurred to Spencer. Thus, (Ill. of Prog. 396): "The last and perhaps the most important distinction" between an animal and society, "is, that while in the body of an animal, only a special tissue is endowed with feeling; in a society, all the members are endowed with feeling." Thus, the *Principle* of Political Corporation seems to have almost occurred to him, but in such an indirect and merely figurative way, as to have passed him by, without any serious attention. Even his whole idea of government, originally was that of a sort of Corporation, and seemed to allow no natural, instinctive, spontaneous, nor elementary rights to society as such; nor scarcely any other rights, than if it were only a voluntary Corporation." (Continuing from *Westminster Review*, Jan. 1860, we quote):—"The community as a whole has no general or CORPORATE consciousness, distinct from those of its components. This is an everlasting reason, why the welfare of citizens cannot rightly be sacrificed to some supposed benefit of the State; but why, on the other hand, the State must be regarded as existing solely for the benefit of citizens. The CORPORATE life must here be subservient to the life of the parts, instead of the life of the parts being subservient to the CORPORATE life."

Again: Spencer has laid down the broad PRINCIPLES, in a general way, whereby the Individual-man and Corporations, react upon each other:—the principles whereby Corporations would provide for and cure, the evils which their own system might give rise to. Although, it seems, that Spencer himself had chiefly in his mind, the organization of Nations, Provinces, Geographical formations, &c. Yet he has repeatedly pointed out the reciprocal actions, of man, on his surroundings; and then of those surroundings, on man; and then of the changed man, again on his surroundings; and then, of those surroundings, again on the man. And these reciprocities of influence reach their climax, of degree, kind, and importance, in the reactions of human SOCIETIES or ASSOCIATIONS, upon each other. Therefore we may infer, that these reactions and reciprocal influences, will "evolve" their greatest results, that is to say, will do their HIGHEST work, in CORPORATIONS. Spencer calls these reciprocal influences or powers, "Factors of Social Phenomena"; and those of the influences which are *above* the physical, and may be termed moral and metaphysical; he would call the "*super*-organic" Factors. But, let us quote, and allow him to speak for himself.

Spencer in Principles of Sociology Part I. chap. ii. § 13, says:—"Recognizing the primary truth, that social phenomena depend, in part on the natures of the Individuals, and in part on the forces the Individuals are subject to; we see that these two fundamentally-distinct sets of factors, with which social changes commence, become progressively involved with other sets, as social changes advance."

And again § 12, he says:—"During social evolutions, these influences are ever modifying Individuals, and modifying society; while being modified by both. They gradually form what we may consider, either, as a non-vital part of the society itself, or else as an additional environment, which eventually becomes even more important than the original environments,—so much more important, that there arises the possibility of carrying on a high type of social life, under inorganic and organic conditions, which originally would have prevented it."

And again § 11, he says:—"Yet a further derivative factor of *extreme importance*, remains. I mean the influence of the *super*-organic environment,—the action and reaction between a society, and neighboring societies. * * * For I may here, in passing, briefly indicate the fact, to be hereafter exhibited in full,—that while the industrial organization of a society, is mainly determined by its inorganic and organic environments; its governmental organization is mainly determined by its *super*-organic environment,—by the action of those *adjacent societies* with which it carries on the struggle for existence."

If the reader should refer to Spencer's Part I., above mentioned, he would find considerable said about the *units* of society, the social units, &c.; and might suppose Mr. Spencer had some idea like our Six Units. But such is not the case. For, Mr. Spencer uses this word Units, ONLY in reference to the INDIVIDUAL: and without explicit definition, that conception runs all through it. See §§ 6, 13, 14, 21, 22, 24, 25: and all along; thus, in his three great divisions (in separate chapters), "the physical, emotional, and intellectual, traits of primitive man": also § 49, and so on. But although *he* has no reference to any other unit than the Individual; yet such is the abstract and general nature of his thought and language on society, and so true is the type-theory, of the Individual really being type of all the five Units above it, and so true also is our theory that *all* the Six Units are types of CORPORATION,—that what he says, (all along in his "Data of Sociology"), of the Individual-man, is true also of *all* our Seven Fundamental Elements of society, and therefore is true also of Corporation. And that celebrated generalist, has probably, in some other places, had indistinct and undeveloped reference, to such voluntary association as we would call Corporation. In all the foregoing or other references to Mr. Spencer, I mean nothing else than the profoundest respect for him: yet still it is possible, that the idea of Political Corporations possessing *fundamental* and *inherent* political functions, may have been (as I suppose), *clearly "differentiated"* for the first time, by me.

(*b*) *Guyot.* Guyot also, without knowing it, or without calling special attention to it; anticipates the necessity of Political Corporations; where, after praising the Greek civilization for its Individuality and Precinct-independence, but condemning it for its lack of Nationality; he says, (p. 309):—"The Greek principle is individuality, and not association; and this is still further determined by the race, by the tribe, that is, by nature, AND NOT BY VOLUNTARY AGREEMENT. THIS political and social work is a NEW work, and is entrusted to a new country and a new people:"—evidently meaning, this business of making governments by "voluntary agreement."

(*c*) *Mill.* Mill, Pol. Econ. p. 542, sets forth the rights of Corporations, so far as "commerce or industry is concerned." But the same language appears to be equally true, when applied to any kind of Corporation, to perform almost any function, which either Individuals or society ought to be allowed freedom to accomplish at all:—"If a number of persons choose to associate for carrying on any operation of commerce or industry, agreeing among themselves, and announcing to those with whom they deal, that the members of the association do not undertake to be responsible beyond the amount of the subscribed capital; is there any reason that the law should raise objections to this proceeding, and should impose on them the UNLIMITED responsibility which they disclaim? For whose sake? Not for that of the partners themselves; for it is *they* whom the limitation of responsibility benefits and protects. It must therefore be for the sake of third parties, namely, those who may have transactions with the association, and to whom it may run in debt, beyond what the subscribed capital suffices to pay. But nobody is obliged to deal with the association; still less is any one obliged to give it unlimited credit. The class of persons with whom such associations have dealings, are in general, perfectly capable of taking care of themselves; and there seems no reason that the law should be more careful of their interest, than they will themselves be; provided no false representation is held out, and they are aware from the first, what they have to trust to."

(*d*) *Carey.* Mr. Carey, in Hunt's Merchants' Magazine, May, 1845, speaking of a Corporation of Industry, says:—"Its operations partake in some respects of THE NATURE OF THOSE OF GOVERNMENTS." Again: "A careful examination of the systems of the several States, can scarcely, we think, fail to convince the reader, of the advantage resulting from permitting men to determine among themselves, the terms upon which they will associate; and allowing the associations that may be formed, to contract with the public, as to the terms upon which they will trade together, whether of the limited or unlimited liability of the partners." And this remark, like Mr. Mill's, is as true when applied to Corporations formed for social and for *general* governmental purposes, as to those for any *special* governmental, or for any other purpose. If not; then for whose benefit is the NOT?

(*e*) *Comte.* Comte (Pos. Phil. p. 765), consciously expects a spiritual, a super-material authority IN society; and that it must finally become instituted, have "its political organization, * * * and be regularly constituted." His type evidently is the church.

Whence we may infer, that he looks to some kind of intellectual Corporation as the new super-material power. Again, more pointedly (p. 787) he says:—"Such thinkers may form a positive Council, under one form or another; and act, either by reviewing and renovating all human conceptions, or by instituting seats of education for the advancement of positive knowledge, and for the training of fit coadjutors; or by regulating the application of the system, through unremitting instruction of all kinds; and even by philosophical intervention in the political conflicts, which must arise till the old social action is exhausted."

(*f*) *Ballou.* The first view that we have found in any writer, of a theory of Corporations, approximating ours, is in Adin Ballou's "Christian Socialism." We however had not understood it, nor even seen his book, until after our theory had suggested itself. The two theories are very different. His is a modification and improvement of and upon Fourierism, and all the other proposed social reorganizations; but ours is a development from the Tribe-theory, of the origin of civil government; and arose, because it was found that the Social Circle and the Precinct, by themselves, without the Corporation, did not express the whole of the action of the Tribe-element, in modern society. See Bk. I. Pt. II. Ch. VIII., and Bk. IV. M.D. II. S. D.L. Ch. I. and II.

Our theory originates with the rights of Individuals, Families, and Precincts, according to the German and ancient Greek idea. But Mr. Ballou's theory goes unconsciously upon the assumption of the Roman idea, of centralism, and of government descending from the greater to the less. The same "seven identical circles" are to be in all his Corporations alike; namely, "the adoptive, unitive, preceptive, communitive, expansive, charitive, and parentive." But these circles are *not to be incorporated,* nor even to have any permanent general organization as such. "This," says he, "precludes all the evils of *caste,*" &c.

And what can we think of a civil polity for the United States, —or for any other republican government,—which would require all its members to abstain entirely from participation in civil and political affairs? And what also can we think of requiring of its members, the belief of such a subtlety as the doctrine of Universal Salvation, as one of the "principles of theological truth," *fundamental* to the constitution of society? Such things might be admissible, as repetitions of the small exclusive communities that have so often been tried, but are hardly worthy of a place in Corporations which propose, as his do, to entirely absorb all the functions of civil society. His Corporations are to keep so much aloof from established governments, that they are not even to obtain charters, or legal acts of incorporation, (but he takes care to say, his trustees "shall take the utmost care that all titles to Real Estate shall be so expressed, executed, and RECORDED, as effectually to preclude all ulterior controversies"; and furthermore, "shall execute and cause to be recorded in the *Registry* of *Deeds* for the *County*, a DECLARATION OF TRUST" &c.). No force is to be used; *except* to compel miserably unhappy married people, to live together:—Inflexibly as in the Roman Church, *or even more so*, for there is no Pope there, to grant "dispensations." "Divorce," says he, "shall NEVER be allowable, except for adultery CONCLUSIVELY proved."

His division of Corporations, into two kinds, "Parochial and Rural," is very good. By "Rural" he means what we should call Precinct-Corporation; or, the contrast between Parochial and Rural, might be expressed by the words, Total and Partial, or Social and Local. Then again, his division of Corporations, into "common-stock and joint-stock," is also good; "joint-stock" meaning regular share-holders' companies; and "common stock" meaning unlimited-property-communism. But he does not seem to conceive of the possibility, of so modifying and combining these two kinds of societies, as to give rise to a third kind, which might partly be a compromise between them. In other words, he does not conceive of the idea, that property holders could really give their *incomes* into the common fund; and yet retain, or have allowed to them, the privilege of voting in proportion to such contributions, as if private shares of stock in joint-stock companies. It must be remarked here, that he calls all these different organizations, "communities"; and the totality of them all, he calls a republic.

And we may add here also, that if worthy Corporations would apply to the civil governments, and obtain complete charters and independent rights; such rights would probably be respected in ALL after times, whether by friends or enemies. Perhaps such

Corporations, of a limited communistic kind, are yet to be the principal arks, whereby "the elect" are to be saved from the deluge of LEVELLING fire, that may perhaps sweep over the world, before many centuries have elapsed. But as far as such independent and peace rights, can be obtained from governments, so far of course, the Corporations are bound to abstain from participation in the affairs of the enclosing government. And this is just what our theory, in part, insists upon, namely, the duty of civil governments to GRANT, but not for societies to take without permission.

Mr. Ballou does not use our word Corporation, but we use this word, all along (in speaking of his theory, as also of our own); the better to show the points of connection between the two theories, as we desire to point out their connections, as well as their differences.

Mr. Ballou's ideal was, to transform all the local governments of the whole Nation, into Corporations of persons who should adopt ALL his fundamental principles. And a part of this ideal seems to have been, that its complete success would ultimately dispense with the use of a national government altogether. But this is a fundamental error: the Corporation cannot displace nationality, because the Corporation is a part of the Tribe-element, and therefore cannot fulfill at most, more than all the functions of the Tribe-principle,—and therefore at most, can only fulfill the functions of, or displace, Social Circle and Precinct.

(*g*) *Calvin Blanchard.* As a set-off to Mr. Ballou's views, let us print some of the dying words of Mr. Blanchard, the Positivist, an old *chum* of Greeley. He says, "The 'Philosophers' and 'Literati' will hardly believe my asseveration, that within a few years past, I have sent forth among unassuming, *common sense* people, books and pamphlets to this purport, written by myself, to the extent of more than 250 thousand. * * * Aided by the social architects who have preceded me, I have fully discovered and demonstrated, that the whole world will be united under the government of those who will be guided by the constitution manifested in Human Nature, and by the laws with which they will thoroughly acquaint themselves, in relation thereto,—to the entire exclusion of all other so-called constitutions and laws. * * * By studying the said *true* constitution and laws, they will find out and put into practice, the great Art of Arts, whereby the perfect happiness of every then and thenceforth human being, will be completely secured; as they will also find out, that only by continuing that practice, can they secure their own happiness. So intimately are Mankind connected, *they form one Unitary Being.* * * * The Science of Sciences, and Art of Arts,—the crowning triumph of Nature through Art,—will be the organization of the whole world, including it and all its inhabitants, in one Joint Stock" [*not common stock*] "Corporation, that will guarantee perfect happiness to every human being who shall then exist, or thenceforth come into existence." (!)

The great objections to this view of Mr. Blanchard, are, (1) that it entirely ignores two essential elements of society, namely, Precinct and Nation. Corporation, we admit, is capable of fulfilling nearly all, but yet *not* quite all, of the functions of civil government. And (2) that it seems to give too much prominence to the joint-stock principle, as compared with communism. (3) The greatest error of all, is, in supposing that any *one* Corporation could answer *all* the wants of even any one person. The great good that Corporations can accomplish, is obtainable by their multiplicity, and by the consequent choices which they would thus present to everybody, everywhere. It is even possible, that Corporations may rise in generality, so as to become really world-wide; but not possible nor desirable, that any ONE or even any *very few* Corporations, should absorb all the others. See this train of thought pursued, in the Third Main Division of this article.

(*h*) *School of the French Empire.* In the school of higher studies of the French Empire,—(says the Journal of Social Science of the Am. Assoc. for 1869),—there has been established so lately as January, 1869, in "the section of economic sciences," a course which includes the history "of commercial and industrial ASSOCIATIONS." These of course, virtually are Corporations; and in Europe, pretty "close" ones, too.

SUB-DIVISION II.

RIGHT OF GOVERNMENTAL CORPORATION.

CHAP. I. STATEMENT OF POSITION.

When writers say that citizens have full right to meet and form laws for THEMSELVES; they SAY, for *themselves*, but MEAN, for *each other;* and so, they entirely confuse Individual-obedience with social obedience. What is wanted is, some legal authority; not that would give one class of persons, control over another, nor even one class, control over its own members, without their consent; but that would only give classes and societies, control over their own members, so far as each Individual or Family had first joined any such society, and promised obedience to it, as the civil government he or they would choose and prefer, first among all the possible or convenient ones that were within their opportunities.

Some Corporations have one kind of power, and others another kind; but within only voluntary limits. Churches rule partly over marriage and divorce, partly over morality, and partly over benevolence. Classes and Social Circles rule partly over the same vital points of discipline. And the great fraternal beneficial societies, as Free Masons, Odd Fellows, Orders of Temperance, &c., also exercise their respective shares of authority. The Trade-Corporations, whether of the wage-classes or of the capitalists, govern their respective matters, by rules fast settling into legality. The municipal law cannot put down the trade-unions, and has even to acknowledge the customs of merchants, as constituting "the Law Merchant"; and so on. And then the Municipal boroughs exercise the local municipal authority, over a few external matters, other than those which pertain to the geographical economy; for this geographical economy, in any case, must be left to some local authority, until indeed every Precinct itself becomes a moral unit, by natural segregation,—in which case the difference between abstract Corporation, and local borough, would become eliminated. Now, what our theory of Corporations, asks and argues for, is, the right and freedom for, and the expediency and practicability of, actually introducing Corporations which shall accomplish several or all of these functions, in ONE organization; yet, without destroying the freedom of the Individual, because he would always be left free to change his membership to any other Corporation that would freely accept him. What we ask for then, is, the institution of whole Corporations for whole uses, instead of or beside, only fractional Corporations for only fractional uses.

There is an analogy here, to the argument in Precinct, Part I. Chap. II. § 1. Various Counties and Districts are found existing, and possessing separate special and local "privileges," as of liquor, dogs, sheep, police, &c.; and we asked for every District to be allowed *all* these privileges *at once.* So also there are various Corporations, as we have seen, for securing separate special rights; one Corporation for one right; and another for another right. And we ask, that these and other Corporations may be allowed, which shall combine provisions for guarding and enforcing as many rights in *each one* Corporation, as its members choose voluntarily and fairly, to unite in it for. And such Corporations, therefore, would take cognizance of the "Rights of Persons," as well as also of the "Rights of Things."

Nevertheless, our Corporation-theory does not conflict with the doctrine, that Nations and Precincts are moral personalities; but the theory affords the only method, whereby that doctrine can be justified in principle; or that can sustain the action of the local authorities as Units, in the face of the world's modern doctrine of liberty, and the rights of the Individual. Either the right of special Corporations, must be admitted to entitle to exception from the local authority, in questions of vital importance, wherein Individuals object; or else the doctrine will be forced upon us, that *all* governments are only voluntary Corporations, subject alone, only and entirely, to the stipulated conditions of those who are *members;* for the idea of "subjects" is passing away, with that absolutism of which it was a part.

CHAP. II. RIGHTS IN GENERAL.

Corporations, according to Blackstone, are treated in law, merely as *artificial persons.* Here is where the old theory of law, seems utterly to lack the capacity of appropriating the new theory, or the new organs of society. By the old law, a Corporation is regarded somewhat as a slave used to be; that is, as an Individual without any natural rights; nay, the case is still harder than the slave's, for the very existence itself of a Corporation, and not only its rights, is supposed to be derived from statute law. No progress can be made, of any great importance, until law proceeds on the entirely opposite presumption. namely, until law proceeds on the presumption that Corporation is one of the great and abiding elements of human society; and that men have a natural right to form themselves into Corporations, for all such objects, and in all such manners, as they may choose; except only where law deems it wise to interpose some *special* restrictions. And this freedom of Corporation must be held in its widest extent, from simple partnership upwards.

It follows, as a matter of course, not only that all charters should be general instead of special, but rather that there should be no charters at all, except the legal contract between the parties, perhaps duly recorded. It follows also, that the few restrictions which law may prescribe, to the right of Corporations, should be as general as the nature of the case may admit.

The right of political Corporation, is fully equal to, and fully as extensive, in the abstract, as the right of contract; but in the concrete and in practice, the right can only be acknowledged in proportion as human society becomes convinced, that the allowance of the right will not injure it. The question is not merely whether some Corporations may not attain too much influence in the government; but the question is, whether some other Corporations may not also be raised, more than sufficient to counteract the dangerous ones; and whether freedom of Corporation, like all other freedom of contract, and freedom of internal commerce, and we may even say, *like all other legitimate freedom, promotes the general good, far more than any opposite course could.*

Corporation being voluntary, is an expression of personal conviction, and thus is TESTIMONY. As such, it relieves the mind's passion for the expression and maintenance of earnest convictions. And thus, passions and opinions, which for want of sufficient expression, would drive Individuals, Precincts or Nations, into debates, quarrels and wars,—will steam out, boil over, and then settle down into quiet permanent Corporations.

Just as passions in the Individual settle down, but become all the more efficient, when they become principles; so the passions in society settle down, when they become permanent organizations.

The human intellect and heart, therefore, unite in the powerful conviction, that the right of Corporation ought to be free. In fact, the very claim to *self*-government, is a mere misnomer, a delusion, a disguise for tyranny, until this God-given right is acknowledged and admitted, in all its divine freedom and force.

CHAP. III. RIGHTS OF NATURALNESS.

Political Corporations are really more natural than business-partnerships. For, when persons enter into any business together, it is obviously more natural, to suppose a division of labor, so that some engage themselves in one thing, and some in another; also more natural to suppose that some are managers, and some not,—than to make the contrary supposition. The partnership law, that all the partners are liable for all things, and have right to do all things, is a merely *arbitrary* enactment of "law," which, no doubt, was one among the many means, whereby the old Land-aristocrats used to take advantage of the industrial and commercial classes.

No act or form should ever be construed as meaning more than it fairly expresses, unless when in each case, a special acknowledgment has been made, that such act or form shall have such extended meaning. According to this, all usual or simple partnerships would be limited, and all general partnerships would have to be expressed and published as such. The duty involved by the act of endorsing promissory notes, might at first sight, appear to be an exception to the above rule. But it is not; because, endorsement *means*, from the first, that the last holder received the paper *from* the previous holder, and therefore has recourse to him, if it be not "good." What "the law" arbitrarily does, is, to limit this recourse. Endorsements "ab extra," merely for the sake of guaranteeing, are done for that very purpose impliedly; and we are speaking of meanings, all along here.

Accordingly therefore, even birth and citizenship in any country, without a voluntary acceptance, and the means thereof, should not be construed to involve any more extension of duties or rights, than what are absolutely *necessary* to right government. In all other matters, freedom of choice should be allowed. Accordingly, the free right of Corporation is a legitimate conclusion. We are speaking of natural right; and grant, that there are special exceptions; but for these exceptions, all the *onus* (or burden) of proof, lies upon those who maintain them.

CHAP. IV. RIGHTS OF INDIVIDUAL SELECTION.

Probably the strongest isolated argument for political government by Corporations, is, that it affords by far the best method, to allow of governments being freely chosen and selected by their citizens *individually*. Unless there is acceptance of government by each Individual, spontaneously; in other words, unless some important elements of *unanimity*, enter into the acceptance, and into the organization itself,—there must be considerable self-delusion or sophism, involved in the term SELF-government.

Both Spencer and Ruskin, feeling the injustice of the present organizations of society, in this matter, have suggested that there must be some methods adopted for Individuals to ignore or avoid the state. And the method of government by Corporations, seems to be the simplest and easiest, whereby to meet this difficulty. Instead of liberty to ignore the state, we propose, liberty to change membership of one's official Corporation.

CHAP. V. RIGHTS OF CONSCIENCE.

Freedom of conscience demands the freedom of Corporation. There cannot be permanent peace in the world, and we had almost said there *ought* not to be; until the claim of human beings to tyrannize over each other, has become utterly refuted; and the right established, of men to form themselves freely, according to their own consciences and judgments, into their own political, civil, and municipal organizations. And this can only come to pass, when the right of Corporations is generally admitted, and its practicability and expediency, generally known and acted upon by governments.

The modern conscience in regard to war, demands the freedom of Corporation. The practice and duty of an ordinary government in time of war, is one of peculiar trial, in regard to the treatment of persons who refuse to co-operate in the war. Conscientious objections are easy to urge, in order to escape Individual-duty. Those persons whose declamations had produced the war, those who want to profit by it, and even those who would fight or work on the *other side*, if they had a convenient opportunity,—all, find it easy to urge conscientious scruples. But Peace-Corporations, duly established, present a fair and just means of avoiding the difficulty; and if the country were invaded, would be respected even by the enemy, under the pressure of the sanctions of Christianity, and of International Law. And the knowledge that the enemy *would* respect the Peace-Corporations as neutrals, takes away the strongest inducement of the home-government for impressing their Individual-members into "the service," or of devastating their territory.

Multitudes of our best citizens believe, that government cannot succeed without supporting and teaching religion, and are endeavoring to engraft religion into "the *Law*"; but unless they wish to force their own religions on other people, there only remains, besides separation into Precincts, the resource, of government by voluntary Corporations.

It is only by our system, either of Precincts or of Corporations, that Individuals or societies can easily and legitimately be released, from suffering taxation for works which they utterly reprobate; only thus can the peace-men escape war-taxes; or the members of one religious education, escape the expenses of others; or those who support their own sick or poor, from the expense of supporting the others, &c.

But release from the taxation on foreign imports, could not easily be allowed to Corporations of persons *scattered* as to locality, except for the articles imported for their corporate use, or at any rate, for such as the Corporation itself should take out of the Custom's Bonded Warehouse, or out of their bonded cars or vessels, and should divide to its own members for their use; or such as they divided to others in charity. And perfect relief from the foreign part of the tax, could only be accomplished by the Precinct itself, whose complete knowledge of all the doings of its members, and whose established reputation, would or might make its release from foreign tax, both safe and judicious.

But this is a very transcendental application, neither probable, practicable, nor judicious, for a long time yet to come: although, the United States government has tried the plan of rail-road-cars under custom house locks; but neither human nature, nor political nature, seems to us, good enough yet, for such methods to be allowed in common use.

SUB-DIVISION III.

ADVANTAGES OF GOVERNMENTAL CORPORATIONS.

CHAP. I. ADVANTAGES COMMON TO PRECINCT AND CORPORATION.

§ 1. *In General.*

When considering the Precinct, we found that much of what it involved and demanded, could be explained and obtained by means of Corporation. So now, having come to the latter, we find also that much of what it involves and demands, can be explained and obtained by means of the former. The special arguments for the Precinct were, in nature, of two kinds. One kind, related to locality, and depended on that; the other kind, related to the principles of things, abstract entirely from locality. These latter kind of arguments are they, which are equally as applicable to Corporation as to Precinct.

§ 2. *Recapitulation from the Precinct.*

Let us now recapitulate from the Precinct, in their order, the chief arguments thus applicable to both elements. Demanded by the history of our own country, to ameliorate the ever increasing evils of largeness of population: Allow all necessary adaptations: Derive light and regulation from international law: Admit of Amalgams with other Corporations: Resemble the system of the United States, inasmuch as the Army, the Navy, the Arsenals, the Navy Yards, the Revenue offices, the Post offices, are virtually national Corporations: Encourage Arbitration, both inward and outward of the Corporation: Require temporary Restrictions during the transitional period of their introduction: Separate the special politics and parties, from the national ones: They are elements of the Tribe-principle, and are needed by the theory of the Essential Elements: The natural right of Individuals to form them, is such, that the burden of proof lies upon the persons who would deny it: They make Social Circles practicable:—Produce some of the effects of differences of geographical location: Produce in the world, whatever there is, of progress, in industry, in public works, in chivalry, in religion, in humanity and in cosmopolitan association: The variety in God's creation; parts crossing and intertwining within parts: The progress from homogeneity to heterogeneity: The development of new and special organs for every function: New concentrations of, and diffusions of, power: Sociological experiments: Ready changes of membership, from one to another: The objects and uses of Law: The release from legal force, by cultivating the powers of SELF-government in the Individual: The Preparation in the Family: Moral homogeneity in associations: The spontaneous social punishments: The multitude and minuteness of governmental affairs: Government by the parties directly interested: Uses of competition: Political objects and uses: Making personal acquaintanceship and direct voting, possible: Preventing corruption: Preventing specialties of law by the superior governments: Promote human happiness: Tend to release people from the local sufferings whose causes they have protested against: Cultivate freedom of thought: Secure Individual liberty: Allow a degree of ignoring of the state: Harmonize with human nature, like seeking like; and thus resemble the law of Heaven: Are demanded by, and in turn promote, Morality and Religion: Make personal supervision and visitations, practicable and complete: Foster religious education according to the rights of conscience: Make Ruskin's and others' ideals practicable: Take the sting out of persecution: Introduce the advantages of the Tribe and its relations: Promote "*stirpi-culture*," and the introduction of improved breeds of human beings: Solve the political and legal difficulties about divorce: Are the complements of each other: Corporations mitigate the absoluteness of Precinct separation or segregation, and its consequent narrow-mindedness: They have no opening for the idea of secession; Yet mitigate the absolutism of national power: Make reactions more visible, but less severe: Open the way for cosmopolitan Unions: Have precedent in the Tribe of Levi; And in the various local charters from superior powers: And supply the special needs of large cities.

§ 3. *Power to Resist the oppressive and centralizing tendencies of Modern Society.*

There is a tendency in all Local governments, to suppress individuality, and to oppress the Individual. Mill describes this tendency as follows:—(In Pol. Econ. V. xi. 3, he says):—"A general objection to government-agency is, that every increase of the functions devolving on the government, is an increase of its power, both in the form of authority, and still more, in the indirect form of influence. * * * Experience proves that the depositaries of power, who are mere delegates of the people, that is, of a majority, are quite as ready (when they think they can count on popular support), as any organs of oligarchy, to assume arbitrary power, and encroach unduly on the liberty of private life. The public collectively is abundantly ready to impose, not only its generally narrow views of its interests, but its *abstract opinions, and even its tastes*, as laws binding upon Individuals. And the present civilization tends so strongly to make the power of persons acting in masses, the only substantial power in society; that there never was more necessity for surrounding Individual-independence of thought, speech and conduct, with the most powerful defences; in order to maintain that originality of mind, and individuality of character, which are the only sources of any real progress, and of most of the qualities which make the human race much superior to any herd of animals. * * * Where public opinion is sovereign, an Individual who is oppressed by the sovereign, does not, as in most other states of things, find a rival power, to which he can appeal for relief; or at all events, for sympathy." Hence we say, comes the necessity to allow those persons who sympathize, to segregate themselves freely.

To the position of Mill,—expressed above, and more formally asserted, "On Liberty": namely:—"The tendency of all the changes taking place in the world, is to strengthen society, and to diminish the power of the Individual,"—Mulford, p. 273, replies: "It is presented with no historical evidence." (Mulford has a favorite way of dismissing obstinate objections, by charging them with being "abstractions": pages v. bis, and vi., and 2, 11, bis, 19, 24, etc.; and yet his is the most abstract work on Social Science, perhaps, since Comte's). Mulford asserts—"the age of the higher national development of England, was the age also of Shakespeare, of Raleigh, of Bacon, of Milton"; just as if England's great period of Nationality, namely, the reign of Henry VIII., had not passed away a half a century or more, before these worthies appeared. But after all, it is of little consequence, whether centralization and high nationality, does or does not produce a FEW greatest men. Mill's argument refers, not to effects on isolated Individuals, but to effects on the generality. The two cases are entirely different; and it may be true to some extent, in state, as it is in church, that the periods of highest churchism, are those which develop the very best persons individually; but yet in such few numbers, that the other condition of things is happiest for the generality, in the common course. Judaism produced the prophets, and finally, during its most perverted formalism, developed the Messiah, (humanly speaking). And some of the saints of the Roman Catholic Church, of the middle and later ages, are perhaps not surpassed by any since the closing of the canon. But thenceforth, of what value in comparison, is an occasional Horace or Virgil, a Shakespeare or Dante, to the general happiness, or the general freedom, of a whole people? Mr. Mulford says, "The country may be called the more free, which has roads open through it; but it is not the more free, when one person is always required to take a road through the valley, and one, always to ride on the hills." But we reply, that the same person, when he has a carriage or is on foot, ought to pass a different road, from what he should when he has a dung wagon,—still (it seems to us), the freedom is impaired, if dung wagons are allowed always to travel along the roads where other vehicles, and foot passengers, are going. But the freedom of these centralizers, is, one road for all, namely, the NATIONAL Passenger Railroad, with ONLY ONE TRACK.

CHAP. II. ADVANTAGES PECULIAR TO CORPORATION.

§ 1. *Analogies in Biology.*

Physiology seems to show, that there are floating through all living creatures, both vegetable and animal, certain germs of life, which have the power of reproducing particles like themselves. And, by the freedom of these particles to unite with others, of a like or homogeneous kind, all growth and reproduction are accomplished. All depends upon the perfect freedom of the particles, as they float along in the blood, to unite together easily, according to their own attractions. Just so, every Individual-human being may be regarded, according to our type-theory, as a particle flowing along with the general current; but there can be no growth, and no progress, unless there is freedom for these particles to unite together, drop out of the current, and form new organisms. And *this* means freedom of Corporation.

Corporations are the only political bodies of society, which have the power of generation by "gamogenesis," instead of by "agamogenesis." (For the physical doctrines and illustrations, see Spencer's Biology, 2; 6: 4, 5, 6, &c.) This method is indefinitely less at variance with growth, than the other method. It is also the method whereby all the higher plants and animals generate. To illustrate this:—when a local division takes place, whether of Precinct or of Nation, the sum of the two parts, in each case, is only equal to what the whole was, previous to the division. But it is not so in Corporations. A subdivision will make *both* more efficient, because it introduces division of labor, and more specialty of organ for function. And these are improvements without any counteractive evils, scientifically speaking. Furthermore, the division of Corporations, makes both parts more desirable to the members of other Corporations, some to one part of the division, and some to the other; and this makes both parts draw members from other Corporations. But this is only competition, and therefore only a temporary and transitional good. The former mentioned, is the eternal good. And Individuals can be members of more than one Corporation; just as children have more than one parent, and parents more than one child; reciprocally.

§ 2. *Prevention of War.*

One great and peculiar advantage possessed by Corporations, is, that whereas, revolutions and divisions in Local governments are usually accomplished only through war and blood,—revolutions and divisions in Corporations, are accomplished quite peaceably, and even charitably. The chief reason for this difference, seems to be, that the human propensity to tyrannize, manifests its true nature so much more baldly and nakedly, in Corporations, than in Localities, that it is at once suppressed as a preposterous "vice of blood,"—instead of being nurtured and worshiped as a divine patriotism, or as an Egyptian Cat, or as some other *fetish*:—or as Carlyle might say,—"Jewish old clothes."

The Philadelphia "Ledger," Feb'y 8, 1871, in an article on "Friends' Principles," says, "We accord all honor to the 'singular' men who devote themselves to presenting, in plain terms, plain truths against ingenious sophistry. They are 'advanced pickets,' 'skirmishers' in the struggle for peace: and the main body of the great and peaceful army of thinking men, is fast closing up. *So far as the claims of men as men, whether called citizens or subjects*, are recognized, just so far the hope of the cessation of war is encouraged." We have already presented a similar thought, under the head of *Right of Corporation.*

§ 3. *Inconceivable for Secession.*

Another great and peculiar advantage belonging to Corporation, compared with Precinct, is, that, Corporation not being coextensive with Locality, the secession of Localities is not only impracticable or impossible, as shown under PRECINCT; but also, is really and utterly *inconceivable;* under a system of Corporations, or as an effect or consequent therefrom; and this Element, therefore, is one of the most efficient means of insuring against said secession.

§ 4. *Self-Counteractions, Inherent in all Voluntary Combinations.*

Every class, when left to itself, has its own counteractions within itself; knows what evidences of fact and of veracity to require, and what oscillations to provide for; knows its own temptations, its own protections, and its own moral supports. It is only when the cry is raised of class against class, that all the natural self-regulating powers, are overwhelmed and swept away, by the rush of angry class-animosities. And yet it is equally certain, from the Zo-ological nature of human society, also according to our theory of types, that the interests of each of these classes would evolve suitable forms, each for themselves, under a proper general government, if they were only allowed freely to do so.

§ 5. *Necessary Harmony of all the Parts of Society.*

What Schleiermacher said, and is quoted by Neander, that all the denominations of Christians are necessary, to exhibit the perfect development of Christ and the church,—may be applied equally well to the different Corporations, which, under the freedom of Corporation, would arise among the politicians, and in the state. And all are necessary to exhibit the full and complete development of humanity, and society, and of humanity IN society. Freedom of civil and political Corporations, is equally as right, as necessary, and as practicable, as, of church Corporations.

The church analogy exhibits all the various classes of society as intermingling, sometimes in the same Corporation; and generally in the same one locality, even when the different churches themselves organize according to classes or Social Circles. In this analogy, so long as it shall hold good, we have proof of the success of Corporations during an intermingling era. Hence, if our argument for the gradual passing away of the intermingling era, as presented under Precinct, in II. X. 1, should be entirely rejected,—then our Corporations come in with additional strength of argument, as capable of most of the political advantages of Precincts, yet without interfering with the friendly intermingling.

§ 6. *Culture of the Individual.*

Mr. Mill points out certain needs of human nature, increasing amid the tendencies of modern civilization,—which, we think no other means of satisfying can be discovered, so efficient, as recognizing the freedom of Corporation.

Mr. Mill, (Pol. Econ. p. 573), says:—" Experience proves the extreme difficulty, of permanently keeping up a sufficiently high standard of those qualities, (the diffusion of intelligence, activity and public spirit, among the governed), a difficulty which increases, as the advance of civilization and security, removes, one after another, of the hardships, embarrassments and dangers, against which individuals had formerly no resource but in their own strength, skill and courage. It is therefore of supreme importance, that all classes of the community, down to the lowest, should have much to do for themselves; that as great a demand should be made upon their intelligence and virtue, as it is in any respect equal to; that the government should not only leave, as far as possible, to their own faculties, the conduct of whatever concerns themselves alone, but should suffer them, or rather encourage them, to manage as many as possible of their joint concerns, by voluntary co-operation; since this discussion and management of collective interests, is the great school of that public spirit, and the great source of that intelligence of public affairs, which are always regarded as the distinctive character, of the public of free countries."

Here it seems plain to us, that there are certain needs in human nature, which are increasing so much in modern civilization, that no other means to supply them can be discovered, so efficient as, on the one hand, the Precinct-system that we have proposed, and on the other hand, the system of free Corporations that we are now advocating,—and chiefly the latter, because it is susceptible of such indefinite extension. Thus we see, that civilization is producing new functions; but has already indicated, and begun to put forth, the organs that are necessary to perform them.

§ 7. *The "De-facto" argument.*

In other parts of this work, we endeavor to show, that whatever is a fixed fact in society, ought to be recognized as such, in the laws, and by the government; and that whatever government acts contrary to this principle, only stultifies itself, as an organism, and produces misery to Individuals. Hence, all the instances that we offer, of the existence of virtual Corporations, good, bad, and indifferent,—combine under this principle of government, to prove the right and necessity of their freedom and legal recognition.

All the foreigners of any one Nation are, virtually, Corporations of their own Nation, but dwelling in another. And just as Asiatic Russia is a conglomerate of many *Precincts*, of essentially different nationalities, so the United States is a conglomerate of many virtual *Corporations*, of essentially different nationalities. These Corporations, to be sure, are not recognized in law, otherwise than by publishing legal documents in their different languages; still the distinctions exist, and are even stronger between clans speaking the same English language, than between those speaking different ones. And it must be admitted, with shame to ourselves, that those settlements of foreigners which have been most compact and self-secluded, have preserved their morality best; whatever might be said about their lack of progress.

Civil governments are actually conducted and swayed, by secret leagues and cliques, which are Corporations in fact; and which transmit their authority from age to age, except as displaced, from time to time, by the same kinds of cliques of other parties. There are leagues of persons engaged in "humbugging" the people in their recreations, or poisoning them, in their amusements, with rum or vice. There is also a tyrannical sort of gentlemen, who even incorporate themselves into rings and clubs, as the actual but secret rulers of the community. Much worse than these also, are the permanent cliques of professional criminals, which are known to embrace various distinct classes: as for instance, cliques of counterfeiters; in which, will be manufacturers, wholesale purchasers, retail purchasers, transitory venders: and there are cliques of burglary; professional operators of many grades, transient operators, receivers of stolen goods, of all grades, from large financial securities, down to old iron. All these organizations are of the nature of Corporations. Since then, criminals incorporate themselves to break the laws, and since all the rogues and outlaws, gamblers, and parasites in society, everywhere, make leagues, either formal or actual, for mutual offence and defence, and for bribing legislators, judges and police executive officers;—why should not plain citizens incorporate themselves in their own way, to protect themselves, and to choose government and rulers and laws for themselves, and defend themselves from these barbarians, who make it their business to war upon society, rob industry, and strike down peace and order? and all this, oftentimes, by the connivance of the same wretched gentlemen, who are the loudest in crying "stop thief"; and who *befool* the people with the longest and *tangledest* laws, they can *quibble up* together.

Thus, Corporations are getting to have the actual power; and it would be better to make them legal, else the bad have the *advantage* of them, rather than the good; and the worse the associations are, the more defiant their power becomes. Because, so long as the freedom and right of Corporations, are crippled by law; so long the fearful fact will continue, that the lower down in the moral scale, and the more thoroughly *contrary* to law, each such association is, the more thoroughly compact and efficient its corporate character will be. In other words, so long as law limits the natural and moral right of Corporation, the worse a Corporation is, the more proportional power it will have.

§ 8. *Classes most Needing Separate Political Corporations.*

Persons who are diverse in their sentiments on important or agitating subjects, cannot understand each other; nor can the peculiar results of each party's system, be exhibited, whilst the persons are continually, either checking each other, or annoying each other. Nor can a government for daily life, adopt forms of police and courts and trials and evidence and watching, that can apply, either rightly or effectively, to all these different kinds of people. What to some is galling tyranny, to others is the blessing of self-control; to others, the blessing of civilization; and to others, the blessing of religion: the oaths that some regard, others despise; and the honor that holds some true to humanity, is to others, a nice "chance" for dishonesty, selfishness, or deceit.

Where a government is elected by the people,—any classes of persons who are too distant, in customs, politics, or religion, to receive, read, and enjoy, a proper government-press, giving a fair representation to all sides, and to all views,—are too distant morally, to reside in the same Precinct, or to assemble peacefully and orderly at the same polls. The only other alternative would be, the introduction of this system of Corporations, and its development to its widest capabilities, and highest functions; so that no persons could vote for any councils, or on any matters, affecting the *other* party, or the other religion; except those who could be trusted by their political or spiritual advisers, to read and hear all sides fairly expressed: and on the other hand, those persons who did thus read in common and freely, should not have the control over those who were conscientiously opposed to or afraid of, thus reading; so far at least, as ingenuity and fairness can contrive plans of avoiding such objectionable control, without vitiating the direct operations of government.

The following are some of the portions of society, who are,

or think they are, in most immediate need of the privilege of organizing themselves into plenary political Corporations, especially in the cities and more dense settlements:—Calvinists, Roman Catholics, Methodists, Quakers and other Interiorists, Peace-parties, Spiritualists, Unitarians, Rational religionists, Infidels, Chinese, and perhaps Africans generally. Also, may be added Women in general, if they are to exercise political functions at all; but, do not put respectable women into *Precincts* for females alone. Others needing the separation, are, Disgraced young people born without wedlock; penitent women; reformed criminals, and convicts released from punishment; and in general, all who are particularly good, particularly bad, particularly bigoted, particularly liberal, or otherwise *particularly* singular.

§ 9. *Comparison with Individuals, as Officials.*

We return now to a different train of thought, namely, to Corporations as organs of society, as the exercisers of derived, or bestowed, political functions. Corporations possess many advantages peculiar to themselves, over Individuals, as organs of society. Even in the simplest form of small partnerships, many of these advantages become very apparent. First then; Corporations are the new organs for the new functions of modern society. Thus the old age of society becomes, like its infancy, the restoration of the fullness in unity, of the Tribe. Second; Their officers are free from the over-strong ties of personal interest, which naturally arise against large payments, or onerous duties, especially if unexpected. Third; We have the argument, that history gives us instances, wherein strictly governmental functions have been entrusted to Corporations. Fourth; As all such organizations originate in a free and voluntary action of their corporators, they select themselves really, from a *judgment of their own fitness.* Fifth; And then again, the officers of such organizations are selected by the corporators, with the judgment of persons well able to know about them. Sixth; In this judgment, the corporators necessarily back up and guarantee their judgment, not only by their reputation, but also by the amount of their capitals, or, respective interests invested; and thus make their responsibility perpetual. This is a responsibility seldom imposed upon, and seldom possible in the case of, Individual-officials, and would be reasonably exacted from

Corporations, but not from Individuals. A sufficient application of this rule, would put political Corporations upon their very best efforts to regulate themselves harmoniously, which is far more than can be said of Individual-politicians. Seventh; They are not so liable to be interrupted by death. Eighth; They tend to prevent villany; because no collusions for evil, between different persons, can be so unrestricted, nor so safe from detection, as the secret thought in one man's soul. Although such is their natural tendency, and what might be secured in them, by proper sociological skill; yet, in fact, they often do worse things than an Individual would do. This is partly because their officers are allowed to shield themselves under the plea of official duty. But this very feature might be so made use of, that many of the repulsive works of society might be accomplished by those means, much better, than by the direct action of civil or political rulers.

SUB-DIVISION IV.

PRACTICABILITY OF GOVERNMENTAL CORPORATIONS.

CHAP. I. IN GENERAL.

To discuss the practicability of Corporations perfectly, the subject would divide itself into two parts; one, the method of their action, and the means whereby they manifest their practicability; the other, a series of abstract arguments and analogies, to show this practicability. As to the methods and means of action; they will be treated among the objects in view, and will be again treated in the Third Main Division and its sub-divisions. Nothing need be said of them just now, except this call of attention. As to the abstract arguments; many of them are involved in what has already been said; namely, in the facts of history; in the opinions of the great writers on Social Science; in the doctrines of the right and the expediency; in the analogies of Biology; in the instinctive organizations of Mankind, even the illegitimate ones; and in the classes of men ready and waiting.

And above all other arguments or reasons, we have faith that what is RIGHT, is certainly PRACTICABLE, if we are only willing for it. We now turn to and touch upon, the *abstract* arguments, and the analogies, showing practicability.

CHAP. II. ABSTRACT ARGUMENTS.

§ 1. *Ill Success of Local Governments in Other Businesses.*

Scarcely anything is more certainly agreed upon in Social Science, than the proposition, that whatever business, commercial, literary or social, that men do or can do, with any tolerable success *voluntarily;* they can and will do much better *thus* voluntarily, than government itself can do, or than they themselves would do, by any legal or any other coercion whatever. Now, all that our theory of Corporation proposes to do, is, to accept this well established principle, and to apply it to the business of government itself. We say,—true,—men can conduct any business voluntarily, far better than government can, and therefore they can thus carry on the business or function of government itself, by spontaneous organizations within the Nation, and within the Precinct. Thus Mr. Mill, (Political Economy, Book 5, ch. xi. § 5) says,—"In all the more advanced communities, the great majority of things are done worse by the intervention of government, than the Individuals most interested in the matter, would do them, or cause them to be done, if left to themselves. The grounds of this truth are expressed with tolerable exactness in the popular dictum, that people understand their own business and their own interests, better than the government does, or can be expected to do. This maxim holds true throughout the greatest part of the business of life; and wherever it *is* true, we ought to condemn every kind of government intervention, that conflicts with it. The inferiority of government agency, for example, in any one of the common operations of industry, or commerce, is proved by the fact, that it is hardly ever able to maintain itself, in equal competition with Individual-agency; where the Individuals possess the requisite degree of industrial enterprise, and can command the necessary assemblage of means. All the facilities which a government enjoys, of access to information, all the means it possesses of remunerating and therefore of commanding, the best available talent in the market,—

are not an equivalent for the one great disadvantage of an inferior interest in the result."

"It must be remembered, besides, that even if a government were superior in intelligence and knowledge, to *any single* Individual in the Nation, it must be inferior to all the Individuals of the Nation, taken together. It can neither possess in itself, nor enlist in its service, more than a portion of the acquirements and capacities which the country contains, applicable to any given purpose. There must be many persons equally qualified for the work, with those whom the government employs, even if it selects its instruments with no reference to any consideration but their fitness. Now these are the very persons, into whose hands, in the cases of most common occurrence, a system of Individual-agency naturally tends to throw the work, because they are capable of doing it better, or on cheaper terms, than any other persons. So far as this is the case, it is evident, that government, by excluding or even by superseding Individual-agency, either substitutes a less qualified instrumentality, for one better qualified; or at any rate, substitutes its own mode of accomplishing the work, for all the variety of modes which would be tried by a number of equally qualified persons, aiming at the same end; a competition by many degrees more propitious to the progress of improvement, than *any uniformity* of system."

§ 2. *Intermingling,—Not Confusion.*

The difficulties and confusions that might, at first sight, be supposed to be insuperable—on account of the intermingling in one Locality, of persons belonging to different municipal and political Corporations,—could readily be counteracted; in some things, by artificial regulations, and in other things, by the natural differences that would arise in the course of time. Nothing that man makes, can be perfect at the start. The functions of time must not be forgotten. The same ingenuity, and homogeneity of humanity, that devise Inter-National and Inter-Precinct law, would also devise Inter-Corporation Law.

Perhaps even the residents of adjoining Precincts, should wear different dresses. At any rate, such a custom should be required of all Individuals who were members of different governmental Corporations for general civil purposes, whilst residing in the *same* districts. Varieties of dress, as here proposed, together with such varieties of manners, habits, &c., as would, in time, probably arise and be visible, both as cause and as effect of connection with such Corporations,—would make differences which would be almost as plain to the casual observer, as differences of sex or race; or at least, as are easily perceived between the countryman and the citizen, or between the out-door and in-door workers, &c. And the degree in which the differences could be made plain, would facilitate the duties of the civil government towards each. Instances of the arising of such differences, may be remembered, as characteristic of the Puritans, the early Methodists, and of the Quakers even at the present day. Spencer has also shown how naturally the political differences of men, express themselves in their differences of clothing, gait, and other apparently trivial signs.

§ 3. *Ruskin's Specimen of Methods.*

Mr. Ruskin has a beautiful and practicable picture, of a method of trade Corporations, for preventing cheating in the manufacture or sale of "sham" goods. He says (pp. 87–8);—"The chief difficulty in the matter would be, to fix your standard. This would have to be done by the guild of every trade, in its own manner, and within certain easily recognizable limits. * * * Advisable improvements of varieties in manufacture, would have to be examined and accepted by the trade guild; when so accepted they would be announced in *public* reports; and all puffery and self-proclamation, on the part of tradesmen, absolutely forbidden, as much as making any other kind of noise or disturbance." [We hope the "disturbances" to be stopped, include advertisements in Directories and other such inappropriate places.]—"But observe, this law is only to have force over tradesmen whom I suppose to have joined VOLUNTARILY, in carrying out a better system of commerce. *Outside* of their guild, they would have to leave the rogue to puff and cheat as he chose, and the public to be gulled as *they* chose. All that is necessary is, that the said public should clearly know the shops in which they could get warranted articles; and as clearly, those in which they bought at their own risk." But now, this writer must say, that as yet, unless each such guild had power by law, to punish those of its own members who transgressed and cheated, whilst they were sailing under the flag of the guild;

then the use of the guild would soon be destroyed by the rush of hypocrites into it; and the better its reputation was, before the rogues got into it, the more they could profit by it, until discovered and exposed. And to give the guilds such power, is just what we are asking to be given to one class of Corporations. Mr. Ruskin advocates the punishment to be "confiscation of goods," and this admits the principle we are arguing for; but not at all to the extent that we suppose to be necessary.

CHAP. III. ANALOGOUS COMPLEXITIES SUCCESSFUL.

§ 1. *Analogy with Philadelphia.*

If it be thought that any one of our (or indeed, any other) systems of Corporations, would be top complicated for practical purposes, we would answer; they need not be any more complicated in structure, than our own present government, or than the British. Take for instance, our own city Philadelphia, in the year 1872. It is, somehow, made to consist of an almost unclassifiable multiplicity of Voting Precincts, City Wards, Districts for State Legislature, and for State Senate, for Fires, and for Police, and for Congress of the United States. We vote for our State Governor every three years, and for President every four years. And, in general, the divisions cross each other in a variety of ways, so complicated as to baffle the book learning of foreigners, while in practice they are perfectly familiar to ourselves. We have a series of items, not often multiples of each other in figures, and still less frequently so, in localities; neither are they related to each other as genera and species, nor even as opponents.

Here then, we have a city divided into 28 Wards, with 28 Select, and 58 Common Council-men, 7 Fire Districts, 18 Districts for State Assembly, 4 Districts for State Senate, 5 for United States Representatives, one of which stretches into another county! The city municipal administration is divided into "Departments," "Committees," and "Trusts"; of; Police; Treasury; Control; Tax; Law; Market; Survey; Registry; Highway; Water; Gas; School; Health; Girard; Poor; Prison; Refuge; and Port. The Nation has on the same ground, a Custom House,—(The business in the Custom House alone, is so complicated, and requires to be performed at so many successive "Desks," that a considerable number of persons called custom-house brokers, find ample employment in preparing the papers for sea captains and merchants, and in "putting them through" the rounds):—a Naval Department; a Surveyor's-; an Appraiser's-; an Assistant Treasurer's-; an Internal Revenue-; and a Post-, Office; also a Mint; a Navy Yard; and an Arsenal. All national property and offices, are exempt from city and state interference,—a set of Corporations in the Precinct, yet of Imperial authority. Besides all these regularly instituted organizations; we have an indefinite number of spontaneous and voluntary Social Circles, Party Clubs and Conventions, Temperance, Mechanics' and Beneficial, Societies, Trades-unions, Churches, Communities, Brotherhoods, Militia, and Fire Companies; "Boards" or "Exchanges," of Trade, of Brokers, of Coal, of Corn, of Real Estate, &c. All these *interlap* each other in every conceivable direction.

And now, finally to settle disputes among all these, and the members of them, we have, partly,—the reserved power in the agreements of several of the associations and boards; also a series of legal courts as follows;—The County, (exactly the same geographically as the city,) has, besides the "Row" of officers, a body of Judges, who incorporate themselves into three different forms of County courts, viz.:—Common Pleas, Orphans', and Criminal. Then,—there are a State District Court, a State Supreme Court, and a National Circuit Court, with right of appeal in certain cases to the National Supreme Court at Washington. All this is complicated enough; but we know by experience, "it is nothing when you get used to it." We also know how readily children learn the most complicated languages, when they begin during infancy.

§ 2. *Analogy with the Roman Church.*

But the completest illustration, of a united and harmonious system of Corporations in great multiplicity, is found in the Roman Catholic Church. Here is a system that is not learned in infancy. Omitting those parts of it, which, while adhering to Rome, yet adhere not to the Latin "rite,"—we may divide its organizations purely ecclesiastical, abstract from the civil organs, into FOUR different or main Divisions, all operating *one within another*. We will mention them in an order, such, that each subsequently named one, operates WITHIN ALL the previously named ones, thus; FIRST. The usual church-orders of Priests, Bishops, Archbishops, &c. These have territorial locations, one within another. SECOND. The Corporate Orders. operating within the territories of the above; yet exempt from their jurisdiction, by express *general* authority from the supreme head of their church, but yet dependent upon said territorial officials for their spiritual offices or "faculties." THIRD. The *special* delegates of the supreme authority; as Vicars, Legates, and so on. FOURTH. Appellate authorities, namely, the Pope, and General Councils. All these operating on each other respectively, in the order mentioned. And now, to this complication, let us add a brief summary of the varieties of authorities and operators, IN each of those four main divisions of their authorities.

FIRST Main Division of Authorities. The varieties of the usual orders of Local Officials, or Ordinaries, with their respective councils. First we have a regular gradation, Bishops, Archbishops, Primates. Next we have two sorts of irregular classes, namely, Metropolitans and Patriarchs.

SECOND Main Division of Authorities. The CORPORATE Orders, operating within the territories of the above. These are in three divisions, namely, the Orders of Military Monks, the Religious Orders, and the "Congregation" Orders.

First Division of the Corporate Bodies: The Orders of Military Monks include the Knights of St. John, The Templars, The Teutonic Knights, Orders of Alcantara, &c. But those are not found in the United States.

Second Division of the Corporate Bodies: The Religious Orders, are of four sub-divisions, namely: The Monks Proper; the Friars or Mendicants; the Canons regular; and the Priests called regular Clerks. Of these four sub-divisions, the Monks Proper are of two kinds, of which the Eastern may be omitted here. The Western kind occasionally follow the Eastern rule, namely, of St. Basil; but most always the rule of St. Benedict. This kind are *sub*-divided by a great variety, as, Carthusians, Cistercians, Celestines, Trappists, &c., &c. The second subdivision, the Friars or Mendicants, are divided into Dominicans, Franciscans, Carmelites, Augustinians, &c. The third sub-division, the Canons regular, are priests administering among the people, but yet, associated under special rules and obligations of strictness of life, for the promotion of their own especial personal sanctity. They are of two kinds, differing as to the degree of their abstraction from the world, and as to their resemblance to monks in their private life. The fourth sub-division, consists of Priests called regular Clerks. They differ from the regular Canons, in not following so strict a life, or at least in not taking any such strict vows as the others. Some of these are evidently adapted to secular operations, as for instance the Jesuits; others are followers of a purer and more spiritual interior piety, than is often found in or out of the Roman Church, as for instance, the Theatines.

The *Third* Division of the Corporate Orders, is "the Congregations." These are made a separate order from the "religious orders," by some differences not well understood, but which appear partly only nominal. The "Congregations" exist for various purposes, Education, Asylum, and Missionary. And these divisions for *purposes*, are again to be sub-divided according to the *classes of persons* to be influenced, as the poor, the paying people, the rulers of society, the heathens, the unbelievers or heretics, and finally even the other orders of clergy and of their own religion.

The THIRD Main Division of Authorities, are; The special delegates of the supreme authority, as Vicars, Legates, &c., &c. Of these, some of the Vicars are regular, and located, but extraordinary in their powers. Other Vicars and the Legates are irregular, and only appear on extraordinary occasions, representing the Pope, investigating facts, hearing causes, and pronouncing decisions,—by direct and special authority from the Head. These act in and on, both the foregoing main Divisions. Moreover, the Legates and Nuncios act on and with the civil governments, officially.

FOURTH Main Division of Authorities. The supreme government of all this vast system of Corporations, consists of three elements, namely; *First*, The Pope; *Second*, Three orders of Cardinals, namely, Cardinal Bishops, Cardinal Priests, and Cardinal Deacons; *Third*, The General Council. The Cardinals elect the Pope; and the Pope selects the Cardinals. He also constitutes the General Council, and appoints its times and circumstances; but not all its Individual-members directly, although indirectly, as he appoints or confirms to the offices which constitute membership in the Council.

All this, *theoretically* seems an inextricable tangle, to some people. And when we remember that many of the foregoing orders, are themselves highly organized bodies, with their "mother houses" or head-centers, at Rome,—we have an additional complication, apparently; but the fact is, it is this very thoroughness of the organizations, which prevents complexity in practice. All these different orders, or at least many heterogeneously self-locating ones, exist and operate in the same localities, with one another, and with the "ordinary" clergy, without confusion. No royal family, no constitution, no dynasty, no Nation in a continuous local government, except the Jewish and Chinese, can compare, either for its own durability, or for the certainty of its operations, with this great world-wide governing Corporation. And the only place where real and great practical uncertainty arises, is, where organization is theoretically simplest, namely at the head, —as to which is the superior, the Pope, or the General Council.

CHAP. IV. CONCLUSION OF PRACTICABILITY.

The fact is that a system of Corporations for government, would in all probability, be less complicated IN PRACTICE, than our present civil system. But even if more complicated, it could easily be taught and explained in the public schools, and elsewhere. Moreover, in the last resort we may say that, at any rate, legal proceedings require learned counsel and experienced attorneys, generally. It would be no real objection to the system of Corporation, if ordinary Individuals had to consult "good advice," in order to know even what Corporations they had better connect themselves with; just as they would consult a physician, as to what medicine they should take. The main thing to be attained in law, as in Medicine, in Mathematics or in other sciences,—is, not simplicity, but certainty and uniformity in their results, known to those who study them, and who are able to understand them. We do not complain that we are compelled to resort to Lawyers and Doctors and Clergymen, for advice; but we complain, that the expenses are great, the answers conflicting, and the results uncertain.

MAIN DIVISION II.

GENERAL SURVEY OF ALL KINDS OF CORPORATIONS, ACCORDING TO THEIR SEVERAL NATURES.

SUB-DIVISION I.

RELATIONS TO THE OTHER ELEMENTS OF SOCIAL SCIENCE.

CHAP. I. PREFACE.

Having in the preceding Main Division, treated of the arguments for the propriety, right, and expediency, of Governmental Corporations; and before giving the scientific exhibition and recital of *them*, which are reserved for the Third Main Division; we proceed now to give, as a necessary preparation thereunto, a general survey of ALL KINDS of Corporations, according to their several Natures.

One reason for laboring hard on this subject of Corporation, is, that the right of Corporation includes within it the right of Precinct; because freedom of Politico-governmental Corporation, actually becomes freedom of Precinct, to persons who desire to reside in special Precincts; so that, if the reader has not been satisfied with the arguments for the Precinct, upon the grounds which have been made under that head, he might still be induced to lend assent to the right of Precinct, upon perhaps not so deep foundations, but yet broader and more comprehensive ones.

We lay great stress on governmental or political Corporations, and feel the great dependence of human prosperity and progress, on the proper understanding and practical application of them. Such Corporations seem to give hopes of *real* and absolute progress, instead of hopes always to be disappointed, and hitherto reaching mostly after FORMS of government; whereas, real progress is more and more perceived to be, *not* dependent on forms. Corporation is not any ONE FORM, but a spirit, an eternal element, and an inherent power.

Corporation is the Seventh Element in our *scale* of the Analytics, namely, Individual, Family, Social Circle, Precinct, Nation, and Mankind;—and then as another *genus*, Corporation. Hence, Corporations, as the SEVENTH fundamental or Analytical element of *human society*, are a kind of sabbath of rest,—both to the fundamental Elements of Society, and also to the throes of society itself, laboring to bring forth its ideals of happiness, and to realize its divine origin, and its ultimate ideal.

In a Biological classification, Corporations would correspond to brain and nerve in the Individual; whereas the other Elements of our Analytics would correspond to the less recondite organs. Corporations fulfill functions towards general society, and towards the state,—similar to what the personal mental and moral qualities or peculiarities of the Individual, which give rise to their respective Corporations, fulfill IN the Individual. Thus the delicate sensitiveness of Corporations, and the tolerance given to them by the state, are true indications of the intellectual and moral character of society, and of the state at large; whether for better or for worse.

We have repeatedly hinted, in the Summary Introduction, that our discovery of the Six Great Units of Society, originated in and from *three distinct* lines of thought. These three trains of thought, when brought together and compared, helped to perfect each other severally, and to corroborate the correctness of them all, as thus perfected. And their thus perfecting each other, and thus correcting one another's aberrations, led to the discovery of the Tribe-principle, and to the classifying of Corporation as almost, but *not quite*, another such a Unit.

The order of thought was about as here given. First was discovered the value of several of them as types, for argument and induction. Second, the value of several of them as heads for improved classification. And third, the value of several, as the Great Units of which Society consists. But it was not exactly the same several, whose value was thus discovered, in each case. Towards the *completion* of the discovery, these three severals looked about as in the annexed table, which represents them in parallel columns.

The three trains of thought were about as follows.

As *Types.*	As *Classification.*	As *Units.*
Individual	Individual	Individual
Family	Family	Family
Social Circle	Social Circle	
Corporation	Corporation	
Precinct	Precinct	
	State	
	Nation	Nation
	Mankind	Mankind

The three lines of thought finally became identified as follows.

Types.	*Classification.*	*Elements of Society.*	
Individual	Individual		Individual
Family	Family		Family
Social Circle	Social Circle	Instinctive, i.e. Units	Social Circle
Precinct	Precinct		Precinct
Nation	Nation		Nation
Mankind	Mankind		Mankind
Corporation	Corporation	Deliberative,	Corporation

The differences and aberrations were corrected about as follows. The *Classification* only called for the elimination of State, which was *not* on either side of it; or rather, its identification with Precinct, which was already in two columns; and then it contained the full seven. The *Types* allowed of Mankind being added from both the others, being as Mankind is the ideal anti-type, towards which all those below it, point; and as it, in turn, is typical of other beings in other solar systems, and also typical of God and the Universe. And then, the Types called for Nation as the highest earthly type of Mankind. Thus the Type-line amounted to the full seven. All that then remained therefore, was to settle the Unit-Line. But as Corporation could not be taken as a Unit; both for lack of history for it; and for the reasons given in Bk. I. Pt. II. Chap. VI. § 1; also for the reasons, that Corporation cannot, without remainder, be divided *into* all the Units above it, nor thus evenly be divided *by* all the Units below it; therefore Social Circle and Precinct had to be taken, as the needed Units; and then Corporation had to be disposed of as a separate Grand Classification; and therefore had to be placed last of all; as is done in

Bk. I. Pt. I. Chap. IX. § 4 (*b*), and throughout our whole work. But to justify this, the three had to be co-ordinated in the Tribe-principle.

CHAP. II. CORPORATION AS AN ELEMENT OF TRIBE.

The Tribe-Principle originating and established, as above and as elsewhere mentioned, involves, among other things, the *perpetual recollection* of the principle, that Corporation, for purposes of general or ungeneric classification, belongs up next to Social Circle and Precinct; but has to be placed LAST, only, because of its functions in the Unit-column: and because of being a Fundamental Element of society itself, it has to be placed *apart* from the six Units; and of course it could not be placed before Individual.

This explanation seems necessary, because, from Corporation being placed at the top, in an ascending series, some persons have wondered if we meant to place it above Nation: whereas, since we place it *after Mankind*, they ought rather to have wondered whether we meant to place it above Mankind; and that wonder ought soon to satisfy itself without further explanation: And here we let the matter rest.

It has been repeatedly said, that our theory of types has this extensive meaning, namely, that in the ascending scale of the Six Units, each one is a type of all those that are higher than it. This theory itself is partly an inference from the fact, that in the historical development of human society, as new units are formed, the old ones are still always retained; that is to say, when Families have been formed, the Individuals still exist, and when tribes have been formed, the Families continue to exist; and so on upwards. Hence it follows, that when the tribe resolves itself, in modern society, into the three forms of Social Circle, Precinct and Corporation, all those Elements must always continue in living action. The facility with which these three elements of Tribe, change, one into the other, or substitute themselves one for the other, has been sufficiently remarked upon, in Bk. I. Part II. Chaps. VIII. and IX., and in Bk. II. Part II. Chap. XII. § 1, and elsewhere. Hence then, we must always look for such an abiding activity of the Tribe-principle, and of the Corporation-principle, in civil government.

Moreover, Corporation, as it comes *after* the six, in the order of the Analytics, is, in one sense, more abstract than either of them, and therefore logically more general. In this sense, *they are all types of it*, as well as in the other sense, it is type of them.

CHAP. III. LOGICAL RELATIONS.

The old saying, that government has no rights nor duties over Individuals, except to prevent them from injuring others,—becomes, in our theory, changed to the proposition, that government has no rights nor duties over Precincts, nor over governmental Corporations, whether local or general,—except to prevent them from committing injuries, either on other such Precincts or Corporations, or on those Individuals who have a just claim and right to depart TO such others.

Our object in the treatment of Corporations, is partly, to endeavor to point out, *how*, nearly all the civil relations can be performed *better* by them, than they are by the present consolidated governments of the world: better, in fact, than they can be in any other method, unless perhaps by going forward and giving to the Precinct-governments the investiture of their localities; with that fulness of power which our Precinct-theory endeavors to point out: although it is also partly our object, to develop a complete theory of Corporations, that will apply to their construction *within* the Precinct, so far as they are needed, and even so far as they are possible, there.

Moreover, the variety of *choices* between the different kinds of Corporations, that we point out, becomes important to be remembered, because we thereby obtain different classes of developments from, and of hopes in, the Corporation-theory. And as the density of the world's population increases; nothing is more certain than, that, both the increased density, and also the increased numbers, will require new developments, new evolutions, and new differentiations,—of all the various kinds of associations, political as well as others. And Corporations are the readiest methods, of thus differentiating and evolving; because they do not necessarily require change of residence, nor change of Location for any purpose; and because they arise with much more freedom and directness, from the *voluntary* powers of Individuals, Families, and Social Circles; and with less interference or intervention by "the law."

While pointing out, however, the logical relations above mentioned, we all along incidentally, in the treatment of this subject, endeavor to establish the right, the utility, and the practicability of the General Theory. Furthermore, we endeavor incidentally to point out, for all these general doctrines, the arguments in respect to two other special doctrines, namely; one, that all virtual Corporations ought to be recognized by municipal law; the other, that fractional uses of Corporations ought to be turned into wholes, and that fractional Corporations ought to be superseded *by* wholes. But yet by wholes, we do *not* mean *one* whole Corporation for all departments of government, or for all subject-matters thereof; but mean, *systems* of Corporations, such systems as will *together* make up a whole, and the scientifically organized parts of which, may therefore be called wholes.

CHAP. IV. REAL RELATIONS.

Corporation, though not a *natural* Element of society, in the same sense that the others are, is yet none the less absolutely fundamental, in the *higher* development of society,—and even absolutely necessary, until Mankind arrive at a state of perfection both of the Individual and of society: and even then, although less necessary, it would be quite as safe. It is therefore really none the less a natural Element than the others; although it is *less obviously* so. For, the mere fact that it may be dispensed with in a perfect state, is no argument against its being natural; for the same may be equally true of the Precinct or the Nation or the Social Circle, and as some imagine, of the Family itself. For, to introduce biological illustrations, the chrysalis is only a transition from the egg to the fly; but yet it is a natural state. So also the time of fruitfulness in the female, is merely transitional between puberty and a more advanced state; but still it is natural. Neither can Corporation be deprived of the attribute natural, on the ground of its being voluntary; for the *will* is natural, in every sense that the word natural can be applied to anything metaphysical. Furthermore, even if Corporations could be dispensed with, in a perfect state, yet in that state they are all the more susceptible of the highest developments, and of the highest and most varied uses to Mankind.

Mr. E. H. Hamilton has suggested the idea, of the church itself as THE great Unit of society. But this of course, can only be true of that Catholic ideal-unit, of that ideal society, which is not yet formed. Nevertheless, in a government consisting of Corporations, the fundamental importance of the church, could not be overlooked. The church, that is to say, the SYSTEM of churches, presents us the grandest and most important system of Corporations to be found in modern times; a system of which the Roman Church organization itself, grand as it is, *is only a part and a type.* The great entrance of Christianity consisted in changing the kingdom of God, from a Nation, into a Corporation,—namely, in changing its "base" from rectilinear to circular functions.

Again: The function of *general* administration is more suitable to a Corporation, than is any *single* function of government; not only because local and even national government itself, is a kind of unartificial spontaneous Corporation; but also because a common Corporation, being a leaf, a product, a result, of miscellaneous and compound government, is the best FUNDAMENTAL ANALOGY for it, and the most approved kind of a type of it. To sum it up,—a common Corporation, involving as it does, legislative, executive, and judicial functions; and, both elective and pecuniary arrangements,—is a form more like a complete political government, than almost any other form.

The Declaration of our Independence, says, "All men are *created* equal, *endowed by their Creator with* certain INALIENABLE rights, such as life, liberty and the pursuit of happiness." The term inalienable expresses the idea which Mulford regards as based on a false theory,—and there are others who regard the reference to a *Creator* as based upon a false theory. But there can be no more doubt that the United States national government, is founded upon the theory of *compact,* than it is upon the theory of equality of rights of Individuals, as given by their Creator. Indeed, the two theories amount to one, in the highest generalization. How indeed, would it have been possible, for a Nation, growing up, as ours from its beginning has done, from many Nations,—to be resolvable into any other theory than that of compact? Whatever, therefore, may be the case with other Nations, *ours* is based upon the theory of compact, in which certain rights are made by the Creator, utterly inalienable; and which, no degree of force, and no length of time, and no past consent by the governed, can ever destroy.

CHAP. V. DIFFERENCES BETWEEN CORPORATIONS AND LOCALITIES.

§ 1. *In their Nature.*

Remembering we frequently say, that all kinds of government, are a sort of Corporations for their respective Localities,—the question may now be asked, and answered: What are the differences between the Corporations strictly so called, and Precinct, or Nation, which are as if sorts or *kinds* of Corporations IMPLIED in the fundamental constitution of society?

The historical difference is this, namely; The Precinct is merely a transformation of the neighborhood-element of the tribe. This element of neighborhood, in the first or migratory condition of tribes, was merely a moving organized Social Circle; but subsequently became localized, by the enlargement of the tribe, and by the change from the migratory to the settled and agricultural condition. But social inequalities arise, even in the migratory condition, hence, even then arise the Social Circles. All governments of Localities come chiefly from the feelings, or the emotive part of our nature. But the Corporations arise from the reasoning faculties, from the suggestions of special works, not undertaken by the tribe as a whole, nor by its rulers; and either the works, or the methods, not agreed upon by all the reasoners and thinkers. Those who agree upon any work and method, unite together for that purpose only, and organize for that end.

The essence of the great difference, between Corporation and the other Elements, consists chiefly in this; that the strictly called Corporations *derive* their power from the Instinctive and Fundamental Elements of society; or at least act under their control, and are therefore of a derivative or *subordinate* kind; but the other Elements of the Analytics are instinctive ones, and may be called primitive; and can never be entirely displaced. In other words, and socially speaking, Social Circle, Precinct or Nation, can no more be entirely eliminated, than Family or *Individual* can be.

Therefore, the relation of Corporations to their organic superiors, differs from the relation of Precincts to *their* superiors, in this; that the Precincts own by nature their privileges, *as* Precincts; but the Corporations derive them from the rights of other Units, namely, from the Individual, the Family, or the Social Circle; as admitted or recognized by the superior. And thus, in a certain sense, Corporation-rights may be said to depend upon the superior powers; but Precinct-rights do not so depend; although their actual powers of course do so. In other words, the case is one of Individuals &c., asking for their liberties and rights in one particular *method.* And there arises, therefore, a much greater right of the superior to exercise judgments, especially as to the methods. But this difference need not necessarily be felt very deeply in practice; because a government, or society at large, may spontaneously give to Corporations, many or even *nearly* all the powers of either or of both.

There is, however, another essential difference between Corporations and local organizations, namely; The Precinct itself may often be the superior to a Corporation, although, of course, it could not be superior to itself. Corporations, therefore, although intellectually so great, yet need to be humble before the local governments, the essential and instinctive natural units of society. Morally, they have rights, but not perhaps to be asserted by force, against truly organized systems of local governments, with Precinct-rights duly preserved.

§ 2. *In their Operation.*

The consideration of the Precinct, established rights and principles, which are, in general, equally as demandable and obtainable by Corporation; and sometimes, but only in less degrees, by some of the other Elements. Nevertheless, the Corporation-principle possesses some advantages over the Precinct and Nation; and over their principles and methods of obtaining human rights, and securing human happiness. This Corporation-principle or method, is much more economical, and much less disruptive of the ties of kindred and acquaintance. It allows the parties to continue to reside and intermingle among each other, a policy which in the past has been useful in allaying animosities, and promoting progress.

Being next in naturalness to Precincts, and needing to precede them in the reformation, Corporations, in the mean while, are the substitutes. They are also the procurers of many particular rights of the Precinct: Because, they are the NEXT most natural and most spontaneous Element of human society, in which it is possible for small bodies of men to organize themselves politically; the Element "Nation" being entirely too extensive, and also too radically different, to be thought of as a recourse in this connection, or in this era of the world.

In their primary operations,—while the Precinct-theory provides government for persons who are near to each other, physically or geographically; the Corporation-theory provides government for those who are near to each other metaphysically or morally. And in their fullest development, the Precinct provides companies for Localities; the Corporation provides associations both for metaphysical and moral bases. Thus it is, that the highest and best obtained uses of Precinct, are involved fundamentally in the very idea of the Corporation, and are directly sought for by it.

Thus it is, that, although the physical condition, Locality,—which constitutes the distinction between the former two, namely, Precinct and Nation, and the latter one,—is a condition, the retention of which, facilitates the calculation of the physical and lower phenomena of society, and the attainment of their corresponding objects:—yet its complete *elimination* furnishes a calculus which facilitates the investigation of the metaphysical and transcendental phenomena of society, and the attainment of *their* corresponding objects,—or, which *will* do so, whenever our lower geometry and algebra, have been sufficiently perfected for such a transcendental elimination.

The great points of difference between the two systems, in practice, would be as follows,—the Corporation-system would be easiest and pleasantest for private citizens as Individuals, but the Precinct-system would be easiest for *faithful* government officials: the Corporation-method would be easiest taken advantage of, by dishonest persons, (whether in or out of office) in its actual administration, *after* being fully inaugurated; but the Precinct-system would be most likely to be taken dishonest advantage of, *in* its inauguration.

SUB-DIVISION II.

MISCELLANEOUS CORPORATIONS.

CHAP. I. CLASSIFICATIONS.

§ 1. *Blackstone's Classification.*

A Corporation, according to Blackstone, is defined to be "an artificial person constituted to maintain perpetual succession, and enjoy legal immortality, in order to preserve PERSONAL rights." But in our Social Science, Corporation sometimes means the *principle* whereby citizens of different Localities associate together for special purposes, abstract from locality; at other times it means a particular association, constituted for such a purpose, and consisting of special Individuals of various Localities, and selecting themselves for the purpose, without necessitating change of domicile. The latter part of Blackstone's definition should be kept distinctly in mind—as to the object—namely, "in order to preserve PERSONAL rights"; and he means the rights of the INDIVIDUAL.

Blackstone says, "Corporations may be erected by Custom, by Prescription, or by act of Parliament." When Prescription means the long usage of Corporation-rights by a particular Corporation, its condition before legal recognition constitutes what we call a *virtual* Corporation. When custom means common custom, such as constitutes the common law, it contains an intelligible meaning; but there is no such custom in the United States, except as to virtual Corporations, in whose case there exists enough of the law to prevent the persons engaged from being considered partners. But only legislative enactments, or special proceedings according to such enactments, constitute Corporations in the United States.

Blackstone says Corporations may be divided thus:

Either Aggregate and Sole,
Or Ecclesiastical and Lay,
Or Civil and Eleemosynary.

But this classification is not sufficient for social science; nor indeed do *we* recognize any such thing as a Corporation *sole.* The nearest approach to it, in our classification, is partnership. THAT is the smallest Corporation we can admit of, even in the definition.

§ 2. *Our Preliminaries.*

In order to consider this subject fairly, it is necessary for us to make some classifications very different from the old ones. Furthermore, inasmuch as the term "Corporation" is not commonly understood in that wide extent, or with that wide significance, that we are about to give it;—or perhaps it would be more proper to say, that the classes of Corporations of which we are about to treat principally, are *scarcely ever found,* even in theories or in books; and as the kinds of *uses* also are not common; we will have to introduce several further classifications.

Referring then, to our classification of the fundamental personal Elements of the Analytics, we remember, that whilst we had *six* Instinctive, we had only *one* Deliberative, Element. There is therefore nothing in the classification of the Analytics, so unique, and without sub-divisions, as Corporation; unless indeed it be the Summary Introduction, on Social Science in general. Corporations have to be classified somewhat like,—GENUS HOMO,—*species man.* This singularity however, refers only to their location as a whole, or as an Element. But when we come to their sub-divisions, the exactly opposite characteristic becomes apparent; and Corporations open up more diversified and complicated sets of classifications, than either of the other divisions. And although they have their historical origin in the tribe and its principles, yet their susceptibilities of almost indefinite development and application, entitle them, in the classification, to a position of almost unparalleled importance. Hence we now propose to give a classification of the classifications, embracing Ten different mentionable characteristics; the last one of which will be the basis in our Third Main Division; and several of the other nine, will aid in understanding that Division.

CHAP. II. CORPORATIONS CLASSIFIABLE ACCORDING TO TEN MENTIONABLE CHARACTERISTICS.

§ (A) *Classification of the Characteristics.*

Corporations need to be looked at in many different views; and in each view, it would be possible to make a separate classification of them all according to their different Characteristics. We will present Ten such different views or Characteristics of possible classifications, with a few remarks upon each, before proceeding to the consideration of those Corporations which are expressly governmental. *First:* Classifiable as to their relations to "the Law"; namely, Legal or Virtual. *Second:* Classifiable as to secrecy; namely secret or not secret. *Third:* Classifiable as to monopolization; namely, whether monopoly or not monopoly. *Fourth:* Classifiable as to their relations to personal intercourse; namely, whether associations involving *sociable* intercourse; or companies not involving sociable intercourse. *Fifth:* Classifiable as to the official nature of Individuals; whether membership constitutes office, or whether it does not. Those in which membership itself does constitute office, are only *Semi*-Corporations; as for instance, Partnerships and possibly Families. *Sixth:* Classifiable as to their objects in view:—These objects may be divided into Physical or Metaphysical; The Physical may be for Pleasure, or Trade, or Transportation, or Currency. The Metaphysical, might also be called Transcendental, and may be for Morality, or Religion, or Charity, or Education. *Seventh:* Classifiable according to their nature, whether simple or compound. *Eighth:* Classifiable as to the means they may use, whether Governmental, or Voluntary, or Mixed. The Governmental, may be either for Civil, or for Political objects. The Voluntary may be either for Morals, for Property, or for Person. The Mixed may be either for Uniformity, for Obedience, or for Separation. The Mixed mean those which are of a *Semi-Family* nature. *Ninth:* Classifiable as to their relations to, or control over, Localities,—whether embracing or governing their localities, or whether NOT embracing or governing them. This classification is general enough, to embrace the Governmental Corporations, which we treat at length in the Third Main Division; and was the classification formerly adopted by us for them. *Tenth:* Classifiable as to their Governmental and Political nature, namely, whether Governmental, or not.

The Governmental ones constitute, as just said, the Third Main Division. We, therefore, only need say here, that they are classified into two Sub-Divisions, namely, First, a Lower or Derivative order, exercising special functions under present governments. And second, a higher order, exercising inherent political functions; and based upon ideas. This higher order would require, and involve, a very considerable reorganization of society.

Now let us make a few general remarks on each of the before-mentioned Ten Characteristics of Corporations.

§ 1. *As Related to "The Law."*

The first and simplest basis of classification of Corporations (for the present purpose), is, that which rests upon their relation to "The Law,"—their authority in the law, to exist. Because, whilst one kind is legal, duly authorized by statute; the other kind is only virtual. A Corporation of the latter kind, is real and efficient to its own members, within certain limits; but is not so to the outside world; and is always liable to disorders, from its abnormal relation to the law. Such a Corporation is in the same relation to law, that ancient Corporations were, whilst in the incompleted process of establishment by "prescription." "AND NOW," in the United States, several of the communes, although operating without charters, and without even that *legal sacrament*, "a common seal,"—have undergone suits, and come out victorious, upon the very ground affirmed by the civil courts, that they are not partnerships, but, virtual corporations.

Our theory, in regarding partnerships as a sort of Corporations, is confirmed by the fact, that the chief or only difference which "the law" makes, between Corporations, is the same that it makes between partnerships; namely, the differences based on the degree of liability of the Individual members; namely, Limited, or Unlimited.

The old English law, until very lately, was as arbitrary and absurd, about Corporations, as *it* was, and as *ours* still is, about partnerships; namely, refusing to allow the *limited* responsibility of the Individual members, according to their own free choice and judgment; as arranged between them and their creditors, spontaneously and voluntarily. J. S. Mill has shown the complete justice, and expediency of such a freedom for partnership. And it is equally as demonstrable for Corporation: and will be seen to be so, when the old despotic policy of tyrannical or avaricious law-makers, shall cease its wretched course, of doling out human rights drop by drop; and only at all, lest blood should flow, or lest *they* should lose their offices.

The difference between Limited and Unlimited Corporations is so great, that probably it ought to have been made by us, into a separate classification, additional to the Ten. But that perhaps it is virtually included in our Fifth class,—namely, as to whether membership therein, of itself constitutes office, or not. (See § 5 below.) Because, no partnership nor Corporation ought to involve unlimited liability, without also, and *at least*, constituting each such accountable member, an officer and ruler of it, *per se;* and not merely a stock voter. Society and law should always extend their saving power and wisdom, to counteract the evils of their own producing.

§ 2. *As to Secrecy.*

The question of secrecy is always one of degree. Secrecy is justifiable or otherwise; according to its object, and according to the right of other people, to know. There is an imperfection in all human character, that will not justify an uncovering of our hearts to other persons, only in proportion as they are in, not only corresponding, but also suitably perfect degrees, both of affection and intelligence. For, without affection, men despise the faults in others, which they themselves possess; and without intelligence, they would despise the confidences of intellect. This principle, in its utmost activity, is *one* of the principles that require simple marriage and personal privacy. In all governments, whether Families, societies, cliques, parties, or even Nation itself, the innermost "wheel within wheel," is a silent, a secret, an "Unknown power." On the other hand, secrecy may be based upon a design to do *wrong* things, and, which we are really ashamed or afraid should become known. Or it may be based on a design to do *mutually selfish* things, namely, for the members to help each other *especially*, whilst at the same time receiving help from non-members, the same as if non-members themselves. And, thirdly, secrecy may be merely the provision of means of recognition, whereby persons mutually acting together in purposes, but separated in localities, may become known to each other, on occasion. In this case, the ultimate object of the association, and also its surrounding circumstances, are to be considered.

But when we would apply the thought to Politics, there is a difficulty to reconcile the universal approval of secret ballot, with the general opposition to secret societies. This much, however, can safely be said, that in proportion as the rights of all the Fundamental Elements of society are practically acknowledged; and especially the rights of Individuals, Precincts, and Corporations; and so far as the forms of legal and social proceedings, are improved generally; just so far, all good reasons or excuses for the secrecy of political associations will be removed. And finally, a completely prevalent communism, would remove the uses of secret *recognition* in the good and moral secret societies; and there would then remain as justifiable secrecies, only those between marital partners, or those between choicest friends.

§ 3. *As to Monopolization.*

All that occurs to say of this, is, that the monopolization, if any, should always be of limited duration; and in proportion to population; and if of an internal Corporation, its charter or rights should NOT be more difficult to alter by the authority of the Government, than the *Constitution* of the Government itself: nevertheless, in all forced alterations, compensation for financial injuries should be made, as truly as to Individuals. These principles apply to the monopolization of governmental and political power, by Precincts and Nations, in the displacement of tribes and governmental Corporations; as well as to common organizations. Corporations for building roads, need a limited monopoly; but Banks on a proper commodity basis, would not need any; but only, evidence of the possession of a sufficiency of the BASIS, and of morality.

§ 4. *As to Relations to Personal Intercourse.*

One of the most evident differences between Corporations, is made upon the principle, whether they involve personal social intercourse, or not. Those which do involve social and sociable intercourse, we may call associations, because the members are associates. We might include, under this head, such of the functions of the Family as belong under the head of Corporation, inasmuch as their members associate together. But we postpone them to another head, which seems to us more appropriate.

Those Corporations which do *not* involve personal social intercourse, are called companies; the members *accompanying* each other in the special occupation for which they are incorporated, but not associating together; at least, not as a matter of course. Partnerships, if they come under the head of Corporations at all, as we endeavor to show that they do, might be placed here; inasmuch as the members are not necessarily associates in the relations of private life. But we reserve them also to a place further on, which seems more appropriate.

Associations are much more complex and special, than companies. They involve that difficult subject, the Social Circle; and many societies therefore fail, because they attempt to be associations, when they might succeed, if they only attempted to be companies. It is obvious, however, that a company might exist, which would accomplish the more complex and especial functions of an association, by sub-dividing itself into two or more associations, according to the different Social Circles of which it consisted.

§ 5. *As to the Relation of Membership, to Office in them.*

(*a*) *In General.* In classifying Corporations, according to specialty of organ for function, and according to objects in view; one principle of the division might be, whether membership in itself constitutes office, or not. Those in which membership *does* constitute office, consist of partnerships on the one hand, and Families on the other. These might be called Semi-Corporations, inasmuch as only a *part* of their nature can be investigated under this head.

Most societies, as they allow all the members an equal right *to speak,* are *partly* of the nature here expressed; especially was this the case originally in the society of "Friends" or Quakers, in which, membership carried with it the right of being a "minister," a speaking-officer; although subsequently the right required confirmation by other officers. But it was only the right of a speaking-officer (an officer *peculiar* to the Christian churches, and existing in most of *them*); it was not the right of a ruling-officer, which is the only thing of much account in direct politics.

Whenever membership in a Corporation involves unlimited liability of the Individual, the law ought to empower him to be, *per se*, a ruling officer in the concern; and that too, even if he was willing and should agree to forego his claim thereunto. See above under § 5.

(*b*) *Partnership.* Here we might say a few words to the legists, who of course will dispute our theory of Corporations "*in toto*"; and in particular, will probably ridicule the very idea of including partnerships under the head of Corporations. And now, gentlemen, pray tell us, what is a limited or special partnership? and what is the difference between it and a Corporation? Ah! It has no corporate seal. Alas, indeed! But we answer: regarding the active members of a partnership as the officers of the concern, then the limited partners are merely stockholders, without having the amount of their investments divided up into a formal and arbitrary number of shares; except under the general name of so many dollars, or so many pounds; so that the difference is not in essence, but only in form; yea, and only in the form of the name. But what the partnership lacks in form, it more than makes up in spirit; because the officers, in this case, seldom find themselves able to cheat the stockholders with trickery, book-keeping, and "long-winded" reports.

The folly of the present law of partnership, in not recognizing it as a Corporation, is, that ordinarily it makes all the partners responsible without limit, for the acts of either one of them.

The principal thing which Social Science has to investigate, in regard to partnerships, is, their further and enlarged capacity to fulfill functions that Corporations now have, or might have, entrusted to them. The head of the government of Rome once consisted of a triumvirate of three partners, and of late years the government of France was a consulate of two parties, so that history does not entirely desert us in this theory. But still, these were not permanent Corporations, nor was the concurrence the result of free selection by the Individuals. The problem for Social Science here is, to fit free, voluntary partnerships, for all the various functions of Corporations; including also governing and political functions.

(*c*) *The Family.* By including the Family under the head of Corporation, all that is meant, is to recall the fact, that *some* of the functions of the Family are of a corporate nature, and belong to Corporation; because it is an institution organized for special purposes, by the voluntary *agreement* of the parties. And as we intimated in the Summary Introduction, Part I. Chap. IX., § 1, in reference to classifications, that a truly scientific one, ought to be general enough to allow all parties to arrange their ideas under its order: and not seek to forestall freedom, or to establish doctrines, by cunning contrivances. It is better to meet the question purely on its own merits, when it comes up under its proper "book,"—The FAMILY, in another volume.

Another thought however, belongs here under this head, namely, that the more, marriage and the Family-organization are entered upon voluntarily and deliberately, as in Modern Society; and consequently the less they are entered upon by mere animal propensity,—the less the principles and rights and duties of mere instinct or feeling, apply to them; and the more like voluntary CORPORATIONS they may become, without violence either to expediency, morality, or the will of God. This idea sheds more light on the evidently changing views of the most civilized peoples, relative to divorce, than anything we have yet thought of.

We have seen in the Introduction, that the deliberative and ratiocinative grounds of the Family, created a difficulty in the Highest Main Division;—that between the instinctive and the deliberative Elements of society. We there unhesitatingly adopted the term instinctive, for the first division, and included the Family in it. But still, it would not be justice to the *whole* truth; nor to the views of a large class of social scientists, nor to the generalness of a strictly scientific classification, to omit the Family entirely from the deliberative Elements.

We must also bear in mind here, according to our type-theory, that Family is type of Corporation; and Corporation, in turn, is type of Family: and that therefore *both* throw light upon each other reciprocally.

We find everywhere in history, Families, which do, in fact, conduct certain mercantile, banking, insurance, and other businesses. And we also find many instances of Families whose members do, in fact, exert a controlling influence in politics, for generations, even in the United States. But this principle has not as yet found any method of expressing itself by corporate organization, according to Republican principles, except in one or two instances of communism.

Here the question arises, whether it is possible to entrust to Families, AS SUCH, any of the functions of Corporations. The political and civil functions seem to have been entrusted to Families, in a certain limited way, in hereditary governments; but that is not at all what we mean. We mean no further hereditary principle, than in the limited degree, which the laws of the United States now allow to property. The question is, in regard to parents and their immediate children or issue. But, after Social Science shall have given to partnerships, all *their* rights, and worked out their problem; then the problem of the corporate uses of Families, may perhaps become plainer. We are not able, as yet, to do anything with it.

§ 6. *As to Objects in view.*

These would be almost endless, unless we take a few COMBINATIONS of chief objects, as portrayed in the latter part of the Third Main Division of this "book." But they may here be classified into Physical and Metaphysical, and then their respective Sub-Divisions might be as follows:—

(*a*) *The Physical.* The physical Corporations and objects, may be divided into Trade, Transportation, and Currency.

As to Trade or Business matters, our modern world is so full of them, that we need only say a little. One thing is, that as governments have proved so inefficient to attend to their own business-matters, or to obtain Individuals to attend hereunto for them,—it would be well for them to authorize large Corporations for all such purposes, as fast as the governments can be made honest enough to resist the large bribes of such Corporations. Another thing to be suggested here, is, that there is some radical defect in some of the American social laws, which tend to hinder, rather than promote, the keeping of all the members of a Family usually in the same business, as is common in Europe. The Family is a Corporation made by nature, able to conduct a business economically and happily, in mutual love and confidence.

As to Transportation and Roads, the first error seems to be, the ignoring *entirely*, the peculiar rights of the *adjacent* land-owners. Because those owners *virtually* and locally are a part of the Corporation of the road. If, after a street or common road was graded, and ordered by law to be opened,—if the final legal process to open, involved under general law, the incorporation of the land-holders *along the street or road*,—then the work over the road would be accomplished at vastly less expense, either in money or in morals, and would be much better done. Moreover, even in the case of turnpikes and Railroads, it would be better if the land-owners, as such, along the line, were invested with some small *proportion* of the stock, even if the public paid for their proportions thereof. Because, all lands ought to carry with them some share of control over the roads adjacent to them,—independent of the interest in their original construction, which sometimes is, but sometimes is *not*, worth considering.

The Precincts in which roads lie, should also have a small right of ownership in the Road-Corporations, and for the same reasons as the adjacent land-owners should have.

We must admit that the Railway companies are terribly corrupting powers over governments; but it is equally as clear, that they *can* do their work far better and far cheaper, than governments do. But a question arises here, and is left for subsequent thinkers; can Corporations for transportation be obtained, without chartering *especially* for the purpose, and merely by employing organs already in existence?

If every Railroad-ownership consisted of two separate companies,—one of the Road-way, and the other of Transportation, and under due legal regulations, by principles, not by details; perhaps things would be better, as each such Corporation would serve as a check to the other. But the main source of improvement would be, for both law and public opinion, to prevent any Railroad-officer from reaping *indirect* profits for himself at the expense of the company, no matter what were the methods or the *circumlocutions* thereof. The Express Companies that avail themselves of the Road-Companies, are *generally* found more reliable, and less risky, as transporters, than the Road-Companies themselves. Hence the conclusion, that the mails could be thus carried, better, safer and more economically, than by the government, and with less corruption of the government. Besides, they would conveniently be responsible for losses as common carriers, or otherwise, which the United States government refuses to be. The Road-Companies themselves are also accountable in this sense; and some of the best of them are perfectly irreproachable, in doing their own express business.

For the protection of travelers and their property, a special Corporation is formed in England, and is evidently necessary elsewhere; because the great power of the Road-Companies, and the smallness of most of the particular losses, generally shut out redress beyond all hope, except in the generosity of the company's officers.

A general principle is evolved from these cases, namely, that every large Corporation needs, that an opposing or corresponding Corporation should be formed or authorized, for every *class* who do business with it, whether, as customers or as employes or as opponents: and the same may be said of every large *system* of Corporations, although each one of them might be of small importance.

Nothing but Corporation can resist Corporation. Corrupt therefore as Corporations sometimes become, they yet counteract each other's evils, and help regulate society; and are all the more necessary to be legitimized in this country; because the disorderly persons *do* and *will* form into virtual, although illegal, Corporations, and into legal Corporations with secret ulterior objects; suppressing personal liberty, and interfering with the natural course of commerce and manufactures. Just as in former times, Corporations were the only powers that could resist the feudal nobility, and the kings; so in modern times, Corporations are the only powers that can resist the mobs, and the demagogues, in their various clubs and associations. Nor, are the large Corporations any more corrupt than the less and more popular ones, or than the disorderly mob-ones,—many of which are quite as much perverted by their leaders, from the real or avowed objects of their members, as are the larger ones.

An important question here is, what are the real causes of the corruption of the large road and transportation companies? One reason seems to be, that their geographical nature, and common use, make them well known to the public, so that they *seem* to be old acquaintances; and therefore the public readily LENDS them money in permanent loans. Banks are more secure than the transportation companies. The reason is, they have *no permanent* loans, because, both as to their discount and circulation, they may be called upon for payment of them at any time, without notice. When Banks meant to swindle, they formerly located in some "wild cat" region, where they could not easily be called upon, for payment.

One method to cure the evil in the Transportation-Companies therefore, would be, to constitute all the bond-holders a *Corporation* separate from the share-holders; and with a right to be the sole administrative power, as soon as a road became unable to pay its obligations promptly.

But a still better method would be, to do away entirely with permanent loans at a *fixed* interest, and convert them into some kind of preferred stock, with only a limited dividend as a maximum. A simpler rule would be, to have *equal* amounts of common stock and preferred stock, issued, subject to equal power in voting: but the common stock never to have dividends allowed, until a certain dividend, at a certain prescribed rate, had been allowed and paid to the preferred stock, and all arrearages, if any, had been made up thereunto. The rate for the preferred stock, to be not fixed by law in a given figure, but to be, say, *the average, actual and legal rate, usual in other safe and preferred investments*, as bonds, mortgages, and municipal loans, &c. Arrearages should also be at *compound* interest, at this rate.

Or, if such an arrangement is too far ahead of the age, perhaps it would be practicable, to have the rate of interest for preferred stock fixed for a given number of years, say 25 or 50 years. And at every expiration of said term, to have the owners of one kind of stock, appraise the total value of the company, and the owners of the other kind, to choose whether to buy or sell at that rate;—the party buying, would of course be the new common stockholders, and would raise new preferred stock in sufficient amount for the next term of 25 or 50 years, at a rate of interest *then* satisfactory to capitalists.

Another reason for the corruption of these companies, is the accomplishment of their elections, by general tickets; whereby, even at best, the entire board is elected by a mere majority of all those voting for boards of directors, instead of by the principle, that each director shall be elected by his own fractional proportion of the stock.

To impute their evils to the system of voting by proxy, is wrong; because the proxy is a *just* principle; and its abolition would place the companies under *still smaller* cliques than now. But distant proxies should be allowed only from old holders.

Another reason of the corruption of these companies, is, their being instituted by special, instead of general charters; so that often there is bribery in their origin, bribery in their progress, and bribery to prevent the chartering of rival lines, so that *some* at least of the officers of some such successful roads, *must* be skillful *Generals* in bribery.

The Postal Organ is of doubtful position in the classification, inasmuch as IT, compared with "express" companies, or other forwarders, performs a much larger proportional amount of *local office* work. For instance. The office expenses of other forwarders, will perhaps only be one-twentieth of their amounts paid for freight; but the office-expenses of the Postal Organ, would perhaps be almost or quite equal to the amounts paid for freight. Hence, the Mail-service, although really a kind of transportation, comes rather under the principles of a *local* business. It is well known that private persons, or Corporations, would do the Mail-business cheaper and more satisfactorily to the public, and would at the same time be responsible for losses as Common carriers; which the government refuses to be, even for registered letters. And a further advantage would be, the withdrawal of the vast power, which the filling of the Post Office gives, to every political administration. Besides, its management has always been *sectional;* formerly in the interests of the South; now in the interests of the West. For one letter weighing one fourth of an ounce, to charge two cents from one street to another, in the same city or county,—and then, for a newspaper weighing four ounces, to carry all the way from Maine to California, for the same price! We would not object so much to charging the cities *as* high as the country, provided the profits thereof were expended IN the cities, in counteracting their vices, miseries, and general ill health. But as it is, the system is unjust, and is another of the methods taken to stimulate the premature settlement of the public lands; and to promote scatteration generally.

The same kind, although a less extensive, superiority of private enterprise, is equally certain in Telegraphy. But some persons are arguing for a postal telegraph. Perhaps the newspaper-men want this "improvement," (of a postal telegraph); or perhaps the land-speculators want it. Or perhaps it is desired to have the Postal Telegraph "run" as the Post Office itself is "run." Or perhaps the Lines want to sell out at a good profit: "Government is rich." Or perhaps what is wanted is, increase of official patronage; or else a monopoly of facilities for getting advantage of the earliest news. But cheap telegraph news at the public expense, answers for a popular cry. Perhaps cheap expressage at the public expense, will be the next cry; and then, perhaps free travel; and then, what next? Perhaps:—Free property?—or what? Or; do these tendencies arise, not so much from the propensity to break down the rights of property; as from the propensity to increase the CENTRAL power? It may be both together: and then the power of the latter might be used, all the more effectually, to break down the rights of the former.

As to currency, we can readily imagine how different would have been the *finale* of the United-States Government-Loans, in the war of the Rebellion, if the government, instead of selecting an organ already possessing a well-established reputation, and in good working order, had attempted to organize, in the haste of war, banking firms or companies, expressly for the purpose. No doubt, banking Corporations *could* be formed, that would at least be safe,—by taking time and care in their construction. But after being constituted, it is not easy to reform their errors, or to change them. Whereas, an agency well selected from among *existing* ones, if it should prove unsatisfactory upon trial, could be changed at once, unless some foolish agreement had been entered into, preventing the change. But the main thing here, after all, is, to endeavor to find how Corporations for all the various purposes of this, and of the subsequent divisions, can be induced to grow up spontaneously, like the metaphysical or transcendental ones hereafter spoken of; which first arise to fulfill the functions themselves voluntarily, and are afterwards availed of by government, for the fulfillment of similar functions to those for which they had originally been incorporated. And yet, the tendency of modern laws in the

United States, is, to forbid all spontaneous attempts of this kind; nor would the free allowance of them probably be safe, so long as either gold or the precious metals with their consequents, and paper, are made the basis of currency: or perhaps also, so long as anything else is made such a basis, except well-selected and transportable merchandise; a plan for which, we have given in the Summary Introduction, and is to be resumed under the head of PROPERTY.

Then the whole matter of Currency would be so simplified, as to be nothing very different from any other kind of a credit commerce.

The question of currency, although so generally treated as a governmental one, is in principle, one only of trade or business. Governments, except in the United States, have generally used the function of coining money, as one method of taxation.

No *supreme* or national government yet established, is perfect enough to be entrusted with the *absolute* power of fixing and *altering* the currency; whether of paper or of coin. All that the supreme governments are perfect enough to have to do with it, is, to regulate and control and enforce the *contracts for it*, the same as for any other articles. And restrictions on governmental-power, are *more* needed in reference to currency, than in reference to any other articles of *contract;* because the currency is the substance and expression of ALL contracts. Nearly all the great Nations of the world have repeatedly debased or deteriorated their coins. In 1834 the United States government deteriorated their gold coins about six per cent. But only three years subsequently, came the great panic of 1837. But only six months previously, the silver coin had been deteriorated nearly one per cent. Again, in 1854, the government deteriorated the silver coins, about seven per cent. further. And again in about three years came the panic of 1857. The last named deterioration was made to the *silver* coin, in consequence of the sudden and large increase of *gold* receipts from California and Australia, which cheapened gold greatly, in comparison with silver, and which were even cheapening ALL money, at nearly the rate of one per cent. per annum,—and when, therefore, the *strictly* just course would have been, to have increased the value of the gold coin to its former value of 1834, instead of again reducing the silver.

Now, as supreme or national governments are not perfect enough to be entrusted with the *absolute* control over currency; and as Individuals have not sufficient continuity of existence, nor sufficient impartiality; therefore Corporations are much better instrumentalities for the purpose; and they, to be held accountable by the NATION, as for the performance of other contracts. We admit that contracts for currency should be held as of *national* concern, and therefore should be subject to the Nation's supervision.

The only proper governmental tamperings with the currency, even including the one of altering the standard of coin, are founded only on temporary reasons, and as expedients of relief for extraordinary cases. They are all at best only bungling methods of doing what might be much better accomplished by a simple law authorizing *specified discounts* to be deducted, in the payment of all debts contracted previous to a specified time; or what is sometimes still better, a stay-law, under adequate security, or by a combination of both methods. Because, debased coins are scarcely ever restored; and debased government-paper is restored, if at all, only with the greatest difficulty, and after the lapse of unnecessary years.

(*b*) *The Metaphysical.* The sub-divisions of the Metaphysical or Transcendental objects, would be Morality, Religion, Charity and Education. But these are objects of such importance, as to require consideration as elements of society, under the heads of Intellectuals and Morals, in the Synthetics; and are, for the most part, deferred to that branch of the subject. We may, however, say here, that they are the most important objects that Mankind, whether as Individuals or societies, can seek; yet the experience of ages has thus far proved, that the more the political governments "leave these affairs alone," the better the affairs prosper. This however is not owing to any universal principle in the nature of things; but partly, to the general corruptness of political government, and partly to the error of attempting to promote transcendental objects, by COMMON FORCE. But yet we see, that society spontaneously puts forth organizations, which accomplish these special purposes by voluntary means, better than governments could do by their coercion. Now, when society has spontaneously put forth appropriate and efficient organs for these purposes, political governments ought to be wise enough to perceive the fact, and to AID the institutions, so far as they can reasonably do, without corrupting them. The various political governments of the United States, do, in fact, pursue this method with moral, charitable and educational societies. But when they come to religion, they seem to lose their senses; and argue, because men have different preferences in religion, that government must therefore do nothing for it; just as if men had not preferences and differences, on moral, and on charitable, and on educational questions. Accordingly, if England aids the Catholic church in Ireland, or the Hindoostanee establishment in India; all Protestantism is in excitement. And here, even a public school must not have any law, except the prejudices or partialities of the Directors, to allow religious services in it.

But waiving for the present, the question of religion, it is evident in general, that society has learned a lesson here, which it will find of the greatest use to apply to all this class of Corporations, whether political or not political, and whether metaphysical or physical,—the lesson of *aiding* organizations spontaneously existing, and thus using them as its own organs. By this method, governments would obtain the services of organizations, that had already proved their efficacy and merits, by their own spontaneous success.

§ 7. *As to their Nature; whether Simple or Compound.*

The Simple Corporations would be those for Morality, Religion, Charity, Education, and Productive Business. The Compound would be Beneficial Associations, Insurance Companies, Churches, Theological Seminaries, Publication and Distribution Societies, Hospitals, Asylums and Educational Institutions; also Corporations for Transportation and Currency; also the Governmental Corporations, if there were no special classification for them.

§ 8. *As to the Means they may use.*

The next basis of classification of Corporations, is, upon the kinds of power they may employ:—(1) Whether they may employ only voluntary, i.e. moral power, or whether they may resort to distraint on property, or whether to coercion of the person. (2) As to whether the force used is to be of a Semi-Family nature; and whether, under it, they are to seek conformity, in the sense of uniformity and harmony, or whether, to seek absolute obedience, or whether, to resort to the alternative of separation and dismission. (3) As to whether the force used is to be of a civil governmental kind, namely, whether in addition to applying coercion to the Individual, it also is to attempt to *punish*, in order to exert an influence on others. This part of the classification would also include political power, and the relations of the Corporation to the other political Elements, namely, Precinct and Nation.

§ 9. *As to their relations to Locality.*

(*a*) *Corporations* NOT *embracing and governing their Localities.* In general, the law of Corporations without political power, ought to be the same as that of Individuals, except that their officers should be free from personal liability; and the common law is thus far correct, in calling them artificial persons.

The first principle to be considered now, in regard to Corporations, is the simple fact of their existence in or out of the Locality or Precinct in which they are intended to transact their business. And by the pre-supposition, this class is the one which has NO relation to the exercise of political functions in the Precinct of its location. In regard to this class, it is evident, that those which act wholly within the Precinct in which they are located, ought to be almost entirely free from all national and all other outside interferences; whatever the nature or business of such a Corporation might be, provided it does not have a *direct* tendency to interfere with the rights of persons, or organizations, outside of the Precinct or Locality. This principle against interference, becomes more and more absolute, exactly in proportion to the social power actually exerted, of confining the influence of such Corporations substantially to the Precinct in which they are located, so far as it is reasonable to suppose that the influence of *Individuals*, may be confined to or within the same limits; but no farther restrictions. Even then, there will remain this difference, of greater power of government over Corporations than over Individuals; inasmuch as from the very nature of Corporations, they cannot remove, like Individuals, to other Localities, that is, to other Precincts, inasmuch as such a removal might forfeit the charter, or essentially change the nature, of a Corporation organized expressly to act wholly within its own Precinct; and that is the kind of Corporation we are now considering.

But it may be asked, What would you do about Corporations organized expressly for immoral or irreligious purposes? We would reply, we would just do with them, what free governments now do with irreligious organizations, and even what the United States ought to have done with rebellious organizations, before they proceeded to any overt act of rebellion; namely, allow them to be COUNTERACTED by OTHER CORPORATIONS, and by Individuals. We would let them alone; but with this difference in favor of our theory, that it only applies to freedom *within* the Precinct; and then in that case, the Precinct itself would be held morally accountable, in the judgment of the Nation and of Mankind; and with this other difference, that other Precincts have a full and equal right to exclude all such Corporations, and even their emigrants, their advocates, and their literature, from their respective localities: so far as they choose to do so, and be amenable to the same moral judgments of Nation and Mankind. These and other various practical means would soon bring them to justice.

Again, you may ask, What would you do about Corporations of this evil class, if established EXPRESSLY for criminal purposes? The answer would be, that those criminal purposes which are private in their nature, and have no direct tendency to injure others, except by example, might safely, according to the principles just before mentioned, be left to the action of their own Precinct; for, that is the locality that sees the example, and suffers by it. And it is fundamental to our theory, that the right of free removal from one Precinct to another, of persons with their property, should be maintained; so that if all good citizens should disapprove of any given proceedings, and should despond of the probability of the Precinct being reformed,—they could readily remove to another. But it is to be borne in mind here, that what one age or denomination, judges criminal, another does not; and this difference of opinion is another argument for the freedom of Corporations.

But, as to that other class of criminal purposes, which are not private, and which are direct aggressions against established rights, and which would tend to foster a class of criminals, who would prey upon the rights of persons or property situate *outside* of the Precinct; such purposes are of course excluded by the nature of our supposition. And Corporations established for any such purposes, could not at all be considered in the class of those who transact their business entirely within the Precinct. And it is hardly conceivable, that any such criminal organizations would be allowed expressly to act within the Precinct itself. And no Precinct recognizes the virtue of another, only as it chooses to.

Now, as to that class of Corporations which transact their business, partly within and partly out of, their own Precinct; why, so far as they act within their Precinct, they come under the class just above mentioned; and so far as they act out of their Precinct, they come under the principles of the class we are next to discuss.

Now, as to that other class of Corporations, which are to act *wholly out* of the Precinct or Locality in which they are situated, they are a singular and curious class. For instance, the state of New York charters a Corporation *located* (?) in the city of New York, to build a Railroad across the Isthmus of Panama, or a telegraph line on the coast of China, or to conduct some business in the territory of Montana, or in the city of Philadelphia. In any of these cases, there ought to be no difficulty in seeing the true principles of fairness. By the comity of Precincts, such as now exist in the United States, and also by express statute, a charter given by one Precinct to a Corporation that is to act in another Precinct, should be valid in all other Precincts, as to the *fact* of the existence of the Corporation, and the official character of its officers. But on the other hand, such a Corporation, as to its action in those other Precincts, should have no rights of operation whatever, but what are given by the laws of the Precinct IN which it is acting. And this state of the case refers us again to Corporations WITHIN their Locality. Because a charter from an outside Precinct, should do *no more* than recognize the mere *fact* of the artificial personality, and real existence, of the Corporation; but is not thereby bound to, either allow or enforce, any of the proceedings thereof within its own domestic Locality; and perhaps, not even in any other Locality than that of the home itself of the said outside Corporation. The case is just the same as the *nativity* of an Individual. The nativity of an Individual only constitutes it a human being, but does not necessarily give it official or political rights in outside Localities, only so far as the latter approve of so doing.

(*b*) *Corporations Embracing and Governing their Localities.* There is a class of Corporations, which exercise only a partial degree of political or government-power, of a secondary kind, that is to say, a kind that refers to some one idea or combination of ideas; and only derived by express grant from original governing bodies in the Locality. The consideration of those will be taken up in the Third Main Division of Corporations. We are now speaking of that kind of Corporations which embrace their Localities *as a whole*, and are the local governing power thereof. For convenience, they might be called Federations. The kind of powers which they may rightly exercise, is that which in general, is now considered as bestowed upon townships, boroughs, and counties.

Here would be the place to arrange for and treat, "States" and Large Cities; if the reader were not satisfied with our locating them under PRECINCT, Part II. Chap. XII.

But every ordinary form of civil government, whether over a township, or a confederation, or an Empire of Nations, is a *sort* of Corporation of the kind here mentioned, namely, the kind which governs the Locality which it embraces. But when we speak in a more restricted sense, only "states" and large cities would come under this category. But we have already considered these under the head of Precinct, where they more properly belong: for according to our theory, governmental Corporations consist essentially of persons disseminated in various inherently political Localities, and can only be considered as co-extensive with Localities, in the final success of a system of Corporations.

This class of Corporations might be divided into two kinds: one of which is positively regarded, by most persons, as a government; for instance, boroughs, counties, towns, &c. The other of which, is not yet so regarded generally, because they only perform, here and there, one or more special functions of government. But the distinction, after all, is hardly scientific but popular rather. The consideration of this class will be deferred to the Third Main Division. This is the same class which has been mentioned above, as possessing only derivative powers, or exercising only derivative functions.

The smaller geographical divisions, do, according to our theory, possess, not a secondary or granted degree of power; but original inherent rights, at least especially the smallest of these divisions; being what we regard as one of the eternal Units, the Precinct. But the kind of power which is usually attributed to them, is merely the power we, in our theory, would attribute to Provinces, Cities, and what in the American Union are called "states." The writer's theory of "state rights," knows of nothing of this higher kind of power in "states," except as in Precincts or in Nations. The American "states" are merely incorporated bodies with *double* charters. In their case, the charter must be considered as originating from and ratified, both by the Nation above them, on the one hand, and by the Precincts of which they are composed, on the other hand.—In other words, they are governmental political Corporations, with double charters.

Very nearly the same principles apply to the rights of large cities. The intimate providential and balancing relations, which exist between these Corporations called "states" and cities, were pointed out when treating of cities, under the head of Precinct: Part II. Chap. XII.

§ 10. *As to Governmental and Political Functions.*

The next important classification would be; into Corporations which are for governmental and political purposes; and those which are not for such purposes. This division is only mentioned here, in order to complete *scientifically* the plan, as it appears in the analysis, of treating of all kinds of Corporations, in a general way, in this Main Division. If we were to enlarge upon it, we should have to take up the governmental or political ones here, also in a general way, before making another Main Division. But that would make a useless break in the main subject of this article, namely, the subject of Governmental or Political Corporations; therefore we place them, both general and special, in the next, namely, the Third Main Division.

MAIN DIVISION III.

CORPORATIONS WITH POLITICO-GOVERNMENTAL FUNCTIONS.

SUB-DIVISION I.

PRELIMINARIES.

CHAP. I. CLASSIFICATIONS.

§ 1. *Analytical Table of Politico-Governmental Corporations.*

III MAIN DIVISION. Corporations exercising Governmental and Political functions	Lower or Derivative Order; exercising functions under present Governments	For Single functions	Treatment of Criminals
			Collection of Taxes
			Police (and Military)
			Civil-Executive
			Judicial
			Deliberative
		For General functions	General Administrative; namely, for general functions
	Higher order; exercising Inherent functions: and Based on Ideas	A Multiplicity. Based on isolated or single ideas	
		A Few. Based on a few principal combinations of ideas	

CHAP. II. DEFINITION.

The doctrine of Governmental or political Corporations, stated in the abstract, is, that there may exist a variety of bodies-politic, operating upon the same grounds,—each attending to its own civil and political duties. These would be governmental Corporations. When these Corporations differ only as to their functions, we have the First Sub-Division, namely, those which exercise functions *derived* from the Governments of Localities. But when these Corporations differ as to the classes of Individuals whom they are to govern, each governing its own members, and letting all others alone,—then we have the Second Sub-Division, namely, those which exercise *inherent* functions based on ideas.

All the objects and functions considered under this general head, belong to, and may properly be considered as referring to, all the different kinds of Corporations; and even to the great Units of society; inasmuch as they partake of the nature of these. Hence, most of the remarks to be made under this head, will apply to all Corporations, and partly even, to all other government-organs: although the particular organs of society, first to be discussed, are supposed to have only *some* of the functions, and to aim at only *some* of the objects of government. In other words, we are now to consider the newly developed special organs, that are, from time to time, putting forth, each to accomplish its own object; in accordance with the great biological law, that, the higher we rise in the scale of the development of being, the more we find, that every different function has its own organ, specially for its particular purpose. Corporations are the new organs, which, as governments develop, must be put forth, so that each function may have its own *special* organs; and so that each organ or each set of organs, may be different from every other organ or set. But sometimes, one function calls for several organs, as the perspiring skin has its thousands of pores, and the nutritive organs have their hundreds of lacteals; and often, the organs for each function, come in pairs, corresponding to the duality in nature. And in a few cases, each function has only one organ.

CHAP. III. GOVERNMENTS SHOULD SELECT RATHER THAN CREATE THEIR CORPORATIONS.

One important suggestion here is, that government should do as little as possible towards the *direct* or actual creation of Political Corporations; but do as much as would be consistent with safety and incorruptness, to induce societies to organize of their own accord, for somewhat similar purposes. Government should endeavor to call forth its needed Corporations, rather by *encouraging* their formation, than by actually creating them. To carry this principle into practice, the greatest freedom of forming Corporations would be indispensably necessary.

CHAP. IV. PROMOTIONS OF CORPORATIONS.

Another suggestion is, that Corporations might be promoted from one function to another; but of course, not only in a merely outward or formal way. There is first to be considered, an outward promotion, namely, the promotion of a Corporation from acting for a Precinct, to the office of performing the same functions for a larger Locality, or a much higher generality. But this is not the main promotion we refer to, although it should by no means be undervalued. But the kind of promotion we chiefly mean, is one, that elevates to higher kinds of function,—one, that is performed by an inward and living process, the like of which is not found in any science less spiritual or metaphysical than Biology, and only there found, by close observation, and in a *few* cases. For instance, the surplus life-power which seems, in infancy, to produce growth, does, after puberty, turn to a power to reproduce its kind. And at a still later age, the generative power passes away, whilst the life-power is all concentrated in maintaining the life of the Individual.

And it is not inconceivable, nor even entirely absurd, to hope, that the time may come, in the case of human Biology, when this life-power may be turned to complete the perfection, and perhaps even the undying longevity, of the Individual-man. Such a hope is, for some reason or other, entertained by the Prussian naturalist Karl Ernst von Baer, and by J. H. Noyes and his coadjutors. But, if not the Individual, perhaps the race may become perpetual, by means of promotions of functions.

It would be presumptuous, to attempt to foretell exactly the *order*, in which the promotions of *Corporations* could take place; but we may presently offer some suggestions as to them, in connection with the other particulars.

CHAP. V. CORPORATIONS, TO BE PROGRESSIVE WITH THE PRECINCT.

Although the theory of Corporations is abstract from Locality, nevertheless, whatever exists at all, must exist *somewhere;* and therefore any actual system of Corporations must have some Locality, whether that of Precinct, Nation or Whole Earth. And as, the smaller the Locality is, the more any actually new system of Political Corporations, wou'd be likely to be adopted; therefore the Precinct-system seems necessary, in order to give perfect practicability to the Corporations. Nevertheless, a large system of Precincts is not necessary to precede, because the success of the Corporations, in a few select Precincts, might be accepted as a sufficient proof of their practicability in the Nation as a totality. On the other hand, the highest differentiations of the Corporation-system, seem to require the pre-existence of the Precinct-; so that both systems can only develop together, which, as Spencer says, is the method of the development of the sciences generally.

SUB-DIVISION II.

CORPORATIONS WITH DERIVATIVE POLITICAL FUNCTIONS.

CHAP. I. EXPLANATION.

The class of Corporations we are now to consider, are, first, those exercising functions *derived* from political government-organizations, namely; those which exercise only a *partial* degree of political or governmental power, of a derivative kind, obtained by express grant from original governing bodies; and to perform some of their functions, which would otherwise be deputed to government persons or officers. Although the real difference between these and other Corporations, (subsequently to be considered), so far as rights are concerned, consists rather in the first kind being regarded by the people *generally*, as a civil government; and the other, not *yet* so regarded. So that the distinction of their rights is popular rather than scientific. Thus, this Division of Corporations, bears the same relation to Corporations as a whole, that *they* bear to the Local Governments. This is so, both in their derivative nature, and in their popular non-apprehension. This division may also be distinguished from the second, by the consideration, that *this* is for *functions*, and *that* is for *ideas*.

CHAP. II. CORPORATIONS FOR SINGLE FUNCTIONS.

§ 1. *In General.*

Corporations should not act for only *one* employer or principal, but each such Corporation should, as far as possible, be so constituted, that it would perform somewhat similar functions for a variety of employers or principals, or on its own account also. This latter condition, in selecting and constituting them, —would be similar in principle to, although different in origin from,—availing, of Corporations already existing for their own business-purposes. And when this cannot, from the nature of the case, be done; the one Corporation should be allowed to fulfill its own peculiar government-functions, for several Precincts or Localities, so far as possible. This creates opportunity of comparison, on the one hand. On the other hand, a Corporation, if ill used, or if too independent to allow itself to be used as a political tool, by one Precinct or Locality, may be free to dispense with the patronage of that one, having other Precincts or Localities, upon which to fall back for employment. All this is simply introducing the common experience and wisdom of the business world, into political government.

The full accomplishment of this, requires the constitution, we have elsewhere maintained, of a large number of small semi-independent, or State-Precincts; although most of this principle might be applied by the present organizations of townships and counties, if they were not too much given to requiring those who work for them, to *reside* in the district of their operations. For evidently, if, for instance, a police, whether of Individuals or of Corporations, is to act for several Precincts, it must be left free from the necessity of *residing* in its place of occupation.

But what shall we say of the possible application of these principles, by national governments? We answer; first; that the principles just set forth, for application by Precincts, may be applied by Nations, when that national organ called patriotism, shall have become a minimum, or shall have been partly absorbed or divided away, among Precincts and Corporations; so that one Nation could trust the Individuals and Corporations of or from another Nation, to perform some of its political or governmental functions; just as Precincts or Corporations now do; just as the time has passed away (except among Turks and Chinese, &c.), when a foreigner was thought not fit even to be trusted with the privilege of a common merchant, much less of a landholder. But, second, and mainly; we answer; that these ideas are to be applied to national affairs, by adhering to the principle, but reversing it:—just as the mucous membrane is one with the outside skin, but is reversed. Instead of one Corporation working for several governments, we may need to have the national government adopting several Corporations to fulfill the same one function,—a plurality of organs,—two, if that bring sufficient *comparison;* but if not, then as many more as may be needed. If the functions to be performed are too few for more than one Corporation in a given Locality, then let them operate in alternate or neighboring Localities, throughout some given field; just as government has policy enough, in the merely material matters of Railroads, &c., to grant its lands away in alternate sections, all along the routes; instead of all in one Locality, which the road or company might select.

§ 2. *For Treatment of Criminals.*

The object of the punishment of criminals, is becoming evidently more and more resolvable into the object, "treatment of the erring," and so far as this is true, it is manageable by the Corporations for the transcendental purposes, namely, Morality, Religion, Charity and Education. The little of personal spontaneous guilt then remaining, in excess of that which is generally allowed to run loose in society, would require the introduction of an element scarcely yet to be found in voluntary Corporations. Such an element would therefore have to be derived from governments, by special charter, or by some more express and special grant than the others: and in this case, both the duties and the restrictions, might be clearly set forth by the government; and a special acceptance thereof, be required from the Corporation.

As a basis then, to begin the promotions with, observe, that some governments have already introduced into the management of criminals, a considerable degree of the power of the benevolent and moral Corporations, (namely, those for Morality, Religion, Charity and Education.) Suppose then, some government were to try the experiment, in a limited field, of giving the control of criminals almost entirely into the hands of the moral and benevolent societies, subject only to the restrictions, that the criminals should not be turned loose on the community, without the consent of the political government; and that the criminals should not be treated any more severely than "the law" for prisons allowed. And suppose such experiments were actually to prove, in the end, undoubted successes; as indeed there is hardly any doubt that they would. Here is a basis to begin with. Then a successful Corporation of that kind, might be promoted to the function of managing professional paupers. The managers might be readily induced, voluntarily to undertake the new function, in addition to the old one, by giving them separate buildings, and separate sub-organizations for each function, at the public expense, of course. Such experiments also, we have no doubt, would prove *stupendous* successes, if the governments would only grant the managers sufficient power. But we cannot admit that criminals should have the higher or promoted order of care, even if it be true that they require more scientific treatment: because *justice* must ever be preferred to merely *apparent* policy.

The next step would be to select the most successful of these already promoted Corporations, and relieve them altogether from the care of criminals, so that they might devote themselves exclusively to the "unfortunates," and the paupers, and to restoring *them* to honor and usefulness. By unfortunates we mean, the five classes, Fallen women, Habitually intemperate persons, Paupers, Persons accused of crime but not yet convicted, and *Youths* in danger of being involved in habitual crime. And each of these five classes of persons, should of course be placed in charge of a different Society. Promotion, as to these five, might begin with the last named one, and perhaps end with the first named; as that is the *order* of *difficulty* of the work to be done in each case. But more probably, the treatment of only one of these classes would be sufficient, in order to qualify for promotion to some higher governmental functions. And voluntary societies would not be profited by, nor consent to, very frequent changes of their functions, unless organized for that object.

Those societies which had proved themselves reliable and efficient, in the management and reforms, of criminals, and professional paupers, and other unfortunates,—would certainly exhibit and *prove* a high degree of Legislative, Police, and Judicial wisdom. We will then pause here, for the present, with their promotions, and take up another line of thought; confident of this at least, that their wisdom and power *can* be utilized in *some* higher forms, whenever we are ready for them.

§ 3. *For Collection of Taxes.*

As to the collection of taxes; all persons ought to know, how difficult it is to ascertain each Individual's share thereof; and how, by false swearing and other means, much of our taxation is really, in the end, more of a tax on honesty and veracity, than it is on the income, importation, or business, of the Individual. Hence, we need not wonder so much, that Rome adopted the policy of selling out the privilege of taxation to the highest bidder! And the successful bidder would probably be the smartest man in finding out the real valuation. But we, in modern times, ought to improve on that method, and even upon our own.

Probably the best method for first trial, would be, to intrust the whole business of collection of taxes, to those Corporations that had already obtained a superior and long-established character as financial organs, that is, the Banks or the Trust Companies. This would be going to the Physical non-political elements, selecting an approved organ, and promoting it to a political function, something in the same manner as we have just before been considering, in the case of the metaphysical. And in both cases, there would in time, probably grow out of the new and promoted society, a division, according to the principles of the division of labor, whereby, one part would devote itself entirely to the new function. Even the very evils and troubles of the combined stages, would hasten the time of the division, when the old "fogies" would return to their first work, and allow the new part of the organ to go on more freely with its own functions.

§ 4. *For Police-and-Military Functions.*

Our theory does not recognize war very gladly, nor at all, only so far as war is a "necessary evil," as if indeed it ever could *really* be either necessary or expedient at all. Therefore we must regard the military power, at best, as only a development from the police, in fact, as a promoted order of police officers. Hence it is only to a very limited extent, and for a FEW persons, that we could appropriate into our theory, the idea of an exclusively theoretical military education. But all that is good, in the high spirit that prevails among military men, might be passed over to the police, although not necessarily to all the present Individuals therein. But, by presenting the idea, that police services were necessary to promotion in the regular army, and gradually even requisite to other executive offices; and by supplying police officers freely, with the preparatory military, and other executive education, necessary to aid them in those professions; and by corresponding examinations of fitness,—the spirit and self-respect of the order would be highly raised, and better classes of men would be drawn into the organization. All this would happen, by making the outward organization correspond, as far as practicable, to the inward theory and spirit,—by maintaining that justifiable war, and even other executive force, are only extended functions of police-duty.

The proposition has already been made, to incorporate companies for the purpose of detective police, but we do not know with what success. But if they be possible, then there might in time grow out of them, the possibility of military authority being vested in a Corporation.

§ 5. *For Civil-Executive Functions.*

Executive functions naturally belong to the police and military class, although of course, executive faculties are required and developed by the headship of every department of government, and of every association. The veto-power is a conglomerate thing, a mixture of executive with legislative functions, and ought to be withdrawn, to have substituted instead of it, a specified largeness of majority. On this basis, then, there is a probability that a Corporation could, if required, fulfill executive functions. But, as the Corporation itself must select its Individuals, the institution and the Individual would both be performing the same functions, and therefore, it is possible that Corporations might be dispensed with, under this head.

The principle involved in this argument, is one reason why a Corporation can never perfectly fulfill all the functions of a Nation. For a Nation is, in spirit, the executive power of the sum of all its Localities, namely, its Locality as a whole.

§ 6. *For Judicial Functions.*

In regard to judicial functions, it is not yet easy to see, how these could be advantageously entrusted to a Corporation, in any other way than indirectly, namely, as being involved in the functions of Corporations previously established for other purposes.

§ 7. *For Deliberative Functions.*

Although Legislatures themselves may not be constituted as Corporations, yet the political bodies who *nominate* and *elect* them, might easily be so constituted. We allude to elementary spontaneous political organizations. We find in the United States, spontaneously originated organizations, of every ward county and state, as well as of the whole country, for nominating and electing candidates. It cannot be doubted that this vast outgrowth, can be trained in and directed to further purposes, and at the same time, be so controlled as to accomplish those purposes better than they now fulfill their proposed ends. By refining them into a suitable system of political clubs, we hope hereafter to show (mainly in the article on Civil Government and Elections) that this element, voluntary political clubs, can be turned into the function of direct election of representatives, whereby the voice of every Individual would continue to be heard, each for himself; instead of those organizations only nominating candidates for a majority representation, and a conglomerate decision. By thus making the influence and functions of these voluntary political clubs, *direct* instead of indirect, we afford a chance for some of them to establish, for themselves, a permanent reputation for political fairness, honesty, and wisdom,—a reputation that might be maintained, generation after generation.

Supposing, then, a reputation for such a character, to have been sufficiently established, surely it could be utilized somewhere, and for some higher end, and in some higher method. It is too soon yet to see just how, and for what immediate ends, this utilization should take place. But it is evidently possible, that out of it, ultimately might grow up a great system of civil government, by Corporations over their own voluntary members; and thereby *to that extent*, releasing them from the local or general political governments; just as ancient Rome allowed foreigners, resident there, to judge themselves by their own laws and proceedings. More will be said of this, in a subsequent part of this article. In the character, then, established by such voluntary political clubs, there is a ground of promoting some of them to some higher purpose, to be afterwards discovered.

CHAP. III. CORPORATIONS FOR GENERAL FUNCTIONS.

§ 1. *Classifications.*

If it were not for the fact, that in the United States, the terms *general administration* apply to the National government, this class ought to be called Corporations of General Administration. These are the last and highest kind the world has yet seen, of political Corporations, as defined by their objects, namely, those for General Administration. These, though apt to be confounded with the executive office, are entirely different; for they combine and exercise several, or all, the different functions of government,—the different kinds above mentioned. But the last named class, namely, those for deliberative functions, might possibly be included under this more general head, because the deliberative function relates to all the others, and even relates to itself also: like the power of thought, which studies thinking, as well as other things.

This class, for General Political Administration, readily passes into that of Corporations embracing and governing their Localities; but must be distinguished also from them. They, we found, were cities and states; they derive their origin partly from the Localities in which they exist; and are so intimately connected with the Precincts which they include, that they belong rather to the head of Precinct, where we have placed them, than to Corporation. But these Corporations we are now speaking of, namely, those for general political functions, do not necessarily correspond with the Locations which they govern, nor do they derive their authority from them. The British East India, and Hudson's Bay, and Dutch East India, Companies, are instances in point; so also, are the colonization-companies of various ages. These colonization-companies, after becoming permanent in their adopted Locations, gradually pass over into Corporations actually embracing and governing their Localities. But the two are not, on that account, to be confused, any more than the citizenships of two different countries should be confused by an Individual changing his citizenship from one to another; nor, for instance, than Normandy must be confused with England, by William of Normandy becoming King of England.

§ 2. *Uses.*

The function of *general* administration, is more suitable to a Corporation, than any single function; because, as has been already said, that element is the best type of civil government; which, in all forms, is a kind of unartificial Corporation constituted by nature, in general, and especially in the United States.

History helps us more with examples of this kind, than with those that exercise only one political function. In fact, both for the formation of new settlements, and for the government of permanent colonies, History shows, how much better and more successful, the plan of Corporations is; than either the plan of direct home-government, or of deputy governors, or of private action and Individual enterprise. If the United States had conducted its settlements in the West, on this principle of Corporations, all the blessings of civilization might have been carried steadily forward, with the settlements. Indian wars might have been prevented, the Indians themselves absorbed in the Corporations; and by preventing the immediate and irritating *causes* of the Southern Rebellion, that great war itself might have been prevented.

§ 3. *Genesis.*

Let us premise here, however, that, even if we fail to show the practicability of, or the methods of, producing and cultivating Corporations for general political purposes; it would still be very premature to suppose, that they never could be cultivated or produced: for, perhaps it may not be possible, to point out how the combined organizations can be developed, until after the Corporations for the various special and elementary functions before mentioned, shall have been *separately produced.* For, as has been said in the Introduction, the true science of society, cannot go very far in advance of the progress of the foremost phases of society itself.

The Corporations that we have already mentioned, would, by their variety, and their promotions, have produced the men and the methods, from which might be selected the various elements to form these Corporations for general administration. Those previous ones, should also have produced the wisdom and the disposition, for the successful combination of the elements. It is scarcely to be expected of this high kind of Corporations, that they could be formed, like some that have already been mentioned, namely, by the direct combination of pre-existing organizations. Perhaps, for this high kind of Corporations, all that can be expected from the previous ones, is, the men, the dispositions, and the ideas.

It is possible, that sometimes these Corporations might grow out of a combination of the developments of Insurance and Police,—that is to say, Corporations might be entrusted with governmental powers, by undertaking to insure the public against Individual losses, either from their own errors, or from rogues; and by assuming the expenses and duties of the detection of criminals. But of course, to be balanced by leaving their punishment or treatment, to the organs that should approve themselves capable of those separate functions; and of course, not to be judges in their own cases, or even in cases involving similar Corporations.

The actual realization of a Corporation of this kind, involving as it would, the exercise of combined functions, would require and presuppose, that there should be a union of two separate organizations; one of which, should have grown up from a fully approved insurance organization, and the other from a fully approved police Corporation. Then, nearly all that would remain to do, would be to get them to combine, in one business or in one function. I do not know whether the analogy for this, that is for the combination of two organs into one, can be found in physical biology. The combination of sex might be compared, but that is in reality metaphysical, so far as we yet know. And in metaphysical objects, we can find other and ample analogies, as of ideas and feeling and will, uniting into one *mentality*.

The very *idea* of voluntary governmental Corporations, seems to have originated with the *religious* element of human nature: the religions of most countries and of all ages, having spontaneously embodied themselves in organizations tantamount to Corporations.

The perception, but misunderstanding of this truth, is what has induced some writers, to charge the religious element with producing caste, and secret associations, in ancient times. But the general principle really budding into existence, could not be understood until the true theory of Corporations became manifested.

The Corporations of the Catholic church, in Catholic countries, developed them pretty fully; but politico-religious Corporations of all ages, have been conducted chiefly for the protection of religious *officials*, rather than of the people,—excepting, however, the Catholic "*communities*" or recluse-houses. Perhaps therefore, the religious element of human nature, may develop such Corporations, especially when at work in recluse association. Either the churches themselves might ultimately receive again, as in former ages, a restored power over their own members; or, if it be necessary to retain perpetually the distinction between the religious and secular powers, the churches might give rise to other Corporations which would exercise such functions,—just as they have given rise to their respective Bible, Tract, Mission, Hospital, and Poor, Societies. It is also possible, that the Temperance, Masonic and other such Societies, might produce such Corporations for political purposes.

SUB-DIVISION III.

CORPORATIONS WITH INHERENT POLITICAL FUNCTIONS.

CHAP. I. NATURE OF THIS SUB-DIVISION.

§ 1. *Justification of the Speculative, and the Abstract.*

Many of the ideas of this division, especially of the first parts of it, are very abstract; and AS YET, our direct interest in it may arise chiefly from the true love of theory or scientific speculation. In this division we have found but little aid from books, and but little encouragement, other than the love of the study, and the necessity of this Sub-Division, to complete a harmonious view of the whole subject,—together with moral faith in the necessity of some higher Corporations than now exist; and in the ultimate usefulness of speculative reasoning, to lead to them. The love of intellectual and systematic beauty, is just as entrancing to scientific theorists, as music is, to its amateurs and devotees; but with the additional consciousness, that the scientific beauty LEADS CERTAINLY TO HIGHER TRUTHS.

For thus adhering to the speculative, rather than the immediately practical enjoyments and uses; and, to the abstract conceptions, rather than to the concrete organizations,—we appeal for further justification, to Comte, (Pos. Phil., p. 810–812.) Of the division "between speculation and practice," he says:—"In all the six provinces of knowledge, we find the first condition of mental progress, to be, the INDEPENDENCE of theory; as no conceptions could have been formed, if the theoretical point of view had been inseparable from the practical. We see, too, how *both* must have entire FREEDOM,—the theoretical spirit, to retire into its condition of analytical abstraction; and the practical, to occupy itself with specialities. If either repressed the other, the consequences would be fatal to progress. *A priori* considerations are very efficacious, if wisely instituted and conducted; but the first condition of their utility, is, that when applied, * * * they should be applied by the practical spirit, in each concrete case."

"The division between the two kinds of contemplation,—the scientific and the æsthetic,—is much less disputed, (though it is less marked)— * * * through the fundamental relation which connects the sense of the beautiful, with the knowledge of the true: * * * Art affording to Science, in return for a secure basis, not only intellectual solace and moral stimulus, but *much reactive aid* in perfecting its philosophical character."

"A more modern, but wholly indispensable division, remains to be noticed; that between abstract and concrete science. * * * Scientific progress has been guided by it for two centuries past; for, as we have seen throughout, concrete science, or natural history properly so called, could not be even undertaken, till abstract science was instituted, in regard to all the orders of elementary phenomena concerned; every concrete inquiry involved the combination of the two; * * * and it is therefore not surprising, that the *great* scientific speculations between Bacon's time and ours, have been of an abstract character,—the concrete speculations during the same interval, having been necessarily *impotent.* * * * The simplest, most general, and highest point of view, attainable by the philosophical spirit, has been reached by a gradual process of abstraction; discarding, first, practical requirements, then æsthetic impressions, and finally, concrete conditions. In the simplest cases, even those of astronomical phenomena, we have seen that *no general law* could be established, while bodies were considered in their collective concrete existence;—from which it was necessary to detach a leading phenomenon, and then to subject IT to abstract examination, * * * leaving all apparent anomalies to be reduced to principle afterward. * * * The maintenance of the division is necessary here, for the same reasons as in regard to the two others, under the penalty of lapse into * * * confused views and desultory speculations: * * * and if this seems to remove the theoretical view too far from the practical, there will be a compensation, in a superior generality, testifying to the necessity of the political and philosophical separation, * * * as the basis of modern reorganization." "These," (namely, Speculative, Scientifico-æsthetic, and Theoretical,) "are the three stages of successive abstraction, the combination of which, determines the gradual institution of the positive method;—in a spontaneous manner at first, and afterward systematically. * * * The method is neither more nor less than, a philosophical extension of popular wisdom to abstract speculation." This latter thought and explanation of science, has been adopted also by Spencer, and elevated into a high position by him.

Here I may mention a singular coincidence between my three divisions of Political Corporations, and the foregoing divisions of Comte's. We (the writer) had already divided the remaining part of this article, as it now stands; and afterward (as is our usual course) sought authorities and quotations in other writers, for miscellaneous supports; and in that seeking, we made the foregoing extracts from Comte. And, when we came to search for the best place wherein to locate them, and not till then, we observed the coincidence, namely;—our First Main Division of Political Corporations is derived directly from the Practical, by the Speculative interest; the Second Main Division was pursued for the sake of the Scientifico-æsthetic enjoyment, and also for the scientific necessity for it, to complete the subject artistically; and the Third Main Division is pre-eminently abstract, and is our main THEORY; and might properly be called THE THEORY OF A NATION OF CORPORATIONS; *which, indeed, was the heading we formerly gave to it.*

§ 2. *Relation to the Other Elements or Parts.*

This kind of Corporations, as possessing inherent political functions, and based upon ideas, includes all the kinds treated of in the foregoing Division, as only *special* cases under it,—or at least it would do so, as soon as it was legally acknowledged. Because it is conceivable, that either of the foregoing special functions,—namely, Treatment of Criminals, Political actions, Collection of Taxes, Police, Civil-Executive, Judicial, Legislative, or General administrative—might at times become the special object, the accomplishment of one or another IDEA of which, might be adopted by some Corporations as their basis of organization. Hence, the investigation of these Corporations based on ideas, is an investigation of general formulas, containing all the others incidentally, and without requiring any further special allusion to them. A partial exception to this, is the last one of the former Division, namely, that for General Political Functions. That is the connecting link between the Lower and the Higher order of Political Corporations, and could, without much violence, be placed in either.

This Division, namely, Corporations for General Political purposes based upon ideas, differs from the Political Clubs treated some pages above, partly in this, that the clubs are included under this latter, it being by two grades the more general head; and partly this, that the ones we are now about to consider, would require a pretty thorough reorganization of society; but the clubs as before proposed, are only a variation in the method of choosing representatives to the usual political nominating and legislative bodies. And moreover, the present Division points out a multiplicity of new organs, for performing the new functions, which organs, the progress of Mankind is continually calling upon society to put forth. But this Division resembles the political clubs in one thing, namely, that one principle of its institution is, to allow to all persons, perfect freedom in their Individual-relations thereunto; namely, for instance, to allow to all persons the same freedom in choosing and in changing their political government, according to their own views, that they now have, of changing their church, their party, or other corporate relations; excepting, of course, that considerable time and notice might be required, before changing from one such political Corporation to another; and that the fulfillment of past obligations should be required.

§ 3. *General Statement of the Theory.*

This whole Division, of Corporations possessing or entitled to inherent governmental or political functions, is based upon the principle of ideas, namely, that Individuals might form and select their Corporations, according to one or more particular political ideas MOST approved by them, and make such ideas the basis of the structure.

As is mentioned below, it would be theoretically *possible*, for governments to organize by Corporations, almost to the exclusion of local divisions, so that the local divisions of a government (whether Precinct or Nation) might almost be replaced, by divisions of organizations based upon different degrees of generality in the scale of sociological ideas. And then, from this condition of things it results, that such Corporations, as a whole, might displace distinct Precinct and National civil governments, and the congress of their national union might become the Unit, identical with Nation: although, such extended application is not necessary to the principle itself. And out of these, again, it is *conceivable* as possible, that *inter*national societies might grow up, that would leave almost as little for Confederations to do, as the former arrangements had left to the Nations; and as little, also, for the local government of an empire of the whole earth, if any such should ever be formed.

Such a transformation of the government of a Nation or Precinct, from a congeries of local centres, to that of a system of Corporations, founded on voluntary and spontaneous selection, would be a change as great in the social world, as the spiritual Regeneration is in the Individual-world. And if there could be added an equal transformation of *all* the national governments of Mankind, into Corporations, the change would be almost as great socially, as the Resurrection is to be, individually. This is suggested merely for the sake of illustrating the abstractness and generality of the principle. Because every degree of the Corporation-system, rightly introduced, would produce its *proportional* amount of wonderful transformations.

Some of us are looking and hoping for a return of the days, when all the residents of a Locality would again be of ONE church: but instead thereof, or *before* that comes, we may look and hope for the time when the *civil* organizations will follow the example of the churches,—re-form themselves spontaneously; and all men voluntarily choose their governmental Corporations, as they now choose their churches.

We suppose then, the possibility, that (for most purposes), government might prescribe a certain SMALL NUMBER OF KINDS of associations, and require every man to join one of every kind; yet allowing in each class a *no-government* association, for dissenters of that class; also allowing the females, either altogether, or, of every class, when in sufficient proportions,—to form separate Corporations. And the representatives of the whole Locality, Nation, or Precinct, of each association, on each subject, should or might be the legislature to decide questions, and enact laws, on *that subject*, (in accordance of course with a suitable constitution).

The representatives of any lower division, in coming into a higher or more general one; might, in some cases, have to rearrange themselves; so that when, in some districts, the sub-division of any one class, had been multiplied beyond that provided for in the higher division; two or more such sub-divisions would have to unite into one. And on the contrary, the representatives from a lower division, coming into a higher, might sometimes be entitled to sub-divide, in order to meet a greater multiplicity already established in the superior order,—although, in this case, it would seem to be the part of duty and wisdom, for the lower division to know and foresee this result,—and therefore itself choose its representatives in or for the proper sub-divisions.

§ 4. *Classifications.*

This sub-division of Corporations, presents two entirely different kinds, or *sub-sub-divisions.* The first one of such kinds would exist, by establishing in every Locality a separate Corporation, based upon, and to take cognizance of, every SINGLE different important idea, object, or civil relation, coming under the regulation of civil law. The conception of this kind is necessary, because the instincts of personal association and of civil government, give rise to local divisions, which are a sort of Corporations for local purposes; just so, the love of ideas impels, so that every important idea of human beings, can, as has been said, be taken up by Corporations, and then the Corporations could arrange themselves according to their views of that idea. These we call *Corporations based on Single Ideas.*

The other kind, or *sub-sub*-division, would exist by establishing in each Locality, only a *few* Corporations; each one of which should be based upon some popular or natural COMBINATION of ideas; and should take cognizance of all, or nearly all affairs, usually or properly coming under civil law, relating to those ideas.

We will take up the first kind, first, after finishing these classifications; and leave the second kind to occupy us most of the remainder of the time.

We might, to be sure, present other divisions, some of them intermediate between these two. One intermediate division is conceivable, which being based on single ideas, would yet take cognizance of all affairs. But this would evidently be a stretching of the applications, indefinitely beyond the principle involved, or the basis built upon. Another intermediate division is also conceivable, which, being based upon a combination of ideas, would have cognizance *only* of the affairs of the several ideas upon which it was based. But this division scarcely needs a separate treatment, as it would not differ from the First one mentioned, and to be treated; except in merely ascertaining the combinations of ideas that would probably be popular. Moreover, the agreement of men in a combination of most important political ideas, is something more than a fact; it is a strong presumptive proof of *general* agreement in political affairs, sufficient to constitute them into a harmonious body-politic. Both the foregoing intermediates are therefore omitted from any special treatment in our general investigations. But their principles are treated in the sub-divisions given.

Again, we may suppose two different systems of Corporations on ideas:—in one system, every Individual would be a member of only one Corporation:—in the other system, every Individual would be a member of several.

Again, whether the system adopted be, for each person to be a member of many Corporations, or, of only one,—in either case, there are two principles of organization:—by one principle, government would prescribe the variety of choices, namely, of single ideas in the one case, or of the combination of ideas in the other case:—by the other principle, Individuals would be left free to select for themselves, the variety of choices.

Again, organizations on ideas, whether of the first sub-sub-division, or of the second; and of whatever kind or system; could arrange themselves in their relation to Locality, or could generalize themselves, in either of two ways. In one way, all the Corporations in a given Locality, whether Precinct or Nation, might co-operate in a government for the Locality. In the other way, all the Corporations *of one ideal, or on one basis,* in many Localities, might unite in a system of gradations, such as is common in various societies; and then the union of the highest ones of these special Corporate organizations, might constitute the local government for the whole.

These two ways of organization give another division, namely, into two kinds of Corporations, according to their ways of organization. Both kinds may be conceived of, as having the same general relation to one another, as Social Circle, Precinct and Nation have, to each other; understanding these relations as not based chiefly on ties of locality or geography, but, on principles or ideas:—so that the more general the Corporation, the *less special* its ideas.

But *whichever* way, or whichever of the two kinds of organization, we may take *first,* to rise in the generality, the top organization reached at last, *is precisely the same in either case,* namely, the civil or political organization of any Precinct or Nation, or of Mankind, in such a way, that the Land's or Earth's local or natural supreme civil power, and the supreme Corporation,—would be identical. And the same is true also, of either of the divisions we have named above.

This unity of the last result in highest generalization, may be seen, by adopting a general formula, whereby to express both those divisions, and both these kinds of organizations at once; as follows. Both divisions and both kinds, are those which make up a government, by bringing into combination, in any one Locality, (ranging from Precinct to Mankind), all the various political Corporations in it, of the same class or kind. Here, is a combination of Corporations, in and for the government of a Locality,—the generalization and combination of Corporations carried so high, that nothing remains that is more general, or that could include them. Thus, they become the political administration itself, of their LOCALITY, whether Precinct, Nation, Other Corporation, or Mankind.

§ 5. *Methods of Political Expression.*

From the great variety of methods, which the varied combinations of the foregoing might produce; perhaps the following four are the principal ones, by which Corporations might be allowed political expression.

One method would be, to allow every Corporation of whatever kind, to have, in some new or special department of government,—a voting power in proportion to its membership, or in some other uniform proportion prescribed by government. By this method, a man would have more or less power, according as he belonged to more or fewer Corporations. And IDEAS AND OBJECTS, would have more or less preponderance in the government, according as they were embodied in more or fewer Corporations. Then the science of such a Society or Nation, would be, so to arrange the number and proportion of these different objects, and of the associations based on them, that the resultant would produce the most fair and equable constitution.

A second method would be, for government to prescribe a few convenient kinds of Corporations, such that every man would or might belong to *one of every* such kind. This would directly equalize the political power of Individuals therein, because all persons would be represented in an equal number of ways.

A third method would be, for government to prescribe some one particular kind of Corporations, of such a kind that *ordinarily* no man would be apt to belong to more than one of that kind; for instance, as the faculty of a college, &c.

The churches would make the best Corporations of this kind, IF they would abstain from efforts to control each OTHER, or to get a preference, one over another. Political clubs, such as were established in France in the time of the Revolution, might answer, if of a kind, of which it is not likely a man would be a member of more than one. And as there might be some persons who would have refused to be enrolled in any of these prescribed Corporations; all such persons should be enrolled as members of the one *non-government* Corporation, which therefore should be allowed its share of political power also, in some manner afterwards to be determined.

A Fourth method would be, for government to allow every man to *select* and designate what Corporation he desired to be enrolled in, as THE ONE in which, if accepted by it, he desired to exercise his amount of the political influence of the corporate kind. For instance, one man might, for this purpose, desire to be enumerated in the church, another might prefer to be enumerated in some college, and another, in some moral or beneficent society. This plan seems to be the fairest, if men could be prevented from fraudulently having themselves enrolled in more than one Corporation for such purposes, (or in more than other men were enrolled in for such purposes; because, it might be best to allow all men to choose two or more such Corporations).

The class of Corporations to which these complicated questions relate, we make a second sub-sub-division of;—namely, those *Based on a Few Chief Combinations of Ideas.*

CHAP. II. FIRST SUB-SUB-DIVISION:—CORPORATIONS BASED ON SINGLE OR SEPARATE IDEAS.

§ 1. *Specimens of the Ideas.*

The more special and concrete the idea is, upon which each Corporation bases itself, the more numerous must the Corporations become, in order to include the whole range of important human ideas. Of course, therefore, we can only give a few *specimens.* Let us then particularize, by adducing, merely as instances, some special ideas that might probably be made the bases.

One basis for each Individual to select his or her Corporation by, ought to be the particular shade of opinion on the subject of war or fighting,—a voluntary Corporation for persons of each shade of opinion, from the absolute non-resistants, to the *lovers* and worshipers of force, violence and riot.

Another basis or principle on which each Individual could select his or her own Corporation, might be, its laws and sanctions of the Family constitution, including marriage and divorce:—the Corporation, to administer said laws, and to guarantee the maintenance of the Families needing help, if any.

Perhaps such Corporations would be better than churches, as the bases, when these churches were without any special Family-idea as one of their doctrines. They can be conceived of as providing for all shades of opinions, from no divorce whatever, down to divorce for almost any cause,—a voluntary Corporation on each idea.

Probably the most suitable basis for women, and the one most likely to be adopted by them, for *their* Corporations, if they were to vote, would be some certain or uncertain ideas of the Family-constitution, in its relation to property; but of *their* future action, perhaps men can only "guess"!

In short, all the prominent social and political ideas, might be adopted, by different persons, as the bases of their political organizations; perhaps as many as 1296, as will presently be shown.

The usual basis for *virtual* societary Corporations now, all the world over, is social position; making virtual Corporations of Social Circles. Yet there are but few *men* who regard this element as so preponderating, as to require its enumeration among the *one-idea* bases, such as we are just now considering. But it comes up as a natural sub-division, into perhaps three kinds (among the occupations), as presently to be mentioned. But women would be apt to introduce Social Circles into greater prominence (as divisions) than men would.

§ 2. *Assumption of Fixed Localities.*

To investigate in a thorough and abstract way, the great multiplicity of *possible* Corporations based upon ideas, would require a Calculus almost equal to W. R. Hamilton's "Quaternions." Therefore, we must get more into the concrete, even in this very general division. At any rate, we must assume the LOCALITIES to be fixed or given, so as to bring the calculation into homogeneity with our two elements of Precinct and Nation. Otherwise, we should have to express the theory in the sixth power, namely, in terms general enough to include all the Six Units; and even indefinitely higher, because Corporation, unlike Mankind, does not consist of any given number of fundamental social elements, but is susceptible of any required number. Whereas, the two just named, are enough for us, and the branch of Quadratics, or second power, is about as high as it is useful for us freshmen and tyros in social science, to go on with.

Therefore, to make the calculation practicable; we suppose that the various Corporations, in forming themselves into organizations of rising degrees of generality, rise in order of superiority, collaterally or correspondingly with the local divisions. For instance, we have every particular trade or craft, forming itself into a Corporation for its craft purposes. Then, we have the Corporations of the different crafts, forming into "unions," to help eaoh other, and thus spontaneously repeating the principles operating in the formation of the American Union of States. Just as the various Temperance and Free Mason societies, and the churches, in fact, generally do. Here then we arrive at some solid ground. Our Six Fundamental Units appear rising up out of chaos.

Hitherto our article on Corporations, has been rising in abstraction and generality, higher and higher, like a balloon; but here it enters its descending node, and commences to diminish its exponents in the series, and becomes more and more special, concrete, and practical.

§ 3. *Statement; with Fixed Localities.*

Thus it is conceivable, that by any of the foregoing methods, based upon single ideas, a whole Nation might gradually come to arrange itself fully into civil Corporations, correlative with all the Localities; so that every citizen and every Family, would be members of some kind or class of Corporation, and so that one person could be a member of only one, or some given number, of such,—just as he now can be a citizen of only one Nation, State, District, or Precinct; and yet every person select his or her own Corporations, by means of the multitude of different kinds existing everywhere.

In case it was deemed best to keep the Local and the Corporate governments distinct, even in the highest generalization,—the constitution of any Locality, whether Precinct or Nation, might perhaps be subject to the revision of the joint ballot, of all the representatives chosen by all these associations, or of delegates selected, in their due proportions, from all, (representing minorities fairly, of course.)

It is even conceivable, that the variety of Corporations might be so great, that each Individual would only need to be a member of one. But, although it is possible to conceive of such systems of Corporations, yet they are at present impracticable; for, the differences of human opinions, feelings, prejudices, interests and so on, are too great to allow of the generality of Individuals finding the satisfaction of all their earnest, political hopes and ideas, in any one, or even in a few organizations, based on *single* ideas, without multiplying the organizations in every location, almost indefinitely. Hence it becomes necessary to enter, in a subsequent division, into some complicated calculations for a reasonable and satisfactory, yet ATTAINABLE variety, of Corporations, for each Individual to select from.

CHAP. III. SECOND SUB-SUB-DIVISION:—CORPORATIONS BASED ON A FEW CHIEF COMBINATIONS OF IDEAS.

§ 1. *Nature of this Sub-Sub-Division.*

All that has gone before, in this whole article on Corporation, is to be considered as partly *introductory* to this which we are now commencing to treat. This is so with the First and Second Main Divisions; also with the First and Second Sub-Divisions of this Third Main Division; also with the first Sub-Sub-Division of this Second Sub-Division. The pith of the matter, and the greatest and highest *practical object* regarding Corporations, in Social Science, for this and the next age,—is to consider investigate and find, a few principal *combinations* of ideas, that will answer as the bases for voluntary governmental organizations; and, to consider, how best to enable them to perform their various functions.

This Sub-Sub-Division, we formerly headed, "Theory of a Nation of Corporations." But subsequently we found it necessary to change the heading, in order to show the connection with the former class,—namely, those based upon single or isolated ideas. One of the most general of all political speculations, now tones down into a practicable theory, accompanied with due attention and regard to all the possible needs, wants, and actions, of Mankind.

In the former Sub-Divisions, we came down from the exceedingly general conception, of all possible Corporations erected on ideas, to the variety of possible ones, corresponding with Units of Locality. Just so again, we come down now, from these latter, to only a small and definite number; although we do not propose to determine *absolutely*, what that definite number shall be; nor *exactly*, their bases, but only illustrations thereof.

Some considerable multiplicity of Corporations is required, and made practicable, by the increasing number and density of human population: And the multiplicity must continue to increase, with the increase of population. Hence, their ultimate number and sub-divisions cannot possibly be given at present.

It is certain however, that, practically, the number of Corporations would be regulated spontaneously, like the number of parties, and would not grow beyond easy ability to calculate and provide for. A similar, although not so great multiplicity is *conceivable*, as to the number of denominational churches, or schools, that might be needed in every Locality; but practically, nature, left to itself, might succeed as well in selecting the variety of political Corporations, as it has, the ecclesiastical.

§ 2. *Probable Bases or Kinds of Classes: namely, Occupations, Moralities, and Polities.*

(a) *In General.* Passing on, then, to the *probable special* bases, we can only give a statement of the multiplicity, sufficient to give an illustration of the idea,—a multiplicity that would now be practicable in the cities or thickly populated rural districts.

PERHAPS THREE DOZEN DIFFERENT CORPORATIONS BASED ON OCCUPATION, HALF A DOZEN EACH, ON MORALITY, AND POLITICAL FORMS, would be an ample number to afford every reasonable variety of choice. These added together would give a maximum number of 48. Yet it is not to be supposed that there would, or must be, that large number in any one Locality.

Because, *if you multiply* together, for instance, all the differences of religious opinions, that have been prominent in church divisions, you would make a possibility of several hundreds; whereas practically, even in the largest cities, there do not exist over about twenty-five different denominations; and *most* of them have only one or two organizations. And even only *adding* totals, there are perhaps 60 religious denominations in the United States, but not more than 25 different kinds, even in the two largest cities; and as smaller cities are taken, the variety becomes less, always being *checked by the proprieties and urgencies of the local circumstances.* Here the system of Corporations based on Combinations of Ideas we are now proposing, shows its almost indefinitely greater practicability, compared with the former sub-division,—that based upon Single Ideas. For, in that division, these numbers, 36, 6 and 6, would have to be *multiplied*, in order to give a Corporation for each idea; and thereby 1296 separate Corporations, would be called for as possible, and *some hundreds* therefore would be actually wanted.

Let us now inquire more minutely, what would probably be the actual principles, and bases, and number, of the classifications for combinations of Ideas.

Sex is not likely to become a basis of the classifications, until density of population enables the classes to be VERY numerous. Then, when each occupation has its own Corporation, those occupations which engage both sexes, would or might naturally give rise to the two classes of Corporations accordingly.

Nevertheless, there might be, and probably soon would be, a Corporation of those women who have "women's rights on the brain;" but it is not likely to draw in, any large proportion of women. In other words, the generality of women will not be apt to form Corporations for themselves, as such, but only as they are led thereto by their avocations, out of the Family-relation.

We suppose then, that the wage-classes, and even all but the really wealthy, being dependent on their trades for MAINTENANCE, would naturally account their trade-relations as among those of the utmost importance to them; and therefore generally would adopt, as their political Corporations, their various guilds or trade-unions. In general, one Corporation for each trade, in its Locality; although some very large trades might form two or more in a place, while some of the smaller closely related trades, might unite into one. In very large cities, "the retail men" of different trades might be in sufficient numbers, to form their Corporations; and even one or two classes of capitalists also; but, as a general thing, in the present density of population, in some places, the capitalists thereof of all the trades together, would only be numerous enough to make one Corporation, i.e., of furnishers of capital, whether little or much, (of course, for their own ends only.)

Social Circle, it is true, *might* itself be considered as a combination of ideas, suitable for another or fourth great basis. But considered apart from religious and moral associations, the Social Circle-divisions might be reduced to three, and come in only as sub-divisions of occupation,—that is to say, each different occupation or class of kindred occupations, instead of forming only one Corporation, might probably form into three different Corporations, according to social-position, and position in the occupation.

But even if the Social Circle were made a distinct and fourth combination of ideas, for a basis, then the divisions upon occupations might be reduced to twelve. This would make $12 + 3 + 6 + 6 = 27$, say only 27 instead of 48 kinds; whilst the number based on single ideas, namely, the former class, would still be the *product* of those numbers multiplied together, and therefore, as before, be 1296. Or if we retain **48** combinations, then the 36 might be resolved into factors in any way the reader pleases, between Occupations, and Social Circles, without altering the result in the number of bases of single ideas. Or the 36 might be divided into sums, the *addition* of which would always be 36, thus retaining the same number under the plan of Combination of Ideas.

Accordingly the following comparisons will show the advantages of the combination-basis, over that of single ideas.

Combinations.		Single Ideas.
$2 + 34 = 36$	. . . . .	$2 \times 34 = 68$
$3 + 33 = 36$	. . . . .	$3 \times 33 = 99$
$6 + 30 = 36$	. . . . .	$6 \times 30 = 180$
$10 + 26 = 36$	. . . . .	$10 \times 26 = 260$
$18 + 18 = 36$	. . . . .	$18 \times 18 = 324$

Either to be added to, or multiplied by 12.—Either 48 or 3888.

And different Localities probably would actually divide in various proportions, according to their own preferences. But the idea is, that each person is to be a member of one out of each of the three, four, or five, Combination-Corporations; but not of all (the 36 or rather) 48 mentioned.

But the few combination-divisions mentioned above, although they would comprise the generality of persons, nevertheless would *not be quite* sufficient for ALL. There would be Individuals having hobbies, and prevalent ideas. Some would have a moral idea, say on religion; some on peace, some on divorce, some on temperance, and some on dress, or Sunday, or amusements, or other subject. Others again would have some political form, for their hobby or prevalent idea; some manner of voting, or taxing, or administering, or constituting, political government. In each case, we would see Individuals from all or several Social Circles, and from the foregoing classes of society, uniting together and forming Corporations, on one and another of these different hobbies,—as its basis; for hobbies are *great* in breaking down social distinctions.

Yet, these ideas could only be the BASIS; they could not be the *sole business*, of the Corporation. Yet still, with several, or a reasonable variety of, Corporations, of each of, say three four or five different kinds mentioned, namely, of Trades, of Morals, and of Political forms, &c.,—it is possible that every person might be sufficiently accommodated, by membership, in *all* of those few different and really independent Corporations, AT ONCE; the independence of which was such, that his choice to or in one, would not materially affect his choice to or in either of the others. These *kinds* taken together, might be called Amalgam or Conglomerating Corporations, in allusion to our Precinct-theory, wherein several taken together for certain purposes, are called Amalgams or Conglomerates. And then, the few particular ones selected, one from each of these kinds, might be called the Amalgam or Conglomerate set, for the Individual so selecting. But many persons would find all their different wants supplied, perhaps in only one, say their Business-Corporation, which would be *plenary* to them. In each case of this kind, a special or plenary Corporation had better be formed; otherwise, the set of the usual or Amalgam conglomerating Corporations, would suffer a political or moral bias, and would exert a seriously disturbing influence, on those of its members who adhered to it for its trade-purposes, but whose moral or political proclivities were in some entirely different direction from that of the generality of persons in it. Besides the few kinds of Amalgam conglomerating Corporations, then, we would have the corresponding three to five kinds of *plenary* ones, thus proposed.

(*b*) *Statement of their Functions.* Now of the (say) three kinds of Conglomerating Corporations, every Individual would be a member of a set, consisting of one of each kind. And each of these Corporations would have the entire function, of enacting judging and executing laws, in relation to the several subjects proper to them, respectively. Each business Corporation would exercise all the legal functions over its own members, for all the physical and material interests included under the term business. Each moral Corporation would exercise the legal functions over its own members, in all matters relating to morality; and to all control over property arising out of the just claims of morality, which the membership had agreed to, whether arising from Liquor, or War, or Religion, or Divorce, or other of the moral bases of the society. The third kind of Corporation, namely, the political, would have also its own legitimate function to perform, of providing for the regulation of its own members, and to accomplish the special objects laid down in its basis. But it must be remembered, that sometimes a Corporation of this kind, although based on harmony of political views, is not necessarily adapted nor intended, for *general* civil administration over its own members, who organize themselves thus, but mainly for some *special* political purposes; yet on the basis of *general harmony* of political feeling, and upon the idea that such harmony is the great basis of the social organization. For such persons, separate Corporations for general political government, are needed, just as much as by the Corporations based on trades, or on morals: and ought to advance to such functions, although beginning only as political clubs.

And, on a little further reflection, we see, that such a "separate" kind of the political ones, is the only kind the Political basis easily admits of; because the idea of a society establishing itself on the basis of political forms over its own members, implies, that there must be some other and objective ideas and measures, in relation to which its political forms are established, and are to be applied. If it be suggested, that the political Corporations alone ought to have the administration of Localities; we would have to reply, no! because the administration over Localities may sound very innocently, but means, administration over all the persons of all the *other* Corporations:—and this would be simply to nullify our whole theory of Corporations, and indeed of right civil government itself. Hence, these political Corporations, being of the kind called separate and plenary, must merely be classed with those separate business or separate moral Corporations, which are exceptional to our general theory, because, although based on one idea, they yet really intend to apply to all kinds of political administration, and to all other ideas. This general administration is only to be sought, in some *union* of all the three several kinds of Corporations here mentioned; or in some new combinations not yet needing investigation.

§ 3. *Operation in "Law."*

(*a*) *The Units to Govern the Geography.* Here come in for consideration, the Local Units, and their combinations; namely, Precinct; Combination thereof into Large City or State; Nation; and Confederation. Instead of political Corporations to rule over all *other* persons, not their own members, and in all matters of daily life,—our theory preserves and presents local elements, and asks that the civil government of each of those elements, shall exercise no other functions over the Locality thereof, than pertain to the Locality itself. This function of Locality does not refer merely to roads, and buildings, and other geographical and engineering subjects: but refers to the more important matter, of who shall or shall not sojourn or reside in the Locality. Thus the function of the local organs is restricted to geographical matters.

(*b*) *Corporations of Occupation, Not to control Property Out of the occupation.* In general, all legal "actions" regarding personal conduct, are usually made to involve also, questions of property, where the Individuals have property to make them responsible. But it will not do to leave such questions to uncertain or unscientific decisions, because morality and religion are the highest interests of Mankind; and because sometimes Locality is the only party supremely interested;—but more than for those reasons; because, often, a part of the very basis and intention, of the agreement in entering a Corporation, may be, that property shall *not* be made responsible for personal actions; and that personal offence shall not go excused for lack of property to pay fines,—in other words, some moral Corporations may be formed expressly, to make person responsible for person, and property for property; and then again, some Corporations may have received from members, an insurance premium or fee, guaranteeing the Individual-fulfillment, by their members, of their obligations, whether financial, material, or local; and as a condition thereof, it may have been agreed that the Corporation, in such a case, should have the jurisdiction over the matter of property. In short, questions of property, as such or in GENERAL, cannot be assigned over to the jurisdiction of the business or trade Corporations; but only, matters of BUSINESS *or* TRADE. If, for instance, marriage be avowedly made as a matter of business, then the jurisdiction of marital questions belongs to the trade Corporations; but not otherwise,—so, also, of the place of location. But such suppositions are out of the question. Questions of jurisdiction are only to be decided by reference to the *main* objects, intentions, and basis, of a Corporation. If these are bad, let the Corporation be made to suffer, but not the innocent or unfortunate Individuals. Thus holding the Corporations accountable, would compel them to be more careful in their selection of members, according to their own principles; until the different principles of different Corporations, would so fully show their effects, that bad principles in the basis, would be voluntarily abandoned by the Corporations themselves. For, Corporations should be held to two kinds of accountability; one, for the actual consequences of their principles, and the other, for actions according to their *declared* principles, and according to the avowed objects of their organization.

(c) *Disputed Jurisdiction.* Now arises the question, what is to be done in regard to affairs, or cases, about which there is doubt, as to which Corporation the jurisdiction of them belongs. And the disputes about jurisdiction might be of two kinds; one, as to which organization should *judge* the cause; and the other, as to which should enforce decision. To illustrate,—a suit or legal "action," as for instance, of divorce, might involve questions both as to the morality of any given truth, and also as to the disposition of property thereunder,—so also in legal actions, in regard to change of Locality, and to many other objects. For, no system of government can be devised, that will not present cases of uncertainty and doubt, as to the form or the organ, of jurisdiction; which yet must be decided SOME way, or there would be NO jurisdiction. In cases of disputed jurisdiction then, we would have to propose the following resources. According to the principles already laid down, under the head of Precinct, and also under International Law, the local authorities would have cognizance of the *forms* of proceeding, to some extent. But, for the most part, the principle of arbitration should be introduced, between the two or more Corporations claiming jurisdiction; or else a court established of equal numbers from each, which is in fact a subtle realization, and a legal form, of arbitration. The higher kinds of arbitration, are our principal judicial resource generally, and will be explained fully, under "Civil Government": and have already been mentioned in the Summary Introduction, Pt. II., Chap. X., under the head of Arbitration-Juries.

Again, the question arises, how are disputes to be settled between Individuals belonging to different Corporations; and again, the answer is,—by arbitration.

Furthermore, where several different Corporations exercised jurisdiction on the same ground or Locality, as our theory proposes,—there might arise a fear, lest disputes would be multiplied, and injustice increased;—But *that* altogether depends on the efficacy of the system in detecting wrong, and punishing it. And while we affirm, that the proposed system would be almost indefinitely better than the present common one, both for punishing wrongs, and for securing rights,—yet this affirmation can only be demonstrated by actual EXPERIMENT.

Another point in jurisdiction, is, that there must always be some power which is *supreme*, in each particular case; some kind of power, also, supreme over the whole organism. What is the supreme power in this system? It cannot be any merely temporary, or special, council of arbitration. Furthermore, it cannot be any of these artificial combinations called Corporations. The supreme power which controls the whole organism, is the power of Locality. Because, nothing can be done otherwise than IN some Locality. And what is prevented in *every* locality, cannot be done at all. But this organ is to enforce its authority, not by interfering with the agreements of the parties, nor with the right of Corporation, but by adhering strictly to its own rights, as governing Localities. The Precinct, when disobeyed, would,—

after due notice and under due regulations, as set forth under that head,—order the departure of the offending party. And every supreme or more general local government, up to Nation, or even up to Confederation,—would have the same kind of authority; to be exercised under similar restrictions, of righteous principles in the methods of its enforcement.

It is also the duty of the superior power, to compel the Precincts and Corporations to *fulfill* the obligations which they voluntarily undertake.

§ 4. *Divine Morality, the Great General of All the Bases.*

(*a*) *Comte's Generality-Principle, with a New Turn.* In a complete, or even in a practical classification of co-ordinations,—Comte (Pos. Phil. p. 775), affirms, that the basis will always be one and the same; that is, the basis of all classifications; even when carried into practical life; namely, "THAT OF THE DEGREE OF GENERALITY, AND SIMPLICITY, OF THE SUBJECT. * * * The same principle was tested, (he says), in its application, in the interior of each science; and, when we were applying it in Biology, we found it assuming a more active character, indicating its social destination. Transferred from ideas and phenomena, to actual beings, it became the principle of zoölogical classification. We then found it to be the basis of Social Statics; and our dynamical inquiry showed us, that it [namely, this generality-basis of all classification], has determined all the elementary evolutions of modern social practice. * * * It will always be found working identically, in every system which consists of homogeneous elements,—subjecting all orders of activity to their due classification, according to their respective degrees of abstractness and generality. This was the principle of classification, in old societies; and we see vestiges of it yet, in the military organization, where the very terms of office [i.e., General, Major General, &c.,] indicate that the less general, are subordinated to the more general, functions. It needs no proof then, that, in a regenerated society, homogeneous in its elements, —the change that will take place, will be found to be, not in the elements, but, in their classification."

Now we feebly strike in, and say;—But, it is obvious, that this spontaneous classification by human beings, into right orders, and by obedience thereunder,—depends largely on the MORAL-

ITY of Individuals, and, of Governments. For, the order actual in the world, is neither right nor harmonious, unless in matters wherein men's lives are immediately in danger, as is the case in military and naval, and in some other extraordinary affairs. DIVINE morality therefore, that is to say, religion, must be looked to, as the *highest generalization;* and at the same time, the completest abstraction; in all practical thought. Instead, therefore, of that generality which Comte has in mind, namely, of Employer to Employe, of Wholesaler to Retailer, of General physicist to Special physicist, &c., we, in our equation, will have to substitute, *at least for a time,* Divine Morality.

Of that one kind of classification, therefore, we may be sure, that the system based upon Divine Morality, would ultimately enable the distinction to be manifested, and to prevail,—between the two great classes of persons into which all the world may be divided, namely, those who are children of God, and those who are not;—and that some how or other, gradually but surely, the two great and all absorbing classes of Corporations, would be the two now mentioned. And the more free the right, and the more thoroughly the organizations, were discovered and provided for, to allow this freedom to develop; the more clearly this great distinction would rise above all others, or in all others; and especially above all those, so called, religious falsities, and sectarian and formal misunderstandings, which now involve the true Israel with the non-Israel, in a common reputation and a common fate.

(*b*) *Scripture Arguments.* But did not our Saviour say, "let both grow together until the harvest"? So he did: but he said this to those violent puritans, who *would* go directly to work in an unscientific and *outward* way, to *judge* between others, as to who were the true "Israelites" and who were not. He was not speaking to those who would provide a method, whereby his people and the worldly, would *voluntarily,* and with mutual consent, indirectly and upon independent and different grounds, segregate themselves. And his very words, "let BOTH grow together until the harvest," imply the admission and perception of the difference between them; at least in a general way. But there was then, as there is yet; a great deal too much bigotry, narrow-mindedness, and unspiritual conceptions, as to who are the good, and who the bad,—to enable one set of men to judge of the spiritual acceptance of another set of men,—much less, to authorize them to use coercion in enforcing the difference. Furthermore, the method or system of Corporations, does not separate the good from the bad, much more than the present system, as to Social Circle; nor separate them at all, as to Locality; but mainly, as to political and civil government. And even in these respects, it does not separate them as much as, (although it does so much more *easily* than) the Precinct-system.

But we may readily turn this allusion to the Saviour, into an argument bearing directly on our system. The Saviour came to establish a "*kingdom*" (or polity), among his followers; and St. Paul reproves Christians for "going to law before unbelievers," and carrying their disputes to worldly judges. But no satisfactory method has ever been devised, whereby these Christian principles can be brought into practical life, other than by our, or some similar, theories,—namely, by Corporations, first and most readily, and finally, by Precincts.

The Saviour, all through his *official* career, idealizes himself into the character of a Ruler of a Corporation,—talks about his "kingdom," and his society (ekklesia), as the same thing,—and continually gives rules, *neither practicable nor obligatory*, except in some such governmental Corporations as our theory of Corporation contemplates. See also the definitions of State and *Civitas*, under NATION, pp. 243 and 244.

§ 5. *Operation in the Social Circle.*

The relation between Corporations and Social Circles, is Mutual and Reciprocal; sometimes Social Circles giving rise to Corporations, and at other times Corporations producing Social Circles. Inasmuch as maintenance and life, are generally held to be *more* important than Social Circles, the business Corporations would affect and reorganize Social Circles; so also with organizations on morality, on marriage, and some, on politics. But inasmuch as most religious or denominational opinions, are frequently held to be *less* important than Social Circles,—organizations based upon these circles, would often supersede those based merely upon denominational opinions. This does not mean that Social Circles would supersede religion or church; but only, that Social Circle would determine the particular society or form, of the religious denomination; just as now, it very often determines the particular church which an Individual would join. And this view has no absolute reference to the *intentions* or self-consciousness of the Individuals, but only to the course which they do *in fact* pursue.

As Social Circle generally has reference to *producing* marriage; almost all civil Corporations on the bases of Social Circle, would have reference, among their general objects, to controlling *divorce*, or to prescribing its conditions, in the Corporation. And as human happiness, after a mere physical subsistence is obtained, depends more upon the relationships of Family, and of Friendship, than upon nearly all other considerations combined; and as both, the Social Circles and the Corporations, wisely look at least a generation in advance,—look, namely, to the marital interests of *grand-children*,—it follows, that there is a peculiar propriety in allowing the Social Circles, more and more to become parallel, with governmental and political Corporations for their own voluntary members. But, the circumstances whereby this may come to pass, will produce almost as great regeneration and reorganization of Social Circles, and of Individuals therein, as our Corporation-system itself, proposes, in relation to the common legal and political organizations. Under such an improved system, Social Circles would be based more on morality, and less on property; more on intentions, and less on success; more on virtue, and less on intellect; more on the Spirit of God, and less on opinions about Him, or on forms of worshiping Him; more upon the ability of the Individual to be happy within one's self, and less upon his ability to get the government of, or advantage over others; more upon marriages of affection or of wisdom, and less upon those of business or speculation. And so far as based upon property at all, Social Circles would be established, more according to a man's savings, and less according to his expenditures. But the main difference would be, that the power of property in the Social Circle would be vastly diminished, because its power to control unjustly, those who did not possess it, would be diminished; whilst yet its power to enjoy itself in its own way, and to "reap" in itself the fruits thereof, would *not* be diminished.

§ 6. *Applications. Concrete Instances.*

(*a*) *The Churches.* But, after stating the aforesaid theory, in its most general form; let us give a method or two, of corporate political action, so concrete and particular, that they might easily be adapted to any present idea, by society as at present constituted; that is to say, by society without any radical or thorough reformation, either in spirit, or in forms of government, in other respects. They also serve as the illustrations, to make intelligible the foregoing brief general statements of the theory. And that is the principal reason for giving them.

All Corporations of the moral elements, that is to say, churches, and the usual moral societies, are, in the order of time, the very *last* ones to which general political powers, should be entrusted, *in fact;* nevertheless, because of their having already so long and so well established themselves, in the exercise of a certain class of functions, they afford the readiest and best organizations to cite, as ILLUSTRATIONS. And, for the regulation of the two matters, Divorce and War; we shall elsewhere argue, that they ought to be committed to these or some other moral societies, but, only under express conditions.

Let us *suppose* then, that government, in the plenitude of its wisdom and goodness, were really to grant freedom of conscience, not only in religious, but also in personal and political matters; and to that end, let us suppose, it decided to grant to all religious and moral societies, the privilege of exercising political and civil functions, for and over such of their members as would *accept* of their plan. The following then might be the basis.

All societies claiming, should be considered churches, which were at the time, and had been popularly so considered before the proposal to the legislature, of the law granting these privileges. But other moral societies, avowedly such, should have the same privileges, after the necessary years of existence *as such,* to be prescribed by statute. Some years' existence should be required, to entitle to these privileges; besides being regularly recorded. The societies should not have cognizance of any circumstance occurring previous to the organization thereof; unless by consent of all parties interested; nor, authority over any Individual-members, who had not signed the special and subsequent agreement, to abide thereby. This would require a general signing, by the members of any church, in order to start the plan in it. Proper forms for this obligation, should constitute both the signers and their minor children, members of such churches. Adults, immediately upon arriving at twenty-one years of age, should of course have the privilege of changing their membership, without any notice, or without as much notice as was required of other persons.

Appeals should be allowed to civil courts, only in case of clear evidence, that a person had changed his church or society, only for the purpose of getting unjust benefit of this privilege of changing; or, that injustice, of a kind plainly recognized as injustice by the society itself, had been done by the decision appealed from; or that the constitution of the State, or the Corporation's rights, had been violated. The lists of members should be published very frequently, and very conspicuously. The duty should be expressed, of providing for children, legitimate or illegitimate; and for widows; also, of aid for divorced women. Also the duty of efficient prison and criminal arrangements for securing their own criminals. Also, that the health and safety of the community should not be endangered by the Corporation's neglect or inefficiency.

(*b*) *The Communities.* Communities are a much less objectionable element, than the churches, that is the usual moral societies, to be entrusted with general political functions over their own members; in fact, they are good and proper ones; because, communism itself could not exist and be maintained, much longer than it could preserve itself from moral and political corruption. It proceeds from a striving to be free from corruption; and also takes away the wants and needs that produce corruption. It does not take human nature as you find it, in the generality of Mankind; but selects the best, and is selected by them. A sort of civil government is actually exercised, over their members, by the Catholic communities: and Protestants should certainly have as full a share of rights. The Catholic communities and the Shakers, have equated the problem of property. They are the types and exemplars of social progress for all time. But a different system is necessary, when you eliminate the celibacy element, in the case of those persons who do not feel called thereunto. Moreover, there are even now, a few communities in the United States, wherein marriage is *honorable*, and some wherein it is merely allowed. These will be mentioned near the conclusion of Book V. which will be devoted wholly to the subject of a proposed new ideal,—Limited Communism.

Limited or Christian Communism is the Divine Resurrection of the Tribe-Element, into modern society. From what, in the Summary Introduction, has been said of the Tribe-Principle, it is settled, that the three Elements, namely, Social Circle, Precinct, and Corporation, must always continue in living action; although we find them continually separated, in modern times. But it is not necessary, that these activities should always continue in separation. On the contrary, the three Elements may combine themselves into one again, just as they had been originally derived from one, namely, the Tribe. This conception seems only possible to be realized, in Limited Communism. In it, the Tribe-principle becomes resuscitated into a living, bodily, and holy element of society; and then, set free from slavery to politicians, and political law, association will manifest the true nature of sainthood, and of the Kingdom of God.

SUB-DIVISION IV.

PARTIAL ADOPTION UNDER CONTRACTS AND TRUSTS.

The Precinct was concluded by an Application, showing, that when its fundamental rights and advantages, cannot be gained for its own sake, as an essential Unit of society; nevertheless, they may, to a considerable degree, be acquired, for other reasons, namely, as *special grants from superior powers.* In a similar way, we may now conclude the Corporation, with an *Application*, (but in this case very brief), showing that when its fundamental rights and advantages cannot be gained on its own ground, as a fundamental element, as we have considered under the Second Sub-division; nor by *general* grant, as we have considered under the First Sub-division; nevertheless, they may to a considerable degree, be acquired on other grounds, namely, by the means of special *contracts* between the parties as Individuals. For, it can hardly be denied, that many, at least, of the advantages of self-selected government, can be obtained by special contracts among a large number of Individuals. Indeed, almost every contract takes more or less of its affairs from under the control of law. Of this, the following quotation, from a widely circulated public journal, is both a proof and an illustration:—

"There is too much of law, and too little of justice. But in this, as in almost everything else, the evil being carried to the extreme, works its own cure. * * * Such is likely to be the case with the outrageous trifling with justice, by the New York judges, in the name of law. * * * Disgusted with the quibblings of lawyers, and the inevitable delay in obtaining decisions in the courts, the merchants long since agreed to submit disputes between them, to a committee of arbitration composed of members of the Chamber of Commerce, and to abide by its decision. These associations, if court decisions continue to trifle with right and justice, are likely to multiply, until they include all the leading pursuits, as they may readily do; with much more of satisfaction as to results, than through the courts, and certainly at a great saving of expense."

Since the above appeared in print, the New York merchants have had their arbitration courts established more firmly, by legislative enactments.

In civil and political affairs, contracts, although they may reach common business-transactions, cannot reach the deeper interests, where the rights of persons are involved; nor where the rights of property follow the decisions as to persons. And some contracts are not legal, as such, even when the parties making them, would take all the responsibility, and jointly guarantee against apprehended evils. It is even doubtful, if a contract to make one's "will" in any particular manner, would be binding in law, even if mutual. This inefficacy is true, of all those deeper social interests, whose laws, and the consequences of whose violation, can only be traced through *long* courses of time. And yet, these are superior interests, claiming the rights and advantages of Corporation, even more than the lower interests.

Sometimes in law, more can be accomplished by TRUSTS, than

by any other method. Trustees, appointed in consequence of Individual-contracts, and subsequently approved by additional contracts, might accomplish much. But a great difficulty arises here, namely, that in order to cover property by trust, the property itself would have to be first transferred to the Trustees; and this raises new dangers and new difficulties, seriously interfering with private business, and with the interests of heirs. No doubt, as far as safety is concerned, there are Individuals and Trust Companies, to be found, who are quite responsible; but such parties would not be willing to undertake trusts, whose accordance with the civil law was doubtful; and even if they did, they would then make the fees and other expenses, consume too much of or nearly all, the profits of the estates committed to them. Add to this also, the complicated difficulties both legal and practical, of enabling a man to conduct his own business, with his own capital, yet all the time acting as agent for his Trustee. Therefore, Individual contracts can never approach as near to accomplishing Corporation-functions, as we have found that charters could approach, to the accomplishment of Precinct-functions.

In a subtle way, the lust for property underlies most of the complications of "the law," even those which *seem* only to apply to persons. St. Paul was right also POLITICALLY, when he said "the love of money is the root of all evil":—and "covetousness * * * is idolatry."

The tangle of our real estate laws, originated, as J. S. Mill says, from the propensity of the spendthrift landed aristocracy, to hold on to the lands, and to keep their creditors out: and in our day, the tangle of our laws as to person and property, originates largely from the covetousness of those, who having nothing, desire and hope ultimately to get something "by law," if not for themselves, at least for the *classes* with whom they sympathize.

And stronger even than the covetousness of property, is the covetousness of POWER, the lust for ruling over and FORCING other people. History proves that even when property has been divided, and ranks leveled, the lust of rule continues as active and as virulent as ever. And the world has yet to decide, whether the cry for freedom, has been only an instinctive ruse of the "*outs*" against the "*ins*," a mere deluded prayer of the covetousness of power;—or whether it is the voice of real justice, and of human rights, for all sides equally: And whether, the call even for freedom of conscience in RELIGION, was only for freedom for the caller's religion, or whether really for freedom for all. If the latter, then the rights both of Precinct and of Corporation will surely prevail; and the result will be voluntary and Limited Communism; cheerfully and voluntarily accepted by the rich as well as by the poor; because the sense of mutual justice will be stronger than the covetousness, either of property or of power, either by those who have either, or by those who have not. *That* would be a real regeneration, honorable alike to God and man.

BOOK V.

LIMITED COMMUNISM.

MAIN DIVISION I.

NATURE OF COMMUNISM.

SUB-DIVISION I.

IDEA OF COMMUNISM.

CHAP. I. RELATION TO OUR GENERAL THEORY OF SOCIAL SCIENCE, AND TO THE OTHER ELEMENTS.

THE reader has perhaps already observed, in the table of contents of this Article, an unusual abundance of headings. The apology is, that most of the article is an *abridgment* and synopsis of a longer one, in manuscript, prepared by us a few years ago. And in abridging, it seemed best to retain the headings mostly, just as they were. The same reason, together with a desire to avoid abstractions here, and to be easily understood, explains some of the imperfections of style hereof.

This essay resumes the subject of the general principles of Social Science, which in the Summary Introduction were considered among the Most General Social Laws. And the present object is, to consider the origin, success, and failure of Communities, by reference to fundamental principles, and the nature of things; and to suggest an improved ideal.

This subject would not come up until the last or Sixteenth Element, in our social science;—but that its exhibition in this first volume, seems necessary in order to give a fair view of our new theory of the science. This is Synthetics, but all the previous parts of this volume are Analytics. See Bk. I. I. IX.

We have sketched the contrast between ours and the Paris

Communism, in our article on the Precinct. Our whole theory is entirely different from the Parisian, scientifically, metaphysically, morally and theologically.

Some people think that a Commune is only a place for the poor and idle to "sponge" upon the rich, or for the lazy to be parasites on the industrious. But really, a Commune is a Civil Government, expressly organized for the cultivation and self-control of the higher moral, intellectual and spiritual faculties. Communism is not merely nor chiefly a tenure of property, but rather a form of government, for a Corporation or even for a Precinct; in which the highest attainable perfection of human nature, is supposed to be the chief object of the Individual, and is established as the chief object of the society; and only with a view to that object, and so far as consistent with that object, the new tenure of property is introduced.

The object is not to lessen labor, so much as to make it pleasant. Thus one of the incidental designs is (like that of the kindergarten), to make all play work, and all work play; that is, to eliminate the distinction between play and work; which is the result the Fourierites long for, under their name "attractive industry."

The Community-life may be sought from four different directions, or, sources of motives. One direction is, from the desire of a higher and perfect life; another direction is, from the desire of improved civil government, such as is possible only in voluntary Corporation; and another is, from a desire for pecuniary gain; and the other is, from a desire for pleasure,—for an easy idle or tasteful and pleasant life. These sources are valuable in the order just set down. Either one of them *except the last*, may be sufficiently overpowering, to hold suitable persons together awhile. But the desire for idleness, or the gratification of taste above one's means, or past habits, is itself contrary to contentment or goodness, and leads to decay. And the desire for pecuniary gain is of too low or self-interested a kind, to give permanency; but being good in itself, it may, in community, lead to such moral and spiritual improvements, as will gradually glide into the higher motives just mentioned. But, as to the second source, namely, desire for the highest political improvement under Corporations, we may say, that when it is merely a demagogic frenzy, tending to leveling any righteous or necessary distinctions, it will soon, of itself, destroy any government which it can establish,—not less certainly than, that nearly all the republics of history, have gone down by intestine broils. Successes and misfortunes alike drive the members to dissatisfaction, cabal, tyranny, and dissolution.

In monarchical countries, the desire for political improvement would be apt to have the tendency towards equality and fraternity; but in democratic countries, this communistic desire for political improvement would be apt to have the tendency towards strong government; not indeed towards the old sort of aristocracies, but, either to some sort of theocracy, or partly to joint stockism, or other reaction against demagogery. Its demands will be for justice and fraternity. Its mottoes will be the fatherhood of God, and the brotherhood of man; and if successful, would thus lead up to the insinuation and adoption, of higher motives than those with which it had been begun. But no Communism which does not, at least, *tend* towards becoming an institution for the promotion of the higher moral life, need be expected to succeed long.

On the side of religion, a Commune may be defined to be, a civil society of religious persons whose *rule* is perfection in all duties towards their fellow-beings, and whose *aim* is perfection in all duties individually towards each other. On the side of government, a Commune may be defined to be a civil and political Corporation, having for its constant aim, its ideal of political government: and whatever else it is, it must be a *highly obeyed* system of government, both in one's Individual-soul, and in the association.

On the side of property, a Commune may be defined to be, a civil and social Corporation, in which the property owners agree to furnish, to non-property holders, an equal share of the net profits; and the non-property holders agree, in return, to allow the others to have an equal share in the government of the concern.

In the totality, the definition would be, a Commune is a progressive social organization, whose aim is the identification of church and state, in the love and choice of every Individual: and whose organization is a high type and partial realization of its holy aim, and which does not disregard the faith that the *full* realization is possible, only in the Millennium, or perhaps, only in Heaven itself.

But a Commune differs from a Church, by not presupposing a profession of religion, any farther than is implied in devotion to perfect morality; and differs (in an opposite direction,) by having the attainment of perfect religion as its chief object; and having unselfishness and communism as parts of its religion.

Communism is one of the methods and means whereby Social Science in general, is to be attained and promoted; and the Communistic theorizers and experimenters are prominent, among those to whom we are to look, for the development of the most general theories of society. Communities are exemplifications of the general social laws, and are types of society itself. Just as the perfection of human society will probably be, that all good Individuals will arrange themselves in Communities,—so also, the culmination of Social Science will be, such systems as will make those Communities practicable; even if not practicable sooner; but the rights of the other Units,—Individual, Family, &c., must be maintained.

In its strictest sense, the Locus of Intersection of Communism with the rest of our Science, is in the voluntary element of civil government,—Corporations, and especially with those founded on the moral basis: because, it is now well ascertained, that only the religious or moral element can make a Commune succeed. Communes strictly belong to the third or highest class of Corporations, namely, those having Inherent Political Functions. See Book IV. Corporation, Main Division III., Sub-Division III.

Again, the other Elements of Tribe, namely, Social Circle and Precinct, also enter essentially into the nature of a Commune; and must be respected by it.

A Commune must be founded in the Tribe-principle, sufficiently, to retain in voluntary membership the GENERALITY of the children born and raised in it. Hence, neither the Individual nor the Family Element, and neither self-will nor Family affection, can be supreme in Communism; nor can those persons succeed, who assume as an axiom, that either the Individual or the Family, is the sole or supreme Unit of society, the sole rock on which it is founded.

The fundamental ideas of Communism may be summed up in two analogous principles: one, relating to the conditions of Individual-membership; and the other, to the objects of the association. The conditions of membership are, the perfect performance of all duties to our fellow-beings; the objects of the association are, to assist one another in the performance of all duties, to God and men.

CHAP. II. CLASSIFICATIONS.

There are now existing in the United States, thirty-two successful Protestant Communities, containing altogether about 13,000 persons, besides the large number of Catholic recluse houses. There have also been many *unsuccessful* attempts among Protestants, of which the twelve most important, lasted from two to eighteen years each. See Main Div. IV., Sub-Div. III. of this article.

Mr. J. H. Noyes formally divides the *unsuccessful* Communes into two kinds,—one, in which Owen's ideal was prominent, namely, home, and thence Communism; the other, in which Fourier's ideal predominated, namely, the joint stock idea. But he (N.) seems to make a third class, i.e. the spiritualistic. We think the *successful* Communes in the *United States*, possessed all three of the following qualifications: namely, they had their religious leader as their communistic leader; their poverty led them to seek chiefly a livelihood; and they had a high sense of honor in the *little* matters of daily life; but those which failed seemed to lack one or another of these elements.

The successful Communities in *every age* of the world, have included *nearly* all the following principles: (1) that the Community-life is to be sought as a means of perfection; (2) that the government of them is to be in the hands of good men; (3) that the governors are supposed to be saints, or to be leading lives of some sort of inspiration, or peculiar consecration.

All Communities that can be permanently successful, may be classified into: (1) those in which the principal element is religious reverence; (2) those in which that element is some kind of human reverence; (3) in which it is complete consecration to perfect human duty; and (4) complete consecration to the perfection of *all* duties, human and divine.

In our Part IV. of this article or "book" we divide the successful Communes of the United States thus ;—Catholic; and Protestant :—The Protestant are sub-divided into,—Those which have regular marriage,—and Those which do *not* have regular marriage. —And these latter are divided into celibate,—and mixed-love.

There are not (we think) any Catholic Communities in the United States, allowing marriage; but in the Middle Ages in Europe, there were several such, and all were military orders, —(established to war against the anti-Christian nations),— namely, "Knights of St. James of the Sword,"—"Order of Calatrava,"—Of Avis,—Of Jesus Christ,—Of St. Michael,— And of Alcantara.

All *possible* Communes may be divided into two classes, good and bad; and two divisions of each class; namely, one, on the basis of social equality, the other, on the opposite practice,— making four divisions in all. But no really bad Commune is likely to prosper, or exist, any great length of time by itself.

CHAP. III. IDEALS.

There is but one way, in the actual course of a Nation, and equally so in the study of Society, to succeed in developing truth, and in making real progress; viz., by constantly aiming to make them perfect. The ideal of hope is necessary to the formation of a true science, and to the actual aim of Nations and government. Every man's Social Science must vary, according as his religion varies, and as his highest ideal of morality. The great want of human society to-day, is a good ideal. Men are tired and sick of temporary expedients, and political corruption; and have therefore become discouraged in their efforts to improve Society. The case is as Samuel Johnson says,—that "worshiping ideals is the *condition* of spiritual life, and that losing a belief that there is somewhere a better than ourselves, is gravitating downwards to what is worse than ourselves." What is an Individual or a Society or a Nation or even Mankind itself,— without an ideal of what it hopes for, and what it aims to be? The thing wanted, therefore, is an entirely new prospect, and that means an entirely new ideal.

Communism is the ideal of Social Science; but it is not necessary that the ideal should be unalterably fixed in the beginning.

Yet, for the beginning, we know, that as Social Science comes in place of the obsolete or scholastic theology (which needed a monastic or contemplative life to develop it), so the modern Communism, also requires a CONTEMPLATIVE life for *its* development and maturity.

The ideal of a completely happy State or Society, is probably all contained in the two objects,—"mutual assurance" of life, property, business, education, and enjoyment: and *co-operation in all things*, instead of competition.

The essentials of Communism may be summed up in these two; namely, fulfilling duties to our neighbor perfectly; and sufficient agreement as to *what* these duties are, and how its *government* is to be constituted. In other words, the two requirements would be, to be unselfish in spirit, and to be harmonious in principal opinions.

The truly "catholic" father Baker, in "Sancta-Sophia," sums it up finely thus, the only essential for membership in a Community is, "to follow the objects of it, according to the spirit of it." This, we take it, requires that any scientific and homogeneous system of Communism is a *compromise*, and therefore must be adopted *as a whole*, if at all, and like any other Government.

CHAP. IV. NECESSITY OF LIMITATIONS.

Most persons do not need exhortations or arguments unto taking care of themselves. But students and theoretical sympathizers with Communism, *do* sometimes stand in need of such arguments. In other words, sympathizers with Communism want proofs to justify them for *limiting* it. The main reasons for so limiting it, are found, in the rights, necessities, and peculiarities of the Individual—the personality of Individual souls. The following reasons may be suggested for taking care of one's self.—Other persons mostly do not know our real needs and wants. Each one's self is his *nearest* neighbor, to be loved and cared for; and is *given in charge* for that purpose by the Lord. "A charge to keep I have." Other persons will take care of themselves, and we would be treated with gross injustice, and worn out and destroyed by them, unless we did take care of ourselves. Only thus can we prevent the wicked from triumphing over the righteous; only thus can we "come to the help of the Lord against the mighty." Only thus can we obtain the means to be useful, and help good causes: except in the case of those who are specially *called* to a different order of life (as Quakers &c.). Others are on the watch to take advantage of the weak, the generous, and the sympathetic. They resort to threats as well as to entreaties, and to false and artful tales. Silence under deliberate injury, makes others believe in its justice, and stimulates to further injustice; but proper criticism checks them; and seemingly ignorant criticisms are often well received,—that is by well-meaning people. But we must take care, not to injure ourselves by criticisms at unfavorable times, and not to put ourselves under the power of others; for they will have hatred for good intentions, and will take advantage of sympathetic consolations. The generality of people are *principled* in their selfishness, and do not believe it to be wrong, and think themselves *smart* in taking advantage, by legalities and opportunities.

Religion in its INDIRECT influence, is a necessity, and preserves the world, and also in the long run preserves the individual life; but in its DIRECT influence it is taken advantage of as excuse and indulgence for sin. Hence individually, religiousness is no proof of fitness for Communism, nor the reverse.

The Family-relations of sex and children also require limitations of Property-Communism. Hence, nearly all the successful Communes have limited the Family-relations. And the "Complex Family" of Oneida, or the free love of the Paris Communists and others, were it peaceable, would be most as consistent as absolute total Communism of property, whilst retaining the necessary and right order of the Family-relation.

The rearing and training of children, and the *inherited* differences, also the differences of long-continued habits, preclude unlimited Communism. It is difficult to decide the ratio or relative rates to be appropriated to individuality and to inheritance. But in the apportionment, individuality has reference, *not* to an equality or a ratio that must *continue through life*, and so would require continually repeated equalizations; but this individuality has reference only once to each Individual, once to each, as each is born only once. And in that apportionment, inheritance also has reference to the amount received but once, and from the parental estates.

But if we were to consider the question of a ratio, which should demand to be continually preserved (and repeated) through life, we would have to speak still stronger for the share due to inheritance, than to that due to individuality; first, because inheritance gives *blood*, which is not much alterable by any one's own Individual-activity; and second, because the cravings of inheritance are given to us from others, and we are comparatively free from *moral* accountability for them; and third, because inheritance betokens the training and *habits* of early life, and all those things which are "second nature," and whose cravings and wants are more durable than those acquired in after years.

Moreover, unlimited Communism is *not possible*, because men's educations, talents, and needs are unequal. Moreover, Absolute Communism even of CAPITAL or of principal, is a physiological impossibility: and those who demand it, are either selfish or one-sided in their views. The difficulty is this. It is impossible for all men to share equally the capital of their BRAINS. They can share the use or measure thereof, but they cannot share the absolute possession. Brains and education WILL have their influence in the government of the Commune, and in a willingness to break it up, and in their portability and susceptibility of being carried away by their owner, after the breaking up.

For instance, two men, and to omit the consideration of inherited differences, say brothers, may enter a Commune,—one with ten thousand dollars in money, the result of a hard life of farming or of commerce,—the other brother may have preferred to pass his early life among books, and so, may have an education and a learned profession, which altogether may have cost ten thousand dollars. This product is in his brains, and physiologically cannot be shared by the Commune, but only its use. But if the man leaves, or the Commune breaks up, he takes his capital with him. Whereas, the other one's ten thousand, having been given to the Commune, might be either lost in business, or squandered, or divided among all the members. This would be doubly unjust, because, in most cases, the education itself had been paid for by the parents, and paid for out of money which would otherwise have descended, and produced its share or part to the other brother. Consider, also, that the acquirement of education is a means of making people nervous, and weakening them as to their ability to make a livelihood, other than by mental labor. Consider, also, that the advantages of brain and education, inure too much to the *male* sex. Consider, also, that those who spend, have *had* the enjoyments and the personal influence, which spending obtains, and thus have had their share.

Hence, also, even supposing a Commune to be eternally existent, and eternally just, but never to form colonies,—still, capital has as good a right to its share in the management, as brains have, or education, or general social qualities and influence.

The ignoring of *our* basis, and the founding of Communes, on capital instead of on incomes, is one reason why some of the existing successful Communes, have to be governed by such iron-hearted and despotic inflexibility, and attain their full capacity soon after their organization; and why some others are going into decay.

But practically, no Commune can be found, scarcely, which does not allow *some* sort of private property among its members. All the Protestant Communes with marriage, allow and authorize *some* little private property, such as chickens, bees, &c. The Oneida Community also has lately adopted a plan, to allow its women thirty-three dollars a year's worth of dress! The surplus to be expended as they please. The Aurora also limits them.

As absolute Communism is therefore a mental and physical impossibility, it is probably inferable, that the call on capitalists for their principal, is one of the methods whereby restless intellect, not satisfied with the power it already possesses, aims to acquire also the power that property ought to have. And if such a rule were established, the already excessive rush into the learned professions, would be largely increased, whenever the current towards Communism became general. For every one would be anxious to invest as much of his property as possible, in his head, whence it could not be demanded, except as income in daily use.

There should be a union of Communism, with freedom from force. There should be a return to, or rather a continuance in, that union of fellowship with freedom, in which successful Communes generally have *started;* although afterwards changing from it. In short, the Communism must be of income and labor, not of principal, as it is commonly called, nor of capital. Such has been the actual course of successful Communes, at their origin. Their later deviations from it, are partly a return to the forcing principles of the world, and partly a good object, namely, a necessity to free men from devoting themselves to their isolated business. The latter object ought of course to be as fully secured as possible; but the return to the force-methods, is an error utterly irreconcilable with right principles, or with ultimate prosperity.

Communism of capital is not right. Human nature is not perfect enough yet; human artificial associations are not permanent enough, to justify persons of wealth or of possessions much above common, to alienate their principal beyond their own control. Parents who have tried it with their own children even, have found its ill effects. Besides, this course presents too many temptations to those who are seeking easy times, of selfishness and self-indulgence, and thus becomes a curse to the Community itself. The Protestant Communities *generally promise* to return seceders their capital: but ten have failed, to one that has succeeded.

Unlimited and absolute Communism of property, would neither be practical nor right, unless that abnormal development, Communism of sex, also could rightfully accompany it. But we cannot admit that.

Unlimited and absolute Communism destroys individuality, and also destroys the motives to activity, or else turns those motives, too much, into the channel of vanity, and of love of *present* approbation; which motives destroy the pleasure and the existence of a Commune. Christ himself, in his suffering life, had reference to the joys that were set *before* him (*in the future*).

Limitations therefore are absolutely necessary, yet I cannot but consider that the *employment* of laborers by a Commune, is an *unnecessary* limitation, and an essential subversion of the very idea of Communism. And every Commune ought to be so skillfully and liberally managed, as to attract enough of *all* the kinds of laborers needed, and especially of unskilled and world-degraded laborers. Failure in this, is probably owing to not presenting fair inducements to capitalists, whereby laborers could afford to be admitted also.

SUB-DIVISION II.

FOUNDATIONS OF COMMUNISM.

CHAP. I. BENEVOLENCE.

Benevolence is, to some extent, the foundation of Communism, and must in all cases be the active *spirit:* because there is no hope that Communism can ever succeed, when demanded on the ground of JUSTICE, but only, when placed on the basis of Christian kindness and benevolence.

We grant of course, that some better apportionment of profits should be given to labor, than what comes from the usual "grab-game" of society,—that is, as soon as the laborer is *morally* fit to have more pay and more leisure. But co-operation and joint-stockism, can furnish all the improvements that are demanded by simple justice. Therefore Communism, even limited more strictly than we propose, requires some of the elements of benevolence and religion, as chief bases and motives. Nevertheless, the benevolence and religion of some people, will naturally "take the *turn*" of Communism, as well as any of the other various *turns* open before them: and in so doing, will be at least AS free from self-seeking of any kind, as the benevolence and religion of Mankind, can be, in any other direction. Nevertheless, the *Fundamental* principle is not mere benevolence; as readily appears from our whole view of the subject.

CHAP. II. THE CONDITIONAL MUTUAL PRINCIPLE.

The power that first works in the improvement of society, is the conditional and mutual improvement principle; viz., that a man will do right to those who will do right to him; and both parties may then follow their own united ideal.

It would be unreasonable for Individuals who are far in the rear of others morally, to expect those who are far in advance of them, to become so much allied to them, and so liable to their influence, as to seriously retard their *own* improvement, and perhaps involve the risk of retrogression. The necessity for organization or form, in societies for self-improvement is, that thus their sentiment or ideal, then becomes distinctly avowed, and also becomes distinctly the care and the LAW of the organization. They take idea and sentiment embodied in words, not only as their government, but also as their GOVERNOR. This governor is a principle, an ideal, and is one chosen not *merely* by a majority, even a large majority, but it is a ruler actually chosen voluntarily by each and every member individually.

Thus self-improvement requires men to be freed from outward hindrances, and to have the necessary opportunities. This implies the selecting and constituting of some sort of select societies, whether formal organizations, or only spontaneous arrangements. Thus, unanimity in main objects is necessary. And then, many collateral influences arise, to aid the main objects, and to prevent breaking good resolutions; such as reason, deliberation, sympathy, &c.

The three difficulties which occur are; (1) the new society, its organs and officers, become temptations; (2) men try to gain little special advantages; (3) most men estimate themselves above their real value. Hence, the necessity that each one be willing to yield largely, what SEEM TO HIM to be his own rights, for the sake of peace. Only thus, can the rule of doing to others as we would be done by, be made practicable in this world. For lack of this little allowance, for the lee-way of differences of opinions, the best-meaning Christians often disagree bitterly. But we must differentiate between what *seem* to *us*, our rights, and what are absolutely such. And this practically means, that we must fill the measure "full and running over." Thus treating other persons severally, a little better than they treat us, (being a little more just, candid and truthful, &c.) is giving an entirely *scientific* turn to the practical *emotional* maxim, "Do unto others as ye would that they should do unto you."

By this means the "weaker" or worse members DO get a little advantage, and a little help incidentally, but *only* incidentally; because the main ground and basis, ever is *mutuality*.

CHAP. III. RELATION TO CO-OPERATION.

In England and Germany, co-operation in single businesses, has succeeded admirably. But *general* co-operation has not yet succeeded permanently, except in Communities, either in the United States or in Europe. But what are called "*Mutual*" Life-Insurance Companies, are really co-operative; so also are certain *subscription* Fire-Insurance Companies, which, without much or any stock capital, assess losses in proportion to subscriptions of assurance.

A report recently made by a British-government officer, shows, that there are in England nearly one thousand co-operative work and trade societies, with over 250,000 members, and with nearly $8,000,000 of capital, of which over $1,000,000 was loaned out. Co-operative stores are but little known in the United States, and yet in England, eight hundred reported their businesses, amounting to a total capital of ten millions, with loans of a million,—goods bought for thirty-five millions, and sold for over forty millions, and showing a net profit of three millions. Of this sum, twenty thousand dollars were spent in furnishing libraries, reading-rooms, and other means of education.

The best field of comparison is Germany, where co-operative stores and societies have raised labor from a low to a high position. In that country there are nearly 2000 savings banks, 300 co-operative societies, and nearly 1000 co-operative stores, with between 300,000 and 400,000 members; doing a business of $150,000,000, on a capital of $12,000,000. Germany, the Land which is first in Theology, is first also in co-operation.

The true starting-place for Communism, seems to be co-operating *boarding-houses*, for persons in a similar moral and religious position. By such associations, one business may be joined to another, and finally, all interests united or guaranteed. Then there would be a complete Commune.

CHAP. IV. SPIRITUAL REWARDS INSTEAD OF WORLDLY ONES.

Christian Communism is not intended nor expected, to do away with the principle, that "every man is to be rewarded according to his works"; ultimately so, even in this life. But it is expected to do away with that principle in a measure, so far as merely *external* works are meant, without regard to moral disposition. It desires to take moral character, moral influence, and a good spirit, into the account, in the apportionments of rewards. It aims also to do away with that principle, of reward of works, so far as applied to the outward works merely, without regard to the position, or physical *ability*, or the necessities of the co-operators. When there is a lack only of the ability, not of the disposition; it desires to reward them by the principles of the gospel, as God does, "according to what a man hath, and not according to what he hath not."

Notwithstanding this brotherhood-fellowship, it must also take into consideration mental ability, and make a difference of rewards according to IT; not chiefly so far as mind is power, but so far as, and because, mind is a *sign* of higher refinement of physical organization; and hence, needs more of the comforts and refinements of life, and has less bodily ability to work its way, or to endure its sufferings. This reason will stand, a rock of truth, against the theories of those who would hold ALL things in common without any difference whatever. They would give, to the plain stout hardy laborers, the same apportionment, as to the delicate refined intellectual cultivated thinkers, students, and managers. They would give the man who needs three or four dollars' worth of comforts a day, no more, than to him who needs and would be equally as well off with, less than one-fourth this amount. They overlook the fact, that under that system, they not only fail to obtain the *membership* of the cultivated and the capable; but that even could *that* be obtained, they must necessarily fail in obtaining their *best intellectual* efforts. These comforts and ease and even *leisure*, to such, are necessary, in order to allow their minds to work freely, and to good advantage. And the respect they deserve, is necessary to obtain their hearty co-operation. And without heart-work head-work is comparatively feeble and incomplete.

But Christian Communism, whilst allowing these differences of rewards according to works; yet, endeavors to keep the motives and feelings of self-interest and self-love, in the background of its thinking, and out of practical use, as much as possible. Like the rewards of Heaven, they are requisite to justice, and the knowledge of them is requisite to religion; yet, the best men are they who keep these rewards out of their motives as much as possible. This keeping these motives out of notice, is possible, not by an arbitrary effort of will, but by means of keeping other, and more divine motives and feelings, before the mind, and by becoming more and more transformed into the divine image. The knowledge of righteous apportionments according to works, is a sort of *military base,* in operating for goodness, and to that base it is necessary to return, or to communicate with it from time to time, until our forces become successful enough, and the country through which we are passing becomes rich and full enough, to enable us to live entirely on the angels' food that we can pick up along our way.

An objection to this may be made, that the American mind seeks *absolute* equality, and will not be happy without it. We can only answer, that persons thus determined, are not as yet fit for Communism. Those who are not able to understand, or are not willing to allow, the peculiar needs and comforts required by the delicate, the refined, the cultivated, and the thinkers, and supporters of the enterprise; such persons are *out* of the spiritual experience and enlargement, necessary to comprehend even *true equality* of rights and of needs itself: for true equality of rights and needs is NON equality of actual distribution. This will be seen to be so, when spiritual and moral ideas obtain their proper supremacy over merely corporeal or material things. To grant to every man his need and his right, is much nearer a maxim of true equality, than to grant to each one the same amount of food, dress, delicacies, or respect. And those who are not willing to allow this, have as yet their wills in bondage to material things, or else to selfishness and falsity. Either their heaven is in this world's things, for the sake of the things themselves, or else they are determined to have by force or deception, what they know to be more than their due share of it. But a right will, a right hope, here, is essential as the very starting-point of Communism. These reasonings are somewhat abstruse. But the wise conclusions to which they lead, are often understood by the true and good *heart,* without much intellectual culture.

CHAP. V. UNION OF HIGH MORAL AND INTELLECTUAL CONDITIONS.

Christian fellowship in general should be founded on the

essential idea, that there are three principles which constitute goodness: (1) the virtue of the right use of one's real moral freedom; (2) proper mental acquirements; (3) favorable external circumstances.

Communism does not destroy free will, nor moral probation; but places them on higher and more interior things.

Moral virtue, as a virtue of the will, consists in the habit of doing, thinking and feeling aright, fully to the *best of a person's moral ability*, according to the degree of *spontaneity* and really free will, and the amount of his disenchantment from servitude to evil circumstances, evil blood, or evil habits. For, habitual completeness according to the degree of one's real spontaneity, is all that any of us are capable of, and is all that a good God would require, and is what constitutes real moral virtue. But after all, there is an objective quality in goodness, even if there never had been and never would be, any really free will, as to right and wrong. And goodness is lovable in itself; and can be promoted by circumstances. And a good Commune is supposed to furnish the most favorable external circumstances, and the necessary or proper intellectual culture, especially as to moral relations.

The foundations of a Commune must be, partly those of superior moral will, or virtue, and partly those of suitable enlightenment in moral duties. Moral virtue consists in doing right, to the best of one's ability. This is a completeness, that Jew, Christian and heathen, are alike capable of. But a degree of mental culture also is required, to enable morally complete persons to harmonize. "How can two walk together, unless they be agreed?" Communism requires harmony of mind and heart, also sympathy and mutual confidence, upon the principal points likely to occupy the hearts and conduct of the members. These points are, religion, honesty, veracity, industry, sex and family-relations, personal habits, mental culture, customs (or fashions), and regard for customs. It must contain a church, or some moral or spiritual society, distinct from its social and civil organization; and based on the idea, that love to man, and faith in God and in goodness, are the essence of all religion. It also requires, in virtue and moral intelligence, a practical respect for, and obedience to, leaders. All the requisites may be summed up in being honest, truthful, good-tempered, and orderly.

CHAP. VI. RELATION TO STRICT RIGHTEOUSNESS, OR PERFECTIONISM.

Whoever would enter fully into religious Communism, must possess an unusual spirit and experience, and some degree of progress in the *real interior* life. Most Christians would speak of a person in such a state, as one who desired, above all things, to live free from sin. Some enthusiasts would even dare to call it "perfection." The mystics and interiorists themselves would call it contemplation, or walking with God.

By perfectionism, we mean, acceptance with God AS IF without sin, and a consciousness by faith, of such acceptance. Perhaps our idea of perfectionism would be summed up sufficiently in the phrase, life of interior righteousness by faith, or life in Christ.

A Christian Commune is a shell, to hold and receive life from a church of interiorists and saints. But, it is not desirable as a condition to joining a Commune, that any should profess having actually entered fully into an interior life; but that they *desire, above all things,* to live free from sin, and to progress in righteousness. Requiring high professions, is only offering a premium for hypocrisy.

There is plenty of experience and testimony, to prove, that such a state of guiltless acceptance or entire assurance with God, is attainable *temporarily*. The great thing to be done, and to be proved, is, the preserving of such a state *continuously*. The real practicability of sainthood, has been the avowed doctrine of more than nine-tenths of Christendom, since the time of Christ. The common Protestant reaction against the doctrine, is merely a polemical extreme.

But the religious Communes are too apt to overlook the real and objective *moral* pre-requisites. Thus, Mr. Finney's settlement at New Oberlin was commenced in the spirit of religious Communism, based on some of the common church theories of perfectionism. But not going on to the perfection of duties to other men, their spirit of Communism gradually evaporated. The two religious perfectionist women-friends of Mr. Wesley, astounded him, when they told him, they could scarcely live together in peace in the same house. But Communism is not possible except on the foundation, that members are *not* to indulge themselves either knowingly or carelessly, in trespasses upon the rights of their neighbors, however small or indirect those trespasses may be; nor can they be allowed frequently, even in unblamable ignorance.

This higher life, after all, probably consists, not mostly in superiority of inward character, but rather in diminished force of temptations, and in improved providential circumstances generally. And this is one of the very grounds of the importance of Communism, namely, because it diminishes the force of temptation, and affords the most favorable providential circumstances for obedience. But then it must also be remembered, that any actual release from sin, should be allowed its true expression in the heart, so that the heart may be really allowed to feel and enjoy as much subjective freedom from the consciousness of sin, as consists with the full realization, that this freedom is itself the result of *God's ordained circumstances*, and that therefore the glory is entirely due to him,—and as much of this freedom as, but no more than, is consistent with the additional consciousness and deep conviction, that objectively and inwardly, we are still sinners, needing confession, atonement and sanctification: and perhaps it may also be said, that natural faults, namely, the remains of indwelling sin, may even require repentance.

If the time has come when we understand the meaning of the Saviour's saying, (Matthew vii. 12,) "All things whatsoever ye would that men should do to you, do ye even so to them; for this is the law and the prophets"; and St. Paul's saying, (Romans xiii. 8 and 9,) "For he that loveth another hath fulfilled the law, * * * and if there be any other commandment, it is briefly comprehended in this saying, namely, Thou shalt love thy neighbor as thyself"; then the time has come when some class or society may arise, which will base itself on duty and love *to man*, as its real and only visible foundation. And this implies, that such a society will or should *reject all other foundations* that have been or may be offered, different from this one, of love and duty *to man*. Therefore they will not allow their basis to be any kind of forms or ceremonies. They will not allow their basis to be the profession of religion, nor of any particular doctrines,—nor any profession nor enactment of religious duty *upon religious grounds;* neither a duty of outward action, nor of inward feeling. True religion lies too deep within the soul, to be judged of, in the last analysis, by any other tests than those which inspiration itself lays down as the *supreme tests* thereof.

CHAP. VII. RELATION TO NATURAL THEOLOGY.

Any community, to succeed in this enlightened age, and where reverence for persons is *not* the governing power, must be founded on a cultivated *natural* religion: this is commonly called natural theology. The kingdom of evil is eminently one of intellectual culture. Men cannot avoid its influence if they would, and would not if they could; hence, culture in truth is needed, to counteract the influence of culture in error. Indeed in the most interior light, we find that all human learning is of very little use, religiously, except to counteract the errors of previous false learning. The age when men were governed by blind faith, has passed away. Even if men know the voice of God, they will not now obey him, unless he actually manifests to their intellects, that he *deserves* to be and must be obeyed. The former age has passed away; and men are no longer willing to stake their all, for time and eternity, upon a literature alone, although inspired. The progress of history does not tend to increase general faith in any mere literature, as such, however ancient. But the progress of science *does* tend to increase faith in nature, in natural law, and in natural doctrine. Hence there arises the great necessity for a cultivated natural theology. Even the Christian now bases his strongest evidence, that is, his strongest external or intellectual evidence, of the divine authority of our own religion, and of the books containing it,—upon the ever increasing proofs derived from philosophy and natural science. The authority of character is gone, and in its place has come, the authority of philosophy and natural science,—in other words, the authority of natural religion.

Now the direct application of these ideas to Communism, is first, that the essential and indispensable basis of Communism, is the absolute certainty of moral laws; and next, the consequent dependence of all, upon moral means as distinct from compulsory ones.

A Community is the quintessence of refined misery, when chiefly held together by any other means than voluntary ones. And this can only be avoided, when the absolute certainty of moral laws is established, also the superiority of moral to physical or formal considerations, as influences on the daily life. These moral laws, of course, include provisions for repentance, reformation, faith, and spiritual life. In fact, they include *every thing*, even in theology itself. But moral laws are as unchangeable as physical ones; the interpretation being found always in this, that men may choose to forfeit the rewards of obedience, but then must fall under consequences, which will always be indefinitely worse than the pain of present obedience. And it seems clear that the only effective external, i.e. intellectual means, to produce firm conviction of this certainty of moral laws, as yet discovered, is found in the study of the natural sciences, and of mental and *moral* philosophy. Miracles, regeneration, divine union, are all found to be not contrary to, but in accordance with moral and spiritual laws,—laws that are as fixed as the character of God himself. It becomes evident that God governs the world, and all his creatures, angels and devils, saints as well as sinners, by strict moral laws; including of course *spiritual* laws. Thus moral character and moral excellencies, become evidently the objects of highest, deepest, and nearest daily importance. The man who would rather be right than be Emperor of the World, is no longer felt to be a fanatic. Such an one IS fast becoming Emperor of the World, both of the living and of the departed, namely, the founder of Christianity. All these things are settled and felt to be true, notwithstanding the practicability of repentance and restoration by the transgressor. And, obedience by the heart, obedience in all things, obedience in little things, is felt to be the highest good, and the highest joy.—Only thus can Communism be a joy; only thus can a Commune hope to become permanent; unless perchance, it may have the special providence of Satan, for a while.

Then again, natural religion furnishes, not only the doctrine and motives of righteousness; it also aids the *power* of actual righteous living. As it gives the strongest grounds for faith in, and submission to the God of the Universe; so it lays before us the ideas well calculated to excite to the service of righteousness, which is the service of God—and gives the *intensest desire* of obedience, which is the true prayer of the heart. And then again, natural religion gives us the strongest proofs, and one of the best outward aids, to the interpretation of divine revelation; and thus becomes the most effective real producer of the love and worship of God. Thus it becomes evident, how valuable natural religion is, even to those ordained saints who, being in the divine union, have no more need of laws for their control,—if or when any are such.

CHAP. VIII. SYMPATHY WITH THE GENERAL CHRISTIAN CHURCH.

Sectarianism itself is the result of human finiteness and ignorance, but the *evils* of sectarianism are the results of selfishness. In fact, the subtle and refined form which, selfishness, self-will, self-conceit and self-interest, take, in the church, is active sectarianism. But Communism is essentially unselfish. Therefore a Commune must be truly catholic and liberal, based on sympathy with, not in opposition to, the general Christian church; nor against their doctrines and writings generally. Nothing that is so based, will ultimately prosper. This implies a recognition of the truly and equally Christian character, of credibly professing Christians in the churches generally. It also implies a recognition of the higher life, in sects and parties credibly professing such interior and higher life. A sectarian or exclusive or self-conceited organization, sets itself against the life of Christ in general; and the end thereof will not be blessed. Such may spring up rapidly at first, and show *signs* of the divine life; and in some peculiar moral climates may flourish well for a while; but that is all of the good they do, and if they become great—Alas! for the evil!

Communism *means* fellowship. The very same original word is used for both, in the New Testament. How then could it be possible for a Community to succeed, one of whose distinguishing principles was *un*fellowship with the Christian church in general, or with interiorists in general, and with other Communists? Any kind of sectarian exclusiveness is strong proof, either of excessive narrow-mindedness, or of great deficiency of Christian love,—generally, is proof of both. It also generally contains a large amount of self-conceit and self-will, showing that selfishness is not all subdued. And when the fervor of pietism, or the *esprit du corps*, subsides, or the great leader dies; the unsubdued self that hitherto might have been, at least in pecuniary matters, previously disinterested and generous, now breaks forth for self-interest. And "thus endeth" its inward virtue.

The true principles of Christian interiorism, are in close harmony with the good in those called "the religious mystics." And these again are found to be in remarkable harmony with one another, in all the cultivated or literary religions of *all* the World, Christian, Mahometan, East Indian, and Heathen, alike. Among all these, and in all times, there have been numbers who, penetrating within and beyond the veil of popular details, have found a higher theory, without opposing the lower, and a higher life and love, without hating the other. Thus the Christian interiorists find themselves a part of the WORLD'S real catholic religion; and give us the nearest approximation to the absolute in religion, that is attainable in this life. This general agreement as to ideas and experience, is noticed by Ullman in "Reformers before the Reformation"; and by Vaughan in "Hours with the Mystics," and by others.

Sympathy with the general Christian church, of course means,—with the church of *all* ages, Greek and Roman, as well as Protestant; and in antiquity as well as in the present. The *vast majority* of the church has always believed in a sort of perfectionism or sainthood: and has been *without* the Bible among the people. That is a luxury brought about partly by reaction against the corruptions of past churches, and partly by the art of printing. But the common use of the whole Bible is no part of the practice of the universal Christian church in the past. Neither is it to be, of the future. Heb. viii. 10 and 11, says; "The covenant * * * I will make with the house of Israel * * * I will put my laws into their mind, and write them in their hearts. * * * And they shall not teach every man his neighbor, * * * saying, 'Know the Lord,' for all shall know me, from the least to the greatest."

Therefore a Commune is not likely to succeed, which abounds with *Bibliolaters*, idolaters of the Book, disputing all the time, with and about the Scriptures, and expecting to settle every thing with a text or two; with but little regard to history, experience, science, or natural religion.

CHAP. IX. THE NON-FORCING PRINCIPLE.

A Commune must be based upon moral suasion; and not upon forcing others against their will. It grants reasonable liberty to all others, and acts upon the maxim of doing to others as we would be done by. When a person is found habitually to need force, and to be persistently ungovernable, or unimprovable, or disturbing to the association, he or she is unfit for Communism.

The true peace-principle is, not to use force except to *resist force;* and only then, according to the importance of resistance at all, and the *necessity* and importance of force as a *means* of resistance.

The true life of God in the soul, has a tendency to submit its own will to others, and to submit events to Divine providence. It has long suffering, and rejoices exceedingly in the reformation of a transgressor, for which it labors and prays. But it feels itself justified in prompt resistance to the attempts of unfit persons, to obtain, by force or fraud, the rule of its Society; and requires that the aggressor should ever remember, that its acquiescence or quietism is *not due* to man as a human duty, but to God, and only and so long as He demands it; and perhaps as a kind of "*meritum ex congruo,*" or work for stars in our crown.

CHAP. X. ANTI-WAR PRINCIPLES.

Strong and clear, but reasonable anti-war principles, ought to be enunciated and adhered to. The following should be announced as the least reasons that could be required, in order to allow war:—(1) that a war be really defensive; (2) that the attack be itself actual, real and violent; (3) that the attack be unjust; (4) that the attack be known to the attackers themselves to be unjust; (5) that no efforts of Christian forbearance or kindness, will avert or terminate the war; (6) that the arguments requiring war in *that case,* are plain and clear beyond reasonable doubt. Nearly all the successful Protestant communes are non-resistants.

CHAP. XI. ORDER, DISCIPLINE AND PUNISHMENT.

Next come the PRINCIPLES of the treatment of criminals by government, of children by parents and teachers, and of refractory members by a Commune. The principles are, that all lawful means necessary to prevent society or Individuals from being trampled on, are justifiable; and therefore the attempt of unfit persons to get the rule over a society by fraud or force, justifies resistance. But, as far as consistent with this, all reasonable kindness and privileges should be shown to offenders.

Punishment, if necessary, should be administered to the passion or propensity or faculty, that offends. The main reliances for communistic and affectionate government or discipline, are, criticism, the fellowship of truth, the exclusion of temptation, and the gratification of all RIGHT human wants and needs.

Yet as punishments may sometimes be necessary, it is best to have several classes; and we propose the following. First class. Special lessons for study in morality and righteousness, and in the principles and objects and reasons of punishments. Second class. Private reprimands, fines and charges,—sometimes recorded, sometimes not. Third class. Debar from social gatherings for recreation and conversation. Debar parents and children from seeing each other; also husbands and wives. Debar from table, and from certain meals, or for a specified time. Debar from any new clothes, except necessary for health. Fourth class. Debar from all social employment, or appoint the most disagreeable work. Order confinement to room, except for necessity and meals. Fifth class. Order a peculiar dress; prohibit visitors; allow general censure. Sixth class. Remand to a lower order. Seventh class. Give notice of early expulsion, unless the required acknowledgments, promises, and reforms are made. Suspension (or an order to leave), without absolute expulsion. Eighth class. Expulsion.

We may also add to these general punishments, non-participation in recreations, and non-intercourse, except with near relations. Debar from the company of the other sex, and defer the time of marriage. And in regard to children, confinement to room, and even whipping if necessary, although we doubt the necessity of it. A system of rewards for doing well, might do away with much disobedience and consequent punishment; and with the young, the prospect of early marriage for the orderly and obedient, might be highly successful.

In trials there might be arbitration,—or a committee might be appointed, one-half by the accused, and the other half by the society.

CHAP. XII. RESORT TO LAW, AND OF HOLDING POLITICAL OFFICES.

We are prohibited from law, only by the two principles,—moral suasion, and anti-war. In all other cases, Interiorists have the same right to resort to law, as other persons. Interiorists, or Communists, have the same right to seek offices, as other men; when those offices can be successfully sought and administered, by gospel means, and in the Lord. But inasmuch as church officials had better keep out of political affairs, and as all Interiorists are a sort of volunteer officials in the Universal Catholic church, it becomes most expedient for them not to seek political offices.

The Shakers say they have never had a lawsuit, (previous to the year 1871.) And those Communities that have had suits, have probably parted with unsuitable persons at the wrong time; having borne with them too long in quietness, and then arisen against them too violently. But the suit against the Shakers, seems to have been instituted to obtain children previously given to their Community.

CHAP. XIII. FELLOWSHIP OF TRUTH.

§ 1. *Confession.*

Another essential of Communism is fellowship of truth, combining the principles of Family, and of Sacrament; and implying strict veracity and frankness, also a willingness to acknowledge one's faults.

The Communities generally make much account of confession, or acknowledgment of error. And such a practice would doubtless be very important and useful, IF it could be made truly harmonious with Protestantism, and rendered as certain of secrecy, as is confession in the Roman church: or if damages were recoverable from the *Individual*-person or officer who would betray confidence; but, not from the Society.

But to require public confession before the Society, of serious matters, is more than the world, even of Communism, is fitted for; and would sometimes involve other parties, and lead to entangling lawsuits. Full confessions cannot be expected, in the origin of any Community; but only gradually, and as its own reliability becomes established.

§ 2. *Information.*

Again, fellowship of truth requires a sort of Christian or Family tale-bearing, according to the command of Christ. When a brother or offender does wrong, another must tell him of it privately, for the offender's good. If that does not succeed, he must take another member with him; and as a last resort, tell the matter to the officers. It is *only* in a Community, that this command of Christ admits of common practical application.

§ 3. *Criticism.*

It is absolutely essential that members be willing to receive criticism, as to their general habits and character, and that the leaders be able to give such criticism wisely. Criticism should at first be administered privately, and should not be turned into laudation, except where encouragement is needed. Officers should be subject to criticism, but only by and in the presence of other officers.

But there is a limitation to criticism, which is too apt to be disregarded by those who overlook its sacramental character, and *indulge it as the spontaneous expression of feeling.* Interiorists qualified to criticise wisely, will be able to govern their own tongues. Unless there is a willingness to suffer much for others, by silence, as also by other means, Community-life is apt to become a place-of-torment on earth. The Oneida Community is able to give, and owes to the world, a scientific work on criticism.

CHAP. XIV. HONOR.

Another basis of Communism is high-toned HONOR, such as prevails among real gentlemen. The necessity of this element, honor, is what gives hope of success of those Communes which might consist of the two Social Circles, namely, genteel and subaltern. But this honor is not merely what exists between friends, or persons of the same class or clique; but is what exists between opponents, and even between enemies. And in a Commune, the honor must be especially and above all, to the Commune itself, just as patriotism exists for the whole Nation, or the whole Precinct.

CHAP. XV. COMMUNITY-OCCUPATIONS.

Each Community must have its own especial and peculiar characteristics, either of business, study, or benevolence. Suppose the special moral aim of a Community, be, as sometimes it has really been, devotion to Theology, or Social Science; and its members should say, We would study to know best how to live. We would live retired lives, and open our doors to others who sincerely desired to reap the benefits of such a life,—in order that we might do them good. These special moral ideas would then have to be the *bases* to collect members.

The business of the Commune must depend upon the acquirements, and means, of those who compose it. Perhaps it would facilitate Communism, to adopt the business first, and collect as members, those in one business, chiefly.

The number of members must be restricted by the amount of income, and the profits likely to arise from the occupations engaged in; and upon the proportion of students and children, non-contributors, and others not immediately productive. Of course those businesses are most suitable, which employ nearly an equal number of both sexes; or else, such a combination of several businesses, that some will employ one sex, and some the other sex. One good start might be made with students well qualified to study any desired sciences, and with an aggregate income sufficient for their support; and with such other persons as can co-operate by aiding, as agriculturists, manufacturers of wearing apparel, house-workers, &c. The publishing business is peculiarly inviting to Communes, either by itself, or in connection with intellectual occupations,—also the seminary or boarding-school occupation, life insurance, annuity and trust companies; also companies to furnish capital or labor, in special partnership with Individuals, or with Communes. These would answer for outside members.

CHAP. XVI. RELIGIOUS EXERCISES.

The best religious means would probably be, to employ, *in turn*, the common prayer of the Episcopal church, the litanies of the

Moravians, the class- or band-meetings of the Methodists, and the silent congregational meetings of the Friends (Quakers). There should also be lectures or readings on Moral Science, Natural Theology, Evidences of Revealed Religion, and exegetical readings of the Scriptures. If desired, "confessors" and "spiritual" directors could be appointed by the Community, or selected by Individuals.

If there were regularly authorized ministers in the Commune, they would probably administer baptisms and communions. True catholic mutual liberty should be allowed in these things. But the *communion of bread and wine* would probably soon become obsolete. Sunday should be faithfully, but not pharisaically nor literally, observed, as a day of rest from ordinary business, and of special religious opportunities: if not for one's own sake, then for the sake of others.

For Religion we suggest four kinds of meetings. One, a Sunday-School, conducted in the usual manner, with prayer, singing, Scripture-lessons, and so on—perhaps with part of the prayers selected from the Episcopal prayer-book, but with some slight revision. Another kind might be for the *adult* study of religion, natural and revealed, accompanied by *discussions.* Another meeting perhaps might be for religious experience. Another meeting might be for worship purely, and should therefore be entirely *silent.*

If however, a Commune should arise among and out of any ONE religious denomination, it would naturally continue the forms of its denomination, in a general way, but in a more liberal manner. But such an arising seems not likely soon, unless the seekers of some kind of higher life, become much more numerous than they are; because they are now so few, that they are acting on Christian-union principles; and these principles indeed, are the natural expression of the higher and unselfish life. But, several denominations are quite large enough to develop Communities, each within itself, if their minds and hearts were turned in that direction. Besides the Catholics, the Episcopals have them in this country, and the Lutherans in Germany; but the Protestants, merely as sisters of charity.

CHAP. XVII. COMMUNISM OF LABORS AND INCOMES.

§ 1. *Plan, In General.*

Some hints on the rights of property, have been already given in Sub-Division I. Chap. IV. of this article: and if the writer be spared long enough, a fuller treatment of that subject may be expected from him, in a future book or article, on PROPERTY, one of the Fourteen Great Elements of Social Science. Property must have its own, and *only* its own, right share in the distribution. Evidently however, some new scientific and moral adjustment between capital and labor, is necessary, and must be POSSIBLE. Because the let-alone theory—and strikes by laborers, and pinching down wages by capitalists—are merely grab-game methods, which must find their final adjustment, not by force of arms, or numbers, or stubbornness of will or of capital; but by reason and morality, and by eternal principles of right.

Our plan of adjustment is, as has been said, the Communism of incomes and labors, but not of capital nor principal.

But Communism, when thus limited to incomes and labors, only, may seem very little different from Fourierist association. But, both the principles and the methods are very different, in all the various great points, as follows. Our theory requires, instead of splendor and luxury, plainness and simplicity, in house and dress and food; and authorizes *no* aristocracy, nor evidence of wealth, in the customs, clothes or food. Again, our theory lays stress on the necessity of early and natural and moral satisfaction of the sexes, by childhood-marriages. And to make such marriages happy and moral, as well as useful, should form a great part of the motive and object, of the government and customs and architecture of a Commune.

Again, Fourier proposes to make industry pleasant, by means of beautifying its surroundings, of home and grounds and clothes, also by music and drill and so on. But our theory proposes to make industry attractive, partly by the principles of the Kindergarten, namely by thoroughly useful education, made pleasant by arranging the plays of children scientifically; promoting the idea of utility, thus to prepare for instructive industries; and partly by stimulating the other great, good motives to industry; and partly by removing the causes of idleness.

And in general, where Fourier proposes to produce happiness by gratifying the sense of beauty, we propose instead, to cultivate the sense of the useful, and the dutiful. Again, Fourier avowedly and intentionally stimulates competition, throughout all his groups and classes, but our theory avoids competition as much as possible, and puts it into the background among the unconscious motives; because its very principle and life are destructive of Communism.

Furthermore, Association in order to succeed, must be something *more generous* than any thing which can be furnished by the Fourier or Joint-stock principle. For the financial economies are counterbalanced by the social discords.

On the other hand, Association must pay some regard to the different proportions of stock contributed, or else it will not be able to attract capital voluntarily. Then again, the regard thus paid to property, must consist at least partly, of something else than mere dividends; for such institutions do not present very strong inducements to the seekers of dividends; and if they did present inducements to such, the institutions would become of a mercenary, or at best, of a business character. The Fourierite proposition of rewarding capitalists by honors and by prominent positions, appeals also to the selfish sentiments too much, if the positions were anything more than merely empty honors; and to suppose that sensible men would be satisfied with empty honors is an absurdity. Moreover, it is impossible to conceive of honors or positions that would not be empty, unless they were positions of POWER in the management. Moreover, power in the management is one of the requisites that are necessary in order to convince capitalists that their property would be safe: neither in fact would their property be safe, if entirely under the power of persons without property; for there is no fact nor argument that can prove the fitness of men to preserve property, so well as the fact of actually having done so.

The plan of merely retaining power instead of honor, for capitalists, not only suits them better, but also suits fair-meaning people who are not capitalists, better. Because it leaves the official positions, and the honors of administration, open to the non-capitalists: and practically does away with the feelings of distinction, both in the actual management, and in the social life, almost entirely; whereas, the plan of giving capitalists ostentatious honors, although even empty ones, tends to keep alive social distinctions, in very unpleasant ways.

The case stands thus: Mankind are entangled in a net-work of circumstances, the results of sin; and which are of such an inveterate nature, that the rights which labor and morality have in property, are largely ignored; neither are the workmen yet fitted to enjoy them fully. And at the same time, the case is so inveterate, that no wisdom of laws, nor government-*force*, can make things better; but every forcing attempt rather makes them worse. In this emergency, (we suppose) property-holders, or at least some of them, come forward voluntarily, and do their share towards the rectification of things, in a limited field, and in a reasonable way. Now, will some workmen come forward, equally generously on the other side?

The case then is thus: Capitalists step in and offer to resign a part of the profits of capital, and a part of the control of it; whilst those without capital, accepting the actions of the other party, to be proofs both of wisdom and of goodness, give up a part of their control over the society's affairs. And the question then to decide is, whether it is for the best interests, as well as the ultimate happiness, of both parties, to enter into the arrangement.

The way to arrange about the stock, so as to avoid the two opposite difficulties, of tempting members to leave, by allowing them to take the value of their stock, and the other difficulty, of debarring their heirs from it *altogether*,—would be, perhaps, to have two kinds of stock, common and preferred, and to decide as time progresses, the proportion of each, to each member: Common stock to revert to the Community at death or at leaving, whilst preferred might continue private property in either case. But all Commune-stock in excess of a certain amount, might revert to issue or the mother thereof, where there was either left to inherit. And the Commune should have the right to prescribe its own laws of inheritance.

In the case of Communes of long or well established financial responsibility: it would perhaps be best to substitute life-annuities, instead of actual principal, for those who withdrew. The amounts of the annuities, to be in proportion to the amounts of capital of course, but NOT necessarily calculated as to age. In other words, merely pay legal or usual or liberal interest, during the life of the party; the Community reserving the privilege of paying the principal instead, if it thought best so to do for its own good.

As to the dissolution of a Commune, speaking of it as distinct from an equitable division of it into two or more Communes:—a decision of dissolution should require the consent separately, of the board of trustees, and of the board of representatives, and a majority of the votes of the stock of full members, as well as of Individuals entitled to vote for representatives, and also a majority of the females over eighteen years of age. In a dissolution, children's shares and interests should be appropriated to their use, or given to their parents; and divorced women's be held in trust for them. This and all other financial matters, should be regulated solely by the *responsible* trustees, representing the stock of those who were full members at the time of the vote for dissolution.

§ 2. *Directors and Government.*

The objects to be accomplished and the difficulties to be overcome, may all be summed up in these two things,—to get good leaders, and to get the members to follow them cheerfully. In order to these objects, the government should be such as to require the consent, of both Capital and Individuals. This is best accomplished by having two equal boards elected, one, a board of trustees chosen by the stock-holders who are resident or full members; the other, a separate board of representatives chosen by Individuals. Of this latter, one half should be chosen by men, the other half by women. These two boards together would constitute the directors. These directors should have all the power of law-making, and appointment of officers.

Immediately upon being chosen, the new directors, trustees and representatives, should elect new officers, and the official terms of all other officers should cease. All appointments and selection of officers, should require the joint consent of the boards of trustees, and of representatives; except the Treasurer, who should be chosen by the trustees alone.

Stockholders who are not full or resident members, should be entitled to their due proportion of profits, but not entitled to vote, or have any voice in the management. Property-qualification should not be admitted in government, unless as one of several in a balance of powers,—nor even then, unless it participates in all the responsibilities, and knows the advantages, by resident membership.

All Communes contain different grades of members virtually, whether avowedly or not. And it is better to have them avowed and organized. Such an organization of them, lessens the power of Individuals within, and keeps out unsuitable members. But the particular grades would vary in different Communes. It would seem most probable, however, that with the balances we propose, nearly or quite all classes of members, of sufficient age, might be allowed to vote.

§ 3. *Property, Shares and Dividends.*

The way to arrange the stock, would perhaps be, as before said, to have two kinds,—common and preferred, and to decide, as time progresses, the proportion of each, to each member,—one kind of stock is to revert to the Community at death, or at leaving; while the other kind is to continue private property in either case.

The capital of the Community, besides the original stock, should consist of all the unengaged or free incomes and profits of all its members. And for the surplus of each one's income over his expenses, certificates of stock should be issued. This is an encouragement for all to produce much, and to consume little. The certificates of stock would be available to the member's heirs, or to himself or herself, in case of secession or dissolution of the association. And in the case of male members, their stock would be liable to deductions for the benefit of their children, or the mothers thereof.

No interest or usance should be allowed on the capital stock. But wages should be allowed to each one, according to his or her industry, at the rates allowed for like services in the world, as near as may be; allowing for benefits in case of sickness, death, &c.: and stock might be issued for the surplus of production over consumption.

In regard to the difficult matter of division of profits, the theoretical idea is, that regard should be had to several things: mental *ability*, moral character, necessities of age, *infirmity* or *sex*, and capital stock invested. But as mental ability would be allowed for in the allotment of world's wages, it may be omitted entirely in distributing profits. It is always apt to get more than its share, under any arrangement, and in every association on earth.

There would then result the principle of dividing one half of the profits to Share-holders, in proportion to stock, and the other half of the profits, to Individuals,—allowing women, say twice as much as men, and children under fourteen years of age, an increasing sum, increasing regularly as they were younger than fourteen, so that a child under one year of age, would have allowed for it a sum fourteen times as much as one of the age of fourteen years. But these allotments of profits for children should be made, not to them as to Individuals, but to a trust-fund for them collectively, in such a way that this trust-fund would decrease in its proper ratio from year to year, if there were a proportional decrease of children. In short, these allotments for children would substantially be, merely something provided ahead for their maintenance and tuition.

Our Saviour said "sell all," but added "and give" (not to a Community, but give) "to the poor"—*give* it away. It is even worse for a Community to accumulate wealth, than for an Individual: hence it is as much for the Community's own interests, as for its women and children, that their portions, shares and interests should be, as far as convenient, secured for them in special trusts. As then there would be but little inducement to the licentious, or the greedy, to break up the Commune. The truly poor, are simply they who need; and this is pre-eminently true of young children.

In course of time, and after success, all stock votes might be, not in proportion to shares owned at the time; but in proportion to the average number of shares owned during membership.

Government ought to be in the hands of the best men,—those who possess most fully the transcendental elements. Communism tests men as to their morality, and their intellectual character, and should offer promotion. There must be different grades or orders of membership, based on age, and spiritual experience, rather than on smartness of talk, or shrewdness of policy.

CHAP. XVIII. RELATIONS OF FAMILY AND SEX.

Idolatrous Family love, either of a married partner, or of a child, is entirely subversive of Community-life. But the Family relation itself must be retained.

In some stages of experience, the sexes should seldom meet; but when the married did meet, they should come together with freedom and seclusion. Marriage, particularly early marriage, should be made a privilege, and a reward of good conduct. In some stages of experience, the sexes, when arrived at near puberty, whether married or not, should reside, eat and work entirely by themselves; and not meet, except on the occasion of the regular meeting, say once or twice a week. If the Commune is large enough, the married and single of each sex, in this stage of experience, might again be separated. The daily meetings for religion and criticism, should be conducted in adjoining rooms, one for each sex; or perhaps entirely apart.

But in other stages of experience, and where years, or knowledge, or sanctification, or good early habits, will justify it, the best safest, and happiest course will be, constant virtuous and chaste intercommunings between the sexes. And this is greatly facilitated, by intercommunings between the youth of one sex, and the aged and experienced of the other sex. In the highest experience and knowledge, nothing earthly contributes so much to chastity of *heart* and life, as the constant presence of loving and beloved ones, of the opposite sex.

Every care should be taken to retard precocity in children; but they should be so trained to useful industry, as to be fitted for early marriage. They should also receive specific instruction, in regard to those matters now too often neglected, which instruction is one of the necessities of modern civilization. The demand for early marriages is imperative; but they cannot be either prudent or safe, except in Communism, wherein alone they can be properly made temperate.

The great cause of liquor intemperance, probably, is sexual excess. For this, the only effectual cures would be, early marriages, and frequent temporary separation of the sexes, in Communes of mutual friends.

Although freedom of sex is no essential part of true and perfect Communism, and is not the equitable nor highest development of sex on earth; nevertheless, some part of the world, in its *selfish* attachment to fashions, forms and outward things, may *possibly* have to pass through a period of "complex marriage," or even of freedom of sex, in its *transition* to the perfect state beyond. For, it may be true, that nothing but the realization of human equality, through the all-powerful bond of sex, will ever enable the commonalty of Mankind to realize the truth of that equality *at all;* and perhaps nothing else will break up the Family-idolatry of children, and Family-selfishness in general. Hence, the best thing that can be done to prevent "complex marriage" &c., is to establish Communes with usual marriage, and reasonable divorce, and thus anticipate against the other development. Fourier saw the coming evil, but not seeing its final cause, he proposed to legitimate the evil, as a good, permanently.

Marriage should be placed upon the plane of the gospel, and upon morality and love; and women and children should be protected. Other matters can safely be left to moral suasion, and the church-principles of the Commune. The true interests of society call for amelioration of the *forcing-principle* in marriage, as fast as practicable. These interests must be the care of every Commune; especially, because the Family is one of the Six fundamental Units of society. All persons who are on the lookout to catch beaux, or girls, or to make fine matches, *in reliance upon the binding and forcing laws in marriage*, are entirely unfit for Communism. But Communism presents a remedy, namely, the desirable peculiarity of enabling divorces to take place, without separating parents from their children, and without injuring the woman. So then, after a Commune had established a good character, and shown that it was able to properly take care of its women and children, it should be granted, by the laws of the land, the power of divorce among its own members. In general, no divorced woman should be expelled, unless under peculiar reasons, or for peculiar atrocity; and should ever be considered as a ward or pensioner of the society—as a person indissolubly married to the society, or as its perpetual infant or ward.

CHAP. XIX. MANNERS AND CUSTOMS.

In these; divine *utility* should be the leading idea; mere fashions or styles, and mere amusements, whether bodily or mental, should not be allowed; nor in dress, anything either in shape, color, material or complexity, that is not useful. All stimulants, narcotics and gormandizing, should be strongly discouraged. Luxury, finery, and emulation, should not be allowed among resident members. Music and the fine arts (perhaps except vocal music), should only be encouraged in those having special talent therefor, and as methods of utility to others.

No one should be encouraged to enter a Commune for any selfish worldly advantages; otherwise, parasites might come in, in oppressive numbers. Neither should the prospect of ease, luxury, or amusement, be presented to induce any to adopt Communism. Economy and almost asceticism are necessary, for the good of the Commune itself, and to exclude the unsuitable. The admirers of beauty always overlook this policy.

General vegetarianism and abstemiousness in diet, also ample ventilation, will promote chastity and continence. This is proved by the instincts and experience of the Shakers and other celibates; and the peculiarities of old maids are necessary and reasonable.

Criticism, instead of minute book-keeping, should be applied, to aid in determining the value of each member's service, and the cost of his maintenance, by a system of grade marks. A record should be kept of each member's grading of others, *so that partiality and prejudice in bad grading, could also come under criticism.*

There should be some arrangement of different orders or degrees, of intellect and spirit; but persons in a lower degree, should *wait* for promotion, until called to a higher.

It is not necessary to delay the starting of Communities, until men become fit for entire equality. There might be one kind of Communities of "gentlefolks" with their "help," and another kind of mechanics, tradesmen, &c., *without* any domestic help. One of the principal difficulties in starting a Commune, is, in regard to the ladies; partly of inducing them to labor, which is a necessity in Communes based upon social equality; and partly, that women make much more of marriage than men, but all like to marry into a superior social condition. Therefore, until Communes obtain the right of divorce, (and the right would prevent the necessity of using it),—these disparities of social distinction seem necessary to be continued. The objection to labor is founded chiefly, on a false idea that there is something socially degrading about it. And the customs of the Commune must break up that falsity.

CHAP. XX. INDUSTRY.

We need say but little of industry, because, in successful Communes, overwork has to be criticised more than idleness; and also, because all the rules very strongly, though indirectly, promote industry. The thinkers of the Community especially, should not be overworked. The Community-life should make labor both honorable and attractive; and should not allow, either persons or customs that tended to degrade labor.

Again, the necessity of labor varies with the property of the Commune. In this age, increased "Production" is not the chief want of society; but improved "Distribution" of the fruits of industry. Still, every person is morally bound to be industrious, mentally or bodily, in proportion to ability and health. The greatest practical difficulty is, to induce members to do the unhealthy, dirty, and world-despised works. This may be remedied, partly by banishing the worldly feeling which despises labor, and partly by a higher rate of profits or honors, for repulsive kinds of work; or fewer hours of labor, with more hours for literary culture, and even by amusements and journeys not allowed to others at all. But, if unskilled physical laborers, unfit for the higher industries, were unwilling to perform hard or rough labor, they would thereby prove themselves unfit for Communism. And if Communism was to be absolutely unlimited, there would be no possibility of extra pay, for the peculiar services, and no use for such extra pay, to the receivers of it.

CHAP. XXI. THE DISPOSITIONS AND SOURCES OF DANGER.

The features of human nature from which all sin and disorder arise, are self-will, self-conceit, and self-interest. These applied to Community-life require various special precautions,—as against social or class prejudices, the forming of cliques of discontent, ambition to rule in excess of contributions or talent, emulation, vanity, contrariness, licentiousness, alcohol, gossip, amusements, idleness, fondness for dress, &c., &c. All these sources of danger combine in such various proportions, that they cannot be provided for in detail, but should be guarded against as well as may be, when they manifest themselves.

Those persons who are most to be dreaded, and who have been most troublesome about money matters, in Communes, have been those who have contributed but limited amounts, (from one to three thousand dollars.) Such persons, on leaving, often demand the whole principal and also interest, besides wages for their own labor. Large contributors do not usually make any such preposterous claims.

CHAP. XXII. THE SELF-SACRIFICE REQUISITE.

"Though Communism is a precious thing, it has its cost, and persons should find out before joining, whether they are willing to pay the price. Joining the Community cuts a person off from such worldly ties and connections as stand in the way of improvement, substituting spiritual relations for merely natural ones. It implies the giving up of trivial habits and tastes; the sacrifice of freedom to come and go, *irrespective* of others; and the submitting of ambition, amativeness, and philoprogenitiveness, to a discipline which renders them unselfish, and obedient to science and to God." * * * "Joining the Community is in fact so far like the 'straight and narrow way' of the gospel, that it is intended to exclude *all* the liberty of the old *carnal* life." * * * "In Community there is the largest liberty for love and generosity, but the smallest liberty for selfishness and seeking one's own. But those persons who enter, with their eye mainly on private luxury and pleasure-seeking, are courting special disappointment. True Communism is the worst hell such persons can easily find. It has nothing for them but arrest and crucifixion, till their motive is changed." J. H. Noyes. Also see the writings of other Communists, whether marital or celibate.

MAIN DIVISION II.

THE COMMUNITY'S PRECAUTIONS AND GUARDS AGAINST INDIVIDUALS.

SUB-DIVISION I.

WAYS AND METHODS OF PRECAUTION.

CHAP. I. IN GENERAL.

The whole structure of the Commune should take the necessary precautions for the protection of itself and its *good* members; otherwise, prudent and good men cannot easily be induced to join. For, the greatest difficulty in Communism, is to get, not members, but good members. We have aimed to make our whole theoretical structure a safeguard against probable dangers: —Therefore this MAIN DIVISION will be rather brief.

Even our third general Main Division—viz.,—the Individual's guards against the Community, acts indirectly, but yet most powerfully, in maintaining the safety of the Commune; for prudent and good men cannot be easily induced to join a Community in which their own rights are not amply guarded, and means taken to protect them from injustice, either from the Community or its officers. The Community best protects itself by providing ample protection from its Individual-members; thus presenting inducements to the most prudent to join it, and *not* presenting much opportunity for the selfish to impose upon others.

CHAP. II. BY CHARTER.

A legal charter should be provided at the outset. This will tend to secure the co-operation of capitalists, and prevent unjust lawsuits by outsiders or seceders. It would also tend to hold the society together, if there were much property. Most of the property of any association may be so arranged by charter, that it may be retained by those members, however few, who remain faithful to the society and its chartered objects: but equity would not allow a Commune to push such a rule too far.

Charters might probably be obtained, granting incorporation to co-operative publishing societies, or other trades, co-operative boarding-houses, life and trust companies, beneficial associations, a Community church, or even *pairs* of monastic institutions. A fully developed charter should contain a selection of the powers usually granted to each or most of the above-named societies.

All donations and bequests to the Commune, and such portions of their shares for each stockholder, as ought properly to revert to the Commune at death, and many incidentals, should be bound for the perpetuation of the original Commune, under the charter.

Seceding shareholders might sell such shares as were in excess of a certain defined amount; but in a general secession, shares would have a very low value. Thus, the attempt of even a majority, to break up the Commune, might in the end result in increasing the pecuniary means of those who remained faithful. But this does not apply to the equitable division of a Commune, next to be spoken of.

Equitable provision should be made in the charter, for a minority, of reasonable strength, to secede in an orderly way, and form themselves into an independent Community, taking their full share of property and responsibilities. Because, if men or women in reasonable numbers and strength, were forcibly restrained from seceding, they would be apt to find some way to break up the Commune, or vex it greatly.

CHAP. III. SUBSTITUTES FOR EXPLICIT CHARTERS.

As it may sometimes occur that legal charters could not be obtained, when the objects were known, it may then be advisable to have the affairs conducted in the name of, and by *trustees*, legally constituted. But this is not so safe from Individual-liability. In other cases perhaps it may be advisable to obtain a charter as a Life and Trust and Health Company, or as a Building Association, or as a Co-operative Store, Factory, Farm or Boarding-house, or other co-operative enterprise for some business which the Community intends to and will actually follow; or, obtain several of such charters; and under such charters it might also accomplish most of the schemes of a worthy Commune, except divorces. Also some of the dangers may be guarded against by making contracts with members, for full services at low wages, and for incomes and loans at a merely nominal interest, and signing a full release in consideration of board and the other privileges:—and by capitalists giving powers of attorney to the trustees to collect income; and so on. Nothing illegal is here proposed; but only the best legal methods and counsel suggested to be sought, whereby to avoid the present unnatural and unjust difficulties of obtaining *corporate* existence. See Corporation.

SUB-DIVISION II.

APPLICATION AND RECEPTION OF NEW MEMBERS.

CHAP. I. PREPARATORY STEPS TOWARDS MEMBERSHIP.

Besides the regular members, there might be allowed an outside "contributing" membership, made up of those giving not less than one-tenth of their income. This might be invested either in the common stock of the association, or for its life insurance fund, or for the maintenance of its women and children. Not much dependence could be placed on this outside membership, although it might often lead persons to become full members.

The applicant for regular membership should present, in writing, an application to be a boarder or employe, with a brief sketch of his life, and a list of his relatives and friends, —the object being, to set forth the persons to whom he refers, and the opportunities such referees have had of knowing about him.

Unworthy persons are very shrewd, in concealing all reference to the very persons whom the society wants most to see; and worthy persons are apt to overlook those whom it is best to see. Certain officers should be appointed to give advice to applicants desiring admission. Great care is required as to the application; because, after a person knows that his application has been received at a regular meeting of the Commune, it should then be utterly improper for him to urge the society any further in regard to the matter, but he should quietly await the result,—acceptance, or being dropped, as the case may be. If approved, two or a few examiners should question the applicant on his knowledge of the principles of the society.

Among the terms of admission should be the prescribed society pledges, (anti-rum, anti-tobacco, &c.) including absolute abstinence from the betrayal of the rights of Family or Sex. There should also be pledges to prefer the Commune to any other society or social obligation (next to the Family), or else to notify the Commune immediately of any change to the contrary thereof: and immediately to leave unless requested by the Community to remain.

A male over twelve years of age, should seldom be received, unless when he has some very near female relative received, either at the same time, or previously; or when he can deposit good security. Purity requires some such rules.

Excellent character should be proved, for order, morals, virtue, truth, kindness, and reverence; also contentment with the station in life. He should also *prove* non-extravagance, non-use of spirits, tobacco, or other drugs; should believe in a few fundamental religious principles, and in the silent worship, as one good method; and resolve to obey all the commandments of God, and the order of the Commune.

Health reform is a preparation, and the health reforming "homes" are beginnings and types of the modes of life.

CHAP. II. PROBATIONARY RESIDENCE AND LIFE-EXPERIENCE.

If approved, the applicant might become a probationer, a boarder, a boarding scholar, or an employe, upon signing pledges of good order, and upon depositing as security, such reasonable sum as he could.

The applicant should not make any request for admission, during the probationary state. If he tires in waiting the decision of the society, he can withdraw; and the society may refund his pledges and release him, say nine or twelve months after his withdrawal, and after deducting charges and expenses.

If approved on probation, the member might be invited to a conference with two or three special officers, men of religious experience, and of reliable secrecy, to hear his experience or life-statement.

CHAP. III. AFFIRMATIONS, OATHS AND COVENANTS.

If the officers deem the statement sincere and satisfactory, they should so report, and the full pledges of the society should be presented and signed. The pledges should furthermore provide, that the member will forever abstain from all force and law against the society, or against any member, for any matter occurring during said membership; and of desiring to live a life of sinless faith and pure love. The pledge should also contain a promise against using any disorderly or tricky means against the harmony of the society, at any time, and especially in case of dissatisfaction or desire to leave; and if dissatisfied, that he will leave quietly and honorably, and that he will faithfully endeavor to follow the rules of the association, as long as he continues a member. He should also state briefly, his principal reasons for joining the order: and should pledge that he does and will give the claims of this society, the preference over those of any other voluntary society, or Corporation:—or failing in that,—will leave voluntarily, unless requested by the society to remain notwithstanding.

He should also pledge himself to have all disputes settled by arbitration in the agreed manner. The pledge or covenant should be made so as to stand as "good in law" as it was possible to be made, and be as binding on honor and conscience also. But perhaps bona-fide *loans* (not being security for good behavior) to the association, might be excepted from these terms of the covenant for arbitration.

A sealed agreement should be made in regard to all children entitled to the benefits of the society, that their parents do and will bind them to the association, to the full ages allowed by law, or else repay to the association all costs and charges, before taking them away.

CHAP. IV. ACTUAL INITIATION.

After taking the oath or affirmation, and agreement, the applicant should subscribe and pay, for as many shares of stock as had been agreed upon.

The actual admission of every member should be under a ritual and set form, and with the solemnity of marriage, or of joining church. In the rites, the general pledges of the member (above mentioned) should be read, and avowed by him in detail. The rite and form ought to contain plain and artless solemnities, calculated to discourage unsuitable persons from joining. Higher grades of membership and initiation, might be provided for afterwards, if desired. And the pledges should be "upon honor" as well as upon conscience and religion.

CHAP. V. DISCERNMENT OF CHARACTER.

In this sort of judgment, the instinctive spirit of God must perhaps be mainly looked to, for guidance. Every religious society is bound to do good to others; and therefore, a real willingness on the part of the applicant, to receive good influences, is worthy of some consideration.

It will probably be found, that some members can detect some spiritual characteristics; whilst others, again, can detect other spiritual characteristics. The signs of human character, as set forth in Phrenology and Physiognomy, also in gait, dress, manners, handwriting, &c., should be studied. But a scientific knowledge of human nature is yet unattained; and many of the worst persons can make themselves very agreeable. The study of human nature belongs to that part of our science which we call "The Individual."

CHAP. VI. INSTRUCTION NEEDED CONCERNING COMMUNISM.

Communism is so entirely different from the worldly life, that it can be understood only as a collective whole. It is difficult to enable even religious people to understand the peculiar nature of religious Communities. The Fourierite and Socialistic schemes are apt to be understood. Then, either materialistic economies, or spiritualistic licentiousness, are chiefly expected.

All human institutions, even the worst, contain equilibrata or balancing powers. Persons brought up from childhood, in good Communities, would understand and appreciate these balancing powers, and mutual advantages; but, other persons would need to have pretty thorough and deep instruction about them,—an instruction nearly as new and great, as converts from heathenism need, in regard to Christianity itself. Everything is so different from their preconceived ideas, that one scarcely knows where to *begin* the explanation.

Among the best means of diffusing the true light on these subjects; one, would be the composition of CATECHISMS OF COMMUNISM, giving synoptical views of the main principles. The answers should be simple, yet comprehensive. Another means would be New Testaments, with revisions and comments as the new light requires; so that Christians may prove and confirm these deeply scriptural ideas, by their daily devotional readings.

CHAP. VII. SUMMARY OF PRECAUTIONS.

The Community's principal protection from unsafe applications, will probably be found, in adhering with great closeness, to a purely moral and religious basis; yet making that basis sit closely upon Natural Theology, and upon the practical "mystic" (so-called), that is, the interior life.

In examining applicants, the object is to judge of their fitness. The examinations should be searching, and contain cross-examinations; remembering, that what persons are least willing to have discussed, are the very things that the society is aiming to find out, namely, the worst faults. But persons without faults, are not to be expected. The great difficulty is, that while rewards ought to be ready for the devoted, yet the knowledge thereof would open the way to pretenders. We would obviate this, by *not* making *direct* devotion either to God or the Community, a practical test; but by endeavoring to find a few easy, yet strong tests; and by having customs in the Commune, which would be distasteful to seekers of worldliness or selfish pleasures, but desirable and helpful to the earnestly devoted ones.

SUB-DIVISION III.

GENERAL TESTS AND QUALIFICATIONS.

CHAP. I. CHOICE-COMBINATIONS OF VIRTUES.

§ 1. *Harmony of Kindness and Truth.*

The particular point of this chapter, is, to select such peculiar combinations of virtues, as will prove the most excellence, from the fewest number of elementary virtues in the combination.

The point now is, not so much, that the single virtues here brought together, would, if taken separately, be pre-eminent above all others; but that the peculiar combination of them in the same Individual, is what is so rare, and so convincing.

Let us take as our first combination, the co-existence of kindness and truth. The whole gospel is summed up by St. John, into grace and truth. Grace implies love to man, and at least reverence to God. And these two are desired to be found co-existing with an uncommon degree of truthfulness. But in the world, kind people are very apt to be insincere and untrue; whilst truthful people are apt to be rough, harsh and unfeeling. But when the two co-exist, there is a desired and rare combination of virtues.

§ 2. *Doing to and Expecting from Others, as We would They should do, as to Us.*

This rule requires a harmony of soul between our expectations from others, and our degree of readiness to fulfill our duties to them. Most all of the tests expressing harmony and balance, between things which are generally out of balance, are very strong; so that one or two of those harmonies seem to express a person's fitness for the first steps of Communism. In the world, those who expect the most, fulfill the least.

§ 3. *Attention to Inward Character, together with the Outward.*

Another test is, whether a person is seeking to improve only his outward life, or that, and his inward life also. This can be determined in a brief way, (as a general thing), only by the candid statements of the applicant himself. But time will reveal even this.

§ 4. *Combination of Purity and Humility.*

Another pair of tests is, sexual purity together with spiritual humility. Earnest religious people often err, by escaping from sins against one of these, to sins against the other one. But it is useless to speak of these things by particulars.

§ 5. *Intellectual Appreciation and Affection, both needed.*

The Communist should have high intellectual appreciation, either of the moral principles of the Commune, or else of the personal character of its members, especially of its leaders. He should also have one active emotional love, either for the moral principles of the Commune, or for its chief members. He should also be found to have, both, one intellectual and one emotional preparation; that is, if he loves the persons engaged, he should appreciate the principles; or if he only appreciates the persons, he should love the principles, at the first.

§ 6. *Attachment to the Spirit, and Detachment from the Form.*

One rare combination of good qualities, is, attachment to the spirit, and detachment from the form. Persons who have a blind attachment to forms and ceremonies, could succeed only in such a Community as was composed of persons of the same denomination, and that, too, a pretty formal one. Other persons are apt to neglect, both the form and the spirit. What marks the man fit for the best Christian society, is a combination of attachment to the spirit and detachment from the letter: not scrupulousness in little things, with carelessness about the great matters of duty.

§ 7. *Solitude and Sociability.*

Most great and good men, and most of the ancient Communities, exhibit much of this valuable combination, namely solitude and sociability; and the same is true of the successful modern ones, generally. Solitude is sought because it is quiet, and favorable to spiritual rest and growth, and to the soul's communings with God, and to hearing His voice within. But the solitude, that is thus valuable, comes not from misanthropy, or scorn, or secret designs on our fellow-beings; and consequently, appreciates society when thrown into it, and is quite congenial. It realizes the full advantages and enjoyments of morally good society, and all the more, as change from habitual solitude. It is particularly marked, by enjoying society itself, *without* conversation, and by mere sympathy, instinct, and company-presence: yet loves to listen as well as talk, not chiefly for knowledge to accomplish designs, but for love of seeing and helping others to enjoy themselves.

CHAP. II. DISCONNECTED TESTS.

§ 1. *Insincerity purged by Secession in Communism.*

Sincerity is to be proved, by willingness to endure the frowns of fortune, or the contempt of the world. The history of the world shows, that nearly all progress has been, by revolutions against established prejudices, and against religious governments,

—by revolutions, whether physical or moral, led by small bands of enthusiasts. The most successful means of progress thus far, have been the formation of new and despised bands of earnest spiritual men, with new ideas. But in proportion as rulers and majorities rely more on moral suasion, and less on force; just so, may we indulge hope of the dawn of a new era. A Community therefore should allow and provide for reasonable secessions.

One good way to hinder secessions, is to endeavor to correct its own faults, and to perfect the Commune, and ever to keep it open for progress and improvement. But the way must be left open for new Communes to separate from the old, on equitable terms.

§ 2. *Freedom from Selfish Prejudices.*

Another general test of fitness, is, finding persons who have nearly overcome the prejudices peculiar to their own locality, sex, or class of society,—also their church, and political party. This test is more certain, when such freedom is the result of humility, and of respect and affection for Mankind; and is not misanthropy. Such men will of course be rather cosmopolitan and "unfashionable."

§ 3. *Virtuous Habits Independently of seeking Communism.*

Another test is, that the applicant, before entering a Commune, should have an established character for the principal habits or virtues necessary, so far as virtues are easily attainable in the usual state of society.

§ 4. *Continual Aim for Individual-Improvement in All Things.*

This is another general test; and this tendency in the Individual, strives to do things PERFECTLY. The habit of endeavoring to improve, must however, be carefully distinguished from that concealed effort to rule, and to be great, which is apt to assume and counterfeit the real virtue of improvement.

§ 5. *Personal Compatibility.*

Another test is, compatibility of temper with those already constituting the Commune; for persons may possess great virtues, and yet not be compatible for intimate association. The degree of incompatibility can only be ascertained by practical acquaintance; and this might be obtained, either by boarding in a co-operative boarding-house, or by transacting business with members of the Commune, as special partners.

§ 6. *Obedience.*

Nothing can compensate for incompatibility, except reverence for and obedience to the Commune; and personal good temper, in the Individual. The three great requisites of the Roman orders are, chastity, poverty, and obedience. In modern times, unselfishness will stand instead of poverty; married virtue and moderation will fulfill chastity; but nothing can be a substitute for obedience. Some persons might be admitted, who would enter a Commune as good *pupils,* willing to obey discipline, and desirous to learn. To such, a suitable Commune would be the best of schools. It would be a real UNIVERSITY.

§ 7. *Contentment.*

As contentment is one of the primal virtues, able to fit men for Communism, it must happen that people's desire for Communism will generally be in the *inverse* proportion to their fitness for it. Hence candidates must be sought out and called, even as Jesus called his first followers, namely, singly and in particular. St. John says, Jesus "knew what was in man." Doubtless Jesus was a superior and instinctive judge of human and Individual character. And to this, probably, was owing much of his success. Children and men of childlike disposition, are often very superior instinctive judges of character. Nor is the final desertion by Judas, any proof of mistake by Jesus: for Judas probably, until a very late period of Jesus' career, was "the right man in the right place." And Dr. Adam Clarke thinks that Judas was finally "saved." But we cannot accept that, in the sense the Dr. meant it.

§ 8. *Living according to Utility.*

A life that is really guided according to utility, manifests that important qualification, in several ways. The person acts and performs and loves,—and judges things and persons, according as *they* act and perform and love,—in accordance with utility, —and *not* in accordance with mere "looks," or appearances. Beauty that cannot prove its *high* utility, will have but small favor in his eyes.

Such a life must necessarily be founded upon, or be accompanied by, a strong *Desire to be Useful.* This desire to be useful, is one of the great tests of fitness for Communism; and manifests itself in taking voluntarily and contentedly, whatever position a person's character, and past deeds, intellectual and moral, qualify him for. But persons "brimful" of the theory, that all are equal, of all sexes and ages and conditions; but who have no superiority in learning, talents or wealth, ought to be kindly admonished that they would not feel themselves at home in a Community; or if *they* would, *nobody* else in it, would.

§ 9. *Doing Unpleasant Duties.*

The habit of present self-denial, for greater future gratification, is a good sign; as it exhibits the self-providing faculties at work in the right direction. The Commune should be specially informed of the particulars, in which the applicant has been in the habit of cheerfully performing unpleasant duties. Duty-seekers, not pleasure-seekers, are who are wanted.

§ 10. *Purity of Bodily Health.*

A strong test of fitness, is the existence of general and habitual fair health, or at least freedom from positively *foul* diseases; yet without rough robustness. This purity, when truly a Christian virtue, is connected with diminishing faith in Doctors or medicines, and with increasing faith in the curative power of resignation and obedience. Some have called it the prayer-cure or the faith-cure.

§ 11. *Applicants to Agree with the Proposed Society, more than with Any Other.*

As before said, all the qualifications for a Communist, are well summed up by that eminent Catholic, "Father Baker," saying, that "*he* is fit for a Community, who follows the object of it, by living according to the spirit of it." Hence, when it can be shown that any Community is nearest to the views and aims of the applicant, *then* there is strong ground to believe, that the duty of the Commune is to receive him.

§ 12. *Tests should be Stringent in Proportion to Intellect of Applicant.*

Much more correctness should be required in the Doctrines of Morals, of Christianity, and of Communism, of persons whose ambition and education cause them to lead others, than of uninfluential persons. It would however be an error, to allow less strict actual morality, in the subaltern, or in any. As to morality, all must be equal before ITS demands. For further suggestions see pp. 70 to 76.

CHAP. III. OF SPECIAL TESTS.

There are a large number of special tests, some examples of which might be given, if there were time and convenience; but it would not be desirable for any Commune to give to the public, too minute a description of its tests, as that might assist parasites to counterfeit or pretend to them, and thus to obtain wrong entrance into it. Besides, these special tests would vary, according to the varied aims of the Association.

We will only give some suggestions, as to the number and classification of these special tests now spoken of.

Of the two sexes, no doubt remains of their distinctness in many traits of character. As to ages, three classes can be considered; viz., (1) youths below puberty, without completed education; (2) persons in the prime of life; (3) persons in the decline of life, who are looking forward to a state of dependence on others. Then, as regards social position, we cannot count less than three classes; viz., (1) those who employ domestic help; (2) those who are the domestic helpers; (3) and those who are neither, but who live an independent or semi-civilized sort of a life; doing their own work, but not the work of any one else. All of these classes may be more or less sub-divided; and the various sub-divisions would range from thirty to sixty; and might be considered under the head of "Social Circle."

The moderate consideration of all the tests, should occupy the attention of the leaders of any progressive movement; and the substance of them should be written and preserved among the oldest and best tried leaders. The possession of such knowledge should be held as sacred, as, of other family-secrets, and also be secured by covenants "good" in religion, in honor, and "*in law.*"

CHAP. IV. PRACTICAL SIMPLICITY COMING OUT OF THIS MULTIPLICITY.

In regard to each of these different classes, it is quite probable that there might easily be pointed out, a few virtues, that would fully prove the Individuals in that class to be fit for Communism, which would not at all prove fitness in other classes. And so also, one or a few *vices* might be pointed out, that would evidently betoken unfitness in one class, that would not be conclusive proofs for unfitness in the other classes.

Thus it will be observed, that both here when we seek *Special* Tests, as well, as before, when seeking the *General* Tests, we aim to find one, or a few tests, which shall alone be sufficient for the particular Individual-person to whom they are to be applied. Thus we avoid requiring ourselves to enter into an almost endless examination of details: and out of multiplicity, aim to bring simplicity; and out of width of theory, aim to bring directness of practical application.

MAIN DIVISION III.

THE INDIVIDUAL'S GUARDS AND PROTECTION AGAINST THE COMMUNE.

SUB-DIVISION I.

FROM THE COMMUNE AS A SOCIETY.

CHAP. I. GENERAL APPLICATION TO THIS USE, OF ALL THE FOREGOING TREATISE.

All that has been said before, in this article headed "Limited Communism," may be re-read with this object, namely,—to see how far this security is guarded. The General IDEA, and The FOUNDATIONS of the Commune, should both provide protection for the Individual, as well as for the Commune. Hence this Third MAIN DIVISION will be very brief.

There should be a suitable and legal charter, and a *paid-up capital*, as in other human Corporations. Such things constitute a security against the non-success of the association, and against fraudulent Individuals.

If the Commune is successful in protecting itself from improper members, it will, in itself, possess a character and an excellence, furnishing a strong security for Individual-rights. The Commune must, as before said, also furnish adequate facility for reasonable secession. This itself is one of the strongest protections of Individuals and of minorities. Even expulsion should never forfeit any member's property, further than for actual expenses, damages, or other liabilities. No member should be tried by any rule or principle, which he had not previously assented to; nor which he dissents from, if within a reasonable time after its adoption, he protests, and gives notice of his intention to withdraw on account of it.

The whole organization of the Commune, should give evidence that it does not want property, but persons, and affections; and that it even does not want *them* in a selfish way.

The rights and feelings of all, must be respected. A Commune should not allow any of such coercive power over inmates, preventing their withdrawal, as is said to be exercised by some Communities. Coercion or force is against one of *our* first principles, and against the first principles of unselfishness.

The Commune should aim, in principle, to be like a large Christian FAMILY, where benevolence and mutual good feelings, hold all together voluntarily, and cheerfully. Care must be taken against the love of power, or exercising it for its own sake.

SUB-DIVISION II.

PROTECTION OF THE INDIVIDUAL-MEMBERS FROM THE RULERS AND OFFICERS, AS PERSONS.

CHAP. I. EACH OF THE DIFFERENT POWERS SHOULD HAVE ITS SHARE OF OFFICERS.

The principal danger is from improper officers, or from their improper conduct. Quite often, the worst men get the highest offices. The chief prevention is, forming a government of separate parts, so that each of those parts shall represent different rights, and different interests; not a balance of legalities, but a balance of powers.

CHAP. II. OFFICERS SHOULD BE SUPERIOR IN THE SPECIAL VIRTUES.

Of course, all the virtues specially fitting for Communism, should be found in the officers, in a high degree. Probably the special religious organizations within the Commune, might be allowed simply a *veto* on all, or on some, movements or laws. But it would be unwise to allow any, or much, direct legislation, or many appointments, to be made by the church-power.

CHAP. III. THE GOVERNMENT OF THE OFFICERS SHOULD BE VIRTUAL, BEFORE IT IS FORMAL.

If the Commune succeed in obtaining a sufficient proportion of *suitable* members, they would produce a feeling and a tendency, to love and honor the influence of the most suitable persons. Thus the good and the wise would be virtually and morally the leaders, before they were officially so.

CHAP. IV. GENERAL LIST OF THE VIRTUES REQUIRED.

Good leaders should possess most of the following qualifications:—able in the criticism of Individual-character; not given to their own crotchets; able to brook opposition charitably; averse to all kinds of evil; parental in their rule, self-sacrificing, free from the lust of rule; acquainted, themselves, with many sorrows; free contributors to the Commune; who really seek assistants devoted to the Commune's special ideas; prompt to welcome other leaders; fond of personal improvement; previously successful in obtaining virtuous distinction; humble, unselfish, and desirous of the success of the enterprise, according to the will of God.

CHAP. V. KNOWLEDGE OF SOCIAL SCIENCE.

As Communism is the quintessence of all Social Science; therefore a highly important test for the leaders of *thought*, is leadership in, and a competent knowledge of, the fundamental principles of Social Science; and, even for the *executive* officers, a common sense instinctive knowledge of this science, is needed.

CHAP. VI. OFFICERS SHOULD BE TALENTED IN SELECTING NEW MEMBERS.

The most important and difficult work, is, to *select* new members. It will not *do* for officers or examiners to adhere to an exact and lengthy code of rules. Neither should they proceed utterly without rules. Choosing applicants by the light of general rules, selected according to the foregoing tests, to be personally applicable, seems to be the medium. Some of the leaders should be men of wide and cosmopolitan sympathies, even about religion,—in order to fit them for selecting. Because, as yet, Romanism, Buddhism, and crotchety and *liberal* Christianity, have practically done more for Communism, than our common or general evangelical Protestantism.

Most or all of the Protestant Communes have been too restrictive, and too selfish; so that some have already become mere fossils; and perhaps only two of them are on the increase. But yet, it would seem, that their frequent efforts to open their doors more liberally to new members, have endangered their own peace, or continuity. This proves the great need of more talent in the selecting of new members, or else the need of more social science, or of both.

CHAP. VII. THE ERA PRODUCING THE BEST LEADERS, HAS NOT YET COME.

As the leaders of the successful Communes, have nearly all been theologians, it is not necessary to commend theology as a fit preparation for them; yet the leaders should be well trained in Social Science also. But as this science has not yet attained much definiteness, nor complete development, it is hardly possible that thoroughly competent leaders could yet arise. Therefore, Communities ought not to be discouraged by the failure of many immature experiments. The duty is to walk by faith. A Commune that "walks by sight but not by faith," and a selfish Commune, can never become of much use, except as special examples or illustrations of some special principles or methods.

MAIN DIVISION IV.

USES, INCLUDING ARGUMENTS AND STATISTICS OF COMMUNISM.

SUB-DIVISION I.

ARGUMENTS FROM SCRIPTURE.

CHAP. I. TEACHINGS IN SCRIPTURE.

St. Paul says, "Set your affections on things above, and not on things on the earth."

Christ taught, in Matthew, chap. vi., "Lay not up for yourselves treasures on earth, for where your treasure is, there will your heart be also." "Ye cannot serve God and mammon." In Luke xii., "Provide for yourselves bags which wax not old, a treasure in the heavens, that faileth not." Also in Luke ix. 23 and 24, we find, "whosoever will save his life, shall lose it; but whosoever will lose his life for my sake, [and the gospel's] the same shall find it. For what is a man advantaged, if he gain the whole world, and lose himself, or be cast away?" And in Matthew xix. 21, 22, "Jesus said" unto the rich young man, "If thou wilt be perfect, go and sell that thou hast, and give to the poor, and thou shalt have treasure in heaven; and come and follow me. But when the young man heard that saying, he went away sorrowful, for he had great possessions." See also Luke xvi. 19 to 31, concerning Dives and Lazarus.

The sermon on the mount, and many other of Jesus' discourses and sayings and injunctions, seem applicable only to a true Christian Commune; and such is what Jesus seems to have had in his mind, frequently, under the term kingdom of God: an ideal, which seems to underlie the teachings and discourses of his whole life, generally; and this explanation, at once turns his apparently wildest figures, into real and tangible directions for a new practical life. See Renan's Life of Jesus, chap. xix. And then, as "The Circular" has shown, the "Lord's prayer" is essentially Communistic. OUR father—THY kingdom come—AS in heaven *so* on earth—Give us *daily* bread (not wealth but sharing income)—Lead us not into temptation—Deliver us from evil (this evil world, also).

St. Paul (2 Cor. vi. 17 and 18), combines together *several* passages from the Old Testament, into one grand climax, thus;—"Wherefore come out from among them, and be ye separate, saith the Lord; and touch not the unclean thing; and I will receive you; and will be a Father unto you, and ye shall be my sons and daughters, saith the Lord Almighty."

St. Paul, the Apostle to the Gentiles; that is, to all the world besides the Jews, and therefore, to us,—is the best commentator upon Jesus. Accordingly, the foregoing words of the Apostle, are the best commentary ever yet written, on those wonderful words of Jesus, about the ever blessed virgin, his mother; and his (so called) "brethren." See Matth. xii. 49 and 50. Mk. iii. 34 and 35. And Luke viii. 21:—"And he stretched forth his hand toward his disciples, and said; Behold, my mother and my brethren! For whosoever shall do the will of my Father who is in Heaven, the same is my brother, and sister, and mother." These passages give the marrow of the whole subject, namely, the true Christian and Limited Commune, is a FAMILY of associated disciples. And this reminds us of that other beautiful passage of St. Paul, Eph. iii. 15:—"Of whom the whole FAMILY in Heaven and Earth is named." And still more politico-governmental is the passage, Eph. ii. 19:—"Now therefore ye are no more strangers and foreigners, but fellow-citizens (συμπολιται) with the saints; and, (not, as in the usual version, 'OF the household of God,' but, οικειοι) householders, or domestics, or fellow-inmates, "of God," built together, &c.

Again; St Paul, agreeing with Jesus, says, "And if there be any other commandment, it is briefly summed up in this—thou shalt love thy neighbor as thyself." But those who clamor for total Unlimited Communism, forget that the neighbor owes duties *to us*, as well as we to him. St. Paul in 1 Cor. vi. also says "Dare any of you having a matter against another, go to law before the unjust, and not before the saints? If then ye have judgment of things pertaining to this life, set them to judge, who are least esteemed in the Church." But we know that such a system of rights, as St. Paul here mentions, if given to the church by the civil law, would, by the love of gain, corrupt the church, unless in a condition of Communism. St. Paul also says "Covetousness is idolatry."

And then there is the repeated scripture-doctrine, "the friendship of the world is enmity with God": and "if any man love the world, the love of the Father is not in him." Such things point to separation from the world, "yet without going altogether out of it": and that means Limited Communism.

CHAP. II. PRACTICES IN SCRIPTURE.

The apostles had a common purse; and Judas was treasurer. "He was provoked to his final crime of selling his Master, by the dispute about the alabaster box, which Christ decided against him. He went immediately from that dispute, and made a contract to sell his Master." Bible Communism, p. 121. Thus his crime was not love of his own money, but self-will in the disposition of the association's money.

After the resurrection, the apostles and their friends, all lived together. (Acts i. 13, 15.) And then, after Pentecost,—Acts ii. 44 and 45,—"And all that believed were together, and had all things common; and sold their possessions and goods, and parted them to all men, as every man had need." See also chap. iv. 32 to 35. In Acts, chap. v. it is related, how Ananias and Sapphira were struck dead, for pretending to give in their goods to the common stock, when they withheld a part; the only instance of such vengeance in all the New Testament. In Acts vi. 1 and 2, are signs of a common table, one of the seven superintendents of which, was St. Stephen, the "first martyr." There are also allusions to a common table, in 2 Thessalonians, chap. iii.—"If any will not work, neither shall he eat":—also there are signs of a communistic meal in 1 Corinthians, (besides the sacrament.) The Mosaic semi-centennial distribution of all the lands of the Nation, is plainly of a Communistic tendency, that is to say, is a form of Limited Communism. The same may also be said of the Mosaic law forbidding farmers to glean their own fields, but allowing the poor to do it. So also, was the gathering of the manna. In fact, the church, whether Jewish or Christian, has always been largely communistic, without being totally or fanatically so. Furthermore; in Chap. IV. of this Sub-Division,—see our theory of 1 Tim. chap. v. Everybody admits that this passage recognizes the existence of a Commune of widows, perhaps deaconesses; but we claim for it a regularly organized but Limited Commune of both sexes.

The 2 Thess. chap. iii. is fairly susceptible of Communistic interpretation, as well as 1 Tim. v. And vs. 11, "walk disorderly * * * working not at all * * * busybodies," &c., all remind us of 1 Tim. v. 13. Communistic also are the phrases (vs. 10) "if any would not work, neither let him eat"; and (vs. 14) "if any man obey not our word by this epistle, note that man, and have no *company* with him," says our translation; but literally, συναναμιγνυμι means to mix up with, which seems to include much more than merely not having company with: especially as vs. 15 says, "count him not as an enemy, but admonish him as a brother." Then the "walking disorderly" of vs. 6 and 11, and rejecting St. Paul's example of working, seem to point to idleness in the Commune. And the "unreasonable men" of vs. 2, (ατοποι means *out of place*, and is a choice word here), would be those who expected to live in idleness, and upon the Commune; and so St. Paul, vs. 8, says "neither did we eat any man's bread for nought" &c.; which is the very thing he quotes in the next verse, as his example to them.

CHAP. III. SCRIPTURAL LIMITATIONS.

The Communism of Christ and of the early church, was a Limited Communism. This may be inferred from the following considerations. First: The conflicting nature of the texts and evidences usually produced, shows, that their customs then were partly Communistic, and partly not. Even Joseph of Arimathea, and the good Lydia, retained their private property. In some passages we hear the Christians spoken of as giving all away; in others, we see them only giving alms liberally. Second: When mention is made of giving all away, it is not for the purpose of sharing *capital*, as capital, to be retained; but only of selling what was immediately wanted, and giving away to the really needy. Thus, Acts ii. 45, they "parted them all as every man had need," and Acts iv. 35, "distribution was made to every man according as he had need." And even now, in any rare cases, if large numbers of fellow-Christians were suffering for the necessaries of life, the same duty would devolve upon us, of selling whatever capital was needed for the emergency. Third: We nowhere in the New Testament, read of a single case of any person actually selling or contributing *all* his property, neither of the rich young man, nor of Barnabas, nor of Ananias, nor of any other (except the widow with the two mites). Fourth: The apostles, and the rich women who traveled about with Jesus, and ministered to his necessities, only shared labors and incomes. The apostles did not sell their nets nor boats; nor the women their property nor valuables, (as far as the record goes). Fifth: Admitting that immediately after Pentecost, there was a more liberal distribution than at other times, yet the circumstances were peculiar, the like having never occurred before or since. The first disciples had been almost as one Family, for years. The mother of Jesus was still with them, and nearly all of them took to preaching, for the time: and Acts i. 14 says they "all continued with one accord." And ii. 46—"They continued daily with one accord in the temple, and breaking bread from house to house; and did eat their meat with gladness and singleness of heart." And v. 32—"The multitude of them that believed, were of one heart and one soul." They were filled with the Holy Ghost, to a marvelous degree. This both gave wisdom for the distribution, and kept aloof the hypocrites and avaricious speculators. Even Ananias and Sapphira, in Acts v. 3, were struck dead, not for withholding of their property, but for lying, and attempting to cheat the apostles by a false pretense. Sixth: Yet even in those perturbed times, and as recorded in the strongest communistic passages, there is latent evidence that the Communism was neither entire, nor absolute. Thus Acts ii. 44—"were together and had all things common,"—that is, not capital, but such things as were portable, and as they would naturally have with them, when they "were together" at a distance from their homes. And vs. 45—"sold their possessions and goods, and parted them to all as every man had need." That is, sold one thing after another, as it happened to be needed for immediate use. And Acts v. 4—"While it remained, was it not thine own? and after it was sold, was it not in thine own power?"

were words spoken to Ananias; clearly showing that the sale itself was entirely voluntary, and that he could himself personally have distributed whatever part of it he chose, if he so preferred; but he had no right to pretend to give all of that property to the apostles, when he was not doing so. Besides, the principal evil after all, perhaps, was not even the simple lie, but the *conspiracy with his wife* to do so—because Family-conspiracies are the chief bane, and most dangerous temptation, in good Communes. In Communism "they that have wives must be as though they had none," so far as impartiality goes. And the same also as to their children.

Seventh: The foregoing principles seem all touched upon at once, in a passage Acts v. 11–14, immediately after the death of Ananias and Sapphira: thus, "And great fear came upon all the church, and upon as many as heard these things. And by the hands of the apostles were many signs and wonders wrought, among the people; (and they were all with one accord in Solomon's porch. And of the rest, durst no man join himself to them. And believers were the more added to the Lord, multitudes both of men and women.")

Eighth: Nearly all the Communistic passages of the Bible, plainly show a Communism not of capital nor principal, but of labors and of board and of income. Plainly so in the Gospels and Acts; and truly so elsewhere. So with the Israelites under Moses, with the manna from heaven; and so with St. Paul, who says "If any will not work, neither let him eat."

CHAP. IV. THEORY OF 1 TIM. V. 1-25.

This difficult passage of Scripture cannot be explained by a running commentary, but only by some theory announced first, and then the texts picked out to suit it. Even the Roman explanations, although the best as yet, do not explain *all* the difficulties. My theory is, that the WHOLE chapter refers to a limited Commune, where the members resided and boarded usually, but went out into the world for their occupations, (the Commune having mixed functions),—and were supported partly by the church, for church work; and where the ministers (and their Families) frequently resided, and Timothy also. I cannot prove exactly, that *full* incomes were what the rich shared, but *that* is more likely than any other portion that can be guessed. The proof, like as in all points of science, is not demonstrative, but only cumulative; and that the proposed theory solves all the difficulties, better than any other theory as yet proposed.

But first, let us give a paragraph on a corroborative text about rich men. In 1 Tim. vi. 18. The English version is erroneous. *Ευμεταδοτους* does *not* mean "READY to distribute"; but means good givers or right givers: Alford says free givers. My theory is, that it means those who, belonging to the Commune, gave the right share, not keeping back any: (giving probably the promised portion of income). *Κοινωνικους* might mean free Communers, or persons having a *tendency* to become full Communists. In "*good* works," *καλοις* means fine or extra (works): and *εργοις* "works" means not merely deeds, but extra deeds, as achievements, &c. Then, the idea of something extra is implied, both in the adjective, and in the noun. And then the phrase "rich in good works" becomes, *rich* in *extra achievements.* In vs. 17, "God who giveth us *richly* all things *to enjoy*," may mean, limiting the Communism to current expenses, and to current consumption; the same as seems meant in the passages in Acts, mentioned above. The words to Timothy, "Them that are rich in this world," seem to mean those that have large incomes, (without regard to their capital), because,—" not trust in uncertain riches" certainly and literally means, *not hope on* (or *for*) *the uncertainty of riches;* and therefore seems to apply to men who are *not* as yet rich, but who have the opportunity to become so. This is confirmed by the hint in vs. 19, thus,—"laying up in store for themselves a good foundation against the time to come."

Now let us return to our explanation of 1 Timothy, chap. v. In vs. 8—"If any provide not for his own, and especially for those of *his own house*," *Οικειων* means domestic, belonging to a household, familiar, *friendly*, intimate, appropriate, and sometimes property, and sometimes one's home or country,—just the Greek work for a Family-Commune. The Latin has it, domesticorum, which the Rheims, translates "*domesticals.*" The Syriac has it "*them who are of the household of faith*": Murdock. The German has it, hausgenossen, i.e., "Family, lodgers, domestic-servants," literally house-fellows. That all these point to the *Syriac* as the FULLEST meaning, as it is also historically far the most ancient, (being of the second century),—is also confirmed by what follows, namely, that he who does not provide for those of his own religious Commune, " hath denied the faith, and is worse than an (infidel, i.e.) unbeliever." The *limited* Communistic interpretation is, that the members of the church must contribute, *as they are able,* to the support of their poor relations, and not leave them entirely dependent on the Commune.

The phrase in vs. 3, " *Honor* widows," means, receive them into the Commune: therefore in vs. 17, "Let the elders be counted worthy of double honor," seems to include, as one part of the double honor, the being received into its membership also. This seems to bring the " elder" of vs. 1, to be also a member of the Commune: and this again makes *all* the persons, young and old, of vss. 1 and 2, to be members of it; and this explains the otherwise *apparent jumble* there, of elders official, and elders by age; and the apparent confusion of the official *elderesses,* and the young women. All were on a par, as members of the Commune. This explains also the *apparent jumble* vs. 19 and 20—"Against an elder" &c.;—and the words "them that sin, rebuke before all," seeming to mean, not officers only, but anybody. And the phrase, "them that sin, rebuke before all, that others also may fear," seems to refer most properly, to proceedings before the Commune. This relation to the Commune, explains also, vs. 23, telling Timothy what he should drink for his "stomach's sake."

Now it would appear, that these aged widows over sixty, were not by any means the only residents of the Commune, but were like the *ministers* therein; and were to be devoted to a mixed work, of taking care of the children, and of strangers, washing the saints' feet, relieving the afflicted, &c., vs. 10. They were also expected, vs. 5, to "continue in supplications and prayers, night and day," evidently so, therefore, for the Commune, and for the church, but *not* for themselves only. And then in vs. 11, the refusal as to the younger widows, was not a refusal of them, as applying to be members of the Commune, (vss. 2 and 14), but merely a refusal to enroll (and ordain) them as *official widows,* vs. 13. The *younger ones,* (not women, as in English version, but the widows of vs. 11), were to marry and to do the house-work and govern, literally be house-masters, (vs. 14); but the elder ones were to take charge of the children, vs. 10, and to do the out-door going, instead of the young ones, vs. 13. Vs. 15 would then simply mean, that some young women had previously been enrolled for this church-work, but had thrown up their ordination vows thereunto. In vs. 6, the "living in pleasure" cannot mean merely being married, because St. Paul *directs* the younger ones to marry, vs. 14. The phrase therefore is general, and directs marital temperance among the members of the Commune.

The charge in vs. 9, that these accepted and aged official widows, should have been "the wife of one man," i.e. should not have been divorced women, and thus perhaps have had one or more divorced husbands still living,—was, to prevent the claims which such divorced husbands (who were probably heathens, or not members of the Commune) might have had upon the Commune, with the heathen civil law, or perhaps only with the sympathies of unruly mobs, which the Acts call "lewd fellows of the baser sort." It is not likely that the words "wife of one man," mean a widow whose former husband had *died* before the widowhood in question, because St. Paul approves of second marriages of the young ones, vs. 14. This interpretation is confirmed by, because it throws light upon, the charge in iii. 2, that a bishop also must be a one-wife-man, i.e. not a divorced man with a living wife in heathendom. See also Sub.-Div. III. Chap. IV. § 4. Also Sub.-Div. I. Chap. II. on 2 Thess. Chap. iii. See also our immediately following meditation on celibacy.

CHAP. V. RELATIONS TO CELIBACY.

§ 1. *On General Principles.*

When we come to the STATISTICS, we will observe the peculiarity, that all the Protestant celibate Communities, have *both* sexes in the same buildings. And the great secret of all this wonder, is, that they have discovered by instinct and experience, the great happiness which the two sexes confer upon each other, by their mere presence and association; and the great aid thereby obtainable to holy living. A prominent Shaker officer and gentleman (Elder Evans) expresses the feeling as one of "indescribable joy." It is probably somewhat like the comfort or exhilaration which very virtuous and holy "lovers" enjoy, during courtship. Whether we call it "magnetism," or what, its purity and power cannot be questioned. It differs from the celibate feeling, when the sexes are separated, by *this* being more magnetic, soothing and restful; whereas the *other*, rather tends to stimulation and unrest and discontent. Both history and experience confirm the idea, that the presence of both sexes gives courage *to both*, and not to the woman only; and is therefore the result of mutual *instinct*, rather than merely of a desire to please the other sex. And the only Catholic devotees allowed to marry, are the Military Orders. Also the presence of women in military and other hospitals, throws considerably more light upon this subject, of the power of their *simple presence* and attendance, to strengthen, comfort and encourage, than is generally supposed. Jesus himself was fond of Martha and Mary.

Accordingly, the common arguments for a select few in the consecrated life, to follow celibacy, are so strong, as to justify, and perhaps often to require it, when the persons are residing in the common "world," out of Communes: but IN Communes, are the very positions where celibacy would neither be necessary, nor be required; yet would be easiest to practice virtuously.

There must also be an admission here, of the great and peculiar *Individual*-strength, comfort and joy, obtained by virtuous celibacy when the sexes are *apart*,—an exhilaration like as from wine, without intoxication. Its joys are corroborated by both Catholic and Protestant celibates. And to this must also be added the increased devotion to moral and divine uses, made possible by being freed from the *usual worldly* relations.

But *Communes really allow* of such arrangements as would promote, *almost* as much freedom from Family-cares and trammels, as does the entirely celibate life. And the "life and health" guarantees of successful Communism, would fully justify an abandonment of all anxiety about wife or children, in case the man should die, or fail in health. But we must carry the subject to an entirely higher plane of thought.

Right marriage is a *divine sacrament* to *both* parties,—that is, such marriage as St. Paul describes in that same passage wherein he alludes to it as a sacrament (Eph. v. 21–33). And marriage is particularly the sacrament *unto unselfishness*, vs. 28, "he that loveth his wife loveth *himself*." Of the sacramental marriage which St. Paul describes, he says, "as Christ is the head of the church * * * the Saviour of the body; * * * church, subject unto

Christ, so let the wives be to their own husbands in every thing," (vs. 23 and 24). And vs. 33,—the husband is to love his wife (that is, such a wife as that?), and the wife is to reverence her husband. The 32d verse concludes it to be a sacrament, by saying, "This is a great mystery." The word, and the only word, in Greek, for sacrament, is mystery. And what *we* call sacraments, the Greek church calls mysteries.

Marriage therefore, being the express mystery or sacrament of unselfishness, and of producing mutual love, is peculiarly a proper ordinance for Communism:—just as, on the other hand, the powerful tendency to idolatry in marriage, specially needs Communism to counteract it, for the sake of the higher life. And this argument does not depend on the scripture texts *alone*, but is founded on nature and on history; and therefore it is placed here among the Arguments on *General* Principles.

Again, marriage is the sacrament of unselfishness, by cultivating the *parental feelings*. The parental feelings, when held in moderation, are truly divine, and are powerful cultivators of the divine life in the soul. How many hardened parents there are, who are restored to lives of virtue, by the influence of their children! And how many are withheld from lives of crime, by the fear of disgracing their children! The temperate love of children, comes nearest the love of God for Mankind, and best exemplifies that love in the soul, of all human instrumentalities. The great thing to be done in this, as in the love between husband and wife, is, to keep it so modified that it shall not become idolatrous. The love of children, however, is a love which those can partake of, who have no children of their own; namely, by devoting themselves to the care of other people's children. And this is a pre-eminent argument why Family-Communes should exist, such as we advocate, and suppose are spoken of in 1 Tim. chap. v. For in these, even the celibates may fulfill and enjoy their celibacy, and still partake of some of the greatest uses and joys of the Family-life. And by thus dividing the cares and joys and affections, of training children, the parental idolatry would cheerfully and happily be much subdued. Family-Communes are the only places where are possible, happy schools for children; keeping them under observation and control, all the time; yet in joy and freedom, as the Kindergartens *aim* to do.

Again, the writer cannot see why the best and most improved Individuals, of the human race, or those supposed to be the best, should set themselves against marriage; and disdain to perpetuate their *better kind.* For if the grace of God is as good and efficient, as it is generally supposed to be, it ought to be able to conquer selfishness in the Family, as well as out of it. In fact, until the grace of God *does* that, it must be considered as not yet having its perfect influence.

The celibate tendency in the higher life, is, to be sure, partly a reaction against intemperance and idolatry, and partly an instinctive shrinking from the usual and well-known selfishness, in married or Family life; and thus, is an expression of the moral weakness of human nature, in Individuals and associations; but most of all, it is an attempt to make transient emotions, the permanent habits of life; as indeed the "revivalists" do, in religion generally.

But another reason against celibacy in the Communes, at least in the Protestant ones, is, the inability to perpetuate the Commune itself, unless by its natural increase of population. Because, in modern times and among a people trained in the *natural* sciences, there cannot be that reverence for celibacy, there formerly was; considered as a virtue in itself: and hence, the celibate Communes fail to draw adult members, in sufficient numbers to maintain their own prosperity; and the taking of children does not succeed, because Communism is itself a development suited rather to the more mature conditions of mind, and morals, and requires *parents to lead* their children into it.

§ 2. *On Scripture Grounds.*

It is said that *the Scriptures teach celibacy.* Let us examine the alleged texts. (1.) Argument: Matth. i. 18 and Luke i. 34,—are understood to teach that Jesus was "born of a virgin." Answer; Yes; but that virgin was *married;* and so at the very time of the *birth.* (2.) Argument: Jesus never married. Answer; the scripture does *not say* so; but, admitting that he was not, yet Peter was, and Paul, 1 Cor. ix. 5, claimed the right to be, if he chose to.

(3.) Argument: Matth. xxii. 30,—"In the resurrection they neither marry nor are given in marriage, but are as the angels of God." Answer; But that is spoken of the state *after* death and resurrection; and Luke xx. 36 adds the evidently philosophical reason, "neither do they die any more." (4.) Argument: Luke xx. 34 and 35 speak in a way that might easily be interpreted of high and low spiritual conditions in *this* world. Answer; Yes, but those phrases are to be interpreted by the parallel passage in Matthew, and by the 36th, the very next verse, in Luke himself, and by the context in both places. (5.) Argument: Yes, but this vs. 36 also speaks of the celibates as being "equal unto the angels" and as being "the children of God." Answer; But immediately he adds "being children of the resurrection." (6.) Argument: But this latter phrase "children of the resurrection" may also be figurative: Answer; Hardly; because the whole parable here, is upon the subject of a LITERAL resurrection, and is to prove that the marriages of this life do *not* necessarily affect or reach to the life beyond. (7.) Argument: Well, if the parable is *mainly* to prove that the marriages of this life, do not reach to the life beyond; then those persons are *wrong* who, from the words, "in the resurrection they neither marry nor are given in marriage," infer that there will *not be any* marriage in Heaven. Answer; Perhaps so; but we have no means of knowing certainly. The Swedenborgians hold to a doctrine of eternal marriage in Heaven. And as sex seems to pervade all nature, their hypothesis is probable. But, observe, the *scripture* says nothing about it; and *that* is what we are talking about now.

(8.) Argument: Mark x. 29 and 30, say, "There is no man that hath left house, or brethren, or sisters, or father, or mother, or wife, or children, or lands, for my sake and the gospel's; but he shall receive a hundredfold now in this time, houses, and brethren, and sisters, and mothers, and children, and lands, with persecutions; and in the world to come, eternal life." Observe, says the celibate, that in vs. 30, wives are omitted from the rewards "in this time." Answer; As the Saviour in vs. 29 is speaking in the *plural,* if he had said wives, plural, it might have been construed as teaching polygamy, or some sort of "complex marriage." The parallel passages Matth. xix. 29 and Lk. xviii. 29, speak in the *singular;* but do not particularize *at all,* as to the rewards. Perhaps Mark (in x. 29 and 30) changed the form from singular to plural, of his own memory; and so, of his own judgment, had to omit "wives" from the rewards, to avoid misinterpretations of polygamy or "complex marriage." (9.) Argument: 1 Cor. vii. 8, 26, 32, 33, 34 and 38, seem to teach the advantage of celibacy. Answer; Repeatedly there, St. Paul insists that he speaks *not* by command of the Lord, but only by permission: see vs. 6, 25, 26 and 40. And there St. Paul spoke chiefly on account of the peculiarity of the age, when Christians were persecuted unto death. In vs. 26 St. Paul says, "I suppose therefore that this is good for the present distress."

(10.) Argument: 1 Tim. v. 9, says, "Let not a widow be taken into the number, under threescore years old": and vs. 11, "But the younger widows refuse: for when they have begun to wax wanton against Christ, they will marry." Answers; (*a*) It is folly to apply this, to the case of any *under* 60 years of age, by St. Paul's own limitation: (*b*) It is often supposed that in vs. 9, the woman must have never had only one husband, but yet vs. 11 expressly orders the young widows to marry a second time: and therefore it means wife of only one man at a time; (*c*) vs. 3, 8, and 16, clearly show, that these widows were to be supported by the church. And it would never do for a *poor* church, to undertake to support all its poor widows, with privilege to marry again and thereby have families, children, and perhaps worthless husbands, or quarrelsome husbands, who would entangle them in lawsuits with the heathen, and so on, and perhaps all to be dependent on the church. (*d*) The arrangement seems probably to have been a mere peculiarity (like the advice not to marry, spoken of above), for the then existing distress. The covenant of the Commune may have been simply this: A poor and persecuted church agrees to take and support a few widows, such as absolutely have no one else to depend upon; but in order to limit the number and responsibility, it imposes the condition of 60 years of age, and a promise not to enter into any Family-arrangements again; (two conditions which may properly go together), and then a third condition, namely, that they would devote themselves to the Lord's work, as compensation for being thus received. (*e*) Remember that St. Paul repeatedly commands the bishops and elders and deacons, to be married. (See Tim. and Titus.) Therefore, celibacy for itself, is not necessary to church officials; and therefore, some other reason than that, must be the ground of this charge about the widows, even if at this late day we cannot tell what that particular reason is. But for an additional explanation, see Theory of 1 Tim. v., Sub-Div. I., Chap. IV.

(11.) Argument: Rev. xiv. 4, says, "These are they which were not defiled with women, for they are virgins." Answers; (*a*) This passage is spoken, of a choice *select* number of the saved: vs. 4—" the first fruits unto God and to the Lamb," and vs. 5—" without fault and without guile." (*b*) It is useless for persons who have faults and guile, or are *not the "first* fruits," to quote this passage. (*c*) It explains, itself, the meaning of virgin, namely, "*not defiled*"; but the scripture nowhere teaches that marriage or its affections defile; but says, "marriage is honorable *in all*," etc. *Read* Heb. xiii. 4.

(12.) Argument: Some argue that because Adam and Eve needed garments, immediately after their fall, therefore their sin was a violation of duty as celibates. Answers; (*a*) Sins of eating and drinking are quite sufficient to affect the passions, without anything further. (*b*) Sin in perfect beings would be *as* likely to take this, as its first development, anyhow. (*c*) Even if there had been a premature violation of celibacy, it would not prove, that God had intended their celibacy to endure any longer than their probation. (*d*) God made them, as all other animals, and even vegetables, subject to marital conditions, and therefore intended such, sooner or later.

SUB-DIVISION II.

ARGUMENTS FROM THE UTILITIES OF COMMUNISM.

CHAP. I. ITS GOOD TENDENCIES IN GENERAL.

The principal general argument for Limited Communism, is its tendency to promote the highest good of human nature. In putting down selfishness, it leads to a higher Christian life. It combines the elements of church, state, and Family; furnishes several trades, and a vast amount of the comforts and refinements of life. It gives a life-insurance to each member, as against ill success, ill health, large Family, &c. It makes the separation by death, far less agonizing; and in marriage, does not separate the young couples from the old parents; nor, separate Families in divorce. It makes the interests of ordinary life, go hand in hand with the best Christian usefulness. It harmonizes class enmities, aims to provide for every want, and is itself (Limited Communism) a felt want of the age.

A Limited and Christian Communism, is the great means in a republic, to help to find out who are the most suitable leaders, and to induce the people to accept them, and also to induce the best men to accept official leadership. In ancient times, the war as to who should be Pope, was voluntarily referred to a retired Communist monk, St. Bernard, who made it his life business to found "Communities."

Among Mankind, as among other animals, it is necessary from time to time, to raise improved kinds and tribes. Communism is one method of accomplishing this end.

One of the uses of Communistic *theories* would be, to elaborate the true principles of the Family. This would also enable the various members of the same Family, to continue to be members of the same united household, after marriage. The reason why good people often have bad children, is, because of the examples of home selfishness. Communism will have much of its success in the world, by being more prolific of *healthy* offspring, and more successful in rearing children, and in *training* them.

Strong Communes afford the last hope for the reform of the erring,—whether inebriates, prostitutes, or criminals. Such persons, by assembling in such Communities (each class by itself, without necessarily separating sexes) would avoid public disgrace, and the temptations that are peculiar or dangerous to themselves. But such Communes must be of two Social Circles, —and the superior division, be either,—*unfallen*, or *thoroughly* reformed.

Limited Communism gives the advantages of poverty, without its sufferings; the advantages of wealth, without its luxuries or temptations. It honors and rescues from disgrace, a life of poverty and toil, which must so long yet be the lot of the mass of Mankind. It is the only thing that can save Christian nations from the fate of Greece and Rome, caused by the luxurious evils of a people, highly developed in intellect and sensibility, without corresponding moral and religious principle.

Another use of Communism, is its aid to Social Science as a science, and may be expressed thus; Social Science comes in place of obsolete or scholastic Theology (see Summary Introduction), and that Theology in its day, needed a recluse or contemplative life to develop and mature it; just so, Social Science requires a recluse and contemplative life to develop and mature IT. Because the honors, contentions, and pressure, of immediate schemes, preclude politicians and even statesmen, from that coolness and impersonal reflection, and gradual accumulation of knowledge, —which are necessary; and the more so, as Social Science has been as yet so little developed.

Communities are the true experiments of Sociology. No experiment can be real, which does not flow out of personal convictions, as these societies do.

CHAP. II. REGENERATION OF LABOR AND STUDY.

Communism makes industry attractive, and makes study a "Kindergarten for adults": and accomplishes both these results, by acting on labor and learning *both together*, and by allowing plenty of rest. Because the alternations of labor, study and rest, are nature's alleviatives for a healthy and useful life. All the other usual suggestions for "attractive industry," only stimulate feelings utterly at variance with the highest human morality. The thing to be done is, to banish pride, emulation, selfishness, and trifling play; and then to make all labors and all studies so interesting, as to be like amusements, getting people to love them; but not compelling any to perform them, only *when* willing to.

To make labor attractive is certainly possible; because the successful Communes generally give it as their experience, that they usually have no difficulty whatever in that respect. See Horace Greeley's account of this peculiarity. Education can also be made attractive. The science of education has succeeded in making the training and studies of children delightful to them. The Kindergarten, object-teaching, teaching the concrete earlier than the abstract; the simplified reading-books lately invented, the discovery that children love great ideas in simple words, elective studies, especially in the more advanced;—all these things have proved learning to be, and made it, no longer a misery, but a pleasure. And our theory gives good prospect of success, in making both education and labor interesting; because it joins the two, and thus increases almost indefinitely the variety of choices of the changes.

The following may be given as an outline of the principles, whereby labor may be made attractive. First, Negative ones; Second, Positive ones.

First, the Negative ones consist in:—Removing the causes of idleness, namely, infirmity of body; inapplication of mind; carelessness of youth and habit; false pride against work, especially as compared with virtue; false opinion that labor is a curse; early expectations, training children among the idle and vicious; financial and civil instability, disturbances, and changes.

Second, the Positive principles of making labor attractive, consist, partly of inducements for both Education and Work. These inducements are, variety and change of each, and from Work to Study, or *vice-versa*, alternations of rest and labor. These make both work and study interesting, by their accompaniments, by their abundant instruments, by their healthful places, arrangements, and methods; and by their times and seasons; and by giving to each and all, the studies and labors which *they* would perform most *cheerfully*. But every person able to work manually, should do enough of it to uphold its honor and dignity; as also to promote his health without being compelled to resort to amusements. He or she who despises labor, ruins the community. Add sufficient compensation, and thereby social power and votes; and in the early stages, perhaps, honors and grades. As far as possible, have all things done in company with other persons, and sometimes with both sexes, and accompanied by the children, they also working when practicable.

The changes when merely from one kind of work to another, may be made very various, as for instance; from out-door to in-door; from sedentary to ambulatory; from quick to slow; from easy to heavy; and from nervous or sensitive to muscular. Make people happy whilst AT their work; and give them sufficient motives, such as compensations, honors, just power, dependent families, duty, &c.; and then make their subsequent rest also happy; keep them healthy and temperate, not precocious, nor with too much confinement to books or otherwise,—and treat contempt of labor, as the crime it really is,—and labor will become fully attractive.

Communism is true economy, because it introduces division and distribution of labor, in domestic and household affairs; and because it purchases by wholesale; and because it has its dwellings, work-shops, stores, recreation-halls, and church, all on the same ground and in close contiguity; and because it makes labor attractive, and makes learning pleasant, and because it banishes extravagant and fashionable expenditures.

CHAP. III. PRACTICABILITY.

The principal practical hindrances to Communism, are as follow:—One is, the disposition of average human beings, to take advantage of unselfishness, leniency, kindness, benevolence, &c.; instead of accepting them, and returning for them an equal or greater amount of the same excellencies. This tendency is ever ready, even from those who love us, as also from those who can only be governed by fear. The direct remedy for it, might be a high sentiment of honor on the subject,—a sentiment that would recoil as strongly against the very idea of returning selfishness for unselfishness, as it would of violating its sacred honor in any other trust. And what can be more base, than returning selfishness for unselfish trust? And all unselfishness IS trust.

Another great practical hindrance is, the egotistical and over-conceited conception of most young Individuals, especially in the United States, that they can succeed better than others can succeed,—the egotistical conceited conception, of so many, that they are smarter than others. This notion necessarily being generally false, tends to produce disappointment, and then roguery. But old folks get over this in part.

There is a third great practical difficulty, namely, the fact that human nature will exert itself more under a stimulus of self, than under any other inducement. The direct antidote to this part truth, is a higher cultivation of the social feelings,—feelings which crave partnership for business, rather than Individual-action or Individual-responsibility,—feelings which may grow, from a craving for small partnerships, to larger ones, and so on up to business and home Corporations, and then Communes. Thus Limited Communism becomes the culmination of civilization in industry.

There are also special difficulties in the United States. Nearly all of the successful Protestant Communes, and many or most of the Roman Catholic ones, have had their origin in the old world, and consist chiefly of foreigners, and their immediate descendants. But the number of UNsuccessful American Protestant Communes (about seventy) is so large, that we can hardly help fearing, that Communism (as Noyes somewhere says) is somehow uncongenial to America. "The first are (sometimes) last, and the last first." And there can be no better final test, of the soundness of American principles of civil government, than their ultimate tendencies in preparing for and producing, not merely the ambition for, because there is plenty of that, but the realization of, successful Christian Limited Communes.

That most of the Communities which have succeeded, have consisted of foreigners,—is not final proof of the unsuitableness of Communism for this country. The same comparative difference exists in regard to co-operation.

To the objection that the American mind seeks absolute equality, in order to happiness,—we answer, that such claimants are not as yet fit for Communism; not having the *spiritual* experience and enlargement, necessary to understand the meaning of true equality. The true equality of Real Communism, does not give to each person an equal amount, of dollars, or of things: but it gives to each one, what *he needs*.

But a general present prevalence of Communism, cannot be expected, in a country thinly settled, and with every material in abundance. Yet a vast change *may* take place, in all these conditions, in less than half a century. But if not, then the decrease in the hiring and purchasing power of property, as well as of the rate of interest of money, may compel the wealthy, formerly aristocratic, to resort to a Limited Communism for their own economy, and to avoid the vexation and indecent treatment, arising under the old system.

Nordhoff seems to think that Communism is practicable, or useful, only for the very poorer and "laboring" classes: but we think it quite as well adapted for the refined and wealthy; so they could do their own house-work, without the annoyances and dissatisfaction of house-help, and with much less expense. For, evidently the troubles and expenses of housekeeping, in this country, are driving the refined, and even the wealthy, into large boarding-houses; from which the way to co-operative boarding, is not distant; and from that, some limited forms of Communism may be developed.

CHAP. IV. ANTICIPATIONS IN HISTORY.

History is foreshadowing Limited Communism, by anticipating its different elements separately. All insurance companies are of the nature of co-operation; and all the mutual companies are Communistic, each for its own function, whether, fire, marine, life, health or accident; even a boarding-house is Communistic. Schools and colleges are Communistic, especially the "public" ones. So also are the beneficiary departments of those not fully public.

All the Protestant churches in the land, are Communistic to a certain extent, and are daily becoming more so. Free churches, as to church property, are Communistic among all who are recognized as members; and their management is Communistic. So also with the Odd-Fellows, and the Temperance and other "orders."

The custom of men (i.e. the male sex) assembling by themselves, in clubs and taverns, shows a want in human nature. The same want of the company of their own sex, exists in women. These wants are best realized in a Commune.

CHAP. V. THE SEMI-RECLUSE LIFE NEEDED FOR THE HIGHER SPIRITUAL ATTAINMENTS.

Nearly all the great ideal-forms, hopes, and aspirations, of human society, are evidently practicable only in Communism. Such ideals ought not to be called failures, until they have been fairly tried; with all the combinations of appliances, that the best instincts of the uneducated, the highest generalizations of genius, and the furthest developments of science, can contribute, and can adapt to the true *art* of reforming society: in other words, until Social Science has become well developed, and has produced a reformed politics.

Christianity, and even Heaven, are based essentially upon Communistic principles. In Heaven, the sameness will much outweigh all the differences. The millennial saints (Rev. chap. ix.) are all arrayed alike, and in beautiful simplicity; with white robes for dresses, and white stones for jewels.

Perfect truth and candor are practicable and *obligatory, only* in Communism. The sacrifices of property and wages, generally required, to live a perfectly good life, are such as to need co-operation in a Commune. This world is a world of suffering for Christians: "yea all that will live godly in Christ Jesus, shall suffer persecution." But "when they persecute you in one city," (or in one form of civilization), "flee ye to another."

Association of the good, makes it easier to carry out the *higher* commands of Christ; such as, "Labor not for the meat which perisheth;" "Take no thought, saying, What shall we eat, or what shall we drink, or wherewithal shall we be clothed?" "Resist not evil," &c.

There is a condition of spiritual life, when a person has too much grace to be happy in the world,—too much grace to enjoy its follies, and yet not enough, to enjoy God, and trust in him. When this condition is *habitual*, it seems to require, at least for a time, the cure of a semi-recluse life,—the cure of a *College for Piety*, such as a good Commune would naturally be.

As Beecher says:—"There is, in almost every event, some subtle element, that may be sweet to those who know how to extract the sweetness,—to those who have the *art*, (for, it becomes an art), or the *education*, (for, we have to be educated into every thing that is not animal), of finding the sweet, the good, in whatever we have to do with. And in a corresponding sense, gratitude is an art, an art which is seldom learned, but which, if it were universal, would transform the world, in a day. If it could be given to men as an immediate experience, * * * it would dry up half the tears on the globe to-day. It would destroy half the temptations to which men are subject."

Piety is something to be learned,—a training of the affections, and familiarity with good examples. The early Christians were called, in their own language, learners or pupils. That is what the word "disciples," means. Then, may not seminaries or boarding-institutions be established, for learning or training in piety? Those who need moral help, and who sincerely desire it, should place themselves as moral children, or apprentices, under the care and control of their moral superiors, who love them, and who sincerely desire to help them. A moral religious Community is the very place to impart the necessary discipline; but some little degree of such discipline, must have first been attained in the Family, or in the world.

Yea, more, we think it may safely be said, that a Communistic life is needed, to secure, even a *decently* good Christian life, among Mankind *ordinarily*. A good Communist must hate injustice and selfishness, everywhere, and of every kind. He must be a "good hater,"—of evil. But the common ideas of Christianity, represent (whether truly or falsely, we cannot say), forgiveness of sins, as a very easy thing to obtain; and consequently, the sense of the evil of sin, is undermined in the heart. And in order to counteract this, the only greatly efficient means, perhaps, are religious persecution, endangering life; or Communism. And now that we are, happily, not in danger of our lives, for religion's sake, the power of a Limited Communism seems almost the only means remaining, to promote among Mankind generally, a due sense of the value of righteousness for its own sake, and for its own *immediate* consequences, its own little heavens upon earth; where, worldliness being for the most part shut out, and temptations reduced to a minimum, the whole structure of things, tends to uphold the value of morality and righteousness, for their own sakes.

CHAP. VI. NEED OF RELEASE FOR CHRISTIANS, FROM POLITICAL GOVERNMENTS.

Communism is needed, to give men a partial escape from the despotic injustice, and immorality, of earthly governments. Even our own country is becoming more and more corrupt. The evil influences of a sinful world, contaminate the law-courts, pervert juries, and pollute justice and legislation. The righteous are persecuted by the unrighteous, the honest by the wicked, and the truthful by the perjurers.

The time has come, when Christians, and all moral persons, may openly claim exemption from the tyranny and injustice of their worldly oppressors, and may modestly petition for the privilege of showing to the world, their faith in, and the real virtue of, their divine principles.

The revivification of Christianity, in modern times, is becoming more and more the revivification of Christian Communism; and this involves a chartered freedom from earthly control; so that moral societies may govern their own members; for only thus can men really govern themselves. All other forms of so-called self-government, are only delusions; and instead of men governing themselves, they are governed by the professional politicians, and their "rings": and therefore, the churches are subject to the civil power in those respects.

It is very desirable that the laws of the land, should fully release all members of religious peace-societies and Communities, from all claims for any kind of involuntary service, in military affairs. The civil power has never had, from God, any power to judge for, and order Christians to fight; and the time is coming, when such assumptions can only be looked upon, as outrageous invasions of the rights of private conscience.

And just as much, does the great moral sacrament of marriage, need to be delivered from political control, and placed among the voluntary and religious duties; excepting of course, the duty of maintaining offspring, and the reasonable preferences due to the woman, as being the principal loser by a *first* divorce. All this can be done only, or far best, in Communities. In *them;* the civil and social right of divorce, left to Individual judgment and conscience, under the *moral* rule of the permanent obligation of marriage, so long as it could possibly be made happy,—and even in divorce, to continue bound for the children,—would tend to prevent hasty or injudicious marriages: and thus would purify the marriage relation; just as deliverance of the church from alliance with the state, purified it, and ennobled religion. And there would be much fewer divorces, under the proposed system, than under the present; especially, after the young had been trained up to take care to *fit* themselves for, and to *deserve, permanency* in marriage.

CHAP. VII. THE KINDS OF PERSONS NEARLY READY.

The successful Communities are loaded and worried, with the great number of applications for membership. But they do not feel called to devote as much attention to them, or to the discovery of suitable tests, as seems to us advisable. A full enumeration of all the important classes of persons, that would be immediately benefited by Communism, would require a reconsideration of all the preceding parts of this essay. The following only will be added :—

Persons who so love truth in common or daily life, as to be determined to speak it, and to live where they can have it spoken to them: persons who deeply desire to have their Families nurtured and trained, with the advantages, but without the vices and temptations, of civilization; this is the most important of all the general uses:—Orthodox and conservative people, who are in sympathy with reform; persons earnestly desirous of being saved *from sin,* or of doing to others *entirely* as they would be done by; students and business-people, desirous of consecrating themselves to God; those having sympathy for the limited wages, and real temptations of women; foundlings; those who have been deeply crossed in love, or whose married life is unhappy; religiously benevolent persons of wealth or talent; professional business men, with too much conscience for this world; work-people of moral and industrious habits, but without sufficient tact or administrative ability, or with too numerous a family to "succeed" in life; married persons unable to live moderately of their own accord, under the usual customs; intelligent, good and orderly young lads and misses, who desire or need early marriage; persons willing to make sacrifices for good health and morality; persons in various ranks, desiring to lead good lives, but conscious that their failure comes from opposing circumstances; persons who have had enough of this "*life*"; persons whose early peculiarities, or subsequent circumstances, have left them with few friends or acquaintances; and in general, all those whom society in its fashions, follies, and moral nonsense, would trample on *singly;* those who are tired of the trickery of the world; politicians disgusted with bribery demagogism and war, and so on. And doubtless there are many other persons ready, could they only get knowledge of each other, and see the evidences necessary to entitle them to confide in each other. Verily now, as of old, publicans and harlots could enter the kingdom of God, before the pharisees;—the pharisees, who now, as of old, "will neither enter the kingdom themselves, nor allow others to enter who would."

SUB-DIVISION III.

STATISTICS.

CHAP. I. A SELECTION OF COMMUNES THAT HAVE DISSOLVED, IN THE UNITED STATES.

A large number, say about seventy-five Communes, have been commenced and then dissolved, in the United States. The following is a selection of the most interesting of them. See The Circular, also American Socialisms by J. H. Noyes, also Communistic Societies of the United States by Charles Nordhoff.

	Greatest Population.	Years Duration.
Alphadelphia Phalanx, Mich.	450	1½
Bishop Hill (Jansenites) Illinois	1100	7
Brook Farm, Mass.	115	5
Hopedale, Mass. (Adin Ballou's)	200	18
Marlborough Association, Ohio	24	4
New Harmony, Ind. (Robert Owen's) . .	900	3
Nashoba, Tenn. (Frances Wright's) . . .	15	3
North Am. Phalanx (Monmouth Co.) N. J.	112	13
Northampton Association, Mass.	130	4
Prairie Home, Ohio	130	1
Skaneateles, New York	150	3½
Sylvania Association, Pa. (Alb. Brisbane's) .	145	2
Spring Farm Association, Wisconsin . . .	50	3
Wisconsin Phalanx	100	6

CHAP. II. OF SUCCESSFUL COMMUNES, IN GENERAL.

Partial developments of good Communism, have taken place in all ages of the world, and in many countries. Some features thereof may be found among the Tuscans, and among the Pitcairn-Islanders; and in former governments of Paraguay by the Jesuits. The fullest political developments, are in Switzerland, where there are a large number of towns or townships, fully Communistic in *many* respects. The ancient Essenes were religious Communists, so also a part of the modern Moravians.

CHAP. III. CATHOLIC COMMUNITIES IN THE UNITED STATES.

In the United States, the Roman Catholics have about one hundred and thirty monasteries, and about three hundred nunneries; altogether, with a membership of about thirty thousand; but as these are all living a professedly celibate life, and are of a peculiar religion, they seem not usually to be cited as an example towards Communism, but rather are used as an example towards asceticism; whereas, the real want of human nature, that now lies, and always has lain, at the bottom of the Roman recluse and celibate life, is the desire of a higher life, in retired association, namely, spirituality in Communism. And our Protestant writers have as much to learn, both of the higher life, and of Community-management, from the "Catholic" monastic writers, as from all others; if only a suitable selection were made. And remembering that the thing really involved in, and necessary under, the idea of celibacy,—that is, necessary, either to the higher life, or to Communism,—is, *not* the celibacy or abstinence itself, but the subjection of all the Family-passions and partialities, to piety and wisdom, and to the advices of persons able to instruct, and manage, those who need *to be* instructed and managed.

CHAP. IV. PROTESTANT COMMUNITIES IN THE UNITED STATES, WITHOUT REGULAR MARRIAGE.

§ 1. *The German Seventh-Day Baptist Monastic Society.*

The "denomination," and the monastic society, arose together: but the denomination once numbered several thousands, whilst the monastery never reached 300, even including outside members. Jacobi in "American Socialisms," confusing the two, speaks as if the "colony" or the Community once numbered "thousands." The denomination is found, chiefly, in central and southern-central Pennsylvania, and is less numerous now than formerly. They are a secession from the Tunkers.

Their founder, Beissel, adopted seventh-day views, in 1725; and finding little tolerance among his denomination, he retired, secretly and alone, to a neighboring *cell* abandoned by some previous hermit. After some years he was discovered. Other Tunkers gradually settled around him; and thus, in A.D. 1733, at Ephrata, Lancaster Co., Pa., arose their monastery: just as the first monasteries had arisen, in the early Christian ages. It adopted the Capuchin, or white friar's garb; both sexes residing together, as celibates, but without any vows. It was a Limited Community of labors and incomes, not of capital, although *some* threw in all they had, of course. "The property which belonged to the society, by donation, and the labor of the single brethren and sisters, was common stock; but none were obliged to throw in their own property, or give up any of their possessions." (See Rupp's Hist. Relig. Denom. U. S.) The outside or neighboring membership, married, and were aided in so doing, and some inside members occasionally left, and were married; but they considered celibacy as more conducive to holiness, and *entire* consecration to God.

The denomination grew, but the Commune did not; but rather dwindled; until now, it perhaps does not contain a dozen. But another of their Communes has started, namely, at Snowhill, Franklin Co., Pa.; and probably numbers about 40 inside members.

In religion they are Trinitarian Baptists, but are "open communion." They had a Sabbath school from about A. D. 1745 to 1777, and were a more liberal people than the Tunkers, except perhaps, that we do not find any mention among them, of the final restoration of all Mankind, as among the Tunkers. They have also declined much, in spirit and zeal. Nordhoff omits all notice of them, even in his map. But, notwithstanding a few omissions, Nordhoff's book on the Successful Communities in the United States, was very much wanted, and is very cheerful. For, of all the sad books that you will easily find, the saddest, is the series in The Circular, afterwards published as "American Socialisms;" because their scope and plan give so little attention to most of the Communes that *did* succeed. But sadder than it, are, the record of the *dissolution* of Bishop Hill; the *decline* of the Ephrata Community, and of the Zoar Commune; and the *stolid pertinacity* with which the New Harmony society, already dwindled from 800 to 110, still persists in refusing to marry, or to perpetuate so noble and pious a people.

§ 2. *The Shaker Societies.*

The Shakers have associations in Maine, New-Hampshire, Connecticut, Massachusetts, New-York, Ohio and Kentucky;

with headquarters at New Lebanon, Columbia Co., N. Y. The Society was founded in 1792, with nine members. It reached its highest number in 1824, namely, 4500. Its present number is 2400. They have eighteen villages, and each village is divided into Sub-societies, or "Families," living in different buildings, so that every Family consists of about seventy-five persons. Both sexes reside in the same building, but at different ends of it. They believe that Christ is both male and female, and that the female appeared in Ann Lee, their founder. They believe in continual communion with spirits. They are strictly celibates, yet keep their two sexes more or less together; worship together, and join in their worship-dance together, each sex in alternate rows. The different sexes visit and converse occasionally, especially on Sunday.

§ 3. *The New-Harmony Society.*

This Society, at Economy, Pa., was founded in 1805, with 700 members. Its highest number was in 1820, when it reached 800. Its present number is 110. Its greatest use in the world seems to have been, in furnishing members as a nucleus for the Bethel and Aurora Communes, presently to be mentioned. They believe that God is dual, male and female; that Adam was dual also, and that original sin consisted in Adam desiring to have the female separated from the male. They believe in the early coming of the Millennium, and the final salvation of all Mankind; but after a future probation and purification, for ordinary sinners. They are a pious, moral, and upright people; but bear every evidence of being near their end, unless they adopt numerous children. The two sexes intermingle freely in society, and in industry, but sit apart, in worship. They are conscientious celibates.

§ 4. *The Oneida Community.*

This Community has three united associations, one at Oneida, N. Y., one near it, at Willow Place, and one at Wallingford, Conn. As their statistics are scattered through many volumes, we shall have to give them from memory. The association began about A.D. 1838, with 6 or 8 members, as a partnership, or Commune only of incomes and labors. But in 1846, with about 40 members, it guardedly began its Restricted Communism of persons, as well as property. Although Mr. Noyes himself absolutely repudiates the term Communism as applicable to them previous to this time, namely 1846. But that seems to be merely because he rejects *Limited Communism.* Its highest numbers were about A.D. 1868, consisting of a little over 300. Its present number is given by Nordhoff, as 283, and by its own weekly paper "The Circular," at 269. But Nordhoff's is probably the correct number. Much of the time, the members' experience or life, is the same as the celibates', at least so they claim; and includes continence of a very peculiar kind. It believes in perfection from selfishness and sin; and, in communion with Christ, and the primitive Church of Saints, who it believes were raised from the dead about A.D. 70; that is, previous to the destruction of Jerusalem; and that Christ's *second* coming occurred then; but yet, that he will have a future or third coming, to raise the rest of Mankind. It believes, like the Shakers, that God is male and female, and that Christ is the female thereof. The members publicly "criticise" one another's errors, with fearful plainness; and even think to cure their diseases by deep criticism, and by faith and prayer.

Besides the foregoing Communes, there are a few other Families in the United States, attempting to be Communes; but as yet, are not large enough to need particularizing in this hasty sketch. See Nordhoff; and "The Circular," and other publications, for the last several years.

CHAP. V. COMMUNITIES IN THE UNITED STATES, WITH REGULAR MARRIAGE.

§ 1. *The Icaria Association.*

Icaria in Iowa, was commenced in 1848, with a "vanguard" of about 70, brought to America by E. Cabet, a popular French socialist. Many others gradually followed him to Illinois, so that the highest number ultimately reached 1500, according to Nordhoff: ("American Socialisms" says 365). But they rapidly declined. The remnant, about 55 persons, removed to Iowa in 1856. Their present number is about 65. They are nearly all French, and Deists; their principal religion is Communism. They *require* marriage, or as Nordhoff says, "command it under penalties"; and avoid a Unitary Home; both of which, seem to be very wise provisions in a deistical Commune.

§ 2. *The Bethel and Aurora Communities.*

For the Statistics of this Community, we rely upon Nordhoff *alone*, as we do not find them mentioned by anybody else.

This Society exists in two associations, Bethel, Shelby Co., in Missouri, and Aurora, near Portland, in Oregon. The Community was founded in 1844 by a Dr. Keil, with a considerable number, (probably about 200?) followers, who had seceded from the New-Harmony association, on account of its celibacy; and adopted marriage. They soon increased, and now number about 600. They are Germans and "Pennsylvania Dutch," and in their religion are as near like Hicks-dox Quakers, as could easily be, except that they use the Bible much. They also are peacemen, have weekly Sunday-School, and semi-weekly preaching. They remind one forcibly of the Hicks-dox Community, "Prairie Home," in Ohio, mentioned in "American Socialisms,"—began in 1843 with about 130 members, but lasted scarcely one year; and having very little order or authority, but dependent chiefly on moral suasion, and on the feeling of what is right, in each Individual. But Bethel and Aurora have a leader, who is, at least, a Bible-politician, and a doctor; and many of their original members had been disciplined, for years, in a well-regulated and pious Community; namely, the New-Harmony Society. See Ch. IV. § 3. And then, they are a plain, unambitious, "Dutch"-like people; and expect all to work industriously. They even allow seceded members to reside among them. They have but little education, and use but few books, except the Bible. They marry early; do to others as they would be done by; and are contented and prosperous. They are the most perfect specimen that we know of, of a common-sense, practical and upright Community, not founded on either, any particular religious, or anti-religious ideas.

§ 3. *The Zoar Separatists' Community.*

This Society is in Tuscarawas Co., Ohio, and was founded in 1819, with about 225 members. It reached its highest number in 1840, about 600. Its present number is about 300. They are Germans, have but little education, live close to nature, and use homeopathy. In religion they are very like the *Orthodox Quakers*, and were aided considerably by the Quakers, in their emigration from Germany. Poverty compelled them to abstain from marriage, for the first ten years of their settlement; and from the experience obtained then, they have adopted some notions about celibacy being more pious, or commendable, than marriage; although they generally marry, but not early in life; and hold that intercourse except for the perpetuation of the race, is sin. Their young people frequently leave them. If they would learn by experience, and by their great decline already, the impossibility of their succeeding, with some of their peculiar notions, they might have quite as glorious a success as, or more so than, Bethel and Aurora.

§ 4. *The Amana Inspirationists' Community.*

This Society consists of seven small Communes, a few miles apart, in Iowa. It was founded in 1844, with 600 members. It remained at Eben-Ezer, near Buffalo, N. Y., several years, before going to Iowa. Its present number appears to be its highest, namely, about 1500, Nordhoff says 1450, although we have seen it set down as 3000, in some publications. They are Germans, use homeopathy, and publish a good many books. Nordhoff calls them Inspirationists. They, too, are very much like the Orthodox Quakers, in religion; although with less of the Quietist, but with rather more of the mystic elements; and with more subservience to their leaders as inspired, than either the Quakers, or Zoarites. They also hold to occasional sacramental communions of bread and wine. Their leaders occasionally administer caustic, "inspired", public reproofs, to certain members who do not seem to give outward proof, of being any worse than others. At such times their leaders are pungent revivalists. They have marriage, but consider it as, generally, a fall from the highest condition; and as requiring time to rise again to the unselfishness of the former condition. They have several orders, or grades of membership. They refuse American applicants for membership, but get recruits directly from Germany; and with their natural increase, perhaps, are growing slowly. They will probably be a great society, some day; and a great example of *possibilities.* Governor Carpenter of Iowa, said to the writer—"they are a grand success."

§ 5. *The Brocton Community.*

This Society is in Brocton, Chautauqua Co., N. Y. It commenced in 1867. The different accounts of its numbers are very conflicting, varying from 50 up to 200. It is partly Swedenborgian, with some Universalism, and with some modifications and additions, made by its founder Mr. Harris, about internal inspiration and respiration; and claims to be exquisitely sensitive against the approach of unchaste persons, but yet does not live at all ascetically. It represents a transient, but active and brilliant, phase of Christian experience.

It was founded by T. L. Harris, (an ex-Universalist preacher, and attaché of the U. S. embassy to Japan), together with a British nobleman, Lawrence Oliphant, M. P. Its "rank and file" consist mostly of English people. The widowed mother of Oliphant joined it subsequently. "The Circular" of Nov. 24, 1873, says the Oliphants have left it. Mr. Noyes classes it as an offshoot of the spiritual Communities: but *that*, perhaps, is because he considers Swedenborgianism as Spiritualism. It has other members of wealth, or high social position,—Americans. Nordhoff omits all mention of this Community, except on his "map of Communities." Yet "American Socialisms" had dwelt upon it, at great length, especially upon the *probabilities* of its final success and permanency, or its fall.

§ 6. *Conclusion.*

Here we may give a reason, for having introduced into this volume, so much matter about Communism of any kind. The justification is, that small writers ought to be at liberty to follow the example of the great ones. And nearly all the great Social Scientists treat Communism with attention and respect, and maintain one or another of its elements. Plato does so, very decidedly. Fourier does so, of course. Comte was originally a St. Simonian. Spencer advocates the tenure of land by the State. And Mill, all along in his article on Property, which is his "Book II.,"—treats Communism sympathetically and argumentatively; especially in his Chap. VIII., §§ 3 and 4, in defense of the Metayer, in preference to the Cottier system; and in Chap. I., §§ 2, 3, and 4, on Communism, and Fourierism.

Few, though the successful and regular-marriage Communes are, yet we must remember, that what *some* men have done, and are doing,—other men also *can* do. Even one successful and permanent experiment, proves what *can* be done, and *prophesies* what will be, and gives hope and faith, in more determined efforts for repeated and even grander successes. Nor is there anything very peculiar about any of these successful Communes, other than seeking the higher moral life, instead of financial advantages,—little other than a Quaker-like simplicity of customs and of religion, and a Quaker-like reliance on the inward spirit. In fact, there are only enough religious peculiarities about either of them, to suffice to hold a people together, and isolated from the world,—during a formative period.

Let us thank God for the Communities that *do* exist, whether Catholic, Protestant, heretic, or infidel; and pray to Him for more of them. And if this volume shall have no other effect, than a tendency to improve those already existing, or to incite to or assist in forming, additional ones; it *ought* to be a sufficient reward to the writer, for all his toils and pains in working it out. But the reward which he would *like to hope for*, is, that it may promote virtue, liberty and harmony, in church and state, both in and out of Communism. For, the Rule is the Ideal; and is very brief:—"All things whatsoever ye would that men should do to you, do ye even so to them: for this is the Law and the Prophets."

Δοξα τῳ Θεῳ. Αμην.

www.ingramcontent.com/pod-product-compliance
Lightning Source LLC
LaVergne TN
LVHW021257110826
845150LV00003B/411

9781425561260